Houghton
Mifflin
Harcourt

GEORGIA
collections

Cover, Title Page Photo Credits: © Michel Leynaud/Corbis

Printed in the U.S.A.

ISBN 978-0-544-09317-1

X0706000575686

4 5 6 7 8 9 10   0868   22 21 20 19 18 17 16 15

4500536289   B C D E F G

Houghton
Mifflin
Harcourt

GEORGIA collections

GRADE 11

Program Consultants:

Kylene Beers

Martha Hougen

Carol Jago

William L. McBride

Erik Palmer

Lydia Stack

About Our Program Consultants

Kylene Beers Nationally known lecturer and author on reading and literacy; 2011 recipient of the Conference on English Leadership Exemplary Leader Award; coauthor of *Notice and Note: Strategies for Close Reading*; former president of the National Council of Teachers of English. Dr. Beers is the nationally known author of *When Kids Can't Read: What Teachers Can Do* and coeditor of *Adolescent Literacy: Turning Promise into Practice*, as well as articles in the *Journal of Adolescent and Adult Literacy*. Former editor of *Voices from the Middle*, she is the 2001 recipient of NCTE's Richard W. Halley Award, given for outstanding contributions to middle-school literacy. She recently served as Senior Reading Researcher at the Comer School Development Program at Yale University as well as Senior Reading Advisor to Secondary Schools for the Reading and Writing Project at Teachers College.

Martha Hougen National consultant, presenter, researcher, and author. Areas of expertise include differentiating instruction for students with learning difficulties, including those with learning disabilities and dyslexia; and teacher and leader preparation improvement. Dr. Hougen has taught at the middle school through graduate levels. Recently her focus has been on working with teacher educators to enhance teacher and leader preparation to better meet the needs of all students. Currently she is working with the University of Florida at the Collaboration for Effective Educator Development, Accountability, and Reform Center (CEEDAR Center) to improve the achievement of students with disabilities by reforming teacher and leader licensure, evaluation, and preparation. She has led similar efforts in Texas with the Higher Education Collaborative and the College & Career Readiness Initiative Faculty Collaboratives. In addition to peer-reviewed articles, curricular documents, and presentations, Dr. Hougen has published two college textbooks: *The Fundamentals of Literacy Assessment and Instruction Pre-K–6* (2012) and *The Fundamentals of Literacy Assessment and Instruction 6–12* (2014).

Carol Jago Teacher of English with 32 years of experience at Santa Monica High School in California; author and nationally known lecturer; and former president of the National Council of Teachers of English. Currently serves as Associate Director of the California Reading and Literature Project at UCLA. With expertise in standards assessment and secondary education, Ms. Jago is the author of numerous books on education, including *With Rigor for All* and *Papers, Papers, Papers*, and is active with the California Association of Teachers of English, editing its scholarly journal *California English* since 1996. Ms. Jago also served on the planning committee for the 2009 NAEP Framework and the 2011 NAEP Writing Framework.

William L. McBride Curriculum specialist. Dr. McBride is a nationally known speaker, educator, and author who now trains teachers in instructional methodologies. He is coauthor of *What's Happening?*, an innovative, high-interest text for middle-grade readers and author of *If They Can Argue Well, They Can Write Well*. A former reading specialist, English teacher, and social studies teacher, he holds a master's degree in reading and a doctorate in curriculum and instruction from the University of North Carolina at Chapel Hill. Dr. McBride has contributed to the development of textbook series in language arts, social studies, science, and vocabulary. He is also known for his novel *Entertaining an Elephant*, which tells the story of a veteran teacher who becomes reinspired with both his profession and his life.

Erik Palmer Veteran teacher and education consultant based in Denver, Colorado. Author of *Well Spoken: Teaching Speaking to All Students* and *Digitally Speaking: How to Improve Student Presentations*. His areas of focus include improving oral communication, promoting technology in classroom presentations, and updating instruction through the use of digital tools. He holds a bachelor's degree from Oberlin College and a master's degree in curriculum and instruction from the University of Colorado.

Lydia Stack Internationally known teacher educator and author. She is involved in a Stanford University project to support English Language Learners, *Understanding Language*. The goal of this project is to enrich academic content and language instruction for English Language Learners (ELLs) in grades K-12 by making explicit the language and literacy skills necessary to meet the Common Core State Standards (CCSS) and Next Generation Science Standards. Her teaching experience includes twenty-five years as an elementary and high school ESL teacher, and she is a past president of Teachers of English to Speakers of Other Languages (TESOL). Her awards include the TESOL James E. Alatis Award and the San Francisco STAR Teacher Award. Her publications include *On Our Way to English, Visions: Language, Literature, Content*, and *American Themes*, a literature anthology for high school students in the ACCESS program of the U.S. State Department's Office of English Language Programs.

Additional thanks to the following Program Reviewers

Stacy Bagwell
Cumming, Georgia

Rosemary Barnes
Atlanta, Georgia

Sean C. Bennett
Fayetteville, Georgia

Lynne Bruschetti
Peachtree City, Georgia

Cheryl Lynn Daniels
Perry, Georgia

Allen Edwards
Moultrie, Georgia

Kathy Franks
Fayetteville, Georgia

Barbara G. James
Fayetteville, Georgia

Shery Sheppard Kearney
Peachtree City, Georgia

Thomas E. Lewis
College Park, Georgia

Sarah Loftus
Cumming, Georgia

Catherine B. Nix
Brooks, Georgia

Joliene Hutto Price
Fayetteville, Georgia

Portia N. Rhodes
Newnan, Georgia

Sharme Ridley
Peachtree City, Georgia

Courtney E. Russell
Peachtree City, Georgia

Carol L. Saboda
Fayetteville, Georgia

Justin D. Spencer
Fayetteville, Georgia

Sheryl Stalvey
Moultrie, Georgia

Margaret A. W. Walls
Peachtree City, Georgia

COMMON CORE

COLLECTION 1
Coming to America

Exploration and Settlement ⏵ 3

ANCHOR TEXT | **HISTORICAL ACCOUNT**
from Of Plymouth Plantation — William Bradford ⏵ 5

HISTORY WRITING
Coming of Age in the Dawnland
from 1491 — Charles C. Mann ⏵ 23

Introduction to *The Tempest* 36

DRAMA
from The Tempest — William Shakespeare ⏵ 37

Media Versions of *The Tempest* 71

COMPARE TEXT AND MEDIA | **FILM VERSION**
The Tempest — BBC Shakespeare ⏵ 71

PRODUCTION IMAGES
The Tempest 73

SHORT STORY
Balboa — Sabina Murray 77

ARGUMENT
"Blaxicans" and Other
Reinvented Americans — Richard Rodriguez 87

POEM
New Orleans — Joy Harjo 97

COLLECTION PERFORMANCE TASK
Write an Argument 103

KEY LEARNING OBJECTIVES

Cite text evidence.
Determine central ideas.
Determine themes.
Support inferences.
Determine meaning of words/phrases.
Analyze language.

Analyze story structure.
Understand point of view and irony.
Analyze and evaluate an argument.
Determine author's purpose.
Analyze drama interpretations.
Analyze foundational texts.

Close Reader

HISTORICAL NARRATIVE
from The General History of Virginia   John Smith

ESSAY
Mother Tongue   Amy Tan

POEM
Indian Boy Love Song (#2)   Sherman Alexie

eBook *Explore It!*

 Video Links   **eBook** *Read On!* Novel list and additional selections   **Visit hmhfyi.com** for current articles and informational texts.

Building a Democracy

A New American Nation ⊙ 109

COMPARE ANCHOR TEXTS

PUBLIC DOCUMENTS
The Declaration of Independence   Thomas Jefferson ⊙ 111

from The United States Constitution: Preamble *and* Bill of Rights ⊙ 121

ARGUMENT
The Federalist No. 10   James Madison ⊙ 129

HISTORY ARTICLE
Thomas Jefferson:
The Best of Enemies   Ron Chernow 141

Colonial American Poetry ⊙ 151

COMPARE TEXTS

POEMS
To the Right Honorable
William, Earl of Dartmouth   Phillis Wheatley 152

On Being Brought from
Africa to America   Phillis Wheatley 154

On the Emigration to America and
Peopling the Western Country   Philip Freneau 155

SHORT STORY
A Soldier for the Crown   Charles Johnson 159

MEDIA ANALYSIS

DOCUMENTARY FILM
Patrick Henry: Voice of Liberty   A&E ⊙ 167

COLLECTION PERFORMANCE TASK
Write an Informative Essay 169

KEY LEARNING OBJECTIVES

Analyze and compare themes and topics.
Analyze ideas and sequence.
Analyze language.
Understand a key term.
Analyze style.
Analyze structure.

Analyze and evaluate an argument.
Analyze point of view.
Analyze a video.
Evaluate constitutional principles.
Analyze foundational documents.

Close Reader

PUBLIC DOCUMENT
from The United States Constitution

PUBLIC DOCUMENT
Petition to the Massachusetts
General Assembly   Prince Hall

HISTORY WRITING
Abigail Adams' Last Act of Defiance   Woody Holton

eBook *Explore It!*

 ▶ **Video Links**   **eBook** *Read On!*
Novel list and additional selections

 fyi hmhfyi.com **Visit hmhfyi.com**
for current articles and
informational texts.

COMMON CORE

COLLECTION **3**

The Individual and Society

A Distinctly American Voice   175

ANCHOR TEXT | **POEMS**
from Song of Myself   Walt Whitman   177

ESSAY
Growing Up Asian in America   Kesaya E. Noda   187

Poems of Emily Dickinson   199
POEMS
The Soul selects her own Society   Emily Dickinson   200
Because I could not stop for Death   Emily Dickinson   201
Much Madness is divinest Sense   Emily Dickinson   202
Tell all the truth but tell it slant   Emily Dickinson   203

ESSAY
from Walden   Henry David Thoreau   207

ANCHOR TEXT | **ARGUMENT**
Against Nature   Joyce Carol Oates   221

American Romanticism   234

COMPARE TEXTS | **SHORT STORY**
The Minister's Black Veil   Nathaniel Hawthorne   235
SHORT STORY
The Pit and the Pendulum   Edgar Allan Poe   ▶   249

COLLECTION PERFORMANCE TASKS
Write a Narrative   267
Debate an Issue   271

KEY LEARNING OBJECTIVES

Cite text evidence.
Summarize.
Determine central ideas.
Determine themes.
Analyze ideas and events.
Analyze language.

Interpret symbols.
Analyze structure.
Analyze structure and mood.
Determine author's purpose.
Evaluate purpose and style.

Close Reader

POEM
I Hear America Singing   Walt Whitman

POEM
A Noiseless Patient Spider   Walt Whitman

ESSAY
from Nature   Ralph Waldo Emerson

ESSAY
from Self-Reliance   Ralph Waldo Emerson

ESSAY
Spoiling Walden: Or, How I
Learned to Stop Worrying and
Love Cape Wind   David Gessner

eBook *Explore It!*

 Video Links

eBook *Read On!*
Novel list and additional selections

 Visit hmhfyi.com for current articles and informational texts.

COLLECTION 4
A New Birth of Freedom

Civil War and Reconstruction   ▶ 277

ANCHOR | **SPEECH**
TEXT | Second Inaugural Address   Abraham Lincoln   ▶ 279

SPEECH
What to the Slave
Is the Fourth of July?   Frederick Douglass   ▶ 285

PUBLIC DOCUMENT
Declaration of Sentiments   Elizabeth Cady Stanton   295

HISTORY WRITING
Building the
Transcontinental Railroad   Iris Chang   301

MEDIA | **DOCUMENTARY FILM**
ANALYSIS | The 54th Massachusetts   HISTORY   ▶ 315

POEM
Runagate Runagate   Robert Hayden   ▶ 317

COLLECTION PERFORMANCE TASK
Present a Persuasive Speech   323

KEY
LEARNING
OBJECTIVES
Cite text evidence.
Analyze ideas and events.
Analyze language.
Analyze structure.

Analyze author's point of view.
Analyze author's purpose.
Integrate and evaluate information.
Evaluate seminal texts.

Close Reader

LEGAL DOCUMENT
The Emancipation Proclamation   Abraham Lincoln

PUBLIC DOCUMENT
from The Iroquois Constitution   Dekanawida

NEWSPAPER ARTICLE
Bonding Over a Mascot   Joe Lapointe

Image Credits: ©Bettmann/Corbis

eBook *Explore It!*

 Video Links

 eBook *Read On!*
Novel list and additional selections

 Visit hmhfyi.com
for current articles and
informational texts.

COLLECTION 5
An Age of Realism

America Transformed ▶ 329

ANCHOR TEXT | **SHORT STORY**
To Build a Fire — Jack London — 331

COMPARE TEXTS | **NOVEL**
from The Jungle — Upton Sinclair — 351
INVESTIGATIVE JOURNALISM
Food Product Design
from Fast Food Nation — Eric Schlosser — 359

ESSAY
The Lowest Animal — Mark Twain — 373

Tenements and the "Other Half" — 383

COMPARE TEXT AND MEDIA | **ESSAY**
Genesis of the Tenement — Jacob Riis — 384
IMAGE COLLECTION
Tenement Photos — Jacob Riis — 389
REPORT
Child Mortality Rates — 391
VIDEO
AMERICA The Story of Us: Jacob Riis — HISTORY ▶ 392

SHORT STORY
The Story of an Hour — Kate Chopin — 395

POEM
The Fish — Elizabeth Bishop — 401

COLLECTION PERFORMANCE TASK
Write an Analytical Essay — 405

KEY LEARNING OBJECTIVES		
Cite text evidence.		Analyze irony and point of view.
Analyze technical terms.		Determine author's purpose.
Interpret symbols.		Determine author's point of view.
Analyze structure.		Evaluate use of satire.
Analyze author's choices.		Integrate and evaluate information.

Close Reader

SHORT STORY
The Men in the Storm   Stephen Crane

SCIENCE WRITING
The Yuckiest Food in the Amazon   Mary Roach

SHORT STORY
A Journey   Edith Wharton

POEM
Ode to a Large Tuna in the Market   Pablo Neruda

Image Credits: ©Nick Norman/National Geographic/Getty Images

eBook *Explore It!*

 Video Links

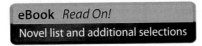 **eBook** *Read On!*
Novel list and additional selections

 Visit hmhfyi.com
for current articles and
informational texts.

COLLECTION 6
The Modern World

Life in a Global Society ⊙ 411

ANCHOR TEXT | **SHORT STORY**
Winter Dreams   F. Scott Fitzgerald   413

The Harlem Renaissance 438
Poems of the Harlem Renaissance 439

COMPARE TEXTS | **POEMS**
Song of the Son   Jean Toomer   440
From the Dark Tower   Countee Cullen   441
A Black Man Talks of Reaping   Arna Bontemps   442

POEMS
Mending Wall   Robert Frost   445
The Death of the Hired Man   Robert Frost   447

Modern American Drama 456

ANCHOR TEXT | **DRAMA**
The Crucible   Arthur Miller   ⊙ 457

Media Versions of *The Crucible* 543

COMPARE TEXT AND MEDIA | **AUDIO VERSION**
The Crucible   ⊙ 543
PRODUCTION IMAGES
The Crucible 545

OPINION AND DISSENTS
Tinker v. Des Moines Independent Community School District   Supreme Court of the United States   549

SCIENCE ESSAY
The Coming Merging of Mind and Machine   Ray Kurzweil   569

SHORT STORY
Reality Check   David Brin   581

KEY LEARNING OBJECTIVES

Cite textual evidence to support inferences.
Analyze character motivation.
Analyze science fiction.
Analyze drama elements.
Analyze language.
Analyze structure.

Analyze structure of an argument.
Analyze author's point of view.
Analyze drama interpretations.
Delineate and evaluate an argument.
Analyze foundational works.

ARGUMENT
The Ends of the World as
We Know Them   Jared Diamond   587

POEM
The Universe as Primal Scream   Tracy K. Smith   597

COLLECTION PERFORMANCE TASKS
Write an Argument   601
Participate in a Panel Discussion   605

Close Reader

SHORT STORY
Ambush   Tim O'Brien

ESSAY
How It Feels to Be Colored Me   Zora Neale Hurston

POEM
The Weary Blues   Langston Hughes

DRAMA
from The Crucible, from Act One   Arthur Miller

ESSAY
Science, Guided by Ethics   Freeman Dyson

eBook *Explore It!*

 Video Links

 eBook *Read On!*
Novel list and additional selections

 Visit hmhfyi.com for current articles and informational texts.

Image Credits: ©Bek Shakirov/Images.com/Corbis

Student Resources

Performance Task Reference Guide	R2
Writing Arguments	R2
Writing Informative Texts	R4
Writing Narratives	R6
Conducting Research	R8
Participating in Collaborative Discussions	R12
Debating an Issue	R14
Reading Arguments	R16
Analyzing an Argument	R16
Recognizing Persuasive Techniques	R17
Analyzing Logic and Reasoning	R18
Identifying Faulty Reasoning	R19
Evaluating Persuasive Texts	R21
Strategies for Evaluating Evidence	R21
Strategies for Evaluating an Argument	R22
Grammar	R23
Quick Reference:	
Parts of Speech	R23
The Sentence and Its Parts	R25
Punctuation	R26
Capitalization	R29
Grammar Handbook:	
1 Nouns	R30
2 Pronouns	R30
3 Verbs	R33
4 Modifiers	R35
5 Prepositions, Conjunctions, and Interjections	R38
6 The Sentence and Its Parts	R39
7 Phrases	R40
8 Verbals and Verbal Phrases	R41
9 Clauses	R42
10 The Structure of Sentences	R43
11 Writing Complete Sentences	R44
12 Subject-Verb Agreement	R45

Vocabulary and Spelling	R49
1 Using Context Clues	R49
2 Analyzing Word Structure	R50
3 Understanding Word Origins	R51
4 Understanding the English Language	R52
5 Synonyms and Antonyms	R53
6 Denotation and Connotation	R53
7 Analogies	R54
8 Homonyms and Homophones	R54
9 Words with Multiple Meanings	R54
10 Specialized Vocabulary	R55
11 Preferred and Contested Usage	R55
12 Using Reference Sources	R56
13 Spelling Rules	R56
14 Commonly Confused Words	R59
Glossary of Literary and Informational Terms	R61
Pronunciation Key	R83
Glossary of Academic Vocabulary	R84
Glossary of Critical Vocabulary	R85
Index of Skills	R89
Index of Titles and Authors	R102
Acknowledgments	R103

DIGITAL OVERVIEW
Connecting to Your World

Every time you read something, view something, write to someone, or react to what you've read or seen, you're participating in a world of ideas. You do this every day, inside the classroom and out. These skills will serve you not only at home and at school, but eventually (if you can think that far ahead!), in your career.

The digital tools in this program will tap into the skills you already use and help you sharpen those skills for the future.

Start your exploration at my.hrw.com

DIGITAL COLLECTIONS

Writing and
Speaking & Listening

Communication in today's world requires quite a variety of skills.
To express yourself and win people over, you have to be able to
write for print, for online media, and for spoken presentations.
To collaborate, you have to work with people who might be sitting
right next to you or at the other end of an Internet connection.

Available Only in Your eBook

*Interactive
Lessons*

**The interactive lessons in these collections will
help you master the skills needed to become
an expert communicator.**

What Does a Strong Argument Look Like?

Read this argument and answer the questions about how the writer states
and supports his position.

Tip

Pitching Perfect Pitch
by José Alvarez

Did you know that when you are listening to your favorite
vocalist, you might be hearing a computer-generated pitch?
Many record companies use pitch-correction software to ensure
that their performers are pitch-perfect. While perfectionism
is an admirable goal, there is a fine line between using
technology to enhance music and using it to make
performers into something they're not. Whether recording
in the studio or playing a live performance, musicians
should not use pitch-correction software. ●

Music production has become a digital experience. Producers
use software to cut and paste pieces of music together, just like
you cut and paste words together in your word-processing
software. ○ When editing these different things together
digitally, slight imperfections can occur where the pieces are
joined. Enter the correction software. What began as a method to
streamline the digital editing process has turned into an almost
industry-wide standard of altering a musician"s work. "Think of it
like plastic surgery," says a Grammy-winning recording engineer.

What is the writer's position, or **claim**, on the
use of pitch-correction software?

☐ Musicians should learn to live with their
imperfections.

☑ Musicians should never use the software.

☐ Musicians should use the software to enhance
live performances only.

Writing Arguments

Master the art of proving your point.

COMMON CORE ELACC11-12W1, ELACC11-12W10

Interactive Lessons

1. Introduction
2. What Is a Claim?
3. Support: Reasons and Evidence
4. Building Effective Support
5. Creating a Coherent Argument
6. Persuasive Techniques
7. Formal Style
8. Concluding Your Argument

Writing Informative Texts

Shed light on complex ideas and topics.

COMMON CORE ELACC11-12W2, ELACC11-12W10

Interactive Lessons

1. Introduction
2. Developing a Topic
3. Organizing Ideas
4. Introductions and Conclusions
5. Elaboration
6. Using Graphics and Multimedia
7. Precise Language and Vocabulary
8. Formal Style

Writing Narratives

A good storyteller can always capture an audience.

COMMON CORE ELACC11-12W3, ELACC11-12W10

Interactive Lessons

1. Introduction
2. Narrative Context
3. Point of View and Characters
4. Narrative Structure
5. Narrative Techniques
6. The Language of Narrative

Writing as a Process

Get from the first twinkle of an idea to a sparkling final draft.

COMMON CORE ELACC11-12W4, ELACC11-12W5, ELACC11-12W10

Interactive Lessons	
1. Introduction	4. Revising and Editing
2. Task, Purpose, and Audience	5. Trying a New Approach
3. Planning and Drafting	

Producing and Publishing with Technology

Learn how to write for an online audience.

COMMON CORE ELACC11-12W6

Interactive Lessons	
1. Introduction	3. Interacting with Your Online Audience
2. Writing for the Internet	4. Using Technology to Collaborate

Conducting Research

There's a world of information out there. How do you find it?

COMMON CORE ELACC11-12W6, ELACC11-12W7, ELACC11-12W8

Interactive Lessons	
1. Introduction	5. Conducting Field Research
2. Starting Your Research	6. Using the Internet for Research
3. Types of Sources	7. Taking Notes
4. Using the Library for Research	8. Refocusing Your Inquiry

Evaluating Sources

Approach all sources with a critical eye.

COMMON CORE ELACC11-12W8

Interactive Lessons	**1.** Introduction **2.** Evaluating Sources for Usefulness	**3.** Evaluating Sources for Reliability

Using Textual Evidence

Put your research into writing.

COMMON CORE ELACC11-12W7, ELACC11-12W8, ELACC11-12W9

Interactive Lessons	**1.** Introduction **2.** Synthesizing Information **3.** Writing an Outline	**4.** Summarizing, Paraphrasing, and Quoting **5.** Attribution

Participating in Collaborative Discussions

There's power in putting your heads together.

COMMON CORE ELACC11-12SL1

Interactive Lessons	**1.** Introduction **2.** Preparing for Discussion **3.** Establishing and Following Procedure	**4.** Speaking Constructively **5.** Listening and Responding **6.** Wrapping Up Your Discussion

Analyzing and Evaluating Presentations

Is there substance behind the style?

COMMON CORE ELACC11-12SL2, ELACC11-12SL3, ELACC11-12SL6

Interactive Lessons

1. Introduction
2. Analyzing a Presentation
3. Evaluating a Speaker's Reliability
4. Tracing a Speaker's Argument
5. Rhetoric and Delivery
6. Synthesizing Media Sources

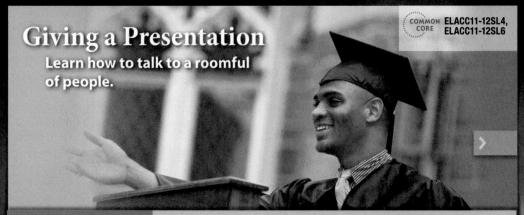

Giving a Presentation

Learn how to talk to a roomful of people.

COMMON CORE ELACC11-12SL4, ELACC11-12SL6

Interactive Lessons

1. Introduction
2. Knowing Your Audience
3. The Content of Your Presentation
4. Style in Presentation
5. Delivering Your Presentation

Using Media in a Presentation

If a picture is worth a thousand words, just think what you can do with a video.

COMMON CORE ELACC11-12SL5

Interactive Lessons

1. Introduction
2. Types of Media: Audio, Video, and Images
3. Using Presentation Software
4. Practicing Your Presentation

Supporting Close Reading, Research, and Writing

Understanding complex texts is hard work, even for experienced readers. It often takes multiple close readings to understand and write about an author's choices and meanings. The dynamic digital tools in this program will give you opportunities to learn and practice this critical skill of close reading—and help you integrate the text evidence you find into your writing.

 Close Read

Learn How to Do a Close Read

An effective close read is all about the details; you have to examine the language and ideas a writer includes. See how it's done by accessing the **Close Read Screencasts** in your eBook. Hear modeled conversations about anchor texts.

 Close Read

of the birds, how they soared and glided overhead. He pointed out the slow, graceful sweep of their wings as they beat the air steadily, without fluttering. Soon Icarus was sure that he, too, could fly and, raising his arms up and down, skirted over the white sand and even out over the waves, letting his feet touch the snowy foam as the water thundered and broke over the sharp rocks. Daedalus watched him proudly but

Soon Icarus was sure that he, too, could fly and, raising his arms up and down, skirted over the white sand and even out over the waves, letting his feet touch the snowy foam as the water thundered and broke over the sharp rocks.

There might be a sense of danger here.

Daedalus watched him proudly but with misgivings. He called Icarus to his side and, putting his arm round the boy's shoulders, said, 'Icarus, my son, we are about to make our flight. No human being has ever traveled through the air before, and I want you to listen carefully to my instructions.

Annotate the Texts

Practice close reading by utilizing the powerful annotation tools in your eBook. Mark up key ideas and observations using highlighters and sticky notes.

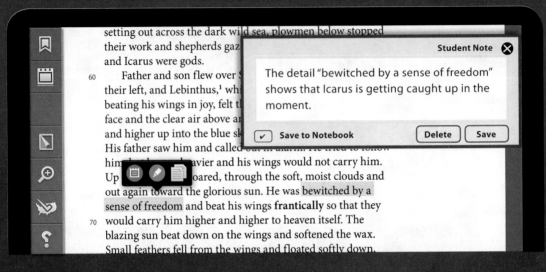

myNotebook

Collect Text Evidence

Save your annotations to your notebook. Gathering and organizing this text evidence will help you complete performance tasks and other writing assignments.

Find More Text Evidence on the Web

Tap into the *FYI* website for links to high-interest informational texts about collection topics. Capture text evidence from any Web source by including it in your notebook.

Integrate Text Evidence into Your Writing

Use the evidence you've gathered to formulate interpretations, draw conclusions, and offer insights. Integrate the best of your text evidence into your writing.

Navigating Complex Texts

By Carol Jago

Reading complex literature and nonfiction doesn't need to be painful.

But to enjoy great poetry and prose you are going to have to do more than skim and scan. You will need to develop the habit of paying attention to the particular words on the page closely, systematically, even lovingly. Just because a text isn't easy doesn't mean there is something wrong with it or something wrong with you. Understanding complex text takes effort and focused attention. Do you sometimes wish writers would just say what they have to say more simply or with fewer words? I assure you that writers don't use long sentences and unfamiliar words to annoy their readers or make readers feel dumb. They employ complex syntax and rich language because they have complex ideas about complex issues that they want to communicate. Simple language and structures just aren't up to the task.

Excellent literature and nonfiction—the kind you will be reading over the course of the year—challenge readers in many ways. Sometimes the background of a story or the content of an essay is so unfamiliar that it can be difficult to understand why characters are behaving as they do or to follow the argument a writer is making. By persevering—reading like a detective and following clues in the text—you will find that your store of background knowledge grows. As a result, the next time you read about this subject, the text won't seem nearly as hard. Navigating a terrain you have been over once before never seems quite as rugged the second time through. The more you read, the better reader you become.

Good readers aren't scared off by challenging text. When the going gets rough, they know what to do. Let's take vocabulary, a common measure of text complexity, as an example. Learning new words is the business of a lifetime. Rather than shutting down when you meet a word you don't know, take a moment to think about the word. Is any part of the word familiar to you? Is there something in the context of the sentence or paragraph that can help you figure out its meaning? Is there someone or something that can provide you with a definition? When we read literature or nonfiction from a time period other than our own, the text is often full of words we don't know.

Each time you meet those words in succeeding readings you will be adding to your understanding of the word and its use. Your brain is a natural word-learning machine. The more you feed it complex text, the larger vocabulary you'll have and as a result, the easier navigating the next book will be.

Have you ever been reading a long, complicated sentence and discovered that by the time you reached the end you had forgotten the beginning? Unlike the sentences we speak or dash off in a note to a friend, complex text is often full of sentences that are not only lengthy but also constructed in intricate ways. Such sentences require readers to slow down and figure out how phrases relate to one another as well as who is doing what to whom. Remember, rereading isn't cheating. It is exactly what experienced readers know to do when they meet dense text on the page. On the pages that follow you will find stories and articles that challenge you at a sentence level. Don't be intimidated. By paying careful attention to how those sentences are constructed, you will see their meanings unfold before your eyes.

Another way text can be complex is in terms of the density of ideas. Sometimes a writer piles on so much information that you find even if your eyes continue to move down the page, your brain has stopped taking in anything. At times like this, turning to a peer and discussing particular lines or concepts can help you pay closer attention and begin to unpack the text. Sharing questions and ideas, exploring a difficult passage together, makes it possible to tease out the meaning of even the most difficult text.

> **"Your brain is a natural word-learning machine. The more you feed it complex text, the larger vocabulary you'll have."**

Poetry is by its nature particularly dense and for that reason poses particular challenges for casual readers. Don't ever assume that once through a poem is enough. Often, seemingly simple poems in terms of word choice and length—for example an Emily Dickinson, Mary Oliver, or W.H. Auden poem—express extremely complex feelings and insights. Poets also often make reference to mythological and Biblical allusions which contemporary readers are not always familiar with. Skipping over such references robs your reading of the richness the poet intended. Look up that bird. Check out the note on the page. Ask your teacher.

You will notice a range of complexity within each collection of readings. This spectrum reflects the range of texts that surround us: some easy, some hard, some seemingly easy but hard, some seemingly hard but easy. Navigating this sea of texts should stretch you as a reader and a thinker. How could it be otherwise when your journey is in the realms of gold? Please accept this invitation to an intellectual voyage I think you will enjoy.

Understanding the Common Core State Standards

What are the English Language Arts Common Core State Standards?

The Common Core State Standards for English Language Arts indicate what you should know and be able to do by the end of your grade level. These understandings and skills will help you be better prepared for future classes, college courses, and a career. For this reason, the standards for each strand in English Language Arts (such as reading informational text or writing) directly relate to the College and Career Readiness Anchor Standards for each strand. The Anchor Standards broadly outline the understandings and skills you should master by the end of high school so that you are well-prepared for college or for a career.

How do I learn the English Language Arts Common Core State Standards?

Your textbook is closely aligned to the English Language Arts Common Core State Standards. Every time you learn a concept or practice a skill, you are working on mastery of one of the standards. Each collection, each selection, and each performance task in your textbook connects to one or more of the standards for English Language Arts listed on the following pages.

The English Language Arts Common Core State Standards are divided into five strands: Reading Literature, Reading Informational Text, Writing, Speaking and Listening, and Language.

Strand	What It Means to You
Reading Literature (RL)	This strand concerns the literary texts you will read at this grade level: stories, drama, and poetry. The Common Core State Standards stress that you should read a range of texts of increasing complexity as you progress through high school.
Reading Informational Text (RI)	Informational text includes a broad range of literary nonfiction, including exposition, argument, and functional text, in such genres as personal essays, speeches, opinion pieces, memoirs, and historical and technical accounts. The Common Core State Standards stress that you will read a range of informational texts of increasing complexity as you progress from grade to grade.
Writing (W)	The Writing strand focuses on your generating three types of texts—arguments, informative or explanatory texts, and narratives—while using the writing process and technology to develop and share your writing. The Common Core State Standards also emphasize research and specify that you should write routinely for both short and extended time frames.
Speaking and Listening (SL)	The Common Core State Standards focus on comprehending information presented in a variety of media and formats, on participating in collaborative discussions, and on presenting knowledge and ideas clearly.
Language (L)	The standards in the Language strand address the conventions of standard English grammar, usage, and mechanics; knowledge of language; and vocabulary acquisition and use.

Common Core Code Decoder

The codes you find on the pages of your textbook identify the specific knowledge or skill for the standard addressed in the text.

COMMON CORE

ELACC 11-12 W 1a

These letters stand for **English Language Arts Common Core.**

Indicates that this standard is for students in grades 11 and 12.

Indicates that this standard is from the **Writing strand.**

Identifies the standard number and standard subpart for the knowledge or skill.

English Language Arts Common Core State Standards

Listed below are the English Language Arts Common Core State Standards that you are required to master by the end of grade 11. We have provided a summary of the concepts you will learn on your way to mastering each standard. The CCR anchor standards and high school grade-specific standards for each strand work together to define college and career readiness expectations—the former providing broad standards, the latter providing additional specificity.

College and Career Readiness Anchor Standards for Reading

Common Core State Standards

KEY IDEAS AND DETAILS

1. Read closely to determine what the text says explicitly and to make logical inferences from it; cite specific textual evidence when writing or speaking to support conclusions drawn from the text.

2. Determine central ideas or themes of a text and analyze their development; summarize the key supporting details and ideas.

3. Analyze how and why individuals, events, and ideas develop and interact over the course of a text.

CRAFT AND STRUCTURE

4. Interpret words and phrases as they are used in a text, including determining technical, connotative, and figurative meanings, and analyze how specific word choices shape meaning or tone.

5. Analyze the structure of texts, including how specific sentences, paragraphs, and larger portions of the text (e.g., a section, chapter, scene, or stanza) relate to each other and the whole.

6. Assess how point of view or purpose shapes the content and style of a text.

INTEGRATION OF KNOWLEDGE AND IDEAS

7. Integrate and evaluate content presented in diverse formats and media, including visually and quantitatively, as well as in words.

8. Delineate and evaluate the argument and specific claims in a text, including the validity of the reasoning as well as the relevance and sufficiency of the evidence.

9. Analyze how two or more texts address similar themes or topics in order to build knowledge or to compare the approaches the authors take.

RANGE OF READING AND LEVEL OF TEXT COMPLEXITY

10. Read and comprehend complex literary and informational texts independently and proficiently.

Reading Standards for Literature, Grades 11–12 Students

The College and Career Readiness Anchor Standards for Reading apply to both literature and informational text.

Common Core State Standards	What It Means to You
KEY IDEAS AND DETAILS	
1. Cite strong and thorough textual evidence to support analysis of what the text says explicitly as well as inferences drawn from the text, including determining where the text leaves matters uncertain.	You will use strong evidence from a text to support your analysis of its central ideas—both those that are stated directly and those that are suggested—and to show where the text leaves matters uncertain.
2. Determine two or more themes or central ideas of a text and analyze their development over the course of the text, including how they interact and build on one another to produce a complex account; provide an objective summary of the text.	You will analyze the development of at least two of a text's key ideas and themes by showing how they progress and interact throughout the text. You will also summarize the text as a whole without adding your own ideas or opinions.
3. Analyze the impact of the author's choices regarding how to develop and relate elements of a story or drama (e.g., where a story is set, how the action is ordered, how the characters are introduced and developed).	You will analyze the author's choices related to setting, plot structure, and characterization in a story or drama.
CRAFT AND STRUCTURE	
4. Determine the meaning of words and phrases as they are used in the text, including figurative and connotative meanings; analyze the impact of specific word choices on meaning and tone, including words with multiple meanings or language that is particularly fresh, engaging, or beautiful. (Include Shakespeare as well as other authors.)	You will analyze specific words and phrases in the text to determine both their figurative and connotative meanings, as well as how they contribute to the text's tone and meaning as a whole. You will also consider multiple-meaning words and vivid language.
5. Analyze how an author's choices concerning how to structure specific parts of a text (e.g., the choice of where to begin or end a story, the choice to provide a comedic or tragic resolution) contribute to its overall structure and meaning as well as its aesthetic impact.	You will analyze the ways in which the author has chosen to structure and order the text and determine how those choices shape the text's meaning and affect the reader.
6. Analyze a case in which grasping a point of view requires distinguishing what is directly stated in a text from what is really meant (e.g., satire, sarcasm, irony, or understatement).	You will understand a point of view in which what is really meant is different from what is said or stated.

Common Core State Standards	What It Means to You
INTEGRATION OF KNOWLEDGE AND IDEAS	
7. Analyze multiple interpretations of a story, drama, or poem (e.g., recorded or live production of a play or recorded novel or poetry), evaluating how each version interprets the source text. (Include at least one play by Shakespeare and one play by an American dramatist.)	You will compare and contrast multiple interpretations of a story, drama, or poem, and analyze how each draws from and uses the source text.
8. (Not applicable to literature)	
9. Demonstrate knowledge of eighteenth-, nineteenth- and early-twentieth-century foundational works of American literature, including how two or more texts from the same period treat similar themes or topics.	You will analyze, compare, and contrast important eighteenth-, nineteenth-, and early-twentieth-century works of American literature.
RANGE OF READING AND LEVEL OF TEXT COMPLEXITY	
10. By the end of grade 11, read and comprehend literature, including stories, dramas, and poems, in the grades 11–CCR text complexity band proficiently, with scaffolding as needed at the high end of the range.	11. You will read and understand grade-level appropriate literary texts by the end of grade 11.

Reading Standards for Informational Text, Grades 11–12 Students

Common Core State Standards	What It Means to You
KEY IDEAS AND DETAILS	
1. Cite strong and thorough textual evidence to support analysis of what the text says explicitly as well as inferences drawn from the text, including determining where the text leaves matters uncertain.	You will use details and information from the text to support your analysis of its central ideas—both those that are stated directly and those that are suggested—and to show where the text leaves matters uncertain.
2. Determine two or more central ideas of a text and analyze their development over the course of the text, including how they interact and build on one another to provide a complex analysis; provide an objective summary of the text.	You will analyze the development of at least two of a text's key ideas by showing how they progress and interact throughout the text. You will also summarize the text as a whole without adding your own ideas or opinions.

Common Core State Standards	What It Means to You
3. Analyze a complex set of ideas or sequence of events and explain how specific individuals, ideas, or events interact and develop over the course of the text.	You will analyze the specific interactions among a set of ideas, individuals, or a sequence of events in a text.

CRAFT AND STRUCTURE

4. Determine the meaning of words and phrases as they are used in a text, including figurative, connotative, and technical meanings; analyze how an author uses and refines the meaning of a key term or terms over the course of a text (e.g., how Madison defines *faction* in *Federalist No. 10*).	You will analyze specific words and phrases in the text to determine their figurative, connotative, and technical meanings, as well as to uncover how an author uses them throughout a text.
5. Analyze and evaluate the effectiveness of the structure an author uses in his or her exposition or argument, including whether the structure makes points clear, convincing, and engaging.	You will examine a text's structure and evaluate whether it makes the author's claims clear, convincing, and interesting.
6. Determine an author's point of view or purpose in a text in which the rhetoric is particularly effective, analyzing how style and content contribute to the power, persuasiveness, or beauty of the text.	You will understand the author's purpose and perspective on a topic and analyze how the author uses language to affect the reader.

INTEGRATION OF KNOWLEDGE AND IDEAS

7. Integrate and evaluate multiple sources of information presented in different media or formats (e.g., visually, quantitatively) as well as in words in order to address a question or solve a problem.	You will integrate multiple and varied sources of information to address a question or solve a problem.
8. Delineate and evaluate the reasoning in seminal U.S. texts, including the application of constitutional principles and use of legal reasoning (e.g., in U.S. Supreme Court majority opinions and dissents) and the premises, purposes, and arguments in works of public advocacy (e.g., *The Federalist*, presidential addresses).	You will analyze the reasoning and underlying principles of important historical U.S. texts for their support of the principles of democracy.

Common Core State Standards	What It Means to You
9. Analyze seventeenth-, eighteenth-, and nineteenth-century foundational U.S. documents of historical and literary significance (including The Declaration of Independence, the Preamble to the Constitution, the Bill of Rights, and Lincoln's Second Inaugural Address) for their themes, purposes, and rhetorical features.	You will read and analyze important eighteenth-, nineteenth-, and early-twentieth-century documents pertaining to American history to determine their themes, purposes, and use of language.

RANGE OF READING AND LEVEL OF TEXT COMPLEXITY

Common Core State Standards	What It Means to You
10. By the end of grade 11, read and comprehend literary nonfiction in the grades 11–CCR text complexity band proficiently, with scaffolding as needed at the high end of the range.	You will demonstrate the ability to read and understand grade-level appropriate literary nonfiction texts by the end of grade 11.

College and Career Readiness Anchor Standards for Writing

Common Core State Standards
TEXT TYPES AND PURPOSES
1. Write arguments to support claims in an analysis of substantive topics or texts, using valid reasoning and relevant and sufficient evidence.
2. Write informative/explanatory texts to examine and convey complex ideas and information clearly and accurately through the effective selection, organization, and analysis of content.
3. Write narratives to develop real or imagined experiences or events using effective technique, well-chosen details, and well-structured event sequences.
PRODUCTION AND DISTRIBUTION OF WRITING
4. Produce clear and coherent writing in which the development, organization, and style are appropriate to task, purpose, and audience.
5. Develop and strengthen writing as needed by planning, revising, editing, rewriting, or trying a new approach.
6. Use technology, including the Internet, to produce and publish writing and to interact and collaborate with others.
RESEARCH TO BUILD AND PRESENT KNOWLEDGE
7. Conduct short as well as more sustained research projects based on focused questions, demonstrating understanding of the subject under investigation.
8. Gather relevant information from multiple print and digital sources, assess the credibility and accuracy of each source, and integrate the information while avoiding plagiarism.

Common Core State Standards
9. Draw evidence from literary or informational texts to support analysis, reflection, and research.

RANGE OF WRITING
10. Write routinely over extended time frames (time for research, reflection, and revision) and shorter time frames (a single sitting or a day or two) for a range of tasks, purposes, and audiences.

Writing Standards, Grades 11–12 Students

Common Core State Standards	What It Means to You
TEXT TYPES AND PURPOSES	
1. Write arguments to support claims in an analysis of substantive topics or texts, using valid reasoning and relevant and sufficient evidence.	You will write and develop arguments with strong evidence and valid reasoning that include
a. Introduce precise, knowledgeable claim(s), establish the significance of the claim(s), distinguish the claim(s) from alternate or opposing claims, and create an organization that logically sequences claim(s), counterclaims, reasons, and evidence.	a. a clear organization of precise claims and counterclaims
b. Develop claim(s) and counterclaims fairly and thoroughly, supplying the most relevant evidence for each while pointing out the strengths and limitations of both in a manner that anticipates the audience's knowledge level, concerns, values, and possible biases.	b. relevant and unbiased support for claims that incorporates audience considerations
c. Use words, phrases, and clauses as well as varied syntax to link the major sections of the text, create cohesion, and clarify the relationships between claim(s) and reasons, between reasons and evidence, and between claim(s) and counterclaims.	c. use of transitional words, phrases, and clauses and varied sentence structures to link information and clarify relationships
d. Establish and maintain a formal style and objective tone while attending to the norms and conventions of the discipline in which they are writing.	d. a tone and style that is appropriate and that adheres to the conventions, or expectations, of the discipline
e. Provide a concluding statement or section that follows from and supports the argument presented.	e. a strong concluding statement or section that summarizes the evidence presented

Common Core State Standards	What It Means to You

TEXT TYPES AND PURPOSES

2. Write informative/explanatory texts to examine and convey complex ideas, concepts, and information clearly and accurately through the effective selection, organization, and analysis of content.

You will write clear, well-organized, and thoughtful informative and explanatory texts with

   a. Introduce a topic; organize complex ideas, concepts, and information so that each new element builds on that which precedes it to create a unified whole; include formatting (e.g., head-ings), graphics (e.g., figures, tables), and multimedia when useful to aiding comprehension.

   a. a clear introduction and an organization that builds on each successive idea, including formats, headings, graphic organizers (when appropriate), and multimedia

   b. Develop the topic thoroughly by selecting the most significant and relevant facts, extended definitions, concrete details, quotations, or other information and examples appropriate to the audience's knowledge of the topic.

   b. a sufficient variety of support and background information

   c. Use appropriate and varied transitions and syntax to link the major sections of the text, create cohesion, and clarify the relationships among complex ideas and concepts.

   c. appropriate and varied transitions and sentence structures

   d. Use precise language, domain-specific vocabulary, and techniques such as metaphor, simile, and analogy to manage the complexity of the topic.

   d. precise language, relevant vocabulary, and the use of comparisons to express complex ideas

   e. Establish and maintain a formal style and objective tone while attending to the norms and conventions of the discipline in which they are writing.

   e. an appropriate tone and style that adheres to the conventions, or expectations, of the discipline

   f. Provide a concluding statement or section that follows from and supports the information or explanation presented (e.g., articulating implications or the significance of the topic).

   f. a strong concluding statement or section that logically relates to the information presented in the text and that restates the importance or relevance of the topic

Common Core State Standards	What It Means to You

TEXT TYPES AND PURPOSES

3. Write narratives to develop real or imagined experiences or events using effective technique, well-chosen details, and well-structured event sequences.

You will write clear, well-structured, detailed narrative texts that

   a. Engage and orient the reader by setting out a problem, situation, or observation and its significance, establishing one or multiple point(s) of view, and introducing a narrator and/or characters; create a smooth progression of experiences or events.

   a. draw your readers in with a clear topic, well-developed point(s) of view, a well-developed narrator and characters, and an interesting progression of events or ideas

   b. Use narrative techniques, such as dialogue, pacing, description, reflection, and multiple plot lines, to develop experiences, events, and/or characters.

   b. use a range of literary techniques to develop and expand on events and/or characters

   c. Use a variety of techniques to sequence events so that they build on one another to create a coherent whole and build toward a particular tone and outcome (e.g., a sense of mystery, suspense, growth, or resolution).

   c. have a coherent sequence and structure that create the appropriate tone and ending for readers

   d. Use precise words and phrases, telling details, and sensory language to convey a vivid picture of the experiences, events, setting, and/or characters.

   d. use precise words, sensory details, and language in order to keep readers interested

   e. Provide a conclusion that follows from and reflects on what is experienced, observed, or resolved over the course of the narrative.

   e. have a strong and logical conclusion that reflects on the topic

PRODUCTION AND DISTRIBUTION OF WRITING

4. Produce clear and coherent writing in which the development, organization, and style are appropriate to task, purpose, and audience.

You will produce writing that is appropriate to the task, purpose, and audience for whom you are writing.

5. Develop and strengthen writing as needed by planning, revising, editing, rewriting, or trying a new approach, focusing on addressing what is most significant for a specific purpose and audience.

You will revise and refine your writing, using a variety of strategies, to address what is most important for your purpose and audience.

Common Core State Standards	What It Means to You
6. Use technology, including the Internet, to produce, publish, and update individual or shared writing products in response to ongoing feedback, including new arguments or information.	You will use technology to share your writing, provide links to other relevant information, and to update your information as needed.

RESEARCH TO BUILD AND PRESENT KNOWLEDGE

7. Conduct short as well as more sustained research projects to answer a question (including a self-generated question) or solve a problem; narrow or broaden the inquiry when appropriate; synthesize multiple sources on the subject, demonstrating understanding of the subject under investigation.	You will engage in short and more complex research tasks that include answering a question or solving a problem by using multiple sources. Your understanding of the subject will be evident in the product you develop.
8. Gather relevant information from multiple authoritative print and digital sources, using advanced searches effectively; assess the strengths and limitations of each source in terms of the task, purpose, and audience; integrate information into the text selectively to maintain the flow of ideas, avoiding plagiarism and overreliance on any one source and following a standard format for citation.	You will effectively conduct searches to gather information from a variety of print and digital sources and will evaluate each source in terms of the goal of your research. You will appropriately cite your sources of information and will follow a standard format for citation, such as the MLA or APA guidelines.

Common Core State Standards	What It Means to You
RESEARCH TO BUILD AND PRESENT KNOWLEDGE	
9. Draw evidence from literary or informational texts to support analysis, reflection, and research.	You will paraphrase, summarize, quote, and cite primary and secondary sources, using both literary and informational texts, to support your analysis, reflection, and research, for purposes including
a. Apply *grades 11–12 Reading standards* to literature (e.g., "Demonstrate knowledge of eighteenth-, nineteenth- and early-twentieth-century foundational works of American literature, including how two or more texts from the same period treat similar themes or topics").	a. written analysis of themes, author's choices, or point of view in American literature
b. Apply *grades 11–12 Reading standards* to literary nonfiction (e.g., "Delineate and evaluate the reasoning in seminal U.S. texts, including the application of constitutional principles and use of legal reasoning [e.g., in U.S. Supreme Court Case majority opinions and dissents] and the premises, purposes, and arguments in works of public advocacy [e.g., *The Federalist*, presidential addresses]").	b. written analysis of central ideas, text structure, word choice, point of view, or reasoning in American literary nonfiction
RANGE OF WRITING	
10. Write routinely over extended time frames (time for research, reflection, and revision) and shorter time frames (a single sitting or a day or two) for a range of tasks, purposes, and audiences.	You will write a variety of texts for different purposes and audiences over both short and extended periods of time.

College and Career Readiness Anchor Standards for Speaking and Listening

Common Core State Standards
COMPREHENSION AND COLLABORATION
1. Prepare for and participate effectively in a range of conversations and collaborations with diverse partners, building on others' ideas and expressing their own clearly and persuasively.
2. Integrate and evaluate information presented in diverse media and formats, including visually, quantitatively, and orally.
3. Evaluate a speaker's point of view, reasoning, and use of evidence and rhetoric.

Common Core State Standards

PRESENTATION OF KNOWLEDGE AND IDEAS

4. Present information, findings, and supporting evidence such that listeners can follow the line of reasoning and the organization, development, and style are appropriate to task, purpose, and audience.

5. Make strategic use of digital media and visual displays of data to express information and enhance understanding of presentations.

6. Adapt speech to a variety of contexts and communicative tasks, demonstrating command of formal English when indicated or appropriate.

Speaking and Listening Standards, Grades 11–12 Students

Common Core State Standards	What It Means to You

COMPREHENSION AND COLLABORATION

1. Initiate and participate effectively in a range of collaborative discussions (one-on-one, in groups, and teacher-led) with diverse partners on grades 11–12 topics, texts, and issues, building on others' ideas and expressing their own clearly and persuasively.	You will actively participate in a variety of discussions in which you
a. Come to discussions prepared, having read and researched material under study; explicitly draw on that preparation by referring to evidence from texts and other research on the topic or issue to stimulate a thoughtful, well-reasoned exchange of ideas.	a. have read any relevant material beforehand and have come to the discussion prepared with background research
b. Work with peers to promote civil, democratic discussions and decision-making, set clear goals and deadlines, and establish individual roles as needed.	b. work with others to establish goals, processes, and roles within the group in order to have reasonable discussions
c. Propel conversations by posing and responding to questions that probe reasoning and evidence; ensure a hearing for a full range of positions on a topic or issue; clarify, verify, or challenge ideas and conclusions; and promote divergent and creative perspectives.	c. ask and respond to questions, encourage a range of positions, and relate the current topic to other relevant information and perspectives
d. Respond thoughtfully to diverse perspectives; synthesize comments, claims, and evidence made on all sides of an issue; resolve contradictions when possible; and determine what additional information or research is required to deepen the investigation or complete the task.	d. respond to different perspectives, summarize points of agreement or disagreement when needed, help to resolve unclear points, and set out a plan for additional research as needed

Common Core State Standards	What It Means to You
2. Integrate multiple sources of information presented in diverse formats and media (e.g., visually, quantitatively, orally) in order to make informed decisions and solve problems, evaluating the credibility and accuracy of each source and noting any discrepancies among the data.	You will integrate multiple and varied sources of information, assessing the credibility and accuracy of each source to aid the group-discussion process.
3. Evaluate a speaker's point of view, reasoning, and use of evidence and rhetoric, assessing the stance, premises, links among ideas, word choice, points of emphasis, and tone used.	You will evaluate a speaker's argument and analyze the nature of the speaker's reasoning or evidence.
PRESENTATION OF KNOWLEDGE AND IDEAS	
4. Present information, findings, and supporting evidence, conveying a clear and distinct perspective, such that listeners can follow the line of reasoning, alternative or opposing perspectives are addressed, and the organization, development, substance, and style are appropriate to purpose, audience, and a range of formal and informal tasks.	You will organize and present information, evidence, and your perspective to your listeners in a logical sequence and style that are appropriate to your task, purpose, and audience.
5. Make strategic use of digital media (e.g., textual, graphical, audio, visual, and interactive elements) in presentations to enhance understanding of findings, reasoning, and evidence and to add interest.	You will use digital media to enhance understanding and to add interest to your presentations.
6. Adapt speech to a variety of contexts and tasks, demonstrating a command of formal English when indicated or appropriate.	You will adapt the formality of your speech appropriately, depending on its context and purpose.

College and Career Readiness Anchor Standards for Language

Common Core State Standards
CONVENTIONS OF STANDARD ENGLISH
1. Demonstrate command of the conventions of standard English grammar and usage when writing or speaking.
2. Demonstrate command of the conventions of standard English capitalization, punctuation, and spelling when writing.

Common Core State Standards

KNOWLEDGE OF LANGUAGE

3. Apply knowledge of language to understand how language functions in different contexts, to make effective choices for meaning or style, and to comprehend more fully when reading or listening.

VOCABULARY ACQUISITION AND USE

4. Determine or clarify the meaning of unknown and multiple-meaning words and phrases by using context clues, analyzing meaningful word parts, and consulting general and specialized reference materials, as appropriate.

5. Demonstrate understanding of word relationships and nuances in word meanings.

6. Acquire and use accurately a range of general academic and domain-specific words and phrases sufficient for reading, writing, speaking, and listening at the college and career readiness level; demonstrate independence in gathering vocabulary knowledge when considering a word or phrase important to comprehension or expression.

Language Standards, Grades 11–12 Students

Common Core State Standards	What It Means to You
CONVENTIONS OF STANDARD ENGLISH	

1. Demonstrate command of the conventions of standard English grammar and usage when writing or speaking.
   a. Apply the understanding that usage is a matter of convention, can change over time, and is sometimes contested.
   b. Resolve issues of complex or contested usage, consulting references (e.g., *Merriam-Webster's Dictionary of English Usage, Garner's Modern American Usage*) as needed.
	You will correctly use the conventions of English grammar and usage, including
	
	   a. demonstrating that usage follows accepted standards and can change or be contested
	
	   b. using references to resolve disagreements or uncertainty about usage

2. Demonstrate command of the conventions of standard English capitalization, punctuation, and spelling when writing.
   a. Observe hyphenation conventions.
   b. Spell correctly.
   c. Correctly use punctuation, capitalization, and spelling in legible work.
	You will correctly use the conventions of standard English capitalization, punctuation, and spelling, including
	   a. hyphens
	   b. spelling
	   c. legible writing

Language Standards, Grades 11–12 Students, continued

Common Core State Standards	What It Means to You
KNOWLEDGE OF LANGUAGE	
3. Apply knowledge of language to understand how language functions in different contexts, to make effective choices for meaning or style, and to comprehend more fully when reading or listening.	You will apply your knowledge of language in different contexts to guide choices in your own writing and speaking by
a. Vary syntax for effect, consulting references (e.g., Tufte's *Artful Sentences*) for guidance as needed; apply an understanding of syntax to the study of complex texts when reading.	**a.** using appropriate references for guidance to vary your syntax and to understand syntax in complex texts
VOCABULARY ACQUISITION AND USE	
4. Determine or clarify the meaning of unknown and multiple-meaning words and phrases based on grades 11–12 reading and content, choosing flexibly from a range of strategies.	You will understand the meaning of grade-level appropriate words and phrases by
a. Use context (e.g., the overall meaning of a sentence, paragraph, or text; a word's position or function in a sentence) as a clue to the meaning of a word or phrase.	**a.** using context clues
b. Identify and correctly use patterns of word changes that indicate different meanings or parts of speech (e.g., *conceive, conception, conceivable*).	**b.** applying various forms of words according to meaning or part of speech
c. Consult general and specialized reference materials (e.g., dictionaries, glossaries, thesauruses), both print and digital, to find the pronunciation of a word or determine or clarify its precise meaning, its part of speech, its etymology, or its standard usage.	**c.** using reference materials to determine and clarify word meaning, part of speech, etymology, and standard usage
d. Verify the preliminary determination of the meaning of a word or phrase (e.g., by checking the inferred meaning in context or in a dictionary).	**d.** inferring and verifying the meanings of words in context

Language Standards, Grades 11–12 Students, continued

Common Core State Standards	What It Means to You
VOCABULARY ACQUISITION AND USE	

5. Demonstrate understanding of figurative language, word relationships, and nuances in word meanings.
  a. Interpret figures of speech (e.g., hyperbole, paradox) in context and analyze their role in the text.
  b. Analyze nuances in the meaning of words with similar denotations.
	You will understand figurative language, word relationships, and slight differences in word meanings by
	  a. interpreting figures of speech in context
	
	  b. analyzing slight differences in the meanings of similar words

6. Acquire and use accurately general academic and domain-specific words and phrases, sufficient for reading, writing, speaking, and listening at the college and career readiness level; demonstrate independence in gathering vocabulary knowledge when considering a word or phrase important to comprehension or expression.	You will develop and use a range of vocabulary at the college and career readiness level and will demonstrate that you can successfully acquire new vocabulary independently.

Coming to America

❝ [In America] individuals of all nations are melted
into a new race … whose labors … will one day
cause great changes in the world. ❞

— Michel-Guillaume Jean de Crèvecoeur

Coming to America

In this collection, you will explore how America has always been a land shaped by immigrants.

hmhfyi.com

COLLECTION

PERFORMANCE TASK Preview

At the end of this collection, you will have the opportunity to complete a task:

- Write an argument about why people come to America or what significant changes occur when they do.

ACADEMIC VOCABULARY

Study the words and their definitions in the chart below. You will use these words as you discuss and write about the texts in this collection.

Word	Definition	Related Forms
adapt (ə-dăpt´) *v.*	to make something suitable for a particular situation; to adjust to an environment	adaptable, adaptability, adaptation
coherent (kō-hîr´ənt) *adj.*	holding together in an orderly, logical, or consistent way	cohere, coherence, coherently, cohesive
device (dĭ-vīs´) *n.*	a literary technique used to achieve a certain effect; something made for a specific purpose	devise
displace (dĭs-plās´) *v.*	to move or force from one place or position to another	displaceable, displacement
dynamic (dī-năm´ĭk) *adj.*	characterized by change, movement, or activity	dynamics, dynamically, dynamism, dynamo

VIDEO

COMMON CORE ELACC11-12RI3,
ELACC11-12RI7,
ELACC11-12RI10

Exploration and Settlement

Although the Portuguese ushered in the age of European exploration in the early 1400s, Spain, England, and France were the countries that explored and settled most of the Americas. These Europeans encountered a rich variety of native cultures in the New World, creating a mixture of cultures that has shaped American history.

EUROPEAN CONTACT WITH NORTH AMERICA Christopher Columbus's voyage to the Caribbean in 1492 marked the beginning of contact between Europeans and Native Americans. Soon, explorers, fishermen, and traders began making contact from Canada down through South America. When the Europeans first arrived, millions of Native Americans were living on the land, in small villages and in large cities such as the Aztec capital of Tenochtitlán, the site of present-day Mexico City. People had been living in the Americas for many thousands of years, adapting to its diverse environments. At first, Native Americans were generally helpful to the Europeans. Before long, however, it became clear that the newcomers intended to take control of their land. And the firearms were not their most dangerous weapons: the settlers brought new diseases that killed millions.

ENGLISH SETTLEMENTS Although the English were not the first Europeans to explore or colonize North America, their settlements along the Eastern seaboard became the thirteen colonies that later formed the United States. England relied on private trading companies to establish a presence in North America. One of these groups, the Virginia Company, established the first permanent English settlement in Jamestown, Virginia, in 1607. Those who settled in New England were Puritans, Protestant reformers who wanted to "purify" the Church of England. Their efforts met with little success, and some Puritans wanted to separate completely from the English Church. Among them was William Bradford, who helped organize the voyage of the *Mayflower*, bringing nearly a hundred people to Massachusetts in 1620. John Winthrop brought others to Boston in 1630 to set up what he called "a City upon a Hill," a godly society that would be an ideal for others to follow. The Puritans' religious beliefs influenced all aspects of their lives, and the values of hard work, thrift, and responsibility led to thriving settlements and financial success.

1513
Balboa "discovers" the
Pacific Ocean in Panama.

1539–41
De Soto explores the region
between Florida and the
Mississippi River.

1400

1492
Columbus lands at
Hispaniola in the
Caribbean.

1521
Cortés conquers the
Aztecs at Tenochtitlán
(Mexico City).

Exploration and Settlement   **3**

SPAIN AND FRANCE IN NORTH AMERICA The territory of New Spain covered all the land under Spanish control north of the Isthmus of Panama and included territory in what became the southeastern and southwestern United States, including California. The Spanish wanted to gain glory and riches in the New World and to convert the natives to Christianity. Spanish settlements were strongest in central Mexico, where the government was located. However, the Spanish also established settlements at St. Augustine, Santa Fe, and the Caribbean, as well as a large number of missions and forts throughout the frontier regions of North America. Spanish language and culture has had a lasting impact in the region. But the Spanish desire to exploit the riches of their territories through mining and ranching led to forced labor and many other abuses of Native Americans.

After early fishing expeditions beginning in the 1520s, France established settlements along the St. Lawrence River in eastern Canada in the early 1600s. French settlers were far fewer than English or Spanish settlers in the Americas. Many of the French who came were trappers and fur traders. In 1673, French explorers and missionaries became the first Europeans to explore the upper Mississippi River. In 1682, the French explored all the way down to the Gulf of Mexico, claiming the entire river valley for King Louis XIV and naming it Louisiana. Because the French had fewer permanent settlers, they were less likely to come into conflict with Native Americans than the Spanish or English were.

EARLY AMERICAN LITERATURE Although few Native American cultures employed written language, all possessed strong oral cultures and a rich tradition of storytelling. Histories, myths, and legends had been passed down for thousands of years, but many of them were lost as people died from European disease and conquest. Some of these old stories have survived, and contemporary Native American writers, like Joy Harjo, often weave them into their writing. Much of what we know about Native American societies comes from the observations of Europeans, who recorded their experiences in America in diaries, letters, and reports back home, beginning with the journals of Christopher Columbus. William Bradford's *Of Plymouth Plantation* records the early years of the Plymouth colony and its relations with the Indians. Bradford and other Puritan writers were motivated by their beliefs about their role in God's plan. Their writings included historical narratives, sermons, and poems written in a generally plain style.

1620
Mayflower Pilgrims
found Plymouth colony
in Massachusetts.

1700

1607
First permanent English
settlement is founded in
Jamestown, Virginia.

1676
English settlers defeat
Native Americans in King
Philip's War.

1682
France claims the
Mississippi River Valley and
names it Louisiana.

Background *Born in England in 1590,* **William Bradford** *became involved in the Protestant Reformation while still a boy. He joined the Puritans, reformers who wanted to purify the Church of England and eventually separate from it. With other Puritans, he migrated to Holland in search of religious freedom. He helped organize the journey on the* Mayflower *in 1620 that brought about 100 people—half of them his fellow "Pilgrims"—to the New World. His* History of Plymouth Plantation, 1620–1647 *describes this journey and provides a glimpse of the settlers' life in what became New England.*

from
Of Plymouth Plantation

Historical Account by William Bradford

AS YOU READ Pay attention to how Bradford describes the settlers' first encounters with Native Americans.

CHAPTER IX

Of their Voyage, and how they Passed the Sea; and of their Safe Arrival at Cape Cod

September 6 These troubles[1] being blown over, and now all being compact together in one ship, they put to sea again with a prosperous wind, which continued **divers** days together, which was some encouragement unto them; yet, according to the usual manner, many were afflicted with seasickness. And I may not omit here a special work of God's providence. There was a proud and very profane young man, one of the seamen, of a lusty,[2] able body, which made him the more haughty; he would always be condemning the poor people in their sickness and cursing them daily with grievous execrations;[3]

10 and did not let to tell them that he hoped to help to cast half of them

divers
(dī´vərz) *adj.*
numerous.

---

[1] **troubles:** the transfer of passengers to the Mayflower after one of the other ships became unseaworthy.
[2] **lusty:** energetic; robust.
[3] **execrations:** angry words; curses.

overboard before they came to their journey's end, and to make merry with what they had; and if he were by any gently reproved,[4] he would curse and swear most bitterly. But it pleased God before they came half seas over, to smite this young man with a grievous disease, of which he died in a desperate manner, and so was himself the first that was thrown overboard. Thus his curses light on his own head, and it was an astonishment to all his fellows for they noted it to be the just hand of God upon him.

After they had enjoyed fair winds and weather for a season, they were encountered many times with cross winds and met with many fierce storms with which the ship was shroudly[5] shaken, and her upper works made very leaky; and one of the main beams in the midships was bowed and cracked, which put them in some fear that the ship could not be able to perform the voyage. So some of the chief of the company, perceiving the mariners to fear the sufficiency of the ship as appeared by their mutterings, they entered into serious consultation with the master and other officers of the ship, to consider in time of the danger, and rather to return than to cast themselves into a desperate and inevitable peril. And truly there was great distraction and difference of opinion amongst the mariners themselves; fain[6] would they do what could be done for their wages' sake (being now near half the seas over) and on the other hand they were loath[7] to hazard their lives too desperately. But in examining of all opinions, the master and others affirmed they knew the ship to be strong and firm under water; and for the buckling of the main beam, there was a great iron screw the passengers brought out of Holland, which would raise the beam into his place; the which being done, the carpenter and master affirmed that with a post put under it, set firm in the lower deck and otherways bound, he would make it sufficient. And as for the decks and upper works, they would caulk them as well as they could, and though with the working of the ship they would not long keep staunch,[8] yet there would otherwise be no great danger, if they did not overpress her with sails. So they committed themselves to the will of God and resolved to proceed.

In **sundry** of these storms the winds were so fierce and the seas so high, as they could not bear a knot of sail, but were forced to hull[9] for divers days together. And in one of them, as they thus lay at hull in a mighty storm, a lusty young man called John Howland, coming upon some occasion above the gratings was, with a seele[10] of the ship, thrown into sea; but it pleased God that he caught hold of the topsail

sundry
(sŭn´drē) *adj.* various or assorted.

---

[4] **reproved:** reprimanded.

[5] **shroudly:** shrewdly, used here in its archaic sense of "wickedly."

[6] **fain:** archaic for "gladly."

[7] **loath:** reluctant.

[8] **staunch:** watertight.

[9] **hull:** to float without using the sails.

[10] **seele:** sudden lurch to one side.

halyards[11] which hung overboard and ran out at length. Yet he held his hold (though he was sundry fathoms under water) till he was hauled up by the same rope to the brim of the water, and then with a boat hook and other means got into the ship again and his life saved. And though he was something ill with it, yet he lived many years after and became a profitable member both in church and commonwealth. In all this voyage there died but one of the passengers, which was William Butten, a youth, servant to Samuel Fuller, when they drew near the coast.

60   But to omit other things (that I may be brief) after long beating at sea they fell with that land which is called Cape Cod;[12] the which being made and certainly known to be it, they were not a little joyful. After some deliberation had amongst themselves and with the master of the ship, they tacked about and resolved to stand for the southward (the wind and weather being fair) to find some place about Hudson's River[13] for their habitation. But after they had sailed that course about

---

[11]**halyards:** ropes for raising a sail.

[12]**Cape Cod:** They sighted Cape Cod in present-day Massachusetts at daybreak on November 9, 1620.

[13]**Hudson's River:** They were trying to reach Manhattan Island. Henry Hudson had made his voyage in 1609 and had claimed the area for the Dutch, but the English did not recognize the Dutch claim.

half the day, they fell amongst dangerous shoals and roaring breakers, and they were so far entangled therewith as they conceived themselves in great danger; and the wind shrinking upon them withal, they resolved to bear up again for the Cape and thought themselves happy to get out of those dangers before night overtook them, as by God's good providence they did. And the next day they got into the Cape Harbor[14] where they rid in safety....

Being thus arrived in a good harbor, and brought safe to land, they fell upon their knees and blessed the God of Heaven who had brought them over the vast and furious ocean, and delivered them from all the perils and miseries thereof, again to set their feet on the firm and stable earth, their proper element. And no marvel if they were thus joyful, seeing wise Seneca was so affected with sailing a few miles on the coast of his own Italy, as he affirmed, that he had rather remain twenty years on his way by land than pass by sea to any place in a short time, so tedious and dreadful was the same unto him.

But here I cannot but stay and make a pause, and stand half amazed at this poor people's present condition; and so I think will the reader, too, when he well considers the same. Being thus passed the vast ocean, and a sea of troubles before in their preparation (as may be remembered by that which went before), they had now no friends to welcome them nor inns to entertain or refresh their weatherbeaten bodies; no houses or much less towns to repair to, to seek for **succour**. It is recorded in Scripture[15] as a mercy to the Apostle and his shipwrecked company, that the barbarians showed them no small kindness in refreshing them, but these savage barbarians, when they met with them (as after will appear) were readier to fill their sides full of arrows than otherwise. And for the season it was winter, and they that know the winters of that country know them to be sharp and violent, and subject to cruel and fierce storms, dangerous to travel to known places, much more to search an unknown coast. Besides, what could they see but a hideous and desolate wilderness, full of wild beasts and wild men—and what multitudes there might be of them they knew not. Neither could they, as it were, go up to the top of Pisgah[16] to view from this wilderness a more goodly country to feed their hopes; for which way soever they turned their eyes (save upward to the heavens) they could have little solace or content in respect of any outward objects. For summer being done, all things stand upon them with a weatherbeaten face, and the whole country, full of woods and thickets, represented a wild and savage hue. If they looked behind them, there was the mighty ocean which they had passed and was now as a main bar and gulf to separate them from all the civil parts of the world. . . .

succour
(sŭk´ər) *n.* help and comfort.

---

[14] **Cape Harbor:** now called Provincetown Harbor.

[15] **Scripture:** In the Acts of the Apostles (Chapter 28), shipwrecked Christians were helped by the "barbarous people" of Malta.

[16] **Pisgah:** mountain from which Moses first viewed the Promised Land.

CHAPTER X

Showing How they Sought out a place of Habitation; and What Befell them Thereabout

110   Being thus arrived at Cape Cod the 11th of November, and necessity calling them to look out a place for habitation (as well as the master's and mariners' importunity[17]); they having brought a large shallop[18] with them out of England, stowed in quarters in the ship, they now got her out and set their carpenters to work to trim her up; but being much bruised and shattered in the ship with foul weather, they saw she would be long in mending. Whereupon a few of them **tendered** themselves to go by land and discover those nearest places, whilst the shallop was in mending; and the rather because as they went into that harbor there seemed to be an opening some two or three
120   leagues off, which the master judged to be a river. It was conceived there might be some danger in the attempt, yet seeing them resolute[19], they were permitted to go, being sixteen of them well armed under the conduct of Captain Standish, having such instructions given them as was thought meet.[20]

tender
(tĕn´dər) *v.* to offer or present.

They set forth the 15th of November; and when they had marched about the space of a mile by the seaside, they espied[21] five or six persons with a dog coming towards them, who were savages; but they fled from them and ran up into the woods, and the English followed them, partly to see if they could speak with them, and partly
130   to discover if there might not be more of them lying in ambush. But the Indians seeing themselves thus followed, they again forsook[22] the woods and ran away on the sands as hard as they could, so as they could not come near them but followed them by the track of their feet sundry miles and saw that they had come the same way. So, night coming on, they made their **rendezvous** and set out their **sentinels**, and rested in quiet that night; and the next morning followed their track till they had headed a great creek and so left the sands, and turned another way into the woods. But they still followed them by guess, hoping to find their dwellings; but they soon lost both them and
140   themselves, falling into such thickets as were ready to tear their clothes and armor in pieces; but were most distressed for want of drink. But at length they found water and refreshed themselves, being the first New England water they drunk of, and was now in great thirst as pleasant unto them as wine or beer had been in foretimes.

rendezvous
(rän´dā-voo´) *n.* meeting place.

sentinel
(sĕn´tə-nəl) *n.* a lookout person or guard.

---

[17]**importunity:** urgent demand.
[18]**shallop:** a heavy sailboat with two masts.
[19]**resolute:** determined.
[20]**meet:** appropriate.
[21]**espied:** saw for a brief moment; glimpsed.
[22]**forsook:** left or abandoned.

Afterwards they directed their course to come to the other shore, for they knew it was a neck of land they were to cross over, and so at length got to the seaside and marched to this supposed river, and by the way found a pond of clear, fresh water, and shortly after a good quantity of clear ground where the Indians had formerly set corn, and some of their graves. And proceeding further they saw new stubble where corn had been set the same year; also they found where lately a house had been, where some planks and a great kettle was remaining, and heaps of sand newly paddled with their hands. Which, they digging up, found in them divers fair Indian baskets filled with corn, and some in ears, fair and good, of divers colours, which seemed to them a very goodly sight (having never seen any such before). This was near the place of that supposed river they came to seek, unto which they went and found it to open itself into two arms with a high cliff of sand in the entrance but more like to be creeks of salt water than any fresh, for aught they saw; and that there was good harborage for their shallop, leaving it further to be discovered by their shallop, when she was ready. So, their time limited them being expired, they returned to the ship lest they should be in fear of their safety; and took with them part of the corn and buried up the rest. And so, like the men from Eshcol, carried with them of the fruits of the land and showed their brethren;[23] of which, and their return, they were marvelously glad and their hearts encouraged.

After this, the shallop being got ready, they set out again for the better discovery of this place, and the master of the ship desired to go himself. So there went some thirty men but found it to be no harbor for ships but only for boats. There was also found two of their houses covered with mats, and sundry of their implements in them, but the people were run away and could not be seen. Also there was found more of their corn and of their beans of various colours; the corn and beans they brought away, purposing to give them full satisfaction when they should meet with any of them as, about some six months afterward they did, to their good content.

And here is to be noted a special providence of God, and a great mercy to this poor people, that here they got seed to plant them corn the next year, or else they might have starved, for they had none nor any likelihood to get any till the season had been past, as the sequel did manifest. Neither is it likely they had had this, if the first voyage had not been made, for the ground was now all covered with snow and hard frozen; but the Lord is never wanting unto His in their greatest needs; let His holy name have all the praise.

The month of November being spent in these affairs, and much foul weather falling in, the 6th of December they sent out their shallop again with ten of their principal men and some seamen, upon

---

[23] **Eshcol . . . their brethren:** In the biblical book of Numbers (Chapter 13), Moses sends spies to explore the Promised Land. They return from the Valley of Eshcol with grapes and other fruit.

further discovery, intending to **circulate** that deep bay of Cape Cod.
190 The weather was very cold and it froze so hard as the spray of the sea
lighting on their coats, they were as if they had been glazed. Yet that
night betimes they got down into the bottom of the bay, and as they
drew near the shore they saw some ten or twelve Indians very busy
about something. They landed about a league or two from them,
and had much ado to put ashore anywhere—it lay so full of flats.
Being landed, it grew late and they made themselves a barricado[24]
with logs and boughs as well as they could in the time, and set out
their sentinel and betook them to rest, and saw the smoke of the fire
the savages made that night. When morning was come they divided
200 their company, some to coast along the shore in the boat, and the rest
marched through the woods to see the land, if any fit place might be
for their dwelling. They came also to the place where they saw the
Indians the night before, and found they had been cutting up a great
fish like a grampus,[25] being some two inches thick of fat like a hog,
some pieces whereof they had left by the way. And the shallop found
two more of these fishes dead on the sands, a thing usual after storms
in that place, by reason of the great flats of sand that lie off.

So they ranged up and down all that day, but found no people,
nor any place they liked. When the sun grew low, they hasted out of
210 the woods to meet with their shallop, to whom they made signs to
come to them into a creek hard by, the which they did at high water;
of which they were very glad, for they had not seen each other all that
day since the morning. So they made them a barricado as usually they
did every night, with logs, stakes and thick pine boughs, the height of
a man, leaving it open to leeward, partly to shelter them from the cold
and wind (making their fire in the middle and lying round about it)
and partly to defend them from any sudden assaults of the savages, if
they should surround them; so being very weary, they betook them
to rest. But about midnight they heard a hideous and great cry, and
220 their sentinel called "Arm! arm!" So they bestirred them and stood to
their arms and shot off a couple of muskets, and then the noise ceased.
They concluded it was a company of wolves or such like wild beasts,
for one of the seamen told them he had often heard such a noise in
Newfoundland.

So they rested till about five of the clock in the morning; for the
tide, and their purpose to go from thence, made them be stirring
betimes. So after prayer they prepared for breakfast, and it being day
dawning it was thought best to be carrying things down to the boat.
But some said it was not best to carry the arms down, others said they
230 would be the readier, for they had lapped them up in their coats from
the dew; but some three or four would not carry theirs till they went

---

[24]**barricado:** a structure quickly assembled to keep enemies out; archaic form of "barricade."

[25]**grampus:** dolphin.

circulate
(sûr´kyə-lāt´) *v.*
to move or travel
around or in a circular
path.

themselves. Yet as it fell out, the water being not high enough, they laid them down on the bank side and came up to breakfast.

But presently, all on the sudden, they heard a great and strange cry, which they knew to be the same voices they heard in the night, though they varied their notes; and one of their company being abroad came running in and cried, "Men, Indians! Indians!" And withal,[26] their arrows came flying amongst them. Their men ran with all speed to recover their arms, as by the good providence of God they did.

240   In the meantime, of those that were there ready, two muskets were discharged at them, and two more stood ready in the entrance of their rendezvous but were commanded not to shoot till they could take full aim at them. And the other two charged again with all speed, for there were only four had arms there, and defended the barricado, which was first assaulted. The cry of the Indians was dreadful, especially when they saw their men run out of the rendezvous toward the shallop to recover their arms, the Indians wheeling about upon them. But some running out with coats of mail on, and cutlasses in their hands, they soon got their arms and let fly amongst them and quickly stopped

250   their violence. Yet there was a lusty man, and no less valiant, stood behind a tree within half a musket shot, and let his arrows fly at them; he was seen [to] shoot three arrows, which were all avoided. He stood three shots of a musket, till one taking full aim at him and made the bark or splinters of the tree fly about his ears, after which he gave an extraordinary shriek and away they went, all of them. They left some to keep the shallop and followed them about a quarter of a mile and shouted once or twice, and shot off two or three pieces, and so returned. This they did that they might conceive that they were not afraid of them or any way discouraged.

260   Thus it pleased God to vanquish their enemies and give them deliverance; and by His special providence so to dispose that not any one of them were either hurt or hit, though their arrows came close by them and on every side [of] them; and sundry of their coats, which hung up in the barricado, were shot through and through. Afterwards they gave God solemn thanks and praise for their deliverance, and gathered up a bundle of their arrows and sent them into England afterward by the master of the ship, and called that place the First Encounter.

---

[26]**withal:** immediately after that.

THE SECOND BOOK

The rest of this history (if God give me life and opportunity) I
270 shall, for brevity's sake, handle by way of annals, noting only the
heads of principal things, and passages as they fell in order of time,
and may seem to be profitable to know or to make use of. And this
may be as the Second Book.

CHAPTER XI

The Remainder of Anno 1620

[The Mayflower Compact]

I shall a little return back, and begin with a combination made
by them before they came ashore; being the first foundation of their
government in this place. Occasioned partly by the discontented and
mutinous[27] speeches that some of the strangers amongst them had let
fall from them in the ship: That when they came ashore they would
use their own liberty, for none had power to command them, the
280 **patent** they had being for Virginia and not for New England, which
belonged to another government, with which the Virginia Company
had nothing to do. And partly that such an act by them done, this their
condition considered, might be as firm as any patent, and in some
respects more sure.

The form was as followeth:
In the Name of God, Amen.

We whose names are underwritten, the loyal subjects of
our dread Sovereign Lord King James, by the Grace of God
of Great Britain, France, and Ireland King, Defender of the
290 Faith, etc.

Having undertaken, for the Glory of God and
advancement of the Christian Faith and Honour of our
King and Country, a Voyage to plant the First Colony in the
Northern Parts of Virginia, do by these presents solemnly
and mutually in the presence of God and one of another,
Covenant and Combine ourselves together into a Civil
Body Politic, for our better ordering and preservation and
furtherance of the ends aforesaid; and by virtue hereof
to enact, constitute and frame such just and equal Laws,
300 Ordinances, Acts, Constitutions and Offices, from time
to time, as shall be thought most meet and convenient for
the general good of the Colony, unto which we promise all
due submission and obedience. In witness whereof we have
hereunder subscribed our names at Cape Cod, the 11th of

patent
(păt´nt) *n.* an official
document granting
ownership.

---

[27]**mutinous:** rebellious.

November, in the year of the reign of our Sovereign Lord King James, of England, France and Ireland the eighteenth, and of Scotland the fifty-fourth. Anno Domini 1620.

After this they chose, or rather confirmed, Mr. John Carver (a man godly and well approved amongst them) their Governor for that 310 year. And after they had provided a place for their goods, or common store (which were long in unlading for want of boats, foulness of the winter weather and sickness of divers) and begun some small cottages for their habitation; as time would admit, they met and consulted of laws and orders, both for their civil and military government as the necessity of their condition did require, still adding thereunto as urgent occasion in several times, and as cases did require.

> **"When they came ashore they would use their own liberty, for none had power to command them."**

In these hard and difficult beginnings they found some discontents and murmurings arise amongst some, and mutinous speeches and carriages in other; but they were soon quelled and 320 overcome by the wisdom, patience, and just and equal carriage of things, by the Governor and better part, which clave faithfully together in the main.

[The Starving Time]

But that which was most sad and lamentable was, that in two or three months' time half of their company died, especially in January and February, being the depth of winter, and wanting houses and other comforts; being infected with the scurvy[28] and other diseases which this long voyage and their inaccommodate condition had brought upon them. So as there died some times two or three of a day in the foresaid time, that of 100 and odd persons, scarce fifty

---

[28] **scurvy:** a disease caused by a lack of vitamin C in the diet.

330 remained. And of these, in the time of most distress, there was but
six or seven sound persons who to their great commendations, be it
spoken, spared no pains night nor day, but with abundance of toil
and hazard of their own health, fetched them wood, made them
fires, dressed them meat, made their beds, washed their loathsome[29]
clothes, clothed and unclothed them. In a word, did all the homely and
necessary offices for them which dainty and queasy stomachs cannot
endure to hear named; and all this willingly and cheerfully, without
any grudging in the least, showing herein their true love unto their
friends and brethren; a rare example and worthy to be remembered.

340 Two of these seven were Mr. William Brewster, their reverend Elder,
and Myles Standish, their Captain and military commander, unto
whom myself and many others were much beholden in our low and
sick condition. And yet the Lord so upheld these persons as in this
general calamity they were not at all infected either with sickness or
lameness. . . .

[Indian Relations]

All this while the Indians came skulking about them, and would
sometimes show themselves aloof off, but when any approached near
them, they would run away; and once they stole away their tools
where they had been at work and were gone to dinner. But about

350 the 16th of March, a certain Indian came boldly amongst them and
spoke to them in broken English, which they could well understand
but marveled at it. At length they understood by discourse with him,
that he was not of these parts, but belonged to the eastern parts where
some English ships came to fish, with whom he was acquainted and
could name sundry of them by their names, amongst whom he had
got his language. He became profitable to them in acquainting them
with many things concerning the state of the country in the east
parts where he lived, which was afterwards profitable unto them; as
also of the people here, of their names, number and strength, of their

360 situation and distance from this place, and who was chief amongst
them. His name was Samoset. He told them also of another Indian
whose name was Squanto, a native of this place, who had been in
England and could speak better English than himself.

Being, after some time of entertainment and gifts dismissed, a
while after he came again, and five more with him, and they brought
again all the tools that were stolen away before, and made way for the
coming of their great Sachem,[30] called Massasoit. Who, about four or
five days after, came with the chief of his friends and other attendance,
with the aforesaid Squanto. With whom, after friendly entertainment

370 and some gifts given him, they made a peace with him (which hath
now continued this 24 years) in these terms:

---

[29]**loathsome:** offensive or disgusting.

[30]**Sachem:** chief.

1. That neither he nor any of his should injure or do hurt to any of their people.
2. That if any of his did hurt to any of theirs, he should send the offender, that they might punish him.
3. That if anything were taken away from any of theirs, he should cause it to be restored; and they should do the like to his.
4. If any did unjustly war against him, they would aid him; if any did war against them, he should aid them.
5. He should send to his neighbours confederates[31] to certify them of this, that they might not wrong them, but might be likewise comprised in the conditions of peace.
6. That when their men came to them, they should leave their bows and arrows behind them.

380

---

[31] **confederates:** allies; persons who share a common purpose.

After these things he returned to his place called Sowams, some 40 miles from this place, but Squanto continued with them and was their interpreter and was a special instrument sent of God for their good beyond their expectation. He directed them how to set their corn, where to take fish, and to procure other commodities, and was also their pilot to bring them to unknown places for their profit, and never left them till he died. He was a native of this place, and scarce any left alive besides himself. He was carried away with divers others by one Hunt, a master of a ship, who thought to sell them for slaves in Spain. But he got away for England and was entertained by a merchant in London, and employed to Newfoundland and other parts, and lastly brought hither into these parts by one Mr. Dermer, a gentleman employed by Sir Ferdinando Gorges and others for discovery and other designs in these parts. . . .

[First Thanksgiving]

They began now to gather in the small harvest they had, and to fit up their houses and dwellings against winter, being all well recovered in health and strength and had all things in good plenty. For as some were thus employed in affairs abroad, others were exercised in fishing, about cod and bass and other fish, of which they took good store, of which every family had their portion. All the summer there was no want; and now began to come in store of fowl, as winter approached, of which this place did abound when they came first (but afterward decreased by degrees). And besides waterfowl there was great store of wild turkeys, of which they took many, besides venison, etc. Besides they had about a peck a meal a week to a person, or now since harvest, Indian corn to that proportion. Which made many afterwards write so largely of their plenty here to their friends in England, which were not feigned but true reports.[32]

---

[32] **reports:** Although the specific day of the Plymouth colonists' first Thanksgiving is not known, it occurred in the fall of 1621. For three days, Massasoit and almost a hundred of his men joined the Pilgrims for feasts and games.

COLLABORATIVE DISCUSSION How did the relationship between the English and the Native Americans change over time? With a partner, discuss how the relationships evolved and why they developed as they did. Cite specific textual evidence from the narrative to support your ideas.

Determine Central Ideas

The main or **central ideas** of a text are the most important ideas that the author communicates. Sometimes an author states a central idea directly in the introduction or conclusion to a text. Often, however, the central ideas are implied. In that case, readers must look at the details the author presents and **infer,** or draw logical conclusions about, the central ideas based on those details. Important details should be closely related to the central ideas and provide support for them. Headings can also provide clues to the central ideas because they hint at the topic of each section of text.

In understanding a long, complex text like *Of Plymouth Plantation*, it is often helpful to **paraphrase** by restating the text in your own words. Determining the central idea of each paragraph or section of the text will then allow you to write an objective summary that conveys the central ideas of the text as a whole.

Analyze Foundational Texts: Historical Accounts

Of Plymouth Plantation is a **historical account**—it tells a true story about events that happened in the past. The events are told mainly in chronological order, or the order in which they happened. The text is also a **primary source,** because the author, William Bradford, observed the events personally. Bradford's vivid details and chronological structure give readers the sense that they are experiencing events right along with the Plymouth settlers.

Bradford's narrative is a **foundational text** because of its great significance in U.S. history. It provides a rare first-hand account of experiences from the early seventeenth century, when Europeans were establishing some of their first permanent settlements in North America. You can better understand Bradford's account by looking at the following elements.

Purposes	Themes	Rhetorical Features
Purpose is the reason why an author writes a particular text. The purpose might be to inform, to entertain, to express one's beliefs or feelings, or to persuade. Many texts have more than one of these purposes. In order to craft a text that will achieve a particular purpose, an author must consider his or her audience, or the people who will read the work.	A **theme** is a central idea or message about life that the author wants to communicate. To identify themes in *Of Plymouth Plantation,* think about the details that Bradford chooses to include. What impression of the settlers and their activities do these details create? Also look for ideas that are emphasized or repeated.	**Rhetorical features** include all the methods a writer uses to communicate ideas to readers. Literary devices such as **repetition** (repeating a word, phrase, or idea) and allusions are examples of rhetorical features. An **allusion** is a reference to something that the author expects will be familiar to readers, for example, the Bible for Bradford's audience.

Analyzing the Text

COMMON CORE

ELACC11-12RI1,
ELACC11-12RI2,
ELACC11-12RI5,
ELACC11-12RI9,
ELACC11-12W3d

Cite Text Evidence   Support your responses with evidence from the selection.

1. **Summarize** Review the last paragraph of Chapter IX (lines 83–109). What is the central idea that Bradford communicates in this paragraph?

2. **Cite Evidence** Locate and analyze two examples of Bradford's use of allusions to the Bible and of references to God's intervention in events. What purpose might these devices serve in his account?

3. **Connect** How might Squanto's experiences with the English (lines 389–399) relate to the Pilgrims' first encounter with the Indians (lines 125–144)? What do the details in these passages tell you about the ways in which early European settlers and Indians made contact with one another?

4. **Analyze** In what way does Bradford change the structure of his narrative at the beginning of Chapter XI? Why might he have chosen to make this change? What effect does this change have on the narrative?

5. **Analyze** What does the Mayflower Compact explicitly say? What does it suggest through its careful **diction,** or word choice, and use of imagery?

6. **Evaluate** Paraphrase the terms of the treaty between Massasoit and the Pilgrims (lines 372–385). Then evaluate whether the treaty is equally fair to both sides.

7. **Analyze** Which beliefs most contributed to the colonists' willingness to face hardships together? What passages best reveal those beliefs?

8. **Synthesize** What is the overall central idea of Bradford's account? How does this reflect his purpose in writing it?

PERFORMANCE TASK

Writing Activity: Journal Entry and Letter Bradford's account describes how the Pilgrims adapted to life in New England. Explore that experience in two brief writing tasks.

1. Choose one event that Bradford describes and write a journal entry in the character of one of the other English participants in the event. Consider how a personal journal might be different from Bradford's narrative written for publication.

2. In the character of one of the Pilgrims who survived the first year in New England, write a letter to someone back in England describing your current situation and how it has improved.

Base both pieces of writing on details from the text to create a coherent narrative. As much as possible, mirror the seventeenth-century style that Bradford uses.

Critical Vocabulary

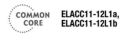 COMMON CORE   ELACC11-12L1a, ELACC11-12L1b

divers	sundry	succour	tender
rendezvous	sentinel	circulate	patent

Practice and Apply Choose the alternative in each sentence that best relates to the Critical Vocabulary word and explain your choice.

1. If you and your friends have **divers** opinions about what to eat, is it easy or difficult to choose a restaurant?

2. If someone offered you **succour,** would you be angry or grateful?

3. If you **tender** your resignation, do you quit your job or are you fired?

4. Would **sundry** pairs of shoes be all the same or different?

5. Is a **rendezvous** more like a plan to go with friends to a specific movie or an accidental meeting with them at the mall?

6. Are **sentinels** more like security guards or construction workers?

7. If you **circulate** a lake in a boat, do you travel along the shore or across the middle?

8. Did the *Mayflower* passengers' **patent** decide where they would live or what they would eat?

Vocabulary Strategy: Archaic Vocabulary

Of Plymouth Plantation contains many examples of **archaic vocabulary**—words that are no longer commonly used. The Critical Vocabulary word *divers,* for example, was common until the end of the 17th century but has now been almost completely replaced by *diverse*. English usage and vocabulary have changed a great deal over time. Here are some strategies you can use to help understand archaic vocabulary.

- Notice if the word is similar to a current, familiar word and try substituting the current word to make a meaningful sentence.
- Use context clues as much as possible when reading a selection that contains archaic vocabulary. Don't stop at every unfamiliar word, but read on to see if you can understand the whole sentence or paragraph.
- Look up archaic words in a dictionary. Many dictionaries include notes for archaic words or for archaic meanings of familiar words; this information is often at the end of an entry and is labeled with the word *archaic* or *obsolete*.

Practice and Apply Use the strategies to determine the meaning of the following archaic vocabulary from *Of Plymouth Plantation*.

1. foretimes (line 144)

2. betimes (line 192)

3. betook (line 198)

4. bestirred (line 220)

5. clave (line 321)

Language and Style: Active and Passive Voice

COMMON CORE ELACC11-12L3a

The **voice** of a verb tells whether its subject performs or receives the verb's action. If the subject performs the action, the verb is in the **active voice:** *Liam mailed the letter.* If the subject receives the action, the verb is in the **passive voice:** *The letter was mailed.* In Bradford's writing, the Pilgrims or the Indians are most often active subjects who perform the action. Sometimes, however, the subject of a sentence or clause receives the action.

Consider this example from the narrative.

> **But it pleased God before they came half seas over, to smite this young man with a grievous disease, of which he died in a desperate manner, and so was himself the first that was thrown overboard. (lines 13–16)**

Note how Bradford combines the active and passive voice in this sentence. Almost all of the clauses in this complex sentence are in the active voice ("it pleased God . . . to smite," "they came half seas over," and "he died"). In the final clause, however, Bradford switches to the passive voice: "[he] was himself the first that *was thrown* overboard." Bradford's style choice obscures who or what exactly throws the "profane young man" overboard.

Although it's fairly clear from context that his fellow passengers threw the body overboard, shifting to the passive voice has two effects. First, following right after a description of God's wrath, it suggests that God is ultimately responsible. Second, it allows Bradford to downplay the idea of formerly-abused passengers tossing the man's body into the open ocean. Choosing the active or passive voice, therefore, is a matter of deciding what you want to emphasize as a writer: Do you want to stress who did something? Or do you want, instead, to focus on the fact that something happened?

This chart shows some reasons you may choose to use the passive voice.

Reason	Example
To emphasize the receiver of an action	The president was elected by a small margin.
When the doer is unknown	The windows were broken last night.
When the doer is unimportant	Smoking was banned.

Practice and Apply Return to the journal entry and letter you wrote in response to this selection's Performance Task and review them to see how often you have used the active and passive voices. Check each instance of the passive voice and see if it is better to rewrite the sentence in the active voice. Choose two examples of active voice and rewrite those sentences in passive voice to compare the strength and clarity of writing in each voice.

Background *In his 2005 book,* 1491: New Revelations of the Americas Before Columbus, *science journalist* **Charles C. Mann** *reviews and synthesizes the work of recent scholars who have studied early Native American societies. Christopher Columbus's voyage to the Caribbean in 1492 marked the beginning of contact between native people in the Americas and Europeans. By 1620, Native Americans in coastal New England had been trading on a limited basis with Europeans for about a hundred years. The man named Tisquantum in this excerpt from Mann's book is the person whom William Bradford called Squanto.*

Coming of Age
in the
Dawnland
from 1491

History Writing by Charles C. Mann

AS YOU READ Notice how Mann's descriptions or explanations of Native American life compare with your prior knowledge of the subject.

Consider Tisquantum, the "friendly Indian" of the textbook. More than likely Tisquantum was not the name he was given at birth. In that part of the Northeast, *tisquantum* referred to rage, especially the rage of *manitou*, the world-suffusing spiritual power at the heart of coastal Indians' religious beliefs. When Tisquantum approached the Pilgrims and identified himself by that sobriquet,[1] it was as if he had stuck out his hand and said, Hello, I'm the Wrath of God. No one would lightly adopt such a name in contemporary Western society. Neither would anyone in seventeenth-century indigenous society.

10 Tisquantum was trying to **project** something.

Tisquantum was not an Indian. True, he belonged to that category of people whose ancestors had inhabited the Western Hemisphere for thousands of years. And it is true that I refer to him as an Indian, because the label is useful shorthand; so would his descendants, and for much the same reason. But "Indian" was not a category that Tisquantum himself would have recognized, any more than the

project
(prə-jĕkt´) *v.* to communicate or put forth.

---

[1] **sobriquet** (sō´brĭ-kā´): nickname.

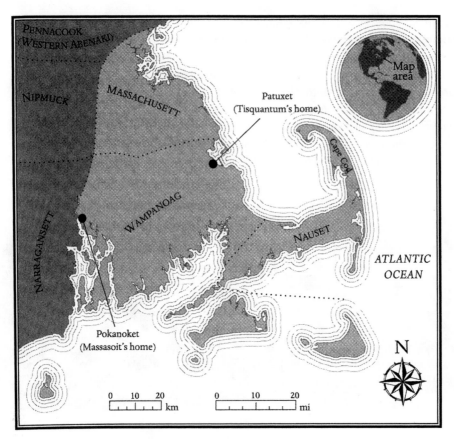

MASSACHUSETT ALLIANCE, 1600 A.D.

inhabitants of the same area today would call themselves "Western Hemisphereans." Still less would Tisquantum have claimed to belong to "Norumbega," the label by which most Europeans then
20 referred to New England. ("New England" was coined only in 1616.) As Tisquantum's later history made clear, he regarded himself first and foremost as a citizen of Patuxet, a shoreline **settlement** halfway between what is now Boston and the beginning of Cape Cod.

    Patuxet was one of the dozen or so settlements in what is now eastern Massachusetts and Rhode Island that comprised[2] the Wampanoag confederation. In turn, the Wampanoag were part of a tripartite alliance with two other confederations: the Nauset, which comprised some thirty groups on Cape Cod; and the Massachusett, several dozen villages clustered around Massachusetts Bay. All of these
30 people spoke variants of Massachusett, a member of the Algonquian language family, the biggest in eastern North America at the time.

settlement
(sĕt´l-mənt) *n.* a small community in a sparsely populated area.

---

[2] **comprised:** made up of.

(Massachusett thus was the name both of a language and of one of the groups that spoke it.) In Massachusett, the name for the New England shore was the Dawnland, the place where the sun rose. The inhabitants of the Dawnland were the People of the First Light.

Ten thousand years ago, when Indians in Mesoamerica and Peru were inventing agriculture and coalescing into villages, New England was barely inhabited, for the excellent reason that it had been covered until relatively recently by an ice sheet a mile thick. People
40　slowly moved in, though the area long remained cold and uninviting, especially along the coastline. Because rising sea levels continually flooded the shore, marshy Cape Cod did not fully lock into its contemporary configuration until about 1000 B.C. By that time the Dawnland had evolved into something more attractive: an ecological crazy quilt of wet maple forests, shellfish-studded tidal estuaries,[3] thick highland woods, mossy bogs full of cranberries and orchids, fractally[4] complex snarls of sandbars and beachfront, and fire-swept stands of pitch pine—"tremendous variety even within the compass of a few miles," as the ecological historian William Cronon put it.
50　In the absence of written records, researchers have developed techniques for teasing out evidence of the past. Among them is "glottochronology," the attempt to estimate how long ago two languages separated from a common ancestor by evaluating their degree of **divergence** on a list of key words. In the 1970s and 1980s linguists applied glottochronological techniques to the Algonquian dictionaries compiled by early colonists. However tentatively, the results indicated that the various Algonquian languages in New England all date back to a common ancestor that appeared in the Northeast a few centuries before Christ.
60　The ancestral language may derive from what is known as the Hopewell culture. Around two thousand years ago, Hopewell jumped into prominence from its bases in the Midwest, establishing a trade network that covered most of North America. The Hopewell culture introduced monumental earthworks and, possibly, agriculture to the rest of the cold North. Hopewell villages, unlike their more egalitarian[5] neighbors, were stratified,[6] with powerful, priestly rulers commanding a mass of commoners. Archaeologists have found no evidence of large-scale warfare at this time, and thus suggest that Hopewell probably did not achieve its dominance by conquest.
70　Instead, one can speculate, the vehicle for transformation may have been Hopewell religion, with its intoxicatingly elaborate funeral rites. If so, the adoption of Algonquian in the Northeast would mark an era

divergence
(dĭ-vûr´jəns) *n.*
a difference or variation.

---

[3] **estuaries:** tidal inlets.

[4] **fractally:** with an infinitely repeating pattern of geometric shapes.

[5] **egalitarian:** based on the principal of equality.

[6] **stratified:** arranged in layers.

of spiritual **ferment** and heady conversion, much like the time when Islam rose and spread Arabic throughout the Middle East.

Hopewell itself declined around 400 A.D. But its trade network remained intact. Shell beads from Florida, obsidian from the Rocky Mountains, and mica from Tennessee found their way to the Northeast. Borrowing technology and ideas from the Midwest, the nomadic peoples of New England transformed their societies. By the end of the first millennium A.D., agriculture was spreading rapidly and the region was becoming an unusual patchwork of communities, each with its preferred terrain, way of subsistence, and cultural style.

Scattered about the many lakes, ponds, and swamps of the cold uplands were small, mobile groups of hunters and gatherers—"collectors," as researchers sometimes call them. Most had recently adopted agriculture or were soon to do so, but it was still a secondary source of food, a supplement to the wild products of the land. New England's major river valleys, by contrast, held large, permanent villages, many nestled in constellations of suburban hamlets and hunting camps. Because extensive fields of maize, beans, and squash surrounded every home, these settlements sprawled along the Connecticut, Charles, and other river valleys for miles, one town bumping up against the other. Along the coast, where Tisquantum and Massasoit lived, villages often were smaller and looser, though no less permanent.

Unlike the upland hunters, the Indians on the rivers and coastline did not roam the land; instead, most seem to have moved between a summer place and a winter place, like affluent snowbirds alternating between Manhattan and Miami. The distances were smaller, of course; shoreline families would move a fifteen-minute walk inland, to avoid direct exposure to winter storms and tides. Each village had its own distinct mix of farming and foraging—this one here, adjacent to a rich oyster bed, might plant maize purely for variety, whereas that one there, just a few miles away, might subsist almost entirely on its harvest, filling great underground storage pits each fall. Although these settlements were permanent, winter and summer alike, they often were not tightly knit entities, with houses and fields in carefully demarcated[7] clusters. Instead people spread themselves through estuaries, sometimes grouping into neighborhoods, sometimes with each family on its own, its maize ground proudly separate. Each community was constantly "joining and splitting like quicksilver[8] in a fluid pattern within its bounds," wrote Kathleen J. Bragdon, an anthropologist at the College of William and Mary—a type of settlement, she remarked, with "no name in the archaeological or anthropological literature."

---

[7] **demarcated:** defined with boundaries.
[8] **quicksilver:** mercury, a liquid metal.

> **Around two thousand years ago,** Hopewell jumped into prominence . . . establishing a trade network that covered most of North America. **"**

In the Wampanoag confederation, one of these quicksilver communities was Patuxet, where Tisquantum was born at the end of the sixteenth century.

Tucked into the great sweep of Cape Cod Bay, Patuxet sat on a low
120 rise above a small harbor, jigsawed by sandbars and shallow enough that children could walk from the beach hundreds of yards into the water before the waves went above their heads. To the west, maize hills marched across the sandy hillocks[9] in parallel rows. Beyond the fields, a mile or more away from the sea, rose a forest of oak, chestnut, and hickory, open and park-like, the underbrush kept down by expert annual burning. "Pleasant of air and prospect," as one English visitor described the area, Patuxet had "much plenty both of fish and fowl every day in the year." Runs of spawning Atlantic salmon, shortnose sturgeon, striped bass, and American shad annually filled the harbor.
130 But the most important fish harvest came in late spring, when the herring-like alewives swarmed the fast, shallow stream that cut through the village. So numerous were the fish, and so driven, that when mischievous boys walled off the stream with stones the alewives would leap the barrier—silver bodies gleaming in the sun—and proceed upstream.

Tisquantum's childhood *wetu* (home) was formed from arched poles lashed together into a dome that was covered in winter by tightly woven rush mats and in summer by thin sheets of chestnut bark. A fire burned constantly in the center, the smoke venting through
140 a hole in the center of the roof. English visitors did not find this arrangement peculiar; chimneys were just coming into use in Britain, and most homes there, including those of the wealthy, were still heated

---

[9] **hillocks:** small hills.

by fires beneath central roof holes. Nor did the English regard the Dawnland *wetu* as primitive; its multiple layers of mats, which trapped insulating layers of air, were "warmer than our English houses," sighed the colonist William Wood. The *wetu* was less leaky than the typical English wattle-and-daub house, too. Wood did not conceal his admiration for the way Indian mats "deny entrance to any drop of rain, though it come both fierce and long."

150   Around the edge of the house were low beds, sometimes wide enough for a whole family to sprawl on them together; usually raised about a foot from the floor, platform-style; and always piled with mats and furs. Going to sleep in the firelight, young Tisquantum would have stared up at the diddering[10] shadows of the hemp bags and bark boxes hanging from the rafters. Voices would skirl[11] up in the darkness: one person singing a lullaby, then another person, until everyone was asleep. In the morning, when he woke, big, egg-shaped pots of corn-and-bean mash would be on the fire, simmering with meat, vegetables, or dried fish to make a slow-cooked dinner

160 stew. Outside the *wetu* he would hear the cheerful thuds of the large mortars and pestles[12] in which women crushed dried maize into *nokake*, a flour-like powder "so sweet, toothsome, and hearty," colonist Gookin wrote, "that an Indian will travel many days with no other but this meal." Although Europeans bemoaned the lack of salt in Indian cuisine, they thought it nourishing. According to one modern

---

[10] **diddering:** trembling.

[11] **skirl:** make a high-pitched sound, like bagpipes.

[12] **mortars and pestles:** bowl-shaped containers and blunt tools for grinding and crushing.

reconstruction, Dawnland diets at the time averaged about 2,500 calories a day, better than those usual in famine-racked Europe.

Pilgrim writers universally reported that Wampanoag families were close and loving—more so than English families, some thought.
170 Europeans in those days tended to view children as moving straight from infancy to adulthood around the age of seven, and often thereupon sent them out to work. Indian parents, by contrast, regarded the years before puberty as a time of playful development, and kept their offspring close by until marriage. (Jarringly, to the contemporary eye, some Pilgrims interpreted this as sparing the rod.) Boys like Tisquantum explored the countryside, swam in the ponds at the south end of the harbor, and played a kind of soccer with a small leather ball; in the summer and fall they camped out in huts in the fields, weeding the maize and chasing away birds. Archery practice began at age two.
180 By adolescence boys would make a game of shooting at each other and dodging the arrows.

The primary goal of Dawnland education was molding character. Men and women were expected to be brave, hardy, honest, and uncomplaining. Chatterboxes and gossips were frowned upon. "He that speaks seldom and opportunely, being as good as his word, is the only man they love," Wood explained. Character formation began early, with family games of tossing naked children into the snow. (They were pulled out quickly and placed next to the fire, in a practice reminiscent of Scandinavian saunas.) When Indian boys came of age,
190 they spent an entire winter alone in the forest, equipped only with a bow, a hatchet, and a knife. These methods worked, the awed Wood reported. "Beat them, whip them, pinch them, punch them, if [the Indians] resolve not to flinch for it, they will not."

Tisquantum's **regimen** was probably tougher than that of his friends, according to Salisbury, the Smith College historian, for it seems that he was selected to become a *pniese*, a kind of counselor-bodyguard to the sachem. To master the art of ignoring pain, future *pniese* had to subject themselves to such miserable experiences as running barelegged through brambles. And they fasted often, to
200 learn self-discipline. After spending their winter in the woods, *pniese* candidates came back to an additional test: drinking bitter gentian juice until they vomited, repeating this bulimic process over and over until, near fainting, they threw up blood.

Patuxet, like its neighboring settlements, was governed by a sachem, who upheld the law, negotiated treaties, controlled foreign contacts, collected tribute, declared war, provided for widows and orphans, and allocated farmland when there were disputes over it. (Dawnlanders lived in a loose scatter, but they knew which family could use which land— "very exact and punctuall," Roger Williams,
210 founder of Rhode Island colony, called Indian care for property lines.)

regimen
(rĕj´ə-mən) *n.* a system or organized routine of behavior.

Most of the time, the Patuxet sachem owed fealty[13] to the great sachem in the Wampanoag village to the southwest, and through him to the sachems of the allied confederations of the Nauset in Cape Cod and the Massachusett around Boston. Meanwhile, the Wampanoag were rivals and enemies of the Narragansett and Pequots to the west and the many groups of Abenaki to the north. As a practical matter, sachems had to gain the consent of their people, who could easily move away and join another sachemship. Analogously, the great sachems had to please or bully the lesser, lest by the **defection** of small communities they lose stature.

defection
(dĭ-fĕkt´shŭn) *n.* the abandonment of one social or political group in favor of another.

> **"** Pilgrim writers universally reported that
> Wampanoag families were
> close and loving—
> more so than English families,
> some thought. **"**

Sixteenth-century New England housed 100,000 people or more, a figure that was slowly increasing. Most of those people lived in shoreline communities, where rising numbers were beginning to change agriculture from an option to a necessity. These bigger settlements required more centralized administration; natural resources like good land and spawning streams, though not scarce, now needed to be managed. In consequence, boundaries between groups were becoming more formal. Sachems, given more power and more to defend, pushed against each other harder. Political tensions were constant. Coastal and riverine New England, according to the archaeologist and ethnohistorian Peter Thomas, was "an ever-changing collage of personalities, alliances, plots, raids and encounters which involved every Indian [settlement]."

---

[13] **fealty:** obedient loyalty.

Armed conflict was frequent but brief and mild by European standards. The *casus belli*[14] was usually the desire to avenge an insult or gain status, not the wish for conquest. Most battles consisted of lightning guerrilla raids by ad hoc companies in the forest: flash of black-and-yellow-striped bows behind trees, hiss and whip of stone-tipped arrows through the air, eruption of angry cries. Attackers
240 slipped away as soon as retribution had been exacted. Losers quickly conceded their loss of status. Doing otherwise would have been like failing to resign after losing a major piece in a chess tournament—a social irritant, a waste of time and resources. Women and children were rarely killed, though they were sometimes abducted and forced to join the winning group. Captured men were often tortured (they were admired, though not necessarily spared, if they endured the pain **stoically**). Now and then, as a sign of victory, slain foes were scalped, much as British skirmishes with the Irish sometimes finished with a parade of Irish heads on pikes. In especially large clashes, adversaries
250 might meet in the open, as in European battlefields, though the results, Roger Williams noted, were "farre less bloudy, and devouring then the cruell Warres of Europe." Nevertheless, by Tisquantum's time defensive palisades[15] were increasingly common, especially in the river valleys.

stoically
(stō´ĭk-lē) *adv.*
without showing
emotion or feeling.

Inside the settlement was a world of warmth, family, and familiar custom. But the world outside, as Thomas put it, was "a maze of confusing actions and individuals fighting to maintain an existence in the shadow of change."

And that was before the Europeans showed up.

---

[14] *casus belli* (kā´səs bĕl´ī): Latin: cause for war.
[15] **defensive palisades:** fortified walls of tall stakes.

COLLABORATIVE DISCUSSION With a partner, discuss two interesting or unexpected details from Mann's description of pre-Columbian Native America. Explain why they were surprising, citing specific passages in your discussion.

Determine the Meaning of Words and Phrases

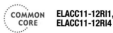

To understand a sophisticated text like "Coming of Age in the Dawnland," you must determine the meanings of words and phrases as the author uses them. These meanings may be literal or nonliteral. The chart provides some examples.

Technical Terms	Figurative Language	Connotations
Mann draws on evidence from a variety of social scientists, and some of the language he uses comes from those specialized fields of study. Examples include *tidal estuaries* and *glottochronology.* Mann defines some of these terms in the text; others you must look up in footnotes or in a dictionary.	**Figurative language** uses words in a nonliteral way to make fresh, interesting comparisons. A **simile,** for example, compares two things using the word *like* or *as*. Mann says an Indian failing to acknowledge a loss in a fight was "like failing to resign after losing a major piece in a chess tournament." This simile helps readers understand an unfamiliar topic by comparing it to something familiar.	To convey subtle shades of meaning, authors choose words with particular **connotations,** or associated feelings. For example, describing bedtime for a Native American family, Mann uses the words *firelight* and *lullaby.* These words have pleasant, homey connotations that help readers connect with the lives of Tisquantum's people.

Determine Author's Purpose

Purpose is the reason why an author writes a particular piece. The author might seek to inform readers, to entertain them, or to persuade them to agree with his or her point of view. An author's purpose is not usually stated in the text. Instead, readers must **infer** the purpose, or draw a logical conclusion based on strong evidence in the text.

No matter what the purpose, an effective piece of writing must have an appealing **style.** Elements of style include word choice, **tone** (the writer's attitude toward the topic), and **imagery** (words and phrases that appeal to readers' senses). Well-chosen content—the facts and ideas that the author includes—also contribute to a powerful text. Use these questions to help you analyze "Coming of Age in the Dawnland" and determine the author's purpose:

- Think about what the text says explicitly. What ideas does the author state directly, and what facts and examples does he include?

- Analyze the author's style. What words and images do you find especially powerful? What tone does his writing convey?

- Based on your analysis, what can you infer is Mann's purpose in this excerpt?

COMMON CORE

ELACC11-12RI1,
ELACC11-12RI2,
ELACC11-12RI4,
ELACC11-12RI6,
ELACC11-12W1

Analyzing the Text

Cite Text Evidence   Support your responses with evidence from the selection.

1. **Infer** In lines 87–90, Mann writes that "New England's major river valleys . . . held large, permanent villages, many nestled in constellations of suburban hamlets and hunting camps." What words in this sentence have strong connotations? How might these feelings affect readers' impression of Native American life in this time and place?

2. **Analyze** Note the sensory details that Mann uses to describe life in Patuxet at the end of the sixteenth century (lines 119–135). What impression of the community does this imagery create for readers?

3. **Cite Evidence** Mann includes evidence from primary sources written by Europeans in the seventeenth century. Identify examples of this evidence and explain what it reveals about these Europeans' opinions of Native American life.

4. **Analyze** Locate at least three examples of scholarly experts that Mann quotes in his writing. Why does he include this content?

5. **Analyze** Mann says the coastal Indians who moved inland in the winter were "like affluent snowbirds alternating between Manhattan and Miami." What purpose might he want to achieve with this simile comparing the Indians to a group of modern Americans?

6. **Draw Conclusions** What is the central idea about Native American societies in the Dawnland that Mann communicates in this excerpt?

7. **Cite Evidence** What evidence does Mann provide to support the idea that Indians in sixteenth-century New England lived in a dynamic world?

8. **Synthesize** What do you think was Mann's overall purpose for writing this text? Cite reasons and evidence for your answer.

PERFORMANCE TASK

Writing Activity: Argument This selection presents Mann's view of Indian societies in New England. Evaluate how successfully he achieves his purpose by writing a brief argument.

- Write a statement that summarizes Mann's purpose for writing.
- Decide whether you think he succeeded or failed in achieving that purpose. Are the style and content of his writing strong and persuasive? Your position on that question is the claim of your argument.
- If you think Mann achieved his purpose, cite evidence that supports that claim. If you think he failed, provide reasons for your opinion.
- Present your reasons and evidence in a logical order.

Critical Vocabulary

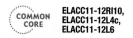

project	settlement	divergence	ferment
regimen	defection	stoically	

Practice and Apply Use a complete sentence to answer each question and demonstrate that you understand the meaning of each Critical Vocabulary word.

1. When an Indian acted **stoically** during torture, what image did he hope to **project**?

2. Why would a sachem be concerned about the **defection** of a small **settlement**?

3. How might a time of religious **ferment** cause a **divergence** of beliefs?

4. Why did young Indians have to endure their training **regimen stoically**?

Vocabulary Strategy: Specialized Vocabulary

Mann uses evidence from several different fields to support his ideas. He cites an ecological historian, an archaeologist and ethnohistorian, and an anthropologist. Many of the words he uses are examples of **specialized vocabulary,** or words that are related to a particular field of study. For example, the Critical Vocabulary word *settlement* is used in a specalized sense of "a place where people live, especially in an area where few people have lived before." This is an example of a specialized meaning for a word that you might already be familar with. The following strategies can help you determine the meaning of specialized vocabulary.

- Look it up! If a complex text is about a specialized topic that you are unfamilar with (for example, vulcanology, the study of volcanos), you should *expect* to see specialized vocabulary that you will need to look up.
- Try to guess the meaning. Use context clues, including the word's part of speech and its use in the sentence, to help determine the meaning. Very often specialized vocabulary will helpfully be defined in the text for readers.
- For very technical words, use specialized reference works, such as an atlas or the glossary in a book on a specialized topic, to get more specific information.

Practice and Apply Work with a partner to complete the following activities.

1. Using prior knowledge and context clues from Mann's writing, identify the subject of each of these fields of study: anthropology, archaeology, and ecology. Check your answers by looking up these words in a dictionary or other reference work.

2. Now that you have a clearer idea of these fields of study, begin to identify and classify some of the specialized vocabulary that appears in this text. You might focus first on the passages where Mann quotes various experts. Determine which words are examples of specialized vocabulary and then classify each word according to the list of fields in step 1. Lastly, prepare a definition for each word, consulting appropriate reference materials. Try to get at least three words for each field.

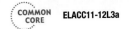

Language and Style:
Dependent (or Subordinate) Clauses

All **clauses** contain a subject and a verb. A **dependent** or **subordinate clause** is not able to stand alone as a sentence but depends on or is subordinate to an independent clause. Using dependent clauses skillfully allows Charles Mann to vary the **syntax** or pattern of his sentences.

> Consider these examples from "Coming of Age in the Dawnland."
>
> **And it is true that I refer to him as an Indian, because the label is useful shorthand. . . .**
>
> **Although Europeans bemoaned the lack of salt in Indian cuisine, they thought it nourishing.**

In each of these complex sentences, the dependent clause begins with a **subordinating conjunction** (*because* and *although*). The conjunction reveals a relationship between the two clauses. The word *because,* for example, indicates a cause-and-effect relationship between two factors. *Although* indicates a concession or exception to the point that Mann makes. Using subordinating conjunctions allows Mann to make nuanced and detailed arguments appropriate for his topic. From a style perspective, it allows him to create a varied rhythm in his prose, making it more engaging and easier to read.

This chart shows some common subordinating conjunctions and the relationships they signal.

Type of Relationship	Subordinating Conjunctions
Causal (i.e., Making Something Happen)	because, since
Concession/Contrast	although, as, as much as, than, though, while
Place	where, wherever
Purpose	in order that, so that, that
Time	after, as, as long as, as soon as, before, since, until, when, whenever, while

Practice and Apply Look back at the argument you wrote in response to this selection's Performance Task. Revise it by combining some simple sentences into complex sentences. Use appropriate subordinating conjunctions to show the relationships between ideas. Vary the placement of dependent clauses at the beginning, the middle, and the end of sentences to create varied sentence structure and a smooth, flowing rhythm.

Introduction to *The Tempest*

O, brave new world, That has such people in 't!

—*The Tempest* (Act V, Scene 1)

Shakespeare's World Shakespeare's world was Elizabethan England. Named after Queen Elizabeth I, who ruled from 1558–1603, this dynamic era was a time of enormous change in the arts, in social order, and in international affairs. England became a commercial and naval power as explorers such as Sir Francis Drake and Sir Walter Raleigh helped expand England's territories all the way to the Americas. The establishment of the first successful colony at Jamestown, Virginia, in 1607 marked the beginning of a process that ultimately brought thousands of people from England to North America, inspired by dreams of commercial gain or of religious liberty in the New World.

Sources for *The Tempest* Shakespeare wove this growing interest in the New World into *The Tempest* (1611). In fact, real events of the time may have influenced the play's plot. The play opens with a storm that causes a shipwreck, stranding a group of noblemen on an unfamiliar island. In 1609 a fleet of ships financed by the Virginia Company set sail for Jamestown with hundreds of colonists on board. Shakespeare knew the company's leaders and likely read the vividly detailed reports of this event that circulated in 1610. During a violent storm off the Bermudas, one of the company's ships, the *Sea Venture,* was separated from the fleet. While the other ships reached Jamestown within a few weeks, the *Sea Venture* was assumed to be lost at sea. A year later, however, its passengers arrived in Jamestown on two small ships that they had built after being shipwrecked in Bermuda.

Another possible source for elements of *The Tempest* is Michel de Montaigne's 1603 essay "Of Cannibals," which focuses on Europe's problematic perception of the New World's "barbaric" native populations and their customs. Similarly, Shakespeare may have created the character of Caliban, a half-man, half-beast, to comment on British colonialism and slavery in the Americas and elsewhere. Scholars speculate that Caliban— whose name is basically an anagram, or rearrangement of the letters in the word *cannibal*—reveals the degree to which England viewed various native groups as uncivilized or less than human.

from The Tempest

Drama by William Shakespeare

William Shakespeare *(1564–1616) was born in 1564 in Stratford-upon-Avon, a market town in central England. His father was a prosperous tradesman. Shakespeare probably attended Stratford's grammar school, where he would have studied Latin and read classical authors. In 1582 he married Anne Hathaway. The next year she gave birth to a daughter, Susanna. Their twins Hamnet and Judith followed in 1585. Sometime during the next seven years, Shakespeare found work in London as an actor; he also began to write plays. His early success aroused the envy of Robert Greene, who in 1592 described him as "an upstart crow." In 1594 Shakespeare joined the Lord Chamberlain's Men, which became the most prestigious theater company in London. Shakespeare soon grew affluent from his share in the company's profits.*

The Height of His Career *Shakespeare's rhetorical gifts and poetic power, as well as his profound psychological insight, would have allowed him to become a great writer in any age. To please the varied tastes of Elizabethan audiences, he mastered all forms of drama. In the 1590s, he focused on comedies and English history plays, such as* A Midsummer Night's Dream *and* Henry IV. *Between 1600 and 1607, he wrote his greatest tragedies, including* Hamlet, Macbeth, *and* King Lear. *The final phase of his career saw the creation of the darker comedies, such as* A Winter's Tale *and* The Tempest.

His Legacy *Shakespeare died in Stratford in 1616. At the time, some of his plays existed in cheap, often very flawed editions; others had never appeared in print. In 1623, two theater colleagues published a collected edition of his plays known as the First Folio, which ensured the survival of his work. Ben Jonson, a rival playwright, wrote an introduction for the volume in which he declared that Shakespeare "was not of an age, but for all time." Four centuries after Shakespeare's death, his plays continue to be performed around the world.*

Image Credits: (c) ©Brooklyn Museum/Corbis Motion; (t) ©Robert Fesus/Shutterstock; (r) ©Dynamic Graphics/Jupiterimages/Getty Images

The Scene: A barren island in the Mediterranean Sea

CHARACTERS
(IN ACT I, AND ACT II, SCENE 1)

Prospero, the former duke of Milan, now a magician on a Mediterranean island

Miranda, Prospero's daughter

Ariel, a spirit, servant to Prospero

Caliban, an inhabitant of the island, servant to Prospero

Ferdinand, prince of Naples

Alonso, king of Naples

Antonio, duke of Milan and Prospero's brother

Sebastian, Alonso's brother

Gonzalo, councillor to Alonso and friend to Prospero

Courtiers in attendance on Alonso:

Adrian

Francisco

Shipmaster

Boatswain

Mariners

Act I

Scene 1

[*A tempestuous noise of thunder and lightning heard. Enter a* Shipmaster *and a* Boatswain.]

Master. Boatswain!

Boatswain. Here, master. What cheer?

Master. Good, speak to th' mariners. Fall to 't yarely or we run ourselves aground. Bestir, bestir!

[*He exits.*]

[*Enter* Mariners.]

5   **Boatswain.** Heigh, my hearts! Cheerly, cheerly, my hearts! Yare, yare! Take in the topsail. Tend to th' Master's whistle.—Blow till thou burst thy wind, if room enough!

[*Enter* Alonso, Sebastian, Antonio, Ferdinand, Gonzalo, *and others.*]

Alonso. Good boatswain, have care. Where's the
10   Master? Play the men.

Boatswain. I pray now, keep below.

Antonio. Where is the Master, boatswain?

Boatswain. Do you not hear him? You mar our labor. Keep your cabins. You do assist the storm.

15   **Gonzalo.** Nay, good, be patient.

Boatswain. When the sea is. Hence! What cares these roarers for the name of king? To cabin! Silence! Trouble us not.

Gonzalo. Good, yet remember whom thou hast aboard.

20   **Boatswain.** None that I more love than myself. You are a councillor; if you can command these elements to silence, and work the peace of the

1 Boatswain: a low-ranking ship's officer (pronounced "bosun")

2 What cheer?: How goes it with you?

3 Good: good fellow; **Fall to 't yarely:** proceed quickly.

4 Bestir: get moving.

5 hearts: hearties; **Cheerly:** heartily.

6 Tend: pay attention.

7–8 Blow . . . enough: The storm can blow its hardest as long as we have enough room to sail safely.

10 Play the men: Act like men.

16–17 What cares . . . king?: What do these roaring waves care about a king's rank?

21 councillor: adviser or member of the king's council.

present, we will not hand a rope more. Use your authority. If you cannot, give thanks you have lived
25 so long, and make yourself ready in your cabin for the mischance of the hour, if it so hap.—Cheerly, good hearts!—Out of our way, I say!

[*He exits.*]

Gonzalo. I have great comfort from this fellow. Methinks he hath no drowning mark upon him.
30 His complexion is perfect gallows. Stand fast, good Fate, to his hanging. Make the rope of his destiny our cable, for our own doth little advantage. If he be not born to be hanged, our case is miserable.

[*He exits with* Alonso, Sebastian, *and the other courtiers.*]

[*Enter* Boatswain.]

Boatswain. Down with the topmast! Yare! Lower,
35 lower! Bring her to try wi' th' main course. [*a cry within*] A plague upon this howling! They are louder than the weather or our office.

[*Enter Sebastian, Antonio, and* Gonzalo.]

Yet again? What do you here? Shall we give o'er and drown? Have you a mind to sink?

40 **Sebastian.** A pox o' your throat, you bawling, blasphemous, incharitable dog!

Boatswain. Work you, then.

Antonio. Hang, cur, hang, you whoreson, insolent noisemaker! We are less afraid to be drowned than
45 thou art.

Gonzalo. I'll warrant him for drowning, though the ship were no stronger than a nutshell and as leaky as an unstanched wench.

Boatswain. Lay her ahold, ahold! Set her two courses.
50 Off to sea again! Lay her off!

[*Enter more Mariners, wet.*]

Mariners. All lost! To prayers, to prayers! All lost!

[*Mariners exit.*]

Boatswain. What, must our mouths be cold?

Gonzalo. The King and Prince at prayers. Let's assist them, for our case is as theirs.

55 **Sebastian.** I am out of patience.

21–23 command . . . present: quiet the wind and waves and establish order.

23 hand: handle.

26 mischance of the hour: impending disaster; **hap:** happen.

29–30 An allusion to the proverb "He that is born to be hanged shall never be drowned."

32 cable: anchor cable; **doth little advantage:** is of little use.

35 Bring . . . course: Use the mainsail to bring the ship close to the wind (keep it away from the island by sailing at an angle into the wind).

36–37 They are . . . office: The passengers make more noise than the storm and us as we work.

38 give o'er: give up.

40 A pox o': a curse on.

46 warrant him for: guarantee him against; **though:** even if.

48 unstanched wench: unclean or immoral woman.

49 Lay . . . courses: Keep the ship close to the wind. Set the foresail and mainsail.

Antonio. We are merely cheated of our lives by drunkards. This wide-chopped rascal—would thou mightst lie drowning the washing of ten tides!

[*Boatswain exits.*]

Gonzalo. He'll be hanged yet, though every drop of
60 water swear against it and gape at wid'st to glut him.

[*A confused noise within:* "Mercy on us!"—"We split, we split!"—"Farewell, my wife and children!"—"Farewell, brother!"—"We split, we split, we split!"]

Antonio. Let's all sink wi' th' King.

Sebastian. Let's take leave of him.

[*He exits with* Antonio.]

Gonzalo. Now would I give a thousand furlongs of sea for an acre of barren ground: long heath, brown
65 furze, anything. The wills above be done, but I would fain die a dry death.

[*He exits.*]

56 merely: utterly.

57 wide-chopped: bigmouthed.

57–58 Antonio exaggerates the traditional punishment for pirates, which was to hang them at the shore and leave their corpses until three tides had washed over them.

60 gape . . . him: open wide to swallow him.

64 heath: heather.

65 furze: a shrub.

66 fain: willingly.

Scene 2

[*Enter* Prospero *and* Miranda.]

Miranda. If by your art, my dearest father, you have
Put the wild waters in this roar, allay them.
The sky, it seems, would pour down stinking pitch,
But that the sea, mounting to th' welkin's cheek,
5 Dashes the fire out. O, I have suffered
With those that I saw suffer! A brave vessel,
Who had, no doubt, some noble creature in her,
Dashed all to pieces. O, the cry did knock
Against my very heart! Poor souls, they perished.
10 Had I been any god of power, I would
Have sunk the sea within the earth or ere
It should the good ship so have swallowed, and
The fraughting souls within her.

Prospero.   Be collected.
No more amazement. Tell your piteous heart
15 There's no harm done.

Miranda.   O, woe the day!

Prospero.   No harm.
I have done nothing but in care of thee,
Of thee, my dear one, thee, my daughter, who
Art ignorant of what thou art, naught knowing
Of whence I am, nor that I am more better
20 Than Prospero, master of a full poor cell,
And thy no greater father.

Miranda.   More to know
Did never meddle with my thoughts.

Prospero.   'Tis time
I should inform thee farther. Lend thy hand
And pluck my magic garment from me.

[*putting aside his cloak*]

                                    So,
25 Lie there, my art.—Wipe thou thine eyes. Have
    comfort.
The direful spectacle of the wrack, which touched
The very virtue of compassion in thee,
I have with such provision in mine art
So safely ordered that there is no soul—
30 No, not so much perdition as an hair,
Betid to any creature in the vessel
Which thou heard'st cry, which thou saw'st sink.

1 art: magic, skill.

3 pitch: a tarlike substance used for waterproofing ships.

4 welkin's: sky's.

6 brave: fine.

11 or ere: before.

13 fraughting souls: passengers.

14 amazement: bewilderment; **piteous:** compassionate.

18 naught knowing: knowing nothing.

19 whence I am: where I come from; **more better:** of higher rank.

20 full poor cell: very humble dwelling.

22 meddle with: enter.

26 direful spectacle: terrible display.

27 virtue: essence

28 provision: foresight.

30 perdition: loss.

31 Betid: happened.

Sit down,
For thou must now know farther.

[*They sit.*]

Miranda.   You have often
Begun to tell me what I am, but stopped
35   And left me to a bootless inquisition,
Concluding "Stay. Not yet."

Prospero.   The hour's now come.
The very minute bids thee ope thine ear.
Obey, and be attentive. Canst thou remember
A time before we came unto this cell?
40   I do not think thou canst, for then thou wast not
Out three years old.

Miranda.   Certainly, sir, I can.

Prospero. By what? By any other house or person?
Of anything the image tell me that
Hath kept with thy remembrance.

Miranda.   'Tis far off
45   And rather like a dream than an assurance
That my remembrance warrants. Had I not
Four or five women once that tended me?

Prospero. Thou hadst, and more, Miranda. But how is it
That this lives in thy mind? What seest thou else
50   In the dark backward and abysm of time?
If thou rememb'rest aught ere thou cam'st here,
How thou cam'st here thou mayst.

Miranda.   But that I do not.

Prospero. Twelve year since, Miranda, twelve year since,
Thy father was the Duke of Milan and
55   A prince of power.

Miranda.   Sir, are not you my father?

Prospero. Thy mother was a piece of virtue, and
She said thou wast my daughter. And thy father
Was Duke of Milan, and his only heir
And princess no worse issued.

Miranda.   O, the heavens!
60   What foul play had we that we came from thence?
Or blessèd was 't we did?

Prospero.   Both, both, my girl.
By foul play, as thou sayst, were we heaved thence,
But blessedly holp hither.

35 bootless inquisition: useless inquiry.

37 ope: open.

41 Out: fully.

43 Of anything . . . me: describe to me anything.

45–46 an assurance . . . warrants: a certainty that my memory guarantees to be true.

50 backward: past; **abysm:** abyss.

51 aught ere: anything before.

53 Twelve year since: twelve years ago.

56 piece of virtue: model of chastity.

59 no worse issued: no less nobly born.

63 holp hither: helped here.

Miranda. O, my heart bleeds
To think o' th' teen that I have turned you to,
65 Which is from my remembrance. Please you, farther.

Prospero. My brother and thy uncle, called Antonio—
I pray thee, mark me—that a brother should
Be so perfidious!—he whom next thyself
Of all the world I loved, and to him put
70 The manage of my state, as at that time
Through all the signories it was the first,
And Prospero the prime duke, being so reputed
In dignity, and for the liberal arts
Without a parallel. Those being all my study,
75 The government I cast upon my brother
And to my state grew stranger, being transported
And rapt in secret studies. Thy false uncle—
Dost thou attend me?

Miranda. Sir, most heedfully.

Prospero. Being once perfected how to grant suits,
80 How to deny them, who t' advance, and who
To trash for overtopping, new created
The creatures that were mine, I say, or changed 'em,
Or else new formed 'em, having both the key
Of officer and office, set all hearts i' th' state
85 To what tune pleased his ear, that now he was
The ivy which had hid my princely trunk
And sucked my verdure out on 't. Thou attend'st not.

Miranda. O, good sir, I do.

Prospero. I pray thee, mark me.
I, thus neglecting worldly ends, all dedicated
90 To closeness and the bettering of my mind
With that which, but by being so retired,
O'erprized all popular rate, in my false brother
Awaked an evil nature, and my trust,
Like a good parent, did beget of him
95 A falsehood in its contrary as great
As my trust was, which had indeed no limit,
A confidence sans bound. He being thus lorded,
Not only with what my revenue yielded
But what my power might else exact, like one
100 Who, having into truth by telling of it,
Made such a sinner of his memory
To credit his own lie, he did believe
He was indeed the Duke, out o' th' substitution
And executing th' outward face of royalty

64 o' th' teen: of the trouble.

65 from: absent from.

68 perfidious: treacherous; **next:** next to.

71 signories: lordships; **first:** foremost.

72 prime: most important.

77 rapt: engrossed.

79 Being once perfected: having mastered; **suits:** petitions.

81 trash: restrain; **overtopping:** exceeding their authority.

82–83 or changed ... formed 'em: either changed their allegiance or created new officials.

85 that: so that.

87 verdure: sap; vitality.

90 closeness: privacy.

91–92 but by ... rate: was more valuable than the public could appreciate merely because it was so secluded.

94 did beget of him: produced in him.

97 sans bound: without limit.

105 With all prerogative. Hence, his ambition growing—
Dost thou hear?

Miranda. Your tale, sir, would cure deafness.

Prospero. To have no screen between this part he played
And him he played it for, he needs will be
110 Absolute Milan. Me, poor man, my library
Was dukedom large enough. Of temporal royalties
He thinks me now incapable; confederates,
So dry he was for sway, wi' th' King of Naples
To give him annual tribute, do him homage,
115 Subject his coronet to his crown, and bend
The dukedom, yet unbowed—alas, poor Milan!—
To most ignoble stooping.

Miranda.   O, the heavens!

Prospero. Mark his condition and th' event. Then tell me
If this might be a brother.

Miranda.   I should sin
120 To think but nobly of my grandmother.
Good wombs have borne bad sons.

Prospero.   Now the condition.
This King of Naples, being an enemy
To me inveterate, hearkens my brother's suit,
Which was that he, in lieu o' th' premises
125 Of homage and I know not how much tribute,
Should presently extirpate me and mine
Out of the dukedom, and confer fair Milan,
With all the honors, on my brother; whereon,
A treacherous army levied, one midnight
130 Fated to th' purpose did Antonio open
The gates of Milan, and i' th' dead of darkness
The ministers for th' purpose hurried thence
Me and thy crying self.

Miranda.   Alack, for pity!
I, not rememb'ring how I cried out then,
135 Will cry it o'er again. It is a hint
That wrings mine eyes to 't.

Prospero.   Hear a little further,
And then I'll bring thee to the present business
Which now 's upon 's, without the which this story
Were most impertinent.

Miranda.   Wherefore did they not
140 That hour destroy us?

108–110 To have . . . Milan: To have no barrier between himself and his role, he must become the duke of Milan without any restrictions.

110 Me: for me.

111 temporal royalties: worldly powers.

112–117 confederates . . . stooping: Antonio was so thirsty for power that he formed an alliance with the king of Naples, agreeing to make annual payments, to declare his obedience, and to turn Milan into a subject state.

123 hearkens . . . suit: listens to my brother's proposal.

124–128 in lieu . . . brother: In return for Antonio's agreement to pay homage and tribute, the king of Naples was to immediately remove Prospero and his family from Milan and give the dukedom to Antonio.

132 ministers: agents

135 hint: occasion.

139 impertinent: irrelevant; **Wherefore:** why.

Prospero.   Well demanded, wench.
My tale provokes that question. Dear, they durst not,
So dear the love my people bore me, nor set
A mark so bloody on the business, but
With colors fairer painted their foul ends.
In few, they hurried us aboard a bark,
Bore us some leagues to sea, where they prepared
A rotten carcass of a butt, not rigged,
Nor tackle, sail, nor mast; the very rats
Instinctively have quit it. There they hoist us
To cry to th' sea that roared to us, to sigh
To th' winds, whose pity, sighing back again,
Did us but loving wrong.

Miranda.   Alack, what trouble
Was I then to you!

Prospero.   O, a cherubin
Thou wast that did preserve me. Thou didst smile,
Infusèd with a fortitude from heaven,
When I have decked the sea with drops full salt,
Under my burden groaned, which raised in me
An undergoing stomach to bear up
Against what should ensue.

Miranda. How came we ashore?

Prospero. By providence divine.
Some food we had, and some fresh water, that
A noble Neapolitan, Gonzalo,
Out of his charity, who being then appointed
Master of this design, did give us, with
Rich garments, linens, stuffs, and necessaries,
Which since have steaded much. So, of his gentleness,
Knowing I loved my books, he furnished me
From mine own library with volumes that
I prize above my dukedom.

Miranda.   Would I might
But ever see that man.

Prospero [*standing*]. Now I arise.
Sit still, and hear the last of our sea-sorrow.
Here in this island we arrived, and here
Have I, thy schoolmaster, made thee more profit
Than other princes can, that have more time
For vainer hours and tutors not so careful.

Miranda. Heavens thank you for 't. And now I pray
  you, sir—

141 durst: dared.

145 few: brief; **bark:** ship.

147 butt: barrel or tub.

148 Nor . . . nor: having neither . . . nor.

151–152 sighing back . . . wrong: the wind's sympathetic sighing wronged us by blowing the boat out to sea.

156 decked: adorned.

157–158 which raised . . . bear up: your smiling gave me the courage to endure.

166 stuffs: materials.

167 have steaded much: have been very useful; **gentleness:** nobility.

174 made thee more profit: made you profit more.

175 princes: royal children.

For still 'tis beating in my mind—your reason
For raising this sea storm?

Prospero.   Know thus far forth:
180 By accident most strange, bountiful Fortune,
Now my dear lady, hath mine enemies
Brought to this shore; and by my prescience
I find my zenith doth depend upon
A most auspicious star, whose influence
185 If now I court not, but omit, my fortunes
Will ever after droop. Here cease more questions.
Thou art inclined to sleep. 'Tis a good dullness,
And give it way. I know thou canst not choose.

[Miranda *falls asleep.* Prospero *puts on his cloak.*]

Come away, servant, come. I am ready now.
190 Approach, my Ariel. Come.

[*Enter* Ariel.]

Ariel. All hail, great master! Grave sir, hail! I come
To answer thy best pleasure. Be 't to fly,
To swim, to dive into the fire, to ride
On the curled clouds, to thy strong bidding task
195 Ariel and all his quality.

Prospero.   Hast thou, spirit,
Performed to point the tempest that I bade thee?

Ariel. To every article.
I boarded the King's ship; now on the beak,
Now in the waist, the deck, in every cabin,
200 I flamed amazement. Sometimes I'd divide
And burn in many places. On the topmast,
The yards, and bowsprit would I flame distinctly,
Then meet and join. Jove's lightning, the precursors
O' th' dreadful thunderclaps, more momentary
205 And sight-outrunning were not. The fire and cracks
Of sulfurous roaring the most mighty Neptune
Seem to besiege and make his bold waves tremble,
Yea, his dread trident shake.

Prospero.   My brave spirit!
Who was so firm, so constant, that this coil
210 Would not infect his reason?

Ariel.   Not a soul
But felt a fever of the mad, and played
Some tricks of desperation. All but mariners
Plunged in the foaming brine and quit the vessel,
Then all afire with me. The King's son, Ferdinand,
215 With hair up-staring—then like reeds, not hair—

Was the first man that leaped; cried "Hell is empty,
And all the devils are here."

Prospero.   Why, that's my spirit!
But was not this nigh shore?

218 nigh: near.

Ariel.   Close by, my master.

Prospero. But are they, Ariel, safe?

Ariel.   Not a hair perished.
220 On their sustaining garments not a blemish,
But fresher than before; and, as thou bad'st me,
In troops I have dispersed them 'bout the isle.
The King's son have I landed by himself,
Whom I left cooling of the air with sighs
225 In an odd angle of the isle, and sitting,
His arms in this sad knot.

[*He folds his arms.*]

220 sustaining garments: garments that helped them float.

221 bad'st: commanded.

222 troops: groups.

225 odd angle: out-of-the-way corner.

Prospero.   Of the King's ship,
The mariners say how thou hast disposed,
And all the rest o' th' fleet.

Ariel.   Safely in harbor
Is the King's ship. In the deep nook, where once
230 Thou called'st me up at midnight to fetch dew
From the still-vexed Bermoothes, there she's hid;
The mariners all under hatches stowed,
Who, with a charm joined to their suffered labor,
I have left asleep. And for the rest o' th' fleet,
235 Which I dispersed, they all have met again
And are upon the Mediterranean float,
Bound sadly home for Naples,
Supposing that they saw the King's ship wracked
And his great person perish.

231 still-vexed Bermoothes: always stormy Bermudas.

233 with a . . . labor: under the combined effects of my spell and their exhaustion.

236 float: sea.

Prospero.   Ariel, thy charge
240 Exactly is performed. But there's more work.
What is the time o' th' day?

Ariel.   Past the mid season.

241 mid season: noon.

Prospero. At least two glasses. The time 'twixt six
and now
Must by us both be spent most preciously.

242 two glasses: two o'clock (two hourglasses past noon).

Ariel. Is there more toil? Since thou dost give me pains,
245 Let me remember thee what thou hast promised,
Which is not yet performed me.

244 pains: tasks.

245 remember: remind.

Prospero.   How now? Moody?
What is 't thou canst demand?

Ariel.   My liberty.

Prospero. Before the time be out? No more.

Ariel.   I prithee,
Remember I have done thee worthy service,
250 Told thee no lies, made no mistakings, served
Without or grudge or grumblings. Thou did promise
To bate me a full year.

Prospero.   Dost thou forget
From what a torment I did free thee?

Ariel.   No.

Prospero. Thou dost, and think'st it much to tread the ooze
255 Of the salt deep,
To run upon the sharp wind of the north,
To do me business in the veins o'th'earth
When it is baked with frost.

Ariel.   I do not, sir.

Prospero. Thou liest, malignant thing. Hast thou forgot
260 The foul witch Sycorax, who with age and envy
Was grown into a hoop? Hast thou forgot her?

Ariel. No, sir.

Prospero. Thou hast. Where was she born? Speak. Tell me.

Ariel. Sir, in Argier.

Prospero.   O, was she so? I must
265 Once in a month recount what thou hast been,
Which thou forget'st. This damned witch Sycorax,
For mischiefs manifold, and sorceries terrible
To enter human hearing, from Argier,
Thou know'st, was banished. For one thing she did
270 They would not take her life. Is not this true?

Ariel. Ay, sir.

Prospero. This blue-eyed hag was hither brought with child
And here was left by th' sailors. Thou, my slave,
As thou report'st thyself, was then her servant,
275 And for thou wast a spirit too delicate
To act her earthy and abhorred commands,
Refusing her grand hests, she did confine thee,
By help of her more potent ministers
And in her most unmitigable rage,
280 Into a cloven pine, within which rift

248 prithee: beg of you.

251 or … or: either … or.

252 bate me: deduct from the time of my service.

257 veins o'th' earth: mineral veins or underground streams.

258 baked: hardened.

261 grown into a hoop: bent over.

264 Argier: Algiers.

269–272 Sycorax was exiled rather than killed, probably because she was pregnant (blue eyelids were thought to be a sign of pregnancy).

275 for: because.

277 hests: commands.

278 ministers: agents.

Imprisoned thou didst painfully remain
A dozen years; within which space she died
And left thee there, where thou didst vent thy groans
As fast as mill wheels strike. Then was this island
285 (Save for the son that she did litter here,
A freckled whelp, hag-born) not honored with
A human shape.

Ariel.   Yes, Caliban, her son.

Prospero. Dull thing, I say so; he, that Caliban
Whom now I keep in service. Thou best know'st
290 What torment I did find thee in. Thy groans
Did make wolves howl, and penetrate the breasts
Of ever-angry bears. It was a torment
To lay upon the damned, which Sycorax
Could not again undo. It was mine art,
295 When I arrived and heard thee, that made gape
The pine and let thee out.

Ariel.   I thank thee, master.

Prospero. If thou more murmur'st, I will rend an oak
And peg thee in his knotty entrails till
Thou hast howled away twelve winters.

Ariel.   Pardon, master.
300 I will be correspondent to command
And do my spriting gently.

Prospero. Do so, and after two days
I will discharge thee.

Ariel.   That's my noble master.
What shall I do? Say, what? What shall I do?

305 **Prospero.** Go make thyself like a nymph o' th' sea.
    Be subject
To no sight but thine and mine, invisible
To every eyeball else. Go, take this shape,
And hither come in 't. Go, hence with diligence!

[Ariel *exits*.]

Awake, dear heart, awake. Thou hast slept well.
310 Awake.

[Miranda *wakes*.]

Miranda. The strangeness of your story put
Heaviness in me.

Prospero.   Shake it off. Come on,
We'll visit Caliban, my slave, who never
Yields us kind answer.

284 as mill wheels strike: as the blades of mill wheels strike the water.

285 litter: give birth to.

291 penetrate the breasts: arouse the sympathy.

300 correspondent: obedient.

301 spriting: spiriting; **gently:** willingly.

311 Heaviness: drowsiness.

Miranda [*rising*].   'Tis a villain, sir,
I do not love to look on.

Prospero.   But, as 'tis,
315 We cannot miss him. He does make our fire,
Fetch in our wood, and serves in offices
That profit us.—What ho, slave, Caliban!
Thou earth, thou, speak!

Caliban [*within*].   There's wood enough within.

Prospero. Come forth, I say. There's other business
    for thee.
320 Come, thou tortoise. When?

[*Enter* Ariel *like a water nymph.*]

Fine apparition! My quaint Ariel,
Hark in thine ear.

[*He whispers to* Ariel.]

Ariel.   My lord, it shall be done.

[*He exits.*]

315 miss: do without.

316 serves in offices:
performs duties.

321 quaint: ingenious;
elegant.

Prospero [*to* Caliban]. Thou poisonous slave, got by the
  devil himself
Upon thy wicked dam, come forth!

[*Enter* Caliban.]

325 **Caliban.** As wicked dew as e'er my mother brushed
With raven's feather from unwholesome fen
Drop on you both. A southwest blow on you
And blister you all o'er.

Prospero. For this, be sure, tonight thou shalt have
  cramps,
330 Side-stitches that shall pen thy breath up. Urchins
Shall forth at vast of night that they may work
All exercise on thee. Thou shalt be pinched
As thick as honeycomb, each pinch more stinging
Than bees that made 'em.

Caliban.   I must eat my dinner.
335 This island's mine by Sycorax, my mother,
Which thou tak'st from me. When thou cam'st first,
Thou strok'st me and made much of me, wouldst
  give me
Water with berries in 't, and teach me how
To name the bigger light and how the less,
340 That burn by day and night. And then I loved thee,
And showed thee all the qualities o' th' isle,
The fresh springs, brine pits, barren place and fertile.
Cursed be I that did so! All the charms
Of Sycorax, toads, beetles, bats, light on you,
345 For I am all the subjects that you have,
Which first was mine own king; and here you sty me
In this hard rock, whiles you do keep from me
The rest o' th' island.

Prospero.   Thou most lying slave,
Whom stripes may move, not kindness, I have
  used thee,
350 Filth as thou art, with humane care, and lodged thee
In mine own cell, till thou didst seek to violate
The honor of my child.

Caliban. O ho, O ho! Would 't had been done!
Thou didst prevent me. I had peopled else
355 This isle with Calibans.

Miranda.   Abhorrèd slave,
Which any print of goodness wilt not take,
Being capable of all ill! I pitied thee,
Took pains to make thee speak, taught thee each hour

323 **got:** fathered.

324 **dam:** mother.

326 **fen:** bog.

327 **southwest:** Winds
from the southwest were
considered unhealthy.

330 **Urchins:**
hedgehogs or goblins.

331 **forth at vast:** go
forth during the long
stretch.

332–333 **Thou shalt . . .
honeycomb:** The
pinches on your body
will be as dense as the
cells in a honeycomb.

337 **strok'st:** stroked.

339 **bigger light:** the
sun; **the less:** the moon.

343 **charms:** spells.

346 **sty me:** pen me up
like a pig.

349 **stripes:** lashes;
used: treated.

354 **I had peopled else:**
otherwise I would have
populated.

356 **Which any . . . take:**
upon whom goodness
cannot make any
impression.

357 **capable of all ill:**
inclined to every evil.

One thing or other. When thou didst not, savage,
360 Know thine own meaning, but wouldst gabble like
A thing most brutish, I endowed thy purposes
With words that made them known. But thy vile race,
Though thou didst learn, had that in 't which
    good natures
Could not abide to be with. Therefore wast thou
365 Deservedly confined into this rock,
Who hadst deserved more than a prison.

Caliban. You taught me language, and my profit on 't
Is I know how to curse. The red plague rid you
For learning me your language!

Prospero.   Hagseed, hence!
370 Fetch us in fuel; and be quick, thou 'rt best,
To answer other business. Shrugg'st thou, malice?
If thou neglect'st or dost unwillingly
What I command, I'll rack thee with old cramps,
Fill all thy bones with aches, make thee roar
375 That beasts shall tremble at thy din.

Caliban.   No, pray thee.
[aside] I must obey. His art is of such power
It would control my dam's god, Setebos,
And make a vassal of him.

Prospero.   So, slave, hence.

[Caliban exits.]

[Enter Ferdinand; and Ariel, invisible, playing and singing.]

[song]

Ariel.
    Come unto these yellow sands,
380   And then take hands.
    Curtsied when you have, and kissed
        The wild waves whist.
    Foot it featly here and there,
        And sweet sprites bear
385   The burden. Hark, hark!
[burden dispersedly, within:] Bow-wow.
        The watchdogs bark.
[burden dispersedly, within:] Bow-wow.
        Hark, hark! I hear
390   The strain of strutting chanticleer
        Cry cock-a-diddle-dow.

Ferdinand. Where should this music be? I' th' air, or
    th' earth?
It sounds no more; and sure it waits upon

362 **race:** natural disposition.

368 **red plague:** plague that causes red sores; **rid:** destroy.

369 **Hagseed:** witch's offspring.

371 **answer other business:** perform other tasks.

373 **rack ... cramps:** torture you with the cramps of old people.

377 **Setebos:** a god that was worshiped in Patagonia, a region of South America.

378 **vassal:** servant or slave.

382 **whist:** into silence.

383 **Foot it featly:** dance nimbly.

384–385 **bear ... burden:** sing the refrain.

390 **strain:** tune; **chanticleer:** a rooster.

393 **waits:** attends.

Some god o' th' island. Sitting on a bank,
395 Weeping again the King my father's wrack,
This music crept by me upon the waters,
Allaying both their fury and my passion
With its sweet air. Thence I have followed it,
Or it hath drawn me rather. But 'tis gone.
400 No, it begins again.

[*song*]

Ariel.
    Full fathom five thy father lies.
      Of his bones are coral made.
    Those are pearls that were his eyes.
      Nothing of him that doth fade
405   *But doth suffer a sea change*
    Into something rich and strange.
    Sea nymphs hourly ring his knell.
[*burden, within:*] *Ding dong.*
    Hark, now I hear them: ding dong bell.

410 **Ferdinand.** The ditty does remember my drowned
    father.
This is no mortal business, nor no sound
That the earth owes. I hear it now above me.

Prospero [*to* Miranda]. The fringèd curtains of thine
    eye advance
And say what thou seest yond.

Miranda.   What is 't? A spirit?
415 Lord, how it looks about! Believe me, sir,
It carries a brave form. But 'tis a spirit.

Prospero. No, wench, it eats and sleeps and hath
    such senses
As we have, such. This gallant which thou seest
Was in the wrack; and, but he's something stained
420 With grief—that's beauty's canker—thou might'st
    call him
A goodly person. He hath lost his fellows
And strays about to find 'em.

Miranda.   I might call him
A thing divine, for nothing natural
I ever saw so noble.

Prospero [*aside*].   It goes on, I see,
425 As my soul prompts it. [*to* Ariel] Spirit, fine spirit,
    I'll free thee
Within two days for this.

397 passion: sorrow; suffering.

398 air: melody

401 Full fathom five: fully five fathoms (30 feet) deep.

407 knell: funeral bell.

410 ditty: song.

411 mortal: human.

412 owes: owns.

413 fringèd curtains: eyelids; **advance:** raise.

416 brave form: splendid appearance.

418 gallant: fine gentleman.

419 but: except that; **something:** somewhat.

420 canker: infection; spreading sore.

424 It goes on: my plan proceeds.

Ferdinand [*seeing* Miranda]. Most sure, the goddess
On whom these airs attend!—Vouchsafe my prayer
May know if you remain upon this island,
And that you will some good instruction give
430 How I may bear me here. My prime request,
Which I do last pronounce, is—O you wonder!—
If you be maid or no.

Miranda.   No wonder, sir,
But certainly a maid.

Ferdinand.   My language! Heavens!
I am the best of them that speak this speech,
435 Were I but where 'tis spoken.

Prospero.   How? The best?
What wert thou if the King of Naples heard thee?

Ferdinand. A single thing, as I am now, that wonders
To hear thee speak of Naples. He does hear me,
And that he does I weep. Myself am Naples,
440 Who with mine eyes, never since at ebb, beheld
The King my father wracked.

Miranda.   Alack, for mercy!

Ferdinand. Yes, faith, and all his lords, the Duke
    of Milan
And his brave son being twain.

Prospero [*aside*].   The Duke of Milan
And his more braver daughter could control thee,
445 If now 'twere fit to do 't. At the first sight
They have changed eyes.—Delicate Ariel,
I'll set thee free for this. [*to* Ferdinand] A word,
    good sir.
I fear you have done yourself some wrong. A word.

Miranda. Why speaks my father so ungently? This
450 Is the third man that e'er I saw, the first
That e'er I sighed for. Pity move my father
To be inclined my way.

Ferdinand.   O, if a virgin,
And your affection not gone forth, I'll make you
The Queen of Naples.

Prospero.   Soft, sir, one word more.
455 [*aside*] They are both in either's powers. But this
    swift business
I must uneasy make, lest too light winning
Make the prize light. [*to* Ferdinand] One word
    more. I charge thee

---

427 **Vouchsafe:** grant.

428 **May know:** that
I may know; **remain:**
dwell.

430 **bear me:** conduct
myself.

432 **maid:** a girl
(as opposed to a
supernatural being).

434 **the best:** highest
in rank.

437 **a single thing:** one
and the same.

438 **Naples:** king of
Naples.

440 **at ebb:** dry.

443 **twain:** two.

444 **control:** refute.

446 **changed eyes:**
exchanged loving looks.

448 **done yourself
some wrong:** spoken
in error.

453 **your affection not
gone forth:** not already
in love with someone
else.

454 **Soft:** wait a minute.

455 **either's:** each
other's.

456 **uneasy:** difficult;
light: easy.

457 **light:** cheap.

That thou attend me. Thou dost here usurp
The name thou ow'st not, and hast put thyself
460 Upon this island as a spy, to win it
From me, the lord on 't.

Ferdinand.   No, as I am a man!

Miranda. There's nothing ill can dwell in such a temple.
If the ill spirit have so fair a house,
Good things will strive to dwell with 't.

Prospero [*to* Ferdinand].   Follow me.
465 [*to* Miranda] Speak not you for him. He's a traitor.
    [*to* Ferdinand] Come,
I'll manacle thy neck and feet together.
Sea water shalt thou drink. Thy food shall be
The fresh-brook mussels, withered roots, and husks
Wherein the acorn cradled. Follow.

Ferdinand.   No,
470 I will resist such entertainment till
Mine enemy has more power.

[*He draws, and is charmed from moving.*]

Miranda.   O dear father,
Make not too rash a trial of him, for
He's gentle and not fearful.

Prospero.   What, I say,
My foot my tutor?—Put thy sword up, traitor,
475 Who mak'st a show, but dar'st not strike, thy
        conscience
Is so possessed with guilt. Come from thy ward,
For I can here disarm thee with this stick
And make thy weapon drop.

Miranda.   Beseech you, father—

Prospero. Hence! Hang not on my garments.

Miranda.   Sir, have pity.
480 I'll be his surety.

Prospero.   Silence! One word more
Shall make me chide thee, if not hate thee. What,
An advocate for an impostor? Hush.
Thou think'st there is no more such shapes as he,
Having seen but him and Caliban. Foolish wench,
485 To th' most of men this is a Caliban,
And they to him are angels.

458–459 Thou dost . . . not: You are unlawfully claiming the title of king, which is not rightly yours.

462 such a temple: Ferdinand's handsome exterior.

468 fresh-brook mussels: freshwater mussels (which are inedible).

470 entertainment: treatment.

Stage direction— *charmed from moving:* put under a spell that immobilizes him.

472 rash a trial: strong a test.

473 gentle: noble.

474 My foot my tutor: Should I let my inferior (Miranda) teach me how to act?

476 ward: fencer's defensive posture.

477 stick: magician's staff.

480 his surety: responsible for him.

485 To: compared to.

Miranda.   My affections
Are then most humble. I have no ambition
To see a goodlier man.

Prospero [*to* Ferdinand]. Come on, obey.
Thy nerves are in their infancy again
490 And have no vigor in them.

Ferdinand.   So they are.
My spirits, as in a dream, are all bound up.
My father's loss, the weakness which I feel,
The wrack of all my friends, nor this man's threats
To whom I am subdued, are but light to me,
495 Might I but through my prison once a day
Behold this maid. All corners else o' th' earth
Let liberty make use of. Space enough
Have I in such a prison.

Prospero [*aside*].   It works.—Come on.—
Thou hast done well, fine Ariel.—Follow me.
500 [*to* Ariel] Hark what thou else shalt do me.

Miranda [*to* Ferdinand].   Be of comfort.
My father's of a better nature, sir,
Than he appears by speech. This is unwonted
Which now came from him.

Prospero [*to* Ariel].   Thou shalt be as free
As mountain winds; but then exactly do
505 All points of my command.

Ariel.   To th' syllable.

Prospero [*to* Ferdinand]. Come follow. [*to* Miranda]
   Speak not for him.

[*They exit.*]

489 **Thy nerves . . .
again:** your sinews are
like those of a baby.

494 **but light:** of little
importance.

496 **All corners else:** all
other places.

502 **unwonted:**
unusual.

504 **then:** if that is to
occur.

Act II

Scene 1

[*Enter* Alonso, Sebastian, Antonio, Gonzalo, Adrian, Francisco, *and others.*]

Gonzalo [*to* Alonso]. Beseech you, sir, be merry. You
    have cause—
So have we all—of joy, for our escape
Is much beyond our loss. Our hint of woe
Is common; every day some sailor's wife,
5 The masters of some merchant, and the merchant
Have just our theme of woe. But for the miracle—
I mean our preservation—few in millions
Can speak like us. Then wisely, good sir, weigh
Our sorrow with our comfort.

Alonso.   Prithee, peace.

10 **Sebastian** [*aside to* Antonio]. He receives comfort like
cold porridge.

Antonio. The visitor will not give him o'er so.

Sebastian. Look, he's winding up the watch of his wit.
By and by it will strike.

15 **Gonzalo** [*to* Alonso]. Sir—

Sebastian. One. Tell.

Gonzalo. When every grief is entertained that's offered,
comes to th' entertainer—

Sebastian. A dollar.

20 **Gonzalo.** Dolor comes to him indeed. You have spoken
truer than you purposed.

Sebastian. You have taken it wiselier than I meant
you should.

Gonzalo [*to* Alonso]. Therefore, my lord—

25 **Antonio.** Fie, what a spendthrift is he of his tongue.

Alonso [*to* Gonzalo]. I prithee, spare.

Gonzalo. Well, I have done. But yet—

Sebastian [*aside to* Antonio]. He will be talking.

Antonio [*aside to* Sebastian]. Which, of he or Adrian,
30 for a good wager, first begins to crow?

Sebastian. The old cock.

3 beyond: greater than; **hint:** occasion.

6 just: exactly

11 cold porridge: pease porridge (a pun on Alonso's cry for "peace").

12 visitor: a person responsible for comforting the sick in their homes; **give him o'er so:** abandon him.

16 One: It has struck one; **Tell:** Keep count.

17 entertained: held in the mind.

18 entertainer: person who holds the grief.

19 A dollar: a pun on the meaning of entertainer as "someone who is paid to amuse others."

20 Dolor: sorrow. This is a play on the word *dollar* in line 19.

26 spare: spare your words.

Antonio. The cockerel.

Sebastian. Done. The wager?

Antonio. A laughter.

35 **Sebastian.** A match!

Adrian. Though this island seem to be desert—

Antonio. Ha, ha, ha.

Sebastian. So. You're paid.

Adrian. Uninhabitable and almost inaccessible—

40 **Sebastian.** Yet—

Adrian. Yet—

Antonio. He could not miss 't.

Adrian. It must needs be of subtle, tender, and delicate temperance.

45 **Antonio.** Temperance was a delicate wench.

Sebastian. Ay, and a subtle, as he most learnedly delivered.

Adrian. The air breathes upon us here most sweetly.

Sebastian. As if it had lungs, and rotten ones.

50 **Antonio.** Or as 'twere perfumed by a fen.

Gonzalo. Here is everything advantageous to life.

Antonio. True, save means to live.

Sebastian. Of that there's none, or little.

Gonzalo. How lush and lusty the grass looks! How
55 green!

Antonio. The ground indeed is tawny.

Sebastian. With an eye of green in 't.

Antonio. He misses not much.

Sebastian. No, he doth but mistake the truth totally.

60 **Gonzalo.** But the rarity of it is, which is indeed almost beyond credit—

Sebastian. As many vouched rarities are.

Gonzalo. That our garments, being, as they were, drenched in the sea, hold notwithstanding their
65 freshness and gloss, being rather new-dyed than stained with salt water.

30–32 first begins to crow: will speak first. (Sebastian and Antonio allude to the proverbial saying "The young cock (**cockerel**) crows as he the old hears.")

34 A laughter: Antonio alludes to the saying "He laughs that wins."

36 desert: deserted

44 Temperance: climate (also a woman's name, which inspires Antonio's punning response).

52 save: except for.

54 lush and lusty: abundant and vigorous.

56 tawny: yellowish-brown (parched by the sun).

57 eye: tinge.

60 rarity: exceptional quality.

62 vouched rarities: alleged wonders.

Antonio. If but one of his pockets could speak, would it not say he lies?

Sebastian. Ay, or very falsely pocket up his report.

69 **pocket up:** conceal; suppress.

70 **Gonzalo.** Methinks our garments are now as fresh as when we put them on first in Afric, at the marriage of the King's fair daughter Claribel to the King of Tunis.

71 **Afric:** Africa.

Sebastian. 'Twas a sweet marriage, and we prosper
75 well in our return.

Adrian. Tunis was never graced before with such a paragon to their queen.

77 **to:** for.

Gonzalo. Not since widow Dido's time.

78 **Dido:** a queen of Carthage who, in Virgil's *Aeneid*, commits suicide after Aeneas abandons her.

Antonio. Widow? A pox o' that! How came that
80 "widow" in? Widow Dido!

Sebastian. What if he had said "widower Aeneas" too? Good Lord, how you take it!

Adrian [*to* Gonzalo]. "Widow Dido," said you? You make me study of that. She was of Carthage, not
85 of Tunis.

84 **study of:** think about.

Gonzalo. This Tunis, sir, was Carthage.

86 Tunis was built near the site of Carthage.

Adrian. Carthage?

Gonzalo. I assure you, Carthage.

Antonio. His word is more than the miraculous harp.

90 **Sebastian.** He hath raised the wall, and houses too.

89 **miraculous harp:** In Greek mythology, Amphion used his harp to raise a wall around Thebes. (Antonio suggests that Gonzalo has surpassed this feat by raising an entire city.)

Antonio. What impossible matter will he make easy next?

Sebastian. I think he will carry this island home in his pocket and give it his son for an apple.

95 **Antonio.** And sowing the kernels of it in the sea, bring forth more islands.

95 **kernels:** seeds.

Gonzalo. Ay.

Antonio. Why, in good time.

97 **Ay:** probably an affirmation of his earlier statement that Tunis was Carthage.

Gonzalo [*to* Alonso]. Sir, we were talking that our
100 garments seem now as fresh as when we were at Tunis at the marriage of your daughter, who is now queen.

Antonio. And the rarest that e'er came there.

Sebastian. Bate, I beseech you, widow Dido.

104 **Bate:** except for.

105 **Antonio.** O, widow Dido? Ay, widow Dido.

Gonzalo [*to* Alonso]. Is not, sir, my doublet as fresh as the first day I wore it? I mean, in a sort.

Antonio. That "sort" was well fished for.

Gonzalo [*to* Alonso]. When I wore it at your daughter's
110 marriage.

Alonso. You cram these words into mine ears against
The stomach of my sense. Would I had never
Married my daughter there, for coming thence
My son is lost, and, in my rate, she too,
115 Who is so far from Italy removed
I ne'er again shall see her.— O, thou mine heir
Of Naples and of Milan, what strange fish
Hath made his meal on thee?

Francisco.   Sir, he may live.
I saw him beat the surges under him
120 And ride upon their backs. He trod the water,
Whose enmity he flung aside, and breasted
The surge most swoll'n that met him. His bold head
'Bove the contentious waves he kept, and oared
Himself with his good arms in lusty stroke
125 To th' shore, that o'er his wave-worn basis bowed,
As stooping to relieve him. I not doubt
He came alive to land.

Alonso.   No, no, he's gone.

Sebastian. Sir, you may thank yourself for this great loss,
That would not bless our Europe with your daughter,
130 But rather lose her to an African,
Where she at least is banished from your eye,
Who hath cause to wet the grief on 't.

Alonso.   Prithee, peace.

Sebastian. You were kneeled to and importuned
     otherwise
By all of us; and the fair soul herself
135 Weighed between loathness and obedience at
Which end o' th' beam should bow. We have lost
     your son,
I fear, forever. Milan and Naples have
More widows in them of this business' making
Than we bring men to comfort them.
140 The fault's your own.

Alonso.   So is the dear'st o' th' loss.

Gonzalo. My lord Sebastian,
The truth you speak doth lack some gentleness

107 in a sort: to some extent.

108 sort: lot (in the game of drawing lots).

111–112 against . . . sense: although I am in no mood to hear them.

114 rate: estimation.

119 surges: waves.

124 lusty: vigorous.

125–126 that o'er . . . him: The cliff at the shoreline, eroded at its base by waves, seemed as if it were stooping over to help Ferdinand.

132 Who . . . on't: you who have reason to weep over the sorrow of it.

133 importuned otherwise: begged to change your decision.

134–136 the fair . . . bow: Claribel weighed on a scale (**beam**) her distaste (**loathness**) for the marriage against her wish to obey her father.

140 dear'st: most costly.

And time to speak it in. You rub the sore
When you should bring the plaster.

Sebastian.   Very well.

145   **Antonio.** And most chirurgeonly.

Gonzalo [*to* Alonso]. It is foul weather in us all, good sir,
When you are cloudy.

Sebastian.   Foul weather?

Antonio.   Very foul.

Gonzalo. Had I plantation of this isle, my lord—

Antonio. He'd sow 't with nettle seed.

Sebastian.   Or docks, or mallows.

150   **Gonzalo.** And were the King on 't, what would I do?

Sebastian. Scape being drunk, for want of wine.

Gonzalo. I' th' commonwealth I would by contraries
Execute all things, for no kind of traffic
Would I admit; no name of magistrate;
155   Letters should not be known; riches, poverty,
And use of service, none; contract, succession,
Bourn, bound of land, tilth, vineyard, none;
No use of metal, corn, or wine, or oil;
No occupation; all men idle, all,
160   And women too, but innocent and pure;
No sovereignty—

Sebastian.   Yet he would be king on 't.

Antonio. The latter end of his commonwealth forgets
the beginning.

Gonzalo. All things in common nature should produce
165   Without sweat or endeavor; treason, felony,
Sword, pike, knife, gun, or need of any engine
Would I not have; but nature should bring forth
Of its own kind all foison, all abundance,
To feed my innocent people.

170   **Sebastian.** No marrying 'mong his subjects?

Antonio. None, man, all idle: whores and knaves.

Gonzalo. I would with such perfection govern, sir,
T' excel the Golden Age.

Sebastian.   'Save his Majesty!

Antonio. Long live Gonzalo!

Gonzalo.   And do you mark me, sir?

144 plaster: a medicinal paste applied to the body.

145 chirurgeonly: like a surgeon.

148 Had I plantation: if I were responsible for colonizing. (Antonio's response plays with the meaning "planting.")

149 nettle seed … docks … mallows: types of weeds.

152–153 by contraries … things: carry out everything in a manner opposite to what is customary.

153 traffic: commerce.

155 Letters: writing learning.

156 use of service: employment of servants; **succession:** inheritance.

157 Bourn: boundary; **tilth:** cultivation of land.

158 corn: grain.

164 in common: for communal use.

166 engine: weapon.

168 foison: plenty.

173 'Save: God save.

175 **Alonso.** Prithee, no more. Thou dost talk nothing to me.

Gonzalo. I do well believe your Highness, and did it to minister occasion to these gentlemen, who are of such sensible and nimble lungs that they always use to laugh at nothing.

177 minister occasion: provide an opportunity.

178 sensible: sensitive; **use:** are accustomed.

180 **Antonio.** 'Twas you we laughed at.

Gonzalo. Who in this kind of merry fooling am nothing to you. So you may continue, and laugh at nothing still.

Antonio. What a blow was there given!

185 **Sebastian.** An it had not fallen flatlong.

185 An it ... flatlong: if it had not been given with the flat of the sword (rather than the edge).

Gonzalo. You are gentlemen of brave mettle. You would lift the moon out of her sphere if she would continue in it five weeks without changing.

186 mettle: temperament.

187 sphere: orbit.

[*Enter Ariel, invisible, playing solemn music.*]

Sebastian. We would so, and then go a-batfowling.

189 a-batfowling: hunting birds at night with a stick (Sebastian proposes using the moon for a lantern).

190 **Antonio** [*to* Gonzalo]. Nay, good my lord, be not angry.

Gonzalo. No, I warrant you, I will not adventure my
discretion so weakly. Will you laugh me asleep? For
I am very heavy.

Antonio. Go sleep, and hear us.

[*All sink down asleep except* Alonso, Antonio, *and* Sebastian.]

195 **Alonso.** What, all so soon asleep? I wish mine eyes
Would, with themselves, shut up my thoughts. I find
They are inclined to do so.

Sebastian.   Please you, sir,
Do not omit the heavy offer of it.
It seldom visits sorrow; when it doth,
200 It is a comforter.

Antonio.   We two, my lord,
Will guard your person while you take your rest,
And watch your safety.

Alonso.   Thank you. Wondrous heavy.

[Alonso *sleeps.* Ariel *exits.*]

Sebastian. What a strange drowsiness possesses them!

Antonio. It is the quality o' th' climate.

Sebastian.   Why
205 Doth it not then our eyelids sink? I find
Not myself disposed to sleep.

Antonio. Nor I. My spirits are nimble.
They fell together all, as by consent.
They dropped as by a thunderstroke. What might,
210 Worthy Sebastian, O, what might—? No more.
And yet methinks I see it in thy face
What thou shouldst be. Th'occasion speaks thee, and
My strong imagination sees a crown
Dropping upon thy head.

Sebastian.   What, art thou waking?

215 **Antonio.** Do you not hear me speak?

Sebastian.   I do, and surely
It is a sleepy language, and thou speak'st
Out of thy sleep. What is it thou didst say?
This is a strange repose, to be asleep
With eyes wide open—standing, speaking, moving—
220 And yet so fast asleep.

Antonio.   Noble Sebastian,
Thou let'st thy fortune sleep, die rather, wink'st
Whiles thou art waking.

191–192 adventure . . .
weakly: risk my
reputation by behaving
so weakly.

193 heavy: sleepy.

198 omit: neglect.

208 consent:
agreement.

212 Th'occasion speaks
thee: the opportunity
calls out to you.

214 waking: awake.

221 wink'st: you close
your eyes.

Sebastian.   Thou dost snore distinctly.
There's meaning in thy snores.

Antonio. I am more serious than my custom. You
225 Must be so too, if heed me; which to do
Trebles thee o'er.

Sebastian.   Well, I am standing water.

Antonio. I'll teach you how to flow.

Sebastian.   Do so. To ebb
Hereditary sloth instructs me.

Antonio.   O,
If you but knew how you the purpose cherish
230 Whiles thus you mock it, how in stripping it
You more invest it. Ebbing men indeed
Most often do so near the bottom run
By their own fear or sloth.

Sebastian.   Prithee, say on.
The setting of thine eye and cheek proclaim
235 A matter from thee, and a birth indeed
Which throes thee much to yield.

Antonio.   Thus, sir:
Although this lord of weak remembrance—this,
Who shall be of as little memory
When he is earthed—hath here almost persuaded—
240 For he's a spirit of persuasion, only
Professes to persuade—the King his son's alive,
'Tis as impossible that he's undrowned
As he that sleeps here swims.

Sebastian.   I have no hope
That he's undrowned.

Antonio.   O, out of that no hope
245 What great hope have you! No hope that way is
Another way so high a hope that even
Ambition cannot pierce a wink beyond,
But doubt discovery there. Will you grant with me
That Ferdinand is drowned?

Sebastian.   He's gone.

Antonio.   Then tell me,
250 Who's the next heir of Naples?

Sebastian.   Claribel.

Antonio. She that is Queen of Tunis; she that dwells
Ten leagues beyond man's life; she that from Naples
Can have no note, unless the sun were post—

---

222 distinctly: in a way that can be understood.

225 if heed me: if you pay attention to me.

226 Trebles thee o'er: makes you three times as great.

227–228 To ebb ... me: My natural laziness (**hereditary sloth**) makes me pull back.

229 the purpose cherish: encourage (**nourish**) your intention (**the purpose**).

231 invest it: clothe it.

234 setting: fixed expression.

235 A matter: something important.

236 throes thee much to yield: causes you great pain to give forth.

238 of as little memory: as quickly forgotten.

239 earthed: buried.

240–241 only ... persuade: his only profession is to persuade.

245 that way: of Ferdinand's being alive.

247–248 cannot pierce ... there: cannot set its sight on any higher goal

252 beyond man's life: farther than one could travel in a lifetime.

253 note: information; **post:** the messenger.

The man i' th' moon's too slow—till newborn chins
255 Be rough and razorable; she that from whom
We all were sea-swallowed, though some cast again,
And by that destiny to perform an act
Whereof what's past is prologue, what to come
In yours and my discharge.

260 **Sebastian.** What stuff is this? How say you?
'Tis true my brother's daughter's Queen of Tunis,
So is she heir of Naples, 'twixt which regions
There is some space.

Antonio.   A space whose ev'ry cubit
Seems to cry out "How shall that Claribel
265 Measure us back to Naples? Keep in Tunis
And let Sebastian wake." Say this were death
That now hath seized them, why, they were no worse
Than now they are. There be that can rule Naples
As well as he that sleeps, lords that can prate
270 As amply and unnecessarily
As this Gonzalo. I myself could make
A chough of as deep chat. O, that you bore
The mind that I do, what a sleep were this
For your advancement! Do you understand me?

275 **Sebastian.** Methinks I do.

Antonio.   And how does your content
Tender your own good fortune?

Sebastian.   I remember
You did supplant your brother Prospero.

Antonio.   True,
And look how well my garments sit upon me,
Much feater than before. My brother's servants
280 Were then my fellows; now they are my men.

Sebastian. But, for your conscience?

Antonio. Ay, sir, where lies that? If 'twere a kibe,
'Twould put me to my slipper, but I feel not
This deity in my bosom. Twenty consciences
285 That stand 'twixt me and Milan, candied be they
And melt ere they molest! Here lies your brother,
No better than the earth he lies upon.
If he were that which now he's like—that's dead—
Whom I with this obedient steel, three inches of it,
290 Can lay to bed forever; whiles you, doing thus,
To the perpetual wink for aye might put
This ancient morsel, this Sir Prudence, who
Should not upbraid our course. For all the rest,

255 from: coming from.

256 cast again: cast into new roles.

259 discharge: performance.

263 cubit: an ancient unit of measure varying from 17 to 22 inches.

265 Measure us: travel over our length; **Keep:** stay.

268 that: those who.

269 prate: babble.

271–272 make . . . chat: train a jackdaw (a bird related to the crow) to speak as profoundly.

275–276 how does . . . Tender: what do you think of.

279 feater: more suitably.

282–283 If 'twere . . . slipper: if it were a sore on my heel, it would force me to wear slippers.

285 candied: covered with frost; frozen.

289 steel: sword.

291 To the . . . put: might put to sleep forever.

They'll take suggestion as a cat laps milk.
295 They'll tell the clock to any business that
We say befits the hour.

Sebastian.   Thy case, dear friend,
Shall be my precedent: as thou got'st Milan,
I'll come by Naples. Draw thy sword. One stroke
Shall free thee from the tribute which thou payest,
300 And I the King shall love thee.

Antonio.   Draw together,
And when I rear my hand, do you the like
To fall it on Gonzalo.

[*They draw their swords.*]

Sebastian.   O, but one word.

[*They talk apart.*]

[*Enter Ariel, invisible, with music and song.*]

Ariel [*to the sleeping* Gonzalo]. My master through his
    art foresees the danger
That you, his friend, are in, and sends me forth—
305 For else his project dies—to keep them living.

[*sings in* Gonzalo's *ear:*]

            While you here do snoring lie,
            Open-eyed conspiracy
                His time doth take.
            If of life you keep a care,
310   *Shake off slumber and beware.*
                Awake, awake!

Antonio [*to* Sebastian]. Then let us both be sudden.

Gonzalo [*waking*]. Now, good angels preserve the King!

[*He wakes Alonso.*]

Alonso [*to* Sebastian]. Why, how now, ho! Awake? Why
    are you drawn?
315 Wherefore this ghastly looking?

Gonzalo [*to* Sebastian].   What's the matter?

Sebastian. Whiles we stood here securing your repose,
Even now, we heard a hollow burst of bellowing
Like bulls, or rather lions. Did 't not wake you?
It struck mine ear most terribly.

Alonso.   I heard nothing.

---

294 take suggestion: accept temptation.

295–296 tell the… hour: agree to anything that we say is appropriate.

305 else: otherwise; **them:** Gonzalo and Alonso.

308 His time: its opportunity.

314 Why are you drawn?: Why have you drawn your weapons?

315 Wherefore: why; **ghastly:** fearful.

316 securing your repose: guarding you while you slept.

320 **Antonio.** O, 'twas a din to fright a monster's ear,
To make an earthquake. Sure, it was the roar
Of a whole herd of lions.

Alonso. Heard you this, Gonzalo?

Gonzalo. Upon mine honor, sir, I heard a humming,
325 And that a strange one too, which did awake me.
I shaked you, sir, and cried. As mine eyes opened,   **326 cried:** cried out.
I saw their weapons drawn. There was a noise,
That's verily. 'Tis best we stand upon our guard,   **328 verily:** indeed true.
Or that we quit this place. Let's draw our weapons.

330 **Alonso.** Lead off this ground, and let's make further
    search
For my poor son.

Gonzalo.   Heavens keep him from these beasts,
For he is, sure, i' th' island.

Alonso.   Lead away.

Ariel [*aside*]. Prospero my lord shall know what I
    have done.
So, king, go safely on to seek thy son.

[*They exit.*]

COLLABORATIVE DISCUSSION Which passages about coming to a new
land were most interesting to you? Discuss this question with a partner,
citing specific textual evidence from the play. Explain why the passages drew
your interest and whether you think they reflect the actual experience of
explorers who came to the Americas.

Support Inferences: Draw Conclusions

To understand any work of literature, you must analyze what the text says explicitly or directly. You must also make **inferences,** or logical assumptions, based on details in the text. This chart shows how textual evidence from *The Tempest* could be used to draw conclusions about Prospero's character.

Textual Evidence	Analysis
"Thou art inclined to sleep. 'Tis a good dullness, / And give it way. I know thou canst not choose. [Miranda *falls asleep* . . .]" (I, ii, 187–188)	Prospero tells Miranda she is tired and cannot choose to stay awake; she immediately falls asleep. Readers can infer that Prospero has magical powers and has made his daughter sleep so that he can speak privately with Ariel.
"It was mine art, / When I arrived and heard thee, that made gape / The pine and let thee out." (I, ii, 294–296)	Prospero tells the story of how he freed Ariel from an enchantment. He directly refers to his magic ("mine art"), so the audience knows that he is a powerful magician.

Analyze Language

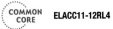

Shakespeare wrote his plays mainly in the poetic form of **blank verse,** unrhymed poetry with the **meter** of iambic pentameter. This meter has five feet or units per line; each unit contains two syllables, the first unstressed and the second stressed. Iambic pentameter is suitable for drama because its rhythm is similar to ordinary spoken English. Here is an example of a line in iambic pentameter from *The Tempest.*

˘ ´ ˘ ´ ˘ ´ ˘ ´ ˘ ´

The sky, it seems, would pour down stinking pitch, (*I, ii, 3*)

This line shows the richness of Shakespeare's language. With just a few words, he creates a powerful image to describe a dark and stormy night: smelly black tar falling from the sky. He also uses the sound device of **alliteration,** repeating the initial consonants *s* (*sky, seems, stinking*) and *p* (*pour, pitch*), to give the line a musical quality.

Shakespeare's text is packed with **figurative language,** or words used in a nonliteral way, often to make fresh comparisons. For example, the simile "They'll take suggestion as a cat laps milk" (II, i, 294) compares weak men who cannot think for themselves to cats that cannot resist a bowl of milk. Other comparisons are more subtle. When Ferdinand describes his eyes as "never since at ebb" (I, ii, 440), he compares his tears over the loss of his father to a tide that keeps bringing forth water.

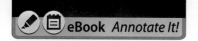 eBook *Annotate It!*

Analyzing the Text

COMMON CORE

ELACC11-12RL1,
ELACC11-12RL4,
ELACC11-12W2,
ELACC11-12W2b

Cite Text Evidence   Support your responses with evidence from the selection.

1. **Cite Evidence** How was Prospero displaced as duke of Milan? Cite evidence from Act I, Scene 2.

2. **Analyze** How would you describe Prospero's relationship with Miranda based on the language that he uses and on his use of magic?

3. **Cite Evidence** Based on the interaction between Caliban and Prospero, what was Caliban's life on the island like before Prospero and Miranda arrived? How and why has their relationship evolved?

4. **Analyze** Several characters in this excerpt from *The Tempest* talk about a desire to rule over others or about the pain of losing their kingdom or freedom. Describe how this comment relates to each of the following characters.

   - Prospero
   - Caliban
   - Sebastian
   - Ariel

5. **Interpret** Review Ariel's song that begins "Full fathom five . . ." (I, ii, 401–409). What is he describing, and how do the words Shakespeare uses help you visualize it?

6. **Infer** The phrase "a sea change" has a literal meaning in Ariel's song but is today used in a more figurative way. What might it mean to say that someone or something has experienced a sea change?

7. **Infer** Review Gonzalo's speech in which he outlines how he would rule the island if he were king of it (II, i, 148–169). How does Gonzalo's approach differ from Prospero's about ruling the island and its inhabitants? What can you infer about Shakespeare's view of the English treatment of the inhabitants of the New World from this contrast?

PERFORMANCE TASK

Writing Activity: Essay Ariel and Caliban are both identified as Prospero's servants, yet they have very different relationships with him. Explore these relationships by writing an explanatory essay following these steps.

- Identify passages that reveal Ariel's and Caliban's character. Look at their own words and actions and what others say about them.
- Identify passages that reveal Prospero's relationship with each of them. Look at his words as well as his actions toward each of them.

- Make inferences from this evidence to explain the reasons for these different relationships.
- Organize your information in a compare-and-contrast structure. Begin with a clear main idea, support your main idea with evidence from the play, and end with a concluding statement that follows from and supports the information you have presented.

MEDIA ANALYSIS

Media Versions of
The Tempest

The Tempest (1980)

Film Version by BBC Shakespeare

AS YOU VIEW Pay attention to the way in which the characters of Prospero, Miranda, and Caliban are portrayed in the film. Write down any questions you generate during your viewing.

COLLABORATIVE DISCUSSION Are the characters in the film what you imagined? With a partner, discuss how they are similar to or different from what you pictured while reading the play. Cite specific images from the video to support your ideas.

Analyze Interpretations of Drama

COMMON CORE   ELACC11-12RL7

Each film or theater director adapts Shakespeare's original text in his or her own way. This clip reveals one director's view of *The Tempest*, Act I, Scene 2, lines 309–378. To understand this vision and how it relates to Shakespeare's text, examine these elements of filmmaking:

Casting is the selection of actors to play roles. Each actor must match the director's vision of the character and his or her traits. What impression of each character is created by the appearance and acting style of the film actors?

Blocking refers to the way the director positions and moves actors around a set. Note where Caliban is positioned in this scene. What does his position suggest? How do the characters move in this scene, and what do their movements communicate?

Lighting and **sound** affect the mood of a scene and the way the audience interprets action and character. What feeling is created by the setting of this scene? How does the director use sound to enhance his or her interpretation?

Costumes may suggest important aspects of a character or reinforce how a director wants a character to be perceived. What does the contrast in attire between Prospero, Miranda, and Caliban tell the audience about them?

Analyzing the Text and Media

COMMON CORE   ELACC11-12RL7,
ELACC11-12W2b,
ELACC11-12W4

Cite Text Evidence Support your responses with evidence from the selections.

1. **Draw Conclusions** What impression of Caliban is created in the film clip? Explain how casting, costume, and make-up all contribute to this characterization.

2. **Analyze** How does the director use Prospero's and Caliban's positions on the set to bring out ideas about their relationship? Are these ideas supported by the text of *The Tempest*? Be specific.

3. **Compare** How do the close-up shots of Caliban affect the emotional impact of the scene? Does Shakespeare's text convey the same effect? Explain.

PERFORMANCE TASK

Writing Activity: Review Based on this scene, would you recommend this film to others? Why or why not?

- Write a review for the school newspaper, presenting your opinion on this interpretation of Shakespeare's play.
- Support your opinion with specific reasons and examples from the film.

- Discuss at lets two of the elements of filmmaking from the chart above.
- Organize your ideas logically and use the conventions of standard written English.

The Tempest (2010)

Production Images from Film Version

AS YOU VIEW Pay attention to details in the images that help you draw conclusions about this film adaptation of *The Tempest*. Write down any questions you generate as you review the images.

Movie poster for *The Tempest* (2010) directed by Julie Taymor and staring Helen Mirren as Prospera.

Caliban confronts Prospera and Miranda in Act I, Scene 2.

Prospera works her magic.

In this scene from Act II, Scene 2, Trinculo and Stephano, two comic characters in the play, make the acquaintance of Caliban.

COLLABORATIVE DISCUSSION What conclusions can you draw about this version of the play based on these images? With a partner, discuss what interests you about this film version and what you might like or dislike about it. Cite specific evidence from the photographs to support your ideas.

Analyze Interpretations of Drama

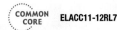
COMMON CORE   ELACC11-12RL7

The movie poster and three production stills from a more recent adaptation of *The Tempest* reveal different visions of the play. Examining some of the same elements in these images that you used to analyze the film clip will give you insight into the director's interpretation.

Casting Directors sometimes cast against type, meaning that they choose an actor who does not explicitly match the character description in the original text. In the play, Prospero is clearly a male character. In this film version, Prospero becomes Prospera, a female character. Think about the qualities that this actor brings to the role and how this shift in gender alters or enhances the play.

Blocking These images clearly show the placement of the actors relative to each other and imply each actor's movements. Note what their body language and positions in regard to each other suggest about their emotions and relationships.

Lighting and Set Design From the photographs, this film appears to have been "shot on location." Consider how the natural setting might affect the audience's understanding of character and action.

Costumes A director may choose costumes from a different time period than that in which the play was conceived. What ideas about characters are conveyed through the choice of modern clothing rather than period costumes?

Analyzing the Text and Media

COMMON CORE   ELACC11-12RL1, ELACC11-12RL7, ELACC11-12W4

Cite Text Evidence   Support your responses with evidence from the selections.

1. **Analyze** In the play, Prospero addresses Caliban by saying, "Thou earth, thou, speak!" (Act I, Scene 2, line 318). Explain how this line relates to the depiction of Caliban in the photographs from this film.

2. **Compare** Examine the photograph of Caliban, Prospera, and Miranda. Explain the impression of Miranda and Prospera conveyed by their position, posture, and gestures. Are these impressions supported by your reading of the play?

3. **Infer** The cloak is a prominent feature of Prospera's costume. What does this cloak add to her characterization? Is it consistent with the descriptions in the text?

PERFORMANCE TASK

Writing Activity: Captions Complete these activities with a partner.

- Write an extended caption for each image that shows a scene in the film.

- Draw from the text of the play to include quotations and other details that provide context for each image and help explain what is happening at that specific moment.

- Share your captions with the class.

Analyzing the Text and Media

COMMON CORE
ELACC11-12RL1,
ELACC11-12RL3,
ELACC11-12RL4,
ELACC11-12RL7,
ELACC11-12SL1

Cite Text Evidence Support your responses with evidence from the selections.

1. **Analyze** Compare the two actors who play Caliban in these media versions. What does each one reveal about the director's interpretation of this character? Which one more closely matches the descriptions of Caliban in the text of the play? Explain.

2. **Compare** Reread lines 309–378 in the text. Describe Prospero's traits as revealed through his dialogue in the play. Drawing from what you have seen in the clip and in the images, explain how in each film Prospero/Prospera does or does not demonstrate these qualities.

3. **Evaluate** In lines 346–348, Caliban says, "and here you sty me / In this hard rock, whiles you do keep from me / The rest o' th' island." How does the film clip convey the physical aspects of this setting as well as the mood evoked by his words?

4. **Compare** How does each director use elements of costume in his or her film to establish or reinforce character?

5. **Analyze** How does the film clip support the idea that Miranda, while innocent and protected, is also a dynamic and strong woman? Cite specific images from the clip to explain.

6. **Synthesize** What are the advantages of seeing more than one version of the same Shakespearean drama? Explain.

PERFORMANCE TASK

Speaking Activity: Debate Do special effects detract from or enhance an audience's appreciation of the original text of Shakespeare's *The Tempest?*

- In a small group, review the trailer for Julie Taymor's version of *The Tempest* (depicted in the photographs) or the actual scene if available on the Internet.

- Identify special effects used in the film. Discuss their function and whether or not they maintain the integrity of Shakespeare's play.

- Organize your ideas logically and present the argument to the class.

- Present specific evidence to support your claim and to counter opposing arguments.

- Speak clearly and concisely, using appropriate tone, volume, and gestures.

- Have groups with opposing views present their arguments. Ask listening classmates to decide which opinion is more convincingly presented.

Background *Vasco Núñez de Balboa (1475–1519) was a Spanish explorer and conquistador who first came to the Americas in 1500 as part of a voyage exploring the coast of present-day Colombia. He is most remembered for being the first European to view the Pacific Ocean in 1513. This event and other facts of Balboa's life form the basis for* **Sabina Murray's** *story, published in her book* Tales of the New World *(2011). Murray lives in western Massachusetts, where she is on the Creative Writing faculty at the University of Massachusetts Amherst.*

Balboa

Short Story by Sabina Murray

AS YOU READ Pay special attention to descriptions of Balboa's relations with the Indians and the Spaniards. Write down any questions you generate during reading.

Vasco Núñez de Balboa ascends the mountain alone. His one thousand Indians and two hundred Spaniards wait at the foot of the mountain, as if they are the Israelites and Balboa alone is off to speak with God. Balboa knows that from this peak he will be able to see the western water, what he has already decided to name the South Sea. He takes a musket with him. The Spaniards have been warned that if they follow, he will use it, because discovery is a tricky matter and he wants no competition. The day is September 25, 1513.

10 　Balboa ascends slowly. His musket is heavy and he would have gladly left it down below, but he doesn't trust his countrymen any more than he trusts the sullen Indians. So he bears the weight. But the musket is nothing. He is dragging the mantle[1] of civilization up the **pristine** slopes, over the mud, over the leaves that cast as much shade as a parasol[2] but with none of the charm.

pristine
(prĭs´tēn´) *adj.* pure or unspoiled.

---

[1] **mantle:** a cloak or robe worn by royalty.
[2] **parasol:** light umbrella.

Balboa is that divining line[3] between the modern and the primitive. As he moves, the shadow of Spain moves with him.

Balboa steps cautiously into a muddy stream and watches with fascination as his boot sinks and sinks. He will have to find another way. Upstream he sees an outcropping of rock. Maybe he can cross there. He tells himself that there is no hurry, but years of staying just ahead of trouble have left him anxiety-ridden. He would like to think of himself as a lion. Balboa the Lion! But no, he is more of a rat, and all of his accomplishments have been made with speed and stealth. Balboa places his hand on a branch and pulls himself up. He sees the tail of a snake disappearing just past his reach. The subtle crush of greenery confirms his discovery and he shrinks back, crouching. In this moment of stillness, he looks around. He sees no other serpents, but that does not mean they are not there. Only in this momentary quiet does he hear his breath, rasping with effort. He hears his heart beating in the arced fingers of his ribs as if it is an Indian's drum. He does not remember what it is to be civilized, or if he ever was. If ever a man was alone, it is he. But even in this painful solitude, he cannot help but laugh. Along with Cristóbal Colón, backed by Isabel I herself, along with Vespucci the scholar, along with the noble Pizarro brothers[4] on their way to claim Inca gold, his name will live—Balboa. Balboa! Balboa the Valiant. Balboa the Fearsome. Balboa the Brave.

Balboa the gambling pig farmer, who, in an effort to escape his debt, has found himself at the very edge of the world.

Balboa stops to drink from the stream. The water is cold, fresh, and tastes like dirt, which is a relief after what he has been drinking— water so green that the very act of ingesting it seems unnatural, as though it is as alive as he, and sure enough, given a few hours, it will get you back, eager to find its way out. He has been climbing since early morning and it is now noon. The sun shines in the sky unblinking, white-hot. Balboa wonders if it's the same sun that shines in Spain. The sun seemed so much smaller there. Even in Hispaniola,[5] the sun was Spanish. Even as he prodded his pigs in the heat, there was Spain all around, men with dice, men training roosters, pitting their dogs against each other. But here…then he hears a twig snap and the sound of something brushing up against the bushes. Balboa stands.

"I give you this one chance to turn back," he says, raising his musket as he turns. And then he freezes. It is not one of the Spaniards hoping to share the glory. Instead, he finds himself face-to-face with

---

[3] **divining line:** point of separation between ideas.

[4] **Cristóbal Colón . . . Pizarro brothers:** Cristóbal Colón is the Spanish name for Christopher Columbus. Isabel I was Queen of Castile (Spain) from 1474 until 1504. Amerigo Vespucci (1451–1512) was an Italian explorer and cartographer. Francisco, Gonzalo, Juan, and Hernándo Pizarro were Spanish conquistadors in Peru.

[5] **Hispaniola:** site of Columbus's first colony; the island containing modern Haiti and the Dominican Republic.

a great spotted cat. On this mountain, he's thought he might find his god, the god of Moses, sitting in the cloud cover near the peaks, running his fingers through his beard. But no. Instead he finds himself face-to-face with a jaguar, the god of the Indians. He knows why these primitives have chosen it for their deity. It is hard to fear one's maker when he looks like one's grandfather, but this great cat
60   can make a people fear god. He hears the growling of the cat and the grating, high-pitched thunder sounds like nothing he has ever heard. The cat twitches its nose and two great incisors show at the corners of its mouth. Balboa raises his musket, ignites the flint,[6] and nothing happens. He tries again and the weapon explodes, shattering the silence, sending up a big puff of stinking smoke. The cat is gone for now, but Balboa knows he hasn't even injured it.

> ❝ **He does not remember what it is to be civilized, or if he ever was.** ❞

And now it will be tailing him silently.
There is nothing he can do about it. He should have brought an Indian with him. The Indians have all seen the South Sea before, so
70   why did he leave them at the foot of the mountain? They have no more interest in claiming the South Sea than they do rowing off to Europe in their dug-out canoes[7] and claiming Spain. But Balboa's hindsight is always good, and no amount of swearing—which he does freely, spilling Spanish profanity into the virgin mountain air—is going to set things straight.
He is already in trouble. His kingdom in Darién on the east coast of the New World is under threat, and not from the Indians, whom he manages well, but from Spain. Balboa had organized the rebellion, **supplanted** the governor—all of this done with great efficiency and
80   intelligence. What stupidity made him send the governor, Martín Fernández de Enciso, back to Spain? Enciso swore that he would have Balboa's head on a platter. He was yelling from the deck of the ship as it set sail. Why didn't he kill Enciso? Better yet, why didn't

supplant
(sə-plănt´) v. to take the place of.

---

[6] **flint:** stone used to create a spark.
[7] **dug-out canoes:** narrow boats made by hollowing out tree trunks.

he turn Enciso over to some Indian tribe that would be glad to have the Spaniard, glad to have his blood on their hands? How could Balboa be so stupid? Soon the caravels[8] would arrive and his days as governor (king, he tells the Indians) of Darién will be over. Unless, Balboa thinks, unless he brings glory by being the first to claim this great ocean for Spain. Then the king will see him as the greatest of his subjects, not a troublemaking peasant, a keeper of pigs.

Unless that jaguar gets him first.

Balboa looks nervously around. The only sound is the trickle and splash of the stream that he is following, which the Indians tell him leads to a large outcropping of rock from which he will see the new ocean. Insects swoop malevolently[9] around his head. A yellow and red parrot watches him cautiously from a branch, first looking from one side of its jeweled head, then the other. Where is the jaguar? Balboa imagines his body being dragged into a tree, his boots swinging from the limbs as the great cat tears his heart from his ribs. He hears a crushing of vegetation and ducks low. He readies his musket again. "Please God, let the damned thing fire." He breathes harshly, genuflecting,[10] musket steady.

The leaves quiver, then part. There is no jaguar.

"Leoncico!" he cries out. Leoncico is his dog, who has tracked him up the slope. Leoncico patters over, wagging his tail, his great wrinkled head bearded with drool. Leoncico is a monster of a dog. His head is the size of a man's, and his body has the look of a lion—shoulders and hipbones **protruding** and muscle pulling and shifting beneath the glossy skin—which is where he gets his name. "Leoncico" means little lion.

"Good dog," says Balboa. "Good dog. Good dog."

He has never been so grateful for the company, not even when he was hidden on board Enciso's ship bound for San Sebastian, escaping his creditors, wrapped in a sail. No one wondered why the dog had come on board. Maybe the dog had been attracted by the smell of **provisions**, the great barrels of salted meat. The soldiers fed him, gave him water. Balboa worried that Leoncico would give him away, but the dog had somehow known to be quiet. He had slept beside Balboa, and even in Balboa's thirst and hunger, the great beast's panting and panting, warm through the sailcloth, had given him comfort. When Enciso's crew finally discovered Balboa—one of the sails was torn and needed to be replaced—they did not punish him. They laughed.

"The Indians massacre everyone. You are better off in a debtors' prison," they said.

Balboa became a member of the crew. When the boat shipwrecked off the coast of San Sebastian (they were rescued by Francisco Pizarro),

protrude
(prō-trōōd´) v. to stick out or bulge.

provision
(prə-vĭzh´ən) n. food supply.

---

[8] **caravels:** small sailing ships with two or three masts.
[9] **malevolently:** with evil intent.
[10] **genuflecting:** bending one knee to the ground.

Enciso had been at a loss as to where to go, and Balboa convinced him to try Darién to the north. Once established there, Enciso had shown himself to be a weak man. How could Balboa not act? Enciso did not
130 understand the Indians as Balboa did. He could see that the Indians were battle-hardened warriors. The Spaniards had not been there long enough to call these armies into existence. Balboa's strength had been to recognize this **discord**. He divided the great tribes, supported one against the other. His reputation spread. His muskets blasted away the faces of the greatest warriors. Balboa's soldiers spread smallpox and syphilis. His Spanish war dogs, great mastiffs and wolfhounds, tore children limb from limb. The blood from his great war machine made the rivers flow red and his name, Balboa, moved quickly, apace[11] with these rivers of blood.

140 Balboa is loved by no one and feared by all. He has invented an unequaled terror. The Indians think of him as a god. They make no **distinction** between good and evil. They have seen his soldiers tear babies from their mothers, toss them still screaming to feed the dogs. They have seen the great dogs pursue the escaping Indians, who must hear nothing but a great panting, the jangle of the dogs' armor, and then, who knows? Do they feel the hot breath on their cheek? Are they still awake when the beasts unravel their stomachs and spill them onto the hot earth? Balboa's dogs have been his most effective weapon because for them, one does not need to carry ammunition, as for
150 the muskets; one does not need to carry food, as for the soldiers. For the dogs, there is fresh meat everywhere. He knows his cruelty will be recorded along with whatever he discovers. This does not bother him, even though one monk, Dominican—strange fish—cursed him back in Darién. He was a young monk, tormented by epileptic[12] fits. He approached Balboa in the town square in his bare feet, unarmed, waving his shrunken fist.

"Your dogs," screamed the monk, "are demons."

As if understanding, Leoncico had lunged at the monk. Leoncico is not a demon. He is the half of Balboa with teeth, the half that eats.
160 Balboa has the mind and appetite. Together, they make one. It is as if the great beast can hear his thoughts, as if their hearts and lungs circulate the same blood and air. What did the monk understand of that? What did he understand of anything? He said that he was in the New World to bring the Indians to God. So the monk converts the Indians, and Balboa sends them on to God. They work together, which is what Balboa told the monk. But the monk did not find it funny.

How dare he find fault with Balboa? Is not Spain as full of torments as the New World? The Spaniards are brought down by smallpox at alarming rates in Seville, in Madrid. Every summer the
170 rich take to the mountains to escape the plague, and in the fall, when

discord
(dĭs′kôrd′) *n.*
disagreement or conflict.

distinction
(dĭ-stĭngk′shən) *n.*
difference in quality.

---

[11]**apace:** fast enough to keep up with something.
[12]**epileptic:** caused by epilepsy, a neurological disorder.

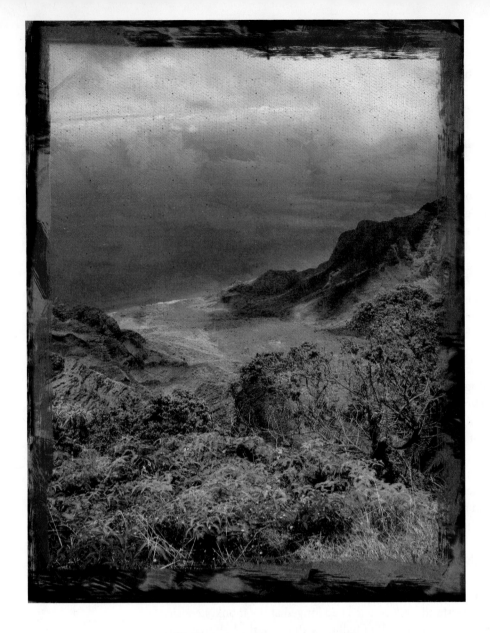

they return, aren't their own countrymen lying in the streets feeding the packs of mongrels? Half of all the Spanish babies die. It is not uncommon to see a peasant woman leave her screaming infant on the side of the road, so why come here and beg relief for these savages? Why not go to France, where, one soldier tells Balboa, they butcher the Huguenots[13] and sell their limbs for food in the street? Why rant over the impaling of the Indians when Spaniards—noblemen among them—have suffered the same fate in the name of God? In fact, the Inquisition[14] has been the great educator when it comes to subduing the Indian population.

180

---

[13] **Huguenots:** French Protestants who were persecuted for their faith in the 16th and 17th centuries.

[14] **the Inquisition:** an investigation by the Roman Catholic Church to identify and punish heretics.

Why take him to task when the world is a violent place?

"May your most evil act be visited on you," said the monk. "I curse you."

The monk died shortly after that. His threats and bravery were more the result of a deadly fever than the words of a divine message. Did the curse worry Balboa? Perhaps a little. He occasionally revisits a particularly spectacular feat of bloodshed—the time Leoncico tore a chieftain's head from his shoulders—with a pang of concern. But Balboa is a busy man with little time for reflection. When the monk delivered his curse, Balboa was already preparing his troops for the great march to the west. His name had reached Spain, and the king felt his authority threatened.

He is the great Balboa.

But here, on the slope of the mountain, his name does not seem worth that much. He has to relieve himself and is terrified that some creature—jaguar, snake, spider—will take advantage of his great heaving bareness.

"Leoncico," he calls. "At attention."

Not that this command means anything to the dog. Leoncico knows "attack," and that is all he needs to know. Leoncico looks up, wags his tail, and lies down, his face smiling into the heat. Balboa climbs onto a boulder. Here, he is exposed to everything, but if that jaguar is still tracking him, he can at least see it coming. He sets his musket down and listens. Nothing. He loosens his belt and is about to lower his pants when he sees it—the flattened glimmer, a shield, the horizon. He fixes his belt and straightens himself. He stares out at the startling bare intrusion, this beautiful nothing beyond the green tangle of trees, the *Mar del Sur*, the glory of Balboa, his gift to Spain.

Balboa, having accomplished his goal, luxuriates in this moment of peaceful ignorance. He does not know that his days are numbered, that even after he returns to Darién with his knowledge of the South Sea, even after he has **ceded** the governorship to Pedro Arias Dávila, even after he is promised Dávila's daughter, he has not bought his safety. Dávila will see that as long as Balboa lives he must sleep with one eye open. With the blessing of Spain, Dávila will bring Balboa to trial for treason, and on January 21, 1519, Balboa's head will be severed from his shoulders. His eyes will stay open, his mouth will be slack, and his great head will roll in the dust for everyone—Indians, Spaniards, and dogs—to see.

cede
(sēd) *v.* to yield or give away.

COLLABORATIVE DISCUSSION Why is Balboa more successful in managing his relationships with the Indians than his relationships with other powerful Spaniards? Discuss with a partner how Murray describes these different relationships. Cite specific evidence from the story to support your ideas.

Determine Themes

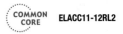

Writers of fiction often use their works to communicate insights about life or human nature. Most of these **themes** are not stated; readers must infer them by looking closely at other elements of the work, especially characters and plot. To identify and trace the development of the themes in "Balboa," answer these questions:

- **Character:** How does the main character change or fail to change? What qualities does the main character possess? How do these qualities determine his or her reaction to the conflict? What message is the author conveying through the way the character's traits influence his or her reactions?
- **Plot:** What is the major conflict in the story? How does this conflict lead to other problems? How is the conflict resolved? Is there a lesson to be learned from the way the conflict is resolved?

Analyze Structure: Flashback and Flash Forward

The **structure** of a story is its organization, or how the action is ordered. Many stories are organized chronologically, following a tale from its beginning to its end. Sometimes, however, authors decide to present the sequence of events out of order to add interest or suspense, or to achieve a more subtle effect. To analyze the structure of "Balboa," look at how the author uses the narrative techniques described in the chart.

Flashback	Flash Forward
A **flashback** is a scene that interrupts the action of a narrative to describe events that took place at an earlier time. Flashbacks often add important background information about characters. This information can help readers gain a new perspective on the character and his or her motives, understand the causes of events, or see the author's message more clearly. The story "Balboa" includes several flashbacks as the main character recalls significant events in his past.	**Flash forward** interrupts the narrative to give readers a look at what will happen after the events in the main plot take place. A flash forward may change readers' outlook on events and characters in the story, affect the mood that is created, or illuminate the meaning of the work. In "Balboa," the author chooses to conclude her story with a flash forward focusing on the end of the main character's life.

Analyzing the Text

COMMON CORE

ELACC11-12RL2,
ELACC11-12RL3,
ELACC11-12RL5,
ELACC11-12RL6

Cite Text Evidence   Support your responses with evidence from the selection.

1. **Interpret** An **allusion** is an indirect reference to a famous person, place, event, or literary work. What allusion is made in the first paragraph of the story? How does this allusion shape readers' understanding of Balboa's character?

2. **Analyze** Balboa could be described as self-aware. Even as he revels in the thought that "his name will live," he is aware of the incongruity that he, a debt-ridden pig farmer, should now be standing "at the very edge of the world." He also assesses his errors in judgment honestly. What is the author's purpose in developing this trait of self-awareness?

3. **Analyze** After Leoncico surprises Balboa on the mountain, the action of the story is interrupted by a flashback. What do readers learn about Balboa from this flashback? What theme does it suggest about the nature of power?

4. **Analyze** At the beginning of the story, the narrator says that Balboa is "dragging the mantle of civilization up the pristine slopes, over the mud, over the leaves" (lines 12–13). What does this image suggest about Balboa and the "civilization" that he is bringing with him?

5. **Interpret** Note the many references to and images of dogs throughout the story. What ideas does the author convey through these references?

6. **Analyze** The vantage point from which a writer tells a story is called the point of view. What point of view did Murray choose for this short story? What does this choice add to the narrative?

7. **Analyze** One form of **irony** is the contrast between expectations and what actually happens. What is ironic about Balboa's first glimpse of the Pacific Ocean? Why does the author present the crowning moment of Balboa's achievement this way?

8. **Analyze** What is revealed by the flash forward at the end of the story? How does this knowledge help bring out a theme of the story?

PERFORMANCE TASK

Writing Activity: Dramatic Monologue Through her portrayal of Balboa, Murray creates a dynamic, multi-dimensional main character. Her characterization enables readers to see him clearly and almost hear his voice. Write a dramatic monologue from the point of view of this fictional Balboa, expressing what he might have said aloud as he stood on the boulder surveying the Pacific Ocean.

- Draw upon the text for details about the path he followed to "the edge of the world."
- Reveal his motives and his feelings upon accomplishing his goal.

- Include his reflections on what his accomplishment really means, incorporating your ideas about the theme.
- Present your monologue to a small group.

Critical Vocabulary

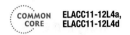 COMMON CORE   ELACC11-12L4a, ELACC11-12L4d

pristine	protrude	discord	cede
supplant	provision	distinction	

Practice and Apply Answer each question, referring to the meaning of each Critical Vocabulary word in your response.

1. If you **ceded** the computer to your younger brother, would that cause **discord**?

2. If both candidates had **pristine** reputations and equal leadership experience, would it be easy to make a **distinction** between them?

3. If the young children in a family **supplanted** their parents in control of the grocery shopping, would the family's **provisions** likely be more or less healthy?

4. If the lawn had many tree roots **protruding** from it, would it be a **pristine** surface?

Vocabulary Strategy: Context Clues

The context of a word is the words, phrases, and sentences that surround it. Looking at the context of an unfamiliar word can help you to define it. For example, read this sentence from the text: "Balboa had organized the rebellion, supplanted the governor. . . ." The word *rebellion* helps you understand that *supplanted,* a Critical Vocabulary word, means "to overthrow or replace." Often key words signal a relationship between the unknown word and others in the sentence that will help you define it.

Key Words	Context Clues
such as, like, for example, including	The unknown word is followed by examples that illustrate its meaning: *We packed provisions, such as fruit, water, and chocolate.*
unlike, but, in contrast, although, on the other hand	The unknown word is contrasted with a more familiar word or phrase: *The tablecloth was pristine before dinner, but it was covered with stains afterwards.*
also, similar to, as, like, as if	The unknown word is compared to a more familiar word or phrase: *The wad of gum protruding from his cheek made him look as if he had the mumps.*
or, that is, which is, in other words	The unknown word is preceded or followed by a restatement of its meaning: *The distinction, or difference, between the identical twins was slight.*

Practice and Apply List four unfamiliar words from the story. Work with a partner to define the words on each of your lists from context. Then check their definitions in a dictionary. Share your words, their context clues, and their definitions with the class.

Richard Rodriguez *is the son of Mexican immigrants and was born in San Francisco in 1944. When he started school, his teachers asked his parents to speak more English at home, and Ricardo became Richard. He planned on an academic career but never completed his Ph.D. dissertation, deciding to write as a journalist and essayist. In the first volume of his autobiography* Hunger of Memory *(1982), Rodriguez describes his assimilation into the majority culture. This 2003 essay followed publication of another volume of memoir,* Brown: The Last Discovery of America, *which explores the issue of race.*

"Blaxicans"
and Other Reinvented Americans

Argument by Richard Rodriguez

AS YOU READ Look for clues that reveal Rodriguez's attitudes toward race and ethnicity as they relate to personal identity.

There is something unsettling about immigrants because…well, because they chatter incomprehensibly, and they get in everyone's way. Immigrants seem to be bent on undoing America. Just when Americans think we know who we are—we are Protestants, **culled** from Western Europe, are we not?—then new immigrants appear from Southern Europe or from Eastern Europe. We—we who are already here—we don't know exactly what the latest comers will mean to our community. How will they fit in with us? Thus we—we who were here first—we begin to question our own identity.

After a generation or two, the grandchildren or the great-grandchildren of immigrants to the United States and the grandchildren of those who tried to keep immigrants out of the United States will romanticize the immigrant, will begin to see the immigrant as the figure who teaches us most about what it means to be an American. The immigrant, in mythic terms, travels from the outermost rind of America to the very center of American mythology. None of this, of course, can we admit to the Vietnamese immigrant who served us our breakfast at the hotel this morning. In another 40 years, we will be prepared to say to the Vietnamese immigrant that he,

cull
(kŭl) *v.* to take from a large quantity.

with his breakfast tray, with his intuition for travel, with his memory
of tragedy, with his recognition of peerless freedoms, he fulfills the
meaning of America.

In 1997, Gallup conducted a survey on race relations in America,
but the poll was concerned only with white and black Americans. No
question was put to the aforementioned Vietnamese man. There was
certainly no question for the Chinese grocer, none for the Guatemalan
barber, none for the tribe of Mexican Indians who reroofed your
neighbor's house.

The American conversation about race has always been a black-
and-white conversation, but the conversation has become as bloodless
as badminton.

I have listened to the black-and-white conversation for most
of my life. I was supposed to attach myself to one side or the other,
without asking the obvious questions: What is this perpetual dialectic[1]
between Europe and Africa? Why does it admit so little reference to
anyone else?

I am speaking to you in American English that was taught me by
Irish nuns—immigrant women. I wear an Indian face; I answer to a
Spanish surname as well as this California first name, Richard. You
might wonder about the complexity of historical **factors**, the collision
of centuries, that creates Richard Rodriguez. My brownness is the
illustration of that collision, or the bland memorial of it. I stand before
you as an Impure-American, an Ambiguous-American.

In the 19th century, Texans used to say that the reason Mexicans
were so easily defeated in battle was because we were so dilute,
being neither pure Indian nor pure Spaniard. Yet, at the same time,
Mexicans used to say that Mexico, the country of my ancestry, joined
two worlds, two competing armies. José Vasconcelos, the Mexican
educator and philosopher, famously described Mexicans as *la raza
cósmica*, the cosmic race. In Mexico what one finds as early as the 18th
century is a **predominant** population of mixed-race people. Also, once
the slave had been freed in Mexico, the incidence[2] of marriage between
Indian and African people there was greater than in any other country
in the Americas and has not been equaled since.

Race mixture has not been a point of pride in America. Americans
speak more easily about "diversity" than we do about the fact that
I might marry your daughter; you might become we; we might
become us. America has so readily adopted the Canadian notion of
multiculturalism because it preserves our preference for thinking
ourselves separate—our elbows need not touch, thank you. I would
prefer that table. I can remain Mexican, whatever that means, in the
United States of America.

factor
(făk´tər) *n.*
component or
characteristic.

predominant
(prĭ-dŏm´ə-nənt) *adj.*
most important or
prevalent.

---

[1] **dialectic:** exchange of opinions and ideas.
[2] **incidence:** occurrence.

> ## "Because of colonial Mexico, I am mestizo. But I was reinvented by President Richard Nixon."

I would propose that instead of adopting the Canadian model of multiculturalism, America might begin to imagine the Mexican alternative—that of a mestizaje society.

Because of colonial Mexico, I am mestizo. But I was reinvented by President Richard Nixon. In the early 1970s, Nixon instructed the Office of Management and Budget to identify the major racial and ethnic groups in the United States. OMB came up with five major
70 ethnic or racial groups. The groups are white, black, Asian/Pacific Islander, American Indian/Eskimo, and Hispanic.

It's what I learned to do when I was in college: to call myself a Hispanic. At my university we even had separate cafeteria tables and "theme houses," where the children of Nixon could gather—of a feather. Native Americans united. African Americans. Casa Hispanic.

The interesting thing about Hispanics is that you will never meet us in Latin America. You may meet Chileans and Peruvians and Mexicans. You will not meet Hispanics. If you inquire in Lima or Bogotá about Hispanics, you will be referred to Dallas. For "Hispanic"
80 is a gringo contrivance,[3] a definition of the world according to European patterns of colonization. Such a definition suggests I have more in common with Argentine Italians than with American Indians; that there is an ineffable[4] union between the white Cuban and the mulatto Puerto Rican because of Spain. Nixon's conclusion has become the basis for the way we now organize and understand American society.

The Census Bureau foretold that by the year 2003, Hispanics would outnumber blacks to become the largest minority in the United States. And, indeed, the year 2003 has arrived and the proclamation of
90 Hispanic **ascendancy** has been published far and wide. While I admit a competition has existed—does exist—in America between Hispanics and black people, I insist that the comparison of Hispanics with blacks will lead, ultimately, to complete nonsense. For there is no such thing as a Hispanic race. In Latin America, one sees every race of the world. One sees white Hispanics, one sees black Hispanics, one sees brown Hispanics who are Indians, many of whom do not speak Spanish

ascendancy
(ə-sĕn′dən-sē) *n.*
a rise in power or influence.

---

[3] **contrivance:** something created to serve a purpose.
[4] **ineffable:** obscure, unknowable.

because they resist Spain. One sees Asian-Hispanics. To compare blacks and Hispanics, therefore, is to construct a fallacious[5] equation.

Some Hispanics have accepted the fiction. Some Hispanics have too easily accustomed themselves to impersonating a third race, a great new third race in America. But Hispanic is an ethnic term. It is a term **denoting** culture. So when the Census Bureau says by the year 2060 one-third of all Americans will identify themselves as Hispanic, the Census Bureau is not speculating in pigment or quantifying according to actual historical narratives, but rather is predicting how by the year 2060 one-third of all Americans will identify themselves culturally. For a country that traditionally has taken its understandings of community from blood and color, the new circumstance of so large a group of Americans identifying themselves by virtue of language or fashion or cuisine or literature is an extraordinary change, and a revolutionary one.

denote
(dĭ-nōt´) *v.* to name or give meaning to.

People ask me all the time if I envision another Quebec[6] forming in the United States because of the large immigrant movement from the south. Do I see a Quebec forming in the Southwest, for example? No, I don't see that at all. But I do notice the Latin American immigrant population is as much as 10 years younger than the U.S. national population. I notice the Latin American immigrant population is more fertile than the U.S. national population. I see the movement of the immigrants from south to north as a movement of youth—like approaching spring!—into a country that is growing middle-aged. I notice immigrants are the archetypal[7] Americans at a time when we—U.S. citizens—have become post-Americans, most concerned with subsidized medications.

I was at a small Apostolic Assembly in East Palo Alto a few years ago—a mainly Spanish-speaking congregation in an area along the freeway, near the heart of the Silicon Valley. This area used to be black East Palo Alto, but it is quickly becoming an Asian and Hispanic Palo Alto neighborhood. There was a moment in the service when newcomers to the congregation were introduced. Newcomers brought letters of introduction from sister evangelical churches in Latin America. The minister read out the various letters and pronounced the names and places of origin to the community. The congregation applauded. And I thought to myself: It's over. The border is over. These people were not being asked whether they had green cards. They were not being asked whether they arrived here legally or illegally. They were being welcomed within a new community for reasons of culture.

---

[5] **fallacious:** untrue; based on faulty reasoning.
[6] **envision another Quebec:** foresee a situation like that in Quebec, a French-speaking province that has sought independence from Canada.
[7] **archetypal:** being a perfect or ideal example.

There is now a north-south line that is theological, a line that cannot be **circumvented** by the U.S. Border Patrol.

140   I was on a British Broadcasting Corporation interview show, and a woman introduced me as being "in favor" of assimilation. I am not in favor of assimilation any more than I am in favor of the Pacific Ocean or clement weather. If I had a bumper sticker on the subject, it might read something like ASSIMILATION HAPPENS. One doesn't get up in the morning, as an immigrant child in America, and think to oneself, "How much of an American shall I become today?" One doesn't walk down the street and decide to be 40 percent Mexican and 60 percent American. Culture is fluid. Culture is smoke. You breathe it. You eat it. You can't help hearing it—Elvis Presley goes in your ear,
150   and you cannot get Elvis Presley out of your mind.

I am in favor of assimilation. I am not in favor of assimilation. I recognize assimilation. A few years ago, I was in Merced, Calif.—a town of about 75,000 people in the Central Valley where the two largest immigrant groups at that time (California is so fluid, I believe this is no longer the case) were Laotian Hmong and Mexicans. Laotians have never in the history of the world, as far as I know, lived next to Mexicans. But there they were in Merced, and living next to Mexicans. They don't like each other. I was talking to the Laotian kids about why they don't like the Mexican kids. They were telling me that
160   the Mexicans do this and the Mexicans don't do that, when I suddenly realized that they were speaking English with a Spanish accent.

On his interview show, Bill Moyers once asked me how I thought of myself. As an American? Or Hispanic? I answered that I am Chinese, and that is because I live in a Chinese city and because I want to be Chinese. Well, why not? Some Chinese American people in the Richmond and Sunset districts of San Francisco sometimes paint their houses (so many qualifiers!) in colors I would once have described as garish: lime greens, rose reds, pumpkin. But I have lived in a Chinese city for so long that my eye has taken on that palette,[8] has come to
170   prefer lime greens and rose reds and all the inventions of this Chinese Mediterranean. I see photographs in magazines or documentary footage of China, especially rural China, and I see what I recognize as home. Isn't that odd?

I do think distinctions exist. I'm not talking about an America tomorrow in which we're going to find that black and white are no longer the distinguishing marks of separateness. But many young people I meet tell me they feel like Victorians[9] when they identify themselves as black or white. They don't think of themselves in those terms. And they're already moving into a world in which tattoo or

---

[8] **palette:** range of colors used to depict a scene.
[9] **Victorians:** people with the outdated opinions and values popular in 19th-century England.

circumvent
(sûr´kəm-vĕnt´) v. to bypass or go around.

180 ornament or movement or commune[10] or sexuality or drug or rave or
electronic bombast[11] are the organizing principles of their identity. The
notion that they are white or black simply doesn't occur.

And increasingly, of course, one meets children who really don't
know how to say what they are. They simply are too many things. I
met a young girl in San Diego at a convention of mixed-race children,
among whom the common habit is to define one parent over the
other—black over white, for example. But this girl said that her mother
was Mexican and her father was African. The girl said "Blaxican."
By reinventing language, she is reinventing America.

190 America does not have a vocabulary like the vocabulary
the Spanish empire evolved to describe the multiplicity of racial
possibilities in the New World. The conversation, the interior
monologue of America cannot rely on the old vocabulary—black,
white. We are no longer a black-white nation.

So, what myth do we tell ourselves? The person who got closest
to it was Karl Marx.[12] Marx predicted that the discovery of gold in
California would be a more central event to the Americas than the
discovery of the Americas by Columbus—which was only the meeting
of two tribes, essentially, the European and the Indian. But when gold

200 was discovered in California in the 1840s, the entire world met. For
the first time in human history, all of the known world gathered. The
Malaysian stood in the gold fields alongside the African, alongside the
Chinese, alongside the Australian, alongside the Yankee.

That was an event without parallel in world history and the
beginning of modern California—why California today provides the
mythological structure for understanding how we might talk about
the American experience: not as biracial, but as the re-creation of the
known world in the New World.

Sometimes truly revolutionary things happen without regard.

210 I mean, we may wake up one morning and there is no black race.
There is no white race either. There are mythologies, and—as
I am in the business, insofar as I am in any business at all, of
demythologizing[13] such identities as black and white—I come to you
as a man of many cultures. I come to you as Chinese. Unless you
understand that I am Chinese, then you have not understood anything
I have said.

---

[10] **commune:** group of unrelated people living together and sharing wealth and
responsibilities.

[11] **bombast:** an arrogant, self-important form of expression.

[12] **Karl Marx:** German political philosopher, author of *The Communist Manifesto*
and *Das Kapital*.

[13] **demythologizing:** replacing myth or legend with fact.

COLLABORATIVE DISCUSSION How does Rodriguez feel about using race or
ethnicity as the main way to determine identity? Discuss this question with a
partner, citing specific textual evidence from the essay to support your ideas.

Analyze and Evaluate Structure: Arguments

COMMON CORE   ELACC11-12RI5

The structure of an **argument** refers to both its organization and the methods by which authors support their **claims,** or positions on an issue. They may choose to persuade their readers by presenting facts, statistics, or expert views. Or, they might illustrate their points with examples and **anecdotes,** brief stories focusing on one episode or event in a person's life. In "'Blaxicans' and Other Reinvented Americans," Rodriguez tells several anecdotes. These stories support important points; they also engage readers by giving them glimpses into Rodriguez's personal experiences.

For example, Rodriguez tells about visiting a community in which Laotians and Mexicans lived unhappily side by side. The Laotians spent the whole time complaining bitterly to him about their Mexican neighbors. But, as he listened to them, Rodriguez noticed that they spoke in a Spanish accent. He includes this anecdote to offer convincing support for his assertion that assimilation, or cultural adaptation, happens regardless of whether we want it to or not.

Determine Author's Purpose: Irony

COMMON CORE   ELACC11-12RI6

A predominant element of Rodriguez's style is **verbal irony.** Although he seems to be stating one idea, he is directing readers to take the opposite meaning from it. This irony is brought out through his choice of words and the context in which they are used as well as the details he includes. His irony affects several elements of his writing.

Tone	Meaning	Purpose
Irony conveys his attitude, or **tone,** toward his topic. For example, he writes in the first paragraph, "Immigrants seem to be bent on undoing America." His irony in this statement brings out the view of many "old" Americans while at the same time conveying his positive feeling that immigrants are, in fact, the "doing" of America.	Irony conveys **meaning.** For example, Rodriguez sees a divide between the official perception of racial identity in America and its reality. In the third paragraph, he reinforces this idea by listing the Americans left out of the 1997 racial survey: "There was certainly no question for the Chinese grocer, none for the Guatemalan barber. . . ."	Irony helps him achieve his **purpose** of persuading readers to agree with him. His ironic words and phrases, such as the statement "I was reinvented by President Richard Nixon," stand out in readers' minds, increasing the effectiveness of his **rhetoric.**

Analyzing the Text

COMMON CORE

ELACC11-12RI1,
ELACC11-12RI2,
ELACC11-12RI4,
ELACC11-12RI5,
ELACC11-12RI6,
ELACC11-12W2b

Cite Text Evidence   Support your responses with evidence from the selection.

1. **Analyze** What is the author's purpose in the first three paragraphs? How does his use of irony help him accomplish this purpose?

2. **Interpret** What does the author mean when he says that the American conversation about race has "become as bloodless as badminton"?

3. **Analyze** Why does Rodriguez call himself "an Impure-American, an Ambiguous-American"? How does the information about his background affect the persuasiveness of his argument?

4. **Analyze** In Rodriguez's discussion of President Nixon, he uses words and phrases such as "learned . . . to call myself a Hispanic," "theme houses," "where the children of Nixon could gather—of a feather," and "gringo contrivance." Why are these word choices significant? How do they affect his tone?

5. **Cite Evidence** How does the author support his point that comparing blacks and Hispanics is "to construct a fallacious equation"?

6. **Draw Conclusions** What are the differences that Rodriguez points out between immigrants and U.S. citizens in lines 113–124? Why is this contrast important to include?

7. **Evaluate** Why does the author include several anecdotes toward the end of his argument? How does each story help him achieve a specific goal?

8. **Analyze** Rodriguez concludes his argument with the statement, "I come to you as Chinese. Unless you understand that I am Chinese, then you have not understood anything I have said." What does this striking statement mean? How does it relate to his central claim?

PERFORMANCE TASK

Writing Activity: Evaluation Do you find Rodriguez's argument convincing? Write a two-paragraph evaluation of his essay:

- In your first paragraph, identify the claim and analyze the author's support of it, offering specific examples from the text to identify areas where you find the argument compelling or uncompelling.

- In the second paragraph, evaluate the effectiveness of his rhetoric, examining aspects such as his use of irony.

Critical Vocabulary

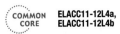

COMMON CORE ELACC11-12L4a, ELACC11-12L4b

cull	predominant	denote
factor	ascendency	circumvent

Practice and Apply Complete each of the following sentence stems in a way that reflects the meaning of the Critical Vocabulary word.

1. The decision whether to launch the jet was influenced by many **factors,** such as . . .

2. Her strong backhand gave her the **ascendancy** over her opponent in the tennis match because . . .

3. **Denoting** racial backgrounds by inventing new words is becoming necessary because . . .

4. They **circumvented** possible objections to their argument by . . .

5. In our state congress, the Republicans are the **predominant** party because . . .

6. The animal was **culled** from the herd and placed in a separate area because . . .

Vocabulary Strategy: The Latin Prefix *circum-*

The Critical Vocabulary word *circumvented* contains the Latin prefix *circum-*, which means "around, about." Many words in English are formed with this prefix. To understand the meanings of these words, use your knowledge of the prefix as well as the context in which the word appears.

Practice and Apply Answer each of these questions in a complete sentence that uses a word from the word web. Use your knowledge of the prefix *circum-* as well as the meanings of any roots that you recognize. Consult a dictionary if necessary.

1. How could a teacher indicate which of the exercises on a page to do?

2. How should a public figure avoid being involved in scandal?

3. How would a seamstress know how big to make the waist of a dress for a client?

4. How could a driver adapt if warned of a road block ahead?

5. What kind of witness testimony would be key for someone accused of a crime?

Language and Style: Using Colons Effectively

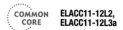

The **colon** is a useful mark of punctuation, having numerous functions related to both form and meaning. Many writers, including Richard Rodriguez, choose to insert colons in their sentences to make their writing clearer and more effective.

Read this sentence from "'Blaxicans' and Other Reinvented Americans":

It's what I learned to do when I was in college: to call myself a Hispanic.

In this sentence, the colon signals readers to pause before reading the phrase. As a result, the phrase stands out and catches readers' attention.

Rather than a colon, the author might have chosen to insert a comma into this sentence:

It's what I learned to do when I was in college, to call myself a Hispanic.

Both are grammatically correct. Although the same words are presented in the same order as in the original version, the comma creates less of a division between the two parts of the sentence. The phrase becomes part of the sentence; readers might not consider it separately or stop to think about its meaning in the same way.

This chart explains the various uses of the colon.

Uses of Colons	
Purpose	**Example**
To join two independent clauses closely related in meaning	*The bride felt cheated: there were no smiling faces watching her entrance and no happy hands applauding her new status.*
To introduce a series or list of ideas or examples that add to the previous statement or illustrate it	*The modern student must master several skills: analysis of text, oral communication of thoughts, written expression of ideas.*
To introduce a quotation that supports or contributes to the previous statement	*As he anticipated the ordeal ahead, a single thought looped through his mind: "Life shrinks or expands in proportion to one's courage."*

Practice and Apply Look back at the evaluation you wrote in response to this selection's Performance Task. Revise your writing to include at least two sentences that use colons. Share your original sentences and your revisions with a partner. Discuss how the insertion of a colon affects your meaning and tone.

Background   *Born in Tulsa, Oklahoma, in 1951 to a Creek father and a Cherokee-French mother,* **Joy Harjo** *is a full member of the Creek Indian tribe. She entered college in New Mexico planning to be a painter before turning her focus to writing. The poem "New Orleans" is from one of her best-known books,* She Had Some Horses *(1983). In the 1830s, hundreds of Harjo's fellow Creek Indians passed through the city of New Orleans during their forced removal from Alabama to present-day Oklahoma.*

New Orleans

Poem by Joy Harjo

AS YOU READ Look for clues that reveal what New Orleans means to the speaker. Write down any questions you generate during reading.

This is the south. I look for evidence
of other Creeks,[1] for remnants of voices,
or for tobacco brown bones to come wandering
down Conti Street, Royal, or Decatur.
5 Near the French Market I see a blue horse
caught frozen in stone in the middle of
a square. Brought in by the Spanish on
an endless ocean voyage he became mad
and crazy. They caught him in blue
10 rock, said
     don't talk.

I know it wasn't just a horse
         that went crazy.

---

[1] **Creeks:** people belonging to a Native American group of the American South.

Nearby is a shop with ivory and knives.
15 There are red rocks. The man behind the
counter has no idea that he is inside
magic stones. He should find out before
they destroy him. These things
have memory,
20   you know.

I have a memory.
                It swims deep in blood,
a delta[2] in the skin. It swims out of Oklahoma,
deep the Mississippi River. It carries my
25 feet to these places: the French Quarter,
stale rooms, the sun behind thick and moist
clouds, and I hear boats hauling themselves up
and down the river.

My spirit comes here to drink.
30 My spirit comes here to drink.
Blood is the undercurrent.

There are voices buried in the Mississippi mud.
There are ancestors and future children
buried beneath the currents stirred up by
35 pleasure boats going up and down.
There are stories here made of memory.

I remember DeSoto.[3] He is buried somewhere in
this river, his bones sunk like the golden
treasure he traveled half the earth to find,
40 came looking for gold cities, for shining streets
of beaten gold to dance on with silk ladies.

He should have stayed home.

                (Creeks knew of him for miles
                before he came into town.
45   Dreamed of silver blades
                and crosses.)

And knew he was one of the ones who yearned
for something his heart wasn't big enough
to handle.
50   (And DeSoto thought it was gold.)

---

[2] **delta:** the mouth of a river, where it flows into a larger body of water.
[3] **DeSoto:** the Spanish conquistador who explored the Mississippi River.

The Creeks lived in earth towns,
     not gold,
  spun children, not gold.
That's not what DeSoto thought he wanted to see.
55 The Creeks knew it, and drowned him in
   the Mississippi River
       so he wouldn't have to drown himself.

Maybe his body is what I am looking for
as evidence. To know in another way
60 that my memory is alive.
But he must have got away, somehow,
because I have seen New Orleans,
the lace and silk buildings,
trolley cars on beaten silver paths,
65 graves that rise up out of soft earth in the rain,
shops that sell black mammy dolls
holding white babies.

And I know I have seen DeSoto,
    having a drink on Bourbon Street,
70   mad and crazy
    dancing with a woman as gold
    as the river bottom.

COLLABORATIVE DISCUSSION Discuss with a partner how Harjo reveals what New Orleans means to the speaker in the poem. Cite specific textual evidence from the poem and explain how these passages reveal the speaker's attitude toward the city.

Analyze Language: Free Verse

 COMMON CORE   ELACC11-12RL1, ELACC11-12RL4

"New Orleans" is an example of **free verse,** or poetry with no set patterns of rhythm and rhyme. When read aloud, free verse sounds more like everyday speech than a conventional poem. However, like other forms of poetry, free verse uses literary devices such as **imagery** and **figurative language** to communicate the author's meaning. The chart will help you analyze these devices in the poem.

Imagery	Figurative Language
Imagery is the use of words and phrases that appeal to the reader's five senses—sight, hearing, touch, taste, and smell. A writer uses imagery to help readers experience places and events in a vivid, sensory way. For example, the speaker describes "a blue horse / caught frozen in stone." Readers can virtually see this blue stone statue and feel its immobility. This image creates a feeling of sadness, since a living animal seems to be trapped in the stone.	**Figurative language** conveys meaning beyond the literal meanings of the words. It often makes a comparison between two things that seem completely unlike each other. A **metaphor** is a kind of figurative language that compares two things without using *like* or *as.* For example, the speaker refers to "blood, a delta in the skin." This metaphor compares the flow of blood through a person's veins to a river's water, constantly on the move.

Determine Themes

 COMMON CORE   ELACC11-12RL1, ELACC11-12RL2

A **theme** is a central idea about life or human nature that a writer wants to communicate to readers. Themes are usually not stated explicitly but must be inferred from clues in the text. To determine the themes in "New Orleans," pay attention to ideas that the poet develops over the course of the poem and how they build on one another. The chart shows textual evidence for one theme in the poem.

Evidence

"Brought in by the Spanish on / an endless ocean voyage he became mad / and crazy."

"DeSoto, . . . / mad and crazy / dancing with a woman as gold / as the river bottom."

"That's not what DeSoto thought he wanted to see. / The Creeks knew it, and drowned him in / the Mississippi River / so he wouldn't have to drown himself."

Theme

Chasing shallow, impossible dreams cannot bring happiness and may even lead to madness.

Analyzing the Text

ELACC11-12RL2,
ELACC11-12RL3,
ELACC11-12RL5,
ELACC11-12RL6

Cite Text Evidence Support your responses with evidence from the selection.

1. **Cite Evidence** Identify examples of color imagery in this poem. What effect does this imagery create?

2. **Infer** In lines 12–13, the speaker says, "I know it wasn't just a horse / that went crazy." What do you think the speaker means? Who else might have gone crazy?

3. **Compare** How does the speaker describe DeSoto and the Creeks in lines 37–57? What do these descriptions indicate about their relationships with one another?

4. **Interpret** In line 64, the speaker refers to "beaten silver paths." To what does this image refer, and how is it connected to the "silver blades and crosses" in lines 45–46?

5. **Draw Conclusions** What does DeSoto represent to the speaker? What particular words or images reveal the most about the speaker's feelings toward DeSoto?

6. **Analyze** The speaker refers to "voices" in line 2 and again in line 32. For what abstract idea are the voices a metaphor? What is the significance of the fact that the voices are "remnants" and "buried in the Mississippi mud"?

7. **Connect** The word *memory* is first used in line 19. Trace the development of the idea of memory through the poem. What possible theme about memory does the poet want to communicate?

8. **Synthesize** Considering the various images and ideas that Harjo develops in this poem about New Orleans, what might be a theme that she wants to communicate about the importance of place?

PERFORMANCE TASK

Speaking Activity New Orleans is clearly a place of significance to Joy Harjo and the Creeks. Explore that significance through research and present your findings in an oral presentation.

- Conduct a short research project to find out more about Creek Indian Removal and its relation to the city of New Orleans. Synthesize at least two sources on the topic.
- Reread "New Orleans" and notice how this new information affects your understanding of the poem. Make note of specific passages that you understand more deeply.

- Create a chart or other graphic display that summarizes your findings.
- Share your findings with a small group.
- Present a clear perspective on Creek Indian Removal and how it affects the interpretation of "New Orleans."

Language and Style: Syntax in Poetry

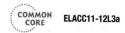 COMMON CORE ELACC11-12L3a

To create particular effects, poets may arrange their words on the page in a variety of ways. These word arrangements, or **syntactical elements,** may affect the sound of the poem, reinforce the poet's meaning, or do both at the same time.

In "New Orleans," Joy Harjo makes use of the techniques shown in the chart.

Syntactical Element	Example
Parallelism is the use of similar grammatical structures to express ideas that are related or equivalent.	"I look for evidence / of other Creeks, for remnants of voices, / or for tobacco brown bones. . . ." (lines 1–3)
Parataxis is the placement of short sentences next to each other without showing how they are related. The sentences lack subordinating conjunctions or transitions, so readers must infer how they are connected.	"Nearby is a shop with ivory and knives. / There are red rocks. The man behind the / counter has no idea that he is inside / magic stones." (lines 14–17)
Ellipsis occurs when a word or phrase that is needed to form a complete grammatical structure is omitted. In the example, the second sentence lacks a subject and verb. Readers might fill in "Maybe I want" at the beginning of the second sentence to complete the thought.	"Maybe his body is what I am looking for / as evidence. To know in another way / that my memory is alive." (lines 58–60)

Poetry, for the most part, follows basic rules of grammar and style. However, it is a condensed form of expression that demands an investment from readers. To create a meaningful whole, readers must connect images and ideas and fill in missing details. Through the use of parataxis and ellipsis, Harjo involves readers in her poem, enriching their poetic experience.

Practice and Apply Complete this activity with a small group.

1. Create a chart similar to the one shown. In the first column, list the terms *parallelism*, *parataxis*, and *ellipsis*.

2. Reread lines 29–41. Fill in examples of each type of syntactical element from this part of the poem in the second column.

3. Discuss with your group how the use of each technique affects the sound and meaning of the poem.

4. Share your examples and insights with the class.

If you need help...
• **Writing Arguments**
• **Using Textual Evidence**

Write an Argument

This collection focuses on how and why Europeans came to the Americas and what happened as they settled in unfamiliar environments. Relocating to the Americas dramatically changed settlers' lives. In turn, the settlers changed the Americas through their interaction with its land and its native populations. Look back at the anchor text, "Of Plymouth Plantation," and at other texts you have read in this collection. Synthesize your ideas about them by writing an argument. Your argument should persuade readers to agree with your claim about how immigration changed America, and how America changes those who come here.

```
COMMON
CORE
```

ELACC11-12W1a–e
Write arguments to support claims in an analysis of substantive topics or texts, using valid reasoning and relevant and sufficient evidence.
ELACC11-12W9 Draw evidence form literary or informational texts to support analysis, reflection, and research.

An effective argument

- identifies a central issue or question
- states a precise claim in response to the question
- develops the claim with valid reasons and relevant evidence, such as examples and quotations from the texts
- anticipates opposing claims and counters them with well-supported counterclaims
- establishes clear, logical connections among claims, counterclaims, reasons, and evidence
- includes an introduction, a logically structured body including transitions, and a conclusion
- maintains an appropriate tone based on its audience and context
- follows the conventions of written English

PLAN

*my*Notebook

Analyze the Text Think about the following questions as they relate to the anchor text, "Of Plymouth Plantation":

- Why did European settlers come to the New World?
- When settlers came to explore and settle the Americas, how did it change their lives?
- What changes did these settlers bring to the Americas?

Choose one question to address in your argument. Then, select three texts from this collection—including "Of Plymouth Plantation"—that provide evidence for your position. These texts might present similar or different views from each other.

ACADEMIC VOCABULARY

As you share your ideas about the role of immigration in American society, be sure to use these words.

adapt
coherent
device
displace
dynamic

You need to formulate a claim for your essay. In order to do this, review your chosen texts and take notes about how each one answers the question you have chosen. List evidence from each text that answers the question. Then form a clear, concise claim that will become the basis of your argument.

Get Organized Organize your notes in an outline to help you create a logical structure for your essay and to make it easier for readers to understand and follow your argument. Begin your outline with a precise statement of your claim, or your position on a question or topic.

Your introduction should

- state your claim as clearly as possible, since it will serve as the foundation of your entire argument
- include an engaging opener (for example, question, comment, or quotation) that helps your audience connect to the topic
- identify the authors and titles of each text

The body of your essay should

- present clear reasons for your claim
- provide relevant and carefully incorporated quotations or examples from each text to support your claim
- anticipate and counter opposing claims as appropriate
- show logical connections among claims, reasons, counterclaims, and evidence

In the conclusion, you should

- restate your claim and summarize your most compelling reasons for it
- end with a fresh insight about settlers in the Americas and their relationship to the New World

PRODUCE

my **WriteSmart**

Write a Draft Use your outline to write an essay that makes a strong argument. The purpose of an argument is to persuade readers that your opinion or belief is correct. Remember to

Write your rough draft in *my*WriteSmart. Focus on getting your ideas down, rather than perfecting your choice of language.

- provide a clear and cohesive introduction, body, and conclusion that your reader can clearly follow and understand
- support your reasons with evidence that clearly connects to your argument
- explain how the evidence supports your claim; don't rely on readers to make all the connections between your claim and the text evidence

- anticipate and respond to opposing claims to strengthen your claim or to acknowledge the complexity of the topic
- use language that is appropriate for your audience
- include transitions to link the major sections of the text

REVISE

my WriteSmart

Have your partner or a group of peers review your draft in *my*WriteSmart. Ask your reviewers to note any reasons that do not support the claim or that lack sufficient evidence.

Improve Your Draft You should now have a rough draft that persuades readers to agree with your claim. It is time to revise your draft so that your readers will clearly understand your argument. Use the chart on the following page to review the characteristics of an effective argument. Your goal is to produce a clear and coherent text. Read your first draft and ensure that it

- has a clearly-developed introduction, body, and conclusion
- makes logical connections among claims, counterclaims, reasons, and evidence
- has sufficient evidence to support these connections
- maintains a formal style and an objective, unbiased tone
- follows the conventions of standard English grammar

Then write a new draft of your essay, incorporating all your revisions.

PRESENT

Exchange Essays When your final draft is completed, exchange essays with a partner. Read your partner's essay and provide feedback. Reread the criteria for an effective argument and ask the following questions

- What is the central claim of your partner's essay?
- Is your partner's essay organized logically?
- Does your partner present sufficient evidence to support the central claim?
- Does your partner include opposing claims and address them effectively?
- Do you agree with your partner's claim?
- If yes, what elements of the essay persuaded you?
- If no, what could your partner have done to persuade you?

Ideas and Evidence	Organization	Language
ADVANCED • The introduction is memorable and persuasive; the claim clearly states a position on a substantive topic. • Valid reasons and relevant evidence from the texts convincingly support the writer's claim. • Opposing claims are anticipated and effectively addressed with counterclaims. • The concluding section effectively summarizes the claim.	• The reasons and textual evidence are organized consistently and logically throughout the argument. • Varied transitions logically connect reasons and textual evidence to the writer's claim.	• The writing reflects a formal style and an objective, or controlled, tone. • Sentence beginnings, lengths, and structures vary and have a rhythmic flow. • Spelling, capitalization, and punctuation are correct. If handwritten, the argument is legible. • Grammar and usage are correct.
COMPETENT • The introduction could do more to capture the reader's attention; the claim states a position on an issue. • Most reasons and evidence from the texts support the writer's claim, but they could be more convincing. • Opposing claims are anticipated, but the counterclaims need to be developed more. • The concluding section restates the claim.	• The organization of reasons and textual evidence is confusing in a few places. • A few more transitions are needed to connect reasons and textual evidence to the writer's claim.	• The style is informal in a few places, and the tone is defensive at times. • Sentence beginnings, lengths, and structures vary somewhat. • Several spelling and capitalization mistakes occur, and punctuation is inconsistent. If handwritten, the argument is mostly legible. • Some grammatical and usage errors are repeated in the argument.
LIMITED • The introduction is ordinary; the claim identifies an issue, but the writer's position is not clearly stated. • The reasons and evidence from the texts are not always logical or relevant. • Opposing claims are anticipated but not addressed logically. • The concluding section includes an incomplete summary of the claim.	• The organization of reasons and textual evidence is logical in some places, but it often doesn't follow a pattern. • Many more transitions are needed to connect reasons and textual evidence to the writer's position.	• The style becomes informal in many places, and the tone is often dismissive of other viewpoints. • Sentence structures barely vary, and some fragments or run-on sentences are present. • Spelling, capitalization, and punctuation are often incorrect but do not make reading the argument difficult. If handwritten, the argument may be partially illegible. • Grammar and usage are incorrect in many places, but the writer's ideas are still clear.
EMERGING • The introduction is missing. • Significant supporting reasons and evidence from the texts are missing. • Opposing claims are neither anticipated nor addressed. • The concluding section is missing.	• An organizational strategy is not used; reasons and textual evidence are presented randomly. • Transitions are not used, making the argument difficult to understand.	• The style is inappropriate, and the tone is disrespectful. • Repetitive sentence structure, fragments, and run-on sentences make the writing monotonous and hard to follow. • Spelling and capitalization are often incorrect, and punctuation is missing. If handwritten, the argument may be partially or mostly illegible. • Many grammatical and usage errors change the meaning of the writer's ideas.

This collection explores how people who are so different can work together to create a unified whole while also protecting the rights of everyone.

hmhfyi.com

COLLECTION

PERFORMANCE TASK Preview

At the end of this collection, you will have the opportunity to complete a task:

- Write an informative essay on how each author, character, or historical figure strikes a balance between preserving individual rights and forming a strong, long-lasting union.

ACADEMIC VOCABULARY

Study the words and their definitions in the chart below. You will use these words as you discuss and write about the texts in this collection.

Word	Definition	Related Forms
contrary (kŏn′trĕr′ē) *adj.*	opposite or opposed in character or purpose	contradict, contrariness
founder (foun′dər) *n.*	someone who sets up, establishes, or provides the basis for something	foundation, founded, fundamental
ideological (ī′dē-ə-lŏj′ĭ-kəl) *adj.*	based on ideas, beliefs, or doctrines	idea, ideologue, ideology
publication (pŭb′lĭ-kā′shən) *n.*	the act of making public in printed or electronic form; the product of this act	public, publish, publisher
revolution	the overthrow and replacement of	

COMMON CORE ELACC11-12RL10, ELACC11-12RI7, ELACC11-12RI10

A New American Nation

In a span of almost two hundred years, a group of British colonies clustered along the Atlantic coast became an independent nation that spread from modern-day New Hampshire to Georgia. United around principles of self-government and liberty, the United States expanded its vision of itself as it began to explore the potential of the country's unique natural resources.

FROM COLONY TO COUNTRY Through the middle of the eighteenth century, the colonists in North America thought of themselves as British. They supported Britain economically and militarily, especially during the French and Indian War (1754–1763), when Britain fought to gain control of all the land east of the Mississippi River. When Britain then tried to recover the costs of the war by taxing the colonists, they rebelled. In 1783, after eight years of the Revolutionary War, the United States won its independence. At first, the founders struggled to govern effectively under the Articles of Confederation. Eventually, however, they created our current form of government under the United States Constitution, which was adopted in 1788.

Ideological debates over the scope and nature of federal power raged throughout the republic's early years. In 1803, President Thomas Jefferson doubled the size of the United States with the purchase from France of the vast Louisiana Territory west of the Mississippi River. The price was $15 million. Jefferson, who normally favored a limited federal government, took this bold step even though the Constitution gave him no explicit authority to do so.

IDEAS OF THE AGE In the 1700s, as the colonists moved toward independence, they drew on traditional Puritan values and on Enlightenment ideals, which questioned previously accepted truths about government. Both sources of inspiration caused people to question traditional authority, eventually leading the colonists to break from Britain's control and embrace democracy. American colonial writers such as Benjamin Franklin, Thomas Paine, and Thomas Jefferson adapted the ideals of the European Enlightenment for their own environment. At the same time, preachers such as Jonathan Edwards called for people to rededicate themselves to the original Puritan vision. This new wave of religious enthusiasm, called the Great Awakening, united geographically and culturally diverse colonists.

1700

1734–1736
Great Awakening begins

1765
Colonists rebel against the Stamp Act

1733
Georgia becomes 13th British colony

1754
French and Indian War begins

WRITING THAT LAUNCHED A NATION As the colonists began to question their relationship with Great Britain, many gifted minds turned to political writing. Between 1763 and 1783, about two thousand inexpensive pamphlets were published, reaching thousands of people and stirring debate and action. *Common Sense* by Thomas Paine was a key pamphlet that helped move the colonists to revolution. Paine's Enlightenment ideas were combined with the Puritan belief that America was destined to be a model of freedom to the world.

Although Thomas Jefferson also wrote pamphlets, his greatest contribution to American government and literature is the Declaration of Independence, adopted by the Second Continental Congress on July 4, 1776. Jefferson's eloquent and stirring articulation of the natural law that would govern America proclaimed the idea that people are born with rights and freedoms that government must protect. While Jefferson's Declaration marked the beginning of the colonies' independence, it was the adoption of the Constitution of the United States of America in 1788 that created the lasting framework for an independent government. Many of the young nation's most outstanding leaders, including Benjamin Franklin, James Madison, Alexander Hamilton, and George Washington, crafted perhaps the country's most important foundational document.

VOICES OF THE PEOPLE Statesmen were joined by poets in examining political and social themes of the day. Among the finest examples of Colonial American poetry are the works of Phillis Wheatley and Philip Freneau. In her poems and letters, Wheatley, a former slave, wrote of the "natural rights" of African Americans. She also pointed out the discrepancy between the colonists' "cry for liberty" and their enslavement of fellow human beings.

Freneau, who became known as the "poet of the American Revolution," wrote verses that harshly criticized the British, such as "The British Prison-Ship," based on his own experience as a prisoner of war. He also celebrated those who fought in the revolutionary cause, including John Paul Jones, whom he exhorted to "bid the haughty Britons know / They to our Thirteen Stars shall bend." After the war, his lyrical poetry continued to build on Enlightenment ideals—celebrating the natural wonders of America while proclaiming that its lands were the ideal site for the growth of freedom.

1783
American Revolution
ends

1776
Declaration of Independence
adopted

1788
U.S. Constitution
adopted

1803
Louisiana Territory
purchased from France

1810

The Declaration of Independence

from The United States Constitution

Public Documents

Background *The Declaration of Independence, adopted July 4, 1776, by the Second Continental Congress, was the culmination of a long process during which the American colonists tried to resolve their differences with Great Britain. Hope for a peaceful resolution still persisted after the outbreak of armed conflict in April 1775. By the spring of 1776, however, most colonists favored a break with Britain. In early June, a committee was formed to draft a statement to support that position, and* **Thomas Jefferson** *took on the task of writing it. Although the Congress made changes to his list of grievances, it did not touch his declaration of rights, which became a lasting statement of "self-evident" truths for the new country and the world.*

In 1787 a Constitutional Convention was called to amend the Articles of Confederation, the first written constitution of the United States. The Articles severely limited the power of the central government and prevented it from meeting many challenges in the country's first years. The Constitution did not have one predominant author because it reflected many compromises needed to resolve differences between large and small states, Northerners and Southerners. The final document sought to create a balance between a strong, workable central government and individual liberty. The Bill of Rights, adopted as the first ten Amendments to the Constitution in 1791, strengthened the original document's protection of individual and states' rights.

Thomas Jefferson *(1743–1826) was one of the most accomplished of our nation's founders. He held a number of important government positions, including governor of Virginia during the Revolutionary War and U.S. minister to France afterward. In addition, he served as the country's first secretary of state, its second vice-president, and its third president. More important than his titles, however, was his vision of liberty and self-government, eloquently expressed in the Declaration of Independence.*

The Declaration of Independence
by Thomas Jefferson

In Congress, July 4, 1776

When, in the course of human events, it becomes necessary for one people to dissolve the political bands which have connected them with another, and to assume, among the powers of the earth, the separate and equal station to which the laws of nature and of nature's God entitle them, a decent respect to the opinions of mankind requires that they should declare the causes which impel them to the separation.

   We hold these truths to be self-evident:—That all men are created equal; that they are endowed by their Creator with certain unalienable
10 rights; that among these are life, liberty, and the pursuit of happiness. That, to secure these rights, governments are instituted among men, deriving their just powers from the consent of the governed; that, whenever any form of government becomes destructive of these ends, it is the right of the people to alter or to abolish it, and to institute a new government, laying its foundation on such principles, and organizing its powers in such form, as to them shall seem most likely to effect their safety and happiness. Prudence, indeed, will dictate that governments long **established** should not be changed for light and transient causes; and, accordingly, all experience hath shown
20 that mankind are more disposed to suffer, while evils are sufferable, than to right themselves by abolishing the forms to which they are accustomed. But, when a long train of abuses and usurpations, pursuing invariably the same object, evinces a design to reduce them under absolute despotism,[1] it is their right, it is their duty, to throw off such government, and to provide new guards for their future security. Such has been the patient sufferance of these colonies; and such is now the necessity that constrains them to alter their former systems of government. The history of the present King of Great Britain[2] is a history of repeated injuries and usurpations, all having, in direct
30 object, the establishment of an absolute tyranny over these States. To prove this, let facts be submitted to a candid world.

establish
(ĭ-stăb´lĭsh) *v.* to formally set up; institute.

---

[1] **despotism:** (dĕs´pə-tĭz´əm) *n.* government by a ruler with unlimited power.
[2] **the present King of Great Britain:** George III, who reigned from 1760 to 1820.

Life, liberty, and the pursuit of happiness. "

He has refused his assent to laws[3] the most wholesome and necessary for the public good.

He has forbidden his Governors to pass laws of immediate and pressing importance, unless suspended in their operation till his assent should be obtained; and, when so suspended, he has utterly neglected to attend to them.

He has refused to pass other laws for the accommodation of large districts of people, unless these people would relinquish the right of
40 representation in the legislature—a right inestimable to them, and formidable to tyrants only.

He has called together legislative bodies at places unusual, uncomfortable, and distant from the depository of their public records, for the sole purpose of fatiguing them into compliance with his measure.

He has dissolved representative houses repeatedly, for opposing, with manly firmness, his invasions on the rights of the people.

He has refused, for a long time after such dissolutions, to cause others to be elected; whereby the legislative powers, incapable of
50 annihilation, have returned to the people at large for their exercise; the State remaining, in the meantime, exposed to all dangers of invasion from without, and convulsions within.

He has endeavored to prevent the population[4] of these States; for that purpose obstructing the laws for the naturalization of foreigners; refusing to pass others to encourage their migration hither, and raising the conditions of new appropriations of lands.

He has obstructed the administration of justice, by refusing his assent to laws for establishing judiciary powers.

---

[3] **refused his assent to laws:** Laws passed in the colonies needed the king's approval; sometimes it took years for laws to be approved or rejected.

[4] **to prevent the population:** to keep the population from growing.

He has made judges dependent on his will alone for the tenure of their offices,[5] and the amount and payment of their salaries.

He has erected a multitude of new offices, and sent hither swarms of officers to harass our people and eat out their substance.[6]

He has kept among us, in times of peace, standing armies, without the consent of our legislatures.

He has **affected** to render the military independent of, and superior to, the civil power.

He has combined with others to subject us to a jurisdiction foreign to our constitutions,[7] and unacknowledged by our laws; giving his assent to their acts of pretended legislation:

For quartering large bodies of armed troops among us;

For protecting them, by a mock trial, from punishment for any murders which they should commit on the inhabitants of these States;

For cutting off our trade with all parts of the world;

For imposing taxes on us without our consent;

For depriving us, in many cases, of the benefits of trial by jury;

For transporting us beyond the seas, to be tried for pretended offenses;

For abolishing the free system of English laws in a neighboring province,[8] establishing there an arbitrary government, and enlarging its boundaries, so as to render it at once an example and fit instrument for introducing the same absolute rule into these colonies;

For taking away our charters, abolishing our most valuable laws, and altering, fundamentally, the forms of our governments;

For suspending our own legislatures, and declaring themselves **invested** with power to legislate for us in all cases whatsoever.

He has **abdicated** government here, by declaring us out of his protection, and waging war against us.

He has plundered our seas, ravaged our coasts, burnt our towns,[9] and destroyed the lives of our people.

He is at this time transporting large armies of foreign mercenaries to complete the works of death, desolation, and tyranny, already begun with circumstances of cruelty and perfidy scarcely paralleled in the most barbarous ages, and totally unworthy the head of a civilized nation.

He has constrained our fellow citizens, taken captive on the high seas, to bear arms against their country, to become the executioners of their friends and brethren, or to fall themselves by their hands.

affect
(ə-fĕkt´) *v.* to cause or influence.

invest
(ĭn-vĕst´) *v.* to grant or endow.

abdicate
(ăb´dĭ-kāt´) *v.* to relinquish or cede responsibility for.

---

[5] **the tenure of their offices:** their job security.

[6] **eat out their substance:** use up their resources.

[7] **subject us . . . our constitutions:** Parliament had passed the Declaratory Act in 1766, stating that the king and Parliament could make laws for the colonies.

[8] **a neighboring province:** the province of Quebec, which at the time extended south to the Ohio River and west to the Mississippi.

[9] **plundered . . . our towns:** American seaports such as Norfolk, Virginia, had already been shelled.

He has excited domestic insurrection amongst us,[10] and has endeavored to bring on the inhabitants of our frontiers the merciless Indian savages, whose known rule of warfare is an undistinguished destruction of all ages, sexes, and conditions.

In every stage of these oppressions we have petitioned for redress,[11] in the most humble terms; our repeated petitions have been answered only by repeated injury. A prince whose character is thus marked by every act which may define a tyrant is unfit to be the ruler of a free people.

Nor have we been wanting in our attentions to our British brethren. We have warned them, from time to time, of attempts by their legislature to extend an unwarrantable jurisdiction over us. We have reminded them of the circumstances of our emigration and settlement here. We have appealed to their native justice and magnanimity; and we have conjured them, by the ties of our common kindred, to disavow these usurpations, which would inevitably interrupt our connections and correspondence.

They, too, have been deaf to the voice of justice and of consanguinity.[12] We must, therefore, acquiesce in the necessity which denounces our separation; and hold them, as we hold the rest of mankind, enemies in war, in peace friends.

---

[10] **excited . . . amongst us:** George III had encouraged slaves to rise up and rebel against their masters.

[11] **redress:** the correction of a wrong; compensation.

[12] **deaf to . . . consanguinity:** The British have ignored pleas based on their common ancestry with the colonists.

We, Therefore, the Representatives of the United
120   States of America, in General Congress assembled, appealing to
the Supreme Judge of the world for the rectitude[13] of our intentions,
do, in the name and by the authority of the good people of these
colonies, solemnly publish and declare, that these United Colonies
are, and of right ought to be, Free and Independent States; that they
are absolved from all allegiance to the British crown, and that all
political connection between them and the state of Great Britain is,
and ought to be, totally dissolved; and that, as free and independent
states, they have full power to levy war, conclude peace, contract
alliances, establish commerce, and to do all other acts and things
130   which independent states may of right do. And, for the support of
this declaration, with a firm reliance on the protection of Divine
Providence, we mutually pledge to each other our lives, our fortunes,
and our sacred honor.

---

[13] **rectitude:** morally correct behavior or thinking.

COLLABORATIVE DISCUSSION What makes a good government? Discuss
this question with a partner, citing specific textual evidence from the
Declaration of Independence to support your ideas.

Analyze Structure: Style and Content

COMMON CORE   ELACC11-12RI6, ELACC11-12L3a

The power of the Declaration of Independence comes not just from *what* it says, or its content, but from *how* Jefferson says it, or his style. **Style** comes from an author's word choice, sentence length, and **tone,** or attitude about the subject. Jefferson's message is complex, so he is careful to arrange the content in an orderly and logical way.

An important element of style is **syntax,** the arrangement of words in phrases, clauses, and sentences. Varying the syntax allows a writer to create variety, emphasis, and a rhythm that helps keep readers engaged. Note how Jefferson begins the Declaration:

> **When, <u>in the course of human events</u>, it becomes necessary for one people to dissolve the political bands which have connected them with another, and to assume, <u>among the powers of the earth</u>, the separate and equal station to which the laws of nature and of nature's God entitle them, . . .**

The two underlined phrases are not strictly needed to convey the meaning of the sentence. Adding them, however, puts in meaningful pauses and adds to the weight of what the colonists are about to do. Reread the sentence without those phrases and see how it affects your response to Jefferson's point. As you analyze the text, be aware of how style and content contribute to the power and persuasiveness of the document.

Analyze Foundational Documents: Theme and Rhetorical Features

COMMON CORE   ELACC11-12RI9

Jefferson wrote the Declaration to justify the move toward independence to the British, represented by the king. He was also writing for the American colonists of his own time and for future generations. His choice of themes and his use of rhetorical features reflect both his purpose and his audience.

Theme	Rhetorical Features
A **theme** is a main message that the author wants to communicate about a topic—in this case, independence. The themes of the Declaration of Independence are relevant to the situation in which the document was written and also speak to broader ideas that are relevant over time.	**Rhetorical features** include all the methods a writer uses to communicate ideas and appeal to readers. • **Repetition** is the technique of repeating words or phrases to reinforce meaning and create rhythm. For example, the repetition of the word *nature* in the first sentence of the Declaration emphasizes the basis for Jefferson's appeal. • **Parallelism** is the use of similar grammatical structures to express ideas that are related or equal in importance. For example, in lines 70–85, Jefferson begins each item in the list with the preposition *for* followed by a gerund, such as *quartering* or *protecting*, to add to the persuasive impact of this section.

COMMON CORE

ELACC11-12RI1,
ELACC11-12RI5,
ELACC11-12RI6,
ELACC11-12RI9

Analyzing the Text

Cite Text Evidence   Support your responses with evidence from the selection.

1. **Analyze** In an argument, a claim is an author's position on an issue. What claim does Jefferson make in the first paragraph, and how does he say he will support that claim?

2. **Infer** What overall reason for the colonies to separate from Britain does Jefferson outline in the second paragraph (lines 8–31)?

3. **Cite Evidence** How do the syntax and rhetorical features that Jefferson uses in the first sentence of the second paragraph (lines 8–10) contribute to the persuasiveness of the document?

4. **Draw Conclusions** What theme about government does Jefferson communicate in the second paragraph?

5. **Cite Evidence** Identify the most striking words that Jefferson chooses to describe the king's actions in lines 22–31. How does this language support his claim?

6. **Evaluate** The list of complaints makes up the largest part of the document's **structure,** or pattern of organization. What does its structure contribute to Jefferson's argument? How does it reinforce his main idea?

7. **Analyze** How do the rhetorical features in the conclusion (lines 119–133) contribute to the power and persuasiveness of the document?

PERFORMANCE TASK

Speaking Activity At the time of its publication, many colonists heard the Declaration of Independence read aloud in public places. Evaluate the effectiveness of this document presented as a speech through the following activity.

1. Work with a partner and take turns presenting the Declaration of Independence as a speech. One partner might read the opening and closing paragraphs and the other might read the list of complaints.

2. As a speaker, use tone of voice and pacing to reflect the rhetorical features of the document and communicate its meaning. As a listener, pay attention to how well you are able to follow the line of reasoning. Notice how the speech appeals to your reason and your emotions.

3. Write an evaluation of how the effectiveness of the Declaration as a speech compares to its effectiveness as a written document. Cite evidence from the document to support your ideas, and consider your experiences as a speaker, a listener, and a reader.

Critical Vocabulary

COMMON CORE ELACC11-12L4c, ELACC11-12L6

established   affected   invested   abdicated

Practice and Apply Create a semantic map like the one below for each Critical Vocabulary word. Use a dictionary or thesaurus as needed. This example is for the word *instituted,* which appears in line 11 of the Declaration of Independence.

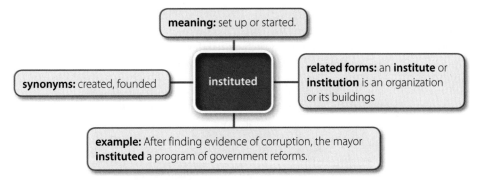

Vocabulary Strategy: Domain-Specific Words

In the Declaration of Independence, Jefferson uses the Critical Vocabulary word *abdicated*. This word is fairly uncommon in general texts but appears more commonly in works of **political science,** or the study of government. Political science has a rich set of terms. Some terms may identify a particular type of government or government function; others, such as *despotism* and *tyranny*, describe the way a government acts. Building a vocabulary of such words will help you read social studies texts and contemporary writing about politics and government to become a better informed citizen. Use these strategies to become familiar with political science words.

- Use context clues to help you determine a word's meaning as it is used in a political text.
- Use a dictionary or other reference work to help you verify a word's meaning and understand its **etymology,** or origin. If a word has multiple meanings, check to see which one most likely applies to a political context.
- When using a reference work, look for related forms of a word and understand how each is used, such as *legislate, legislature,* or *legislative.*

Practice and Apply Work with a partner to investigate the meaning, etymology, and related forms of these domain-specific words using a dictionary or other reference work.

1. sovereign	6. republic
2. despotism	7. democracy
3. tyranny	8. legislative
4. govern	9. executive
5. oligarchy	10. judicial

Language and Style: Parallel Structure

Jefferson makes frequent use of the rhetorical device of parallelism in the Declaration of Independence. **Parallelism** is the use of similar grammatical constructions to express ideas that are closely related or equal in importance. The grammatical constructions may include phrases, clauses, or sentences. Parallel structures are an important element in a writer's **syntax,** or arrangement of words. Consider this example from the Declaration:

> . . . it is the right of the people to alter or to abolish it, and to institute a new government, laying its foundation on such principles, and organizing its powers in such form . . .

First notice the use of three infinitives to describe what people have a right to do: *to alter, to abolish, to institute.* All of these rights are given equal weight. Jefferson then proceeds to use two phrases with parallel grammatical structure: "laying its foundation on such principles, and organizing its powers in such form." Laying the foundation of the new government and organizing its powers are equally important and are part of the same process. The parallel structure makes this close relationship clear.

The chart shows two more examples of parallel structures. Try reading each passage aloud. Note how the parallelism creates rhythm and helps emphasize similarities among related ideas.

Parallel Structure	
parallel phrases	"He has plundered our seas, ravaged our coasts, burnt our towns, and destroyed the lives of our people."
parallel clauses or sentences	"We have warned them, from time to time, of attempts by their legislature to extend an unwarrantable jurisdiction over us. We have reminded them of the circumstances of our emigration and settlement here. We have appealed to their native justice and magnanimity; and we have conjured them, by the ties of our common kindred, to disavow these usurpations, which would inevitably interrupt our connections and correspondence."

Practice and Apply Look back at the evaluation of the Declaration of Independence that you wrote in response to this selection's Performance Task. Cite additional evidence of Jefferson's use of parallelism and explain how it contributes to the effectiveness of the spoken and written versions of the document. Then review your own writing to make any necessary revisions to correct for parallel structure or to add parallelism to strengthen your expression.

AS YOU READ Notice what kinds of rights are protected in the Bill of Rights. Write down any questions you generate during reading.

from The United States Constitution: Preamble and Bill of Rights

Preamble

We the People of the United States, in Order to form a more perfect Union, establish Justice, insure domestic Tranquility, provide for the common defence,[1] promote the general Welfare, and secure the Blessings of Liberty to ourselves and our **Posterity**, do ordain and establish this Constitution for the United States of America.

posterity
(pŏ-stĕr´ĭ-tē) *n.* future generations.

---

[1] **defence:** alternate spelling of *defense*.

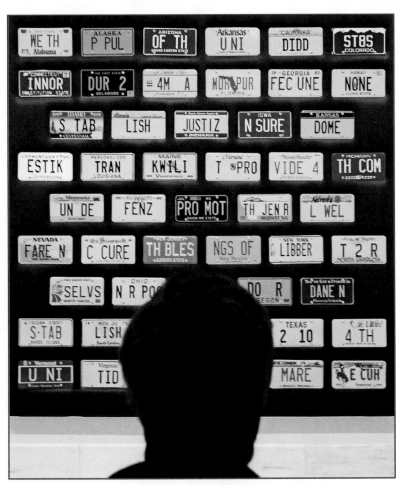

The Bill of Rights

The Preamble to The Bill of Rights

Congress of the United States begun and held at the City of New-York, on Wednesday the fourth of March, one thousand seven
10 hundred and eighty nine.

THE Conventions of a number of the States, having at the time of their adopting the Constitution, expressed a desire, in order to prevent misconstruction or abuse of its powers, that further declaratory and restrictive clauses should be added: And as extending the ground of public confidence in the Government, will best ensure the beneficent ends of its institution.

RESOLVED by the Senate and House of Representatives of the United States of America, in Congress assembled, two thirds of both Houses concurring, that the following Articles be proposed to the Legislatures
20 of the several States, as amendments to the Constitution of the United States, all, or any of which Articles, when ratified by three fourths of the said Legislatures, to be valid to all intents and purposes, as part of the said Constitution; viz.

ARTICLES in addition to, and Amendment of the Constitution of the United States of America, proposed by Congress, and ratified by the Legislatures of the several States, pursuant to the fifth Article of the original Constitution.

Amendment I

Congress shall make no law respecting an establishment of religion, or prohibiting the free exercise thereof; or abridging[2] the freedom of
30 speech, or of the press; or the right of the people peaceably to assemble, and to petition the Government for a redress of grievances.

Amendment II

A well regulated Militia, being necessary to the security of a free State, the right of the people to keep and bear Arms, shall not be **infringed**.

infringe
(ĭn-frĭnj´) *v.* to interfere with; violate.

Amendment III

No Soldier shall, in time of peace be quartered[3] in any house, without the consent of the Owner, nor in time of war, but in a manner to be **prescribed** by law.

prescribe
(prĭ-skrīb´) *v.* to authorize or regulate.

---

[2] **abridging:** limiting.
[3] **quartered:** housed or lodged.

Amendment IV

The right of the people to be secure in their persons, houses, papers, and effects, against unreasonable searches and seizures, shall not be violated, and no Warrants shall issue, but upon probable cause,
40   supported by Oath or affirmation, and particularly describing the place to be searched, and the persons or things to be seized.

Amendment V

No person shall be held to answer for a capital, or otherwise infamous crime, unless on a presentment[4] or indictment of a Grand Jury, except in cases arising in the land or naval forces, or in the Militia, when in actual service in time of War or public danger; nor shall any person be subject for the same offence to be twice put in jeopardy of life or limb; nor shall be compelled in any criminal case to be a witness against himself, nor be deprived of life, liberty, or property, without due process of law; nor shall private property be taken for public use,
50   without just compensation.

Amendment VI

In all criminal prosecutions, the accused shall enjoy the right to a speedy and public trial, by an impartial jury of the State and district wherein the crime shall have been committed, which district shall have been previously ascertained by law, and to be informed of the nature and cause of the accusation; to be confronted with the witnesses against him; to have compulsory process for obtaining witnesses in his favor, and to have the Assistance of Counsel for his defence.

---

[4] **presentment:** presentation of evidence.

Amendment VII

In Suits at common law,[5] where the value in controversy shall exceed
60 twenty dollars, the right of trial by jury shall be preserved, and no fact
tried by a jury, shall be otherwise re-examined in any Court of the
United States, than according to the rules of the common law.

Amendment VIII

Excessive bail shall not be required, nor excessive fines **imposed**, nor
cruel and unusual punishments inflicted.

impose
(ĭm-pōz´) *v.* to charge
or apply.

Amendment IX

The enumeration[6] in the Constitution, of certain rights, shall not be
construed to deny or disparage others retained by the people.

Amendment X

The powers not delegated to the United States by the Constitution, nor
prohibited by it to the States, are reserved to the States respectively, or
to the people.

---

[5] **common law:** laws based on court decisions and individual circumstances
rather than on government legislation.
[6] **enumeration:** the mention or listing.

COLLABORATIVE DISCUSSION How is the Bill of Rights relevant to you as a
high school student in the twenty-first century? Discuss this question with
a partner, citing specific textual evidence from the Bill of Rights to support
your ideas.

Evaluate Seminal Texts: Constitutional Principles

COMMON CORE · ELACC11-12RI8

The U.S. Constitution has influenced the development of U.S. legal history for more than two hundred years. Lawmakers have applied constitutional principles to individual pieces of legislation at the federal and state levels. The Constitution lays out the founders' most basic assumptions about the nature of government and the rights and responsibilities of citizens and their political leaders. At the same time, the Constitution allows for change. The Preamble to the Bill of Rights indicates that amendments may be added "pursuant to the fifth Article of the original Constitution."

The parts of the Constitution presented here are from its very beginning (the Preamble) and from the last section, the list of amendments or additions to the original document. In between the Preamble and the Bill of Rights is the body of the Constitution itself. Here are some examples of constitutional principles found in the body of the document:

- Representative democracy—the people elect others to represent their wishes and carry out the functions of government
- The separation of powers—between legislative, executive, and judicial branches and between the federal and state governments
- A system of checks and balances—each branch imposes limits on the others
- A balance between government authority and individual rights and freedom

As you analyze these excerpts from the Constitution, look for evidence of these principles and for reasons why the Constitution was written in this particular way.

Analyze Foundational Documents

COMMON CORE · ELACC11-12RI5, ELACC11-12RI9

When you analyzed the Declaration of Independence, you paid attention to its **purpose, themes,** and **rhetorical features.** You will focus on these same elements as you analyze the Preamble and Bill of Rights from the U.S. Constitution.

Purpose is the reason why something is written. The preambles to the Constitution and to the Bill of Rights state the purposes of each section of the document.

A **theme** is a main message that the author wants to communicate about a particular topic. Again, the Preamble and the Bill of Rights have separate but related messages to communicate. These themes are related to the purpose of each part of the document.

Rhetorical features include all the methods a writer uses to communicate ideas and appeal to readers. Because the Constitution has a different purpose from the Declaration of Independence, it was written with different rhetorical features. Notice how the responsibilities of government and the rights of citizens are described in the Constitution. How do those descriptions communicate particular ideas and how might they have appealed to the concerns of eighteenth-century Americans?

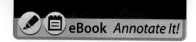

Analyzing the Text

COMMON CORE

ELACC11-12RI5,
ELACC11-12RI8,
ELACC11-12RI9,
ELACC11-12W2a,
ELACC11-12W7,
ELACC11-12W8

Cite Text Evidence   Support your responses with evidence from the selection.

1. **Analyze** What rhetorical features in the Preamble reveal the purpose of the Constitution? What is that purpose?

2. **Infer** How does the Preamble reflect the constitutional principle of representative democracy?

3. **Analyze** What is the purpose of the Bill of Rights? To what part of the Preamble is it most directly related?

4. **Summarize** In your own words, summarize Amendment V. Then describe three present-day situations where this law might give a citizen important protections from a potentially abusive government.

5. **Draw Conclusions** What is an overall theme about government that is communicated by the Preamble and the Bill of Rights?

6. **Identify Patterns** What do Amendments IV–VIII have in common? What do these Amendments reveal about the concerns and anxieties of early Americans about government and authority during this period?

7. **Evaluate** How is the Bill of Rights structured? How effective is this structure in achieving the purpose of the document?

8. **Interpret** How might the rights guaranteed in Amendment I be stated as a basic constitutional principle? What basic principle does it protect?

PERFORMANCE TASK

Media Activity The Bill of Rights contains what the founders considered the most basic and important protections of individual liberties and states' rights. Evaluate the lasting importance of the Bill of Rights by creating a multimedia presentation on its applications to life in the twenty-first century. Follow these steps to complete the activity.

1. Work with a small group and decide which Amendment(s) will be the topic of your presentation. Conduct research to find the most relevant information and examples to develop your topic.

2. Organize your information so that your ideas will build on one another and lead to a logical conclusion.

3. Decide how to most effectively combine text and graphics to aid comprehension of your ideas.

4. Use appropriate software to create your presentation and share it with your classmates.

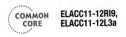

Critical Vocabulary

COMMON CORE ELACC11-12RI9, ELACC11-12L3a

| posterity | infringed | prescribed | imposed |

Practice and Apply For each Critical Vocabulary word, identify which example below best illustrates its meaning. Explain why the example you chose is most accurate.

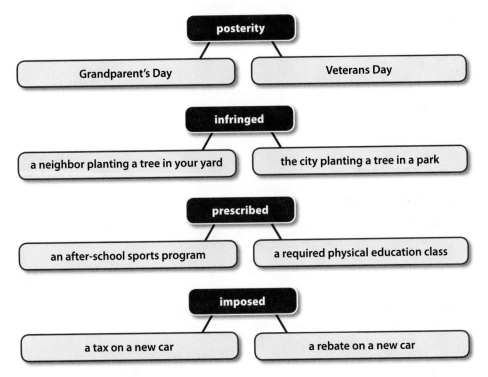

posterity

| Grandparent's Day | Veterans Day |

infringed

| a neighbor planting a tree in your yard | the city planting a tree in a park |

prescribed

| an after-school sports program | a required physical education class |

imposed

| a tax on a new car | a rebate on a new car |

Language and Style: Formal and Informal Style

Style refers to *how* something is written and reflects an author's word choices and sentence structures as well as the tone or attitude toward a subject. **Formal style,** used for most writing, follows all the conventions of the English language in usage and grammar. **Informal style** is more like spoken language. In writing, an informal style might be appropriate in personal exchanges such as letters or emails, in dialogue, or in any context that is appropriate to reflect everyday speech.

The Constitution is an important legal document and reflects a very formal style that is appropriate to that context. Legal documents often contain certain formulations that are not generally used in other formal writing. For example, notice the paragraph in the Preamble to the Bill of Rights that begins with the word *RESOLVED*. This paragraph is the formal, legal way of saying that Congress has agreed to propose these Amendments to the Constitution. Each Amendment was also carefully crafted and written in a formal style that would be appropriate in a legal context.

Practice and Apply Work with a partner to restate three of the Amendments in a slightly less formal style, as if you were paraphrasing it for a classroom assignment. Continue to observe the conventions of standard English usage.

The Declaration of Independence Preamble and Bill of Rights

Analyze Foundational Documents

 COMMON CORE   ELACC11-12RI9

The Declaration of Independence lays the foundation for the United States' existence as an independent country built on specific principles of liberty and self-government. The U.S. Constitution built on that foundation and created the framework for the country's form of government, which has lasted for more than two hundred years. After analyzing each of these documents to determine their **purpose, themes,** and **rhetorical features,** you can now look more closely at the similarities and differences between the two documents. As you compare them, recall the historical context in which each document was written. Review the Background on the two documents as needed.

Analyzing the Text

 COMMON CORE   ELACC11-12RI1, ELACC11-12RI9, ELACC11-12W2, ELACC11-12W9b

Cite Text Evidence   Support your responses with evidence from the selections.

1. **Compare** What are the specific purposes of the Declaration of Independence, the Preamble to the Constitution, and the Bill of Rights?

2. **Synthesize** What is an overall theme about the U.S. government that is communicated by these documents?

3. **Cite Evidence** What rhetorical features do these documents share? Why are there differences in the rhetoric of the Declaration and the Constitution?

4. **Connect** How might the Constitution be seen as fulfilling Jefferson's vision in the Declaration?

PERFORMANCE TASK

Writing Activity: Essay In many ways, the Constitution was built on the foundation of the Declaration of Independence. Explore the details of how the Declaration influenced the Constitution by writing an explanatory essay considering the following questions.

- How might the abuses of the British government have influenced the type of government the United States established and the type of rights it wanted to protect?
- How did the focus on "unalienable rights" in the Declaration specifically influence ideas in the Bill of Rights?

Cite evidence from both documents to support your ideas. Communicate your ideas clearly and accurately using a formal style.

Background *The Federalist No. 10 is the most famous of the Federalist Papers, a series of 85 essays written in 1787–1788 to support ratification of the U.S. Constitution. Originally published in New York newspapers under the pseudonym Publius, the essays were actually written by Alexander Hamilton, John Jay, and* **James Madison***. Madison, the author of No. 10, introduced the Bill of Rights while serving in the House of Representatives and later became the fourth U. S. President. While Madison and other Federalists strongly supported the Constitution, the Anti-Federalists took the contrary position and opposed ratification.*

The Federalist No. 10

Argument by James Madison

AS YOU READ Look for clues that indicate Madison's attitude toward the Anti-Federalists, who are the audience for this argument.

To the People of the State of New York:

AMONG the numerous advantages promised by a well constructed Union, none deserves to be more accurately developed than its tendency to break and control the violence of **faction**. The friend of popular governments never finds himself so much alarmed for their character and fate, as when he contemplates their propensity[1] to this dangerous vice. He will not fail, therefore, to set a due value on any plan which, without violating the principles to which he is attached, provides a proper cure for it. The instability, injustice, and confusion introduced into the public councils, have, in truth, been the mortal

10 diseases under which popular governments have everywhere perished; as they continue to be the favorite and fruitful topics from which the adversaries to liberty derive their most specious declamations. The valuable improvements made by the American constitutions on the popular models, both ancient and modern, cannot certainly be too much admired; but it would be an unwarrantable partiality, to contend

faction
(fak´shən) *n.* an organized subgroup that disagrees with the larger group as a whole.

---

[1] **propensity:** natural tendency or inclination.

that they have as effectually obviated[2] the danger on this side, as was wished and expected. Complaints are everywhere heard from our most considerate and virtuous citizens, equally the friends of public and private faith, and of public and personal liberty, that our governments

20 are too unstable, that the public good is disregarded in the conflicts of rival parties, and that measures are too often decided, not according to the rules of justice and the rights of the minor party, but by the superior force of an interested and overbearing majority. However anxiously we may wish that these complaints had no foundation, the evidence, of known facts will not permit us to deny that they are in some degree true. It will be found, indeed, on a candid review of our situation, that some of the distresses under which we labor have been erroneously charged on the operation of our governments; but it will be found, at the same time, that other causes will not alone account for

30 many of our heaviest misfortunes; and, particularly, for that prevailing and increasing distrust of public engagements, and alarm for private rights, which are echoed from one end of the continent to the other. These must be chiefly, if not wholly, effects of the unsteadiness and injustice with which a factious spirit has tainted our public administrations.

By a faction, I understand a number of citizens, whether amounting to a majority or a minority of the whole, who are united and actuated[3] by some common impulse of passion, or of interest, adversed to the rights of other citizens, or to the permanent and

40 **aggregate** interests of the community.

aggregate
(ăg´rĭ-gĭt) *adj.*
combined.

There are two methods of curing the mischiefs of faction: the one, by removing its causes; the other, by controlling its effects.

There are again two methods of removing the causes of faction: the one, by destroying the liberty which is essential to its existence; the other, by giving to every citizen the same opinions, the same passions, and the same interests.

It could never be more truly said than of the first remedy, that it was worse than the disease. Liberty is to faction what air is to fire, an aliment without which it instantly expires. But it could not be

50 less folly to abolish liberty, which is essential to political life, because it nourishes faction, than it would be to wish the annihilation of air, which is essential to animal life, because it imparts to fire its destructive agency.

The second expedient is as impracticable as the first would be unwise. As long as the reason of man continues fallible,[4] and he is at liberty to exercise it, different opinions will be formed. As long as the connection subsists between his reason and his self-love, his opinions and his passions will have a **reciprocal** influence on each other; and

reciprocal
(rĭ-sĭp´rə-kəl) *adj.*
mutual or shared.

---

[2] **obviated:** avoided or removed.

[3] **actuated:** moved to action.

[4] **fallible:** able to make mistakes.

the former will be objects to which the latter will attach themselves.
The diversity in the faculties of men, from which the rights of
property originate, is not less an insuperable[5] obstacle to a uniformity
of interests. The protection of these faculties is the first object of
government. From the protection of different and unequal faculties of
acquiring property, the possession of different degrees and kinds of
property immediately results; and from the influence of these on the
sentiments and views of the respective proprietors, ensues a division of
the society into different interests and parties.

The **latent** causes of faction are thus sown in the nature of man;
and we see them everywhere brought into different degrees of activity,
according to the different circumstances of civil society. A zeal for
different opinions concerning religion, concerning government, and
many other points, as well of speculation as of practice; an attachment
to different leaders ambitiously contending for pre-eminence and
power; or to persons of other descriptions whose fortunes have been
interesting to the human passions, have, in turn, divided mankind
into parties, inflamed them with mutual animosity,[6] and rendered
them much more disposed to vex and oppress each other than to
co-operate for their common good. So strong is this propensity of
mankind to fall into mutual animosities, that where no substantial
occasion presents itself, the most frivolous and fanciful distinctions
have been sufficient to kindle their unfriendly passions and excite
their most violent conflicts. But the most common and durable source
of factions has been the various and unequal distribution of property.
Those who hold and those who are without property have ever formed
distinct interests in society. Those who are creditors, and those who
are debtors, fall under a like discrimination. A landed interest, a
manufacturing interest, a mercantile interest, a moneyed interest, with
many lesser interests, grow up of necessity in civilized nations, and
divide them into different classes, actuated by different sentiments
and views. The regulation of these various and interfering interests
forms the principal task of modern legislation, and involves the spirit
of party and faction in the necessary and ordinary operations of the
government.

No man is allowed to be a judge in his own cause, because his
interest would certainly bias his judgment, and, not improbably,
corrupt his integrity. With equal, nay with greater reason, a body
of men are unfit to be both judges and parties at the same time; yet
what are many of the most important acts of legislation, but so many
judicial determinations, not indeed concerning the rights of single
persons, but concerning the rights of large bodies of citizens? And
what are the different classes of legislators but advocates and parties
to the causes which they determine? Is a law proposed concerning

latent
(lāt′nt) *adj.*
underlying or hidden.

---

[5] **insuperable:** invincible or unconquerable.
[6] **animosity:** hatred or hostility.

IT IS IN VAIN to say that enlightened statesmen will be able to adjust these clashing interests.

private debts? It is a question to which the creditors are parties on one side and the debtors on the other. Justice ought to hold the balance between them. Yet the parties are, and must be, themselves the judges; and the most numerous party, or, in other words, the most powerful faction must be expected to prevail. Shall domestic manufactures be encouraged, and in what degree, by restrictions on foreign manufactures? are questions which would be differently decided by the
110 landed and the manufacturing classes, and probably by neither with a sole regard to justice and the public good. The **apportionment** of taxes on the various descriptions of property is an act which seems to require the most exact impartiality;[7] yet there is, perhaps, no legislative act in which greater opportunity and temptation are given to a predominant[8] party to trample on the rules of justice. Every shilling with which they overburden the inferior number, is a shilling saved to their own pockets.

apportionment
(ə-pôr′shən-mənt) *n.*
distribution.

It is in vain to say that enlightened statesmen will be able to adjust these clashing interests, and render them all subservient to the public
120 good. Enlightened statesmen will not always be at the helm. Nor, in many cases, can such an adjustment be made at all without taking into view indirect and remote considerations, which will rarely prevail over the immediate interest which one party may find in disregarding the rights of another or the good of the whole.

The inference[9] to which we are brought is, that the *causes* of faction cannot be removed, and that relief is only to be sought in the means of controlling its *effects*.

If a faction consists of less than a majority, relief is supplied by the republican principle, which enables the majority to defeat its sinister[10]
130 views by regular vote. It may clog the administration, it may convulse the society; but it will be unable to execute and mask its violence under the forms of the Constitution. When a majority is included in a

---

[7] **impartiality:** equal treatment.
[8] **predominant:** stronger, more powerful.
[9] **inference:** a conclusion based on facts and reasoning.
[10] **sinister:** evil or harmful.

faction, the form of popular government, on the other hand, enables it to sacrifice to its ruling passion or interest both the public good and the rights of other citizens. To secure the public good and private rights against the danger of such a faction, and at the same time to preserve the spirit and the form of popular government, is then the great object to which our inquiries are directed. Let me add that it is the great desideratum[11] by which this form of government can be
140   rescued from the opprobrium[12] under which it has so long labored, and be recommended to the esteem and adoption of mankind.

By what means is this object attainable? Evidently by one of two only. Either the existence of the same passion or interest in a majority at the same time must be prevented, or the majority, having such coexistent passion or interest, must be rendered, by their number and local situation, unable to concert and carry into effect schemes of oppression. If the impulse and the opportunity be suffered to coincide, we well know that neither moral nor religious motives can be relied on as an adequate control. They are not found to be such on the injustice
150   and violence of individuals, and lose their efficacy in proportion to the number combined together, that is, in proportion as their **efficacy** becomes needful.

> **efficacy**
> (ĕf´ĭ-kə-sē) *n.*
> effectiveness.

From this view of the subject it may be concluded that a pure democracy, by which I mean a society consisting of a small number of citizens, who assemble and administer the government in person, can admit of no cure for the mischiefs of faction. A common passion or interest will, in almost every case, be felt by a majority of the whole; a communication and concert result from the form of government itself; and there is nothing to check the inducements[13] to sacrifice the weaker
160   party or an obnoxious individual. Hence it is that such democracies have ever been spectacles of turbulence and contention; have ever been found incompatible with personal security or the rights of property; and have in general been as short in their lives as they have been violent in their deaths. Theoretic politicians, who have patronized this species of government, have erroneously supposed that by reducing mankind to a perfect equality in their political rights, they would, at the same time, be perfectly equalized and assimilated in their possessions, their opinions, and their passions.

A republic, by which I mean a government in which the scheme
170   of representation takes place, opens a different prospect, and promises the cure for which we are seeking. Let us examine the points in which it varies from pure democracy, and we shall comprehend both the nature of the cure and the efficacy which it must derive from the Union.

---

[11] **desideratum:** a desirable thing.
[12] **opprobrium:** public criticism and disgrace.
[13] **inducements:** rewards or bribes.

The two great points of difference between a democracy and a republic are: first, the delegation of the government, in the latter, to a small number of citizens elected by the rest; secondly, the greater number of citizens, and greater sphere of country, over which the latter may be extended.

180   The effect of the first difference is, on the one hand, to refine and enlarge the public views, by passing them through the medium[14] of a chosen body of citizens, whose wisdom may best discern the true interest of their country, and whose patriotism and love of justice will be least likely to sacrifice it to temporary or partial considerations. Under such a regulation, it may well happen that the public voice, pronounced by the representatives of the people, will be more consonant to the public good than if pronounced by the people themselves, convened for the purpose. On the other hand, the effect may be inverted. Men of factious tempers, of local prejudices, or of
190 sinister designs, may, by intrigue, by corruption, or by other means, first obtain the suffrages,[15] and then betray the interests, of the people. The question resulting is, whether small or extensive republics are more favorable to the election of proper guardians of the public weal;[16] and it is clearly decided in favor of the latter by two obvious considerations:

    In the first place, it is to be remarked that, however small the republic may be, the representatives must be raised to a certain number, in order to guard against the cabals[17] of a few; and that, however large it may be, they must be limited to a certain number,
200 in order to guard against the confusion of a multitude. Hence, the number of representatives in the two cases not being in proportion to that of the two constituents, and being proportionally greater in the small republic, it follows that, if the proportion of fit characters be not less in the large than in the small republic, the former will present a greater option, and consequently a greater probability of a fit choice.

    In the next place, as each representative will be chosen by a greater number of citizens in the large than in the small republic, it will be more difficult for unworthy candidates to practice with success the vicious arts by which elections are too often carried; and the suffrages
210 of the people being more free, will be more likely to centre in men who possess the most attractive merit and the most diffusive[18] and established characters.

    It must be confessed that in this, as in most other cases, there is a mean,[19] on both sides of which inconveniences will be found to

---

[14] **medium:** mechanism or vehicle for doing something.
[15] **suffrages:** votes.
[16] **public weal:** the people's well-being.
[17] **cabals:** secret political groups.
[18] **diffusive:** widely known.
[19] **mean:** middle point.

lie. By enlarging too much the number of electors, you render the representatives too little acquainted with all their local circumstances and lesser interests; as by reducing it too much, you render him unduly attached to these, and too little fit to comprehend and pursue great and national objects. The federal Constitution forms a happy combination in this respect; the great and aggregate interests being referred to the national, the local and particular to the State legislatures.

The other point of difference is, the greater number of citizens and extent of territory which may be brought within the compass of republican than of democratic government; and it is this circumstance principally which renders factious combinations less to be dreaded in the former than in the latter. The smaller the society, the fewer probably will be the distinct parties and interests composing it; the fewer the distinct parties and interests, the more frequently will a majority be found of the same party; and the smaller the number of individuals composing a majority, and the smaller the compass within which they are placed, the more easily will they concert and execute their plans of oppression. Extend the sphere, and you take in a greater variety of parties and interests; you make it less probable that a majority of the whole will have a common motive to invade the rights of other citizens; or if such a common motive exists, it will be more difficult for all who feel it to discover their own strength, and to act in unison with each other. Besides other impediments, it may be remarked that, where there is a consciousness of unjust or dishonorable purposes, communication is always checked by distrust in proportion to the number whose concurrence is necessary.

Hence, it clearly appears, that the same advantage which a republic has over a democracy, in controlling the effects of faction, is enjoyed by a large over a small republic,—is enjoyed by the Union over the States composing it. Does the advantage consist in the substitution of representatives whose enlightened views and virtuous sentiments render them superior to local prejudices and schemes of injustice? It will not be denied that the representation of the Union will be most likely to possess these requisite endowments.[20] Does it consist in the greater security afforded by a greater variety of parties, against the event of any one party being able to outnumber and oppress the rest? In an equal degree does the increased variety of parties **comprised** within the Union, increase this security. Does it, in fine, consist in the greater obstacles opposed to the concert and accomplishment of the secret wishes of an unjust and interested majority? Here, again, the extent of the Union gives it the most palpable[21] advantage.

The influence of factious leaders may kindle a flame within their particular States, but will be unable to spread a general conflagration

comprise (kəm-prīz´) v. contain.

---

[20] **requisite endowments:** necessary qualities.
[21] **palpable:** able to be felt.

through the other States. A religious sect[22] may degenerate into a political faction in a part of the Confederacy; but the variety of sects
260 dispersed over the entire face of it must secure the national councils against any danger from that source. A rage for paper money, for an abolition of debts, for an equal division of property, or for any other improper or wicked project, will be less apt to **pervade** the whole body of the Union than a particular member of it; in the same proportion as such a malady is more likely to taint a particular county or district, than an entire State.

pervade
(pər-vād´) *v.* to spread or exist throughout.

In the extent and proper structure of the Union, therefore, we behold a republican remedy for the diseases most incident to republican government. And according to the degree of pleasure and
270 pride we feel in being republicans, ought to be our zeal in cherishing the spirit and supporting the character of Federalists.
PUBLIUS.

---

[22] **sect:** denomination or group.

COLLABORATIVE DISCUSSION What does Madison think about the Anti-Federalists, and how does he address them? Discuss this question with a partner, citing evidence from the document to support your ideas.

Analyze Language: Defining a Key Term

COMMON CORE

ELACC11-12RI1,
ELACC11-12RI4,
ELACC11-12RI8

In The *Federalist* No. 10, Madison uses the term *faction* repeatedly and refines its meaning over the course of the document. In fact, the entire document could be seen as an extended definition of that key term.

Madison introduces the term in the first sentence with the idea that a "well constructed Union" has a "tendency to break and control the violence of faction." Without knowing the full meaning, the reader begins to understand that factions are harmful. Madison then defines the term in the next paragraph:

> **By a faction, I understand a number of citizens, whether amounting to a majority or a minority of the whole, who are united and actuated by some common impulse of passion, or of interest, adversed to the rights of other citizens, or to the permanent and aggregate interests of the community.**

Understanding this key term and its development over the course of the text is essential to understanding Madison's argument.

Evaluate Seminal Texts:
Purpose and Premises of an Argument

COMMON CORE   ELACC11-12RI8

In an **argument,** an author states a **claim,** or position on an issue, and supports it with reasons and evidence. In the *Federalist* No. 10, Madison very clearly lays out his claim in the first sentence of the text: "Among the numerous advantages promised by a well constructed Union, none deserves to be more accurately developed than its tendency to break and control the violence of faction."

Madison's **purpose,** therefore, is to convince readers to embrace the form of government that he believes is best, the one set out in the Constitution. What is more subtle, however, is the set of **premises,** or general principles, about society and human nature that he assumes his readers will agree with. In a well-reasoned argument, the claim logically follows and depends on the premises.

Madison's argument actually contains a series of tightly linked premises and claims. For example, in the first half of the argument, one of Madison's claims is that the causes of factions cannot be removed. Here is one premise related to this claim:

> **The diversity in the faculties of men, from which the rights of property originate, is not less an insuperable obstacle to a uniformity of interests.**
> **(lines 60–62)**

In other words, Madison states the following general principle: The more abilities you possess, the more property you possess; these differences result in diverse, opposing interests. According to Madison's reasoning, it then follows that people with different economic interests will inevitably join opposing factions.

Evaluating and examining the premises of an argument will give you a fuller understanding of the historical forces that shaped this document.

Analyzing the Text

COMMON CORE

ELACC11-12RI1,
ELACC11-12RI4,
ELACC11-12RI8,
ELACC11-12SL1b,
ELACC11-12SL1c

Cite Text Evidence Support your responses with evidence from the selection.

1. **Cite Evidence** An effective argument acknowledges the claims made by opponents and refutes these claims with counterarguments. In the first paragraph of his argument, what does Madison acknowledge about criticisms of existing governments? How might this appeal to Anti-Federalists?

2. **Interpret** According to Madison's definition of *faction* in lines 36–40, what makes factions harmful to popular or democratic government?

3. **Infer** Why does Madison say that "liberty . . . is essential to [faction's] existence" (line 44)? Why does he put forth the idea of destroying liberty to remove faction?

4. **Cite Evidence** In lines 94-96, Madison says that "No man is allowed to be a judge in his own cause, because his interest would certainly bias his judgment, and, not improbably, corrupt his integrity." How does this premise relate to Madison's main claim about the virtues of representative democracy? What claims in the second half of this publication are based on the premises in this paragraph?

5. **Evaluate** Identify three additional premises that Madison uses to support his claim that "the *causes* of faction cannot be removed" (lines 125–126). The premises may be stated or implied. How effectively do these general principles support the claim?

6. **Compare** Why does Madison conclude that a "pure democracy" (lines 153–156) cannot solve the problems of faction but that a republic can solve them?

7. **Analyze** How does Madison's argument on the benefits of a large republic relate to his claim that a "well constructed Union" can control the problems of factions?

PERFORMANCE TASK

Speaking Activity Madison concludes that factions are a part of a free society and that it can be challenging to deal with the animosity that they create. Work with a small group to promote a civil, democratic discussion about an issue that creates factions by following these steps.

- Brainstorm with your group to choose a topic that creates factions at school, in your community, or in the nation.

- Together, write a set of rules that will guide your discussion.

- In your discussion, pose and respond to questions that will allow a full range of contrary positions to be heard.

- Write a brief evaluation of how well your rules worked.

Critical Vocabulary

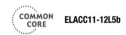

faction	aggregate	reciprocal	latent
apportionment	efficacy	comprised	pervade

Practice and Apply Complete each sentence to reflect your understanding of the Critical Vocabulary word.

1. Rich people and poor people belong to different **factions** because . . .

2. The federal government is able to focus on the **aggregate** interests of the country because . . .

3. Opinions and passions have a **reciprocal** influence on each other because . . .

4. Adopting the Constitution would allow the **latent** benefits of the new government to become obvious because . . .

5. The government wanted the **apportionment** of taxes to closely match the value of property because . . .

6. A faction's **efficacy** in achieving its goals is stronger in a small area because . . .

7. There is more diversity **comprised** in a larger republic because . . .

8. A feeling of harmony **pervades** a group of people with similar interests because . . .

Vocabulary Strategy: Evaluating Nuances in Meaning

In choosing to use the Critical Vocabulary word *faction* as the focus of his essay, Madison was conscious not just of the word's **denotation** or dictionary definition, but also of its **nuances** or shades of meaning. Madison also uses other words in the text with similar denotations, such as *party*, *interest*, and *sect*, to refer to groups or causes. Yet Madison often combines these words, which are more neutral, with adjectives so that the nuances become more similar to *faction*. Consider these examples:

- rival parties
- interfering interests
- ruling passion or interest

The word *faction* has the nuance of promoting conflict, and Madison often uses the related adjective *factious* to attach that nuance to neutral or positive words.

- factious spirit
- factious tempers
- factious combinations
- factious leaders

Practice and Apply With a partner, use the line references to find each word in context. Discuss why Madison chose the word rather than one of the listed synonyms. What nuances of meaning make each word an appropriate choice to convey his precise meaning? Consult a dictionary or thesaurus as needed.

1. declamations (line 12): recitations, speeches

2. alarm (line 31): panic, worry

3. contending (line 73): arguing, brawling

4. cabals (line 198): groups, factions

Language and Style: Transitions

Transitions are words and phrases that show how ideas are related to one another. Using transitions effectively helps an author create **coherence** so that all sentences are related to one another and ideas flow in a logical manner. Transitions can communicate time or sequence, spatial relationships, degree of importance, compare-and-contrast relationships, or cause and effect. James Madison uses a variety of transitions to create coherence in his argument and to help readers follow his reasoning.

Much of Madison's argument is broken into a consideration of alternatives. Notice how he uses transitions to make this structure clear:

> **There are two methods of curing the mischiefs of faction: <u>the one</u>, by removing its causes; <u>the other</u>, by controlling its effects.**

Madison uses the phrases *the one* and *the other* to clarify the two alternatives. In the next example, he uses the word *but* to signal a contrast and *the most* to show a hierarchy of ideas. He points out that while people often come into conflict over trivial matters, inequalities in people's wealth creates deep and long-lasting factions:

> **So strong is this propensity of mankind to fall into mutual animosities, that where no substantial occasion presents itself, the most frivolous and fanciful distinctions have been sufficient to kindle their unfriendly passions and excite their most violent conflicts. <u>But the most</u> common and durable source of factions has been the various and unequal distribution of property.**

The chart shows other transitions that Madison uses to clarify the structure of his argument by pointing out premises and claims.

Uses of transitions in argument		
Purpose	**Transition Words**	**Example**
Signal a premise or cause	*because, since, so, for the reason that, due to, inasmuch as*	No man is allowed to be a judge in his own cause, <u>because</u> his interest would certainly bias his judgment, and, not improbably, corrupt his integrity.
Signal a claim, conclusion, or effect	*therefore, thus, hence, consequently, as a result*	<u>Hence</u>, it clearly appears, that the same advantage which a republic has over a democracy, in controlling the effects of faction, is enjoyed by a large over a small republic,...

Practice and Apply Look back at the evaluation you wrote about your discussion in response to this selection's Performance Task. Revise your writing to include transitions that will help you make the relationships between your ideas clearer and your paragraphs more coherent.

Background *Thomas Jefferson (1743–1826) and Alexander Hamilton (1755/57–1804) were founders of the United States who played different roles in the country's development. In this 2004 magazine article,* **Ron Chernow** *explores how the men's ideological differences brought them into conflict when both served in President George Washington's first Cabinet. Chernow is the award-winning author of several biographies, including* Alexander Hamilton *(2004) and* Washington: A Life *(2010). As a writer, his goal is to make historical figures come alive.*

Thomas Jefferson: The Best of Enemies

History Article by Ron Chernow

AS YOU READ Look for clues that reveal Jefferson's and Hamilton's personalities. Write down any questions you generate during reading.

On March 21, 1790, Thomas Jefferson belatedly arrived in New York City to assume his duties as the first Secretary of State after a five-year ministerial stint in Paris. Tall and lanky, with a freckled complexion and auburn hair, Jefferson, 46, was taken aback by the adulation being heaped upon the new Treasury Secretary, Alexander Hamilton, who had streaked to prominence in his absence. Few people knew that Jefferson had authored the Declaration of Independence, which had yet to become holy writ for Americans. Instead, the Virginian was eclipsed by the 35-year-old wunderkind
10 from the Caribbean, who was a lowly artillery captain in New York when Jefferson composed the famous document. Despite his murky background as an illegitimate orphan, the self-invented Hamilton was trim and elegant, carried himself with an erect military bearing and had a mind that worked with dazzling speed. At first, Hamilton and Jefferson socialized on easy terms, with little inkling that they were destined to become mortal foes. But their clash inside George Washington's first Cabinet proved so fierce that it would spawn the two-party system in America. It also produced two divergent visions of the country's future that divide Americans to the present day.

20   For Hamilton, the first Treasury Secretary, the supreme threat
to liberty arose from insufficient government power. To avert that,
he advocated a vigorous central government marked by a strong
President, an independent judiciary and a liberal reading of the
Constitution. As the first Secretary of State, Jefferson believed that
liberty was jeopardized by concentrated federal power, which he tried
to restrict through a narrow construction of the Constitution. He
favored states' rights, a central role for Congress and a comparatively
weak judiciary.

     At first glance, Hamilton might seem the more formidable figure
30 in that classic matchup. He took office with an ardent faith in the new
national government. He had attended the Constitutional Convention,
penned the bulk of the Federalist papers to secure passage of the
new charter and spearheaded ratification efforts in New York State.
He therefore set to work at Treasury with more unrestrained gusto
than Jefferson—who had monitored the Constitutional Convention
from his post in Paris—did at State. Jefferson's enthusiasm for the
new political order was **tepid** at best, and when Washington crafted
the first government in 1789, Jefferson didn't grasp the levers of
power with quite the same glee as Hamilton, who had no ideological
40 inhibitions about shoring up federal power.

tepid
(tĕp´ĭd) *adj.*
lukewarm; indifferent.

     Hamilton—brilliant, brash and charming—had the self-reliant
reflexes of someone who had always had to live by his wits. His
overwhelming intelligence petrified Jefferson and his followers. As an
orator, Hamilton could speak extemporaneously for hours on end. As
a writer, he could crank out 5,000- or 10,000-word memos overnight.
Jefferson never underrated his foe's **copious** talents. At one point,
a worried Jefferson confided to his comrade James Madison that
Hamilton was a one-man army, "a host[1] within himself."

copious
(kō´pē-əs) *adj.*
extensive.

     Whether in person or on paper, Hamilton served up his opinions
50 promiscuously. He had a true zest for debate and never left anyone
guessing where he stood. Jefferson, more than a decade older, had

---

[1] **host:** an army or large group of troops.

the quiet, courtly manner of a Virginia planter. He was emphatic in
his views—Hamilton labeled him "an atheist in religion and a fanatic
in politics"— but shrank from open conflict. Jefferson, a diffident
speaker, mumbled his way through his rare speeches in a soft, almost
inaudible voice and reserved his most scathing strictures for private
correspondence.

The epic battle between these two Olympian[2] figures began
not long after Jefferson came to New York City to assume his State
Department duties in March 1790. By then Hamilton was in the thick
of a contentious campaign to retire massive debt inherited from the
Revolution. America had suspended principal and interest payments[3]
on its obligations, which had traded as low as 15¢ on the dollar. In
an audacious scheme to restore public credit, Hamilton planned to
pay off that debt at face value, causing the securities to soar from
depressed levels. Jefferson and Madison thought the original holders
of those securities—many of them war veterans—should profit from
that appreciation even if they had already sold their paper to traders
at depressed prices. Hamilton thought it would be impractical to track
them down. With an eye on future U.S. capital markets, he wanted
to enshrine the **cardinal** principle that current owners of securities
incurred all profits and losses, even if that meant windfall gains for
rapacious speculators who had only recently bought the securities.

That skirmish over Hamilton's public credit plan was part of a
broader tussle over the U.S.'s economic future. Jefferson was fond
of summoning up idyllic scenes of an agrarian America peopled by
sturdy yeoman farmers. That poetic vision neglected the underlying
reality of large slave plantations in the South. Jefferson was a fine
populist on paper but not in everyday life, and his defense of Virginia
interests was inextricably bound up with slavery. Hamilton—derided

cardinal
(kär´dn-əl) *adj.* most
important; prime.

---

[2] **Olympian:** like a god; one from Mount Olympus.
[3] **principal and interest payments:** the amount borrowed and the fees charged by
the lender.

as a pseudo aristocrat, an elitist, a crypto-monarchist[4]—was a passionate abolitionist with a far more expansive economic vision. He conceded that agriculture would persist for decades as an essential component of the economy. But at the same time he wanted to foster the **rudiments** of a modern economy—trade, commerce, banks, stock exchanges, factories and corporations—to enlarge economic opportunity.

rudiment
(rōō'də-mənt) *n.* basic form.

Hamilton dreamed of a meritocracy, not an aristocracy, while Jefferson retained the landed gentry's disdain for the vulgar realities of
90   trade, commerce and finance. And he was determined to undermine Hamilton's juggernaut.[5]

Because we celebrate Jefferson for his sonorous words in the Declaration of Independence—Hamilton never matched Jefferson's gift for writing ringing passages that were at once poetic and inspirational— we sometimes overlook Jefferson's consummate skills as a practicing politician. A master of subtle, artful indirection, he was able to marshal his forces without divulging his generalship. After Hamilton persuaded President Washington to create the Bank of the United States, the country's first central bank, Jefferson was aghast
100   at what he construed[6] as a breach of the Constitution and a perilous expansion of federal power. Along with Madison, he recruited the poet Philip Freneau to launch an opposition paper called the National Gazette. To subsidize the paper covertly, he hired Freneau as a State Department translator. Hamilton was shocked by such flagrant disloyalty from a member of Washington's Cabinet, especially when Freneau began to mount withering assaults on Hamilton and even Washington. Never one to suffer in silence, Hamilton retaliated in a blizzard of newspaper articles published under Roman pseudonyms. The backbiting between Hamilton and Jefferson grew so acrimonious
110   that Washington had to exhort both men to desist.

Instead, the feud worsened. In early 1793, a Virginia Congressman named William Branch Giles began to harry Hamilton with resolutions ordering him to produce, on short deadlines, stupendous amounts of Treasury data. With prodigious bursts of energy, Hamilton complied with those inhuman demands, foiling his opponents. Jefferson then committed an unthinkable act. He secretly drafted a series of anti-Hamilton resolutions for Giles, including one that read, "Resolved, That the Secretary of the Treasury has been guilty of maladministration in the duties of his office and should, in the
120   opinion of Congress, be removed from his office by the President of the United States." The resolution was voted down, and the effort to oust Hamilton stalled. Jefferson left the Cabinet in defeat later that year.

---

[4] **crypto-monarchist:** one who secretly supports government rule by a king.
[5] **juggernaut:** an extremely powerful force.
[6] **construed:** interpreted.

Throughout the 1790s, the Hamilton-Jefferson feud continued to fester in both domestic and foreign affairs. Jefferson thought Hamilton was "bewitched" by the British model of governance, while Hamilton considered Jefferson a credulous apologist for the gory excesses of the French Revolution. Descended from French Huguenots on his mother's side, Hamilton was fluent in French and had served as
130   Washington's liaison with the Marquis de Lafayette and other French aristocrats who had rallied to the Continental Army. The French Revolution immediately struck him as a bloody affair, governed by rigid, Utopian thinking. On Oct. 6, 1789, he wrote a remarkable letter to Lafayette, explaining his "foreboding of ill" about the future course of events in Paris. He cited the "vehement character" of the French people and the "reveries" of their "philosophic politicians," who wished to transform human nature. Hamilton believed that Jefferson while in Paris "drank deeply of the French philosophy in religion, in science, in politics." Indeed, more than a decade passed before
140   Jefferson fully realized that the French Revolution wasn't a worthy sequel to the American one so much as a grotesque travesty.[7]

If Jefferson and Hamilton define opposite ends of the political spectrum in U.S. history and seem to exist in perpetual conflict, the two men shared certain traits, feeding a mutual cynicism. Each scorned the other as excessively ambitious. In his secret diary, or Anas, Jefferson recorded a story of Hamilton praising Julius Caesar as the greatest man in history. (The tale sounds dubious, as Hamilton invariably used Caesar as shorthand for "an evil tyrant.") Hamilton repaid the favor. In one essay he likened Jefferson to "Caesar coyly
150   refusing the proffered diadem" and rejecting the trappings, but "tenaciously grasping the substance of imperial domination."

Similarly, both men hid a potent hedonism[8] behind an intellectual **façade**. For all their outward differences, the two politicians stumbled into the two great sex scandals of the early Republic. In 1797 a journalist named James T. Callender exposed that Hamilton, while Treasury Secretary and a married man with four children, had entered into a yearlong affair with grifter Maria Reynolds, who was 23 when it began. In a 95-page pamphlet, Hamilton confessed to the affair at what many regarded as inordinate length. He wished to show that the
160   money he had paid to Reynolds' husband James had been for the favor of her company and not for illicit speculation in Treasury securities, as the Jeffersonians had alleged. Forever after, the Jeffersonians tagged Hamilton as "the amorous Treasury Secretary" and mocked his pretensions to superior morality.

By an extraordinary coincidence, during Jefferson's first term as President, Callender also exposed Jefferson's relationship with Sally Hemings. Callender claimed that "Dusky Sally," a.k.a. the "African

façade
(fə-säd´) *n.* false or misleading appearance.

---

[7] **travesty:** an unreasonable distortion or parody.
[8] **hedonism:** the belief that personal pleasure is the primary goal in life.

Venus," was the President's slave concubine, who had borne him five children. "There is not an individual in the neighborhood of
170   Charlottesville who does not believe the story," Callender wrote, "and not a few who know it." Jefferson never confirmed or denied Callender's story. But the likely truth of the Hemings affair was dramatically bolstered by DNA tests published in 1998, which indicated that a Jefferson male had sired at least one of Hemings' children.

   The crowning irony of the stormy relations between Hamilton and Jefferson is that Hamilton helped install his longtime foe as President in 1801. Under constitutional rules then in force, the candidate with the majority of electoral votes became President; the runner-
180   up became Vice President. That created an **anomalous** situation in which Jefferson, his party's presumed presidential nominee, tied with Aaron Burr, its presumed vice presidential nominee. It took 36 rounds of voting in the House to decide the election in Jefferson's favor. Faced with the prospect of Burr as President, a man he considered unscrupulous, Hamilton not only opted for Jefferson as the lesser of two evils but also was forced into his most measured assessment of the man. Hamilton said he had long suspected that as President, Jefferson would develop a keen taste for the federal power he had deplored in opposition. He recalled that a decade earlier, in Washington's Cabinet,
190   Jefferson had seemed like a man who knew he was destined to inherit an estate—in this case, the presidency—and didn't wish to deplete it. In fact, Jefferson, the strict constructionist, freely exercised the most sweeping powers as President. Nothing in the Constitution, for instance, permitted the Louisiana Purchase.[9] Hamilton noted that with rueful mirth.

anomalous
(ə-nŏm´ə-ləs) *adj.*
unusual.

---

[9] **Louisiana Purchase:** France's 1803 sale of its territory west of the Mississippi River to the United States.

COLLABORATIVE DISCUSSION How might Jefferson's and Hamilton's personal characteristics have affected their ability to work together easily? Discuss this question with a partner, citing evidence from the article to support your ideas.

Analyze Ideas and Events: Sequence

COMMON CORE ELACC11-12RI3

Authors use organizational patterns to help convey information and ideas. For example, a writer might organize a text by using comparison/contrast, problem/solution, or cause-and-effect relationships. Sometimes writers use multiple organizational patterns to achieve their purpose. In this article, Chernow makes use of **chronological order**, a pattern of organization that presents events in the order in which they happened. Chernow uses this structure to follow the sequence of events important to the men's relationship and explore how their ideas about government evolved over time.

In his introduction, Chernow uses sequence references to orient the reader.

On March 21, 1790, Thomas Jefferson belatedly arrived in New York City . . . after a five-year ministerial stint in Paris. . . . Alexander Hamilton, who had streaked to prominence in his absence. . . . who was a lowly artillery captain in New York when Jefferson composed the famous document. . . . At first, Hamilton and Jefferson socialized on easy terms, with little inkling that they were destined to become mortal foes.

Use these strategies when analyzing the sequence of events in an informative text.
- Look for words and phrases that identify times, such as *in a year, three weeks earlier, in 1789*, and *the next day*.
- Look for words that signal order, such as *first, afterward, then, during*, and *finally* to see how events or ideas are related.

Analyze Structure: Comparison and Contrast

COMMON CORE ELACC11-12RI5

The overarching structure of Chernow's article is a point-by-point comparison of Jefferson and Hamilton that shows how and why they became "the best of enemies." In such a structure, a writer discusses a particular point of comparison about both subjects and then moves on to the next point. Chernow follows this structure closely as this beginning of an outline of the article shows.

I. Point 1: View of biggest threat to liberty
A. Hamilton: insufficient federal power
B. Jefferson: concentrated federal power
II. Point 2: Attitude to new national government
A. Hamilton: ardent faith
B. Jefferson: tepid enthusiasm

Chernow uses this structure to make his exposition of complex ideas clear and weaves in narrative elements to make the text more engaging.

Use these strategies when analyzing a text using a compare-and-contrast structure.
- To find similarities, look for words and phrases such as *like, similarly, both, all, every, also*, and *in the same way*.
- To find differences, look for words and phrases such as *unlike, but, on the other hand, more, less, in contrast*, and *however*.

Analyzing the Text

COMMON CORE

ELACC11-12RI1,
ELACC11-12RI3,
ELACC11-12RI5,
ELACC11-12W2

Cite Text Evidence   Support your responses with evidence from the selection.

1. **Compare** How did Hamilton's and Jefferson's different experiences relating to the writing of the Constitution affect their roles as members of Washington's Cabinet?

2. **Analyze** What event sparked the beginning of the conflict between Hamilton and Jefferson? What was the sequence of events that caused the feud to worsen?

3. **Analyze** An author's choice of words, or **diction,** can communicate a great deal about a subject. Reread the passage where Chernow directly describes Hamilton (lines 41–51), paying careful attention to the adjectives and verbs Chernow uses. What words reveal the most about Hamiton's personality and character?

4. **Cite Evidence** How did Hamilton's and Jefferson's different personal styles affect the ways they carried out their feud?

5. **Infer** How does the disagreement over the creation of the Bank of the United States reflect the ideological differences that separated Hamilton and Jefferson?

6. **Interpret** Despite their conflicts, Chernow also emphasizes that the two shared some common traits. In what ways where Jefferson and Hamilton similar, according to Chernow?

7. **Compare** Chernow describes how both politicians "stumbled into the two great sex scandles of the early Republic." What were the scandals? How did each individual respond to the accusations? How were their responses consistent with what you know about them from this text?

8. **Analyze** How does Chernow's point-by-point comparison of these two enemies add to the strength of his concluding paragraph?

9. **Evaluate** How effectively did Chernow combine chronological order and compare-and-contrast structures to portray the idea that Hamilton and Jefferson were "destined to become mortal foes"?

PERFORMANCE TASK

Writing Task: Essay   Chernow states that the clash between Hamilton and Jefferson "produced two divergent visions of the country's future that divide Americans to the present day."

- Write an essay that provides a point-by-point comparison of these two visions, using Chernow's article as a model for the structure and a source of content.

- Conclude your essay with a paragraph that explores how these visions continue to divide Americans, based on prior knowledge or research.

In your essay, include evidence from the text and use the conventions of standard English.

Critical Vocabulary

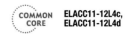 ELACC11-12L4c, ELACC11-12L4d

tepid   copious   cardinal

rudiments   façade   anomalous

Practice and Apply Go on a Critical Vocabulary scavenger hunt to find examples of the words in advertisements, news articles, online, or in your environment. Write your own definition of each word based on at least two examples. Follow these tips.

- If you search online, don't go to a dictionary or other site that defines the word but look for examples by searching for News or Images.
- If you do an online search for *cardinal*, eliminate examples of birds, sports teams, or church officials. You might also find examples of companies that use the word *cardinal* in their name. Eliminate those unless they reflect the meaning of the word.

Vocabulary Strategy:
Consulting General and Specialized Reference Works

Consulting general and specialized reference works such as dictionaries, glossaries, and thesauruses, both print and digital, can provide additional information about unfamiliar words as you read. Here is an example of the entry for the Critical Vocabulary word *copious* from the *American Heritage Dictionary of the English Language*.

> **co·pi·ous** (kō′pē-əs) *adj.* **1.** Yielding or containing plenty; affording ample supply: a copious harvest. See Synonyms at **plentiful**. **2.** Large in quantity; abundant: *copious rainfall*. **3.** Abounding in matter, thoughts, or words; wordy: *"I found our speech copious without order, and energetic without rules"* (Samuel Johnson). [Middle English, from Latin *cōpiōsus*, from *cōpia*, abundance; see **op-** in Indo-European roots.]—**co′pi·ous·ly** *adv.* —**co′pi·ous·ness** *n.*

Here are the important elements of this entry:
- The word is broken into syllables with its pronunciation shown in parentheses using standard symbols to represent different sounds.
- Part of speech is shown next; in this case the word is an adjective.
- Three distinct but related definitions are listed, with an example of how each sense of the word might be used. Note that the first definition also tells readers where to look in the dictionary for synonyms.
- Etymology or word derivation is shown in brackets. This English word is very similar to its Latin origin.
- Related words are shown, indicating how to turn this adjective into an adverb and a noun.

Practice and Apply Consult a dictionary or thesaurus to find additional information about each of these Critical Vocabulary words: *tepid, cardinal, rudiments, façade, anomalous*. Then meet with a partner to discuss how this additional knowledge might help deepen your understanding of the article by Ron Chernow.

Language and Style: Hyphenation

Following the conventions of punctuation is important for clear communication. "Thomas Jefferson: The Best of Enemies" contains several examples of hyphenated words. Using a hyphen joins words into compounds so that their meaning is clear. Hyphenated words can also be a simpler way of saying something.

Consider this phrase from the article.

after a five-year ministerial stint in Paris

The author could instead have written the phrase this way:

after a ministerial stint of five years in Paris

The hyphenated adjective creates a more streamlined sentence. Here are some examples of hyphenation conventions used in the article.

Uses of hyphens	
Purpose	**Example**
join parts of a compound adjective before a noun	two-party system, one-man army, Hamilton-Jefferson feud
join parts of a compound with *all-*, *ex-*, *self-*, or *-elect*	the self-invented Hamilton; the self-reliant reflexes
join parts of a compound number (to ninety-nine)	the 35-year-old wunderkind
join a prefix to a word beginning with a capital letter	anti-Hamilton resolutions
shows two or more compounds are joined to a single base	5,000- or 10,000-word memos
create a new word by adding a prefix or suffix	crypto-monarchist, runner-up

Consult a dictionary if you are unsure whether a compound word should be hyphenated, open, or closed. For example, *cryptographer* is closed and *follow up* as a verb or a noun is open, but the adjective, as in *follow-up phone call* uses a hyphen.

Practice and Apply   Look back at the essay you wrote in response to this selection's Performance Task comparing Hamilton's and Jefferson's visions of the future. Review your writing to see if you have used hyphenation conventions correctly. See if you can add one or two hyphenated words to streamline your writing or make your meaning clearer.

HISTORY | VIDEO

Colonial American Poetry

Phillis Wheatley *was born in West Africa, probably in 1753, and became the first African American to publish a book of poetry. In 1761 she was enslaved, brought to Boston, and purchased by a local merchant, John Wheatley. He named the little girl Phillis and gave her to his wife, Susannah. Phillis learned to read and write English very quickly, and the Wheatley family tutored her in Latin, English literature, and the classics. Wheatley was quickly recognized as a remarkable prodigy and respect for her talents soon grew. Phillis's first published poem appeared in 1767, and by 1770 her work was known throughout the colonies. In 1773 she traveled to London for the publication of her* Poems on Various Subjects, Religious and Moral *but soon returned to Boston.*

Phillis was given her freedom after Susannah Wheatley's death in 1774. Her life, however, became more difficult as revolution spread through the colonies and as her patrons, wealthy Loyalists, fled the city. In 1778 she married John Peters, but the couple fell into extreme poverty. Their children all died in infancy, and Phillis died in 1784.

Philip Freneau *was called the "poet of the American Revolution." He was born in New York City in 1752. Freneau began writing poetry while studying at Princeton. After graduating in 1771, he briefly worked as a teacher before sailing to the Caribbean, where he developed a deep hatred of slavery.*

In 1778 Freneau returned to New Jersey and enlisted in the revolutionary militia. He captained a privateer until he was captured and briefly imprisoned by the British. He started a newspaper in 1790 and supported Thomas Jefferson in his ideological dispute with the Federalists. Freneau left the paper soon after Jefferson became president. He retired to a New Jersey farm and continued to write and publish until his death in 1832.

AS YOU READ Pay attention to details that reveal the tone, or attitude, that the speaker in each poem has toward America.

To the Right Honourable William, Earl of Dartmouth

*His Majesty's Principal Secretary
of State for North America, etc.*

by Phillis Wheatley

Hail, happy day, when, smiling like the morn,
Fair *Freedom* rose *New-England* to adorn:
The northern clime[1] beneath her genial ray,
Dartmouth, congratulates thy blissful sway:[2]
5 Elate with hope her race no longer mourns,
Each soul expands, each grateful bosom burns,
While in thine hand with pleasure we behold
The silken reins, and Freedom's charms unfold.
Long lost to realms beneath the northern skies
10 She shines supreme, while hated *faction* dies:
Soon as appeared the *Goddess* long desir'd,
Sick at the view, she languish'd and expir'd;
Thus from the splendors of the morning light
The owl in sadness seeks the caves of night.

15 No more, *America*, in mournful strain[3]
Of wrongs, and grievance unredress'd complain,
No longer shall thou dread the iron chain,
Which wanton *Tyranny* with lawless hand
Had made, and with it meant t' enslave the land.

20 Should you, my lord, while you peruse my song,
Wonder from whence my love of *Freedom* sprung,
Whence flow these wishes for the common good,
By feeling hearts alone best understood,
I, young in life, by seeming cruel fate
25 Was snatch'd from *Afric's* fancy'd happy seat:[4]
What pangs excruciating must molest,
What sorrows labour in my parent's breast?
Steel'd was that soul and by no misery mov'd
That from a father seiz'd his babe belov'd:
30 Such, such my case. And can I then but pray
Others may never feel tyrannic sway?

---

[1] **clime:** climate region.
[2] **sway:** control or rule.
[3] **strain:** song.
[4] **seat:** location or site.

For favours past, great Sir, our thanks are due,
And thee we ask thy favours to renew,
Since in thy pow'r, as in thy will before,
35 To sooth[5] the griefs, which thou did'st once deplore.
May heav'nly grace the sacred sanction give
To all thy works, and thou for ever live
Not only on the wings of fleeting *Fame,*
Though praise immortal crowns the patriot's name,
40 But to conduct to heav'ns refulgent fane,[6]
May fiery coursers[7] sweep th' ethereal plain,
And bear thee upwards to that blest abode,
Where, like the prophet,[8] thou shalt find thy God.

---

[5] **sooth:** alternate spelling of soothe; relieve or ease pain.

[6] **heav'ns refulgent fane:** a shining temple in the sky.

[7] **coursers:** fast horses.

[8] **prophet:** Elijah; according to the Old Testament, he ascended to heaven in a chariot after overturning an immoral political system.

On Being Brought from Africa to America

by Phillis Wheatley

'Twas mercy brought me from my *Pagan* land,
Taught my benighted[9] soul to understand
That there's a God, that there's a *Saviour* too:
Once I redemption neither sought nor knew.
5   Some view our sable[10] race with scornful eye,
"Their colour is a diabolic die."[11]
Remember, *Christians*, *Negroes*, black as *Cain*,
May be refin'd, and join th' angelic train.

---

[9] **benighted:** ignorant.
[10] **sable:** dark brown or black.
[11] **diabolic die:** an evil or devilish coloring agent (dye).

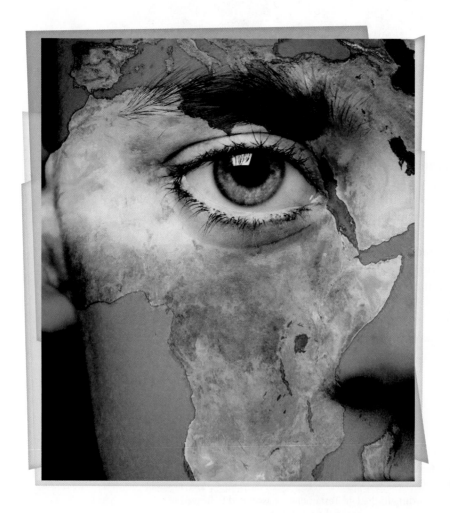

On the Emigration to America and Peopling the Western Country

by Philip Freneau

To western woods, and lonely plains,
Palemon[12] from the crowd departs,
Where Nature's wildest genius reigns,
To tame the soil, and plant the arts—
5 What wonders there shall freedom show,
What mighty states successive grow!

From Europe's proud, despotic shores
Hither the stranger takes his way,
And in our new-found world explores
10 A happier soil, a milder sway,
Where no proud despot holds him down,
No slaves insult him with a crown.

What charming scenes attract the eye,
On wild Ohio's savage stream!
15 There Nature reigns, whose works outvie
The boldest pattern art can frame;
There ages past have rolled away,
And forests bloomed but to decay.

From these fair plains, these rural seats,
20 So long concealed, so lately known,
The unsocial Indian far retreats,
To make some other clime his own,
When other streams, less pleasing, flow,
And darker forests round him grow.

25 Great Sire[13] of floods! whose varied wave
Through climes and countries takes its way,
To whom creating Nature gave
Ten thousand streams to swell thy sway!
No longer shall they useless prove,
30 Nor idly through the forests rove;

Nor longer shall your princely flood
From distant lakes be swelled in vain,
Nor longer through a darksome wood

---

[12] **Palemon:** reference to Polemon I, a first-century Roman noble who escaped to
form a kingdom in the Baltic region.
[13] **Great Sire:** The Mississippi River.

Advance, unnoticed, to the main;[14]
35 Far other ends, the heavens decree—
And commerce plans new freights for thee.

While virtue warms the generous breast,
There heaven-born freedom shall reside,
Nor shall the voice of war molest,
40 Nor Europe's all-aspiring pride—
There Reason shall new laws devise,
And order from confusion rise.

Forsaking kings and regal state,
With all their pomp and fancied bliss,
45 The traveler owns, convinced though late,
No realm so free, so blessed as this—
The east is half to slaves consigned,
Where kings and priests enchain the mind.

O come the time, and haste the day,
50 When man shall man no longer crush,
When Reason shall enforce her sway,
Nor these fair regions raise our blush,
Where still the African complains,
And mourns his yet unbroken chains.

55 Far brighter scenes a future age,
The muse predicts, these States will hail,
Whose genius may the world engage,
Whose deeds may over death prevail,
And happier systems bring to view,
60 Than all the eastern sages knew.

---

[14] **main:** the sea.

COLLABORATIVE DISCUSSION What is the overall tone toward America—as both a place and an idea—expressed in the poems? What are each speaker's reasons for having that attitude? Discuss these questions with a small group, citing textual details to support your ideas.

Colonial American Poetry

The **topic** of a work is what it is about. The three poems in this selection all cover the broad topic of colonial America. Two of them suggest more specific topics in their titles: "On Being Brought from Africa to America" and "On the Emigration to America and Peopling the Western Country." To accurately identify the topic of any poem, you must analyze the details it contains and ask yourself what the poem is mostly about.

Title	Details	Topic
"On Being Brought from Africa to America"	"'Twas mercy brought me from my *Pagan* land, / Taught my benighted soul to understand" "Remember, *Christians*, *Negroes*, black as *Cain*, / May be refin'd, and join th' angelic train."	How coming to America redeemed the speaker's soul through her Christian faith

The **theme** of a work is a message about life or about human nature that the author communicates through details in the text. This deeper meaning is sometimes stated directly, but more often readers must infer it. The final couplet of "On Being Brought from Africa to America" comes close to stating the theme of the poem. What do these two lines suggest about Wheatley's view of life in the Colonies?

The Wheatley and Freneau poems give you the opportunity to compare how several texts from 18th-century America treat similar themes and topics. As you reread the poems, think about what they have in common and how they differ. The chart shows a comparison between two poems that have themes involving the formation of a better society.

Themes about Forming a Better Society	
"To the Right Honourable William, Earl of Dartmouth"	**"On the Emigration to America and Peopling the Western Country"**
Textual detail: "For favours past, great Sir, our thanks are due, / And thee we ask they favours to renew, / Since in thy pow'r, as in thy will before, / To sooth the griefs, which thou didst once deplore." (lines 32–35) **Theme:** What type of leaders does Wheatley think the colonies need? What words might describe that leader?	**Textual detail:** "While virtue warms the generous breast, / There heaven-born freedom shall reside, . . . / There Reason shall new laws devise, / And order from confusion rise." (lines 37–42) **Theme:** What do these lines reveal about Freneau's views on liberty?

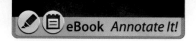

Analyzing the Text

COMMON
CORE

ELACC11-12RL1,
ELACC11-12RL2,
ELACC11-12RL4,
ELACC11-12RL5,
ELACC11-12RL9,
ELACC11-12SL1

Cite Text Evidence   Support your responses with evidence from the selections.

1. **Interpret** Poets use **imagery,** or language that appeals to readers' senses, both to create a vivid experience for readers and to communicate ideas. What imagery does Wheatley use in the first stanza of "To the Right Honourable William, Earl of Dartmouth" (lines 1–14)? How does this imagery express her hopes about the Earl?

2. **Compare** How do Wheatley and Freneau treat themes about being redeemed or saved by coming to America? Compare and contrast how each poem defines or imagines this redemption.

3. **Analyze** Compare Wheatley's description of her enslavement and captivity in both of her poems, especially in lines 20–31 of "To the Right Honourable William . . . ." How might her purpose shape her description in each cases?

4. **Analyze** What words does Freneau use to describe Europe and "the east" in "On the Emigration to America . . ."? What does his diction reveal? Why does Freneau believe that America will break away from these two models of civilization?

5. **Cite Evidence** How does Freneau describe the North American landscape before the arrival of European settlers? What central ideas about Native American culture does he suggest through his diction, imagery, and choice of details?

6. **Analyze** Wheatley ends her poem addressed to the Earl of Dartmouth with an **allusion** to the biblical story of Elijah. Elijah performed bold and miraculous works on God's behalf, after which a fiery horse-drawn chariot transported him to heaven. What meaning does she intend by this allusion, and what effect does she achieve by placing it at the very end of her poem?

7. **Compare** How is the topic of slavery or oppression treated in each of the three poems? How does each poet's personal experiences or political opinions shape their view of slavery or oppression?

PERFORMANCE TASK

Speaking Activity How does each poet's attitude toward authority affect his or her interpretation of life in the colonies? With a partner, discuss similarities and differences.

1. Working independently, review the poems and identify textual evidence for each poet's attitude toward authority.

2. Meet with your partner to review the evidence you have found. Discuss how each poet's view of authority affects his or her view of life in the colonies.

3. Write a brief summary of your discussion that includes the similarities and differences you found between the two poets and key textual evidence that supports your analysis.

Background *As a writer, philosopher, artist, and educator,*
Charles Johnson *has confronted the effects of race and racism.*
"Racism is based on our belief in a division between Self and
Other, and our tendency to measure ourselves against others,"
he says. "Sad to say, it is also based on fear." Johnson was born
in 1948 in Evanston, Illinois, and taught for many years at the
University of Washington. His work has earned a MacArthur
fellowship, the National Book Award for The Middle Passage
(1990), and the American Academy of Arts and Letters Award.

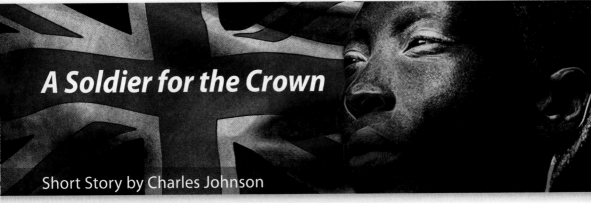

A Soldier for the Crown

Short Story by Charles Johnson

AS YOU READ Pay attention to the concept of liberty and the way in
which personal, social, and ideological differences affect its meaning.

YOU ALWAYS WERE a gambler.
    Before the war broke out, when you were still a servant in
Master William Selby's house, you'd bet on anything—how early
spring thaw might come, or if your older brother Titus would beat
your cousin Caesar in a wrestling match—and most of the time you
won. There was something about gambling that you could not resist.
There was suspense, the feeling that the future was not already written
by white hands. Or finished. There was chance, the luck of the draw.
In the roll of dice or a card game, there was always—what to call it?—
an *openness*, a chance that the outcome would go this way or that. For
or against you. Of course, in bondage to Master Selby there were no
odds. Whichever way the dice fell or the cards came up, you began and
ended your day a slave.
    But did you win *this* time?
    Standing by the wooden rail on a ship bound for Nova Scotia,
crammed with strangers fleeing the collapse of their colonial world—
women and children, whites and blacks, whose names appear in
Brigadier General Samuel Birch's *Book of Negroes*—you pull a long-
shanked pipe from your red-tinted coat, pack the bowl with tobacco,

20 and strike a friction match against a nail in your bootheel. You know you are fortunate to be on board. Now that the Continental Army is victorious, blacks who fought for the crown are struggling desperately to leave on His Majesty's ships departing from New York harbor. Even as your boat eased away from the harbor, some leaped from the docks into the water, swimming toward the ship for this last chance to escape slavery. Seeing them, you'd thought, *That might have been me.* But it wasn't; you've always been lucky that way, at taking risks. Running away from bondage. Taking on new identities. Yet you wonder what to call yourself now. A loyalist? A traitor? A man without a country?

30 As the harbor shrinks, growing fainter in the distance, severing you forever from this strange, newly formed nation called the United States, you haven't the slightest idea after years of war which of these names fits, or what the future holds, though on one matter you *are* clear:

From the start, you were fighting for no one but yourself.

The day after Lieutenant General Sir Henry Clinton promised liberty to all blacks deserting the rebel standard and willing to fight on the side of the British, you learned that Titus and Caesar were planning to flee. In the evening, on your way to the quarters after 40 finishing your duties in the house, Titus stopped you outside the barn, and asked, "Can you go back to the kitchen and sneak out some provisions for us?" Naturally, you'd asked him what for, and he put his fingers to his lips, shushing you. They planned to steal two horses, he said. Then ride to safety behind British lines. "You're leaving?" You were almost speechless with anger. "And you're not taking *me*?"

"How can I?" he asked. "You're only fifteen."

"What's that got to do with anything? I can fight!"

"You ever fired a gun?"

"No, but I can learn!"

50 "Once I'm free, and got the papers to prove it, I'll come back."

"Titus, if you don't take me, I'll *tell*."

For a heartbeat or two, Titus looked as if he might hit you. Grudgingly, he agreed to bring you along, despite your age and his declaration after your parents' deaths that he'd keep you from harm. You did as he requested, returning to the house and filling a sack with food, Master Selby's clothing, even some of the mistress's jewelry that the three of you might barter, then delivered all this to your brother and Caesar in the barn. The three of you left that night on two of the master's best horses, you riding behind Titus, your arms tightly 60 circling his waist until you stopped to make camp in the woods. There, Caesar suggested that it would help if you all changed your names and appearances as much as possible since Master Selby was sure to post your descriptions. Titus said fine, he'd grow a beard and call himself John Free. Caesar liked that, said, "Then I'll be George Liberty." They waited for you to pick a name, poking sticks at the campfire, sending up sparks into the starless sky. "Give me time," you'd said, changing into buckskin breeches, blue stockings, and a checkered, woolen shirt. "I'll shave my hair off, and I'll think of *some*thing before we get there. I don't want to rush." What you didn't tell them that night was how thrilling, how sweet this business of renaming oneself felt, and that you wanted to toy with a thousand possibilities—each name promising a new nature—turning them over on your tongue, and creating whole histories for each before settling, as you finally did, on "Alexander Freeman" as your new identity.

Thus, it was Alexander Freeman, George Liberty, and John Free who rode a few days later, bone weary from travel, into the British camp. You will never forget this sight: scores of black men in British uniforms, with the inscription LIBERTY TO SLAVES on their breasts, bearing arms so naturally one would have thought they were born with a rifle in their hands. Some were cleaning their weapons. Others marched. Still others were relaxing or stabbing their bayonets at sacks suspended from trees or performing any of the thousand chores that kept a regiment well-oiled and ready. When you signed on, the black soldier who wrote down your names didn't question you, though he remarked he thought you didn't look very strong. The three of you were put immediately to work. Harder work, you recall, than anything you'd known working in Master Selby's house, but for the first time in fifteen years you fell to each task eagerly, gambling that the labor purchased a new lease on life.

Over the first months, then years of the seesawing war, you, Titus, and Caesar served His Majesty's army in more **capacities** than you had fingers on the hand: as orderlies[1] to the white officers, laborers, cooks, foragers, and as foot soldiers who descended upon farms abandoned by their white owners, burning the enemy's fortifications and plundering plantations for much-needed provisions; as spies slipping in and out of southern towns to gather information; and as caretakers to the dying when smallpox swept through your regiment, weakening and killing hundreds of men. Your brother among them. And it was then you nearly gave up the gamble. You wondered if it might not be best to take your chips off the table. And pray the promise of the Virginia Convention that black runaways to the British side would be pardoned was genuine. And slink back home, your hat in your hand, to Master Selby's farm—if it was still there. Or perhaps you and Caesar might switch sides, deserting to the ranks of General Washington who, pressured for manpower, **belatedly** reversed his opposition to Negroes fighting in the Continental Army. And then there was that magnificent Declaration penned by Jefferson, proclaiming that "We hold these truths to be self-evident, that all men are created equal, that they are endowed by their Creator with certain **unalienable** Rights, that among these are Life, Liberty and the pursuit of Happiness,"

capacity
(kə-păsˊĭ-tē) *n.* ability to hold or have something; function or role.

belatedly
(bĭ-lāˊtĭd-lē) *adv.* done too late or overdue.

unalienable
(ŭn-ālˊyə-nə-bəl) *adj.* impossible to be taken away.

---

[1] **orderlies:** soldiers who provide personal assistance and perform minor tasks.

words you'd memorized after hearing them. If the Continentals won, would this brave, new republic be so bad?

"Alex, those are just *words*," said Caesar. "White folks' words for other white folks."

"But without us, the rebels would lose—"

"So would the redcoats. Both sides need us, but I don't trust neither one to play fair when this thing is over. They can do that Declaration over. Naw, the words I want to see are on a British pass with my name on it. I'm stayin' put 'til I see *that*."

120   Caesar never did. A month later your regiment was routed by the Continental Army. The rebels fired cannons for six hours, shelling the village your side occupied two days before. You found pieces of your cousin strewn everywhere. And you ran. Ran. You lived by your wits in the countryside, stealing what you needed to survive until you reached territory still in British hands, and again found yourself a pawn in the middle of other men's battles—Camden, where your side scattered poorly trained regulars led by General Gates, then liberated slaves who donned their masters' fancy clothing and powdered wigs and followed along behind Gates as his men pressed on; and the
130   disastrous encounter at Guilford Court House, where six hundred redcoats died and Cornwallis was forced to fall back to Wilmington for supplies, then later abandon North Carolina altogether, moving on to Virginia. During your time as a soldier, you saw thousands sacrifice their lives, and no, it wasn't as if you came through with only a scratch. At Camden you took a ball in your right shoulder. Fragments remain there still, making it a little hard for you to sleep on that side or withstand the dull ache in your shoulder on days when the weather is damp. But, miraculously, as the war began to wind down, you were given the **elusive**, long-coveted British pass.

140   On the ship, now traveling north past Augusta, you knock your cold pipe against the railing, shaking dottle from its bowl, then reach into your coat for the scrap of paper that was so difficult to earn. Behind you, other refugees are bedding down for the night, covering themselves and their children with blankets. You wait until one of the hands on deck passes a few feet beyond where you stand, then you unfold the paper with fingers stiffened by the cold. In the yellowish glow of the ship's lantern, tracing the words with your forefinger, shaping your lips silently to form each syllable, you read:

150   This is to certify to whomſoever it may concern, that the
          Bearer hereof…Alexander Freeman…a Negro, reſorted
          to the Britiſh Lines, in conſequence of the Proclamations
          of Sir William Howe, and Sir Henry Clinton, late
          Commanders in Chief in America; and that the ſaid
          Negro has hereby his Excellency Sir Benjamin Hampton's
          Permiſſion to go to Nova-Scotia, or wherever elſe he may
          think proper…By Order of Brigadier General Ruttledge

elusive
(ĭ-lōō′sĭv) *adj.* difficult to find.

The document, dated April 1783, brings a broad smile to your lips. Once your ship lands, and you find a home, you will frame this precious deed of manumission.[2] At least in this sense, your gamble paid off. And for now you still prefer the adopted name Alexander Freeman to the one given you at birth—Dorothy.

Maybe you'll be Dorothy again, later in Nova Scotia. Of course, you'll keep the surname Freeman. And, Lord willing, when it's safe you will let your hair grow out again to its full length, wear dresses, and perhaps start a new family to replace the loved ones you lost during the war.

---

[2] **deed of manumission:** a document confirming a person's release from slavery.

COLLABORATIVE DISCUSSION Were you surprised by the twist at the end of the story? What does it change about your views on Alexander's struggle for liberation? What specific events now appear in a new light? Cite evidence from the text that supports your ideas.

Analyze Structure: Suspense and Ambiguity

COMMON CORE

ELACC11-12RL1,
ELACC11-12RL5,
ELACC11-12RL6

The **structure** of a story consists of a writer's choices concerning how to organize information. As you analyze the overall meaning and impact of the author's structure in "A Soldier for the Crown," note the following elements:

Suspense is the excitement or tension that readers feel as they wait to find out how a story ends. The author introduces Alexander Freeman as a risk-taker and creates suspense about the story's outcome with statements such as, "But did you win *this* time?" The description of Freeman aboard the ship helps frame the story and raise questions in readers' minds about the events that brought Freeman there.	**Ambiguity** is the uncertainty created when an author leaves elements of a text open to the reader's interpretation. The author builds the story by forcing the reader to put together clues about Alexander Freeman. The reader must then reevaluate these inferences and assumptions about Freeman's identity in the story's surprise ending.

Analyze Point of View: Second Person

COMMON CORE

ELACC11-12RL1,
ELACC11-12RL6

Point of view refers to the method an author uses to narrate a story. Most stories are told in the first-person or third-person point of view. In a work written in the **first-person point of view,** the narrator is a character in the story and shares his or her own thoughts and feelings. When a writer uses the **third-person point of view,** the narrator is not a character in the story but an outside observer. Sometimes a third-person narrator is **omniscient,** meaning he or she knows the thoughts, feelings, and actions of all the characters in a story. A third-person narrator can also be **limited** to one character's thoughts, observations, or experiences.

A more unusual method of narration is the **second-person point of view,** in which the narrator addresses one or more individuals using the pronoun *you.* In "A Soldier for the Crown," the narrator addresses the main character, Alexander Freeman, but often speaks as if he or she has entered the mind of that character. For example, in lines 26–27, the narrator says

> "Seeing them, you'd thought, *That might have been me.* But it wasn't; you've always been lucky that way, at taking risks."

The second-person point of view requires the reader to piece together the information that is revealed by the narrator and to distinguish what is directly stated in the text from what is really meant. In the example, the reader knows that the "you" has been a lucky risk taker in the past. However, even with the clues provided earlier in the story, it isn't yet exactly clear what type of risk taking has led the person to be on board the ship.

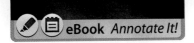

Analyzing the Text

COMMON CORE
ELACC11-12RL1,
ELACC11-12RL5,
ELACC11-12RL6,
ELACC11-12W7,
ELACC11-12W9a,
ELACC11-12W10,
ELACC11-12SL1a,
ELACC11-12SL3

Cite Text Evidence Support your responses with evidence from the selection.

1. **Infer** What evidence does the author provide in the opening sentence of the story and the paragraph that follows to suggest the risks that the main character will take to escape slavery?

2. **Identify** How does the setting contribute to the suspense within the text? Explain, citing details that reveal the setting of the story.

3. **Cite Evidence** What clues in the story hint at Freeman's identity? Provide details from the story in your explanation.

4. **Analyze** What effect does the use of the second-person point of view have on the scene in lines 60–74? What idea is the author able to communicate by using this point of view?

5. **Analyze** Why does the conversation between Caesar and Freeman about the Declaration of Independence leave the reader with a sense of ambiguity, but hold greater significance once Freeman's identity is revealed?

6. **Evaluate** In what ways does Freeman assume a greater risk than other African Americans who join the British side? How does assuming a different gender complicate her situation?

7. **Interpret** What does the narrator mean by the reference to Freeman's deed of manumission, "At least in this sense, your gamble paid off."

8. **Analyze** Why is it **ironic,** or contrary to what you might have expected, that Freeman considers the deed of manumission to be so precious?

PERFORMANCE TASK

Writing and Speaking Activity Alexander Freeman decides to continue fighting for the British in the Revolution after her brother died. However, she had several other options. Prepare for a small group discussion by doing some research and writing an outline of your notes. Complete these steps:

- identify the other alternatives Freeman considers
- research the alternatives by looking for information about the role of African Americans in the Revolutionary War
- write notes about your research, remembering to identify each of your sources
- gather with a small group to discuss and evaluate Alexander Freeman's options
- use your research notes to support your ideas during the discussion
- as a group write a summary of your discussion including whether you agree or disagree about the decision Alexander Freeman made

Critical Vocabulary

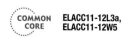

COMMON CORE   ELACC11-12L3a,
ELACC11-12W5

| capacity | belatedly | unalienable | elusive |

Practice and Apply Answer each question. Then discuss your answers with a partner.

1. What do you possess as an individual that is **unalienable**? Explain.

2. Describe a circumstance in which you received something **belatedly.**

3. When have you tried to grasp something that proved **elusive**? Explain.

4. In what **capacity** might you help out at a local animal shelter?

Language and Style: Point of View

In narrating from a particular **point of view,** a writer must use the correct personal pronoun form to refer to the person making a statement, the person being addressed, or the thing the statement is about.

	Nominative	Objective	Possessive
Singular			
First person	I	me	my, mine
Second person	you	you	your, yours
Third person	he, she, it	her, him, it	her, hers, his, its
Plural			
First person	we	us	our, ours
Second person	you	you	you, yours
Third person	they	them	their, theirs

Notice how the personal pronouns would change form if the last paragraph from "A Soldier for the Crown," were rewritten in the first-person or third-person point of view.

First-Person Point of View	Third-Person Point of View
Maybe I'll be Dorothy again, later in Nova Scotia. Of course, I'll keep the surname Freeman. And, Lord willing, when it's safe I will let my hair grow long again to it's full length, wear dresses, and perhaps start a new family to replace the loved ones I lost during the war.	Maybe she'll be Dorothy again, later in Nova Scotia. Of course, she'll keep the surname Freeman. And, Lord willing, when it's safe she will let her hair grow long again to it's full length, wear dresses, and perhaps start a new family to replace the loved ones she lost during the war.

Practice and Apply Look back at your summary of your discussion about Freeman's choices. Rewrite the summary from the second-person point of view. Address the audience as Freeman. Remember to use the correct personal pronoun form.

A&E BIO

Background *Patrick Henry (1736–1799) is remembered for his ringing declaration "Give me liberty or give me death!" Yet, he contributed much more than rhetoric to eighteenth-century politics and to the formation of a new United States. This video excerpt describes the ways in which his efforts helped change the course of American history and the circumstances that led to Henry becoming the "voice of liberty." Henry was born in a frontier region of Virginia, and was raised in a cultured but modest environment. He made several unsuccessful attempts at storekeeping and farming before discovering his true calling: the law and politics.*

MEDIA ANALYSIS

Patrick Henry: Voice of Liberty

Documentary by A&E

AS YOU VIEW Pay attention to the way in which Patrick Henry is portrayed in this video. Write down any questions you generate during your viewing.

COLLABORATIVE DISCUSSION What facts did you learn about Patrick Henry that surprised you?

Analyze Foundational Documents

As one of the leading statesmen of the eighteenth century, Patrick Henry had a significant impact on the political thought of the day as well as on foundational documents, such as the Constitution, that defined the American system of government and articulated the country's principles.

The video excerpt from *Patrick Henry: Voice of Liberty* presents information about the historical context of Henry's life and achievements. To understand the extent of Henry's contribution to the core of American democracy, viewers may analyze relationships between these elements:

- Henry's abilities as a statesman and political decisions that led to the founding of the new country
- Henry's political philosophy and the themes of foundational documents
- the effect that Henry's words had on the founding of the United States and on the early history of the nation

Analyzing the Media

> *Cite Text Evidence*   Support your responses with evidence from the selection.

1. **Analyze** Why was Patrick Henry such an effective speaker? Why do we have so little information on the exact content of Henry's speeches?

2. **Evaluate** Explain the historical significance of Henry's Virginia Stamp Act Resolutions. How did his objections shape or transform the political discussion around the controversy?

3. **Evaluate** Based on this video, in what ways might Henry's Speech to the Second Virginia Convention be considered a foundational U.S. document? What was the historical and literary significance of the speech?

PERFORMANCE TASK

Media Activity: Presentation What is a foundational document for the 21st century? Work with a partner to create a media presentation that responds to this question.

- Choose a book, album, movie, Web site, or even a law that could be considered the equivalent of a foundational document today.

- Explain the impact of this work on society, citing specific details.

- Incorporate your defense of your choice into a media presentation. If possible, use elements similar to those seen in *Patrick Henry: Voice of Liberty*.

Write an Informative Essay

How can a large group of people with widely different backgrounds, beliefs, and interests work together to form one political union? This collection focuses on ways that Americans during and after the revolution envisioned the future of their new nation. Choose three texts you have read in this collection, including the anchor texts—the Declaration of Independence and the U.S. Constitution—and identify how each author, character, or founder finds a balance between preserving individual rights and forming a strong and long-lasting union. Write an informative essay in which you cite evidence from all three texts to support your topic.

Your informative essay should include:

- an introduction with a clear topic statement about the conflict between a strong, centralized government and individualism as explored in the Declaration of Independence, the Constitution, and one other text from the collection

- a logically structured body that thoroughly develops the topic with relevant examples, details, and quotations from the texts

- transitions to clarify the relationships between sections of your essay and to link ideas with the textual evidence that supports them

- a conclusion that follows from the ideas conveyed in the body of the essay

- precise use of language with appropriate tone and style for an informative essay

COMMON CORE

ELACC11-12W2 Write informative/ explanatory texts to examine and convey complex ideas, concepts, and information clearly and accurately through the effective selection, organization, and analysis of content.
ELACC11-12W4 Produce clear and coherent writing in which the development, organization, and style are appropriate to task, purpose, and audience.
ELACC11-12W9 Draw evidence from literary or informational texts to support analysis, reflection, and research.
ELACC11-12SL1 Initiate and participate effectively in a range of collaborative discussions, building on others' ideas and expressing their own clearly and persuasively.

PLAN

Analyze the Texts Reread the Declaration and the Preamble and Bill of Rights from the U.S. Constitution and consider what the texts say about both forming a union and protecting the rights of individuals. Make notes about specific details in the texts. Then review the other texts in the collection to decide which one provides the best material to complement what you have found in the anchor texts. Note relevant details and examples from that text, as well. Be sure to look for evidence that may be contrary to the ideas expressed in the Declaration and the Constitution, as well as evidence that reinforces those ideas.

Share Ideas Once you have thought about your topic and identified evidence in the texts, get together with a group of classmates to share

my Notebook

Use the notebook in your eBook to record examples and quotations on the rights of the individual balanced against the needs of society.

ideas. Be prepared to discuss specific textual evidence and even to reconsider some of your choices. You might decide, for example, that a text you had not planned to use for your essay actually has some strong evidence that you'd like to include.

These questions can guide your discussion:

- What ideas did our nation's founders have to allow people with differing backgrounds, opinions, and interests to work together and form a union?

- In what ways are factions, or groups of people with competing interests, dangerous to a union? Are there any benefits to factions?

- The Preamble states the goal of "[forming] a more perfect Union." Is there any such thing as a perfect union? How have people tried to strike a balance between union and faction, or union and individualism?

Get Organized Organize your details and evidence in an outline.

- Decide what organizational pattern you will use for your essay. For example, you might discuss each text in a separate section, or you might devote each section to an idea and explore how all three texts treat that idea.

- Choose which textual evidence is the most relevant to your topic and your central ideas.

- Use your organizational pattern to sort your textual evidence into a logical order.

- Select an interesting quotation or detail to introduce your informative essay.

- List some ideas for your concluding section.

ACADEMIC VOCABULARY

As you write your informative essay, be sure to use these words.

contrary
founder
ideological
publication
revolution

PRODUCE

Draft Your Report Write a draft of your essay, following your outline.

- Introduce your topic about union and individualism. Present your topic in such a way that your reader will want to continue reading. Remember that you must take an objective perspective on the topic; you are not making an argument or stating your opinion.

- Present your details, facts, quotations, and examples from the texts in logically ordered paragraphs.

- Use appropriate transitions to create cohesion between sections of your essay and to clarify relationships between your topic and the provided evidence.

- Write a concluding section that summarizes your central ideas. Make a closing statement that relates the topic to your audience.

*my*WriteSmart

Write your rough draft in *my*WriteSmart. Focus on creating a clear structure with an introduction, a body, and a conclusion.

Improve Your Draft Revise your draft to make sure it is clear, coherent, and engaging. Use the chart on the following page to review the characteristics of an effective informative essay. Ask yourself these questions as you revise:

Have your partner or a group of peers review your draft in *my*WriteSmart. Ask your reviewers to note places where you might include more effective text evidence.

- Have I introduced my topic clearly? Does my introduction engage the reader?

- Have I presented relevant evidence from the texts to support the central ideas in my essay?

- Is my essay logically organized? Are transitions from section to section smooth and easy to follow? Do I need to clarify how the central ideas are connected to the evidence from the texts?

- Have I maintained an objective viewpoint throughout the essay, avoiding conveying my opinion about the topic?

- Have I used a formal style of English appropriate for an informative essay?

- Does my conclusion follow logically from the body and provide a satisfying ending?

PRESENT

Exchange Essays When your final draft is completed, exchange essays with a partner. Read your partner's essay and provide feedback. Did your partner maintain an objective viewpoint throughout the essay? Be sure to point out aspects of the essay that are particularly strong, as well as areas that could be improved.

Publish Online If your school has a website where you can post your writing, work with your classmates to publish your collection of essays online. First, review your own essay and look for places to add links to other online sources, such as the text of the Bill of Rights, that readers may find helpful. Then, as a group, create a front page that introduces the collection and invites readers to explore the individual essays. You might also consider setting up a blog to allow readers to share their views on the essays.

COLLECTION 2 **TASK**
INFORMATIVE ESSAY

Ideas and Evidence	Organization	Language
ADVANCED • The introduction is intriguing and informative; the controlling idea clearly identifies a compelling topic. • The topic is strongly developed with relevant facts, concrete details, interesting quotations, and examples from the texts. • The concluding section capably follows from and supports the ideas presented.	• The organization is effective and logical throughout the essay. • Transitions are well crafted and successfully connect related ideas.	• The writing reflects a formal style and an objective, knowledgeable tone. • Language is vivid and precise. • Sentence beginnings, lengths, and structures vary and have a rhythmic flow. • Spelling, capitalization, and punctuation are correct. If handwritten, the essay is legible. • Grammar and usage are correct.
COMPETENT • The introduction could do more to attract the reader's curiosity; the controlling idea identifies a topic. • One or two key points could use additional support in the form of relevant facts, concrete details, quotations, and examples from the texts. • The concluding section mostly follows from and supports the ideas presented.	• The organization is confusing in a few places. • A few more transitions are needed to connect related ideas.	• The style is inconsistent in a few places, and the tone is subjective at times. • Vague language is used in a few places. • Sentence beginnings, lengths, and structures vary somewhat. • Some spelling, capitalization, and punctuation mistakes occur. If handwritten, the essay is mostly legible. • Some grammatical and usage errors are repeated in the essay.
LIMITED • The introduction provides some information about a topic but does not include a controlling idea. • Most key points need additional support in the form of relevant facts, concrete details, quotations, and examples from the texts. • The concluding section is confusing and does not follow from the ideas presented.	• The organization is confusing in some places and often doesn't follow a pattern. • More transitions are needed throughout to connect related ideas.	• The style is too informal; the tone conveys subjectivity and a lack of understanding of the topic. • Vague, general language is used in many places. • Sentence structures barely vary, and some fragments or run-on sentences are present. • Spelling, capitalization, and punctuation are often incorrect but do not make reading the essay difficult. If handwritten, the essay may be partially illegible. • Grammar and usage are incorrect in many places, but the writer's ideas are still clear.
EMERGING • The appropriate elements of an introduction are missing. • Facts, details, quotations, and examples from the texts are missing. • The essay lacks an identifiable concluding section.	• A logical organization is not used; information is presented randomly. • Transitions are not used, making the essay difficult to understand.	• The style and tone are inappropriate for the essay. • Language is too vague or general to convey the information. • Repetitive sentence structure, fragments, and run-on sentences make the writing monotonous and difficult to follow. • Spelling, capitalization, and punctuation are incorrect throughout. If handwritten, the essay may be partially or mostly illegible. • Many grammatical and usage errors change the meaning of the writer's ideas.

The Individual and Society

The Individual and Society

In this collection, you will explore how writers in the early 19th century created a new "American" literature.

COLLECTION
PERFORMANCE TASK Preview

At the end of this collection, you will have the opportunity to complete two tasks:

• Write a narrative about the individual's relationship with nature and society.

• Participate in a debate about the way many writers interpret the natural world.

ACADEMIC VOCABULARY

Study the words and their definitions in the chart below. You will use these words as you discuss and write about the texts in this collection.

Word	Definition	Related Forms
analogy (ə-năˊə-jē) *n.*	a comparison that finds a similarity between things that are dissimilar	analogous, analogist, analog
denote (dĭ-nōtˊ) *v.*	to mean something specific; to name	denotation, denotable, denotative
quote (kwōt) *v.*	to cite something word for word	quotation, quotation mark, quotable
topic (tŏpˊĭk) *n.*	the subject of a piece of writing or speech	topical, topic sentence
unique (yo͞o-nēkˊ) *adj.*	one of a kind; unable to be compared	uniqueness, uniquely

A Distinctly American Voice

COMMON CORE

ELACC11-12RL10,
ELACC11-12RI3,
ELACC11-12RI4,
ELACC11-12RI7,
ELACC11-12RI10

In the first half of the 19th century, a distinctly American voice emerged as the United States reaffirmed its independence from Britain politically and economically. The country was expanding geographically, creating diversification in the ways that people worked and lived. Reflecting the optimism of a growing country, writers developed a national literature, speaking for the first time in their own unique voices rather than imitating European authors and styles.

AN ERA OF GROWTH AND CHANGE In 1812, simmering tensions between the United States and Great Britain erupted in a two-year war. Victory in the War of 1812 cemented the reality of American independence—it is sometimes referred to as the second war for American independence—and brought great changes to life in the United States. Because the war interrupted trade, Americans had to produce many of the goods they had imported in the past. This period marked the beginning of the Industrial Revolution in the United States, as the country shifted from its largely agrarian economy to become an industrial powerhouse. The growth of the factory system brought many people from farms into cities, where they worked long hours for low wages, often under harsh conditions. Writers of the period reacted to the negative effects of industrialization—the commercialism, hectic pace, and lack of conscience—by turning to nature and to the self for simplicity, truth, and beauty.

At the same time, following the Louisiana Purchase of 1803, the country experienced change of another kind as settlers moved farther and farther west. As European settlers moved into new territory to make money and gain land, Native Americans who had lived there for generations were displaced. The Indian Removal Act of 1830, for instance, required Native Americans in southeastern regions to relocate west of the Mississippi River. Indians who tried to remain in their homelands were often brutally pushed off their lands.

In the middle of the century, Americans embraced the idea of "manifest destiny"—a belief that the United States was destined to expand to the Pacific Ocean and into Mexican Territory. The United States' annexation of Texas from Mexico in 1845 set off the Mexican-American War (1846–1848). Through treaties and later land purchases from the Mexican government, the United States established the current borders of the 48 contiguous states.

1810

1824
Lowell, Massachusetts, becomes a major textile manufacturing center.

1830
Congress passes the Indian Removal Act.

1812–14
War of 1812 affirms U.S. independence from Great Britain.

1825
Erie Canal links Lake Erie with the Hudson River.

THE INDIVIDUAL AND IMAGINATION American writers of this period were influenced by European Romanticism but soon adapted it to their own culture. The Romantics reacted to what had come before, including both the Enlightenment's emphasis on reason and also the strict doctrines of Puritanism. Romantics were inspired by nature and celebrated the individual human spirit, including the emotions and imagination. An early Romantic, Washington Irving was the first truly American writer who was recognized abroad. As a pioneer of the short story form, he influenced later writers such as Nathaniel Hawthorne.

Ralph Waldo Emerson, a New England writer, nurtured the pride that Americans took in their emerging culture. He led a group focused on transcendentalism—a philosophical and literary movement that emphasized living a simple life and celebrating the truth found in nature and in personal emotion and imagination. Emerson gave this European philosophy a uniquely American spin: he said that every individual is capable of discovering this higher truth on his or her own, through intuition. Unlike the Puritans, the transcendentalists believed that people were inherently good and should follow their own beliefs, however different these beliefs may be from the norm.

In 1842, Emerson called for the emergence of a poet worthy of the new America—a fresh voice with limitless passion and originality. Two poets who began writing in the middle of the century arguably met this challenge: Walt Whitman and Emily Dickinson. Although their lives outwardly were very dissimilar, both Whitman and Dickinson wrote poems that broke with the traditional conventions of poetic form and content. In this way they followed the transcendentalist ideals of individuals discovering the truth through intuition and following their own beliefs.

Not all American Romantics were optimistic or had faith in the innate goodness of humankind, however. Edgar Allan Poe, Nathaniel Hawthorne, and Herman Melville are what have been called "brooding" romantics or "anti-transcendentalists." Their stories are characterized by a probing of the inner life of their characters, and examination of the complex and often mysterious forces that motivate human behavior. These stories are romantic, however, in their emphasis on emotion, nature, the individual, and the unusual. (For more on the dark side of Romanticism, see the introduction titled "American Romanticism" later in this collection.)

1838
John Deere develops a steel plow for the western prairies.

1832
Samuel B. Morse invents the telegraph.

1846–48
Mexican-American War expands western territory of the United States.

1848
Discovery of gold in California leads to the first gold rush.

1850

from
Song of Myself

Poem by Walt Whitman

1 I celebrate myself, and sing myself

6 A child said *What is the grass?*

from **33** I understand the large hearts of heroes

52 The spotted hawk swoops by

Walt Whitman (1819–1892) *in his younger years showed little indication of literary promise as he moved from one job to the next. Finally, in the 1850s, he devoted himself completely to writing his collection of poems entitled* Leaves of Grass. *He printed the volume in 1855. It soon ignited a flurry of reaction from readers because of its content and form, both of which were considered revolutionary. Many early readers scorned his efforts, but, undeterred, Whitman continued working on the book for the rest of his life—revising or rearranging existing poems and adding new poems. It has become recognized as the most influential book of poetry in American literature. Rejecting the rigidity of earlier poetic conventions, Whitman's poetry captures the vitality, optimism, and voice of America in a style that reflects the freedom and vastness of his beloved country.*

Background *"Song of Myself" is a long poem in fifty-two sections that appears in* Leaves of Grass.

AS YOU READ Consider why people in the 1800s found Whitman's poetry so "revolutionary." Write down any questions that you generate during reading.

1 I celebrate myself, and sing myself

I celebrate myself, and sing myself,
And what I assume you shall assume,¹
For every atom belonging to me as good belongs to you.

I loaf and invite my soul,
5 I lean and loaf at my ease observing a spear of summer grass.

My tongue, every atom of my blood, form'd from this soil, this air,
Born here of parents born here from parents the same, and their
    parents the same,
I, now thirty-seven years old in perfect health begin,
Hoping to cease not till death.

10 Creeds and schools in abeyance,²
Retiring back a while sufficed at what they are, but never forgotten,
I harbor for good or bad, I permit to speak at every hazard,
Nature without check with original energy.

---

¹ **assume:** Here, the word *assume* means "take on."
² **abeyance:** temporary suspension; inactivity.

ELACC11-12RL1,
ELACC11-12RL2,
ELACC11-12RL3,
ELACC11-12RL5

Analyzing the Text

Cite Text Evidence   Support your responses with evidence.

1. **Interpret** Explain how lines 1–3 establish the speaker as an individual but also as a representative for all others.

2. **Analyze** How does Whitman's line length and word arrangement in lines 6 and 7 help readers to interpret their meaning?

3. **Infer** In the last stanza, the poet refers to schools of thought that he has considered in the past and has now left behind. What does the last line suggest about his poetic creed, or system of belief?

6 A child said *What is the grass?*

A child said *What is the grass?* fetching it to me with full hands;
How could I answer the child? I do not know what it is any more than
     he.

I guess it must be the flag of my disposition, out of hopeful green stuff
     woven.

Or I guess it is the handkerchief of the Lord,
5 A scented gift and remembrancer designedly dropt,
Bearing the owner's name someway in the corners, that we may see
     and remark, and say *Whose?*

Or I guess the grass is itself a child, the produced babe of the
     vegetation.

Or I guess it is a uniform hieroglyphic,[1]
And it means, Sprouting alike in broad zones and narrow zones,
10 Growing among black folks as among white,
Kanuck, Tuckahoe, Congressman, Cuff,[2] I give them the same,
     I receive them the same.

And now it seems to me the beautiful uncut hair of graves.

Tenderly will I use you curling grass,
It may be you transpire from the breasts of young men,
15 It may be if I had known them I would have loved them,
It may be you are from old people, or from offspring taken soon out of
     their mothers' laps,
And here you are the mothers' laps.

The grass is very dark to be from the white heads of old mothers,
Darker than the colorless beards of old men,
20 Dark to come from under the faint red roofs of mouths.

O I perceive after all so many uttering tongues,
And I perceive they do not come from the roofs of mouths for nothing.

I wish I could translate the hints about the dead young men and
     women,

---

[1] **hieroglyphic:** picture symbol used in a writing system to represent sounds or
words.

[2] **Kanuck, Tuckahoe, . . .Cuff:** *Kanuck, Tuckahoe,* and *Cuff* are slang terms,
now considered offensive, for a French Canadian, an inhabitant of the Virginia
lowlands, and an African American, respectively.

And the hints about old men and mothers, and the offspring taken
      soon out of their laps.

25   What do you think has become of the young and old men?
And what do you think has become of the women and children?

They are alive and well somewhere,
The smallest sprout shows there is really no death,
And if ever there was it led forward life, and does not wait at the end to
      arrest it,
30 And ceas'd the moment life appear'd.

All goes onward and outward, nothing collapses,
And to die is different from what any one supposed, and luckier.

Analyzing the Text

ELACC11-12RL2,
ELACC11-12RL4,
ELACC11-12RL5

Cite Text Evidence   Support your responses with evidence.

1. **Analyze** How does the repetition of the phrase "Or I guess" in lines
4–8 contribute to the sound of this section? What is the relationship
between the repeated elements?

2. **Analyze** Why does the poet choose to present the details in lines
23–26 in the form of a list or catalogue? How does this technique add
to the impact of the conclusion the speaker reaches in lines 27–32?

3. **Interpret** What deeper meaning, or **symbolism,** does the grass have
in this section?

from 33 I understand the large hearts of heroes

I understand the large hearts of heroes,
The courage of present times and all times,
How the skipper saw the crowded and rudderless wreck of the
    steam-ship, and Death chasing it up and down the storm,
How he knuckled tight and gave not back an inch, and was faithful
    of days and faithful of nights,

5 And chalk'd in large letters on a board, *Be of good cheer,*
    we will not desert you;
How he follow'd with them and tack'd with them three days and
    would not give it up,
How he saved the drifting company at last,
How the lank loose-gown'd women look'd when boated from the
    side of their prepared graves,
How the silent old-faced infants and the lifted sick, and the sharp-
    lipp'd unshaved men;
10 All this I swallow, it tastes good, I like it well, it becomes mine,
I am the man, I suffer'd, I was there.

The disdain and calmness of martyrs,
The mother of old, condemn'd for a witch, burnt with dry wood,
    her children gazing on,
The hounded slave that flags in the race, leans by the fence,
    blowing, cover'd with sweat,
15 The twinges that sting like needles his legs and neck, the
    murderous buckshot and the bullets,
All these I feel or am.

I am the hounded slave, I wince at the bite of the dogs,
Hell and despair are upon me, crack and again crack the
    marksmen,
I clutch the rails of the fence, my gore dribs, thinn'd with the ooze
    of my skin,
20 I fall on the weeds and stones,
The riders spur their unwilling horses, haul close,
Taunt my dizzy ears and beat me violently over the head with
    whip-stocks.

Agonies are one of my changes of garments,
I do not ask the wounded person how he feels, I myself become the
    wounded person,
25 My hurts turn livid upon me as I lean on a cane and observe.

I am the mash'd fireman with breast-bone broken,
Tumbling walls buried me in their debris,
Heat and smoke I inspired,[1] I heard the yelling shouts of my
    comrades,
I heard the distant click of their picks and shovels,
30 They have clear'd the beams away, they tenderly lift me forth.

I lie in the night air in my red shirt, the pervading hush is for
    my sake,
Painless after all I lie exhausted but not so unhappy,
White and beautiful are the faces around me, the heads are bared
    of their fire-caps,
The kneeling crowd fades with the light of the torches.

35 Distant and dead resuscitate,
They show as the dial or move as the hands of me, I am the clock
    myself.

I am an old artillerist, I tell of my fort's bombardment,
I am there again.

Again the long roll of the drummers,
40 Again the attacking cannon, mortars,
Again to my listening ears the cannon responsive.

I take part, I see and hear the whole,
The cries, curses, roar, the plaudits for well-aim'd shots,
The ambulanza slowly passing trailing its red drip,
45 Workmen searching after damages, making indispensable repairs,
The fall of grenades through the rent roof, the fan-shaped
    explosion,
The whizz of limbs, heads, stone, wood, iron, high in the air.

Again gurgles the mouth of my dying general, he furiously waves
    with his hand,
He gasps through the clot *Mind not me—mind—the entrenchments.*

---

[1] **inspired:** breathed in.

Analyzing the Text

COMMON CORE ELACC11-12RL4, ELACC11-12RL5

Cite Text Evidence   Support your responses with evidence.

1. **Infer** What words and phrases convey a **mood,** or atmosphere, of
tension and suspense in lines 3–10? Why does Whitman open this
section of the poem with this account?

2. **Analyze** In lines 26–34, what details appeal to the readers' senses?
Explain what effect Whitman intends these details to have on readers.

52 The spotted hawk swoops by

The spotted hawk swoops by and accuses me, he complains
    of my gab and my loitering.

I too am not a bit tamed, I too am untranslatable,
I sound my barbaric yawp[1] over the roofs of the world.

The last scud[2] of day holds back for me,
5 It flings my likeness after the rest and true as any on the shadow'd
    wilds,
It coaxes me to the vapor and the dusk.

I depart as air, I shake my white locks at the runaway sun,
I effuse[3] my flesh in eddies,[4] and drift it in lacy jags.

I bequeath myself to the dirt to grow from the grass I love,
10 If you want me again look for me under your boot-soles.

You will hardly know who I am or what I mean,
But I shall be good health to you nevertheless,
And filter and fiber your blood.

Failing to fetch me at first keep encouraged,
15 Missing me one place search another,
I stop somewhere waiting for you.

---

[1] **yawp:** a loud, harsh cry.
[2] **scud:** windblown mist and low clouds.
[3] **effuse:** spread out.
[4] **eddies:** small whirlwinds.

COMMON CORE ELACC11-12RL4,
ELACC11-12RL5

Analyzing the Text

Cite Text Evidence Support your responses with evidence.

1. **Analyze** Why does Whitman use the word "untranslatable" to describe the speaker? What does "barbaric yawp" suggest about the speaker's message to the world?

2. **Analyze** Explain how Whitman's word choice and line arrangement in lines 4–8 create a feeling of vitality and motion in this section.

COLLABORATIVE DISCUSSION How is Whitman's poetry a departure from the style and subjects of other poems you have read? With a partner, discuss what makes Whitman's work unique. Cite specific textual evidence from "Song of Myself" to support your ideas.

Analyze Structure: Free Verse

Whitman's poetry burst upon the public, startling readers with its use of **free verse.** Free verse is poetry that does not contain regular patterns of rhyme or meter. Because free verse flows more naturally than strictly rhymed, metrical lines, it sounds more like everyday speech. It also gives greater emphasis to some poetic devices that can be used to impose rhythm, heighten emotion, and convey meaning:

- **cataloguing:** frequent lists of people, things, and attributes. Cataloguing is seen in this line from the excerpt from section 33: "The whizz of limbs, heads, stone, wood, iron, high in the air."
- **repetition:** repeated words or phrases. Repetition is seen in lines 14–16 of number 6: "It may be you transpire . . . /It may be if I had known . . . /It may be you are . . ."

Whitman's use of free verse and its accompanying components of cataloguing and repetition help him to achieve exactly the effects he desired.

Determine Themes

COMMON CORE   ELACC11-12RL2, ELACC11-12L5a

The **theme** or themes of a poem are the underlying message or messages that a poet wants to convey. A poet relies on the words themselves and also poetic devices and form to reveal meaning to the reader.

Through these selections from "Song of Myself," Whitman communicates several themes, using elements such as the ones described in the chart:

Elements	How They Reveal Themes
free verse	Look for words that are emphasized by the poet's manipulation of lines. For example, *gab* and *loitering* in line 1of section 52 stand out.
imagery	Think about the types of **images** created by sensory language and why the poet wants readers to "see" these pictures. For example, section 33 relies heavily on imagery: "I clutch the rails of the fence, my gore dribs . . ."
figures of speech	Comparisons in the form of **similes** and **metaphors** tell readers how the poet wants them to view certain ideas. In section 6, the grass is compared to "the handkerchief of the Lord."
symbols	A person, place, or thing that has a meaning beyond itself is often central to the poem's meaning. For example, in section 52, the hawk might symbolize all that is wild and free in nature.
direct statements	Sometimes the poet expresses ideas directly as in this line from section 1: "Nature without check with original energy."

Analyzing the Text

COMMON CORE
ELACC11-12RL1,
ELACC11-12RL2,
ELACC11-12RL4,
ELACC11-12RL5,
ELACC11-12SL4,
ELACC11-12SL6

Cite Text Evidence   Support your responses with evidence from the selections.

1. **Analyze** "I celebrate myself . . ." is the first section of Whitman's poem "Song of Myself." In what ways does "I celebrate myself . . ." serve as an appropriate introduction to the themes and poetic vision described in these excerpts?

2. **Analyze** "The spotted hawk swoops by" completes Whitman's "Song of Myself." What do lines 7–16 suggest about the theme of Whitman's long, multi-part poem? How is section 52 a fitting conclusion to the larger work?

3. **Interpret** Compare the themes brought out by "A child said: *What is the grass?*" and "The spotted hawk swoops by." What insight do they both offer?

4. **Compare** How do "I celebrate myself . . ." and "I understand the large hearts . . ." communicate Whitman's vision of a bond that unites all humanity?

5. **Analyze** Whitman's poetic voice has been described as democratic, inclusive, and encompassing. How is this voice especially evident in the **metaphor** in lines 8–12 of "A child said . . ." and lines 14–25 of "I understand the large hearts . . ."?

6. **Analyze** Think of Whitman's topics and the ideas he expresses in his poetry. Why is free verse the best vehicle for his poetry? Explain.

7. **Cite Evidence** In his preface to *Leaves of Grass*, Whitman describes the American poet: "His spirit responds to his country's spirit . . . he incarnates its geography and natural life . . . For such the expression of the American poet is to be transcendant and new . . . He is the equalizer of his age and land . . ." How well does Whitman live up to his own description? Bring in specific examples from "Song of Myself" to support your ideas.

PERFORMANCE TASK

Speaking Activity: Oral Defense Whitman has been accused of being an "egotist," or overly focused on himself, by some readers of his poetry. Use your reading of the selections from "Song of Myself" to defend him against this charge.

- Prepare speaking notes in which you quote liberally from "Song of Myself" in support of your claim.

- Rehearse your speech in small groups. Have classmates share feedback on both speaking style and content.

- Include opposing claims and counterarguments.

- Present your defense to the class. Have class members evaluate the effectiveness of your argument.

Language and Style: Parallel Structure

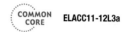 COMMON CORE ELACC11-12L3a

Parallel structure is a very important element in Whitman's poetry. Parallelism—another name for this type of structure—is the use of similar grammatical constructions to express ideas that are closely connected. Whitman uses this technique frequently in his free verse to create a distinct rhythm. Parallel structure can also add emotion to a text through repetition or can emphasize phrases or ideas that are important to an author.

Read these lines from "I celebrate myself and sing myself":

I loaf and invite my soul,
I lean and loaf at my ease observing a spear of summer grass.

Notice that each line begins with the pronoun "I" and two verbs connected by the conjunction "and." In saying these lines aloud, the reader has to linger over the first four words in each line, reinforcing with this leisurely rhythm the meaning of the words themselves. Whitman could have avoided the use of parallel structure, writing the lines this way:

I loaf and invite my soul,
Observing a spear of summer grass at my ease, leaning and loafing.

The removal of parallel structure changes the rhythm. Instead of the lines sounding like someone lazily reflecting on his or her actions, smoothly moving from the first to the second line, the rhythm is forced and less like natural speech.

This chart identifies the elements of sentences that may be used in a parallel construction:

Parallel Structure	
Elements	**Example**
words	He liked Whitman's poetry but not Melville's novels.
phrases	The speaker felt at one with nature and with himself.
clauses	I went to the library to study; I went for the quiet setting.

Practice and Apply Each of these sentences is an example of faulty parallel structure. Rewrite the sentences in a way that correctly uses parallel structure.

1. The speaker in the poem describes himself as being untamed, unable to be translated, and not very civilized.

2. With one hand she gives a gift and then she is taking one away with both hands.

3. I expect that you will finish your paper on Whitman soon and to enjoy reading it.

4. The content is revolutionary; the form has many eccentric features.

Background *The experiences of* **Kesaya E. Noda's** *family reflect those of many Japanese immigrants to the United States in the 20th century. After Japan attacked Pearl Harbor in 1941, over 110,000 Japanese residents in America were relocated to isolated internment camps for the duration of World War II. About 60 percent of them were American-born citizens. Noda's parents married after the war and moved to New Hampshire in 1957 for her father's teaching job at Dartmouth Medical School.*

Growing Up Asian in America

Essay by Kesaya E. Noda

AS YOU READ Look for clues that reveal Noda's feelings about her family. Write down any questions that you generate during reading.

Sometimes when I was growing up, my identity seemed to hurtle toward me and paste itself right to my face. I felt that way, encountering the stereotypes of my race perpetuated by non-Japanese people (primarily white) who may or may not have had contact with other Japanese in America. "You don't like cheese, do you?" someone would ask. "I know your people don't like cheese." Sometimes questions came making allusions to history. That was another aspect of the identity. Events that had happened quite apart from the me who stood silent in that moment connected my face with an

10   incomprehensible past. "Your parents were in California? Were they in those camps during the war?" And sometimes there were phrases or nicknames: "Lotus Blossom." I was sometimes addressed or referred to as racially Japanese, sometimes as Japanese American, and sometimes as an Asian woman. Confusions and distortions **abounded**.

How is one to know and define oneself? From the inside—within a context that is self defined, from a grounding in community and a connection with culture and history that are comfortably accepted? Or from the outside—in terms of messages received from the media

abound
(ə-bound´) *v.* occur or exist in great number.

and people who are often ignorant? Even as an adult I can still
see two sides of my face and past. I can see from the inside out, in
freedom. And I can see from the outside in, driven by the old voices of
childhood and lost in anger and fear.

I am racially Japanese

A voice from my childhood says: "You are other. You are less than. You
are unalterably alien." This voice has its own history. We have indeed
been seen as other and alien since the early years of our arrival in the
United States. The very first immigrants were welcomed and sought
as laborers to replace the dwindling numbers of Chinese, whose influx
had been cut off by the Chinese Exclusion Act of 1882.[1] The Japanese
fell natural heir to the same anti-Asian prejudice that had arisen
against the Chinese. As soon as they began striking for better wages,
they were no longer welcomed.

I can see myself today as a person historically defined by law
and custom as being forever alien. Being neither "free white," nor
"African," our people in California were deemed "aliens, ineligible for
citizenship," no matter how long they intended to stay here. Aliens
ineligible for citizenship were prohibited from owning, buying, or
leasing land. They did not and could not belong here. The voice in
me remembers that I am always a *Japanese* American in the eyes of
many. A third-generation German American is an American. A third-
generation Japanese American is a Japanese American. Being Japanese
means being a danger to the country during the war and knowing how
to use chopsticks. I wear this history on my face.

I move to the other side. I see a different light and claim a different
context. My race is a line that stretches across ocean and time to link
me to the shrine where my grandmother was raised. Two high, white
banners lift in the wind at the top of the stone steps leading to the
shrine. It is time for the summer festival. Black characters are written
against the sky as boldly as the clouds, as lightly as kites, as sharply as
the big black crows I used to see above the fields in New Hampshire.
At festival time there is liquor and rood, ritual, discipline, and
abandonment. There is music and drunkenness and **invocation**. There
is hope. Another season has come. Another season has gone.

I am racially Japanese. I have a certain claim to this crazy place
where the prayers intoned by a neighboring Shinto priest (standing
in for my grandmother's nephew who is sick) are drowned out by the
rehearsals for the pop singing contest in which most of the villagers
will compete later that night. The village elders, the priest, and I stand
respectfully upon the immaculate, shining wooden floor of the outer

invocation
(ĭn´və-kā´shən) *n.*
prayer or incantation.

---

[1] **Chinese Exclusion Act of 1882:** a federal law that prevented Chinese people
from immigrating to the United States and prevented Chinese residents in the
U.S. from becoming citizens.

shrine, bowing our heads before the hidden powers. During the patchy
60   intervals when I can hear him, I notice the priest has a stutter. His
voice flutters up to my ears only occasionally because two men and
a woman are singing gustily into a microphone in the compound,
testing the sound system. A prerecorded tape of guitars, samisens,[2]
and drums accompanies them. Rock music and Shinto prayers. That
night, to loud applause and cheers, a young man is given the award
for the most *netsuretsu*—passionate, burning—rendition of a song.
We roar our approval of the reward. Never mind that his voice had
wandered and slid, now slightly above, now slightly below the given
line of the melody. Netsuretsu. Netsuretsu.
70   In the morning, my grandmother's sister kneels at the foot of
the stone stairs to offer her morning prayers. She is too crippled to
climb the stairs, so each morning she kneels here upon the path. She
shuts her eyes for a few seconds, her motions as matter of fact as when
she washes rice. I linger longer than she does, so reluctant to leave,
savoring the connection I feel with my grandmother in America, the
past, and the power that lives and shines in the morning sun.
     Our family has served this shrine for generations. The family's
need to protect this claim to identity and place outweighs any
individual claim to any individual hope. I am Japanese.

---

[2] **samisens** (săm´ĭ-sĕns´): Japanese stringed instruments.

I am a Japanese American

80 "Weak." I hear the voice from my childhood years. "Passive," I hear. Our parents and grandparents were the ones who were put into those camps. They went without resistance; they offered cooperation as proof of loyalty to America. "Victim," I hear. And, "Silent."

Our parents are painted as hard workers who were socially uncomfortable and had difficulty expressing even the smallest opinion. Clean, quiet, motivated, and determined to match the American way; that is us, and that is the story of our time here.

"Why did you go into those camps," I raged at my parents, frightened by my own inner silence and **timidity**. "Why didn't you 90 do anything to resist? Why didn't you name it the injustice it was?" Couldn't our parents even think? Couldn't they? Why were we so passive?

I shift my vision and my stance. I am in California. My uncle is in the midst of the sweet potato harvest. He is pressed, trying to get the harvesting crews onto the field as quickly as possible, worried about the flow of equipment and people. His big pickup is pulled off to the side, motor running, door ajar. I see two tractors in the yard in front of an old shed; the flat bed harvesting platform on which the workers will stand has already been brought over from the other field. It's early 100 morning. The workers stand loosely grouped and at ease, but my uncle looks as harried and tense as a police officer trying to unsnarl a New York City traffic jam. Driving toward the shed, I pull my car off the road to make way for an approaching tractor. The front wheels of the car sink luxuriously into the soft, white sand by the roadside and the car slides to a dreamy halt, tail still on the road. I try to move forward. I try to move back. The front bites contentedly into the sand, the back lifts itself at a jaunty[3] angle. My uncle sees me and storms down the road, running. He is shouting before he is even near me.

"What's the matter with you," he screams. "What the hell are 110 you doing?" In his frenzy, he grabs his hat off his head and slashes it through the air across his knee. He is beside himself. "Don't you know how to drive in sand? What's the matter with you? You've blocked the whole roadway. How am I supposed to get my tractors out of here? Can't you use your head? You've cut off the whole roadway, and we've got to get out of here."

I stand on the road before him helplessly thinking, "No, I don't know how to drive in sand. I've never driven in sand."

"I'm sorry, uncle," I say, burying a smile beneath a look of sincere apology. I notice my deep amusement and my affection for him with 120 great curiosity. I am usually devastated by anger. Not this time.

During the several years that follow I learn about the people and the place, and much more about what has happened in this California

timidity
(tĭm-ĭd´ĭ-tē) *n.*
showing a lack
of courage or
confidence.

---

[3] **jaunty:** stylishly self-confident.

village where my parents grew up. The issei,[4] our grandparents, made this settlement in the desert. Their first crops were eaten by rabbits and ravaged by insects. The land was so barren that men walking from house to house sometimes got lost. Women came here too. They bore children in 114 degree heat, then carried the babies with them into the fields to nurse when they reached the end of each row of grapes or other truck farm crops.

"Why didn't you do anything to resist? Why didn't you name it the injustice it was?"

130   I had had no idea what it meant to buy this kind of land and make it grow green. Or how, when the war came, there was no space at all for the **subtlety** of being who we were—Japanese Americans. Either/ or was the way. I hadn't understood that people were literally afraid for their lives then, that their money had been frozen in banks; that there was a five-mile travel limit; that when the early evening curfew came and they were inside their houses, some of them watched helplessly as people they knew went into their barns to steal their belongings. The police were patrolling the road, interested only in violators of curfew. There was no help for them in the face of thievery. I had not been able
140   to imagine before what it must have felt like to be an American—to know absolutely that one is an American—and yet to have almost everyone else deny it. Not only deny it, but challenge that identity with machine guns and troops of white American soldiers. In those circumstances it was difficult to say, "I'm a Japanese American." "American" had to do.

   But now I can say that I am a Japanese American. It means I have a place here in this country, too. I have a place here on the East Coast, where our neighbor is so much a part of our family that my mother never passes her house at night without glancing at the lights to see
150   if she is home and safe; where my parents have hauled hundreds of pounds of rocks from fields and arduously planted Christmas trees

subtlety
(sŭt´l-tē) *n.* nuance; fine detail.

---

[4] **issei:** first-generation immigrants from Japan.

and blueberries, lilacs, asparagus, and crab apples; where my father still dreams of angling a stream to a new bed so that he can dig a pond in the field and fill it with water and fish. "The neighbors already came for their Christmas tree?" he asks in December. "Did they like it? Did they like it?"

I have a place on the West Coast where my relatives still farm, where I heard the stories of feuds and backbiting, and where I saw that people survived and flourished because fundamentally they trusted and relied upon one another. A death in the family is not just a death in a family; it is a death in the community. I saw people help each other with money, materials, labor, attention, and time. I saw men gather once a year, without fail, to clean the grounds of a ninety-year-old woman who had helped the community before, during, and after the war. I saw her remembering them with birthday cards sent to each of their children.

I come from a people with a long memory and a distinctive grace. We live our thanks. And we are Americans. Japanese Americans.

I am a Japanese American woman

Woman. The last piece of my identity. It has been easier by far for me to know myself in Japan and to see my place in America than it has been to accept my line of connection with my own mother. She was my dark self, a figure in whom I thought I saw all that I feared most in myself. Growing into womanhood and looking for some model of strength, I turned away from her. Of course, I could not find what I sought. I was looking for a black feminist or a white feminist. My mother is neither white nor black.

My mother is a woman who speaks with her life as much as with her tongue. I think of her with her own mother. Grandmother had Parkinson's disease and it had frozen her gait and set her fingers, tongue, and feet jerking and trembling in a terrible dance. My aunts and uncles wanted her to be able to live in her own home. They fed her, bathed her, dressed her, awoke at midnight to take her for one last trip to the bathroom. My aunts (her daughters-in-law) did most of the care, but my mother went from New Hampshire to California each summer to spend a month living with grandmother, because she wanted to and because she wanted to give my aunts at least a small rest. During those hot summer days, mother lay on the couch watching the television or reading, cooking foods that grandmother liked, and speaking little. Grandmother thrived under her care.

The time finally came when it was too dangerous for grandmother to live alone. My relatives kept finding her on the floor beside her bed when they went to wake her in the mornings. My mother flew to California to help clean the house and make arrangements for grandmother to enter a local nursing home. On her last day at home, while grandmother was sitting in her big, overstuffed armchair, hair combed and wearing a green summer dress, my mother went to her and knelt at her feet. "Here, Mamma," she said. "I've polished your shoes." She lifted grandmother's legs and helped her into the shiny black shoes. My grandmother looked down and smiled slightly. She left her house walking, supported by her children, carrying her pocket book, and wearing her polished black shoes. "Look, Mamma," my mom had said, kneeling. "I've polished your shoes."

Just the other day, my mother came to Boston to visit. She had recently lost a lot of weight and was pleased with her new shape and her feeling of good health. "Look at me, Kes," she exclaimed, turning toward me, front and back, as naked as the day she was born. . . . Her hips were small. I was not a large baby, but there was so little room for me in her that when she was carrying me she could not even begin to bend over toward the floor. She hated it, she said.

"Don't I look good? Don't you think I look good?"

I looked at my mother, smiling and as happy as she, thinking of all the times I have seen her naked. I have seen both my parents naked throughout my life, as they have seen me. From childhood through adulthood we've had our naked moments, sharing baths, idle conversations picked up as we moved between showers and closets, hurried moments at the beginning of days, quiet moments at the end of days.

I know this to be Japanese, this ease with the physical, and it makes me think of an old, Japanese folk song. A young nursemaid, a fifteen-year-old girl, is singing a lullaby to a baby who is strapped to her back. The nursemaid has been sent as a servant to a place far from her own home. "We're the beggars," she says, "and they are the nice people. Nice people wear fine sashes. Nice clothes."

> If I should drop dead,
> bury me by the roadside!
> I'll give a flower
> to everyone who passes.

> What kind of flower?
> The cam-cam-camellia [tsun-tsun-tsubaki]
> watered by Heaven:
> alms water.

The nursemaid is the intersection of heaven and earth, the intersection of the human, the natural world, the body, and the soul. In this song, with clear eyes, she looks steadily at life, which is sometimes so very terrible and sad. I think of her while looking at my mother, who is standing on the red and purple carpet before me, laughing, without any clothes.

I am my mother's daughter. And I am myself.

I am a Japanese American woman.

COLLABORATIVE DISCUSSION Why does Noda have mixed feelings about her family? Discuss this question with a partner, citing evidence from the essay that shows both positive and negative feelings.

Analyze Ideas and Events: Classification

COMMON CORE   ELACC11-12RI3

When a writer presents a complex set of ideas, he or she needs to decide on a clear organizational pattern that will allow readers to trace the development and interaction of those ideas over the course of the text. In her essay, Kesaya Noda uses a pattern of organization called **classification,** in which ideas and information are grouped together based on the characteristics they share. Noda suggests the pattern of organization in her opening paragraph and then explicitly breaks the essay into three sections based on the characteristics that make up her complex identity.

As you reread the essay, look for the types of ideas and events Noda presents in each section, and see how each detail develops the description of her identity.

Determine Author's Purpose

COMMON CORE   ELACC11-12RI6

An author's **purpose** is his or her reason for writing. Usually readers need to infer, or make logical assumptions about, the author's purpose from the content and style of the writing. Use these clues to help you determine Noda's purpose in writing her essay.

Content	Style
Content is what a writer says. Noda includes information from her own experience and from the broader experience of Japanese immigrants. Notice what she says and what others say about her, her family, or Japanese immigrants in general.	Style refers to how a writer expresses the content. One important part of style is **tone,** a writer's attitude toward the subject. Noda's tone shifts in each section from the way she begins to the way she ends. This shift in tone is often signaled by a shift in perspective: "A voice from my childhood says...."" I move to the other side. I see a different light...."

Analyzing the Text

 COMMON CORE ELACC11-12RI1,
ELACC11-12RI3,
ELACC11-12RI6,
ELACC11-12SL1a,
ELACC11-12SL1c

Cite Text Evidence   Support your responses with evidence from the selection.

1. **Interpret** To which part of her identity is Noda referring when she says that "my identity seemed to hurtle toward me and paste itself right to my face" (lines 1–2)?

2. **Analyze** A key part of an author's **style** is word choice. How do the different meanings of the word *alien* used in the third and fourth paragraphs (lines 23–42) contribute to the power of Noda's essay?

3. **Analyze** Noda ends the second part of her essay—I Am Racially Japanese—with a brief paragraph. How does this statement summarize her argument in this section?

4. **Compare** Noda describes a scene (lines 88–92) in which she confronts her parents for being too passive in response to the Japanese internment. How does the section that immediately follows this scene respond to Noda's complaints and show that her view has evolved? Why was Noda not "devastated" by her uncle's anger?

5. **Analyze** Why is Noda's identity as a Japanese American woman the most difficult part of herself to accept?

6. **Interpret** What does Noda mean when she says: "My mother is neither white nor black" (lines 175–176)? How does this statement connect to Noda's larger point about coming to undertand her parents better?

7. **Cite Evidence** How does Noda's identity as a Japanese American woman include the ideas of being racially Japanese and being Japanese American?

8. **Infer** Why did Noda quote from a Japanese folk song (lines 224–231) when she wrote about her mother?

9. **Draw Conclusions** How might Noda have had one purpose in writing this essay for herself and another in writing for a broader audience?

PERFORMANCE TASK

Speaking Activity: Discussion Noda describes different ways in which society affects her individual identity. Explore this topic in a group discussion.

- Reread the essay and look for examples of the role of community and society in shaping the three aspects of Noda's personal identity.

- Prepare notes on your reading to be used in a small group discussion.

- Refer to your evidence to present your ideas. Allow everyone in the group to have a chance to participate in the exchange of ideas.

- Pose and respond to questions to clarify or challenge ideas and conclusions.

Critical Vocabulary

abounded   **invocation**   **timidity**   **subtlety**

Practice and Apply Answer each question based on your own experiences to show that you understand the meaning of each Critical Vocabulary word.

1. Describe a time when something good or bad **abounded** in your life.

2. When and where might you hear an **invocation**?

3. When did you show **timidity**? Why?

4. When did you need to use **subtlety**? Why?

Vocabulary Strategy: Patterns of Word Change

The Critical Vocabulary word *invocation* is formed by adding the noun suffix *-tion* to the verb *invoke*. Note that the *-ke* at the end of *invoke* changes to *-ca* when the suffix *-tion* is added to the word. The chart shows other words that change their spelling when suffixes that form nouns or adjectives are added. Once you become familiar with these patterns of word change, you can use them to more easily recognize unfamilar words by connecting them to more common root words.

Verb form	Noun: *–tion, –sion* "state of being"	Adjective: *–able* "capable of being"
invoke	invocation	
conceive	conception	conceivable
certify	certification	certifiable
concede	concession	

Practice and Apply For each row of the chart, identify one new word that would follow the same spelling pattern. With each word you choose, follow these steps:

1. Identify the verb form and its meaning.

2. Use suffixes to change each verb to a noun and an adjective. Write a definition for each new word. Note that not all verbs can be turned into adjectives with the suffix *–able*. Consult a dictionary if you are unsure.

3. Write a sentence using one form of each word you chose.

Language and Style: Varying Sentence Structure

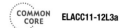 ELACC11-12L3a

An essential part of a writer's style is **syntax,** or how the writer arranges words to construct phrases, clauses, and sentences. Noda uses great variety in sentence structure and length to create an engaging rhythm in her prose. Part of her syntax includes **parallelism,** or the use of similar grammatical structures to express ideas of similar meaning or importance. She sometimes uses sentence fragments to add emphasis or to create an informal, conversational style. Varying her syntax allows Noda to create a unique voice in her writing. Readers can imagine that they are listening to her speak. The chart shows examples from the essay.

Varying Syntax for Effect	
Sentence Structure	**Example**
Simple	Confusions and distortions abounded. (line 14)
Compound	They went without resistance; they offered cooperation as proof of loyalty to America. (lines 82–83)
Complex	His voice flutters up to my ears only occasionally because two men and a woman are singing gustily into a microphone in the compound, testing the sound system. (lines 60–63)
Compound complex	I hadn't understood that people were literally afraid for their lives then, that their money had been frozen in banks; that there was a five-mile travel limit; that when the early evening curfew came and they were inside their houses, some of them watched helplessly as people they knew went into their barns to steal their belongings. (lines 133–137)
Sentence fragment	Woman. The last piece of my identity. (line 169)

Practice and Apply Write a brief essay on the topic of society's effect on Noda's identity using the notes you prepared for the Performance Task discussion. Vary your syntax to create a distinctive voice and an engaging rhythm. Share your essay with a partner and discuss how each of you used varied syntax in your writing.

Poems

by Emily Dickinson

The Soul selects her own Society

Because I could not stop for Death

Much Madness is divinest Sense

Tell all the truth but tell it slant

Emily Dickinson (1830–1886) *lived and died in Amherst, Massachusetts, seldom venturing far from her home. Dickinson's father, Edward, encouraged her love of reading and writing, and it was through reading and writing that Dickinson reached out to the world. As a young adult, she entertained friends and socialized. As a poet, her most productive years were 1858–1865, during some of the most turbulent years in American history. But as she grew older, she became more reclusive and earned a reputation as an eccentric. She died at the age of 55 and was buried in Amherst.*

After her death, her sister discovered nearly 1,800 poems Dickinson had written. Family and friends recognized Dickinson's talent and sought to publish her poetry. In 1890, the first volume of poems was published to great public and critical acclaim. Over time, her remaining poems were published. Emily Dickinson is now considered one of America's greatest poets.

AS YOU READ Look for evidence of Dickinson's perspectives about life in the lines of her poems. Write down any questions that you generate during reading.

The Soul selects her own Society

The Soul selects her own Society—
Then—shuts the Door—
To her divine Majority—
Present no more—

5 Unmoved—she notes the Chariots—pausing—
At her low Gate—
Unmoved—an Emperor be kneeling
Upon her Mat—

I've known her—from an ample nation—
10 Choose One—
Then—close the Valves of her attention—
Like Stone—

Analyzing the Text

COMMON CORE ELACC11-12RL4, ELACC11-12L3, ELACC11-12L5a

Cite Text Evidence   Support your responses with evidence.

1. **Analyze** The poet uses the phrase "shuts the door" in the poem. What does she mean by it? How does it affect the tone of the poem?

2. **Interpret** In the second stanza, the narrator repeats the word *unmoved*. Who is unmoved? What is the effect of repeating the word?

Because I could not stop for Death

Because I could not stop for Death—
He kindly stopped for me—
The Carriage held but just Ourselves—
And Immortality.

5 We slowly drove—He knew no haste
And I had put away
My labor and my leisure too,
For His Civility—

We passed the School, where Children strove
10 At Recess—in the Ring—
We passed the Fields of Gazing Grain—
We passed the Setting Sun—

Or rather—He passed Us—
The Dews drew quivering and chill—
15 For only Gossamer,¹ my Gown—
My Tippet—only Tulle²—

We paused before a House that seemed
A Swelling of the Ground—
The Roof was scarcely visible—
20 The Cornice³—in the Ground—

Since then—'tis Centuries—and yet
Feels shorter than the Day
I first surmised the Horses' Heads
Were toward Eternity—

---

¹ **Gossamer:** thin, soft material.
² **Tippet . . . Tulle:** shawl made of fine netting.
³ **Cornice:** molding at the top of a building.

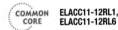

COMMON CORE ELACC11-12RL1, ELACC11-12RL6

Analyzing the Text

Cite Text Evidence Support your responses with evidence.

1. **Interpret** In the third stanza, Death, **personified** as a suitor, takes the speaker past a school and fields. What are these places a reminder of?

2. **Analyze** What is the speaker's attitude about the ride in the first three stanzas? How does the speaker's perception of what is happening to her change in the fourth stanza?

Much Madness is divinest Sense

Much Madness is divinest Sense—
To a discerning Eye—
Much Sense—the starkest Madness—
'Tis the Majority
5 In this, as All, prevail—
Assent—and you are sane—
Demur—you're straightway dangerous—
And handled with a Chain—

Analyzing the Text

COMMON CORE

ELACC11-12RL4,
ELACC11-12L4a,
ELACC11-12L5a

Cite Text Evidence   Support your responses with evidence.

1. **Analyze** According to the speaker in this poem, what are the main criteria for "madness" and "sense"?

2. **Summarize** Paraphrase the last three lines of the poem. How does the poet's diction add power to the poem's closing section?

Tell all the truth but tell it slant

Tell all the truth but tell it slant—
Success in Circuit[1] lies
Too bright for our infirm Delight
The Truth's superb surprise
5   As Lightning to the Children eased
With explanation kind
The Truth must dazzle gradually
Or every man be blind—

_____
[1] **Circuit:** indirect path.

COMMON
CORE
ELACC11-12RL1,
ELACC11-12RL4,
ELACC11-12L3,
ELACC11-12L4a

Analyzing the Text

Cite Text Evidence   Support your responses with evidence.

1. **Interpret** What does the narrator mean by "tell it slant"?

2. **Analyze** To what does the narrator compare circling the truth? Does this comparison work? Explain.

COLLABORATIVE DISCUSSION With a partner, discuss the themes that Dickinson explores in her poetry and how they express her feelings about life. Cite specific textual evidence to support your ideas.

Analyze Language

ELACC11-12RL4,
ELACC11-12L4a,
ELACC11-12L5a

Words are the building blocks of literature. Consequently, writers choose their words carefully, recognizing that specific word choices affect meaning and tone in a literary work. You can analyze the effect of specific word choices in Dickinson's poetry by looking at the following elements.

Denotation and Connotation	Figurative Language	Multiple Meaning Words
Denotation refers to the dictionary definition of a word. A word's **connotation,** however, refers to the ideas and feelings that a word suggests beyond its primary meaning. In her short poems, Dickinson often uses words with strong connotations to shape and expand the themes of her poems.	**Metaphors** are a kind of figurative language in which one thing is said to be another for the sake of a comparison. For example, in "Because I could not stop for Death," Dickinson uses an **extended metaphor**—a metaphor developed over a number of lines or with several examples—to express her ideas about life and death.	**Multiple meaning words** are words that have more than one meaning. Though the primary meaning may be apparent, the influence of a secondary meaning can change the tone. A good example is in the poem "Much madness is divinest sense." In the first line, *divinest* can mean "extremely good" as well as "relating to God."

Determine Themes

ELACC11-12RL2

The **theme** of a poem is its underlying message—the point the poet wants to make about life. In a complex work, poets may even develop two or more themes in a single poem, themes that interact and build on one another to produce a more sophisticated message. Most often, a reader has to infer the theme of a poem after considerable thought. Theme is different from subject. A poem's subject might be "death" or "love," but theme is the statement a poet makes about that subject.

In her nearly 1,800 poems, Emily Dickinson dealt with an abundance of themes, many of which she returned to again and again. Some of these themes center on death, madness or insanity, truth as the poet sees it, the beauty of nature, friendship and love, and God and religion. Readers can determine the theme of a poem by making inferences about the images that the poet creates with words, the speaker's point of view, and the tone that the poet establishes through a careful choice of details.

Analyzing the Text

 COMMON CORE · ELACC11–12RL1, ELACC11–12RL2, ELACC11–12RL4, ELACC11–12RL6, ELACC11–12RL9, ELACC11–12L3, ELACC11–12L5a, ELACC11–12W1, ELACC11–12W4

Cite Text Evidence   Support your responses with evidence from the selections.

1. **Analyze** Dickinson uses dashes freely in her poems. How do the dashes affect the way you read the poem? How do they help clarify the meaning of words or phrases?

2. **Analyze** Sometimes understanding a point of view requires distinguishing what is directly stated in a text from what is really meant. Think about the kindly and courtly behavior of Death in "Because I could not stop for Death." How is Death's character ironic?

3. **Compare** The speaker in "Because I could not stop for Death" is somewhat passive. Think about the speaker in "The Soul selects her own Society." How are the two different?

4. **Infer** In both "Much Madness is divinest Sense" and "The Soul selects her own Society," the poet speaks of the Majority. What does the Majority refer to? What does the poet think of the Majority?

5. **Evaluate** What do the connotations of the words *assent* and *demur* in "Much Madness is divinest Sense" indicate about the individual?

6. **Interpret** A **paradox** is a statement that seems to contradict itself but may nevertheless suggest an important truth. Identify the paradoxes in "Tell all the truth but tell it slant" and "Much Madness is divinest Sense." What truth does each paradox convey?

7. **Analyze** In "The Soul selects her own Society," the poet uses the term *soul* to refer to an individual. Why does she use this term? What themes does this poem and "Because I could not stop for Death" reflect?

8. **Identify Patterns** In "Because I could not stop for Death," what metaphors does Dickinson use to express her ideas and views about death?

PERFORMANCE TASK

Writing Activity: Analysis Emily Dickinson chose each word carefully. But it is up to the reader to determine the impact of specific word choices on meaning and tone. Choose one of Dickinson's poems and write a two-paragraph analysis of it.

1. In the first paragraph, explain, line by line, what the poem means. Include opposing claims and counterarguments.

2. In the second paragraph, explain how specific words and phrases helped you determine the meaning and tone of the poem.

In your writing, include evidence from the text and use the conventions of standard English.

Vocabulary Strategy: Affixes

Affixes are word parts that are added to the beginning or the end of a base word or root. A **prefix** is added to the beginning of a base word or root. A prefix such as *mis–*, *over–*, and *un–* always changes the denotation, or meaning of the base word. A **suffix** is added to the end of a base word or root. **Inflectional suffixes,** like *–ed* and *–ing*, usually just change the tense, the person, or the number of a word (generally a verb). **Derivational suffixes,** like those listed in the chart, change the meaning of a root or base word.

Suffixes	Meanings	Examples
–ity	state of; condition of	immortality
–ous	full of	malicious
–ness	quality or state of being	madness
–tion	condition or state of	attention

You can use derivational suffixes to help you decipher the meaning of unfamiliar words. By identifying the suffix and the root word, you can determine how the suffix changes the word's meaning. For example, in "Because I could not stop for Death," it might be difficult to determine the meaning of *civility* just by relying on the context clues in the poem. However, you can infer the word's meaning by identifying the root word, *civil*, and the suffix, *–ity*, as demonstrated.

Root Word, Meaning	Suffix, Meaning	Full Word, Meaning
civil: polite	*–ity:* state of	*Civility:* polite behavior

Practice and Apply Use the chart as a model to create your own suffix-analysis chart for the following words from Dickinson's poems.

1. eternity

2. explanation

3. majority

4. dangerous

Henry David Thoreau (1817–1862) *of Concord, Massachusetts, was a transcendentalist like his friend and mentor Ralph Waldo Emerson. After graduating from Harvard College and teaching school for a few years, Thoreau decided to become a nature poet. In 1845 he began his two-year experiment living in a cabin that he built in the woods near Walden Pond on property owned by Emerson.* Walden *(1854) is a collection of 18 essays based on his experiences. Thoreau's most famous essay, "Civil Disobedience" (1849), defends the right of an individual to follow his conscience rather than obey unjust laws.*

from Walden

Essay by Henry David Thoreau

AS YOU READ Note the observations Thoreau makes about modern life that still seem relevant today.

from Where I Lived, and What I Lived For

When first I took up my abode in the woods, that is, began to spend my nights as well as days there, which, by accident, was on Independence day, or the fourth of July, 1845, my house was not finished for winter, but was merely a defense against the rain, without plastering or chimney, the walls being of rough weather-stained boards, with wide chinks, which made it cool at night. The upright white hewn studs and freshly planed door and window casings gave it a clean and airy look, especially in the morning, when its timbers were saturated with dew, so that I fancied that by noon some sweet gum would exude from them. . . .

I was seated by the shore of a small pond, about a mile and a half south of the village of Concord and somewhat higher than it, in the midst of an extensive wood between that town and Lincoln, and about two miles south of that our only field known to fame, Concord Battle Ground; but I was so low in the woods that the opposite shore, half a mile off, like the rest, covered with wood, was my most distant horizon. For the first week, whenever I looked out on the pond it

impressed me like a tarn[1] high up on the side of a mountain, its
bottom far above the surface of other lakes, and, as the sun arose, I
20 saw it throwing off its nightly clothing of mist, and here and there, by
degrees, its soft ripples or its smooth reflecting surface was revealed,
while the mists, like ghosts, were stealthily withdrawing in every
direction into the woods, as at the breaking up of some nocturnal
conventicle.[2] The very dew seemed to hang upon the trees later into
the day than usual, as on the sides of mountains. . . .

I went to the woods because I wished to live deliberately, to front
only the essential facts of life, and see if I could not learn what it had
to teach, and not, when I came to die, discover that I had not lived.
I did not wish to live what was not life, living is so dear; nor did I
30 wish to practice resignation, unless it was quite necessary. I wanted
to live deep and suck out all the marrow of life, to live so sturdily
and Spartan-like[3] as to put to rout all that was not life, to cut a broad
swath and shave close, to drive life into a corner, and reduce it to its
lowest terms, and, if it proved to be mean, why then to get the whole
and genuine meanness of it, and publish its meanness to the world; or
if it were sublime, to know it by experience, and be able to give a true
account of it in my next excursion. For most men, it appears to me, are
in a strange uncertainty about it, whether it is of the devil or of God,
and have *somewhat hastily* concluded that it is the chief end of man
40 here to "glorify God and enjoy him forever."

Still we live meanly, like ants; though the fable tells us that we
were long ago changed into men; like pygmies we fight with cranes; it
is error upon error, and clout upon clout, and our best virtue has for its
occasion a superfluous and evitable[4] wretchedness. Our life is frittered
away by detail. An honest man has hardly need to count more than his
ten fingers, or in extreme cases he may add his ten toes, and lump the
rest. Simplicity, simplicity, simplicity! I say, let your affairs be as two or
three, and not a hundred or a thousand; instead of a million count half
a dozen, and keep your accounts on your thumbnail. In the midst of
50 this chopping sea of civilized life, such are the clouds and storms and
quicksands and thousand-and-one items to be allowed for, that a man
has to live, if he would not founder and go to the bottom and not make
his port at all, by dead reckoning, and he must be a great calculator
indeed who succeeds. Simplify, simplify. Instead of three meals a day,
if it be necessary eat but one; instead of a hundred dishes, five; and
reduce other things in proportion. . . .

Why should we live with such hurry and waste of life? We are
determined to be starved before we are hungry. Men say that a stitch
in time saves nine, and so they take a thousand stitches today to save

---

[1] **tarn:** a small mountain lake or pool.

[2] **conventicle:** a secret or unlawful religious meeting.

[3] **Spartan-like:** in a simple and disciplined way, like the inhabitants of the
ancient city-state of Sparta.

[4] **superfluous and evitable:** unnecessary and avoidable.

60 nine to-morrow. As for *work*, we haven't any of any consequence. We have the Saint Vitus' dance,[5] and cannot possibly keep our heads still. If I should only give a few pulls at the parish bell-rope, as for a fire, that is, without setting the bell, there is hardly a man on his farm in the outskirts of Concord, notwithstanding that press of engagements which was his excuse so many times this morning, nor a boy, nor a woman, I might almost say, but would forsake all and follow that sound, not mainly to save property from the flames, but, if we will confess the truth, much more to see it burn, since burn it must, and we, be it known, did not set it on fire,—or to see it put out, and have a

70 hand in it, if that is done as handsomely; yes, even if it were the parish church itself. Hardly a man takes a half hour's nap after dinner, but when he wakes he holds up his head and asks, "What's the news?" as if the rest of mankind had stood his sentinels. Some give directions to be waked every half hour, doubtless for no other purpose; and then, to pay for it, they tell what they have dreamed. After a night's sleep the news is as indispensable as the breakfast. "Pray tell me any thing new that has happened to a man any where on this globe,"—and he reads it over his coffee and rolls, that a man has had his eyes gouged out this morning on the Wachito River; never dreaming the while that he lives

80 in the dark **unfathomed** mammoth cave of this world, and has but the rudiment of an eye himself.

unfathomed
(ŭn-făth´əmd) *adj.*
located at the deepest place.

---

[5] **Saint Vitus' dance:** a disorder of the nervous system, characterized by rapid, jerky, involuntary movements.

For my part, I could easily do without the post-office. I think that there are very few important communications made through it. To speak critically, I never received more than one or two letters in my life—I wrote this some years ago—that were worth the postage. The penny-post is, commonly, an institution through which you seriously offer a man that penny for his thoughts which is so often safely offered in jest. And I am sure that I never read any memorable news in a newspaper. If we read of one man robbed, or murdered, or killed by accident, or one house burned, or one vessel wrecked, or one steamboat blown up, or one cow run over on the Western Railroad, or one mad dog killed, or one lot of grasshoppers in the winter,—we never need read of another. One is enough. . . .

66 I have always been regretting that I was not as wise as the day I was born. 99

Let us spend one day as deliberately as Nature, and not be thrown off the track by every nutshell and mosquito's wing that falls on the rails. Let us rise early and fast, or break fast, gently and without **perturbation**; let company come and let company go, let the bells ring and the children cry,— determined to make a day of it. . . .

Time is but the stream I go a-fishing in. I drink at it; but while I drink I see the sandy bottom and detect how shallow it is. Its thin current slides away, but eternity remains. I would drink deeper; fish in the sky, whose bottom is pebbly with stars. I cannot count one. I know not the first letter of the alphabet. I have always been regretting that I was not as wise as the day I was born. The intellect is a cleaver; it discerns and rifts its way into the secret of things. I do not wish to be any more busy with my hands than is necessary. My head is hands and feet. I feel all my best faculties concentrated in it. My instinct tells me that my head is an organ for burrowing, as some creatures use their snout and fore-paws, and with it I would mine and burrow my way through these hills. I think that the richest vein is somewhere hereabouts; so by the divining rod and thin rising vapors I judge; and here I will begin to mine.

perturbation
(pûr′tər-bā′shən) *n.*
disturbance or agitation.

from **Solitude**

This is a delicious evening, when the whole body is one sense, and imbibes delight through every pore. I go and come with a strange liberty in Nature, a part of herself. As I walk along the stony shore of the pond in my shirt sleeves, though it is cool as well as cloudy and windy, and I see nothing special to attract me, all the elements are unusually **congenial** to me. The bullfrogs trump to usher in the night, and the note of the whippoorwill is borne on the rippling wind from
120 over the water. Sympathy with the fluttering alder and poplar leaves almost takes away my breath; yet, like the lake, my serenity is rippled but not ruffled. These small waves raised by the evening wind are as remote from storm as the smooth reflecting surface. Though it is now dark, the wind still blows and roars in the wood, the waves still dash, and some creatures lull the rest with their notes. The repose is never complete. The wildest animals do not repose, but seek their prey now; the fox, and skunk, and rabbit, now roam the fields and woods without fear. They are Nature's watchmen,—links which connect the days of animated life. . . .
130   Men frequently say to me, "I should think you would feel lonesome down there, and want to be nearer to folks, rainy and snowy days and nights especially." I am tempted to reply to such,—This whole earth which we inhabit is but a point in space. How far apart, think you, dwell the two most distant inhabitants of yonder star, the breadth of whose disk cannot be appreciated by our instruments? Why should I feel lonely? Is not our planet in the Milky Way? This which you put seems to me not to be the most important question. What sort of space is that which separates a man from his fellows and makes him solitary? I have found that no exertion of the legs can bring two minds much
140 nearer to one another. . . .

congenial
(kən-jēn′yəl) *adj.*
agreeable; pleasant.

from **The Pond in Winter**

Every winter the liquid and trembling surface of the pond, which was so sensitive to every breath, and reflected every light and shadow, becomes solid to the depth of a foot or a foot and a half, so that it will support the heaviest teams, and perchance the snow covers it to an equal depth, and it is not to be distinguished from any level field. Like the marmots in the surrounding hills, it closes its eye-lids and becomes dormant for three months or more. Standing on the snow-covered plain, as if in a pasture amid the hills, I cut my way first through a foot of snow, and then a foot of ice, and open a window
150 under my feet, where, kneeling to drink, I look down into the quiet parlor of the fishes, pervaded by a softened light as through a window of ground glass, with its bright sanded floor the same as in summer; there a **perennial** waveless serenity reigns as in the amber twilight sky,

perennial
(pə-rĕn′ē-əl) *adv.*
enduring; long-lasting.

corresponding to the cool and even temperament of the inhabitants. Heaven is under our feet as well as over our heads. . . .

from Spring

One attraction in coming to the woods to live was that I should have leisure and opportunity to see the spring come in. The ice in the pond at length begins to be honey-combed, and I can set my heel in it as I walk. Fogs and rains and warmer suns are gradually melting the snow;
160 the days have grown sensibly longer; and I see how I shall get through the winter without adding to my woodpile, for large fires are no longer necessary. I am on the alert for the first signs of spring, to hear the chance note of some arriving bird, or the striped squirrel's chirp, for his stores must be now nearly exhausted, or see the woodchuck venture out of his winter quarters. . . .

The change from storm and winter to serene and mild weather, from dark and sluggish hours to bright and elastic ones, is a memorable crisis which all things proclaim. It is seemingly instantaneous at last. Suddenly an influx of light filled my house,
170 though the evening was at hand, and the clouds of winter still overhung it, and the eaves were dripping with sleety rain. I looked out the window, and lo! where yesterday was cold gray ice there lay the transparent pond already calm and full of hope as in a summer evening, reflecting a summer evening sky in its bosom, though none was visible overhead, as if it had intelligence with some remote horizon. . . .

We can never have enough of nature. We must be refreshed by the sight of inexhaustible vigor, vast and titanic features, the sea-coast with its wrecks, the wilderness with its living and its decaying trees,
180 the thunder-cloud, and the rain which lasts three weeks and produces freshets.[6] We need to witness our own limits transgressed, and some life pasturing freely where we never wander. We are cheered when we observe the vulture feeding on the carrion which disgusts and disheartens us, and deriving health and strength from the repast. There was a dead horse in the hollow by the path to my house, which compelled me sometimes to go out of my way, especially in the night when the air was heavy, but the assurance it gave me of the strong appetite and inviolable health of Nature was my compensation for this. I love to see that Nature is so rife with life that myriads can be
190 afforded to be sacrificed and suffered to prey on one another; that tender organizations can be so serenely squashed out of existence like pulp—tadpoles which herons gobble up, and tortoises and toads run over in the road; and that sometimes it has rained flesh and blood! With the liability to accident, we must see how little account is to be

---

[6] **freshets:** overflowings of a stream caused by heavy rain or melting snow.

made of it. The impression made on a wise man is that of universal innocence. Poison is not poisonous after all, nor are any wounds fatal. Compassion is a very **untenable** ground. It must be expeditious. Its pleadings will not bear to be stereotyped.[7]

untenable
(ŭn-tĕn´ə-bəl) *adj.*
unsustainable,
insupportable.

from Conclusion

I left the woods for as good a reason as I went there. Perhaps it seemed
200 to me that I had several more lives to live, and could not spare any
more time for that one. It is remarkable how easily and insensibly we
fall into a particular route, and make a beaten track for ourselves. I
had not lived there a week before my feet wore a path from my door
to the pond-side; and though it is five or six years since I trod it, it is
still quite distinct. It is true, I fear that others may have fallen into
it, and so helped to keep it open. The surface of the earth is soft and
impressible by the feet of men; and so with the paths which the mind
travels. How worn and dusty, then, must be the highways of the world,
how deep the ruts of tradition and conformity! I did not wish to take a
210 cabin passage, but rather to go before the mast and on the deck of the
world, for there I could best see the moonlight amid the mountains. I
do not wish to go below now.

---

[7] **pleadings . . . stereotyped:** its defense, or reasons for acting in a certain way,
cannot be easily pinned down or understood.

I learned this, at least, by my experiment; that if one advances confidently in the direction of his dreams, and endeavors to live the life which he has imagined, he will meet with a success unexpected in common hours. He will put some things behind, will pass an invisible boundary; new, universal, and more liberal laws will begin to establish themselves around and within him; or the old laws be expanded, and interpreted in his favor in a more liberal sense, and he will live with the license of a higher order of beings. In proportion as he simplifies his life, the laws of the universe will appear less complex, and solitude will not be solitude, nor poverty poverty, nor weakness weakness. If you have built castles in the air, your work need not be lost; that is where they should be. Now put the foundations under them. . . .

Why should we be in such desperate haste to succeed, and in such desperate enterprises? If a man does not keep pace with his companions, perhaps it is because he hears a different drummer. Let him step to the music which he hears, however measured or far away.[8] It is not important that he should mature as soon as an appletree or an oak. Shall he turn his spring into summer? If the condition of things which we were made for is not yet, what were any reality which we can substitute? We will not be shipwrecked on a vain reality. Shall we with pains erect a heaven of blue glass over ourselves, though when it is done we shall be sure to gaze still at the true ethereal heaven far above, as if the former were not? . . .

However mean your life is, meet it and live it; do not shun it and call it hard names. It is not so bad as you are. It looks poorest when you are richest. The fault-finder will find faults even in paradise. Love your life, poor as it is. You may perhaps have some pleasant, thrilling, glorious hours, even in a poorhouse. The setting sun is reflected from the windows of the almshouse as brightly as from the rich man's abode; the snow melts before its door as early in the spring. I do not see but a quiet mind may live as contentedly there, and have as cheering thoughts, as in a palace. The town's poor seem to me often to live the most independent lives of any. May be they are simply great enough to receive without misgiving.[9] Most think that they are above being supported by the town; but it oftener happens that they are not above supporting themselves by dishonest means, which should be more disreputable. Cultivate poverty like a garden herb, like sage. Do not trouble yourself much to get new things, whether clothes or friends. Turn the old; return to them. Things do not change; we change. Sell your clothes and keep your thoughts. God will see that you do not want society. If I were confined to a corner of a garret all my days, like a spider, the world would be just as large to me while I had my

---

[8] **If a man . . . or far away:** This is one of Thoreau's most famous passages. The "different drummer" evolved from a journal entry describing how Thoreau fell asleep to the sound of someone beating a drum "alone in the silence and the dark."

[9] **misgiving** (mĭs-gĭv´ĭng): a feeling of doubt, mistrust, or uncertainty.

thoughts about me. The philosopher[10] said: "From an army of three divisions one can take away its general, and put it in disorder; from the man the most abject and vulgar one cannot take away his thought." Do not seek so anxiously to be developed, to subject yourself to many influences to be played on; it is all **dissipation**. Humility like darkness
260 reveals the heavenly lights. The shadows of poverty and meanness gather around us, "and lo! creation widens to our view." We are often reminded that if there were bestowed on us the wealth of Croesus,[11] our aims must still be the same, and our means essentially the same. Moreover, if you are restricted in your range by poverty, if you cannot buy books and newspapers, for instance, you are but confined to the most significant and vital experiences; you are compelled to deal with the material which yields the most sugar and the most starch. It is life near the bone where it is sweetest. You are defended from being a trifler. No man loses ever on a lower level by magnanimity on a higher.
270 Superfluous wealth can buy superfluities only. Money is not required to buy one necessary of the soul. . . .

dissipation
(dĭs′ə-pā′shən) *n.* wasteful self-indulgence.

"If a man does not keep pace with his companions, perhaps it is because he hears a different drummer."

The life in us is like the water in the river. It may rise this year higher than man has ever known it, and flood the parched uplands; even this may be the eventful year, which will drown out all our muskrats. It was not always dry land where we dwell. I see far inland the banks which the stream anciently washed, before science began to record its freshets. Every one has heard the story which has gone the rounds of New England, of a strong and beautiful bug which came out of the dry leaf of an old table of apple-tree wood, which had stood in

[10] **philosopher:** Confucius (551–479 B.C.), Chinese teacher of moral living, who had an influence on Thoreau's ideas.
[11] **Croesus:** an ancient king legendary for his great wealth.

280 a farmer's kitchen for sixty years, first in Connecticut, and afterward in Massachusetts,—from an egg deposited in the living tree many years earlier still, as appeared by counting the annual layers beyond it; which was heard gnawing out for several weeks, hatched perchance by the heat of an urn. Who does not feel his faith in a resurrection and immortality strengthened by hearing of this? Who knows what beautiful and winged life, whose egg has been buried for ages under many concentric layers of woodenness in the dead dry life of society, deposited at first in the alburnum[12] of the green and living tree, which has been gradually converted into the semblance of its well-seasoned

290 tomb,—heard perchance gnawing out now for years by the astonished family of man, as they sat round the festive board,—may unexpectedly come forth from amidst society's most trivial and handselled[13] furniture, to enjoy its perfect summer life at last!

I do not say that John or Jonathan[14] will realize all this; but such is the character of that morrow which mere lapse of time can never make to dawn. The light which puts out our eyes is darkness to us. Only that day dawns to which we are awake. There is more day to dawn. The sun is but a morning star.

---

[12] **alburnum** (ăl-bûr′nəm): the part of a tree's trunk through which sap flows.
[13] **handselled:** given as a mere token of good wishes and therefore of no great value in itself.
[14] **John or Jonathan:** John Bull and Brother Jonathan were traditional personifications of England and the United States, respectively.

COLLABORATIVE DISCUSSION Which of Thoreau's descriptions or criticisms of modern life seem most relevant to today's world? In what way? Discuss this question with a partner, citing specific evidence from the text to support your ideas.

Determine Central Ideas: Summarize

Each essay in *Walden* expresses one or more central ideas, while the book as a whole reflects central ideas that the essays have in common. One way to determine a text's central ideas is to write an objective summary of it. When you **summarize,** you restate the central ideas in your own words. A summary is much shorter than the original text and includes only the most important supporting details. For example, you might summarize the opening paragraph of "Where I Lived, and What I Lived For" in a single sentence:

> **In July 1845, Thoreau moved into a newly-built cabin in the woods that pleased him with its rough, simple construction.**

Use these strategies to help you summarize Thoreau's essays.

- Use the essay titles as clues to the central ideas of each section.
- Summarize individual paragraphs or sections first.
- See if a topic sentence, usually at the beginning or end of a paragraph, explicitly states the paragraph's central idea.
- Infer a central idea from the details contained in a paragraph.

Determine Author's Purpose: Style

Readers must usually **infer** an author's **purpose,** or reason for writing, from the content and style of the writing. **Style** refers to how a writer expresses his or her ideas. Thoreau's style has several distinctive characteristics, as shown in the chart.

Elements of Style	Example
Informality: Long sentences but simple language	"The upright white hewn studs and freshly planed door and window casings gave it a clean and airy look, especially in the morning, when its timbers were saturated with dew, so that I fancied that by noon some sweet gum would exude from them. . . ."
Frequent use of **figurative language,** or language used in a nonliteral way.	
• **Simile:** comparison using *like* or *as*	"the mists, like ghosts, were stealthily withdrawing in every direction"
• **Metaphor:** comparison without using *like* or *as*	"Time is but the stream I go a-fishing in."
• **Personification:** giving human characteristics to an animal, object, or idea	"I saw it [the pond] throwing off its nightly clothing of mist. . . ."

Analyzing the Text

 COMMON CORE   ELACC11-12RI1,
ELACC11-12RI2,
ELACC11-12RI3,
ELACC11-12RI6,
ELACC11-12L5a,
ELACC11-12W2

Cite Text Evidence   Support your responses with evidence from the selection.

1. **Summarize** How does Thoreau describe his reasons for moving to the woods in lines 26–40? How do these lines relate to his purpose in writing *Walden*?

2. **Identify Patterns** What is the metaphor that Thoreau uses to describe civilized life in lines 49–54? Where else is a similar metaphor used in the text?

3. **Analyze** In lines 71–81, Thoreau uses a type of figurative language called **hyperbole,** exaggeration of the truth for a particular effect. What is he exaggerating, and what is his purpose for using this figurative language?

4. **Interpret** Summarize what Thoreau has to say on the topic of solitude (lines 113–140). How do his observations about nature help develop his central idea in this section?

5. **Compare** What **analogy,** or comparison, can you make between the central ideas Thoreau expresses in "The Pond in Winter" and in "Spring"? In what ways are the ideas in these two passages similar and different?

6. **Infer** Throeau rejects many thing as inessential or unimportant. List at least three things that *were* important to him, citing specific lines from the essay to support your answers.

7. **Critique** In what ways did Thoreau achieve his goals at Walden Pond? How do the central ideas in the "Conclusion" explicitly connect back to the beginning of the text?

8. **Evaluate** Think about Thoreau's purpose in writing *Walden*. How is Thoreau's particular style of writing effective for achieving his purpose? Explain.

PERFORMANCE TASK

Writing Activity: Essay Transcendentalism emphasized living a simple life and celebrating the truth found in nature, emotion, and imagination. How does *Walden* reflect these key aspects of transcendentalism? Write an essay that answers this question.

- Reread the excerpts and look for the most significant evidence of each aspect of transcendentalism.

- Organize your evidence so that you can develop the topic of your essay into a unified whole.

- Use appropriate transitions, varied syntax, and precise language to maintain a formal style.

- Provide a concluding statement that follows from the evidence presented.

Critical Vocabulary

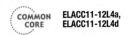 COMMON CORE   ELACC11-12L4a, ELACC11-12L4d

unfathomed	**perturbation**	**congenial**
perennial	**untenable**	**dissipation**

Practice and Apply Choose the alternative in each sentence that best relates to the Critical Vocabulary word and explain your choice.

1. If Walden Pond was **unfathomed,** was it deep or shallow?

2. Many people experience **perturbation** when listening to the news. Does it make them upset or happy?

3. Thoreau found solitude **congenial.** Was he content or lonely?

4. Thoreau noticed the **perennial** peace at the bottom of the pond in winter. Was this an unusual occurrence or something that was always there?

5. Judging nature to be evil is an **untenable** position for Thoreau. Would he make such a judgment or criticize it?

6. A lavish lifestyle can lead to **dissipation.** Are people who follow this lifestyle more likely to work too hard or to party too hard?

Vocabulary Strategy: Context Clues

Using **context clues**—nearby words, phrases, and sentences—can help you figure out the meanings of unfamiliar words. Consider the context for the Critical Vocabulary word *perturbation*:

> **Let us rise early and fast, or break fast, gently and without perturbation. . . .**

The word *without* signals a contrast between *gently* and *perturbation.* You can guess that *perturbation* means "agitation or uneasiness."

Sometimes you have to look at a wider context to find clues to a word's meaning. The word *congenial* appears in this sentence:

> **I see nothing special to attract me, all the elements are unusually congenial to me.**

A reader might conclude that *congenial* means "boring" or "uninteresting." However, other words and phrases in the paragraph let the reader know that that *congenial* denotes something pleasurable or agreeable.

> **This is a delicious evening, when the whole body . . . imbibes delight through every pore. . . . I see nothing special to attract me, all the elements are unusually congenial to me. . . . my serenity is rippled but not ruffled. These small waves . . . are as remote from storm as the smooth reflecting surface.**

Practice and Apply Work with a partner to identify five unfamiliar words from Thoreau's essays and use context clues to determine their meanings. Discuss which context clues were most helpful. Then check your definitions by using a dictionary.

Language and Style: Rhetorical Questions

 COMMON CORE ELACC11-12L3a

A distinctive element of Thoreau's style is his use of **rhetorical questions,** or questions that are asked to make a point and without the expectation of an actual reply. Rhetorical questions require that readers reflect on some aspect of a writer's argument or claim. In many cases, however, they also suggest that the writer's view is obvious or common sense; if readers just consider the issue—properly expressed, of course—they will just naturally agree with the writer. Thoreau often uses rhetorical questions to add emphasis and emotion to his writing. The chart shows several examples.

Rhetorical Questions in *Walden*	
Example	**Purpose**
Why should we live with such hurry and waste of life? (line 57)	To strongly suggest we should live in the opposite way
Why should I feel lonely? Is not our planet in the Milky Way? (lines 135–136)	To suggest he is not lonely; answer to the second question is an obvious "yes"
Why should we be in such desperate haste to succeed, and in such desperate enterprises? (lines 225–226)	To suggest that we should not act in this way
Who does not feel his faith in a resurrection and immortality strengthened by hearing of this? (lines 284–285)	To suggest that everyone should have faith in resurrection, since the expected answer is "no one"

Because *Walden* reflects Thoreau's experiment with living simply and the lessons he learned from that experiment, these questions also suggest the kinds of questions Thoreau asked himself while spending time alone in the woods, reflecting on life. They suggest the internal monologue of someone living in solitude. With their focus on the "big questions" of life, they elevate the book above the level of nature observations to an expression of transcendental philosophy.

Practice and Apply Review the essay you wrote about *Walden* as a reflection of key aspects of transcendentalism in this selection's Performance Task. Revise the essay to make it an argument that includes at least two rhetorical questions. Consider taking one of the three main ideas and stating it as a claim that you support with evidence from *Walden*.

Joyce Carol Oates (b. 1938) *was born in Lockport, New York. She begin writing at a young age, typing out story after story on a typewriter she received as a gift at the age of 14. Oates published her first novel,* With Shuddering Fall, *when she was 26. A subsequent novel,* them, *won the National Book Award. Since 1978, Oates has taught writing in the creative writing program at Princeton. All the while, she has been a terrifically prolific writer, turning out dozens of critically acclaimed novels. Some of her best known include* Bellefleur, The Gravedigger's Daughter, Blonde, *and* We Were the Mulvaneys.

Against Nature

Argument by Joyce Carol Oates

AS YOU READ Identify ways in which Oates tries to persuade the reader.

> *We soon get through with Nature. She excites an expectation which she cannot satisfy.*
> —Thoreau, *Journal,* 1854

> *Sir, if a man has experienced the inexpressible, he is under no obligation to attempt to express it.*
> —Samuel Johnson

The writer's resistance to Nature.

It has no sense of humor: in its beauty, as in its ugliness, or its neutrality, there is no laughter.

It lacks a moral purpose.

It lacks a satiric dimension, registers no irony.

Its pleasures lack **resonance**, being accidental; its horrors, even when premeditated, are equally perfunctory,[1] "red in tooth and claw,"[2] et cetera.

It lacks a symbolic subtext—excepting that provided by man.

10   It has no (verbal) language.

It has no interest in ours.

It inspires a painfully limited set of responses in "nature writers"—REVERENCE, AWE, PIETY, MYSTICAL ONENESS.

It eludes us even as it prepares to swallow us up, books and all.

I was lying on my back in the dirt gravel of the towpath[3] beside the Delaware and Raritan Canal, Titusville, New Jersey, staring up at the sky and trying, with no success, to overcome a sudden attack of tachycardia[4] that had come upon me out of nowhere—such attacks are always "out of nowhere," that's their charm—and all around me

20   Nature thrummed with life, the air smelling of moisture and sunlight, the canal reflecting the sky, red-winged blackbirds testing their spring calls: the usual. I'd become the jar in Tennessee,[5] a fictitious center, or parenthesis, aware beyond my erratic heartbeat of the numberless heartbeats of the earth, its pulsing, pumping life, sheer life, incalculable. Struck down in the midst of motion—I'd been jogging a minute before—I was "out of time" like a fallen, stunned boxer, privileged (in an abstract manner of speaking) to be an involuntary witness to the random, wayward, nameless motion on all sides of me.

Paroxysmal tachycardia can be fatal, but rarely; if the heartbeat

30   accelerates to 250–270 beats a minute you're in trouble, but the average attack is about 100–150 beats and mine seemed about average; the trick now was to prevent it from getting worse. Brainy people try brainy strategies, such as thinking calming thoughts, pseudo-mystic thoughts, *If I die now it's a good death*, that sort of thing, *if I die this is a good place and good time;* the idea is to deceive the frenzied heartbeat that, really, you don't care: you hadn't any other plans for the afternoon. The important thing with tachycardia is to prevent panic! you must prevent panic! otherwise you'll have to be taken by ambulance to the closest emergency room, which is not so

40   very nice a way to spend the afternoon, really. So I contemplated the blue sky overhead. The earth beneath my head. Nature surrounding me on all sides; I couldn't quite see it but I could hear it, smell it, sense it, there is something *there*, no mistake about it. Completely oblivious

resonance
(rĕz′ə-nəns) *n.*
richness of meaning;
the ability to evoke
emotion.

---

[1] **perfunctory:** without interest or enthusiasm.

[2] **"red in tooth and claw":** a reference to the unsentimental violence of the natural world.

[3] **towpath:** a path along a waterway on which animals walk while towing boats.

[4] **tachycardia:** an abnormally rapid heartbeat.

[5] **the jar in Tennessee:** an allusion to Wallace Stevens's poem "The Anecdote of the Jar."

to the predicament of the individual but that's only "natural," after all, one hardly expects otherwise.

When you discover yourself lying on the ground, limp and unresisting, head in the dirt, and, let's face it, helpless, the earth seems to shift forward as a presence; hard, emphatic, not mere surface but a genuine force—there is no other word for it but *presence*. To
50 keep in motion is to keep in time, and to be stopped, stilled, is to be abruptly out of time, in another time dimension perhaps, an alien one, where human language has no resonance. Nothing to be said about it expresses it, nothing touches it, it's an absolute against which nothing human can be measured. . . . Moving through space and time by way of your own volition[6] you inhabit an interior consciousness, a hallucinatory consciousness, it might be said, so long as breath, heartbeat, the body's **autonomy** hold; when motion is stopped you are jarred out of it. The interior is invaded by the exterior. The outside wants to come in, and only the self's fragile membrane prevents it.

60 The fly buzzing at Emily's death.[7]

Still, the earth *is* your place. A tidy grave site measured to your size. Or, from another angle of vision, one vast democratic grave.

Let's contemplate the sky. Forget the crazy hammering heartbeat, don't listen to it, don't start counting, remember that there is a clever way of breathing that conserves oxygen as if you're lying below the surface of a body of water breathing through a very thin straw but you *can* breathe through it if you're careful, if you don't panic; one breath and then another and then another, isn't that the story of all lives?

autonomy
(ô-tŏn´ə-mē) *n.*
freedom
from control;
independence.

---

[6] **volition:** the act of making a choice.
[7] **The fly buzzing at Emily's death:** an allusion to an Emily Dickinson poem that begins, "I heard a Fly buzz—when I died—".

careers? Just a matter of breathing. Of course it is. But contemplate
the sky, it's there to be contemplated. A mild shock to see it so blank,
blue, a thin airy ghostly blue, no clouds to disguise its emptiness. You
are beginning to feel not only weightless but near-bodiless, lying on
the earth like a scrap of paper about to be blown off. Two dimensions
and you'd imagined you were three! And there's the sky rolling away
forever, into infinity—if "infinity" can be "rolled into"—and the
forlorn[8] truth is, that's where you're going too. And the lovely blue isn't
even blue, is it? isn't even there, is it? a mere optical illusion, isn't it? no
matter what art has urged you to believe.

Early Nature memories. Which it's best not to suppress.

. . . Wading, as a small child, in Tonawanda Creek near our house,
and afterward trying to tear off, in a frenzy of terror and revulsion, the
sticky fat black bloodsuckers that had attached themselves to my feet,
particularly between my toes.

. . . Coming upon a friend's dog in a drainage ditch, dead for
several days, **evidently** the poor creature had been shot by a hunter
and left to die, bleeding to death, and we're stupefied[9] with grief and
horror but can't resist sliding down to where he's lying on his belly,
and we can't resist squatting over him, turning the body over.

. . . The raccoon, mad with rabies, frothing at the mouth and
tearing at his own belly with his teeth, so that his intestines spill out
onto the ground . . . a sight I seem to remember though in fact I did
not see. I've been told I did not see.

Consequently, my chronic uneasiness with Nature mysticism: Nature
adoration; Nature-as-(moral)-instruction-for-mankind. My doubt
that one can, with philosophical validity, address "Nature" as a single
coherent noun, anything other than a Platonic, hence discredited, is-
ness.[10] My resistance to "Nature writing" as a genre, except when it is
brilliantly fictionalized in the service of a writer's individual vision—
Thoreau's books and *Journal*, of course, but also, less known in this
country, the miniaturist prose poems of Colette *(Flowers and Fruit)*
and Ponge *(Taking the Side of Things)*—in which case it becomes yet
another, and ingenious, form of storytelling. The subject is *there* only
by the grace of the author's language.

Nature has no instructions for mankind except that our poor
beleaguered humanist-democratic way of life, our fantasies of the
individual's high worth, our sense that the weak, no less than the
strong, have a right to survive, are absurd. When Edmund of *King
Lear* said excitedly, "Nature, be thou my goddess!" he knew whereof he
spoke.

evidently
(ĕv´ĭ-dənt-lē) *adv.*
plainly, or obviously
apparent from
evidence or data.

---

[8] **forlorn:** sad.

[9] **stupefied:** stunned; in a daze.

[10] **a Platonic . . . is-ness:** Plato's idea that there are ideal forms as an absolute and
eternal reality of which the phenomena, or experiences, of the world are an
imperfect and transitory reflection.

110   In any case, where *is* Nature, one might (skeptically) inquire. Who has looked upon her/its face and survived?[11]

But isn't this all exaggeration, in the spirit of rhetorical contentiousness?[12] Surely Nature is, for you, as for most reasonably intelligent people, a "perennial" source of beauty, comfort, peace, escape from the delirium of civilized life; a respite[13] from the ego's ever-frantic strategies of self-promotion, as a way of ensuring (at least in fantasy) some small measure of immortality? Surely Nature, as it is understood in the usual slapdash way, as human, if not dilettante,[14] *experience* (hiking in a national park, jogging on the beach at dawn,
120   even tending, with the usual comical frustrations, a suburban garden), is wonderfully consoling; a place where, when you go there, it has to take you in?—a palimpsest[15] of sorts you choose to read, layer by layer, always with care, always cautiously, in proportion to your psychological strength?

        Nature: as in Thoreau's upbeat Transcendentalist[16] mode ("The indescribable innocence and beneficence of Nature,—such health, such cheer, they afford forever! and such sympathy have they ever with our race, that all Nature would be affected . . . if any man should ever for a just cause grieve"), and not in Thoreau's grim mode ("Nature is
130   hard to be overcome but she must be overcome").

        Another way of saying, not *Nature-in-itself* but *Nature-as-experience.*

        The former, Nature-in-itself, is, to allude slantwise to Melville, a blankness ten times blank;[17] the latter is what we commonly, or perhaps always, mean, when we speak of Nature as a noun, a single entity—something of *ours.* Most of the time it's just an activity, a sort of hobby, a weekend, a few days, perhaps a few hours, staring out the window at the mind-dazzling autumn foliage of, say, northern Michigan, being rendered speechless—temporarily—at the sight of
140   Mt. Shasta, the Grand Canyon, Ansel Adams's[18] West. Or Nature writ small, contained in the back yard. Nature filtered through our optical nerves, our "senses," our fiercely romantic expectations. Nature that

---

[11] **Who has . . . and survived?:** Perhaps an allusion to Exodus 33:20: And [God] said, Thou canst not see my face: for there shall no man see me, and live.

[12] **contentiousness:** tendency to argue.

[13] **respite:** rest or break.

[14] **dilettante:** a person with a superficial interest in an art or an activity.

[15] **palimpsest:** a manuscript that has been written over still-visible erasures.

[16] **Transcendentalist:** one who believes that the material world contains an underlying, perceivable spiritual component.

[17] **to allude . . . ten times blank:** Herman Melville, when writing about Hawthorne's work, compared its "dark half" to the part of the globe that is "shrouded in darkness ten times black."

[18] **Ansel Adams's:** Adams (1902–1984) was an American photographer known for his black-and-white landscapes.

pleases us because it mirrors our souls, or gives the comforting illusion of doing so.

Nature as the self's (flattering) mirror, but not ever, no, never, Nature-in-itself.

Nature is mouths, or maybe a single mouth. Why glamorize it, romanticize it?—well, yes, but we must, we're writers, poets, mystics (of a sort) aren't we, precisely what else are we to do but glamorize and romanticize and generally exaggerate the significance of anything we focus the white heat of our "creativity" upon? And why not Nature, since it's there, common property, mute, can't talk back, allows us the possibility of **transcending** the human condition for a while, writing prettily of mountain ranges, white-tailed deer, the purple crocuses outside this very window, the thrumming dazzling "life force" we imagine we all support. Why not?

Nature *is* more than a mouth—it's a dazzling variety of mouths. And it pleases the senses, in any case, as the physicists' chill universe of numbers certainly does not.

Oscar Wilde,[19] on our subject:

> Nature is no great mother who has borne us. She is our creation. It is in our brain that she quickens to life. Things are because we see them, and what we see, and how we see it, depends on the Arts that have influenced us. To look at a thing is very different from seeing a thing. . . . At present, people see fogs, not because there are fogs, but because poets and painters have taught them the mysterious loveliness of such effects. There may have been fogs for centuries in London. I dare say there were. But no one saw them. They did not exist until Art had invented them. . . . Yesterday evening Mrs. Arundel insisted on my going to the window and looking at the glorious sky, as she called it. And so I had to look at it. . . . And what was it? It was simply a very second-rate Turner, a Turner of a bad period, with all the painter's worst faults exaggerated and over-emphasized.

> ("The Decay of Lying," 1889)

(If we were to put it to Oscar Wilde that he exaggerates, his reply might well be, "Exaggeration? I don't know the meaning of the word.")

Walden, that most artfully composed of prose fictions, concludes, in the rhapsodic chapter "Spring," with Henry David Thoreau's contemplation of death, decay, and regeneration as it is suggested to him, or to his protagonist, by the spectacle of vultures feeding off carrion. There is a dead horse close by his cabin, and the stench of its

transcend
(trăn-sĕnd´) *v.* to go beyond the limits or become independent of.

-----

[19]**Oscar Wilde:** (1854–1900) an Irish author of poems, plays, and prose.

decomposition, in certain winds, is daunting. Yet "the assurance it gave me of the strong appetite and inviolable health of Nature was my compensation for this. I love to see that Nature is so rife with life that myriads can be afforded to be sacrificed and suffered to prey upon one another; that tender organizations can be so serenely squashed out of existence like pulp,— tadpoles which herons gobble up, and tortoises and toads run over in the road; and that sometimes it has rained flesh and blood! . . . The impression made on a wise man is that of universal innocence."

190

Come off it, Henry David. You've grieved these many years for your elder brother, John, who died a ghastly death of lockjaw;[20] you've never wholly recovered from the experience of watching him die. And you know, or must know, that you're fated too to die young of consumption[21]. . . . But this doctrinaire[22] Transcendentalist passage ends *Walden* on just the right note. It's as impersonal, as coolly detached, as the Oversoul[23] itself: a "wise man" filters his emotions through his brain.

200

Or through his prose.

Nietzsche: "We all pretend to ourselves that we are more simple-minded than we are: that is how we get a rest from our fellow men."

> *Once out of nature I shall never take*
> *My bodily form from any natural thing,*
> *But such a form as Grecian goldsmiths make*
> *Of hammered gold and gold enamelling*
> *To keep a drowsy Emperor awake;*
> *Or set upon a golden bough to sing*
> *To lords and ladies of Byzantium*
> *Of what is past, or passing, or to come.*
>
> —William Butler Yeats, *Sailing to Byzantium*

210

Yet even the golden bird is a "bodily form [taken from a] natural thing." No, it's impossible to escape!

The writer's resistance to Nature.

Wallace Stevens: "In the presence of extraordinary actuality, consciousness takes the place of imagination."

Once, years ago, in 1972 to be precise, when I seemed to have been another person, related to the person I am now as one is related, **tangentially**, sometimes embarrassingly, to cousins not seen for decades—once, when we were living in London, and I was very sick,

220

tangentially
(tăn-jĕn´shəl-lē) *adv.*
indirectly or peripherally connected.

---

[20]**lockjaw:** tetanus, which causes muscles in the neck and jaw to stiffen.

[21]**consumption:** tuberculosis.

[22]**doctrinaire:** insisting on a theory without regard to practical problems.

[23]**Oversoul:** a spititual essence or vital force in the universe in which all souls participate and that therefore transcends individual consciousness.

I had a mystical vision. That is, I "had" a "mystical vision"—the heart sinks: such pretension—or something resembling one. A fever dream, let's call it. It impressed me enormously and impresses me still, though I've long since lost the capacity to see it with my mind's eye, or even, I suppose, to believe in it. There is a statute of limitations on "mystical visions," as on romantic love.

    I was very sick, and I imagined my life as a thread, a thread of
230 breath, or heartbeat, or pulse, or light—yes, it was light, radiant light; I was burning with fever and I ascended to that plane of serenity that might be mistaken for (or *is*, in fact) Nirvana, where I had a waking dream of uncanny[24] lucidity:

    My body is a tall column of light and heat.

    My body is not "I" but "it."

    My body is not one but many.

    My body, which "I" inhabit, is inhabited as well by other creatures, unknown to me, imperceptible—the smallest of them mere sparks of light.
240   My body, which I perceive as substance, is in fact an organization of infinitely complex, overlapping, imbricated[25] structures, radiant

---

[24]**uncanny:** strange or mysterious.

[25]**imbricated:** placed in an overlapping pattern.

light their manifestation, the "body" a tall column of light and blood heat, a temporary agreement among atoms, like a high-rise building with numberless rooms, corridors, corners, elevator shafts, windows. . . . In this fantastical structure the "I" is deluded as to its sovereignty, let alone its autonomy in the (outside) world; the most astonishing secret is that the "I" doesn't exist!—but it behaves as if it does, as if it were one and not many.

In any case, without the "I" the tall column of light and heat would die, and the microscopic life particles would die with it . . . will die with it. The "I," which doesn't exist, is everything.

But Dr. Johnson is right, the inexpressible need not be expressed.
And what resistance, finally? There is none.

This morning, an invasion of tiny black ants. One by one they appear, out of nowhere—that's their charm too!—moving single file across the white Parsons table where I am sitting, trying without much success to write a poem. A poem of only three or four lines is what I want, something short, might, mean; I want it to hurt like a white-hot wire up the nostrils, small and compact and turned in upon itself with the density of a hunk of rock from the planet Jupiter. . . .

But here come the black ants: **harbingers**, you might say, of spring. One by one by one they appear on the dazzling white table and one by one I kill them with a forefinger, my deft right forefinger, mashing each against the surface of the table and then dropping it into a wastebasket at my side. Idle labor, mesmerizing, effortless, and I'm curious as to how long I can do it—sit here in the brilliant March sunshine killing ants with my right forefinger—how long I, and the ants, can keep it up.

After a while I realize that I can do it a long time. And that I've written my poem.

harbinger
(här´bĭn-jər) *n.* a person or thing that signals a future occurrence.

COLLABORATIVE DISCUSSION How does Oates try to persuade readers to agree with her point of view on nature and nature writing? Cite specific words, phrases, and examples from the text.

Analyze and Evaluate Structure

Essays may be structured in a number of unique ways, depending on the goal of the author. The three main types of essays are argumentative, informative (or explanatory), and narrative. The chart gives a brief description of each **structure.**

Argumentative	Informative	Narrative
Argumentative writing attempts to convince the reader to think a certain way about a subject. An argument begins with a statement of opinion and includes reasons supported by evidence to back up that opinion.	An **informative essay** is a nonfiction piece that attempts to explain a particular topic. Informative writing includes several central ideas that are supported by facts and examples.	**Narrative writing** relays the events and experiences in a person's life, often in chronological order. Unlike an expository essay, which simply states the events and experiences, a narrative includes the writer's thoughts and feelings.

Oates's essay does not fit neatly into any of these categories. Instead, the author combines forms, mixing all three styles, putting forth a complex set of ideas and developing them over the course of the text. Take for instance the following narrative excerpt:

> **I'd become the jar in Tennessee, a fictitious center, or parenthesis, aware beyond my erratic heartbeat of the numberless heartbeats of the earth, its pulsing, pumping life, sheer life, incalculable.**

The author describes events and the feelings that accompany those events. But in the same essay, she goes on to write this:

> **Paroxysmal tachycardia can be fatal, but rarely; if the heartbeat accelerates to 250–270 beats a minute you're in trouble. . . .**

Here, the author explains the symptoms of an attack in a relatively straightforward manner, adding informative writing to the mix. Sprinkled throughout, however, is opinion writing:

> **Walden, that most artfully composed of prose fictions, concludes, in the rhapsodic chapter "Spring," with Henry David Thoreau's contemplation of death, decay, and regeneration as it is suggested to him, or to his protagonist, by the spectacle of vultures feeding off carrion.**

Here, as elsewhere in the essay, the author's opinion falls into the realm of **literary criticism,** or the interpretation and analysis of literature. Though it is a kind of argumentative writing, literary criticism focuses solely on literature.

To identify an essay's structure, look for the qualities that correspond to each kind of writing. Be aware that, like Oates, authors may mix styles. Nevertheless, their goal is the same: to structure an essay so that it is both clear and engaging.

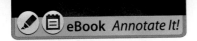
Analyzing the Text

COMMON CORE
ELACC11-12RI1,
ELACC11-12RI2,
ELACC11-12RI3,
ELACC11-12RI5,
ELACC11-12W2,
ELACC11-12W7,
ELACC11-12L4a

Cite Text Evidence Support your responses with evidence from the selection.

1. **Analyze** Look at the list at the beginning of the essay (lines 1–14). In what way does it contribute to the structure of the author's argument?

2. **Analyze** In line 15, the author begins a **narrative** about an experience she had in nature. How does the author use this narrative to engage the reader?

3. **Identify** Attempting to transcend her condition, the author tries to focus on nature as she lies limp in the dirt (lines 46–78). What does she realize about the earth and the sky as she lies there?

4. **Analyze** The author quotes Thoreau in a passage that celebrates the virtues of nature in the decomposition of a dead horse (lines 180–193). Then she addresses Thoreau directly: "Come off it, Henry David." What central idea is developed in lines 194–202? What effect does Oates's **tone,** or attitude toward her subject, in this passage have on the reader?

5. **Interpret** According to the author, how do writers and artists help perpetuate *"Nature-as-experience"* (lines 131–132)?

6. **Analyze** The essay ends with a **narrative** passage about black ants that the author smashes with her forefinger. What do the ants represent? How is the ending a kind of bookend to the narrative at the beginning of the essay?

7. **Evaluate** Is this essay effective as **literary criticism**? Is the structure clear, engaging, and persuasive? Does the author use quotations effectively to support or refute her points? Explain.

PERFORMANCE TASK

Writing Activity: Analysis Review the Oscar Wilde passage that Oates quotes in lines 161–176. Do you agree with the ideas he expresses? Write a brief analysis of the passage and its place in Oates's argument.

- Identify Wilde's central idea and the details he uses to support it. Decide whether you agree with his idea, and why.

- Consider how the passage fits into the structure of Oates's argument. What central idea of hers does the Wilde passage support?

- Write a brief analysis that summarizes your ideas.

Critical Vocabulary

 COMMON CORE ELACC11-12L4b

resonance	autonomy	evidently
transcending	tangentially	harbingers

Practice and Apply Answer the questions by applying each Critical Vocabulary word to your own life.

1. When have you wanted **autonomy**?

2. What have you ever seen or read that had **resonance**?

3. What do you see as a **harbinger** of winter?

4. When have you found yourself **transcending** physical pain to perform a task?

5. What is **evidently** true about you, based on your favorite activities?

6. When have you answered a direct question **tangentially**?

Vocabulary Strategy: Parts of Speech

The Critical Vocabulary word *resonance* is a noun, formed by adding the suffix *-ance* to the root of the verb *resonate*. Specific **suffixes,** word parts at the end of a word or root, identify a word as a noun, verb, adjective, or adverb. These suffixes are patterns of word changes that indicate different parts of speech. Recognizing the part of speech that each suffix represents will help you begin to identify unknown words. Here are some common suffixes you will see in English words, along with their corresponding part of speech:

Suffixes	Part of Speech	Example
–ance, -ence	noun	tolerance
–ly	adverb	tangentially
–ing	verb	transcending
–able	adjective	remarkable

Practice and Apply There are many more suffixes besides the ones in the chart. Create your own comprehensive chart that lists suffixes, their part of speech, and an example word that contains each suffix.

Language and Style: Quotations

Quotations, words taken directly from another text, serve an important purpose in "Against Nature." The author uses them to support her argument, adding evidence to help prove her claims about nature and nature writing.

Read the following sentences from "Against Nature."

Nature *is* more than a mouth—it's a dazzling variety of mouths. And it pleases the senses, in any case, as the physicists' chill universe of numbers certainly does not.

Oscar Wilde, on our subject:

Nature is no great mother who has borne us. She is our creation. It is in our brain that she quickens to life. Things are because we see them, and what we see, and how we see it, depends on the Arts that have influenced us.

The author might well have stated her point and left it at that. But instead, she quotes Oscar Wilde, a noted writer, adding weight and authority to her argument. She also chooses a quotation that is directly relevant to her point, maintaining a continuity of thought.

Quotations can also be used to vary syntax for effect. Rather than repeating or reframing a point, a quotation serves to add interest and variety, to break up a string of monotonous statements. For example, in the following lines, Oates uses a quotation to add variety to the text:

Nature has no instructions for mankind except that our poor beleaguered humanist-democratic way of life, our fantasies of the individual's high worth, our sense that the weak, no less than the strong, have a right to survive, are absurd. When Edmund of *King Lear* said excitedly, "Nature, be thou my goddess!" he knew whereof he spoke.

The author weaves quotations into her text both to bolster her argument and to add literary interest. Her quotations constantly engage and challenge the reader to follow her reasoning.

Practice and Apply Look back at the analysis you wrote in response to this selection's Performance Task. Revise the analysis by adding at least one quotation to support the argument you make and one quotation to vary your prose.

The Minister's Black Veil

Short Story by Nathaniel Hawthorne

The Pit and the Pendulum

Short Story by Edgar Allan Poe

American Romanticism

In the years after winning independence from the British and establishing a new nation, Americans began to form their own cultural identity. Writers calling themselves Romantics helped build this identity, and their work still influences the way Americans view themselves, their society, and the natural world.

Romanticism refers to schools of thought that value feeling and intuition over reason. Developed in part as a reaction against rationalism, Romanticism strongly influenced literature, music, and painting in Europe and the United States from the late eighteenth to the mid-nineteenth centuries. In the wake of the Industrial Revolution, with its squalid cities and miserable working conditions, people had come to realize the limits of reason. The Romantics believed that the imagination allowed people to discern truths that the rational mind could not comprehend. These truths were usually accompanied by powerful emotion and were associated with natural beauty. To the Romantics, imagination, individual feelings, and wild and untamed natural settings held greater value than reason, logic, and sophistication.

THE DARK SIDE OF ROMANTICISM   Not all American writers agreed with the general Romantic notion that the divine is embodied in nature and that people are essentially good. Some felt that these views did not adequately take into account the presence of suffering in the world and the ongoing conflict between good and evil. The **Dark Romantics,** as these skeptics were called, shared with the other Romantics an interest in the spiritual world and a belief in the value of intuition and imagination over rationalism. However, they also sought to explore the darker mysteries of human existence.

During the Romantic period in European literature, a similar division had resulted in the Gothic novel, which emerged in England in the late eighteenth century. These tales of terror, often a set in a medieval Gothic castle, symbolically used their pointed arches and vaults, dark dungeons, and mysterious underground passages to evoke hidden secrets or fears. The term **Gothic** was later expanded to describe any fiction that created a haunting atmosphere and depicted strange and chilling events, including live burials, horrifying torture, and the earthly resurrection of corpses.

Nathaniel Hawthorne *(1804–1864) was born in Salem, Massachusetts. By the time he left for Bowdoin College in 1821, Hawthorne knew he wanted to write. After graduation, he lived alone for 12 years, dedicated to building his literary career. By 1842, he had achieved some success. When times were tough, Hawthorne had well-connected friends set him up with government jobs, whose dull routines choked his imagination and limited his time to write. Hawthorne, however, never stopped writing. Today he is most celebrated for his short stories and for* The Scarlet Letter *(1850).*

The Minister's Black Veil

Short Story by Nathaniel Hawthorne

AS YOU READ Pay careful attention to how the minister's veil affects Mr. Hooper and the community as a whole.

The sexton stood in the porch of Milford meetinghouse, pulling lustily at the bell rope. The old people of the village came stooping along the street. Children, with bright faces, tripped merrily beside their parents, or mimicked a graver gait, in the conscious dignity of their Sunday clothes. Spruce[1] bachelors looked sidelong at the pretty maidens, and fancied that the Sabbath sunshine made them prettier than on weekdays. When the throng had mostly streamed into the porch, the sexton began to toll the bell, keeping his eye on the Reverend Mr. Hooper's door. The first glimpse of the clergyman's
10   figure was the signal for the bell to cease its summons.

    "But what has good Parson Hooper got upon his face?" cried the sexton in astonishment.

    All within hearing immediately turned about, and beheld the semblance[2] of Mr. Hooper, pacing slowly his meditative way towards the meetinghouse. With one accord they started, expressing more

---

[1] **Spruce:** neat and clean.
[2] **semblance:** appearance.

wonder than if some strange minister were coming to dust the cushions of Mr. Hooper's pulpit.

"Are you sure it is our parson?" inquired Goodman[3] Gray of the sexton.

20 "Of a certainty it is good Mr. Hooper," replied the sexton. "He was to have exchanged pulpits with Parson Shute of Westbury; but Parson Shute sent to excuse himself yesterday, being to preach a funeral sermon."

The cause of so much amazement may appear sufficiently slight. Mr. Hooper, a gentlemanly person about thirty, though still a bachelor, was dressed with due clerical neatness, as if a careful wife had starched his band, and brushed the weekly dust from his Sunday's garb. There was but one thing remarkable in his appearance. Swathed about his forehead, and hanging down over his face, so low as to be shaken by his breath, Mr. Hooper had on a black veil. On a nearer view, it seemed
30 to consist of two folds of crape,[4] which entirely concealed his features, except the mouth and chin, but probably did not intercept his sight, farther than to give a darkened aspect to all living and inanimate things. With this gloomy shade before him, good Mr. Hooper walked onward, at a slow and quiet pace, stooping somewhat and looking on the ground, as is customary with abstracted[5] men, yet nodding kindly to those of his parishioners who still waited on the meetinghouse steps. But so wonder-struck were they that his greeting hardly met with a return.

40 "I can't really feel as if good Mr. Hooper's face was behind that piece of crape," said the sexton.

"I don't like it," muttered an old woman, as she hobbled into the meetinghouse. "He has changed himself into something awful, only by hiding his face."

"Our parson has gone mad!" cried Goodman Gray, following him across the threshold.

A rumor of some unaccountable phenomenon had preceded Mr. Hooper into the meetinghouse, and set all the congregation astir. Few could refrain from twisting their heads towards the door; many stood
50 upright, and turned directly about; while several little boys clambered upon the seats, and came down again with a terrible racket. There was a general bustle, a rustling of the women's gowns and shuffling of the men's feet, greatly at variance[6] with that hushed repose which should attend the entrance of the minister. But Mr. Hooper appeared not to notice the perturbation of his people. He entered with an almost noiseless step, bent his head mildly to the pews on each side, and bowed as he passed his oldest parishioner, a white-haired great-

---

[3] **Goodman:** a title equivalent to *mister.*

[4] **crape:** a black, silky fabric worn as a sign of mourning.

[5] **abstracted:** absent-minded; preoccupied.

[6] **at variance:** contrasting.

grandsire, who occupied an armchair in the centre of the aisle. It was
strange to observe how slowly this venerable man became conscious
60 of something singular in the appearance of his pastor. He seemed not
fully to partake of the prevailing wonder till Mr. Hooper had ascended
the stairs, and showed himself in the pulpit, face-to-face with his
congregation, except for the black veil. That mysterious **emblem** was
never once withdrawn. It shook with his measured breath as he gave
out the psalm; it threw its obscurity between him and the holy page, as
he read the Scriptures; and while he prayed, the veil lay heavily on his
uplifted countenance. Did he seek to hide from the dread Being whom
he was addressing?

Such was the effect of this simple piece of crape, that more than
70 one woman of delicate nerves was forced to leave the meetinghouse.
Yet perhaps the pale-faced congregation was almost as fearful a sight
to the minister as his black veil to them.

Mr. Hooper had the reputation of a good preacher, but not
an energetic one: he strove to win his people heavenward by mild
persuasive influences, rather than to drive them thither by the
thunders of the Word. The sermon which he now delivered was
marked by the same characteristics of style and manner as the general
series of his pulpit oratory. But there was something, either in the
sentiment of the discourse itself, or in the imagination of the auditors,
80 which made it greatly the most powerful effort that they had ever
heard from their pastor's lips. It was tinged, rather more darkly than
usual, with the gentle gloom of Mr. Hooper's temperament. The
subject had reference to secret sin, and those sad mysteries which we
hide from our nearest and dearest, and would fain conceal from our
own consciousness, even forgetting that the Omniscient[7] can detect
them. A subtle power was breathed into his words. Each member of the
congregation, the most innocent girl, and the man of hardened breast,
felt as if the preacher had crept upon them, behind his awful veil, and
discovered their hoarded iniquity[8] of deed or thought. Many spread
90 their clasped hands on their bosoms. There was nothing terrible in
what Mr. Hooper said; at least, no violence; and yet, with every tremor
of his melancholy voice, the hearers quaked. An unsought **pathos**
came hand in hand with awe. So sensible were the audience of some
unwonted attribute in their minister, that they longed for a breath of
wind to blow aside the veil, almost believing that a stranger's visage
would be discovered, though the form, gesture and voice were those of
Mr. Hooper.

At the close of the services, the people hurried out with
indecorous[9] confusion, eager to communicate their pent-up
100 amazement, and conscious of lighter spirits the moment they lost

emblem
(ĕm´blǝm) *n.* an
identifying mark or
symbol.

pathos
(pā´thŏs´) *n.*
something that
evokes pity or
sympathy

---

[7] **the Omniscient:** God; literally, the all-knowing.

[8] **iniquity:** sinfulness.

[9] **indecorous:** undignified; inappropriate.

sight of the black veil. Some gathered in little circles, huddled closely together, with their mouths all whispering in the centre; some went homeward alone, wrapped in silent meditation; some talked loudly, and profaned[10] the Sabbath day with **ostentatious** laughter. A few shook their sagacious heads, intimating[11] that they could penetrate the mystery; while one or two affirmed that there was no mystery at all, but only that Mr. Hooper's eyes were so weakened by the midnight lamp as to require a shade. After a brief interval, forth came good Mr. Hooper also, in the rear of his flock. Turning his veiled face from one
110 group to another, he paid due reverence to the hoary[12] heads, saluted the middle-aged with kind dignity, as their friend and spiritual guide, greeted the young with mingled authority and love, and laid his hands on the little children's heads to bless them. Such was always his custom on the Sabbath day. Strange and bewildered looks repaid him for his courtesy. None, as on former occasions, aspired to the honor of walking by their pastor's side. Old Squire Saunders, doubtless by an accidental lapse of memory, neglected to invite Mr. Hooper to his table, where the good clergyman had been wont[13] to bless the food almost every Sunday since his settlement. He returned, therefore, to
120 the parsonage, and at the moment of closing the door, was observed to look back upon the people, all of whom had their eyes fixed upon the minister. A sad smile gleamed faintly from beneath the black veil, and flickered about his mouth, glimmering as he disappeared.

"How strange," said a lady, "that a simple black veil, such as any woman might wear on her bonnet, should become such a terrible thing on Mr. Hooper's face!"

"Something must surely be amiss with Mr. Hooper's intellects," observed her husband, the physician of the village. "But the strangest part of the affair is the effect of this vagary,[14] even on a sober-minded
130 man like myself. The black veil, though it covers only our pastor's face, throws its influence over his whole person, and makes him ghost-like from head to foot. Do you not feel it so?"

"Truly do I," replied the lady; "and I would not be alone with him for the world. I wonder he is not afraid to be alone with himself!"

"Men sometimes are so," said her husband.

The afternoon service was attended with similar circumstances. At its conclusion, the bell tolled for the funeral of a young lady. The relatives and friends were assembled in the house, and the more distant acquaintances stood about the door, speaking of the good
140 qualities of the deceased, when their talk was interrupted by the appearance of Mr. Hooper, still covered with his black veil. It was now

ostentatious
(ŏs′tĕn-tā′shəs) *adj.*
conspicuous and vulgar

---

[10]**profaned:** desecrated; treated irreverently.
[11]**intimating:** revealing.
[12]**hoary:** gray or white.
[13]**wont:** habit.
[14]**vagary:** oddity.

an appropriate emblem. The clergyman stepped into the room where the corpse was laid, and bent over the coffin, to take a last farewell of his deceased parishioner. As he stooped, the veil hung straight down from his forehead so that, if her eyelids had not been closed forever, the dead maiden might have seen his face. Could Mr. Hooper be fearful of her glance, that he so hastily caught back the black veil? A person, who watched the interview between the dead and the living, scrupled[15] not to affirm that, at the instant when the clergyman's features were
150 disclosed, the corpse had slightly shuddered, rustling the shroud[16] and muslin cap, though the countenance retained the composure of death. A superstitious old woman was the only witness of this prodigy. From the coffin, Mr. Hooper passed into the chamber of the mourners, and thence to the head of the staircase, to make the funeral prayer. It was a tender and heart-dissolving prayer, full of sorrow, yet so imbued with celestial[17] hopes, that the music of the heavenly harp, swept by the fingers of the dead, seemed faintly to be heard among the saddest accents of the minister. The people trembled, though they but darkly understood him, when he prayed that they, and himself, and all of
160 mortal race might be ready, as he trusted this young maiden had been, for the dreadful hour that should snatch the veil from their faces. The bearers went heavily forth, and the mourners followed, saddening all the street, with the dead before them, and Mr. Hooper in his black veil behind.

"Why do you look back?" said one in the procession to his partner.

"I had a fancy," replied she, "that the minister and the maiden's spirit were walking hand in hand."

"And so had I, at the same moment," said the other. That night, the handsomest couple in Milford village were to be joined in wedlock.
170 Though reckoned a melancholy man, Mr. Hooper had a placid cheerfulness for such occasions, which often excited a sympathetic smile, where livelier merriment would have been thrown away. There was no quality of his disposition which made him more beloved than this. The company at the wedding awaited his arrival with impatience, trusting that the strange awe, which had gathered over him throughout the day, would now be dispelled. But such was not the result. When Mr. Hooper came, the first thing that their eyes rested on was the same horrible black veil, which had added deeper gloom to the funeral, and could portend nothing but evil to the wedding. Such was
180 its immediate effect on the guests, that a cloud seemed to have rolled duskily from beneath the black crape, and dimmed the light of the candles. The bridal pair stood up before the minister. But the bride's cold fingers quivered in the tremulous[18] hand of the bridegroom,

---

[15] **scrupled:** was reluctant.

[16] **shroud:** a cloth in which people were wrapped before burial.

[17] **celestial:** relating to heaven.

[18] **tremulous:** trembling.

and her death-like paleness caused a whisper that the maiden who had been buried a few hours before was come from her grave to be married. If ever another wedding were so dismal, it was that famous one where they tolled the wedding knell.[19] After performing the ceremony, Mr. Hooper raised a glass of wine to his lips, wishing happiness to the new-married couple, in a strain of mild pleasantry

190   that ought to have brightened the features of the guests, like a cheerful gleam from the hearth. At that instant, catching a glimpse of his figure in the looking glass, the black veil involved his own spirit in the horror with which it overwhelmed all others. His frame shuddered—his lips grew white—he spilt the untasted wine upon the carpet—and rushed forth into the darkness. For the Earth, too, had on her Black Veil.

The next day, the whole village of Milford talked of little else than Parson Hooper's black veil. That, and the mystery concealed behind it, supplied a topic for discussion between acquaintances meeting in the street, and good women gossiping at their open windows. It was

200   the first item of news that the tavern keeper told to his guests. The children babbled of it on their way to school. One imitative little imp covered his face with an old black handkerchief, thereby so affrighting his playmates that the panic seized himself, and he well-nigh lost his wits by his own waggery.[20]

It was remarkable that, of all the busybodies and impertinent people in the parish, not one ventured to put the plain question to Mr. Hooper, wherefore he did this thing. Hitherto, whenever there appeared the slightest call for such interference, he had never lacked advisers, nor shown himself averse to be guided by their judgment.

210   If he erred at all, it was by so painful a degree of self-distrust that even the mildest censure[21] would lead him to consider an indifferent action as a crime. Yet, though so well acquainted with this amiable weakness, no individual among his parishioners chose to make the black veil a subject of friendly remonstrance.[22] There was a feeling of dread, neither plainly confessed nor carefully concealed, which caused each to shift the responsibility upon another, till at length it was found expedient to send a deputation to the church, in order to deal with Mr. Hooper about the mystery, before it should grow into a scandal. Never did an embassy so ill discharge its duties. The minister received

220   them with friendly courtesy, but became silent, after they were seated, leaving to his visitors the whole burden of introducing their important business. The topic, it might be supposed, was obvious enough. There was the black veil, swathed round Mr. Hooper's forehead, and concealing every feature above his placid mouth, on which, at times, they could perceive the glimmering of a melancholy smile. But that

---

[19] **If ever...wedding knell:** In Hawthorne's "The Wedding Knell," funeral bells ring during a wedding ceremony.

[20] **waggery:** silly humor.

[21] **censure:** disapproval or criticism

[22] **remonstrance:** protest.

piece of crape, to their imagination, seemed to hang down before his heart, the symbol of a fearful secret between him and them. Were the veil but cast aside, they might speak freely of it, but not till then. Thus they sat a considerable time, speechless, confused, and shrinking uneasily from Mr. Hooper's eye, which they felt to be fixed upon them with an invisible glance. Finally, the deputies returned abashed to their constituents, pronouncing the matter too weighty to be handled, except by a council of the churches, if, indeed, it might not require a general synod.[23]

But there was one person in the village unappalled by the awe with which the black veil had impressed all beside herself. When the deputies returned without an explanation, or even venturing to demand one, she, with the calm energy of her character, determined to chase away the strange cloud that appeared to be settling round Mr. Hooper, every moment more darkly than before. As his plighted wife,[24] it should be her privilege to know what the black veil concealed. At the minister's first visit, therefore, she entered upon the subject, with a direct simplicity, which made the task easier both for him and her. After he had seated himself, she fixed her eyes steadfastly upon the veil, but could discern nothing of the dreadful gloom that had so overawed the multitude: it was but a double fold of crape, hanging down from his forehead to his mouth, and slightly stirring with his breath.

"No," said she aloud, and smiling, "there is nothing terrible in this piece of crape except that it hides a face which I am always glad to look upon. Come, good sir, let the sun shine from behind the cloud. First lay aside your black veil: then tell me why you put it on."

Mr. Hooper's smile glimmered faintly.

---

[23]**synod:** an assembly or court of church officials.
[24]**plighted wife:** fiancée.

"There is an hour to come," said he, "when all of us shall cast aside our veils. Take it not amiss, beloved friend, if I wear this piece of crape till then."

"Your words are a mystery too," returned the young lady. "Take away the veil from them, at least."

"Elizabeth, I will," said he, "so far as my vow may suffer me.
Know, then, this veil is a type and a symbol, and I am bound to wear it ever, both in light and darkness, in solitude and before the gaze of multitudes, and as with strangers, so with my familiar friends. No mortal eye will see it withdrawn. This dismal shade must separate me from the world: even you, Elizabeth, can never come behind it!"

"What grievous affliction hath befallen you," she earnestly inquired, "that you should thus darken your eyes forever?"

"If it be a sign of mourning," replied Mr. Hooper, "I, perhaps, like most other mortals, have sorrows dark enough to be typified by a black veil."

"But what if the world will not believe that it is the type of an innocent sorrow?" urged Elizabeth. "Beloved and respected as you are, there may be whispers that you hide your face under the consciousness of secret sin. For the sake of your holy office, do away this scandal!"

The color rose into her cheeks, as she intimated the nature of the rumors that were already abroad in the village. But Mr. Hooper's mildness did not forsake him. He even smiled again—that same sad smile, which always appeared like a faint glimmering of light proceeding from the obscurity beneath the veil.

"If I hide my face for sorrow, there is cause enough," he merely replied; "and if I cover it for secret sin, what mortal might not do the same?"

And with this gentle but unconquerable **obstinacy** did he resist all her entreaties. At length Elizabeth sat silent. For a few moments she appeared lost in thought, considering, probably, what new methods might be tried to withdraw her lover from so dark a fantasy, which, if it had no other meaning, was perhaps a symptom of mental disease. Though of a firmer character than his own, the tears rolled down her cheeks. But, in an instant, as it were, a new feeling took the place of sorrow: her eyes were fixed insensibly on the black veil, when, like a sudden twilight in the air, its terrors fell around her. She arose, and stood trembling before him.

"And do you feel it then at last?" said he mournfully.

She made no reply, but covered her eyes with her hand, and turned to leave the room. He rushed forward and caught her arm.

"Have patience with me, Elizabeth!" cried he passionately. "Do not desert me, though this veil must be between us here on earth. Be mine, and hereafter there shall be no veil over my face, no darkness between our souls! It is but a mortal veil—it is not for eternity! Oh! you know not how lonely I am, and how frightened to be alone behind my black veil. Do not leave me in this miserable obscurity forever!"

obstinacy
(ŏb´stə-nə-sē) *n.*
stubbornness

"Lift the veil but once, and look me in the face," said she.

"Never! It cannot be!" replied Mr. Hooper.

"Then, farewell!" said Elizabeth.

She withdrew her arm from his grasp and slowly departed, pausing at the door to give one long, shuddering gaze that seemed almost to penetrate the mystery of the black veil. But even amid his grief, Mr. Hooper smiled to think that only a material emblem had separated him from happiness, though the horrors which it shadowed forth must be drawn darkly between the fondest of lovers.

310   From that time no attempts were made to remove Mr. Hooper's black veil or, by a direct appeal, to discover the secret which it was supposed to hide. By persons who claimed a superiority to popular prejudice, it was reckoned merely an eccentric whim, such as often mingles with the sober actions of men otherwise rational, and tinges them all with its own semblance of insanity. But with the multitude, good Mr. Hooper was irreparably a bugbear.[25] He could not walk the streets with any peace of mind, so conscious was he that the gentle and timid would turn aside to avoid him, and that others would make it a point of hardihood to throw themselves in his way. The impertinence

320 of the latter class compelled him to give up his customary walk, at sunset, to the burial ground, for when he leaned pensively over the gate, there would always be faces behind the gravestones, peeping at his black veil. A fable went the rounds that the stare of the dead people drove him thence. It grieved him to the very depth of his kind heart to observe how the children fled from his approach, breaking up their merriest sports, while his melancholy figure was yet afar off. Their instinctive dread caused him to feel, more strongly than aught else, that a preternatural[26] horror was interwoven with the threads of the black crape. In truth, his own antipathy to the veil was known to be

330 so great that he never willingly passed before a mirror, nor stooped to drink at a still fountain, lest, in its peaceful bosom, he should be affrighted by himself. This was what gave **plausibility** to the whispers that Mr. Hooper's conscience tortured him for some great crime too horrible to be entirely concealed, or otherwise than so obscurely intimated. Thus, from beneath the black veil there rolled a cloud into the sunshine, an ambiguity of sin or sorrow, which enveloped the poor minister, so that love or sympathy could never reach him. It was said that ghost and fiend consorted with him there. With self-shudderings and outward terrors, he walked continually in its shadow,

340 groping darkly within his own soul, or gazing through a medium that saddened the whole world. Even the lawless wind, it was believed, respected his dreadful secret, and never blew aside the veil. But still good Mr. Hooper sadly smiled at the pale visages of the worldly throng as he passed by.

plausibility
(plô´zə-bəl´ĭ-tē) *n.*
likelihood;
believability.

---

[25]**bugbear:** source of irrational fear.

[26]**preternatural:** inexplicable, supernatural.

Among all its bad influences, the black veil had the one desirable effect, of making its wearer a very efficient clergyman. By the aid of his mysterious emblem—for there was no other apparent cause—he became a man of awful power, over souls that were in agony for sin. His converts always regarded him with a dread peculiar to themselves,

350 affirming, though but figuratively, that before he brought them to celestial light, they had been with him behind the black veil. Its gloom, indeed, enabled him to sympathize with all dark affections. Dying sinners cried aloud for Mr. Hooper, and would not yield their breath till he appeared; though ever, as he stooped to whisper consolation, they shuddered at the veiled face so near their own. Such were the terrors of the black veil, even when Death had bared his visage! Strangers came long distances to attend service at his church, with the mere idle purpose of gazing at his figure, because it was forbidden them to behold his face. But many were made to quake ere they

360 departed! Once, during Governor Belcher's[27] administration, Mr. Hooper was appointed to preach the election sermon. Covered with his black veil, he stood before the chief magistrate, the council, and the representatives, and wrought so deep an impression that the legislative measures of that year were characterized by all the gloom and piety of our earliest ancestral sway.

In this manner Mr. Hooper spent a long life, irreproachable[28] in outward act, yet shrouded in dismal suspicions; kind and loving, though unloved, and dimly feared; a man apart from men, shunned in their health and joy, but ever summoned to their aid in mortal

370 anguish. As years wore on, shedding their snows above his sable veil, he acquired a name throughout the New England churches, and they called him Father Hooper. Nearly all his parishioners, who were of a mature age when he was settled, had been borne away by many a funeral: he had one congregation in the church, and a more crowded one in the churchyard; and having wrought so late into the evening, and done his work so well, it was now good Father Hooper's turn to rest.

Several persons were visible by the shaded candlelight in the death chamber of the old clergyman. Natural connections[29] he had none. But

380 there was the decorously grave, though unmoved physician, seeking only to **mitigate** the last pangs of the patient whom he could not save. There were the deacons, and other eminently pious members of his church. There, also, was the Reverend Mr. Clark, of Westbury, a young and zealous divine, who had ridden in haste to pray by the bedside of the expiring minister. There was the nurse, no hired handmaiden of death, but one whose calm affection had endured thus long, in secrecy,

mitigate
(mĭt´ĭ-gāt´) v. to lessen

---

[27]**Governor Belcher:** Jonathan Belcher (1682–1757), governor of Massachusetts Bay Colony from 1730 until 1741.

[28]**irreproachable:** without fault; blameless.

[29]**Natural connections:** relatives, kin.

in solitude, amid the chill of age, and would not perish, even at the dying hour. Who, but Elizabeth! And there lay the hoary head of good Father Hooper upon the death pillow, with the black veil still swathed about his brow and reaching down over his face, so that each more difficult gasp of his faint breath caused it to stir. All through life that piece of crape had hung between him and the world: it had separated him from cheerful brotherhood and woman's love, and kept him in that saddest of all prisons, his own heart; and still it lay upon his face, as if to deepen the gloom of his darksome chamber, and shade him from the sunshine of eternity.

For some time previous, his mind had been confused, wavering doubtfully between the past and the present, and hovering forward, as it were, at intervals, into the indistinctness of the world to come. There had been feverish turns, which tossed him from side to side and wore away what little strength he had. But in the most convulsive struggles, and in the wildest vagaries of his intellect, when no other thought retained its sober influence, he still showed an awful solicitude lest the black veil should slip aside. Even if his bewildered soul could have forgotten, there was a faithful woman at his pillow, who, with averted eyes, would have covered that aged face, which she had last beheld in the comeliness of manhood. At length the death-stricken old man lay quietly in the torpor[30] of mental and bodily exhaustion, with an imperceptible pulse, and breath that grew fainter and fainter, except when a long, deep, and irregular inspiration[31] seemed to prelude the flight of his spirit.

The minister of Westbury approached the bedside.

"Venerable Father Hooper," said he, "the moment of your release is at hand. Are you ready for the lifting of the veil, that shuts in time from eternity?"

Father Hooper at first replied merely by a feeble motion of his head; then, apprehensive, perhaps, that his meaning might be doubtful, he exerted himself to speak.

"Yea," said he, in faint accents, "my soul hath a patient weariness until that veil be lifted."

"And is it fitting," resumed the Reverend Mr. Clark, "that a man so given to prayer, of such a blameless example, holy in deed and thought, so far as mortal judgment may pronounce; is it fitting that a father in the church should leave a shadow on his memory that may seem to blacken a life so pure? I pray you, my venerable brother, let not this thing be! Suffer us to be gladdened by your triumphant aspect, as you go to your reward. Before the veil of eternity be lifted, let me cast aside this black veil from your face!"

And thus speaking, the Reverend Mr. Clark bent forward to reveal the mystery of so many years. But, exerting a sudden energy that made

---

[30] **torpor:** lifelessness, inactivity.

[31] **inspiration:** inhalation of air into the lungs.

all the beholders stand aghast, Father Hooper snatched both his hands from beneath the bedclothes and pressed them strongly on the black veil, resolute to struggle, if the minister of Westbury would contend with a dying man.

"Never!" cried the veiled clergyman. "On earth, never!"

"Dark old man!" exclaimed the affrighted minister, "with what horrible crime upon your soul are you now passing to the judgment?"

Father Hooper's breath heaved; it rattled in his throat; but with a mighty effort, grasping forward with his hands, he caught hold of life,
440 and held it back till he should speak. He even raised himself in bed; and there he sat shivering, with the arms of death around him, while the black veil hung down, awful, at that last moment, in the gathered terrors of a lifetime. And yet the faint, sad smile, so often there, now seemed to glimmer from its obscurity, and linger on Father Hooper's lips.

"Why do you tremble at me alone?" cried he, turning his veiled face round the circle of pale spectators. "Tremble also at each other! Have men avoided me, and women shown no pity, and children screamed and fled, only for my black veil? What, but the mystery
450 which it obscurely typifies, has made this piece of crape so awful? When the friend shows his inmost heart to his friend; the lover to his best beloved; when man does not vainly shrink from the eye of his Creator, loathsomely treasuring up the secret of his sin; then deem me a monster, for the symbol beneath which I have lived, and die! I look around me, and, lo! On every visage a Black Veil!"

While his auditors shrank from one another, in mutual affright, Father Hooper fell back upon his pillow, a veiled corpse, with a faint smile lingering on his lips. Still veiled, they laid him in his coffin, and a veiled corpse they bore him to the grave. The grass of many years has
460 sprung up and withered on that grave, the burial stone is moss-grown, and good Mr. Hooper's face is dust; but awful is still the thought, that it mouldered beneath the Black Veil!

COLLABORATIVE DISCUSSION With a partner, discuss how the black veil changes Mr. Hooper's relationship with the villagers. Cite specific quotes and textual evidence to support your ideas.

Determine Themes: Romanticism

 ELACC11-12RL2

Like other Dark Romantics and Gothic writers of his era, Nathaniel Hawthorne's work explores the ideas of sin and suffering. "The Minister's Black Veil" suggests a moral lesson that the villagers should learn from their reactions to the minister. Answering these questions can help you determine the story's **themes,** or central messages:

- How does the author introduce and develop the characters?
- How do the events of the story build upon a central idea?

Analyze Structure: Symbolism

 ELACC11-12RL5

A **symbol** is a person, place, thing, or event that represents something more than its implicit meaning. Although a symbol may have universal meanings, a writer will usually adapt it in some unique and imaginative way to suggest not just one, but myriad interpretations. Nathaniel Hawthorne is known for his masterful use of symbolism.

Analyzing the Text

 ELACC11-12RL2, ELACC11-12RL3, ELACC11-12RL5, ELACC11-12SL1

Cite Text Evidence   Support your responses with evidence from the selection.

1. **Evaluate** What evidence in the text hints at or suggests Mr. Hooper's reasons for wearing the black veil? What affect does the **ambiguity,** or uncertainty, surrounding the veil add to the overall meaning of the story?

2. **Analyze** Mr. Hooper's conversation with Elizabeth is the first time that readers learn about Mr. Hooper from his own words. What insight does this conversation provide about Mr. Hooper's character?

3. **Interpret** What does the veil symbolize? Cite specific details from the story to support your interpretation.

4. **Analyze** What themes do Mr. Hooper's last words and the final image in the story suggest? Quote and paraphrase the text in your response.

PERFORMANCE TASK

Speaking Activity: Discussion Wearing the black veil leads to Mr. Hooper's separation from his congregation. Based on the following passages, what argument would you make about the real causes of the villagers' discomfort in the minister's presence? Explore your views in a moderated discussion.

- the first sighting of the minister (lines 40–46)

- parishioners' comments after services (lines 124–135)

- the minister's arrival at the wedding (lines 174–179)

- the attempt to confront the minister (lines 214-234)

Critical Vocabulary

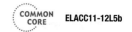

emblem	pathos	ostentatious
obstinacy	plausibility	mitigate

Practice and Apply Complete each of the following sentence stems in a way that reflects the meaning of the Critical Vocabulary word.

1. The painting evoked **pathos** in the viewer because . . .

2. The **obstinacy** of her response was made clear by . . .

3. The runner treasured his race number as an **emblem** of . . .

4. The **ostentatious** display of wealth made visitors uncomfortable because . . .

5. Proponents of the new law sought to **mitigate** opposition by . . .

6. The **plausibility** of her statement was supported by . . .

Vocabulary Strategy: Nuances in Word Meanings

When you analyze nuances in the meaning of words with similar **denotations,** or dictionary meanings, you look for subtle differences in shades of meaning. The **connotation** of a word refers to the feelings or ideas associated with it. For example, consider the connotation of the Critical Vocabulary word *ostentatious* in this sentence from "The Minister's Black Veil":

> Some gathered in little circles, huddled closely together, with their mouths all whispering in the centre; some went homeward alone, wrapped in silent meditation; some talked loudly, and profaned the Sabbath day with ostentatious laughter.

The word *ostentatious* carries a negative connotation of disapproval, in contrast to the synonym *loud*, which has a more neutral connotation. This emphasizes the reproach of the congregants' behavior on their solemn day of worship.

Practice and Apply Work with a partner to explore nuances in word meanings. Follow these steps:

- List five words from the story that have a strongly positive or negative connotation.
- Use a dictionary and a thesaurus to find definitions and synonyms of the words.
- Discuss how synonyms with different connotations would impact meaning.

Edgar Allan Poe (1809–1849) *is considered one of literature's "most brilliant, but erratic stars." Poe explored such distinctive themes as madness, untimely death, and obsession. He was orphaned at an early age, and for most of his life he struggled to earn a living. The 1845 publication of his poem "The Raven" made Poe famous. This success, however, was soon marred by the death of his wife and his own illness. Although Poe's life was brief, his literary influence was great, especially on the development of the horror story and detective fiction.*

The Pit and the Pendulum

Short Story by Edgar Allan Poe

AS YOU READ Notice sensory details that help create a mood of terror in the story.

> *Impia tortorum longos hic turba furores*
> *Sanguinis innocui, non satiata, aluit.*
> *Sospite nunc patria, fracto nunc funeris antro,*
> *Mors ubi dira fuit vita salusque patent.[1]*
>
> *[Quatrain composed for the gates of a market*
> *to be erected upon the site of the Jacobin[2] Club*
> *House at Paris.]*

I was sick—sick unto death with that long agony; and when they at length unbound me, and I was permitted to sit, I felt that my senses
10 were leaving me. The sentence—the dread sentence of death—was the last of distinct accentuation which reached my ears. After that, the sound of the inquisitorial voices seemed merged in one dreamy

---

[1] **Impia . . . patent:** *Latin:* Here the wicked crowd of tormentors, unsated, fed their long-time lusts for innocent blood. Now that our homeland is safe, now that the tomb is broken, life and health appear where once was dread death.

[2] **Jacobin** (jăk´ə-bĭn): a radical political group active in the French Revolution and later known for implementing the Reign of Terror.

indeterminate hum. It conveyed to my soul the idea of *revolution*—perhaps from its association in fancy with the burr of a millwheel. This only for a brief period; for presently I heard no more. Yet, for a while, I saw; but with how terrible an exaggeration! I saw the lips of the black-robed judges. They appeared to me white—whiter than the sheet upon which I trace these words—and thin even to grotesqueness; thin with the intensity of their expression of firmness—of immoveable

20 resolution—of stern contempt of human torture. I saw that the decrees of what to me was Fate, were still issuing from those lips. I saw them writhe with a deadly locution.[3] I saw them fashion the syllables of my name; and I shuddered because no sound succeeded. I saw, too, for a few moments of delirious horror, the soft and nearly imperceptible waving of the sable draperies which enwrapped the walls of the apartment. And then my vision fell upon the seven tall candles upon the table. At first they wore the aspect of charity, and seemed white slender angels who would save me; but then, all at once, there came a most deadly nausea over my spirit, and I felt every fiber in my frame

30 thrill as if I had touched the wire of a galvanic battery,[4] while the angel forms became meaningless specters, with heads of flame, and I saw that from them there would be no help. And then there stole into my fancy, like a rich musical note, the thought of what sweet rest there must be in the grave. The thought came gently and stealthily, and it seemed long before it attained full appreciation;[5] but just as my spirit came at length properly to feel and entertain it, the figures of the judges vanished, as if magically, from before me; the tall candles sank into nothingness; their flames went out utterly; the blackness of darkness supervened; all sensations appeared swallowed up in a mad

40 rushing descent as of the soul into Hades.[6] Then silence, and stillness, and night were the universe.

I had swooned;[7] but still will not say that all of consciousness was lost. What of it there remained I will not attempt to define, or even to describe; yet all was not lost. In the deepest slumber—no! In delirium—no! In a swoon—no! In death—no! even in the grave all *is not* lost. Else there is no immortality for man. Arousing from the most profound of slumbers, we break the gossamer web of *some* dream. Yet in a second afterward, (so frail may that web have been) we remember not that we have dreamed. In the return to life from the swoon there

50 are two stages; first, that of the sense of mental or spiritual; secondly, that of the sense of physical, existence. It seems probable that if, upon reaching the second stage, we could recall the impressions of the first, we should find these impressions eloquent in memories of the gulf

indeterminate
(ĭn´dĭ-tûr´mə-nĭt) *adj.*
not precisely known.

---

[3] **locution:** style of speech.
[4] **galvanic battery:** a device for producing electricity with series of voltaic cells.
[5] **appreciation:** understanding.
[6] **Hades:** in Greek mythology, the underworld where the dead reside.
[7] **swooned:** fainted.

beyond. And that gulf is—what? How at least shall we distinguish its shadows from those of the tomb? But if the impressions of what I have termed the first stage, are not, at will, recalled, yet, after long interval, do they not come unbidden, while we marvel whence they come? He who has never swooned, is not he who finds strange palaces and wildly familiar faces in coals that glow; is not he who beholds floating in midair the sad visions that the many may not view; is not he who ponders over the perfume of some novel flower—is not he whose brain grows bewildered with the meaning of some musical cadence which has never before arrested his attention.

    Amid frequent and thoughtful endeavors to remember; amid earnest struggles to regather some token of the state of seeming nothingness into which my soul had lapsed, there have been moments when I have dreamed of success; there have been brief, very brief periods when I have conjured up remembrances which the **lucid** reason of a later epoch assures me could have had reference only to that condition of seeming unconsciousness. These shadows of memory tell, indistinctly, of tall figures that lifted and bore me in silence down—down—still down—till a hideous dizziness oppressed me at the mere idea of the interminableness of the descent. They tell also of a vague horror at my heart, on account of that heart's unnatural stillness. Then comes a sense of sudden motionlessness throughout all things; as if those who bore me (a ghastly train!) had outrun, in their descent, the limits of the limitless, and paused from the wearisomeness of their toil. After this I call to mind flatness and dampness; and that all is *madness*—the madness of a memory which busies itself among forbidden things.

    Very suddenly there came back to my soul motion and sound— the **tumultuous** motion of the heart, and, in my ears, the sound of its beating. Then a pause in which all is blank. Then again sound, and motion, and touch—a tingling sensation pervading my frame. Then the mere consciousness of existence, without *thought*—a condition which lasted long. Then, very suddenly, thought, and shuddering terror, and earnest endeavor to comprehend my true state. Then a strong desire to lapse into insensibility. Then a rushing revival of soul and a successful effort to move. And now a full memory of the trial, of the judges, of the sable draperies, of the sentence, of the sickness, of the swoon. Then entire forgetfulness of all that followed; of all that a later day and much earnestness of endeavor have enabled me vaguely to recall.

    So far, I had not opened my eyes. I felt that I lay upon my back, unbound. I reached out my hand, and it fell heavily upon something damp and hard. There I suffered it to remain for many minutes, while I strove to imagine where and *what* I could be. I longed, yet dared not to employ my vision. I dreaded the first glance at objects around me. It was not that I feared to look upon things horrible, but that I grew aghast lest there should be *nothing* to see. At length, with a wild

lucid
(lo͞oʹsĭd) *adj.* easily understood

tumultuous
(to͞o-mŭlʹcho͞o-əs) *adj.* stormy, intense

desperation at heart, I quickly unclosed my eyes. My worst thoughts, then, were confirmed. The blackness of eternal night encompassed me. I struggled for breath. The intensity of the darkness seemed to oppress and stifle me. The atmosphere was intolerably close. I still lay quietly, and made effort to exercise my reason. I brought to mind the inquisitorial proceedings, and attempted from that point to deduce my real condition. The sentence had passed; and it appeared to me that a very long interval of time had since elapsed. Yet not for a moment did I suppose myself actually dead. Such a **supposition**, notwithstanding
110 what we read in fiction, is altogether inconsistent with real existence;—but where and in what state was I? The condemned to death, I knew, perished usually at the *autos-da-fé*,[8] and one of these had been held on the very night of the day of my trial. Had I been remanded to my dungeon, to await the next sacrifice, which would not take place for many months? This I at once saw could not be. Victims had been in immediate demand. Moreover, my dungeon, as well as all the condemned cells at Toledo, had stone floors, and light was not altogether excluded.

A fearful idea now suddenly drove the blood in torrents upon my
120 heart, and for a brief period, I once more relapsed into insensibility. Upon recovering, I at once started to my feet, trembling convulsively in every fiber. I thrust my arms wildly above and around me in all directions. I felt nothing; yet dreaded to move a step, lest I should be impeded by the walls of the *tomb*. Perspiration burst from every pore and stood in cold big beads on my forehead. The agony of suspense grew at length intolerable, and I cautiously moved forward, with my

supposition
(sŭp′ə-zĭsh′ən) *n.* a belief or assumption

---

[8] **autos-da-fé** (ou′tōz-də-fā′): Portuguese for *acts of faith*; public executions of people condemned by the Inquisition and carried out by the civil authorities.

arms extended, and my eyes straining from their sockets, in the hope of catching some faint ray of light. I proceeded for many paces; but still all was blackness and vacancy. I breathed more freely. It seemed evident that mine was not, at least, the most hideous of fates.

And now, as I still continued to step cautiously onward, there came thronging upon my recollection a thousand vague rumors of the horrors of Toledo. Of the dungeons there had been strange things narrated—fables I had always deemed them—but yet strange, and too ghastly to repeat, save in a whisper. Was I left to perish of starvation in the subterranean world of darkness; or what fate, perhaps even more fearful, awaited me? That the result would be death, and a death of more than customary bitterness, I knew too well the character of my judges to doubt. The mode and the hour were all that occupied or distracted me.

My outstretched hands at length encountered some solid obstruction. It was a wall, seemingly of stone masonry—very smooth, slimy, and cold. I followed it up! stepping with all the careful distrust with which certain antique narratives had inspired me. This process, however, afforded me no means of ascertaining the dimensions of my dungeon; as I might make its circuit, and return to the point whence I set out, without being aware of the fact; so perfectly uniform seemed the wall. I therefore sought the knife which had been in my pocket, when led into the inquisitorial chamber; but it was gone; my clothes had been exchanged for a wrapper of coarse serge.[9] I had thought of forcing the blade in some minute crevice of the masonry, so as to identify my point of departure. The difficulty, nevertheless, was but trivial; although, in the disorder of my fancy, it seemed at first **insuperable**. I tore a part of the hem from the robe and placed the fragment at full length, and at right angles to the wall. In groping my way around the prison I could not fail to encounter this rag upon completing the circuit. So, at least I thought: but I had not counted upon the extent of the dungeon, or upon my own weakness. The ground was moist and slippery. I staggered onward for some time, when I stumbled and fell. My excessive fatigue induced me to remain **prostrate**; and sleep soon overtook me as I lay.

Upon awakening, and stretching forth an arm, I found beside me a loaf and a pitcher with water. I was too much exhausted to reflect upon this circumstance, but ate and drank with avidity. Shortly afterward, I resumed my tour around the prison, and with much toil, came at last upon the fragment of the serge. Up to the period when I fell I had counted fifty-two paces, and upon resuming my walk, I counted forty-eight more;—when I arrived at the rag. There were in all, then, a hundred paces; and, admitting two paces to the yard, I presumed the dungeon to be fifty yards in circuit. I had met, however, with many

insuperable
(ĭn-sōō′pər-ə-bəl) *adj.* impossible to overcome.

prostrate
(prŏs′trāt′) *adj.* lying down with the head facing downward.

---

9 **serge** (sûrj): a type of woolen fabric.

angles in the wall, and thus I could form no guess at the shape of the vault; for vault I could not help supposing it to be.

I had little object—certainly no hope—in these researches; but a vague curiosity prompted me to continue them. Quitting the wall, I resolved to cross the area of the enclosure. At first I proceeded with extreme caution, for the floor, although seemingly of solid material, was treacherous with slime. At length, however, I took courage, and did not hesitate to step firmly; endeavoring to cross in as direct a line as possible. I had advanced some ten or twelve paces in this manner,

180   when the remnant of the torn hem of my robe became entangled between my legs. I stepped on it, and fell violently on my face.

In the confusion attending my fall, I did not immediately apprehend a somewhat startling circumstance, which yet, in a few seconds afterward, and while I still lay prostrate, arrested my attention. It was this—my chin rested upon the floor of the prison, but my lips and the upper portion of my head, although seemingly at a less elevation than the chin, touched nothing. At the same time my forehead seemed bathed in a clammy vapor, and the peculiar smell of decayed fungus arose to my nostrils. I put forward my

190   arm, and shuddered to find that I had fallen at the very brink of a circular pit, whose extent, of course, I had no means of ascertaining at the moment. Groping about the masonry just below the margin, I succeeded in dislodging a small fragment, and let it fall into the abyss. For many seconds I hearkened to its reverberations as it dashed against the sides of the chasm in its descent; at length there was a sullen plunge into water, succeeded by loud echoes. At the same moment there came a sound resembling the quick opening, and as rapid closing of a door overhead, while a faint gleam of light flashed suddenly through the gloom, and as suddenly faded away.

200   I saw clearly the doom which had been prepared for me, and congratulated myself upon the timely accident by which I had escaped. Another step before my fall, and the world had seen me no more. And the death just avoided, was of that very character which I had regarded as fabulous and frivolous in the tales respecting the Inquisition. To the victims of its tyranny, there was the choice of death with its direst physical agonies, or death with its most hideous moral horrors. I had been reserved for the latter. By long suffering my nerves had been unstrung, until I trembled at the sound of my own voice, and had become in every respect a fitting subject for the species of torture

210   which awaited me.

Shaking in every limb, I groped my way back to the wall; resolving there to perish rather than risk the terrors of the wells, of which my imagination now pictured many in various positions about the dungeon. In other conditions of mind I might have had courage to end my misery at once by a plunge into one of these abysses; but now I was the veriest of cowards. Neither could I forget what I had read of these pits—that the *sudden* extinction of life formed no part of their most horrible plan.

Agitation of spirit kept me awake for many long hours; but at length I again slumbered. Upon arousing, I found by my side as before, a loaf and a pitcher of water. A burning thirst consumed me, and I emptied the vessel at a draft. It must have been drugged; for scarcely had I drunk, before I became irresistibly drowsy. A deep sleep fell upon me—a sleep like that of death. How long it lasted of course, I know not; but when, once again, I unclosed my eyes, the objects around me were visible. By a wild sulphurous luster,[10] the origin of which I could not at first determine, I was enabled to see the extent and aspect of the prison.

In its size I had been greatly mistaken. The whole circuit of its walls did not exceed twenty-five yards. For some minutes this fact occasioned me a world of vain trouble; vain indeed! for what could be of less importance, under the terrible circumstances which environed me, than the mere dimensions of my dungeon? But my soul took a wild interest in trifles, and I busied myself in endeavors to account for the error I had committed in my measurement. The truth at length flashed upon me. In my first attempt at exploration I had counted fifty-two paces, up to the period when I fell; I must then have been within a pace or two of the fragments of serge; in fact, I had nearly performed the circuit of the vault. I then slept, and upon awaking, I must have returned upon my steps—thus supposing the circuit nearly double what it actually was. My confusion of mind prevented me from observing that I began my tour with the wall to the left, and ended it with the wall to the right.

I had been deceived, too, in respect to the shape of the enclosure. In feeling my way around I had found many angles, and thus deduced an idea of great irregularity; so potent is the effect of total darkness upon one arousing from lethargy or sleep! The angles were simply those of a few slight depressions, or niches, at odd intervals. The general shape of the prison was square. What I had taken for masonry seemed now to be iron, or some other metal, in huge plates, whose sutures or joints occasioned the depression. The entire surface of this metallic enclosure was rudely daubed in all the hideous and repulsive devices to which the charnel superstitions[11] of the monks has given rise. The figures of fiends in aspects of menace, with skeleton forms, and other more really fearful images, overspread and disfigured the walls. I observed that the outlines of these monstrosities were sufficiently distinct, but that the colors seemed faded and blurred, as if from the effects of a damp atmosphere. I now noticed the floor, too, which was of stone. In the center yawned the circular pit from whose jaws I had escaped; but it was the only one in the dungeon.

---

[10] **sulphurous luster:** a pale, yellow glow.
[11] **charnel superstitions:** irrational beliefs about death and dying.

"I could no longer doubt the doom prepared for me by monkish ingenuity in torture."

All this I saw distinctly and by much effort: for my personal condition had been greatly changed during slumber. I now lay upon my back, and at full length, on a species of low framework of wood. To this I was securely bound by a long strap resembling a surcingle.[12] It passed in many convolutions about my limbs and body, leaving at liberty only my head, and my left arm to such extent that I could, by dint[13] of much exertion, supply myself with food from an earthen dish which lay by my side on the floor. I saw, to my horror, that the pitcher had been removed. I say to my horror; for I was consumed with intolerable thirst. This thirst it appeared to be the design of my persecutors to stimulate: for the food in the dish was meat pungently seasoned.

Looking upward I surveyed the ceiling of my prison. It was some thirty or forty feet overhead, and constructed much as the side walls. In one of its panels a very singular figure riveted my whole attention. It was the painted figure of Time as he is commonly represented, save that, in lieu of a scythe, he held what, at a casual glance, I supposed to be the pictured image of a huge pendulum such as we see on antique clocks. There was something, however, in the appearance of this machine which caused me to regard it more attentively. While I gazed directly upward at it (for its position was immediately over my own) I fancied that I saw it in motion. In an instant afterward the fancy was confirmed. Its sweep was brief, and of course slow. I watched it for some minutes, somewhat in fear, but more in wonder. Wearied at length with observing its dull movement, I turned my eyes upon the other objects in the cell.

A slight noise attracted my notice, and, looking to the floor, I saw several enormous rats traversing it. They had issued from the well, which lay just within view to my right. Even then, while I gazed, they came up in troops, hurriedly, with ravenous eyes, allured by the scent of the meat. From this it required much effort and attention to scare them away.

---

[12]**surcingle:** a belt used to hold a saddle or pack onto a horse's back.
[13]**dint:** force.

It might have been half an hour, perhaps even an hour, (for I could take but imperfect note of time) before I again cast my eyes upward. What I then saw confounded and amazed me. The sweep of the pendulum had increased in extent by nearly a yard. As a natural consequence, its velocity was also much greater. But what mainly disturbed me was the idea that it had perceptibly *descended*. I now observed—with what horror it is needless to say—that its nether

300 extremity was formed of a crescent of glittering steel, about a foot in length from horn to horn; the horns upward, and the under edge evidently as keen as that of a razor. Like a razor also, it seemed massy and heavy, tapering from the edge into a solid and broad structure above. It was appended to a weighty rod of brass, and the whole *hissed* as it swung through the air.

I could no longer doubt the doom prepared for me by monkish ingenuity in torture. My cognizance of the pit had become known to the inquisitorial agents—*the pit* whose horrors had been destined for so bold a recusant[14] as myself—*the pit*, typical of hell, and regarded

310 by rumor as the Ultima Thule[15] of all their punishments. The plunge into this pit I had avoided by the merest of accidents, and I knew that surprise, or entrapment into torment, formed an important portion of all the grotesquerie of these dungeon deaths. Having failed to fall, it was no part of the demon plan to hurl me into the abyss; and thus (there being no alternative) a different and a milder destruction awaited me. Milder! I half smiled in my agony as I thought of such application of such a term.

What boots it[16] to tell of the long, long hours of horror more than mortal, during which I counted the rushing vibrations of the

320 steel! Inch by inch—line by line—with a descent only appreciable at intervals that seemed ages—down and still down it came! Days passed—it might have been that many days passed—ere it swept so closely over me as to fan me with its acrid breath. The odor of the sharp steel forced itself into my nostrils. I prayed—I wearied heaven with my prayer for its more speedy descent. I grew frantically mad, and struggled to force myself upward against the sweep of the fearful scimitar.[17] And then I fell suddenly calm, and lay smiling at the glittering death, as a child at some rare bauble.

There was another interval of utter insensibility; it was brief; for,

330 upon again lapsing into life there had been no perceptible descent in the pendulum. But it might have been long; for I knew there were demons who took note of my swoon, and who could have arrested the vibration at pleasure. Upon my recovery, too, I felt very—oh,

---

[14]**recusant:** a heretic or dissident.

[15]**Ultima Thule** (ŭl′tə-mə thōō′lē): according to ancient geographers, the most remote region of the world—here used figuratively to mean "most extreme achievement; summit."

[16]**What boots it?:** What good is it?

[17]**scimitar:** a curved sword of Middle Eastern origin.

inexpressibly sick and weak, as if through long inanition.[18] Even amid the agonies of that period, the human nature craved food. With painful effort I outstretched my left arm as far as my bonds permitted, and took possession of the small remnant which had been spared me by the rats. As I put a portion of it within my lips, there rushed to my mind a half formed thought of joy—of hope. Yet what business had I with hope? It was, as I say, a half formed thought—man has many such which are never completed. I felt that it was of joy—of hope; but I felt also that it had perished in its formation. In vain I struggled to perfect—to regain it. Long suffering had nearly annihilated all my ordinary powers of mind. I was an imbecile—an idiot.

The vibration of the pendulum was at right angles to my length. I saw that the crescent was designed to cross the region of the heart. It would fray the serge of my robe—it would return and repeat its operations—again—and again. Notwithstanding its terrifically wide sweep (some thirty feet or more) and the hissing vigor of its descent, sufficient to sunder these very walls of iron, still the fraying of my robe would be all that, for several minutes, it would accomplish. And at this thought I paused. I dared not go farther than this reflection. I dwelt upon it with a **pertinacity** of attention—as if, in so dwelling, I could arrest *here* the descent of the steel. I forced myself to ponder upon the sound of the crescent as it should pass across the garment—upon the peculiar thrilling sensation which the friction of cloth produces on the nerves. I pondered upon all this frivolity until my teeth were on edge.

Down—steadily down it crept. I took a frenzied pleasure in contrasting its downward with its lateral velocity. To the right—to the left—far and wide—with the shriek of a . . . spirit; to my heart with the stealthy pace of the tiger! I alternately laughed and howled as the one or the other idea grew predominant.

Down—certainly, relentlessly down! It vibrated within three inches of my bosom! I struggled violently, furiously, to free my left arm. This was free only from the elbow to the hand. I could reach the latter, from the platter beside me, to my mouth, with great effort, but no farther. Could I have broken the fastenings above the elbow, I would have seized and attempted to arrest the pendulum. I might as well have attempted to arrest an avalanche!

Down—still unceasingly—still inevitably down! I gasped and struggled at each vibration. I shrunk convulsively at its every sweep. My eyes followed its outward or upward whirls with the eagerness of the most unmeaning despair; they closed themselves spasmodically at the descent, although death would have been a relief, oh! how unspeakable! Still I quivered in every nerve to think how slight a sinking of the machinery would precipitate that keen, glistening axe upon my bosom. It was *hope* that prompted the nerve to quiver—the

pertinacity
(pûr′tn-ăs′ĭ-tē) *n.*
firm, unyielding intent.

---

[18]**inanition:** weakness from starvation.

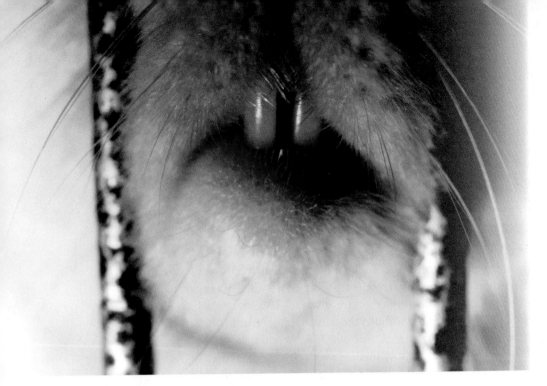

frame to shrink. It was *hope*—the hope that triumphs on the rack[19]—that whispers to the death-condemned even in the dungeons of the Inquisition.

380

I saw that some ten or twelve vibrations would bring the steel in actual contact with my robe, and with this observation there suddenly came over my spirit all the keen, collected calmness of despair. For the first time during many hours—or perhaps days—I *thought*. It now occurred to me that the bandage, or surcingle, which enveloped me, was *unique*. I was tied by no separate cord. The first stroke of the razor-like crescent athwart[20] any portion of the band, would so detach it that it might be unwound from my person by means of my left hand. But how fearful, in that case, the proximity of the steel! The result of the slightest struggle how deadly! Was it likely, moreover,

390

that the minions[21] of the torturer had not foreseen and provided for this possibility! Was it probable that the bandage crossed my bosom in the track of the pendulum? Dreading to find my faint, and, as it seemed, my last hope frustrated, I so far elevated my head as to obtain a distinct view of my breast. The surcingle enveloped my limbs and body close in all directions—*save in the path of the destroying crescent.*

Scarcely had I dropped my head back into its original position, when there flashed upon my mind what I cannot better describe than as the unformed half of that idea of deliverance to which

400

I have previously alluded, and of which a moiety[22] only floated indeterminately through my brain when I raised food to my burning

---

[19] **rack:** a device for torture that stretches the victim's limbs.

[20] **athwart:** across, from one side to the other.

[21] **minions:** followers, servants.

[22] **moiety:** one of two equal parts.

lips. The whole thought was now present—feeble, scarcely sane, scarcely definite,—but still entire. I proceeded at once, with the nervous energy of despair, to attempt its execution.

For many hours the immediate vicinity of the low framework upon which I lay, had been literally swarming with rats. They were wild, bold, ravenous; their red eyes glaring upon me as if they waited but for motionlessness on my part to make me their prey. "To what food," I thought, "have they been accustomed in the well?"

410   They had devoured, in spite of all my efforts to prevent them, all but a small remnant of the contents of the dish. I had fallen into an habitual seesaw, or wave of the hand about the platter, and, at length, the unconscious uniformity of the movement deprived it of effect. In their voracity the vermin frequently fastened their sharp fangs into my fingers. With the particles of the oily and spicy viand[23] which now remained, I thoroughly rubbed the bandage wherever I could reach it; then, raising my hand from the floor, I lay breathlessly still.

At first the ravenous animals were startled and terrified at the change—at the cessation of movement. They shrank alarmedly
420   back; many sought the well. But this was only for a moment. I had not counted in vain upon their voracity. Observing that I remained without motion, one or two of the boldest leaped upon the framework, and smelt at the surcingle. This seemed the signal for a general rush. Forth from the well they hurried in fresh troops. They clung to the wood—they overran it, and leaped in hundreds upon my person. The measured movement of the pendulum disturbed them not at all. Avoiding its strokes they busied themselves with the anointed bandage. They pressed—they swarmed upon me in ever accumulating heaps. They writhed upon my throat; their cold lips sought my own;
430   I was half stifled by their thronging pressure; disgust, for which the world has no name, swelled my bosom, and chilled, with a heavy clamminess, my heart. Yet one minute, and I felt that the struggle would be over. Plainly I perceived the loosening of the bandage. I knew that in more than one place it must be already severed. With a more than human resolution I lay *still*.

Nor had I erred in my calculations—nor had I endured in vain. I at length felt that I was *free*. The surcingle hung in ribands from my body. But the stroke of the pendulum already pressed upon my bosom. It had divided the serge of the robe. It had cut through the
440   linen beneath. Twice again it swung, and a sharp sense of pain shot through every nerve. But the moment of escape had arrived. At a wave of my hand my deliverers hurried tumultuously away. With a steady movement—cautious, sidelong, shrinking, and slow—I slid from the embrace of the bandage and beyond the reach of the scimitar. For the moment, at least, *I was free*.

---

[23]**viand:** food.

Free!—and in the grasp of the Inquisition! I had scarcely stepped from my wooden bed of horror upon the stone floor of the prison, when the motion of the hellish machine ceased and I beheld it drawn up, by some invisible force, through the ceiling. This was a lesson which I took desperately to heart. My every motion was undoubtedly watched. Free!—I had but escaped death in one form of agony, to be delivered unto worse than death in some other. With that thought I rolled my eyes nervously around the barriers of iron that hemmed me in. Something unusual—some change which at first I could not appreciate distinctly—it was obvious, had taken place in the apartment. For many minutes in a dreamy and trembling abstraction, I busied myself in vain, unconnected conjecture. During this period, I became aware, for the first time, of the origin of the sulphurous light which illuminated the cell. It proceeded from a fissure, about half an inch in width, extending entirely around the prison at the base of the walls, which thus appeared, and were, completely separated from the floor. I endeavored, but of course in vain, to look through the aperture.

As I arose from the attempt, the mystery of the alteration in the chamber broke at once upon my understanding. I have observed that, although the outlines of the figures upon the walls were sufficiently distinct, yet the colors seemed blurred and indefinite. These colors had now assumed, and were momentarily assuming, a startling and most intense brilliancy, that gave to the spectral and fiendish portraitures an aspect that might have thrilled even firmer nerves than my own. Demon eyes, of a wild and ghastly vivacity, glared upon me in a thousand directions, where none had been visible before, and gleamed with the lurid luster of a fire that I could not force my imagination to regard as unreal.

Unreal!—Even while I breathed there came to my nostrils the breath of the vapor of heated iron! A suffocating odor pervaded the prison! A deeper glow settled each moment in the eyes that glared at my agonies! A richer tint of crimson diffused itself over the pictured horrors of blood. I panted! I gasped for breath! There could be no doubt of the design of my tormentors—oh! most unrelenting! oh! most demoniac of men! I shrank from the glowing metal to the center of the cell. Amid the thought of the fiery destruction that impended, the idea of the coolness of the well came over my soul like balm. I rushed to its deadly brink. I threw my straining vision below. The glare from the enkindled roof illumined its inmost recesses. Yet, for a wild moment, did my spirit refuse to comprehend the meaning of what I saw. At length it forced—it wrestled its way into my soul—it burned itself in upon my shuddering reason.—Oh! for a voice to speak!—oh! horror!— oh! any horror but this! With a shriek, I rushed from the margin, and buried my face in my hands—weeping bitterly.

490   The heat rapidly increased, and once again I looked up, shuddering as with a fit of the ague.[24] There had been a second change in the cell—and now the change was obviously in the form. As before, it was in vain that I, at first, endeavored to appreciate or understand what was taking place. But not long was I left in doubt. The Inquisitorial vengeance had been hurried by my twofold escape, and there was to be no more dallying with the King of Terrors. The room had been square. I saw that two of its iron angles were now acute— two, consequently, obtuse. The fearful difference quickly increased with a low rumbling or moaning sound. In an instant the apartment

500 had shifted its form into that of a lozenge. But the alteration stopped not here—I neither hoped nor desired it to stop. I could have clasped the red walls to my bosom as a garment of eternal peace. "Death," I said, "any death but that of the pit!" Fool! might I have not known that *into the pit* it was the object of the burning iron to urge me? Could I resist its glow? or, if even that, could I withstand its pressure? And now, flatter and flatter grew the lozenge, with a rapidity that left me no time for contemplation. Its center, and of course, its greatest width, came just over the yawning gulf. I shrank back—but the closing walls pressed me resistlessly onward. At length for my seared and writhing

510 body there was no longer an inch of foothold on the firm floor of the prison. I struggled no more, but the agony of my soul found vent in one loud, long, and final scream of despair. I felt that I tottered upon the brink—I **averted** my eyes—

    There was a discordant hum of human voices! There was a loud blast of many trumpets! There was a harsh grating as of a thousand thunders! The fiery walls rushed back! An outstretched arm caught my own as I fell, fainting, into the abyss. It was that of General Lasalle. The French army had entered Toledo. The Inquisition was in the hands of its enemies.

avert
(ə-vûrt´) *v.* to turn away

---

[24]**ague:** an illness, like malaria, that causes fever and shivering.

COLLABORATIVE DISCUSSION What elements of the story contribute to a mood of terror? Discuss the effectiveness of these elements with a partner. Cite specific examples from the story to support your reasoning.

Determine Themes: Romanticism

COMMON CORE   ELACC11-12RL2

Although Romanticism generally conveys a sense of optimism, Gothic literature exhibits a unique fascination with the darker aspects of human nature. In contrast to Hawthorne's exploration of common fears and everyday behaviors, Poe confronts sheer terror and the grotesque. As you explore the central ideas, or themes, of "The Pit and the Pendulum," consider the following:

- What does the narrator fear most and why?
- How do the narrator's changing states of consciousness affect the story?

Analyze Structure: Atmosphere and Dramatic Tension

COMMON CORE   ELACC11-12RL3, ELACC11-12RL5

A writer's decisions about how to structure a plot contribute to a story's overall meaning and impact. For example, the structure of "The Pit and the Pendulum" helps build dramatic tension and create an atmosphere of terror. As you analyze this structure, consider the impact of Poe's choices about where to begin and end the story and about how to gradually reveal details of the narrator's plight.

Analyzing the Text

COMMON CORE   ELACC11-12RL2, ELACC11-12RL3, ELACC11-12RL5, ELACC11-12SL1

Cite Text Evidence   Support your responses with evidence from the selection.

1. **Interpret** Poe opens "The Pit and the Pendulum" by describing the narrator's sickening agony of awaiting his sentence. How does this beginning contribute to the meaning of the story? Quote vivid details in your interpretation.

2. **Infer** The narrator is often uncertain about how much time has elapsed and about the physical details of the prison. What does this uncertainty suggest about the narrator's state of mind?

3. **Analyze** Poe's narrator tells us almost nothing of his past; his personal qualities are revealed through his responses to the horrors of imprisonment. What do we know about him? What aspects of his personality allow him to survive this ordeal?

4. **Evaluate** Identify elements of Gothic fiction in "The Pit and the Pendulum." Choose one element and explain its importance to one of the story's central ideas.

PERFORMANCE TASK

Speaking Activity: Discussion In his essay "The Philosophy of Composition," Poe writes that "close circumscription of space is absolutely necessary to the effect of insulated incident—it has the force of a frame to a picture." In a small group, discuss how "The Pit and the Pendulum" demonstrates Poe's idea about confined spaces. Quote and analyze specific details to support your response.

Critical Vocabulary

COMMON CORE · ELACC11-12L4a, ELACC11-12L4d

indeterminate	lucid	tumultuous	supposition
insuperable	prostrate	pertinacity	averted

Practice and Apply Indicate whether the words in each pair are synonyms or antonyms.

1. precise/indeterminate
2. supposition/assumption
3. lucid/clear
4. concentrated/averted
5. insuperable/unconquerable
6. erect/prostrate
7. tumultuous/subdued
8. reluctance/pertinacity

Vocabulary Strategy: Context Clues

When you come across an unfamiliar word in a text, you can use **context clues,** or information in surrounding phrases and sentences, to determine the word's meaning. For example, you can use context clues to determine the meaning of the Critical Vocabulary word *indeterminate* in this passage from "The Pit and the Pendulum":

> I was sick—sick unto death with that long agony; and when they at length unbound me, and I was permitted to sit, I felt that my senses were leaving me. The sentence—the dread sentence of death—was the last of distinct accentuation which reached my ears. After that, the sound of the inquisitorial voices merged in one dreamy indeterminate hum.

The word *dreamy* provides a clue that *indeterminate* means "not precisely known." The clause "I felt that my senses were leaving me" in the first sentence also hints at this meaning. In addition, the word *distinct* contrasts what the narrator hears when the sentence is announced from the sound of the voices that follow.

Practice and Apply Work with a partner to use context clues to help determine or clarify the meaning of unknown words. Follow these steps:

- Identify unfamiliar words in the story.
- Look for synonyms, antonyms, and other clues in surrounding words and sentences that help you infer the word's meaning.
- Verify your preliminary determination of each word's meaning by checking the dictionary definition.

Language and Style: Semicolons

A writer's **style** is the particular way in which he or she uses language to communicate ideas. One characteristic of Edgar Allan Poe's distinctive, innovative style is his use of **semicolons** to create long, interrupted sentences that mirror his narrator's frantic or disturbed states of mind. Notice the effects of the semicolon in this sentence from "The Pit and the Pendulum":

> He who has never swooned, is not he who finds strange palaces and wildly familiar faces in coals that glow; is not he who beholds floating in midair the sad visions that the many may not view; is not he who ponders over the perfume of some novel flower—is not he whose brain grows bewildered with the meaning of some musical cadence which has never before arrested his attention.

The semicolons help create a long, digressive sentence that draws attention to double negatives. It also asks the reader to contemplate the joy that people miss by not allowing their minds to wander in and out of varying states of consciousness and reality.

Here are some ways that semicolons function in sentences:

Semicolons	
Purpose	**Example**
to separate two independent clauses that are linked by a conjunction (*and* or *but*), especially when the parts contain a number of commas	How long it lasted of course, I know not; but when, once again, I unclosed my eyes, the objects around me were visible. (lines 224–226)
to separate parts of a compound sentence that are not joined by a coordinating conjunction or an adverb	They shrank alarmedly back; many sought the well. (lines 419–420)
to link an independent clause with another independent clause preceded by an adverb (*then, however, thus,* or *therefore*) to closely connect the two ideas	With the particles of the oily and spicy viand which now remained, I thoroughly rubbed the bandage wherever I could reach it; then, raising my hand from the floor, I lay breathlessly still. (lines 415–417)

Practice and Apply With a partner, discuss Poe's use of semicolons in "The Pit and the Pendulum." Follow these steps:

- Identify passages in which Poe effectively uses semicolons.
- Prepare for the discussion by revising sentences to remove the semicolons and consider how this change affects tone and meaning.

Themes in American Romanticism

 COMMON CORE   ELACC11-12RL9

Comparing works of literature from the same historical period can deepen your understanding of each work's themes and provide an insight into issues and ideas important within the social context of the time. "The Minister's Black Veil" and "The Pit and the Pendulum" are both American short stories written in the first half of the nineteenth century—published in 1836 and 1843, respectively. They represent two different strains of American Romanticism. Poe is considered a master of Gothic literature. Hawthorne's work is more subtle and more psychologically probing.

Romanticism broke with the rigid formality of previous literary movements. It emphasized the power of the individual artist. The artist, once freed from artificial constraints and forms, could explore ideas and emotions that spoke to his or her personal experiences or flowed from a unique imagination.

Analyzing the Texts

COMMON CORE   ELACC11-12RL2,
ELACC11-12RL3,
ELACC11-12RL5,
ELACC11-12RL9,
ELACC11-12W9a

Cite Text Evidence   Support your responses with evidence from the selections.

1. **Cite Evidence** What is the setting of each story? What evidence from the texts reveals the setting? How does each setting relate to ideas and themes the writer presents?

2. **Understand** Compare and contrast the techniques each author uses to characterize, or reveal the distinctive traits of, the main character in each story.

3. **Analyze** Select two short passages from each story and identify details that contribute to a dark and ominous mood. Consider word choice, imagery, and plot details in your response.

4. **Analyze** How does each author use ambiguity or uncertainty to add interest and to advance his themes? Cite an example of ambiguity in each story and describe its effect.

PERFORMANCE TASK

Writing Activity: Analysis Reread the American Romanticism essay on page 234. In a one-page essay, describe how "The Minister's Black Veil" and "The Pit and the Pendulum" both exemplify aspects of Romantic literature. In your analysis, consider the following elements:

- narrative features, such as plot, setting, and descriptive details

- each work's **themes,** or central ideas about life

- the authors' tone as revealed through word choice

- the historical period in which each text was written

COLLECTION 3

PERFORMANCE TASK A

Interactive Lessons

If you need help with...
• **Writing a Narrative**
• **Using Textual Evidence**

Write a Narrative

The texts in this collection focus on the individual and how individuals fit into the larger schemes of nature and society. Consider the following quotation.

> "Trust thyself: every heart vibrates to that iron string."
> (Ralph Waldo Emerson, from "Self-Reliance")

What does this quote really mean and how does it connect to the texts in this collection? Should we all listen to our own internal sense of what is right or wrong, or what is true or untrue? Look back at the anchor text "Song of Myself" and at the other texts in the collection. Then synthesize your ideas about the role of an individual in society by writing a personal, nonfiction, or fictional narrative.

An effective narrative

- introduces a setting and main character and establishes a clear point of view
- engages readers by presenting a conflict, situation, or observation that sets the narrative in motion
- describes a clear and logical sequence of events
- uses a variety of narrative techniques, such as dialogue, pacing, and description
- reveals a significant theme related to one of the quotations
- concludes by resolving the conflict or by conveying the writer's reflection on the experiences described in the narrative

> COMMON
> CORE
>
> **ELACC11-12W3a–e** Write narratives.
> **ELACC11-12W4** Produce clear and coherent writing.
> **ELACC11-12W5** Develop and strengthen writing.
> **ELACC11-12W9a–b** Draw evidence from literary or informational texts.

PLAN

*my*Notebook

Use the notebook in your eBook to record examples and quotations that address each author's ideas about the individual's role in society.

Find Inspiration Take another look at the Emerson quote and start planning your response.

- Review the selections from "Song of Myself" and take notes about how the speaker's experiences reflect themes about the individual, society, and nature. The characters, events, and setting of your narrative should similarly reflect the theme that you want to communicate.
- Review the other stories in the collection: "The Minister's Black Veil" and "The Pit and the Pendulum." What narrative techniques do you find especially effective, and how might you use them in your own writing?

Brainstorm Write down some ideas for your narrative. How does the quotation mirror your own ideas about how individuals fit into society? In response to the quotation, create a word map to generate ideas for your narrative. Include characters, setting, plot (or sequence of events), and conflict. Remember that your narrative can be either fiction or nonfiction. You can base it on events in your own life or on the lives of people you know or have read about. Or if you prefer, you can center your narrative on an entirely fictional situation.

- A short story describes fictional characters and events.
- A nonfiction narrative describes real people and events.
- A personal narrative describes your own experiences and your reflections on them.

Get Organized
Organize your notes, using an outline or a graphic organizer.

- Decide on the structure of your narrative and create an outline or use a story map to reflect your ideas. Look back at the narrative texts in this collection to help you. Ask yourself these questions about each story:
  - » How does the story begin? Identify techniques the writer uses to engage readers and make them want to keep reading.
  - » What is the plot of the narrative? Is there more than one plot line? What is the central conflict?
  - » How does the writer develop the narrative? What is the sequence of events? Map out the rising action, climax, and falling action of the narrative.
  - » How does the writer use setting, characters, conflict, and story events to reveal a theme about individuals and their place in society or nature?
  - » How does the story end? Is the conflict resolved? How?
- Select which point of view you will use in your narrative, and take notes on other narrative techniques in the texts that you plan to use.
- Flesh out your setting and characters with descriptive details. Write down details about your characters' appearance, personality, and anything else that makes them unique.
- Remember that your narrative must reflect the theme that you want to communicate. Record some ideas for revealing your theme.

Draft Your Narrative
Write a draft of your narrative, following your notes, outline, and/or graphic organizers.

my WriteSmart

Write your rough draft in *my*WriteSmart. Focus on getting your ideas down, rather than perfecting your choice of language.

- Begin by introducing your readers to the setting, the main character(s), and a conflict or experience that will be central to the plot or narrative.

- Describe a clear sequence of events. In a short story, it's especially important that these events build toward a climax and a resolution to the conflict.

- Use descriptive details and narrative techniques to make the setting, characters, and events realistic for your readers.

- Provide a satisfying conclusion. A personal or nonfiction narrative should end with reflections on the events and experiences that have been described. A short story should end by resolving the central conflict.

Improve Your Draft
Use the chart on the following page to review the characteristics of an effective narrative. Exchange drafts with a partner. When reading your partner's draft, ask yourself the questions below. Then use feedback from your partner to revise your own draft.

my WriteSmart

Have your partner or a group of peers review your draft in *my*WriteSmart. Ask your reviewers to note any elements of your narrative that might benefit from more concrete details.

- Are the plot, setting, and characters fully developed?

- How could your partner make the narrative more interesting for readers? Suggest additional narrative techniques or descriptive language that could be used.

- Does the narrative move along at a good pace? What might your partner do to speed up the action in sections that feel too slow? Are there any places where your partner should add more descriptive details to slow readers down and give them time to reflect?

- Is the sequence of events clear? Could more transitions help clarify the narrative?

- Do the setting, characters, and events successfully convey the theme your partner intended to express?

Share Your Narrative
When your final draft is completed, read your narrative to a small group. Use your voice and gestures to present a lively reading of the narrative. Be prepared to answer questions or respond to comments from your group members.

COLLECTION 3 TASK A
NARRATIVE

	Ideas and Evidence	Organization	Language
ADVANCED	• The narrative begins memorably, clearly introducing the setting, a main character, and an interesting conflict. • The plot or sequence of events is thoroughly developed. • The narrative reveals a significant theme related to the Emerson quotation. • The narrative ends by resolving the conflict or reflecting thoughtfully on the experience.	• The sequence of events is effective, clear, and logical. • The pace and organization keep the reader curious about the next event. • Effective transitions clearly connect ideas and show the sequence of events.	• The point of view is effective and consistent throughout the narrative. • Vivid descriptive details reveal the setting and characters. • Sentence beginnings, lengths, and structures vary and have a rhythmic flow. • Spelling, capitalization, and punctuation are correct. If handwritten, the narrative is legible. • Grammar and usage are correct.
COMPETENT	• The narrative introduces the setting, a main character, and a conflict, but the opening could be more engaging. • The plot or sequence of events is adequately developed. • The narrative suggests a theme related to the Emerson quotation. • The conflict is resolved, or there is some reflection, but more details are needed to create a satisfying conclusion.	• The sequence of events is mostly clear and logical. • The pace could move along more quickly to hold the reader's interest. • A few more transitions are needed to explain the sequence of events.	• The point of view is mostly consistent. • A few more descriptive details are needed to develop the setting and characters. • Sentence beginnings, lengths, and structures mostly vary. • Several spelling, capitalization, and punctuation mistakes occur. If handwritten, the narrative is mostly legible. • Some grammatical and usage errors are repeated in the narrative.
LIMITED	• The narrative opening is uneventful; it identifies a setting and a main character but only hints at a conflict. • Development of the plot or sequence of events is uneven in a few places. • A theme related to the quotation is only hinted at. • The narrative resolves some parts of the conflict or reflects on some aspect of the experience.	• The sequence of events is confusing in a few places. • The pace often lags. • More transitions are needed throughout to clarify the sequence of events.	• The point of view shifts in a few places. • The descriptive details are ordinary or not used regularly enough. • Sentence structures vary somewhat. • Spelling, capitalization, and punctuation are often incorrect but do not make reading the narrative difficult. If handwritten, the narrative may be partially illegible. • Grammar and usage are incorrect in many places, but the writer's ideas are still clear.
EMERGING	• The opening is missing critical information about the setting and main character and doesn't set up a conflict. • The plot or sequence of events is barely developed. • There is no theme related to the quotation. • The narrative lacks a clear resolution.	• There is no clear sequence of events, making it easy for the reader to lose interest in the narrative. • The pace is ineffective. • Transitions are not used, making the narrative difficult to understand.	• The narrative lacks a clear point of view. • Descriptive details are rarely or never used to develop the setting and characters. • A repetitive sentence structure makes the writing monotonous. • Spelling, capitalization, and punctuation are incorrect throughout. If handwritten, the narrative may be partially or mostly illegible. • Many grammatical and usage errors change the meaning of the writer's ideas.

Debate an Issue

This collection focuses on individualism, imagination, society, and nature. The anchor text "Against Nature" presents a critique of the way many writers have interpreted the natural world, including Henry David Thoreau in his "rhapsodic chapter" on Spring. Do you agree or disagree with Joyce Carol Oates's critical assessment of nature writing? Synthesize your ideas by writing a brief argument and then debating the issue with your classmates.

Participants in an effective debate

- argue for or against Oates's assessment of nature writing
- draw upon evidence from "Against Nature" and at least one other text from the collection
- follow an orderly format in which speakers from each team take turns presenting their claims, counterclaims, reasons, and evidence
- encourage a thoughtful, well-reasoned exchange of ideas in which participants respond to diverse perspectives, build on each other's ideas, and evaluate the reasoning of other speakers

COMMON CORE

ELACC11-12W1 Write arguments.

ELACC11-12W2 Write informative/explanatory texts.

ELACC11-12W9a–b Draw evidence form literary or informational texts.

ELACC11-12SL1a–d Initiate and participate effectively in a range of collaborative discussions.

ELACC11-12SL3 Evaluate a speaker's point of view, reasoning, and use of evidence and rhetoric.

ELACC11-12SL4 Present information, findings, and supporting evidence.

ELACC11-12SL6 Adapt speech to a variety of contexts and tasks.

PLAN

Get Organized To prepare for the debate, collect evidence for an argument in which you will support your opinion of Oates's position.

- Review "Against Nature" and identify the claim Oates makes about nature writing. Notice the way she quotes from other texts to provide evidence for her claim.
- Review other texts in the collection with Oates's claim in mind. Identify passages that could be used to support or refute her claim.
- Based on your review of the collection, decide whether you agree or disagree with Oates's assessment.
- Write a clear statement of your claim. Identify a quotation from another collection text that strongly supports your argument.

my Notebook

Use the notebook in your eBook to record possible quotations that address the relationship between the individual and the natural world.

ACADEMIC VOCABULARY

As you build your argument on the issue of nature writers and how they interpret the natural world, be sure to use these words.

> *analogy*
> *denote*
> *quote*
> *topic*
> *unique*

Build Your Argument Write a brief argument for your position that will form the basis for your participation in the debate.

- Begin with the statement of your claim regarding Oates's view of nature writing.

- Outline several reasons that support your claim.

- Present the quotation you selected from another collection text and explain how it supports your reasoning.

Develop Counterarguments Think of arguments your classmates might make to refute your ideas. Plan the counterarguments you will make to prove your points. Create notes on these counterarguments to which you can refer during the debate.

*my***WriteSmart**

Write your rough draft in *my*WriteSmart. Focus on getting your ideas down, rather than perfecting your choice of language.

Practice for the Debate Use the chart at the end of this Performance Task to review the characteristics of an effective argument presented in a debate. Get together with a partner to practice presenting and defending your argument. If possible, select a partner who takes a different position on Oates's ideas.

- Take turns reading your written arguments to each other.

- When you have both read your arguments, begin an informal debate. One of you might begin by asking a question about the other's reasoning.

- Respond thoughtfully and respectfully to each other's comments and questions. Try to resolve any contradictions between your interpretations of the evidence.

*my***WriteSmart**

Have your partner or a group of peers review your draft in *my*WriteSmart. Ask your reviewers to note any elements of your argument that do not support the claim or that lack sufficient evidence.

Revise Your Argument After your practice debate, review your argument and make any revisions necessary to strengthen it. Consider these questions:

- Does my claim still reflect my opinion on the issue? Could it be stated more clearly so that other participants in the debate will understand it?

- Did my practice partner point out any flaws in my reasoning? Which reasons could be strengthened or replaced?

- Is the quotation I selected the best one to support my argument? If not, what might be a good replacement?

- Did my partner raise some opposing arguments that I should add to my notes?

Hold the Debate Some debates have a very formal structure, but this debate will be more informal. Select a student to serve as moderator, or have your teacher play that role.

- Start the debate by having each member of the class present his or her argument and supporting quotation. Take notes as your classmates are speaking.

- Next, the moderator should invite students to comment on or ask questions about each other's arguments. Allow the debate to flow naturally as students contribute their ideas. The moderator may step in as needed to restore order.

- Listen closely to what everyone says so that you can respond appropriately and build on others' ideas.

- Maintain a respectful tone toward your fellow debaters, even when you disagree with their ideas.

- Conclude the debate by taking a vote on Oates's assessment of nature writing. How many students agree with her, and how many disagree?

Write an Analysis After the debate, write an analysis of the ways writers tend to approach nature. Draw on other students' ideas and quotations as well as your own. Be sure to do the following in your analysis:

- introduce the topic with an interesting observation, quotation, or detail from the debate

- include a clear thesis statement about how writers tend to approach nature

- organize your central ideas in a logically structured body that develops your thesis statement

- use transitions to link sections of the text

- include quotations or examples from the debate that illustrate your central ideas

- write a concluding section that follows logically from the main body of your analysis

	Ideas and Evidence	Organization	Language
ADVANCED	• Argument introduces a precise, knowledgeable claim about the critique presented in "Against Nature." • Claim is developed thoroughly with a relevant quotation from another collection text. • Opposing claims are anticipated and effectively addressed with counterclaims.	• Reasons and evidence are organized consistently and logically throughout the argument. • Varied transitions logically connect reasons and evidence to the writer's claim. • Debaters follow the agreed-upon rules during the activity.	• Argument maintains a formal style and an objective tone. • Debaters use appropriately formal English to express their ideas clearly during the activity. • In writing and in speech, students vary sentence beginnings, lengths, and structures to create a rhythmic flow.
COMPETENT	• Argument introduces a clear claim about the critique presented in "Against Nature." • Claim is supported with a quotation from another collection text. • At least one opposing claim is anticipated and addressed with a counterclaim.	• The organization of reasons and evidence is confusing in a few places. • A few more transitions are needed to connect reasons and evidence to the writer's claim. • Debaters mostly follow the rules during the activity.	• Argument uses an informal style in places and does not always have an objective tone. • Debaters mostly use formal English to express their ideas but sometimes use informal language. • Students' writing and speech contains some variety of sentence beginnings, lengths, and structures.
LIMITED	• Argument begins with a statement about "Against Nature" but does not take a clear position. • A quotation from another collection text is provided but is not clearly relevant to the claim. • At least one opposing claim is anticipated, but it is not addressed logically.	• The organization of reasons and evidence is logical in some places, but it often doesn't follow a pattern. • Many more transitions are needed to connect reasons and evidence to the writer's position. • Debaters have some problems keeping order during the activity.	• The argument's style becomes informal in many places, and the tone is often dismissive of other viewpoints. • Debaters use mostly informal English to express their ideas. • Students' writing and speech contains little variety of sentence beginnings, lengths, and structures.
EMERGING	• Argument does not assert a claim about the critique presented in "Against Nature." • No quotation from another collection text is provided as evidence. • Opposing claims are neither anticipated nor addressed.	• An organizational strategy is not used; reasons and evidence are presented randomly. • Transitions are not used, making the argument difficult to understand. • Debaters do not follow the rules during the activity, resulting in a confusing and disorderly discussion.	• The argument's style is inappropriate, and the tone is disrespectful. • Debaters use informal English and slang, making some of their ideas unclear. • Students' writing and speech is monotonous, with no variety of sentence beginnings, lengths, and structures.

A New Birth of Freedom

❝ My father was a slave and my people died to build this country, and I'm going to stay here and have a part of it. ❞

—Paul Robeson

A New Birth of Freedom

In this collection, you will explore how African Americans and women gained new freedoms after a bloody civil war.

hmhfyi.com

COLLECTION

PERFORMANCE TASK Preview

At the end of this collection, you will have the opportunity to complete a task:

• Write a persuasive speech about a freedom that you believe should be expanded in the world today.

ACADEMIC VOCABULARY

Study the words and their definitions in the chart below. You will use these words as you discuss and write about the texts in this collection.

Word	Definition	Related Forms
confirm (kən-fûrm´) *v.*	to establish the truth or certainty of something	confirmable, confirmation
definitely (dĕf´ə-nĭt-lē) *adv.*	in an exact, certain, or precise way	definite, define, definitive
deny (dĭ-nī´) *v.*	to refuse to see or to allow; to reject	deniable, deniability, denial, denier
format (fôr´măt´) *n.*	the organization or arrangement of parts in a whole	form, formation
unify (yoo´nə-fī´) *v.*	to bring together into a cohesive whole	unity, union, unification, unifiable

COMMON CORE | ELACC11-12RL10, ELACC11-12RI3, ELACC11-12RI7, ELACC11-12RI9, ELACC11-12RI10

Civil War and Reconstruction

In the middle of the 19th century, increasing sectionalism challenged the spirit of nationalism that had characterized the Romantic era. Eventually sectional tensions erupted into the Civil War. After four years of fighting, the country was unified once again, although much of the South was in ruins and many issues remained unresolved. Writers gave voice to the debates throughout the period, sharing personal experiences and lofty ideals of freedom and unity.

A HOUSE DIVIDED For decades, Congress worked to keep a balance between slave states and free states. In the 1850s, compromise became more difficult as new western territories sought statehood. At the same time, slavery became more important to the Southern economy. New inventions such as the cotton gin allowed cotton production to increase greatly after 1793, requiring the labor of more slaves.

By the mid-19th century, many Americans had joined together to fight slavery and other social ills of the time. White and black abolitionists—both men and women— began to work for emancipation. They formed societies, spoke at conventions, published newspapers, and swamped Congress with petitions to end slavery. They also established the Underground Railroad, an informal network of abolitionists who helped slaves escape to freedom in the North. Some former slaves who had escaped related the realities of life under slavery through slave narratives such as Frederick Douglass's *My Bondage and My Freedom* (1855). Abolitionist Harriet Beecher Stowe's 1852 novel about the evils of slavery, *Uncle Tom's Cabin*, became a bestseller and is sometimes cited as a cause of the Civil War. Their work for abolition made many women more aware of how their own rights had been denied. Reformers such as Elizabeth Cady Stanton and Lucretia Mott soon turned their attention to the fight for women's rights, including the right to vote.

In the 1850s the conflict over slavery turned violent in the territory of Kansas and in the halls of Congress. Abraham Lincoln wrote in 1858, "A house divided against itself cannot stand," reflecting the bitter divisions in the country. Lincoln was a political moderate, but his election as president in 1860 ignited war. Enraged at Lincoln's pledge to stop the western spread of slavery, the Southern states seceded to form the Confederate States of America. When the Confederates fired on Fort Sumter in the spring of 1861, the Civil War began.

1857
Supreme Court's *Dred Scott* decision declares slaves are not entitled to rights of U.S. citizens.

1861
Civil War begins with Confederates firing on Fort Sumter.

1850

1850
Fugitive Slave Act forces Northern officials to return escaped slaves to their owners.

1860
Lincoln's election as president leads Southern states to secede from the Union.

VOICES OF WAR AND RECONSTRUCTION Romantic ideals of heroism that were common when the war started soon gave way to a harsher reality after the bloody Union defeat at the Battle of Bull Run in Virginia in July 1861. When the war ended in April 1865, approximately 618,000 men had died, nearly as many as have died in all other wars that the United States has ever fought. Some who gave their lives in the fight to end slavery and save the Union were African Americans, who fought in the Union army starting in 1863.

The United States suffered bitterly during the Civil War, yet it brought the Declaration of Independence's notion of liberty and equality for all closer to reality. Slavery was outlawed by Lincoln's bold Emancipation Proclamation and the Thirteenth Amendment to the Constitution. Lincoln's plans for Reconstruction, the process of addressing the injustices of slavery and re-admitting Southern states to the Union, were cut short by his assassination within days of the war's end. Republicans in Congress imposed martial law on the South and passed laws to give African Americans their rights, including the right to vote. Some African Americans were elected to Congress for the first time. Eventually, Northerners lost interest in Reconstruction, and Southern Democrats gradually took control of Southern state governments, imposing harsh new restrictions on African Americans. A compromise in 1877 allowed Republican Rutherford B. Hayes to become president in exchange for the end of federal control over the South.

As the nation began to rebuild, projects that had been interrupted by the Civil War resumed. Construction of a transcontinental railroad began in 1862, and work from the western end continued during the war. In 1869 a golden spike was driven into the track at Promontory Summit, Utah, marking the completion of the country's first nationwide railroad.

Civil war inevitably divides a nation's voice into factions. Northern and Southern writers, black and white, male and female, high-ranking officers and lowly foot soldiers all expressed different perspectives on their wartime experiences through diaries and letters. These more personal accounts contrasted with the public pronouncements of President Lincoln, whose inspirational Gettysburg Address proved to be one of the most enduring works of the Civil War. After the war, fiction created by realistic writers such as Ambrose Bierce and Stephen Crane focused on the human tragedy of the war.

1865
Civil War ends; Lincoln is assassinated; 13th Amendment abolishes slavery.

1880

1863
Lincoln issues the Emancipation Proclamation.

1869
Transcontinental Railroad is completed at Promontory, Utah.

1877
Compromise allows Hayes to become president and ends Reconstruction.

Abraham Lincoln (1809–1865) *did not favor the abolition of slavery when he became the 16th U. S. president, but he had campaigned to prevent slavery's expansion into new territories. His election in 1860 led to the Civil War. Lincoln issued the Emancipation Proclamation in January 1863. After his re-election, Lincoln successfully pushed Congress to pass the Thirteenth Amendment to the Constitution, which outlawed slavery. Lincoln gave this speech on March 4, 1865, less than six weeks before he was assassinated.*

Second Inaugural Address

Speech by Abraham Lincoln

AS YOU READ Notice how Lincoln describes how the situation in the country has changed since his first inauguration in 1861. Write down any questions you generate during reading.

FELLOW COUNTRYMEN:

At this second appearing to take the oath of the presidential office, there is less occasion for an extended address than there was at the first. Then a statement, somewhat in detail, of course to be pursued, seemed fitting and proper. Now, at the expiration of four years, during which public declarations have been constantly called forth on every point and phase of the great contest which still absorbs the attention and **engrosses** the energies of the nation, little that is new could be presented. The progress of our arms, upon which all else chiefly depends, is as well known to the public as to myself; and it is, I

10   trust, reasonably satisfactory and encouraging to all. With high hope for the future, no prediction in regard to it is **ventured**.

On the occasion corresponding to this four years ago, all thoughts were anxiously directed to an impending civil war. All dreaded it—all sought to avert it. While the inaugural address was being delivered from this place, devoted altogether to saving the Union without war, insurgent agents were in the city seeking to destroy it without war— seeking to dissolve the Union, and divide effects, by negotiation. Both parties **deprecated** war; but one of them would make war rather than

engross
(ĕn-grōs´) *v.* to completely engage the attention or interest.

venture
(vĕn´chər) *v.* to risk or dare.

deprecate
(dĕp´rĭ-kāt´) *v.* to express disapproval.

let the nation survive; and the other would accept war rather than let it
20 perish. And the war came.

One-eighth of the whole population were colored slaves, not
distributed generally over the Union, but localized in the Southern
part of it. These slaves constituted a peculiar and powerful interest.
All knew that this interest was, somehow, the cause of the war. To
strengthen, perpetuate, and extend this interest was the object for
which the insurgents would rend the Union, even by war; while the
government claimed no right to do more than to restrict the territorial
enlargement of it.

Neither party expected for the war the magnitude or the duration
30 which it has already attained. Neither anticipated that the cause of
the conflict might cease with, or even before, the conflict itself should
cease. Each looked for an easier triumph, and a result less fundamental
and astounding. Both read the same Bible, and pray to the same God;
and each invokes his aid against the other. It may seem strange that
any men should dare to ask a just God's assistance in **wringing** their
bread from the sweat of other men's faces; but let us judge not, that
we be not judged. The prayers of both could not be answered—that of
neither has been answered fully.

The Almighty has his own purposes. "Woe unto the world because
40 of offences! for it must needs be that offences come; but woe to that
man by whom the offence cometh." If we shall suppose that American
slavery is one of those offences which, in the providence of God, must
needs come, but which, having continued through his appointed time,
he now wills to remove, and that he gives to both North and South
this terrible war, as the woe due to those by whom the offence came,
shall we discern therein any departure from those divine attributes[1]
which the believers in a living God always ascribe to him? Fondly do
we hope—fervently do we pray—that this mighty scourge of war may
speedily pass away. Yet, if God wills that it continue until all the wealth
50 piled by the bondman's two hundred and fifty years of unrequited toil
shall be sunk, and until every drop of blood drawn with the lash shall
be paid by another drawn with the sword, as was said three thousand
years ago, so still it must be said, "The judgments of the Lord are true
and righteous altogether."

With malice toward none; with charity for all: with firmness in
the right, as God gives us to see the right, let us strive on to finish the
work we are in; to bind up the nation's wounds; to care for him who
shall have borne the battle, and for his widow, and his orphan—to
do all which may achieve and cherish a just and lasting peace among
60 ourselves, and with all nations.

wring
(rĭng) v. to obtain
through force or
pressure.

---

[1] **attributes:** qualities or characteristics.

COLLABORATIVE DISCUSSION How does emphasizing the changes that
have taken place in America strengthen Lincoln's argument?

Evaluate Seminal Texts:
Premises, Purposes, and Arguments

Lincoln delivered his Second Inaugural Address in a particular historical context: the nation had been at war for four years, and recent events on the battlefield were making it look more likely that the war might end soon with a Union victory. Therefore, Lincoln's overall **purpose** in this speech was to persuade his audience to adopt his ideas about how the country could best move forward. This address was Lincoln's opportunity to make his case to the public.

Lincoln's speech presents an argument. In an **argument,** a writer expresses a position on a particular issue and supports that position with reasons and evidence. In analyzing an argument, it is helpful to keep the following definitions in mind.

Parts of an Argument		
Term	**Definition**	**Example**
Claim	writer's position on an issue; a conclusion	The American colonies are justified in fighting for freedom from British rule.
Reasons	declarations that support a claim	The American colonies are oppressed by British rule.
Evidence	specific pieces of information that support a claim or reason	The British have levied unjust taxes on the colonies for ten years.
Premise	a general principle most people agree with; links the reasons and evidence to the claim	People have the right to revolt when oppressed.

As you apply these ideas in analyzing Lincoln's Second Inaugural Address, ask:

- What statements or word choices indicate Lincoln's tone or attitude toward Northerners and Southerners?
- What are some general principles that Lincoln states or implies about Americans' shared values, about slavery, and about the war?
- What are some of the central ideas that Lincoln develops in the speech about slavery and the war?
- How do the rhetorical features in the speech, including word choice and parallelism, or the use of similar grammatical structures to express ideas that are related or equal in importance, reveal which appeals Lincoln makes?

By analyzing how all these elements work together in this seminal text, you can better understand the historical significance of this speech.

Analyzing the Text

COMMON CORE

ELACC11-12RI1,
ELACC11-12RI2,
ELACC11-12RI8,
ELACC11-12RI9,
ELACC11-12SL1a,
ELACC11-12SL1c

Cite Text Evidence Support your responses with evidence from the selection.

1. **Identify** In lines 17–20, Lincoln says that one party "would make war" while the other "would accept war." To whom was Lincoln referring in each part of this sentence? How does this sentence begin to set the **tone** or attitude that Lincoln takes throughout the speech?

2. **Compare** What are the similarities between Northerners and Southerners that Lincoln outlines in the speech? What are their differences? Why does Lincoln highlight these similarities and differences in the speech?

3. **Evaluate** What does Lincoln mean when he says "Neither anticipated that the cause of the conflict might cease with, or even before, the conflict itself should cease" (lines 30–32)?

4. **Analyze** Lincoln makes a moral argument in lines 39–54. Both his premise and claim can be inferred from the Biblical quotations at the beginning and end of the paragraph. What evidence does Lincoln present so that his claim follows logically from the premise?

5. **Infer** How might the statement, "The Almighty has his own purposes" (line 39) relate to Lincoln's purpose in giving this speech?

6. **Evaluate** Why does Lincoln use religious references in his argument?

7. **Analyze** Examine the rhetorical features that Lincoln uses in the concluding paragraph of the speech. How do these features support Lincoln's purpose? What theme does this conclusion express?

PERFORMANCE TASK

Speaking Activity: Discussion As president, Lincoln's goal was to unify the North and the South. Explore how this speech supports that goal through this activity.

- Work with a partner. Have each partner play the role of a person meeting another person who has been on the other side during the Civil War. Decide which partner will represent which side.

- Review Lincoln's speech and discuss how it speaks to your interests and concerns.

- In your discussion, pose and respond to questions that will allow each partner's position to be fully expressed and heard.

- After your discussion, write a summary of how Lincoln's speech promoted unity between the North and the South.

Critical Vocabulary

engross   venture   deprecate   wring

Practice and Apply Working with a partner, answer each question from your own experiences to show that you understand the meaning of each Critical Vocabulary word.

1. What is something that **engrosses** you?

2. When have you **ventured** something?

3. When have you **deprecated** something?

4. When have you engaged in an act of **wringing**?

Vocabulary Strategy: Pronunciation

The Critical Vocabulary word *wringing* has a silent first letter, so it is pronounced just like *ringing*. Someone listening to Lincoln's speech would need to determine the correct word from its context rather than its sound. This example shows why it is helpful to verify the pronunciation of an unfamiliar word by checking a dictionary. In *wringing*, *write*, and all English words that begin with *wr*, the *w* is silent.

Not all words follow such clear patterns. For example, in the word *trough* (a long, narrow container), the *gh* sounds like *f* and the word rhymes with *off*, but in the word *through*, the *gh* is silent and the vowel combination *ou* is also pronounced differently—the word is pronounced like *threw*.

These examples emphasize that words are not always spelled the way they are pronounced, or pronounced the way they are spelled. Using a dictionary to find the correct pronunciation of a word will help you achieve and demonstrate your command of the conventions of written and spoken English.

Practice and Apply Use a dictionary to confirm the pronunciation of each of these words. Then practice the pronunciation by saying the words in sentences with a partner.

1. cliché
2. segue
3. subtle
4. colonel
5. indict
6. epitome
7. aisle
8. circuit
9. silhouette
10. respite

Language and Style: Balanced Sentences

Lincoln's style in the Second Inaugural Address is marked by complex, balanced sentences and paragraphs. **Syntax** is the way an author arranges words in phrases, clauses, and sentences. Lincoln uses his distinctive syntax to support the content of the speech and emphasize particular ideas.

Consider this sentence from the paragraph in which Lincoln makes his strongest moral argument (lines 49–54)

> Yet, if God wills that it continue until all the wealth piled by the bondsman's two hundred and fifty years of unrequited toil shall be sunk, and until every drop of blood drawn with the lash shall be paid by another drawn with the sword, as was said three thousand years ago, so still it must be said "The judgments of the Lord are true and righteous altogether."

Notice that there are two clauses that begin with the conjunction *until*. In each of these clauses, Lincoln presents images of how long the war might last to balance the evils of slavery. In the second clause, there is further balance between "blood drawn with the lash" and "drawn with the sword." He then concludes with another balanced statement about the enduring truth of God's judgments: "as it was said three thousand year ago, so still it must be said." The balanced way this long, complex sentence is constructed helps to make the meaning clear and strongly supports Lincoln's message.

Lincoln also uses this balanced style for the fourth paragraph (lines 29–38), adding to it the repetition of the words *neither*, *each*, and *both* to emphasize the similarities in Northerners' and Southerners' reactions to the war.

> Neither party expected for the war the magnitude or the duration which it has already attained. Neither anticipated that the cause of the conflict might cease with, or even before, the conflict itself should cease. Each looked for an easier triumph, and a result less fundamental and astounding. Both read the same Bible, and pray to the same God; and each invokes his aid against the other. It may seem strange that any men should dare to ask a just God's assistance in wringing their bread from the sweat of other men's faces; but let us judge not, that we be not judged. The prayers of both could not be answered—that of neither has been answered fully.

These stylistic choices support Lincoln's message that it was time for the North and the South to come together once again and to heal the nation's wounds.

Practice and Apply   Look back at the summary you wrote of your earlier discussion in response to this selection's Performance Task. Revise your writing to include balanced sentences and paragraphs to support the ideas you want to express about how Lincoln promoted unity between the North and the South in his speech.

Frederick Douglass (c. 1818–1895) *was born in Maryland and spent his first 21 years in slavery. After his escape, the Massachusetts Anti-Slavery Society hired him as a lecturer. His book* Narrative of the Life of Frederick Douglass, an American Slave *(1845) brought him international fame. Friends raised money to buy his freedom, allowing him to fully pursue his career as a reformer. He advised President Lincoln during the Civil War. In 1852, he spoke at a celebration of the Declaration of Independence.*

What to the Slave Is the Fourth of July?

Speech by Frederick Douglass

AS YOU READ Think about how Douglass answers the question of what the Fourth of July means to African Americans in 1852. Write down any questions you generate during reading.

Fellow-Citizens—Pardon me, and allow me to ask, why am I called upon to speak here to-day? What have I, or those I represent, to do with your national independence? Are the great principles of political freedom and of natural justice, embodied in that Declaration of Independence, extended to us? and am I, therefore, called upon to bring our humble offering to the national altar, and to confess the benefits, and express devout gratitude for the blessings, resulting from your independence to us?

10 Would to God, both for your sakes and ours, that an affirmative answer could be truthfully returned to these questions! Then would my task be light, and my burden easy and delightful. For who is there so cold that a nation's sympathy could not warm him? Who so obdurate[1] and dead to the claims of gratitude, that would not thankfully acknowledge such priceless benefits? Who so stolid[2] and selfish, that would not give his voice to swell the hallelujahs of

---

[1] **obdurate:** inflexible, stubborn.
[2] **stolid:** impassive or unemotional.

a nation's jubilee, when the chains of servitude had been torn from his limbs? I am not that man. In a case like that, the dumb might eloquently speak, and the "lame man leap as an hart."

But, such is not the state of the case. I say it with a sad sense
20 of the disparity between us. I am not included within the **pale** of this glorious anniversary! Your high independence only reveals the immeasurable distance between us. The blessings in which you this day rejoice, are not enjoyed in common. The rich inheritance of justice, liberty, prosperity, and independence, bequeathed by your fathers, is shared by you, not by me. The sunlight that brought life and healing to you, has brought stripes and death to me. This Fourth of July is *yours*, not *mine*. *You* may rejoice, *I* must mourn. To drag a man in fetters into the grand illuminated temple of liberty, and call upon him to join you in joyous anthems, were inhuman mockery and
30 sacrilegious[3] irony. Do you mean, citizens, to mock me, by asking me to speak to-day? If so, there is a parallel to your conduct. And let me warn you that it is dangerous to copy the example of a nation whose crimes, towering up to heaven, were thrown down by the breath of the Almighty, burying that nation in irrecoverable[4] ruin! I can to-day take up the plaintive[5] lament of a peeled and woe-smitten people.

"By the rivers of Babylon, there we sat down. Yea! we wept when we remembered Zion.[6] We hanged our harps upon the willows in the midst thereof. For there, they that carried us away captive, required of us a song; and they who wasted us required of us mirth, saying,
40 Sing us one of the songs of Zion. How can we sing the Lord's song in a strange land? If I forget thee, O Jerusalem, let my right hand forget her cunning. If I do not remember thee, let my tongue **cleave** to the roof of my mouth."

Fellow-citizens, above your national, tumultuous joy, I hear the mournful wail of millions, whose chains, heavy and grievous yesterday, are to-day rendered more intolerable by the jubilant shouts that reach them. If I do forget, if I do not faithfully remember those bleeding children of sorrow this day, "may my right hand forget her cunning, and may my tongue cleave to the roof of my mouth!" To
50 forget them, to pass lightly over their wrongs, and to chime in with the popular theme, would be treason most scandalous and shocking, and would make me a **reproach** before God and the world. My subject, then, fellow-citizens, is AMERICAN SLAVERY. I shall see this day and its popular characteristics from the slave's point of view. Standing there, identified with the American bondman, making his wrongs mine, I do not hesitate to declare, with all my soul, that the character and conduct of this nation never looked blacker to me than on this

pale
(pāl) *n.* boundary or enclosed area.

cleave
(klēv) *v.* stick or adhere.

reproach
(rĭ-prōch´) *n.* a disgrace or a bad example.

---

[3] **sacrilegious:** disrespectful, irreverent.

[4] **irrecoverable:** unable to be remedied or repaired.

[5] **plaintive:** full of sorrow; grieving.

[6] **By the rivers . . . Zion:** The beginning of Psalm 137, which refers to the Babylonian captivity of Jewish people in the 6th century BC.

> # This Fourth of July is *yours*, not *mine*. *You* may rejoice, *I* must mourn.

Fourth of July. Whether we turn to the declarations of the past, or to the professions of the present, the conduct of the nation seems
60 equally hideous and revolting. America is false to the past, false to the present, and solemnly binds herself to be false to the future. Standing with God and the crushed and bleeding slave on this occasion, I will, in the name of humanity which is outraged, in the name of liberty which is fettered, in the name of the constitution and the bible, which are disregarded and trampled upon, dare to call in question and to denounce, with all the emphasis I can command, everything that serves to perpetuate slavery—the great sin and shame of America! "I will not equivocate; I will not excuse;" I will use the severest language I can command; and yet not one word shall escape me that any man,
70 whose judgment is not blinded by prejudice, or who is not at heart a slaveholder, shall not confess to be right and just.

But I fancy I hear some one of my audience say, it is just in this circumstance that you and your brother abolitionists fail to make a favorable impression on the public mind. Would you argue more, and denounce less, would you persuade more and rebuke less, your cause would be much more likely to succeed. But, I submit, where all is plain there is nothing to be argued. What point in the anti-slavery creed would you have me argue? On what branch of the subject do the people of this country need light? Must I undertake to prove that
80 the slave is a man? That point is conceded already. Nobody doubts it. The slaveholders themselves acknowledge it in the enactment of laws for their government. They acknowledge it when they punish disobedience on the part of the slave. There are seventy-two crimes in the state of Virginia, which, if committed by a black man, (no matter how ignorant he be,) subject him to the punishment of death; while only two of these same crimes will subject a white man to the like

punishment. What is this but the acknowledgment that the slave is a moral, intellectual, and responsible being. The manhood of the slave is conceded. It is admitted in the fact that southern statute books are covered with enactments forbidding, under severe fines and penalties, the teaching of the slave to read or write. When you can point to any such laws, in reference to the beasts of the field, then I may consent to argue the manhood of the slave. When the dogs in your streets, when the fowls of the air, when the cattle on your hills, when the fish of the sea, and the reptiles that crawl, shall be unable to distinguish the slave from a brute, then will I argue with you that the slave is a man!

For the present, it is enough to affirm the equal manhood of the negro race. Is it not astonishing that, while we are plowing, planting, and reaping, using all kinds of mechanical tools, erecting houses, constructing bridges, building ships, working in metals of brass, iron, copper, silver, and gold; that, while we are reading, writing, and cyphering, acting as clerks, merchants, and secretaries, having among us lawyers, doctors, ministers, poets, authors, editors, orators, and teachers; that, while we are engaged in all manner of enterprises common to other men—digging gold in California, capturing the whale in the Pacific, feeding sheep and cattle on the hillside, living, moving, acting, thinking, planning, living in families as husbands, wives, and children, and, above all, confessing and worshiping the christian's God, and looking hopefully for life and immortality beyond the grave,— we are called upon to prove that we are men!

Would you have me argue that man is entitled to liberty? that he is the rightful owner of his own body? You have already declared it. Must I argue the wrongfulness of slavery? Is that a question for republicans?[7] Is it to be settled by the rules of logic and argumentation, as a matter beset with great difficulty, involving a doubtful application of the principle of justice, hard to be understood? How should I look to-day in the presence of Americans, dividing and subdividing a discourse, to show that men have a natural right to freedom, speaking of it relatively and positively, negatively and affirmatively? To do so, would be to make myself ridiculous, and to offer an insult to your understanding. There is not a man beneath the canopy of heaven that does not know that slavery is wrong *for him*.

What! am I to argue that it is wrong to make men brutes, to rob them of their liberty, to work them without wages, to keep them ignorant of their relations to their fellow-men, to beat them with sticks, to flay their flesh with the lash, to load their limbs with irons, to hunt them with dogs, to sell them at auction, to sunder their families, to knock out their teeth, to burn their flesh, to starve them into obedience and submission to their masters? Must I argue that a system, thus marked with blood and stained with pollution, is wrong?

---

[7] **republicans:** citizens who govern themselves by electing a president and representatives.

No; I will not. I have better employment for my time and strength than such arguments would imply.

What, then, remains to be argued? Is it that slavery is not divine; that God did not establish it; that our doctors of divinity are mistaken? There is blasphemy in the thought. That which is inhuman cannot be divine. Who can reason on such a proposition! They that can, may; I cannot. The time for such argument is past.

At a time like this, scorching irony, not convincing argument, is needed. Oh! had I the ability, and could I reach the nation's ear, 140 I would to-day pour out a fiery stream of biting ridicule, blasting reproach, withering sarcasm, and stern rebuke. For it is not light that is needed, but fire; it is not the gentle shower, but thunder. We need the storm, the whirlwind, and the earthquake. The feeling of the nation must be **quickened**; the conscience of the nation must be roused; the propriety of the nation must be startled; the hypocrisy of the nation must be exposed; and its crimes against God and man must be proclaimed and denounced.

What to the American slave is your Fourth of July? I answer, a day that reveals to him, more than all other days in the year, the 150 gross injustice and cruelty to which he is the constant victim. To him, your celebration is a sham; your boasted liberty, an unholy **license**; your national greatness, swelling vanity; your sounds of rejoicing are empty and heartless; your denunciations of tyrants, brass-fronted[8]

quicken
(kwĭk´ən) v. to make alive or stimulate.

license
(lī´səns) n. unacceptably unrestrained behavior.

---

[8] **brass-fronted:** cheaply or falsely coated.

impudence; your shouts of liberty and equality, hollow mockery; your prayers and hymns, your sermons and thanksgivings, with all your religious parade and solemnity, are to him mere bombast, fraud, deception, impiety, and hypocrisy—a thin veil to cover up crimes which would disgrace a nation of savages. There is not a nation on the earth guilty of practices more shocking and bloody, than are the
160   people of these United States, at this very hour.

Go where you may, search where you will, roam through all the monarchies and despotisms of the old world, travel through South America, search out every abuse, and when you have found the last, lay your facts by the side of the every-day practices of this nation, and you will say with me, that, for revolting barbarity and shameless hypocrisy, America reigns without a rival.

COLLABORATIVE DISCUSSION According to Douglass, what does the Fourth of July represent to an African American living in the 1850s? Why does he say this is so? Discuss these questions with a partner, citing textual evidence to support your ideas.

Analyze Author's Point of View: Speech

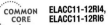
COMMON CORE ELACC11-12RI4, ELACC11-12RI6

Rhetoric is the art of using language effectively and persuasively. The Greek philosopher Aristotle categorized rhetoric into three areas: **ethos, pathos,** and **logos.** As you analyze Douglass's point of view in his speech, consider how the use of these elements contributes to the power of his speech.

Ethos	Pathos	Logos
Ethos, which is the Greek word for "character," refers to an ethical appeal that relies on the credibility of the speaker. An audience must first accept that someone is credible before they will consider him or her to be an authority on a subject. For example, Frederick Douglass has the authority to speak on behalf of slaves because he himself suffered under slavery. If a speaker, however, is unlikable or not respectable, an audience might not want to listen or be persuaded. Audiences may be swayed by two types of ethos:	Pathos means "suffering" or "experience" in Greek. In this method of appeal, a speaker tries to provoke an emotional response from the audience. The following elements can contribute to the effective use of pathos:	Logos, the Greek word for "reason," refers to an appeal through the use of logic and reasoning. A speaker using this type of appeal supports his or her claim with reasons and evidence such as facts, examples, and statistics. Douglass's speech follows a **deductive,** rather than **inductive,** line of reasoning. Instead of leading from specific evidence to a general principle or generalization (an inductive process), he begins with general principles and applies those principles to specific facts about slavery. Ask yourself the following questions as you delineate and evaluate Douglass's reasoning:
• **Extrinsic ethos** refers to the already-existing opinion the audience may have about the speaker. At the time of his speech, Douglass was well respected by his audience of fellow abolitionists.	• **Figurative language,** such as allusions and metaphors, helps an audience imagine an experience with which the speaker wants the audience to identify. Audience members can then apply their feelings about this experience to the subject of the speech. For example, Douglass prompts his audience to relate their feelings about Jewish people who were oppressed in ancient times to slaves in the United States.	• What general principles does Douglass discuss?
• **Intrinsic ethos** refers to what the audience learns about the speaker's character through the speech.	• **Word choice** can trigger emotions through the use of strong connotations. Douglass uses connotative words such as *grievous*, *scandalous*, and *shocking* to prod his audience.	• How does he apply legal concepts to the situation of slavery? • Do the general principles Douglass addresses apply logically to the specific situations he includes?

Analyzing the Text

COMMON CORE

ELACC11-12RI4,
ELACC11-12RI6,
ELACC11-12RI8,
ELACC11-12W4,
ELACC11-12SL1b,
ELACC11-12SL1d

Cite Text Evidence Support your responses with evidence from the selection.

1. **Infer** Describe the tone of Douglass's speech. How does his tone contribute to the appeal that he makes using ethos and pathos?

2. **Analyze** How does Douglass's extrinsic ethos, or reputation, influence the manner in which he addresses his audience? Explain.

3. **Interpret** According to Douglass, how does Virginia law help show that slavery is wrong? What are some of the assumptions, or premises, of Virginia law about African Americans? What type of argument is Douglass making in this section of the text: an appeal to ethos, pathos, or logos?

4. **Analyze** Identify two examples of figurative language that Douglass uses to elicit an emotional response from his audience. Explain how each example contributes to the power of his speech.

5. **Analyze** How does Douglass use word choice and literary references to confirm his credibility?

6. **Evaluate** Tokenism is the practice of making a symbolic gesture toward a goal, such as eliminating slavery, but not actually fulfilling that goal. Why does Douglass view his invitation to speak on the Fourth of July as an act of tokenism?

7. **Analyze** Douglass's use of strong connotative language builds toward the end of the text. Cite some specific examples and describe the effect that each has on the power of his message.

8. **Connect** Reread the second paragraph of the Declaration of Independence (page 112). How have the words of the Declaration influenced and inspired Douglass? How does Douglass use the Declaration to further the aims of the abolitionist cause?

PERFORMANCE TASK

Writing Activity: Outline and Summary How does Douglass persuade his audience by using logos, or logic and reasoning?

1. Work with a partner to analyze Douglass's speech and to create an outline of his argument.

2. Start your outline with a list of the general principles Douglass discusses.

3. Then, determine how Douglass supports each general principle with logical evidence or reasoning.

4. Finally, use your outline to write a summary of the speech that includes only the logic and reasoning Douglass used to persuade his audience to agree with his central ideas.

Critical Vocabulary

COMMON CORE

ELACC11-12L4,
ELACC11-12L4c,
ELACC11-12L4d

pale   cleave   reproach   quicken   license

Practice and Apply Use your knowledge of each Critical Vocabulary word to answer each question. Then discuss your answers with a partner.

1. What kind of action could be perceived as a **reproach**?

2. What types of materials might a collage artist **cleave** together?

3. What movies or stories have you seen or read in which a character was **quickened to take action**?

4. How might officials try to control the **license** of a large, unruly crowd?

5. What are some examples of places in which people would be located within a **pale**?

Vocabulary Strategy: Multiple-Meaning Words

Many words have more than one meaning. For example, when the Critical Vocabulary word *pale* is used as a noun it means "enclosed area," as in this sentence from Douglass's speech:

I am not included within the pale of this glorious anniversary!

The noun *pale* can also refer to a fence or a stake used in a fence. As an adjective, *pale* can mean "light in complexion," "dim," or "weak." *Pale* may also be used as a verb in these senses, meaning "to enclose in pales" or "to become or to cause to become pale." When you come across a familiar word used in an unfamiliar way, follow these steps to determine its meaning:

- Look at the word's context to determine its part of speech and infer the correct meaning.

- Consult a dictionary to look up all the meanings of the word.

- Compare your preliminary determination of the word's meaning to the dictionary definitions to verify the correct meaning of the word as it is used in context.

Practice and Apply Look up the meanings of each Critical Vocabulary word in a dictionary. Then write sentences for each word using its different meanings.

Language and Style: Rhetorical Devices

COMMON CORE   ELACC11-12L3a

Rhetorical devices are ways of using language that increase the power and clarity of a writer's or speaker's message. In his speech, Frederick Douglass makes effective use of many rhetorical devices and questions to keep his audience engaged and to convey the precise meanings and emotions he intends. The chart shows several examples.

Rhetorical Device	Example from Douglass's Speech
An **allusion** is an indirect reference to a famous person, place, event, or literary work.	"And let me warn you that it is dangerous to copy the example of a nation whose crimes, towering up to heaven, were thrown down by the breath of the Almighty. . . ." (This is a reference to the city of Babylon.)
Antithesis presents contrasting ideas in parallel structures.	"*You* may rejoice, *I* must mourn."
A **conceit** is an elaborate comparison between two unlike things.	"To drag a man in fetters into the grand illuminated temple of liberty, and call upon him to join you in joyous anthems, were inhuman mockery and sacrilegious irony."
Rhetorical questions are intended to make a point, not to elicit a direct answer.	"Would you have me argue that man is entitled to liberty? that he is the rightful owner of his own body? You have already declared it."

Rhetorical questions allow a speaker to vary his or her syntax by using different sentence structures. They also make listeners feel as if they are engaged in a conversation with the speaker. Consider this revision to the example in the chart:

Perhaps I should argue that a man is entitled to liberty, or that he is the rightful owner of his own body. However, you have already declared it.

In this version, Douglass is not challenging the audience to think about the absurdity of his situation. He is simply making statements. His use of rhetorical questions does a better job of conveying his bitterly ironic attitude toward the occasion.

The conceit in which Douglass compares himself to "a man in fetters" dragged into a "grand illuminated temple of liberty" (lines 27–30) is a powerful way for him to say that he is offended at being asked to celebrate liberty in a nation where so many are enslaved. Like the allusion that compares the United States to the biblical city of Babylon—which was doomed by its own arrogance—the conceit adds richness and potent imagery to the speech, leaving a lasting impression on listeners or readers.

Practice and Apply Write a paragraph that could be included in a speech about an injustice in today's world. Use at least three rhetorical devices in your paragraph. Then work with a partner and read your paragraphs aloud. Discuss the impact of the rhetorical devices.

Background *The 1848* Declaration of Sentiments *was presented at the Seneca Falls Convention, the birthplace of the women's rights movement in the United States.* **Elizabeth Cady Stanton** *(1815–1902) and* **Lucretia Mott** *(1793–1880) had first discussed the idea for the conference at the World Anti-Slavery Convention in London in 1840. Active abolitionists, the women had been denied the right to participate in the convention because of their gender.*

Declaration of Sentiments

Public Document by Elizabeth Cady Stanton

AS YOU READ Think about what rights women in the United States have today that they did not have in 1848. Write down any questions you generate during reading.

Put forth at Seneca Falls, N. Y., July, 19th *and* 20th, 1848.

WHEN, in the course of human events, it becomes necessary for one portion of the family of man to assume among the people of the earth a position different from that which they have hitherto occupied, but one to which the laws of nature, and of nature's God entitle them, a decent respect to the opinions of mankind requires that they should declare the causes that impel them to such a course.

We hold these truths to be self-evident; that all men and women are created equal; that they are endowed by their Creator with certain inalienable rights; that among these are life, liberty, and the pursuit
10 of happiness; that to secure these rights governments are instituted, deriving their just powers from the consent of the governed. Whenever any form of Government becomes destructive of those ends, it is the right of those who suffer from it, to refuse allegiance to it, and to insist upon the institution of a new government, laying its foundation on such principles, and organizing its powers in such form as to them shall seem most likely to effect their safety and happiness. Prudence,

indeed, will dictate, that governments long established should not be changed for light and **transient** causes; and accordingly, all experience hath shown that mankind are more disposed to suffer, while evils are
20 sufferable, than to right themselves by abolishing the forms to which they are accustomed. But when a long train of abuses and usurpations, pursuing invariably the same object, **evinces** a design to reduce them under absolute despotism, it is their duty to throw off such government, and provide new guards for their future security. Such has been the patient sufferance of the women under this government, and such is now the necessity which constrains them to demand the equal station, to which they are entitled.

The history of mankind is a history of repeated injuries and usurpations on the part of man toward woman, having in direct object
30 the establishment of an absolute tyranny over her. To prove this, let facts be submitted to a candid world.

He has never permitted her to exercise her inalienable right to the elective franchise.[1]

He has compelled her to submit to laws, in the formation of which she had no voice.

He has withheld from her rights which are given to the most ignorant and degraded men—both natives and foreigners.

Having deprived her of this first right of a citizen, the elective franchise, thereby leaving her without representation in the halls of
40 legislation, he has oppressed her on all sides.

He has made her, if married, in the eye of the law, civilly dead.

He has taken from her all right in property, even to the wages she earns.

He has made her, morally, an irresponsible being, as she can commit many crimes with impunity, provided they be done in the presence of her husband. In the covenant[2] of marriage, she is compelled to promise obedience to her husband, he becoming, to all intents and purposes, her master—the law giving him power to deprive her of her liberty, and to administer chastisement.[3]
50 He has so framed the laws of divorce, as to what shall be the proper causes of divorce, in case of separation, to whom the guardianship of children shall be given; as to be wholly regardless of the happiness of women—the law, in all cases, going upon the false supposition of the supremacy of man, and giving all power into his hands.

After depriving her of all rights as a woman, if single and the owner of property, he has taxed her to support a government, which recognizes her only when her property can be made profitable to it.

---

[1] **inalienable right to the elective franchise:** unassailable right to vote.
[2] **covenant:** agreement or contract.
[3] **chastisement:** punishment.

transient
(trăn′zē-ənt) *adj.* temporary; short-term.

evince
(ĭ-vĭns′) *v.* to reveal or give evidence of.

He has monopolized nearly all the profitable employments; and from those she is permitted to follow, she receives but a scanty remuneration.[4]

He closes against her all avenues to wealth and distinction, which he considers most honorable to himself. As a teacher of Theology, Medicine or Law, she is not known.

He has denied her the facilities for obtaining a thorough education—all colleges being closed against her.

He allows her in Church as well as State, but a subordinate position, claiming Apostolic[5] authority for her exclusion from the ministry, and with some exceptions, from any public participation in the affairs of the Church.

He has created a false public sentiment, by giving to the world a different code of morals for man and woman, by which moral **delinquencies** which exclude women from society, are not only tolerated but deemed of little account when committed by man.

He has usurped the prerogative of Jehovah himself, claiming it as his right to assign for her a sphere of action, when that belongs to her conscience and her God.

He has endeavored in every way that he could, to destroy her confidence in her own powers, to lessen her self-respect, and to make her willing to lead a dependent and **abject** life.

Now, in view of this entire disfranchisement of one half the people of this country, their social and religious degradation—in view of the unjust laws above mentioned and because women do feel themselves aggrieved, oppressed and fraudulently deprived of their most sacred rights, we insist that they have immediate admission to all the rights and privileges, which belong to them as citizens of these United States.

In entering upon the great work before us, we anticipate no small amount of misconception, misrepresentation and ridicule; but we shall use every instrumentality within our power to effect our object. We shall employ agents, circulate tracts, petition the State and National Legislatures, and endeavor to enlist the pulpit and the press in our behalf. We hope this Convention will be followed by a series of Conventions, embracing every part of the country.

Firmly relying upon the final triumph of the Right and the True, we do this day affix our signatures to this declaration.

delinquency
(dĭ-lĭng′kwən-sē) *n.*
shortcoming or misbehavior.

abject
(ăb′jĕkt′) *adj.*
miserable and submissive.

---

[4] **scanty remuneration:** minimal payment.
[5] **Apostolic:** from the Apostles, the initial followers of Jesus.

COLLABORATIVE DISCUSSION How do women's rights in the United States today differ from those in 1848? With a partner, discuss the differences that you find most interesting or surprising. Cite specific textual evidence from the Declaration of Sentiments to support your ideas.

Analyze Author's Purpose

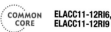

Adaptation means to change the form or content of something to make it appropriate for a new audience, situation, or purpose. For example, stage plays or movies may be adaptations of short stories or novels. Writers may take a classic text such as a Shakespearean play, a Jane Austen novel, or an ancient myth or legend and rewrite the basic story to occur in a different place or time. By adapting a well-known work, writers begin with a certain built-in appeal and audience awareness that can lend power and credibility to the new work.

The Declaration of Sentiments is an adaptation of the Declaration of Independence. After its adoption in 1776, the Declaration of Independence became a powerful and widely circulated foundational American document. It also inspired others fighting for freedom, including abolitionist Sarah Grimké who built on Jefferson's statement that "all men are created equal" when she wrote in 1837 that "men and women were CREATED EQUAL . . . whatever is right for man to do, is right for woman."

As Jefferson did when writing the Declaration of Independence, Elizabeth Cady Stanton drew upon ideas and language used by earlier writers—Sarah Grimké being one of them. However, Stanton went beyond simple adaptation of the content and also adapted the format and style from an earlier document. Keep the three concepts presented in the chart and this question in mind as you analyze the text: How did using the Declaration of Independence as a model help Stanton accomplish her purpose and add to the power and persuasiveness of the Declaration of Sentiments?

Purpose	Theme	Rhetorical Features
Consider the audience that the Declaration of Sentiments was intended to reach and the reason why the document was written. Think about how using the Declaration of Independence as a model might serve Stanton's purpose.	Theme is the central idea or message that an author wants to communicate on a particular topic, in this case the need for women's equal rights. Think about how Stanton's choice of a model allowed her to borrow and build on themes that Jefferson had expressed on the topic of independence and freedom.	Rhetorical features include all the methods a writer uses to communicate ideas and appeal to readers. In the Declaration of Independence, Jefferson made effective use of repetition, repeating words or phrases to reinforce meaning and create rhythm; and parallelism, the use of similar grammatical structures to express ideas that are related or equal in importance. Look for examples in which Stanton makes use of these same rhetorical features.

Analyzing the Text

COMMON CORE

ELACC11-12RI1,
ELACC11-12RI6,
ELACC11-12RI9,
ELACC11-12W2

Cite Text Evidence   Support your responses with evidence from the selection.

1. **Analyze** In an argument, a **claim** is an author's position on an issue. What claim does Stanton make in lines 1–6, and how does she say she will support the claim elsewhere in the document?

2. **Draw Conclusions** Lines 7–10 of Stanton's document exactly repeat the language used in the Declaration of Independence, except for the addition of the phrase "and women" in line 7. How does using this sentence—and the addition of this phrase—contribute to the persuasiveness of her argument?

3. **Interpret** In lines 24–27, Stanton writes, "Such has been the patient sufferance of the women under this government, and such is now the necessity which constrains them to demand the equal station, to which they are entitled." What does this reveal about Stanton's purpose in writing the Declaration of Sentiments?

4. **Infer** In lines 32–33, Stanton refers to "her inalienable right to the elective franchise." What does this statement mean and how is this right connected to the inalienable rights listed in lines 9–10?

5. **Cite Evidence** What rhetorical features does Stanton use throughout the list of facts that she presents, beginning with line 32? How does her rhetoric contribute to the power and persuasiveness of the text?

6. **Draw Conclusions** What specific themes about women's rights in 1848 does Stanton communicate in this document?

7. **Analyze** What rhetorical features in lines 81–93 of the Declaration of Sentiments support Stanton's purpose in writing?

PERFORMANCE TASK

Writing Activity: Comparison What are the similarities and differences between the Declaration of Sentiments and the Declaration of Independence? Write an essay making a point-by-point comparison of the two documents by following these steps.

- Review the text of the Declaration of Independence and compare each section in detail with the Declaration of Sentiments.
- Look for similarities and differences in the language and ideas of the two documents.
- Formulate a central idea that you want to communicate in your essay.

- Select the most significant and relevant points of comparison in order to develop your topic thoroughly.
- Conclude with a statement that confirms your central idea and that flows from the evidence you cited.
- Maintain a formal style and follow the conventions of standard English.

Critical Vocabulary

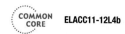

transient	evince	delinquency	abject

Practice and Apply Use your knowledge of the Critical Vocabulary words to respond to each question.

1. Why does Stanton claim that the denial of women's rights has not been a **transient** situation?

2. What does the long list of facts about man's treatment of woman **evince**?

3. When Stanton refers to moral **delinquencies** is she more likely referring to major crimes or social misconduct?

4. How might you describe the living situations of women who have **abject** lives?

Vocabulary Strategy: The Latin Root *ject*

The Critical Vocabulary word *abject* combines the Latin root *ject*, meaning "to throw" and the prefix *ab-*, meaning "from" or "away." The word *abject* originally meant "outcast," someone who is thrown out of society. This root is combined with other prefixes to form several common English words. When you see the root *ject* in a word, you can often use your knowledge of prefixes and context clues to help you determine the meaning of the word.

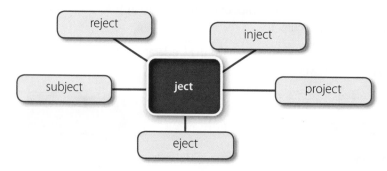

Practice and Apply Choose the word from the word web that best completes each sentence. Consider what you know about the Latin root and the prefixes. If necessary consult a dictionary to confirm the meaning.

1. Stanton believed that many people would _____ her ideas.

2. Stanton and Mott were angry that men wanted to _____ women from the anti-slavery convention.

3. Stanton believed that women should not be _____ to the demands of men.

4. A powerful speaker, Stanton had the ability to _____ her voice in a large hall.

5. By using the Declaration of Independence as a model, Stanton intended to _____ Jefferson's rhetoric into her document.

Background *As a historian,* **Iris Chang** *(1968–2004) sought to shed light on acts of injustice. Her international bestseller* The Rape of Nanking *documents previously unpublished accounts of brutal violence by the Japanese military during their occupation of China prior to World War II. In* The Chinese in America, *Chang traces her ethnic group's immigration experiences and achievements from the mid-nineteenth century to the present day. This chapter from her book details the role of Chinese laborers in building a vital transportation link that fueled westward expansion in the United States.*

Building the Transcontinental Railroad

History Writing by Iris Chang

AS YOU READ Pay attention to details about the accomplishments of Chinese laborers and the hardships they faced. Write down any questions you generate during reading.

From sea to shining sea. In the decade of the 1840s, Americans were consumed by this vision, articulated in the doctrine of Manifest Destiny, which proclaimed it the right and duty of the United States to expand its democratic way of life across the entire continent, from the Atlantic to the Pacific, from the Rio Grande in the south to the 54th parallel in the north. The country was feeling confident (during this decade, it acquired the territories of Texas, California, and Oregon), its population was increasing, and many wanted to push west, especially to California, made famous by gold and Richard Henry Dana's
10 recounting of his adventures there, in *Two Years Before the Mast.*

Making the vision real, however, was dangerous and frustrating. The territory between the coasts was unsettled and there was no reliable transport or route. Crossing the continent meant braving death by disease, brigands,[1] Native Americans, starvation, thirst, heat, or freezing. This was true especially for those headed straight to the

---

[1] **brigands:** bandits.

gold hills of California, but the gold rushers weren't the only ones frustrated by the lack of a safe passage between the settled East and the new state of California in the sparsely populated West. Californians themselves were impatient at waiting months to receive mail and

20 provisions. Washington, too, recognized the economic as well as political benefits of linking the country's two coasts. In the West lay rich farmland waiting for settlement, gold and silver to be mined and taxed. What was needed was a transcontinental railroad to move more people west and natural resources safely and profitably to major markets back east.

There were only two overland routes west—over the Rockies or along the southern route through Apache and Comanche territory— both hazardous. It took longer, but was almost always safer, to get to California from anywhere east of the Missouri by sea. This meant

30 heading east to the Atlantic Ocean or south to the Gulf of Mexico, boarding a ship that would sail almost to the southern tip of South America, passing through the Strait of Magellan, and heading back north to California. The sea voyage could be shortened considerably by disembarking on the eastern coast of Central America, traveling by wagon across the isthmus,[2] and then hitching a ride on the first steamer headed north.[3]

The need for a transcontinental railroad was so strongly argued that Congress, with the support of President Lincoln, passed legislation to finance the railroad with government bonds, even

40 though the country was already at war. Two companies divided the task of actual construction. In 1862, the Central Pacific Railroad Corporation, headed by the "Big Four"—Leland Stanford, Collis P. Huntington, Charles Crocker, and Mark Hopkins—was awarded the contract to lay tracks eastward from Sacramento, while its rival, the Union Pacific, was awarded the path westward from Omaha, Nebraska, which was already connected to the East through existing rail lines. The goal was to meet in the middle, connecting the nation with a continuous stretch of railroad tracks from the Atlantic to the Pacific. The Union Pacific's job—laying track over plains—was much

50 easier, while the Central Pacific had to go over steep mountains. The Central Pacific engineers promised that the **formidable** physical obstacles could be overcome, and to a great extent, it was Chinese labor, and even, here and there, Chinese ingenuity, that helped make the transcontinental railroad a reality.

The first and largest challenge was figuring out how to cut a path through California's and Nevada's rugged Sierra Nevada, which stood as a final barrier to the West. The workers of the Central Pacific had the dangerous task of ramming tunnels through these mountains,

formidable
(fôr′mĭ-də-bəl) *adj.*
difficult and
intimidating.

---

[2] **isthmus** (ĭs′məs): a thin strip of land between two bodies of water.
[3] Eventually, U.S. engineers would build the Panama Canal in the early twentieth century. [Author's note]

and then laying tracks across the parched Nevada and Utah deserts.
60 Some engineers, watching the project from afar, said this was
impossible. In a major recruitment drive for five thousand workers,
the Central Pacific sent advertisements to every post office in the state
of California, offering high wages to any white man willing to work.
But the appeal secured only eight hundred. Why toil for wages when
an instant fortune was possible in the mines? Many men who did sign
on were, in the words of company superintendent James Strobridge,
"unsteady men, unreliable. Some of them would stay a few days, and
some would not go to work at all. Some would stay until payday, get
a little money, get drunk, and clear out." The company thought of
70 asking the War Department for five thousand Confederate prisoners
to put to work, but Lee's surrender at the Appomattox Court House
ended the war and this plan.

Fortunately for the Central Pacific, Chinese immigrants provided
a vast pool of cheap, plentiful, and easily exploitable labor. By 1865,
the number of Chinese in California reached close to fifty thousand,
at least 90 percent of them young men. In the spring of that year, when
white laborers demanded higher pay and threatened to strike, Charles
Crocker, the Central Pacific's chief contractor, ordered Superintendent
Strobridge to recruit Chinese workers. The tactic worked, and the
80 white workers agreed to return, as long as no Chinese were hired, but
by then the Central Pacific had the upper hand and hired fifty Chinese
anyway—former miners, laundry men, domestic servants, and market
gardeners—to do the hard labor of preparing the route and laying
track. Many claimed the railroad did this as a reminder to the white
workers that others were ready to replace them. Needless to say, this
did not contribute to harmony between the whites and the Chinese.

Of course prejudice against the Chinese railroad workers did not
start with the white laborers. Initially, Superintendent Strobridge was
unhappy with their being hired. "I will not boss Chinese!" he roared,
90 suggesting that the Chinese were too delicate for the job. (The Chinese
averaged four feet ten inches in height and weighed 120 pounds.)
Crocker, however, pointed out that a race of people who had built the
Great Wall of China could build a railroad. Grudgingly, Strobridge put
the Chinese to work, giving them light jobs, like filling dump carts.

To the surprise of many—but apparently not the Chinese
themselves—the first fifty hired excelled at their work, becoming
such disciplined, fast learners that the railroad soon gave them other
responsibilities, such as rock cuts. In time, the Central Pacific hired
another fifty Chinese, and then another fifty, until eventually the
100 company employed thousands of Chinese laborers—the overwhelming
majority of the railroad workforce. E. B. Crocker, brother of Charles,
wrote to Senator Cornelius Cole (R-Calif.) that the Chinese were
nearly equal to white men in the amount of work they could do and
far more reliable. Leland Stanford, the railroad's president, and later
the founder of Stanford University, praised the Chinese as "quiet,

peaceable, patient, industrious and economical." (Stanford's position on the Chinese was governed by **expedience**. In 1862, to please the racist sentiments of the state, he called the Chinese in California the "dregs" of Asia, a "degraded" people. A few years later, he was praising

110 the Chinese to President Andrew Johnson and others in order to justify the Central Pacific's mass hiring of Chinese. Later still—notably in 1884, when he ran for the U.S. Senate—he would ally himself with those who favored a ban on Chinese immigration.)

expedience
(ĭk-spē´dē-əns) *n.* a self-interested means to an end.

Delighted by the productivity of the Chinese, railroad executives became fervent[4] advocates of Chinese immigration to California. "I like the idea of your getting over more Chinamen," Collis Huntington, one of the "Big Four" executives at the Central Pacific, wrote to Charlie Crocker in 1867. "It would be all the better for us and the State if there should a half million come over in 1868."

120 The Central Pacific printed handbills and dispatched recruiters to China, especially the Guangdong province, to find new workers. It negotiated with a steamship company to lower their rates for travel. And, fortuitously[5] for the Central Pacific, Sino-American diplomacy would create more favorable conditions for Chinese immigration to the United States. In 1868, China and the U.S. government signed the Burlingame Treaty. In exchange for "most favored nation" status in trade, China agreed to recognize the "inherent and inalienable right of man to change his home and allegiance and also the mutual advantage of free migration and emigration of their citizens and subjects

130 respectively from one country to the other for purposes of curiosity or trade or as permanent residents."

The new Chinese recruits docked at San Francisco and were immediately transported by riverboat to Sacramento, and then by the Central Pacific's own train to the end of the laid tracks, which was a moving construction site. There they were organized into teams of about a dozen or so, with each team assigned its own cook and headman, who communicated with the Central Pacific foreman. The Chinese paid for their own food and cooked it themselves—they were even able to procure special ingredients like cuttlefish, bamboo shoots,

140 and abalone. At night they slept in tents provided by the railroad, or in dugouts in the earth. At the peak of construction, Central Pacific would employ more than ten thousand Chinese men.

The large number of Chinese made white workers uncomfortable. As Lee Chew, a railroad laborer, later recalled in a spasm of national pride, the Chinese were "persecuted not for their vices but for their virtues. No one would hire an Irishman, German, Englishman or Italian when he could get a Chinese, because our countrymen are so much more honest, industrious, steady, sober and painstaking." Crocker explicitly acknowledged this work ethic. After recruiting

---

[4] **fervent:** avid, enthusiastic.

[5] **fortuitously:** luckily; by favorable chance.

> ## 66 The Chinese, without fail, always outmeasured the Cornish miners. 99

150 some Cornish miners from Virginia City, Nevada, to excavate one end
of a tunnel and the Chinese the other, he commented, "The Chinese,
without fail, always outmeasured the Cornish miners. That is to say,
they would cut more rock in a week than the Cornish miners did.
And here it was hard work, steady pounding on the rock, bone-labor."
The Cornish eventually walked off the job, vowing that "they would
not work with Chinamen anyhow," and soon, Crocker recalled, "the
Chinamen had possession of the whole work."

White laborers began to feel that Chinese **diligence** forced
everyone to work harder for less reward. Crocker recalled that one
160 white laborer near Auburn was questioned by a gentleman about
his wages. "I think we were paying $35 a month and board to white
laborers, and $30 a month to Chinamen and they boarded themselves,"
Crocker said. "The gentleman remarked, 'That is pretty good wages.'
'Yes,' says he, 'but begad if it wasn't for them damned nagurs we would
get $50 and not do half the work.' "

Some white laborers on the Central Pacific whispered among
themselves about driving the Chinese off the job, but when Charles
Crocker got wind of this, he threatened to replace all the whites with
Chinese. Eventually the white workers gave up, placated[6] perhaps
170 by being told that they alone could be promoted to the position of
foreman. The more Chinese workers, the fewer whites in the labor
force and the less competition for foreman positions among the whites.
And foremen were paid several times the wages of a Chinese laborer.

In the process of laying the track across northern California,
Nevada, and Utah, hundreds of men—Chinese, Irish, German, and
others—cleared a path through some of the world's largest trees, some
with stumps so deeply rooted that ten barrels of gunpowder were often
needed to unearth them. It was dangerous work—work that loosened
boulders, started landslides, and filled the air with flying debris. Even
180 more dangerous was the work that began upon reaching the Sierra
Nevada.

Ideally, the roadbed[7] through the mountains would be tunneled
through by heavy machinery. This machinery was unavailable,
however, because it was expensive and difficult to transport (entire

diligence
(dĭl′ə-jəns) *n.*
consistent, thorough
effort and dedication.

---

[6] **placated:** made peaceful or less angry.
[7] **roadbed:** the path or foundation on which railroad tracks are laid.

bridges would have had to be rebuilt for such machinery to reach the current site). Thus the Chinese were forced to chisel tunnels through the granite using only handheld drills, explosives, and shovels. In some places they encountered a form of porphyritic[8] rock so hard it was impervious[9] to frontal attack, even with gunpowder. Work proceeded, on average, seven inches a day, at a cost of as much as a million dollars for one mile of tunnel.

In the summer of 1866, to move farther faster, the railroad kept several shifts of men going day and night. Shoulder to shoulder, hour after hour, the Chinese railroad workers chipped away at the rock, breathing granite dust, sweating and panting by the dim flickering glow of candlelight, until even the strongest of them fainted from exhaustion.

Finally, to speed up the process, the Central Pacific brought in nitroglycerin. Only the Chinese—a people experienced with fireworks—were willing to handle this unpredictable explosive, pouring it into the tunnel through holes drilled in the granite. Countless workers perished in accidental blasts, but the Central Pacific did not keep track of the numbers.

Still the workers struggled on. One terrifying challenge lay at Cape Horn, the nickname for a three-mile stretch of gorge above the American River three miles east of Colfax, California, and fifty-seven miles east of Sacramento. Through much of the way, a flat roadbed had to be carved along a steep cliff, and a Chinese headman suggested to Strobridge that they employ an ancient method used to create fortresses along the Yangtze River gorges: they could dangle supplies down to the work site in reed baskets, attached to ropes secured over the tops of mountains.

Reeds were shipped out immediately from San Francisco to Cape Horn. At night the Chinese workers wove them into wicker baskets and fastened them to sturdy ropes. When everything was ready, workers were lowered in the baskets to drill holes and tamp in dynamite, literally sculpting the rail bed out of the face of sheer rock. The lucky ones were hauled up in time to escape the explosions; others, peppered with shards of granite and shale, fell to their deaths in the valley below.

Disease swept through the ranks of the exhausted railroad workers, but the Chinese fared better than whites. Caucasian laborers, subsisting largely on salt beef, potatoes, bread, coffee, and rancid butter, lacked vegetables in their diet, while the Chinese employed their own cooks and ate better-balanced meals. White workers succumbed to dysentery after sharing communal dippers from greasy pails, but the Chinese drank fresh boiled tea, which they kept in whiskey barrels or powder kegs suspended from each end of a bamboo

---

[8] **porphyritic** (pôr´fə-rĭt´ĭk): rock containing relatively large, visible crystals.
[9] **impervious:** immune or resistant.

pole. They also avoided alcohol and, "not having acquired the taste of whiskey," as one contemporary observed, "they have fewer fights and no blue Mondays." Most important, they kept themselves clean, which helped prevent the spread of germs. The white men had "a sort of hydrophobia," one writer observed, whereas the Chinese bathed every night before dinner, in powder kegs filled with heated water.

In the Sierras, the railroad workers endured two of the worst winters in American history. In 1865, they faced thirty-foot drifts and spent weeks just shoveling snow. The following year brought the "Homeric winter" of 1866–67, one of the most brutal ever recorded, which dropped forty feet of snow on the crews and whipped up drifts more than eighty feet high. Power snowplows, driven forward by twelve locomotives linked together, could scarcely budge the densest of these drifts. Sheds built to protect the uncompleted tracks collapsed under the weight of the snow, which snapped even the best timber. On the harshest days, travel was almost impossible; as horses broke the icy crust, sharp edges slashed their legs to the bone. They received mail from a Norwegian postal worker on cross-country skis.

Making the best of the situation, the Chinese carved a working city under the snow. Operating beneath the crust by lantern light, they trudged through a labyrinth of snow tunnels, with snow chimneys and snow stairs leading up to the surface. Meanwhile, they continued to shape the rail bed out of rock, using materials lowered down to them through airshafts in the snow.

The cost in human life was enormous. Snow slides and avalanches swept away entire teams of Chinese workers. On Christmas Day 1866, the *Dutch Flat Enquirer* announced that "a gang of Chinamen employed by the railroad…were covered up by a snow slide and four or five died before they could be exhumed. Then snow fell to such a depth that one whole camp of Chinamen was covered up during the night and parties were digging them out when our informant left." When the snow melted in the spring, the company found corpses still standing erect, their frozen hands gripping picks and shovels.

Winter was only one obstacle. Other conditions also affected the workers. Landslides rolled tons of soil across the completed track, blocking its access and often smothering workers. Melting snow mired wagons, carts, and stagecoaches in a sea of mud. Once through the mountains, the crews faced terrible extremes of weather in the Nevada and Utah deserts. There the temperature could plummet to 50 degrees below zero—freezing the ground so hard it required blasting, as if it were bedrock—or soar above 120, causing heat stroke and dehydration.

The Chinese labored from sunrise to sunset six days a week, in twelve-hour shifts. Only on Sundays did they have time to rest, mend their clothes, talk, smoke, and, of course, gamble.[10] The tedium of their lives was aggravated by the **systematized** abuse and contempt heaped on them by the railroad executives. The Chinese worked longer and harder than whites, but received less pay: because the Chinese had to pay for their own board, their wages were two-thirds those of white workers and a fourth those of the white foremen. (Even the allocation for feed for horses—fifty dollars a month for each—was twenty dollars more than the average Chinese worker earned.) Worst of all, they endured whippings from their overseers, who treated them like slaves.

Finally, the Chinese rebelled. In June 1867, as the Central Pacific tottered[11] on the brink of bankruptcy (Leland Stanford later described a two-week period when there was not a dollar of cash in the treasury), some two thousand Chinese in the Sierras walked off the job. As was their way in a strange land, they conducted the strike politely, appointing headmen to present James Strobridge a list of demands that included more pay and fewer hours in the tunnels. They also circulated among themselves a placard written in Chinese, explaining their rights. In retrospect, it is surprising that they managed to organize a strike at all, for there are also reports of frequent feuds erupting between groups of Chinese workers, fought with spades, crowbars, and spikes. But organize they did.

The Central Pacific reacted swiftly and ruthlessly. An enraged Charles Crocker contacted employment agencies in an attempt to recruit ten thousand recently freed American blacks to replace the Chinese. He stopped payments to the Chinese and cut off the food supply, effectively starving them back to work. Because most of them could not speak English, could not find work elsewhere, and lacked transportation back to California, the strike lasted only a week. However, it did achieve a small victory, securing the Chinese a raise of two dollars a month. More important, by staging the largest Chinese strike of the nineteenth century, they demonstrated to their current and future employers that while they were willing and easily managed workers, if pushed hard enough they were able to organize to protect themselves, even in the face of daunting odds.

Later, the railroad management expressed admiration at the orderliness of the strike. "If there had been that number of whites in a strike, there would have been murder and drunkenness and disorder," Crocker marveled. "But with the Chinese it was just like Sunday. These men stayed in their camps. They would come out and walk around, but not a word was said; nothing was done. No violence was perpetuated[12] along the whole line."

systematize

(sĭs´tə-mə-tīz´) *v.* to form something into an organized plan or scheme.

---

[10] Gambling was as addictive for Chinese railroad workers as whiskey among their white counterparts. Chinese gamblers left their mark on Nevada, where casinos credit the nineteenth-century Chinese railroad workers with introducing the game of keno, based on the Chinese lottery game of *pak kop piu.* [Author's note]

[11] **tottered:** wobbled unsteadily.

[12] **perpetuated:** sustained.

Image Credits: ©Corbis

The Chinese were certainly capable, however, of violence.
As the railroad neared completion, the Chinese encountered the
Irish workers of the Union Pacific for the first time. When the two
companies came within a hundred feet of each other, the Union
Pacific Irish taunted the Chinese with catcalls and threw clods of dirt.
When the Chinese ignored them, the Irish swung their picks at them,
320 and to the astonishment of the whites, the Chinese fought back. The
level of antagonism continued to rise. Several Chinese were wounded
by blasting powder the whites had secretly planted near their side.
Several days later, a mysterious explosion killed several Irish workers.
The presumption was that the Chinese had retaliated in kind. At that
point, the behavior of white workers toward the Chinese immediately
improved.

If relations were often tense between the Chinese and the Irish,
there were also moments of camaraderie.[13] In April 1869, the Central
Pacific and Union Pacific competed to see who could throw down
330 track the fastest. The competition arose after Charlie Crocker bragged
that the Chinese could construct ten miles of track a day. (In some
regions, the Union Pacific had averaged only one mile a week.) So
confident was Crocker in his employees that he was willing to wager
$10,000 against Thomas Durant, the vice president of Union Pacific.
On the day of the contest, the Central Pacific had eight Irish workers
unload materials while the Chinese spiked, gauged, and bolted the
track, laying it down as fast as a man could walk. They broke the
Union Pacific record by completing more than ten miles of track
within twelve hours and forty-five minutes.

340 On May 10, 1869, when the railways from the east and west were
finally joined at Promontory Point, Utah, the Central Pacific had
built 690 miles of track and the Union Pacific 1,086 miles. The two
coasts were now welded together. Before the transcontinental railroad,

---

[13]**camaraderie:** friendly companionship.

trekking across the country took four to six months. On the railroad, it would take six days. This accomplishment created fortunes for the moguls of the Gilded Age, but it also exacted a monumental sacrifice in blood and human life. On average, three laborers perished for every two miles of track laid, and eventually more than one thousand Chinese railroad workers died, with twenty thousand pounds of their bones shipped to China.[14] Without Chinese labor and know-how, the railroad would not have been completed. Nonetheless, the Central Pacific Railroad cheated the Chinese railway workers of everything they could. They tried to write the Chinese out of history altogether. The Chinese workers were not only excluded from the ceremonies, but from the famous photograph of white American laborers celebrating as the last spike, the golden spike, was driven into the ground. Of more immediate concern, the Central Pacific immediately laid off most of the Chinese workers, refusing to give them even their promised return passage to California. The company retained only a few hundred of them for maintenance work, some of whom spent their remaining days in isolated small towns along the way, a few living in converted boxcars.

The rest of the Chinese former railway workers were now homeless as well as jobless, in a harsh and hostile environment. Left to fend for themselves, some straggled by foot through the hinterlands[15] of America, looking for work that would allow them to survive, a journey that would disperse them throughout the nation.

---

[14] Years later, some of the Chinese railroad workers would journey back to the Sierra Nevada to search for the remains of their colleagues. On these expeditions, known as *jup seen you* ("retrieving deceased friends"), they would hunt for old grave sites, usually a heap of stones near the tracks marked by a wooden stake. Digging underneath the stones, they would find a skeleton next to a wax-sealed bottle, holding a strip of cloth inscribed with the worker's name, birth date, and district of origin. [Author's note]

[15] **hinterlands:** remote areas.

COLLABORATIVE DISCUSSION With a partner, discuss examples of how racism contributed to the challenges Chinese laborers endured while building the transcontinental railroad. Cite specific evidence in the text to support your ideas.

Analyze Ideas and Events: Sequence

COMMON CORE ELACC11-12RI3

"Building the Transcontinental Railroad" is a **historical narrative,** an account of real events that occurred in the past. To help readers understand the role of Chinese laborers in building the railroad, Iris Chang presents events in **chronological order.** This structural format allows Chang to develop the sequence of events over the course of the text. Dates and **time-order signal words** such as *finally*, *later*, and *then* help show the connections between a sequence of events. As you analyze the ideas and events Chang presents, you might use a sequence chart like the one below to record important events and dates.

First:

↓

Then:

↓

In June 1867, two thousand Chinese laborers went on strike.

↓

Then:

↓

Finally:

Author's Purpose: Tone and Style

COMMON CORE ELACC11-12RI6

An **author's purpose** is his or her reason for writing. Analyzing elements of a writer's **style** may help you determine an author's purpose. For example, identifying Iris Chang's **tone,** or attitude toward her topic, might help you confirm your inferences about her reasons for telling the story of Chinese laborers who built the transcontinental railroad. Chang's purpose for writing shapes her word choice and the details she chooses to include in her narration of events. An author's purpose also affects the kinds of sources an author consults. For example, an author might use information from primary source documents to add strength to the central ideas of the text. Ask yourself these questions to determine and analyze Iris Chang's purpose:

- What is Chang's attitude toward the treatment of Chinese laborers?
- What details and events does Chang emphasize in the account?
- How do certain descriptions and quotations add power to Chang's message?

Analyzing the Text

 COMMON CORE

ELACC11-12RI3,
ELACC11-12RI4,
ELACC11-12RI6,
ELACC11-12W7,
ELACC11-12SL1a,
ELACC11-12SL3,
ELACC11-12L4a

Cite Text Evidence   Support your responses with evidence from the selection.

1. **Infer** According to Iris Chang, what economic, social, and political forces led the United States to build the transcontinental railroad?

2. **Summarize** What were the main challenges that the Central Pacific faced in completing its part of the transcontinental railroad?

3. **Infer** What is Iris Chang's purpose for writing "Building the Transcontinental Railroad"? Cite evidence from the text that helps you infer her purpose.

4. **Analyze** Identify Iris Chang's tone toward her topic or the various main elements of her topic. Provide examples of word choice that reflects her attitude.

5. **Draw Conclusions** In lines 198–203, Chang refers to the use of nitroglycerin to tunnel through mountains. What context clues help you determine the meaning of this technical term?

6. **Evaluate** How does Chang's use of quotations from primary sources contribute to the effectiveness of her message?

7. **Evaluate** In lines 237–261, Chang provides a detailed description of the "Homeric winter" of 1866–1867. What does the word *Homeric* suggest? How does her description support the central idea of the text as a whole?

8. **Summarize** How does Chang's description of the strike connect to the other events she presents?

PERFORMANCE TASK

Speaking Activity: Discussion "Building the Transcontinental Railroad" describes the role of Chinese workers in creating an infrastructure that transformed the United States. Explore the topic in further depth and evaluate Chang's account through research and discussion.

- Conduct research on the building of the transcontinental railroad. Take notes to compare and contrast your findings with Iris Chang's account. List similarities and differences between Chang's account and the accounts you discover in your research.

- Engage in a collaborative group discussion to evaluate the effectiveness of Chang's account based on the details and events she includes, her links among ideas, and her points of emphasis. Support your opinions with evidence from the text and from your research.

Critical Vocabulary

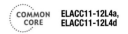

COMMON CORE   ELACC11-12L4a,
               ELACC11-12L4d

formidable   **expedience**   **diligence**   **systematize**

Practice and Apply Use your knowledge of the Critical Vocabulary words in your written responses.

1. Tell about a **formidable** task that you accomplished.

2. Identify an action that someone took that was guided by **expedience.**

3. Describe something you did with **diligence.**

4. Explain how you **systematized** a process for completing a complex project.

Vocabulary Strategy: Context Clues

When you come across an unfamiliar word, **context clues** in surrounding phrases and sentences can help you determine its meaning. Notice how the highlighted context clues in the examples below from "Building the Transcontinental Railroad" can help you determine the meaning of the boldfaced words.

Context Clue	Example
Provides a **definition** of the doctrine of Manifest Destiny	"... the **doctrine of Manifest Destiny,** which proclaimed it the right and duty of the United States to expand its democratic way of life across the continent, ..."
Provides an **example** of Stanford's expedience	"Stanford's position on the Chinese was governed by **expedience.** In 1862, to please the racist sentiments of the state, he called the Chinese in California the 'dregs' of Asia, ..."
Suggests a **similarity:** diligence is hard work	"... Chinese **diligence** forced everyone to work harder for less reward."
Suggests a **contrast:** something that is formidable is difficult to overcome	"The Central Pacific engineers promised that the **formidable** physical obstacles could be overcome, ..."

Practice and Apply Use context clues to help you determine the meaning of unknown words in "Building the Transcontinental Railroad." Follow these steps:

- Identify unfamiliar words in the text.
- Look for context clues that provide a definition or example of the unknown word, or compare or contrast with it.
- Confirm your inferred meaning of the word in a dictionary.
- Write a new sentence for each word.

Language and Style: Avoiding Misplaced Modifiers

COMMON CORE   ELACC11-12L3a

Modifiers are words or groups of words that change or limit the meaning of other words. For example, adjectives modify nouns by telling which one, what kind, how many, or how much. Adverbs modify verbs, adjectives, and other adverbs by telling where, when, how, or to what extent. Chang's careful placement of modifiers contributes to the clarity and readability of her text.

In less professional writing a modifier is sometimes placed so far away from the word it modifies that the intended meaning of the sentence is unclear. To correct a sentence with a misplaced modifier, you must first find the word being modified. Then place the modifying word or phrase as close as possible to the word it modifies.

Read the following sentence with a misplaced modifier:

> **The railroad workers gathered the necessary supplies to finish the tunnel before starting.**

The placement of the prepositional phrase *before starting* creates confusion because it seems to modify the immediately preceding infinitive phrase *to finish the tunnel*. However, finishing the tunnel before starting would be impossible.

Here the sentence has been revised for clarity so that the prepositional phrase properly functions as an adverb modifying the verb *gathered*:

> **Before starting, the railroad workers gathered the necessary supplies to finish the tunnel.**

While it's always important to maintain clarity, writers may intentionally distance modifiers from the words they modify to add information or for stylistic reasons or for effect. For example, read this sentence from "Building the Transcontinental Railroad":

> **Grudgingly, Strobridge put the Chinese to work, giving them light jobs, like filling dump carts.**

While the adverb *grudgingly* could also be placed immediately before the verb it modifies, its placement at the beginning of the sentence helps emphasize the superintendent's reluctance to manage Chinese workers.

Practice and Apply Revise the following sentences to correct the misplaced modifiers. Refer to "Building the Transcontinental Railroad" if you are unsure about the intended meaning of a sentence.

1. Disembarking the ship and crossing the Isthmus of Panama on the sea voyage by wagon could shorten the trip to the West Coast considerably.

2. The Union Pacific Railroad was contracted to build westward from Omaha, Nebraska, across the plains already connected to other railways in the East.

3. Unpredictable and dangerous, many workers were killed by the explosives.

4. Everyone praised the railroad workers' accomplishments at the ceremony.

Background *The 54th Massachusetts Volunteer Infantry was the first black northern regiment in the Civil War. It was formed in 1863, soon after the Emancipation Proclamation was issued. African Americans had served in both the Revolutionary War and the War of 1812, but there were concerns in the North about upsetting border states and about the "effectiveness" of black soldiers. Not only did African American soldiers help the North win the Civil War, but the historical and social significance of their enlistment and of their brave service continues to resonate through the centuries.*

MEDIA ANALYSIS

The 54th Massachusetts

Documentary by HISTORY

AS YOU VIEW Note the controversy engendered by the idea of a black regiment. Write down any questions you generate during your viewing.

COLLABORATIVE DISCUSSION Why was the idea of black enlistment resisted even in the North? With a partner, discuss the objections that delayed the entrance of African Americans into the military.

Integrate and Evaluate Information

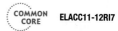

Significant historical events are complex and multifaceted. They normally involve many different people with differing motivations, creating debate or even controversy about how or why events unfolded. To do justice to the formation of the 54th Massachusetts Volunteer Infantry—a milestone on the way to full equality for African Americans—the producers of this video chose to present information using multiple types of media and sources instead of relying on just one source or expert.

To evaluate the effectiveness and validity of the information presented, use these guiding questions:

- What helps to create unity throughout the video?
- How do the interviews with historians enrich your understanding of this time in history and this particular event? Do their insights enhance your impression of the credibility of the video?
- What is the purpose of the excerpts from Frederick Douglass's and Governor Andrew's speeches?
- What ideas are supported by the visual elements?
- Do all of the elements contribute to the same perception of the event? Why or why not?

Analyzing the Media

Cite Text Evidence   Support your responses with evidence from the selection.

1. **Cause/Effect** Explain how the Emancipation Proclamation and the enlistment of African American soldiers were mutually dependent upon each other.

2. **Cite Evidence** Why did Douglass advocate so vigorously for black men to be allowed to fight? Provide specific details from the video to support your response.

3. **Analyze** What is the producers' purpose in this video? Explain which elements are most effective in achieving this purpose.

PERFORMANCE TASK

Speaking Activity: Debate Would the entrance of black soldiers into the Civil War have been as effective if it had taken place earlier?

- In a small group, debate this question, drawing on information and ideas presented in the video.

- As you listen to each debate group, evaluate the way in which group members integrate information from the video and use it to support their views.

Robert Hayden *(1913–1980) endured a childhood marred by poverty, a broken family, and a dysfunctional foster home. Plagued by depression, vision problems, and bullying peers, the Detroit native withdrew into a world of books. He researched African American folklore for the Federal Writers' Project in 1936, published his first book of poems in 1940, and earned a masters degree in English. Hayden then began his own lengthy career as a teacher while continuing to produce volumes of poetry. Much of his award-winning work explores the history and legacy of racial injustice in America.*

Runagate Runagate

Poem by Robert Hayden

AS YOU READ Identify the different voices that appear in the poem and notice the different rhythms of their speech.

I.

Runs falls rises stumbles on from darkness into darkness
and the darkness thicketed with shapes of terror
and the hunters pursuing and the hounds pursuing
and the night cold and the night long and the river
5 to cross and the jack-muh-lanterns[1] beckoning beckoning
and blackness ahead and when shall I reach that somewhere
morning and keep on going and never turn back and keep on going

        Runagate[2]
            Runagate
10   Runagate

---

[1] **jack-muh-lanterns:** a mythical goblin, popular in African-American folklore.
[2] **Runagate:** a fugitive slave.

Many thousands rise and go
many thousands crossing over

O mythic North
O star-shaped yonder Bible city

15 Some go weeping and some rejoicing
some in coffins and some in carriages
some in silks and some in shackles

Rise and go or fare you well

No more auction block for me
20 no more driver's lash for me

If you see my Pompey, 30 yrs of age,
new breeches, plain stockings, negro shoes;
if you see my Anna, likely young mulatto
branded E on the right cheek, R on the left,
25 catch them if you can and notify subscriber.
Catch them if you can, but it won't be easy.
They'll dart underground when you try to catch them,
plunge into quicksand, whirlpools, mazes,
turn into scorpions when you try to catch them.

30 And before I'll be a slave
I'll be buried in my grave

North star and bonanza gold
I'm bound for the freedom, freedom-bound
and oh Susyanna don't you cry for me[3]

35 Runagate

Runagate

II.

Rises from their anguish and their power,

Harriet Tubman,

woman of earth, whipscarred,
40 a summoning, a shining

Mean to be free

And this was the way of it, brethren brethren,
way we journeyed from Can't to Can.

---

[3] **oh Susyanna don't you cry for me:** an allusion to the chorus of "Oh! Susanna"
by Stephen Foster.

Moon so bright and no place to hide,
45 the cry up and the patterollers[4] riding,
hound dogs belling[5] in bladed air.
And fear starts a-murbling, Never make it,
we'll never make it. *Hush that now,*
and she's turned upon us, levelled pistol
50 glinting in the moonlight:
Dead folks can't jaybird-talk,[6] she says;
you keep on going now or die, she says.

Wanted   Harriet Tubman   alias The General
Alias Moses   Stealer of Slaves

55 In league with Garrison   Alcott   Emerson
Garrett   Douglass   Thoreau   John Brown

Armed and known to be Dangerous

Wanted   Reward   Dead or Alive

Tell me, Ezekiel, oh tell me do you see
60 mailed[7] Jehovah coming to deliver me?

---

[4] **patterollers:** people who watched and restricted the movement of black slaves
at night.
[5] **belling:** barking.
[6] **jaybird-talk:** talk like fools.
[7] **mailed:** covered with a flexible armor made of rings or plates.

Hoot-owl calling in the ghosted air,
five times calling to the hants[8] in the air.
Shadow of a face in the scary leaves,
shadow of a voice in the talking leaves:

65   Come ride-a my train

        Oh that train, ghost-story train
        through swamp and savanna movering movering,
        over trestles of dew, through caves of the wish,
        Midnight Special on a sabre track movering movering,
70   *first stop Mercy and the last Hallelujah.*

        Come ride-a my train

            Mean mean mean to be free.

_____

[8] **hants:** ghosts.

COLLABORATIVE DISCUSSION How does the poet unify the many
perspectives presented in the poem? With a partner, identify the poem's
central ideas and discuss how specific lines in the poem help convey them.

Analyze Language: Allusions

An **allusion** is an author's reference to a well-known historical or literary person, event, or composition. It's a figure of speech designed to evoke specific feelings or ideas associated with the thing to which the author refers. Writers try to choose allusions that their readers will definitely understand. Biblical allusions, for example, appear quite frequently throughout traditional Western art and literature—Hayden employs several, including Ezekiel (line 59), in "Runagate Runagate." An allusion, of course, cannot work successfully if nobody recognizes it.

Unlike other genres, though, modern poetry often contains extremely complex literary and cultural allusions. Many poets seem to expect a great deal from their readers. (Ezra Pound, for instance, would allude to classical Greek texts—in Greek!) However, you can still understand and enjoy a good poem without recognizing all of its allusions or cultural references. In fact, some of the best allusions work on both the literal and figurative levels. Consider the following lines from the poem:

> **And this was the way of it, brethren brethren,**
> **way we journeyed from Can't to Can.**

On one level, we can interpret a trip "from Can't to Can" as a movement away from restriction, from slavery to freedom. Yet on another level, the phrase alludes to a famous saying about the long hours of toil that enslaved people endured: "We worked from Can-see to Can't," meaning "from dawn to darkness." If you recognize this allusion, then you can also interpret the line as meaning "we traveled at night." Both interpretations work very well within the context. The best allusions, like this one, amplify meaning rather than simply convey it.

Analyzing Structure: Rhythm and Meaning

The sound produced by the arrangement of stressed and unstressed syllables, along with the intervals of time that fall between them, creates rhythm in language. People respond to rhythm instinctually and on many levels. Poets, like musicians, manipulate rhythm to express ideas and emotions. In English poetry, rhythm has two basic components:

- Accent, the vocal emphasis given to a word or syllable.
- Meter, a repetitive pattern created by small groups of accented and unaccented syllables, called feet.

Like a movie soundtrack, a poem's rhythm enhances its overall meaning and helps create a unified, multisensory experience. A good poet combines rhythm and content in complementary ways by carefully selecting words and controlling line lengths and format. Even the title Hayden chooses for his poem—"Runagate Runagate"—uses rhythm to heighten its meaning. Imagine the difference if the poet had used the word only once or chosen "Escaped Slave" instead. As you think about the meaning of the poem, pay attention to when, how, and why its rhythms rush you along, slow you down, or suddenly make you stop and change direction.

Analyzing the Text

 COMMON CORE

ELACC11-12RL2,
ELACC11-12RL4,
ELACC11-12RL5,
ELACC11-12W2b

Cite Text Evidence   Support your responses with evidence from the selection.

1. **Analyze** The opening stanza portrays a frightened narrator fleeing through darkness. How does its rhythm reflect and enhance its meaning?

2. **Identify** What allusions to religion or the Bible can you find in the poem? Why are religious imagery or Biblical allusions appropriate for this topic?

3. **Analyze** Hayden alludes to "Oh! Susanna" in line 34. Do some independent research on the content and history of this traditional American song. How does this allusion add meaning to the poem?

4. **Interpret** Consider the stanza that begins "And this was the way of it," (lines 42–52). Who are the two speakers in the stanza, and how do the rhythms of their speech reflect the differences in their attitudes?

5. **Analyze** The "wanted poster" for Harriet Tubman (lines 53–58) includes several names. What do these people have in common?

6. **Synthesize** Read the two stanzas in lines 59–64, starting with the one that begins "Tell me, Ezekiel." How do the rhythms in these stanzas differ from most other parts of the poem? How do the rhythms and the meanings of the verses combine to create a certain feeling or to form an allusion?

7. **Infer** Many people escaped from slavery by following the Underground Railroad, a network of hiding places and routes leading north. What words and phrases does Hayden include as allusions to the Underground Railroad?

8. **Draw Conclusions** Explain the figurative and connotative meanings of line 33 ("I'm bound for the freedom, freedom-bound"). How do they reflect the central tension of the poem?

PERFORMANCE TASK

Writing Activity: Essay Compare this poem with lines 17-25 in section 33 of Walt Whitman's "Song of Myself" in Collection 3.

Both Whitman and Hayden imagine the plight of fugitives from slavery. Write a one-page essay exploring similarities and differences in their presentations.

- Consider the background and purpose of each poet.
- List some of the content and imagery the poets choose to achieve that purpose.

- Think about how the rhythms and diction of each poem contribute to its overall structure and meaning.
- Begin with a brief, objective summary of each poem.
- Include specific examples to support your opinions.
- Use conventions of standard written English.

COLLECTION **4**
PERFORMANCE TASK

Present a Persuasive Speech

The texts in this collection focus on the continuing work of bringing freedom and justice to all members of American society. Look back at the anchor text, Lincoln's Second Inaugural Address, and at the other texts in the collection. What messages about freedom—its meaning and its costs—do the texts convey? Synthesize your ideas by preparing a persuasive speech about a kind of freedom you would like to see expanded in today's world. Incorporate rhetorical and literary devices from the collection texts to enhance the power of your speech.

....
COMMON
CORE
....

ELACC11-12SL4 Present information, findings, and supporting evidence.
ELACC11-12W1a–e Write arguments to support claims.
ELACC11-12W9a–b Draw evidence from literary or informational texts.

An effective speech

- identifies a type of freedom to be expanded and states a precise claim about it
- develops the claim with valid reasons and relevant evidence from Lincoln's Second Inaugural Address and two other texts
- anticipates counterclaims and addresses them effectively
- establishes clear, logical relationships among claims, reasons, and evidence
- has a conclusion that follows logically from the body of the speech and makes a persuasive call to action
- engages the audience by including a variety of rhetorical devices and techniques to support the claim
- maintains a formal tone through appropriate word choices and the use of standard English
- maintains audience interest with appropriate emphasis, volume, and gestures

PLAN

*my*Notebook

Make a Claim Review the texts in this collection, including Lincoln's Second Inaugural Address, and identify each writer's message about freedom. Based on the ideas conveyed in the texts, write a clearly worded claim about a type of freedom that you think should be further developed in our current society. Remember that you will need to support this claim with logical reasoning and evidence.

Use the notebook in your eBook to record historical examples of discrimination, noting how society overcame a legacy of inequality. You can use these examples later in your presentation as historical evidence for the benefits of increasing economic and political freedom.

Gather Evidence Choose texts from the collection that provide reasons and evidence most relevant to your argument. Take notes about the meaning and costs of freedom conveyed by each writer, paying special attention to details, quotations, and examples that support your claim.

Identify Rhetorical Devices Review Lincoln's and Douglass's speeches, identifying techniques used to help convey their message and appeal to their audience. Here are some suggestions.

- Find places in the text where rhetorical questions are used to engage the audience in the speaker's argument.

- Look for parallel structure and repetition, used to create emphasis or to show similarities between certain ideas.

- Identify any allusions that draw upon familiar stories to add power to the speaker's message.

Get Organized Use an outline or graphic organizer to organize your speech. Be sure to include your claim, reasons, and evidence. Think of counterclaims that could be made against your claim, and address them with counterarguments. Consider ideas for engaging your audience at the beginning of the speech and inspiring them to act at the end.

ACADEMIC VOCABULARY

As you share your ideas about freedom, be sure to incorporate these words.

confirm
definitely
deny
format
unify

> **PRODUCE**

my WriteSmart

Draft Your Speech Write a clearly organized speech. Think about your purpose and audience as you write. Which rhetorical devices can you use to help convince your audience of your ideas about freedom? Remember to include

Write your rough draft in *my*WriteSmart. Focus on getting your ideas down, rather than perfecting your choice of language.

- an engaging introduction, a logically ordered body, and a persuasive conclusion

- transitions between the main sections of your speech

- details, quotations, and examples from the texts to support your claim

- formal language and sentence structures appropriate for an oral presentation

- a variety of grammatical structures that will keep your audience engaged and interested in your speech *my***WriteSmart**

Have your partner or a group of peers review your draft in *my*WriteSmart. Ask your reviewers to note any reasons that do not support the claim or that lack sufficient evidence.

Practice Your Speech When you deliver your speech to your classmates, you will need to make it come alive with appropriate expressions, volume, and gestures. Read over your draft and mark places in the text where you might want to emphasize a word, insert a pause, or use gestures to convey meaning or emotion. Then practice your speech with a partner. When listening to your partner's speech, ask yourself these questions:

- Does the beginning of the speech draw me in?
- Can I follow the reasoning, organization, and development of the speech?
- Is the claim presented clearly and concisely followed by reasons and evidence to support the claim? Does my partner address counterclaims?
- Does the conclusion make a compelling call to action?
- Does my partner use appropriate tone, emphasis, and gestures?
- Can I hear my partner clearly? Does he or she need to speak more loudly or softly?
- How is my partner's pace? Does he or she need to slow down or speed up in certain sections or throughout the speech?

Evaluate Your Performance After you and your partner have presented your speeches, give each other feedback. Use the chart on the following page to evaluate the substance and style of your partner's speech as well as your own. Mention what your partner did particularly well and what he or she could have done better. Then revise your draft based on your partner's feedback, the rubric, and your own observations of your speech. Make sure that your audience can and will understand it.

Deliver Your Speech Present your speech to the whole class. The audience should listen, take notes, and be prepared to comment and ask questions.

	Ideas and Evidence	Organization	Language
ADVANCED	• The introduction immediately engages the audience; the claim clearly states the speaker's position on expanding a type of freedom. • Valid reasons and relevant evidence convincingly support the speaker's claim. • Counterclaims are anticipated and effectively addressed with counterarguments. • The concluding section effectively summarizes the claim and makes a persuasive call to action.	• The reasons and evidence are organized consistently and logically throughout the speech. • Varied transitions logically connect reasons and evidence to the speaker's claim.	• The speech reflects a formal style and an objective, or controlled, tone. • Sentence beginnings, lengths, and structures vary and have a rhythmic flow. • Grammar, usage, and mechanics are correct.
COMPETENT	• The introduction could do more to capture the audience's attention; the speaker's claim states a position on a type of freedom. • Most reasons and evidence support the speaker's claim, but they could be more convincing. • Counterclaims are anticipated, but the counterarguments need to be developed more. • The concluding section restates the claim and suggests that the audience take action.	• The organization of reasons and evidence is confusing in a few places. • A few more transitions are needed to connect reasons and evidence to the speaker's claim.	• The style is informal in a few places, and the tone is defensive at times. • Sentence beginnings, lengths, and structures vary somewhat. • Some grammatical and usage errors are repeated in the speech.
LIMITED	• The introduction is ordinary; the speaker's claim identifies an issue about freedom, but the position is not clearly stated. • The reasons and evidence are not always logical or relevant. • Counterclaims are anticipated but not addressed logically. • The concluding section includes an incomplete summary of the claim and does not summon the audience to take action.	• The organization of reasons and evidence is logical in some places, but it often doesn't follow a pattern. • Many more transitions are needed to connect reasons and evidence to the speaker's position.	• The style becomes informal in many places, and the tone is often dismissive of other viewpoints. • Sentence structures barely vary, and some fragments or run-on sentences are evident. • Grammar and usage are incorrect in many places, but the speaker's ideas are still clear.
EMERGING	• The introduction is confusing. • Significant supporting reasons and evidence are missing. • Counterclaims are neither anticipated nor addressed. • The concluding section is missing.	• A logical organization is not used; reasons and evidence are presented randomly. • Transitions are not used, making the speech difficult to understand.	• The style is inappropriate, and the tone is disrespectful. • Repetitive sentence structure, fragments, and run-on sentences make the speech monotonous and hard to follow. • Many grammatical and usage errors change the meaning of the speaker's ideas.

Image Credits: ©Nick Norman/National Geographic/Getty Images

An Age of Realism

" Reality is that which, when you stop
believing in it, doesn't go away. "

—Phillip K. Dick

An Age of Realism

In this collection, you will explore how post–Civil War America experienced rapid industrialization, urban growth, and social change.

hmhfyi.com

COLLECTION
PERFORMANCE TASK Preview

At the end of this collection, you will have the opportunity to complete a task:

• Write an analytical essay that examines the ways in which writers in the collection use realism to present and emphasize a variety of themes.

ACADEMIC VOCABULARY

Study the words and their definitions in the chart below. You will use these words as you discuss and write about the texts in this collection.

Word	Definition	Related Forms
ambiguous (ăm-bĭg´yōō-əs) *adj.*	able to be interpreted in more than one way; uncertain	ambiguously, ambiguity
clarify (klăr´ə-fī´) *v.*	to make clearer or more understandable	clarity, clarifies, clarification
implicit (ĭm-plĭs´ĭt) *adj.*	not directly stated or obviously apparent	imply, implicate, implicitly
revise (rĭ-vīz´) *v.*	to change or alter a text; reconsider	revision, revisable, reviser
somewhat (sŭm´wŏt´) *adv.*	to a limited extent	somewhere, somehow

America Transformed

ELACC11-12RL10,
ELACC11-12RI3,
ELACC11-12RI7,
ELACC11-12RI10

At the end of the 19th century, America struggled with a paradox: It was a nation of almost unlimited possibilities and wealth, but it was marked by great poverty and pain for many of its citizens. Reflecting this tension, a new literary movement known as realism emerged, which expressed a view of life that was unsentimental, bitterly ironic, and often harsh or ugly.

ENGINES OF SOCIAL CHANGE In the two decades after the completion of the transcontinental railroad, the rail system brought thousands of settlers to the West. The railroad industry also became an engine for industrial growth as new manufacturing centers grew up around railroad hubs in Pittsburgh, Cleveland, Detroit, and Chicago. New technologies and industrial modernization brought prosperity to large parts of the nation.

The growth of industry caused the growth of cities as more and more people came looking for work. In the early 19th century, Chicago was an average-sized city; by 1910, the population was more than 2 million, making it the country's second largest city after New York. All the new manufacturing centers grew in similar fashion. However, a very small group of men controlled the vast share of this industry, including the enormously profitable steel, railroad, oil, and meatpacking sectors. This era became known as the Gilded Age, and was dominated by captains of industry such as oil tycoon John D. Rockefeller and railroad magnate Cornelius Vanderbilt.

Although ordinary people did not achieve the level of wealth of industry leaders, some of them did have more money, and there were new things to spend it on. City dwellers could take a train to an amusement park and shop in new department stores. Some factory workers could even afford new inventions such as automobiles, telephones, and electricity. However, much of the urban population growth was due to an influx of immigrants who came to America in search of freedom and opportunity. These immigrants lived in crowded tenements and found work in factories, where many of them worked 16-hour days in airless sweatshops for subsistence wages.

1884
Mark Twain publishes
*The Adventures of
Huckleberry Finn.*

1896
Supreme Court upholds
"separate but equal" doctrine of
segregationist Jim Crow laws.

1880

1880
John D. Rockefeller's Standard
Oil Company of Ohio
controls U.S. oil refining.

1892
New York's Ellis Island
becomes entry point for
European immigrants.

This period also was marked by new roles for women. The movement to secure their right to vote was reinvigorated as women sought to have a larger voice in every aspect of public life. Increasing numbers of women achieved the goal of a university education as a step toward their broader role in society.

ORDINARY LIVES AND VOICES Realist writers pursued their goal of showing ordinary lives as they were—without romance or sentimentality—through a variety of genres and forms. Although Americans were glad to move past the divisions of the Civil War, they regretted losing their regional identities and were unsettled by the rapid changes taking place in the country. Some writers began to capture the customs, characters, and landscapes of the nation's distinct regions—a type of writing that came to be called regionalism. Willa Cather, Mark Twain, and Kate Chopin, among others, celebrated America's diversity in settings ranging from the plains of Nebraska to Mississippi River towns and the city of New Orleans. The publication in 1884 of Twain's *The Adventures of Huckleberry Finn* marked the high point of regionalism. Told in Huck's colorful and colloquial voice, the novel is a biting satire that tackles the issue of racism in America.

NATURALISM The social conditions in America's growing industrial cities, with their great disparities of wealth, led to the rise of the literary movement called naturalism, a darker form of realism. Looking to the theories of Charles Darwin and other scientists, writers who favored naturalism, such as Stephen Crane and Jack London, saw human beings as helpless creatures moved by forces beyond their understanding or control. While Crane and others gave voice to ordinary people living in cities, London captured readers with his tales of an arctic world totally outside their everyday experiences. Riveted by the exotic settings and thrilling action of his novels, readers were willing to accept tragic endings. Women writers such as Edith Wharton combined naturalism with their own experiences to portray a culture that trapped women in narrow, restricted lives.

Reform-minded journalists, part of a progressive movement that aimed to restore economic opportunities and correct injustices in American life, expressed these naturalist influences in another way. An immigrant himself, Jacob Riis exposed the plight of tenement dwellers in his book *How the Other Half Lives*. A group of journalists labeled as "muckrakers" sought to expose the political and economic corruption that resulted from the excessive power of large corporations. Among this group was Upton Sinclair, whose novel *The Jungle* helped lead to the passage of new laws regulating the food industry.

1903
Orville and Wilbur Wright make the first flight in an engine-powered airplane.

1898
Spanish-American War results in U.S. control of Guam, Puerto Rico, and the Philippines.

1906
Earthquake and fire destroy much of San Francisco.

1908
Ford Motor Company brings out the first Model T automobile.

1910

Jack London (1876–1916) *not only wrote adventure stories, he lived them. London traveled as a hobo across the United States, tried his luck in the Klondike Gold Rush, escaped a typhoon on a seal-huntng ship, and sailed the South Seas in his own boat, the* Snark. *London's formal education was limited, but he read widely using public libraries. Many of his works, including the story "To Build a Fire," have themes involving survival and humans versus nature. His novel* The Call of the Wild *(1903) brought London fame and is still one of his best-known works. London died in California at age 40.*

To Build a Fire

Short Story by Jack London

AS YOU READ Pay attention to the specific details that London includes to create a vivid, realistic setting. Write down any questions you generate during reading.

Day had broken cold and gray, exceedingly cold and gray, when the man turned aside from the main Yukon trail and climbed the high earth bank, where a dim and little-traveled trail led eastward through the fat spruce timberland. It was a steep bank, and he paused for breath at the top, excusing the act to himself by looking at his watch. It was nine o'clock. There was no sun or hint of sun, though there was not a cloud in the sky. It was a clear day, and yet there seemed an **intangible** pall[1] over the face of things, a subtle gloom that made the day dark, and that was due to the absence of sun. This fact
10 did not worry the man. He was used to the lack of sun. It had been days since he had seen the sun, and he knew that a few more days must pass before that cheerful orb, due south, would just peep above the skyline and dip immediately from view.

    The man flung a look back along the way he had come. The Yukon lay a mile wide and hidden under three feet of ice. On top of this

intangible
(ĭn-tăn´jə-bəl) *adj.*
unable to be defined or understood.

---

[1] **pall:** overspreading atmosphere of gloom and depression.

> **He knew that at fifty below, spittle crackled on the snow, but this spittle had crackled in the air.**

ice were as many feet of snow. It was all pure white, rolling in gentle undulations where the ice jams of the freeze-up had formed. North and south, as far as his eye could see, it was unbroken white, save for a dark hairline that curved and twisted from around the spruce-covered

20 island to the south, and that curved and twisted away into the north, where it disappeared behind another spruce-covered island. This dark hairline was the trail—the main trail—that led south five hundred miles to the Chilkoot Pass, Dyea, and salt water; and that led north seventy miles to Dawson, and still on to the north a thousand miles to Nulato, and finally to St. Michael on the Bering Sea, a thousand miles and half a thousand more.

But all this—the mysterious, far-reaching hairline trail, the absence of sun from the sky, the tremendous cold, and the strangeness and weirdness of it all—made no impression on the man. It was

30 not because he was long used to it. He was a newcomer in the land, a cheechako,[2] and this was his first winter. The trouble with him was that he was without imagination. He was quick and alert in the things of life, but only in the things, and not in the significances. Fifty degrees below zero meant eighty-odd degrees of frost. Such fact impressed him as being cold and uncomfortable, and that was all. It did not lead him to meditate upon his frailty as a creature of temperature, and upon man's frailty in general, able only to live within certain narrow limits of heat and cold, and from there on it did not lead him to the conjectural[3] field of immortality and man's place in the

40 universe. Fifty degrees below zero stood for a bite of frost that hurt and that must be guarded against by the use of mittens, earflaps, warm moccasins, and thick socks. Fifty degrees below zero was to him just

---

[2] **cheechako:** Chinook jargon for "newcomer" or "tenderfoot."
[3] **conjectural:** based on guesswork or uncertain evidence.

precisely fifty degrees below zero. That there should be anything more to it than that was a thought that never entered his head.

As he turned to go on, he spat speculatively. There was a sharp, explosive crackle that startled him. He spat again. And again, in the air, before it could fall to the snow, the spittle crackled. He knew that at fifty below, spittle crackled on the snow, but this spittle had crackled in the air. Undoubtedly it was colder than fifty below—how much colder
50 he did not know. But the temperature did not matter. He was bound for the old claim[4] on the left fork of Henderson Creek, where the boys were already. They had come over across the divide from the Indian Creek country, while he had come the roundabout way to take a look at the possibilities of getting out logs in the spring from the islands in the Yukon. He would be into camp by six o'clock; a bit after dark, it was true, but the boys would be there, a fire would be going, and a hot supper would be ready. As for lunch, he pressed his hand against the protruding bundle under his jacket. It was also under his shirt, wrapped up in a handkerchief and lying against the naked skin. It was
60 the only way to keep the biscuits from freezing. He smiled agreeably to himself as he thought of those biscuits, each cut open and sopped in bacon grease, and each enclosing a generous slice of fried bacon.

He plunged in among the big spruce trees. The trail was faint. A foot of snow had fallen since the last sled had passed over, and he was glad he was without a sled, traveling light. In fact, he carried nothing but the lunch wrapped in the handkerchief. He was surprised, however, at the cold. It certainly was cold, he concluded, as he rubbed his numb nose and cheekbones with his mittened hand. He was a warm-whiskered man, but the hair on his face did not protect the high
70 cheekbones and the eager nose that thrust itself aggressively into the frosty air.

At the man's heels trotted a dog, a big native husky, the proper wolf dog, gray coated and without any visible or temperamental difference from its brother, the wild wolf. The animal was depressed by the tremendous cold. It knew that it was no time for traveling. Its instinct told it a truer tale than was told to the man by the man's judgment. In reality, it was not merely colder than fifty below zero; it was colder than sixty below, than seventy below. It was seventy-five below zero. Since the freezing point is thirty-two above zero, it meant
80 that one hundred and seven degrees of frost obtained. The dog did not know anything about thermometers. Possibly in its brain there was no sharp consciousness of a condition of very cold such as was in the man's brain. But the brute had its instinct. It experienced a vague but menacing **apprehension** that subdued it and made it slink along at the man's heels, and that made it question eagerly every unwonted[5] movement of the man, as if expecting him to go into camp or to seek

apprehension
(ăp´rĭ-hĕn´shən) *n.*
fear or anxiety; dread.

---

[4] **claim:** piece of land staked out by a miner.

[5] **unwonted:** unusual.

shelter somewhere and build a fire. The dog had learned fire, and it wanted fire, or else to burrow under the snow and cuddle its warmth away from the air.

90   The frozen moisture of its breathing had settled on its fur in a fine powder of frost, and especially were its jowls, muzzle, and eyelashes whitened by its crystaled breath. The man's red beard and moustache were likewise frosted, but more solidly, the deposit taking the form of ice and increasing with every warm, moist breath he exhaled. Also, the man was chewing tobacco, and the muzzle of ice held his lips so rigidly that he was unable to clear his chin when he expelled the juice. The result was that a crystal beard of the color and solidity of amber was increasing its length on his chin. If he fell down it would shatter itself, like glass, into brittle fragments. But he did not mind the appendage.[6]

100   It was the penalty all tobacco chewers paid in that country, and he had been out before in two cold snaps. They had not been so cold as this, he knew, but by the spirit thermometer[7] at Sixty Mile he knew they had been registered at fifty below and at fifty-five.

He held on through the level stretch of woods for several miles, crossed a wide flat, and dropped down a bank to the frozen bed of a small stream. This was Henderson Creek, and he knew he was ten miles from the forks. He looked at his watch. It was ten o' clock. He was making four miles an hour, and he calculated that he would arrive at the forks at half past twelve. He decided to celebrate that event by

110   eating his lunch there.

The dog dropped in again at his heels, with a tail drooping discouragement, as the man swung along the creek bed. The furrow of the old sled trail was plainly visible, but a dozen inches of snow covered the marks of the last runners. In a month no man had come up or down that silent creek. The man held steadily on. He was not much given to thinking, and just then particularly, he had nothing to think about save that he would eat lunch at the forks and that at six o'clock he would be in camp with the boys. There was nobody to talk to; and, had there been, speech would have been impossible because of

120   the ice muzzle on his mouth. So he continued monotonously to chew tobacco and to increase the length of his amber beard.

Once in a while the thought reiterated[8] itself that it was very cold and that he had never experienced such cold. As he walked along he rubbed his cheekbones and nose with the back of his mittened hand. He did this automatically, now and again changing hands. But rub as he would, the instant he stopped his cheekbones went numb, and the following instant the end of his nose went numb. He was sure to frost his cheeks; he knew that, and experienced a pang of regret that he had

---

[6] **appendage:** something attached to another object.

[7] **spirit thermometer:** alcohol thermometer. In places where the temperature often drops below the freezing point of mercury, alcohol is used in thermometers.

[8] **reiterated:** repeated.

not devised a nose strap of the sort Bud wore in the cold snaps. Such a strap passed across the cheeks, as well, and saved them. But it didn't matter much, after all. What were frosted cheeks? A bit painful, that was all; they were never serious.

Empty as the man's mind was of thought, he was keenly observant, and he noticed the changes in the creek, the curves and bends and timber jams, and always he sharply noted where he placed his feet. Once, coming around a bend, he shied abruptly, like a startled horse, curved away from the place where he had been walking, and retreated several paces back along the trail. The creek, he knew, was frozen clear to the bottom—no creek could contain water in that arctic winter—but he knew also that there were springs that bubbled out from the hillsides and ran along under the snow and on top of the ice of the creek. He knew that the coldest snaps never froze these springs, and he knew likewise their danger. They were traps. They hid pools of water under the snow that might be three inches deep, or three feet. Sometimes a skin of ice half an inch thick covered them, and in turn was covered by the snow. Sometimes there were alternate layers of water and ice skin, so that when one broke through he kept on breaking through for a while, sometimes wetting himself to the waist.

That was why he had shied in such panic. He had felt the give under his feet and heard the crackle of a snow-hidden ice skin. And to get his feet wet in such a temperature meant trouble and danger. At the very least it meant delay, for he would be forced to stop and build a fire, and under its protection to bare his feet while he dried his socks and moccasins. He stood and studied the creek bed and its banks, and decided that the flow of water came from the right. He reflected awhile, rubbing his nose and cheeks, then skirted to the left, stepping gingerly and testing the footing for each step. Once clear of the danger, he took a fresh chew of tobacco and swung along at his four-mile gait.

In the course of the next two hours he came upon several similar traps. Usually the snow above the hidden pools had a sunken, candied appearance that advertised the danger. Once again, however, he had a close call; and once, suspecting danger, he compelled the dog to go on in front. The dog did not want to go. It hung back until the man shoved it forward, and then it went quickly across the white, unbroken surface. Suddenly it broke through, floundered to one side, and got away to firmer footing. It had wet its forefeet and legs, and almost immediately the water that clung to it turned to ice. It made quick efforts to lick the ice off its legs, then dropped down in the snow and began to bite out the ice that had formed between the toes. This was a matter of instinct. To permit the ice to remain would mean sore feet. It did not know this. It merely obeyed the mysterious prompting that arose from the deep crypts[9] of its being. But the man knew, having achieved a judgment on the subject, and he removed the mitten from

_____

[9] **crypts:** hidden recesses.

his right hand and helped tear out the ice particles. He did not expose his fingers more than a minute, and was astonished at the swift numbness that smote[10] them. It certainly was cold. He pulled on the mitten hastily, and beat the hand savagely across his chest.

At twelve o'clock the day was at its brightest. Yet the sun was too far south on its winter journey to clear the horizon. The bulge of the earth intervened between it and Henderson Creek, where the man walked under a clear sky at noon and cast no shadow. At half past twelve, to the minute, he arrived at the forks of the creek. He was pleased at the speed he had made. If he kept it up, he would certainly be with the boys by six. He unbuttoned his jacket and shirt and drew forth his lunch. The action consumed no more than a quarter of a minute, yet in that brief moment the numbness laid hold of the exposed fingers. He did not put the mitten on, but instead struck the fingers a dozen sharp smashes against his leg. Then he sat down on a snow-covered log to eat. The sting that followed upon the striking of his fingers against his leg ceased so quickly that he was startled. He had had no chance to take a bite of biscuit. He struck the fingers repeatedly and returned them to the mitten, baring the other hand for the purpose of eating. He tried to take a mouthful, but the ice muzzle prevented. He had forgotten to build a fire and thaw out. He chuckled at his foolishness, and as he chuckled he noted the numbness creeping into the exposed fingers. Also, he noted that the stinging which had first come to his toes when he sat down was already passing away.

---

[10] **smote:** powerfully struck.

He wondered whether the toes were warm or numb. He moved them inside the moccasins and decided that they were numb.

He pulled the mitten on hurriedly and stood up. He was a bit frightened. He stamped up and down until the stinging returned into the feet. It certainly *was* cold, was his thought. That man from Sulphur Creek had spoken the truth when telling how cold it sometimes got in the country. And he had laughed at him at the time! That showed one must not be too sure of things. There was no mistake about it, it was cold. He strode up and down, stamping his feet and threshing his arms, until reassured by the returning warmth. Then he got out matches and proceeded to make a fire. From the undergrowth, where high water of the previous spring had lodged a supply of seasoned twigs, he got his firewood. Working carefully from a small beginning, he soon had a roaring fire, over which he thawed the ice from his face and in the protection of which he ate his biscuits. For the moment the cold of space was outwitted. The dog took satisfaction in the fire, stretching out close enough for warmth and far enough away to escape being singed.

When the man had finished, he filled his pipe and took his comfortable time over a smoke. Then he pulled on his mittens, settled the earflaps of his cap firmly about his ears, and took the creek trail up the left fork. The dog was disappointed and yearned back toward the fire. This man did not know cold. Possibly all the generations of his ancestry had been ignorant of cold, of real cold, of cold one hundred and seven degrees below freezing point. But the dog knew; all its ancestry knew, and it had inherited the knowledge. And it knew that it was not good to walk abroad in such fearful cold. It was the time to lie snug in a hole in the snow and wait for a curtain of cloud to be drawn across the face of outer space whence this cold came. On the other hand, there was no keen intimacy between the dog and the man. The one was the toil slave of the other, and the only caresses it had ever received were the caresses of the whiplash and of harsh and menacing throat sounds that threatened the whiplash. So the dog made no effort to communicate its apprehension to the man. It was not concerned in the welfare of the man; it was for its own sake that it yearned back toward the fire. But the man whistled, and spoke to it with the sound of whiplashes, and the dog swung in at the man's heels and followed after.

The man took a chew of tobacco and proceeded to start a new amber beard. Also, his moist breath quickly powdered with white his mustache, eyebrows, and lashes. There did not seem to be so many springs on the left fork of the Henderson, and for half an hour the man saw no signs of any. And then it happened. At a place where there were no signs, where the soft, unbroken snow seemed to advertise solidity beneath, the man broke through. It was not deep. He wet himself halfway to the knees before he floundered out to the firm crust.

He was angry, and cursed his luck aloud. He had hoped to get into camp with the boys at six o'clock, and this would delay him an hour, for he would have to build a fire and dry out his footgear. This was **imperative** at that low temperature—he knew that much; and he turned aside to the bank, which he climbed. On top, tangled in the underbrush about the trunks of several small spruce trees, was a high-water deposit of dry firewood—sticks and twigs, principally, but also larger portions of seasoned branches and fine, dry, last year's grasses. He threw down several large pieces on top of the snow. This served for a foundation and prevented the young flame from drowning itself in the snow it otherwise would melt. The flame he got by touching a match to a small shred of birch bark that he took from his pocket. This burned even more readily than paper. Placing it on the foundation, he fed the young flame with wisps of dry grass and with the tiniest dry twigs.

He worked slowly and carefully, keenly aware of his danger. Gradually, as the flame grew stronger, he increased the size of the twigs with which he fed it. He squatted in the snow, pulling the twigs out from their entanglement in the brush and feeding directly to the flame. He knew there must be no failure. When it is seventy-five below zero, a man must not fail in his first attempt to build a fire—that is, if his feet are wet. If his feet are dry, and he fails, he can run along the trail for a half a mile and restore his circulation. But the circulation of wet and freezing feet cannot be restored by running when it is seventy-five below. No matter how fast he runs, the wet feet will freeze the harder.

All this the man knew. The old-timer on Sulphur Creek had told him about it the previous fall, and now he was appreciating the advice. Already all sensation had gone out of his feet. To build the fire, he had been forced to remove his mittens, and the fingers had quickly gone numb. His pace of four miles an hour had kept his heart pumping blood to the surface of his body and to all the **extremities**. But the instant he stopped, the action of the pump eased down. The cold of space smote the unprotected tip of the planet, and he, being on that unprotected tip, received the full force of the blow. The blood of his body recoiled before it. The blood was alive, like the dog, and like the dog it wanted to hide away and cover itself up from the fearful cold. So long as he walked four miles an hour, he pumped that blood, willy-nilly,[11] to the surface; but now it ebbed away and sank down into the recesses of his body. The extremities were the first to feel its absence. His wet feet froze the faster, and his exposed fingers numbed the faster, though they had not yet begun to freeze. Nose and cheeks were already freezing, while the skin of all his body chilled as it lost its blood.

imperative
(ĭm-pĕr´ə-tĭv) *adj.* of great importance; essential.

extremity
(ĭk-strĕm´ĭ-tē) *n.* the outermost or farthest point or portion; the hand or foot.

---

[11] **willy-nilly:** without choice.

But he was safe. Toes and nose and cheeks would be only touched by the frost, for the fire was beginning to burn with strength. He was feeding it twigs the size of his finger. In another minute he would be able to feed it with branches the size of his wrist, and then he could remove his wet footgear, and, while it dried, he could keep his naked feet warm by the fire, rubbing them at first, of course, with snow. The fire was a success. He was safe. He remembered the advice of the old-timer on Sulphur Creek, and smiled. The old-timer had been very serious in laying down the law that no man must travel alone in the Klondike after fifty below. Well, here he was; he had had the accident; he was alone; and he had saved himself. Those old-timers were rather womanish, some of them, he thought. All a man had to do was to keep his head and he was all right. Any man who was a man could travel alone. But it was surprising, the rapidity with which his cheeks and nose were freezing. And he had not thought his fingers could go lifeless in so short a time. Lifeless they were, for he could scarcely make them move together to grip a twig, and they seemed remote from his body and from him. When he touched a twig, he had to look and see whether or not he had hold of it. The wires were pretty well down between him and his finger ends.

All of which counted for little. There was the fire, snapping and crackling and promising life with every dancing flame. He started to untie his moccasins. They were coated with ice; the thick German socks were like sheaths of iron halfway to the knees; and the moccasin strings were like rods of steel all twisted and knotted as by some conflagration.[12] For a moment he tugged with his numb fingers, then, realizing the folly of it, he drew his sheath knife.

But before he could cut the strings it happened. It was his own fault, or, rather, his mistake. He should not have built the fire under the spruce tree. He should have built it in the open. But it had been easier to pull the twigs from the bush and drop them directly on the fire. Now the tree under which he had done this carried a weight of snow on its boughs. No wind had blown for weeks, and each bough was fully freighted. Each time he had pulled a twig he had communicated a slight agitation to the tree—an imperceptible agitation, so far as he was concerned, but an agitation sufficient to bring about the disaster. High up in the tree one bough capsized its load of snow. This fell on the boughs beneath, capsizing them. This process continued, spreading out and involving the whole tree. It grew like an avalanche, and it descended without warning upon the man and the fire, and the fire was blotted out! Where it had burned was a mantle of fresh and disordered snow.

The man was shocked. It was as though he had just heard his own sentence of death. For a moment he sat and stared at the spot where the fire had been. Then he grew very calm. Perhaps the old-timer on

---

[12]**conflagration:** large fire.

Sulphur Creek was right. If he had only had a trail mate, he would have been in no danger now. The trail mate could have built the fire. Well, it was up to him to build the fire over again, and this second time there must be no failure. Even if he succeeded, he would most likely lose some toes. His feet must be badly frozen by now, and there would be some time before the second fire was ready.

340　　Such were his thoughts, but he did not sit and think them. He was busy all the time they were passing through his mind. He made a new foundation for a fire, this time in the open, where no treacherous tree could blot it out. Next he gathered dry grasses and tiny twigs from the high-water flotsam.[13] He could not bring his fingers together to pull them out, but he was able to gather them by the handful. In this way he got many rotten twigs and bits of green moss that were undesirable, but it was the best he could do. He worked methodically, even collecting an armful of the larger branches to be used later when the fire gathered strength. And all the while the dog sat and watched him, a certain yearning wistfulness in its eyes, for it looked upon him as the

350　fire provider, and the fire was slow in coming.

When all was ready, the man reached in his pocket for a second piece of birch bark. He knew the bark was there, and, though he could not feel it with his fingers, he could hear its crisp rustling as he fumbled for it. Try as he would, he could not clutch hold of it. And all the time, in his consciousness, was the knowledge that each instant his feet were freezing. This thought tended to put him in a panic, but he fought against it and kept calm. He pulled on his mittens with his teeth, and threshed his arms back and forth, beating his hands with all his might against his sides. He did this sitting down, and he stood up to do it; and all the while the dog sat in the snow, its wolf brush

360　of a tail curled around warmly over its forefeet, its sharp wolf ears pricked forward intently as it watched the man. And the man, as he beat and threshed with his arms and hands, felt a great surge of envy as he regarded the creature that was warm and secure in its natural covering.

After a time he was aware of the first faraway signals of sensation in his beaten fingers. The faint tingling grew stronger till it evolved into a stinging ache that was excruciating, but which the man hailed with satisfaction. He stripped the mitten from his right hand and

370　fetched forth the birch bark. The exposed fingers were quickly going numb again. Next he brought out his bunch of sulphur matches. But the tremendous cold had already driven the life out of his fingers. In his effort to separate one match from the others, the whole bunch fell in the snow. He tried to pick it out of the snow, but failed. The dead fingers could neither touch nor clutch. He was very careful. He drove the thought of his freezing feet, and nose, and cheeks, out of his mind,

---

[13] **high-water flotsam:** branches and debris washed ashore by a stream or river during the warm months, when the water is high.

devoting his whole soul to the matches. He watched, using the sense of vision in place of that of touch, and when he saw his fingers on each side of the bunch, he closed them—that is, he willed to close them, for the wires were down, and the fingers did not obey. He pulled the mitten on the right hand, and beat it fiercely against his knee. Then, with both mittened hands, he scooped the bunch of matches, along with much snow, into his lap. Yet he was no better off.

After some manipulation he managed to get the bunch between the heels of his mittened hands. In this fashion he carried it to his mouth. The ice crackled and snapped when by a violent effort he opened his mouth. He drew the lower jaw in, curled the upper lip out of the way, and scraped the bunch with his upper teeth in order to separate a match. He succeeded in getting one, which he dropped on his lap. He was no better off. He could not pick it up. Then he devised a way. He picked it up in his teeth and scratched it on his leg. Twenty times he scratched before he succeeded in lighting it. As it flamed he held it with his teeth to the birch bark. But the burning brimstone went up his nostrils and into his lungs, causing him to cough spasmodically.[14] The match fell into the snow and went out.

The old-timer on Sulphur Creek was right, he thought in the moment of controlled despair that ensued: After fifty below, a man should travel with a partner. He beat his hands, but failed in exciting

---

[14] **spasmodically:** in a sudden, violent manner; fitfully.

any sensation. Suddenly he bared both hands, removing the mittens
400 with his teeth. He caught the whole bunch between the heels of his
hands. His arm muscles, not being frozen, enabled him to press the
hand heels tightly against the matches. Then he scratched the bunch
along his leg. It flared into flame, seventy sulphur matches at once!
There was no wind to blow them out. He kept his head to one side to
escape the strangling fumes, and held the blazing bunch to the birch
bark. As he so held it, he became aware of sensation in his hand. His
flesh was burning. He could smell it. Deep down below the surface he
could feel it. The sensation developed into pain that grew acute. And
still he endured it, holding the flame of matches clumsily to the bark
410 that would not light readily because his own burning hands were in
the way, absorbing most of the flame.

At last, when he could endure no more, he jerked his hands apart.
The blazing matches fell sizzling into the snow, but the birch bark was
alight. He began laying dry grass and the tiniest twigs on the flame.
He could not pick and choose, for he had to lift the fuel between the
heels of his hands. Small pieces of rotten wood and green moss clung
to the twigs, and he bit them off as well as he could with his teeth.
He cherished the flame carefully and awkwardly. It meant life, and it
must not perish. The withdrawal of blood from the surface of his body
420 now made him begin to shiver, and he grew more awkward. A large
piece of green moss fell squarely on the little fire. He tried to poke it
out with his fingers, but his shivering frame made him poke too far,
and he disrupted the nucleus of the little fire, the burning grasses and
tiny twigs separating and scattering. He tried to poke them together
again, but in spite of the tenseness of the effort, his shivering got away
with him, and the twigs were hopelessly scattered. Each twig gushed a
puff of smoke and went out. The fire provider had failed. As he looked
apathetically[15] about him, his eyes chanced on the dog, sitting across
the ruins of the fire from him, in the snow, making restless, hunching
430 movements, slightly lifting one forefoot and then the other, shifting its
weight back and forth on them with wistful eagerness.

The sight of the dog put a wild idea into his head. He remembered
the tale of the man, caught in a blizzard, who killed a steer and crawled
inside the carcass, and so was saved. He would kill the dog and bury
his hands in the warm body until the numbness went out of them.
Then he could build another fire. He spoke to the dog, calling it to
him; but in his voice was a strange note of fear that frightened the
animal, who had never known the man to speak in such a way before.
Something was the matter, and its suspicious nature sensed danger—it
440 knew not what danger, but somewhere, somehow, in its brain arose
an apprehension of the man. It flattened its ears down at the sound of
the man's voice, and its restless, hunching movements and the liftings
and shiftings of its forefeet became more pronounced; but it would not

---

[15] **apathetically:** with little interest or concern; indifferently.

come to the man. He got on his hands and knees and crawled toward the dog. This unusual posture again excited suspicion, and the animal sidled mincingly[16] away.

The man sat up in the snow for a moment and struggled for calmness. Then he pulled on his mittens, by means of his teeth, and got up on his feet. He glanced down at first in order to assure himself that he was really standing up, for the absence of sensation in his feet left him unrelated to the earth. His erect position in itself started to drive the webs of suspicion from the dog's mind; and when he spoke peremptorily,[17] with the sound of whiplashes in his voice, the dog rendered its customary allegiance and came to him. As it came within reaching distance, the man lost his control. His arms flashed out to the dog, and he experienced genuine surprise when he discovered that his hands could not clutch, that there was neither bend nor feeling in the fingers. He had forgotten for the moment that they were frozen and that they were freezing more and more. All this happened quickly, and before the animal could get away, he encircled its body with his arms. He sat down in the snow, and in this fashion held the dog, while it snarled and whined and struggled.

But it was all he could do, hold its body encircled in his arms and sit there. He realized that he could not kill the dog. There was no way to do it. With his helpless hands he could neither draw nor hold his sheath knife nor throttle the animal. He released it, and it plunged wildly away, its tail between its legs and still snarling. It halted forty feet away and surveyed him curiously, with ears sharply pricked forward. The man looked down at his hands in order to locate them, and found them hanging on the ends of his arms. It struck him as curious that one should have to use his eyes in order to find out where his hands were. He began threshing his arms back and forth, beating the mittened hands against his sides. He did this for five minutes, violently, and his heart pumped enough blood up to the surface to put a stop to his shivering. But no sensation was aroused in his hands. He had an impression that they hung like weights on the ends of his arms, but when he tried to run the impression down, he could not find it.

A certain fear of death, dull and oppressive, came to him. This fear quickly became poignant[18] as he realized that it was no longer a mere matter of freezing his fingers and toes, or of losing his hands and feet, but that it was a matter of life and death, with the chances against him. This threw him into a panic, and he turned and ran up the creek bed along the old, dim trail. The dog joined in behind and kept up with him. He ran blindly, without intention, in fear such as he had never known in his life. Slowly, as he plowed and floundered through the snow, he began to see things again—the banks of the creek, the

---

[16] **sidled mincingly:** moved sideways with small steps.

[17] **peremptorily:** in a commanding way.

[18] **poignant:** painfully affecting feelings; touching.

old timber jams, the leafless aspens, and the sky. The running made him feel better. He did not shiver. Maybe, if he ran on, his feet would thaw out; and, anyway, if he ran far enough, he would reach the camp
490 and the boys. Without doubt he would lose some fingers and toes and some of his face; but the boys would take care of him, and save the rest of him when he got there. And, at the same time, there was another thought in his mind that said he would never get to the camp and the boys; that it was too many miles away, that the freezing had too great a start on him, and that he would soon be stiff and dead. This thought he kept in the background and refused to consider. Sometimes it pushed itself forward and demanded to be heard, but he thrust it back and strove to think of other things.

It struck him as curious that he could run at all on feet so frozen
500 that he could not feel them when they struck the earth and took the weight of his body. He seemed to himself to skim along above the surface, and to have no connection with the earth. Somewhere he had once seen a winged Mercury,[19] and he wondered if Mercury felt as he felt when skimming over the earth.

His theory of running until he reached camp and the boys had one flaw in it: He lacked the endurance. Several times he stumbled, and finally he tottered, crumpled up, and fell. When he tried to rise, he failed. He must sit and rest, he decided, and next time he would merely walk and keep on going. As he sat and regained his breath, he noted
510 that he was feeling quite warm and comfortable. He was not shivering, and it even seemed that a warm glow had come to his chest and trunk. And yet, when he touched his nose or cheeks, there was no sensation. Running would not thaw them out. Nor would it thaw out his hands and feet. Then the thought came to him that the frozen portions of his body must be extending. He tried to keep this thought down, to forget it, to think of something else; he was aware of the panicky feeling that it caused, and he was afraid of the panic. But the thought asserted itself, and persisted, until it produced a vision of his body totally frozen. This was too much, and he made another wild run along the
520 trail. Once he slowed down to a walk, but the thought of the freezing extending itself made him run again.

And all the time the dog ran with him, at his heels. When he fell down a second time, it curled its tail over its forefeet and sat in front of him, facing him, curiously eager and intent. The warmth and security of the animal angered him, and he cursed it till it flattened down its ears appeasingly. This time the shivering came more quickly upon the man. He was losing in this battle with the frost. It was creeping into his body from all sides. The thought of it drove him on, but he ran no more than a hundred feet when he staggered and pitched headlong. It
530 was his last panic. When he had recovered his breath and control, he

---

[19] **Mercury:** in Roman mythology, messenger of the gods, who is depicted wearing winged sandals and a winged hat.

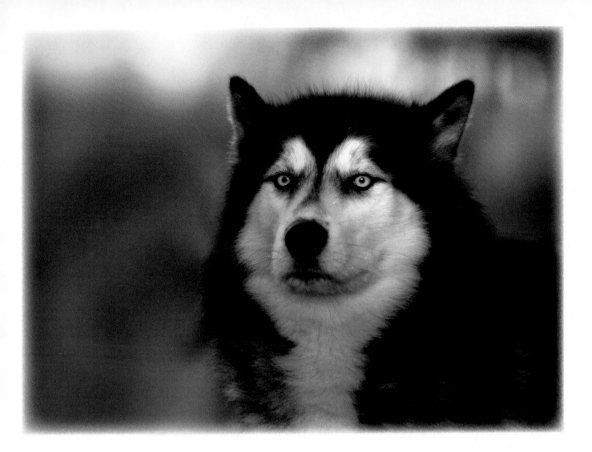

sat up and entertained in his mind the conception of meeting death with dignity. However, the conception did not come to him in such terms. His idea of it was that he had been making a fool of himself, running around like a chicken with its head cut off—such was the simile that occurred to him. Well, he was bound to freeze anyway, and he might as well take it decently. With this newfound peace of mind came the first glimmerings of drowsiness. A good idea, he thought, to sleep off to death. It was like taking an anesthetic.[20] Freezing was not so bad as people thought. There were lots worse ways to die.

540   He pictured the boys finding his body next day. Suddenly he found himself with them, coming along the trail and looking for himself. And, still with them, he came around a turn in the trail and found himself lying in the snow. He did not belong with himself anymore, for even then he was out of himself, standing with the boys and looking at himself in the snow. It certainly was cold, was his thought. When he got back to the States, he could tell the folks what real cold was. He drifted on from this to a vision of the old-timer on Sulphur Creek. He could see him quite clearly, warm and comfortable, and smoking a pipe.

550   "You were right, old hoss; you were right," the man mumbled to the old-timer of Sulphur Creek.

---

[20]**anesthetic:** medication that causes loss of the sensation of pain.

Then the man drowsed off into what seemed to him the most comfortable and satisfying sleep he had ever known. The dog sat facing him and waiting. The brief day drew to a close in a long, slow twilight. There were no signs of a fire to be made, and, besides, never in the dog's experience had it known a man to sit like that in the snow and make no fire. As the twilight drew on, its eager yearning for the fire mastered it, and with a great lifting and shifting of forefeet, it whined softly, then flattened its ears down in anticipation of being

560 chidden[21] by the man. But the man remained silent. Later, the dog whined loudly. And still later it crept close to the man and caught the scent of death. This made the animal bristle and back away. A little longer it delayed, howling under the stars that leaped and danced and shone brightly in the cold sky. Then it turned and trotted up the trail in the direction of the camp it knew, where were the other food providers and fire providers.

---

[21] **chidden:** scolded.

COLLABORATIVE DISCUSSION Why is the setting important in this story? With a partner, discuss how the setting shapes the story's events and how the author creates a clear sense of the setting. Cite specific textual evidence to support your ideas.

Analyze Structure: Realism and Naturalism

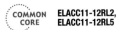 COMMON CORE   ELACC11-12RL2, ELACC11-12RL5

Jack London's "To Build a Fire" can be classified as a work of both realism and naturalism. **Realism** is a style of writing in which the author attempts to show life as it really is. It maintains an objective, detached view of characters and events, allowing readers to draw their own conclusions. **Naturalism** uses many of the same techniques as realism but views human life through the lens of scientific ideas such as Darwin's theory of natural selection. The chart can help you identify specific features of realism and naturalism in the story.

Realism	Naturalism
Realist writers include many specific details about daily life. What details in "To Build a Fire" create a vivid picture of life in the Yukon wilderness?	Naturalist writers observe life and often present the darker side of things. Consider whether this is true in "To Build a Fire."
Stories are set in real places that the authors know well.	Naturalist stories also develop real settings, often in even greater detail than realist works.
Realism focuses on individuals, especially ordinary people. Characters are complex. Their internal thoughts are often explored, as well as their actions. Dialect may be used to portray how people speak in specific places, as when London includes the Chinook term *cheechako*.	Naturalism uses ordinary people as characters. Characters may face staggering odds and be controlled by a larger force, such as their environment or chance. What odds does the man face in London's story?
Word choice is natural, everyday speech with an objective, detached tone. The narrator observes the story but does not comment on it or attach any particular emotion to it. How does London convey such a tone in his story?	Word choice is natural, everyday speech, and the overall tone is often grim. Think about how "To Build a Fire" would be different if London had used more academic or poetic language.

Jack London wrote often about life in the West and Northwest, capturing life in gritty detail. In doing so, he frequently tackled themes involving the survival of the fittest and the power of nature over human life. How do these qualities apply to "To Build a Fire"? As you analyze the story, think about the details you identified as you read, the setting of the story, and the key themes London develops.

Analyzing the Text

 COMMON CORE — ELACC11-12RL2, ELACC11-12RL3, ELACC11-12RL5, ELACC11-12W3, ELACC11-12W5

Cite Text Evidence   Support your responses with evidence from the selection.

1. **Draw Conclusions** Throughout the story, the man remembers "the old-timer on Sulphur Creek" and his advice. Find examples and note the man's response at each point in the story when he remembers the old-timer's advice. What conclusions can you draw about the man's character based on these thoughts?

2. **Compare** Reread lines 27–44 and lines 72–89. How do the dog and the man differ in their understanding of the cold? Which of them seems better adapted to this setting?

3. **Cite Evidence** Cite details from the first two paragraphs of the story that support the idea that it is a work of realism. How do these details contribute to the story's realism?

4. **Draw Conclusions** What purpose does the dog serve in this story? How do London's descriptions of the dog reveal its function in the story?

5. **Analyze** Works of naturalism often address the theme of survival of the fittest. Give examples that show how London's story develops this theme. What message does the story convey about the survival of the fittest?

6. **Evaluate** Naturalism also considers larger forces that control human lives, such as nature or fate. Does London think that the man ever had a chance in this harsh climate, or was he doomed from the start? Explain.

7. **Connect** Think about the two themes you considered in questions 5 and 6. How do these two themes—survival of the fittest and the power of nature or fate—interact and build on each other in this story?

PERFORMANCE TASK

 my WriteSmart

Writing Activity: Narrative Realism and naturalism both feature detailed descriptions of specific places. Write a narrative that incorporates details to describe a place you know well.

1. Write three or four paragraphs about yourself or some other ordinary person experiencing an ordinary event in a specific place. Provide realistic details to develop the setting. Avoid expressing emotion in the text; allow readers to respond naturally to the details you provide.

2. Share your narrative with a partner. Give each other advice on how to improve the writing to be closer to the realist and/or naturalist style.

3. Revise your narrative based on your partner's feedback. Be sure to follow the conventions of standard English in your writing.

Critical Vocabulary

intangible   **apprehension**   **imperative**   **extremity**

Practice and Apply Answer the questions to demonstrate your knowledge of the Critical Vocabulary words.

1. What are some **intangible** characteristics that make some athletes sucessful?

2. Why might you feel **apprehension** right before an important exam?

3. Why is it **imperative** to wear your seatbelt when in a car?

4. Why might it be hard for a country to defend the **extremities** of its territory?

Vocabulary Strategy: Etymology

The **etymology** of a word is its history. Most English words have evolved over time from older words, often from other languages. These older words are the modern word's roots. You can consult general reference materials, such as a good print or digital dictionary, to study a word's etymology. Examining a word's origins can help you clarify and remember the word's precise meaning and also see how it relates to other words with the same roots.

This word map for the Critical Vocabulary word *intangible* shows how to break down a word's meaning.

Practice and Apply Use a dictionary, print or digital, to create a word map like the one above for each of the remaining Critical Vocabulary words.

1. Write the word in the center of the chart.

2. Consult a dictionary to help break down the word, provide meanings for its parts, and choose the most appropriate meaning for its use in "To Build a Fire."

3. Write a sentence that uses the word in an appropriate way.

4. With a partner, discuss how the etymology of each word helps you understand the word's meaning. Think of other words with the same roots and discuss how the meanings are related.

Language and Style: Consistent Tone

COMMON CORE   ELACC11-12RL4, ELACC11-12L3a

Tone is the author's attitude toward the subject or his or her audience. For example, the tone of a work might be serious, ironic, playful, or detached. Diction, or word choice, plays an important role in creating tone.

Read these lines from the story:

> But before he could cut the strings it happened. It was his own fault, or, rather, his mistake. He should not have built the fire under the spruce tree. He should have built it in the open. But it had been easier to pull the twigs from the bush and drop them directly on the fire.

The passage uses a detached, unemotional tone, even though this situation is very dangerous and a key turning point in the story. Notice that the sentences are generally short and objective. London uses realism in this scene to provide detail, but little commentary. The passage continues:

> Now the tree under which he had done this carried a weight of snow on its boughs. No wind had blown for weeks, and each bough was fully freighted. Each time he had pulled a twig he had communicated a slight agitation to the tree—an imperceptible agitation, so far as he was concerned, but an agitation sufficient to bring about the disaster.

These lines continue to focus on realistic detail, explaining the natural forces that are at work whether or not the man pays attention. In the next paragraph, the man reacts:

> The man was shocked. It was as though he had just heard his own sentence of death. For a moment he sat and stared at the spot where the fire had been. Then he grew very calm. Perhaps the old-timer on Sulphur Creek was right. If he had only had a trail mate, he would have been in no danger now. The trail mate could have built the fire.

Consider the effect if London had instead written this:

> The man was shocked. "Yikes," he despaired, "I'm going to die!" For a moment he sat and stared in horror at the spot where the fire had been, where it should be. "Why didn't I listen to that old-timer on Sulphur Creek? If I had someone with me, he could build the fire now. I don't want to die!"

Notice that the second version is much more emotional than London's version. The word choice and the decision to quote the man's thoughts directly create a less detached tone.

Remember that one component of naturalism is a belief that nature is a powerful, unfeeling force with control over human life. That belief in a universe with no compassion for human suffering pairs well with the detached, objective tone London uses.

Practice and Apply   Try to emulate London's style. Choose a terrible event and write about it in a realistic style, using a calm, unemotional tone. Remember that word choice and sentence structure can affect your tone.

from
The Jungle
Novel by Upton Sinclair

Food Product Design
from Fast Food Nation
Journalism by Eric Schlosser

Upton Sinclair (1878–1968) *was sent by the socialist newspaper* Appeal to Reason *to Chicago to investigate working conditions in the stockyards, where animals were processed into meat. Sinclair himself was a socialist, and he believed that the means and products of production should be collectively owned by the workers. He belived that socialism, with its focus on strong government regulation and collective action, could solve many of the inequalities of his era. The result of Sinclair's investigation in Chicago was his most famous novel,* The Jungle *(1906), which he was forced to self-publish after several publishers turned down the manuscript. Jurgis Rudkus, the main character, is a Lithuanian immigrant who works in the stockyards.*

Eric Schlosser (b. 1959) *became a journalist after studying history in college. In 1998, the magazine* Rolling Stone *published his two-part investigative series on the fast-food industry. Schlosser then expanded the articles into a best-selling book,* Fast Food Nation: The Dark Side of the All-American Meal *(2001), which examines the effects of the fast-food industry on workers, consumers, and the landscape. In 2006, Schlosser and writer Charles Wilson published a version of the book for young people,* Chew On This: Everything You Don't Want to Know About Fast Food. *The original book was also made into a movie in the same year, with Schlosser co-writing the screenplay.*

from **The Jungle**
by Upton Sinclair

AS YOU READ Notice how Sinclair's descriptions of the stockyards affect you as a reader. Write down any questions you generate during reading.

Jurgis heard of these things little by little, in the gossip of those who were **obliged** to perpetrate them. It seemed as if every time you met a person from a new department, you heard of new swindles and new crimes. There was, for instance, a Lithuanian who was a cattle butcher for the plant where Marija had worked, which killed meat for canning only; and to hear this man describe the animals which came to his place would have been worthwhile for a Dante or a Zola.[1] It seemed that they must have agencies all over the country, to hunt out old and crippled and diseased cattle to be canned. There were cattle

10 which had been fed on "whiskey malt," the refuse of the breweries, and had become what the men called "steerly"—which means covered with boils. It was a nasty job killing these, for when you plunged your knife into them they would burst and splash foul-smelling stuff into your face; and when a man's sleeves were smeared with blood, and his hands steeped in it, how was he ever to wipe his face, or to clear his eyes so that he could see? It was stuff such as this that made the "embalmed beef" that had killed several times as many United States soldiers as all the bullets of the Spaniards; only the army beef, besides, was not fresh canned, it was old stuff that had been lying for years in

20 the cellars.

Then one Sunday evening, Jurgis sat puffing his pipe by the kitchen stove, and talking with an old fellow whom Jonas had introduced, and who worked in the canning-rooms at Durham's; and so Jurgis learned a few things about the great and only Durham canned goods, which had become a national institution. They were regular alchemists at Durham's; they advertised a mushroom-catsup, and the men who made it did not know what a mushroom looked like. They advertised "potted chicken"—and it was like the boarding-house soup of the comic papers, through which a chicken had walked with

30 rubbers on. Perhaps they had a secret process for making chickens chemically—who knows? said Jurgis's friend; the things that went into the mixture were tripe, and the fat of pork, and beef suet, and hearts of beef, and finally the waste ends of veal, when they had any. They put these up in several grades, and sold them at several prices; but the contents of the cans all came out of the same hopper. And then there was "potted game" and "potted grouse," "potted ham," and "deviled

oblige
(ə-blīj´) *v.* to force or require.

---

[1] **a Dante or a Zola:** Dante Alighieri (1265–1321), Florentine poet who wrote the *Inferno*, about a journey through Hell; Emile Zola (1840–1902), French novelist and playwright who focused on social and political ills.

ham"—de-vyled, as the men called it. "De-vyled" ham was made out of the waste ends of smoked beef that were too small to be sliced by the machines; and also tripe, dyed with chemicals so that it would not
40 show white, and trimmings of hams and corned beef, and potatoes, skins and all, and finally the hard cartilaginous gullets of beef, after the tongues had been cut out. All this **ingenious** mixture was ground up and flavored with spices to make it taste like something. Anybody who could invent a new imitation had been sure of a fortune from old Durham, said Jurgis's informant, but it was hard to think of anything new in a place where so many sharp wits had been at work for so long; where men welcomed tuberculosis[2] in the cattle they were feeding, because it made them fatten more quickly; and where they bought up all the old rancid butter left over in the grocery stores of a
50 continent, and "oxidized" it by a forced-air process, to take away the odor, rechurned it with skim milk, and sold it in bricks in the cities! Up to a year or two ago it had been the custom to kill horses in the yards—**ostensibly** for fertilizer; but after long agitation the newspapers had been able to make the public realize that the horses were being canned. Now it was against the law to kill horses in Packingtown, and the law was really complied with—for the present, at any rate. Any day, however, one might see sharp-horned and shaggy-haired creatures running with the sheep—and yet what a job you would have to get the public to believe that a good part of what it buys for lamb and mutton
60 is really goat's flesh!

There was another interesting set of statistics that a person might have gathered in Packingtown—those of the various afflictions of the workers. When Jurgis had first inspected the packing plants with Szedvilas, he had marveled while he listened to the tale of all the things that were made out of the carcasses of animals, and of all the lesser industries that were maintained there; now he found that each one of these lesser industries was a separate little inferno, in its way as horrible as the killing-beds, the source and fountain of them all. The workers in each of them had their own peculiar diseases. And the
70 wandering visitor might be **sceptical** about all the swindles, but he could not be sceptical about these, for the worker bore the evidence of them about on his own person—generally he had only to hold out his hand.

There were the men in the pickle rooms, for instance, where old Antanas had gotten his death; scarce a one of these that had not some spot of horror on his person. Let a man so much as scrape his finger pushing a truck in the pickle rooms, and he might have a sore that would put him out of the world; all the joints in his fingers might be eaten by the acid, one by one. Of the butchers and floorsmen, the
80 beef boners and trimmers, and all those who used knives, you could

ingenious
(ĭn-jēn´yəs) *adj.*
cleverly inventive.

ostensibly
(ŏ-stĕn´sə-blē) *adv.*
seemingly or
outwardly.

sceptical
(skĕp´tĭ-kəl) *adj.*
having doubts or
reservations.

---

[2] **tuberculosis:** an infectious disease that causes the growth of nodules on lung tissue.

scarcely find a person who had the use of his thumb; time and time
again the base of it had been slashed, till it was a mere lump of flesh
against which the man pressed the knife to hold it. The hands of
these men would be criss-crossed with cuts, until you could no longer
pretend to count them or to trace them. They would have no nails,—
they had worn them off pulling hides; their knuckles were swollen so
that their fingers spread out like a fan. There were men who worked
in the cooking rooms, in the midst of steam and sickening odors, by
artificial light; in these rooms the germs of tuberculosis might live for
90 two years, but the supply was renewed every hour. There were the beef
luggers, who carried two-hundred-pound quarters into the refrigerator
cars, a fearful kind of work, that began at four o'clock in the morning,
and that wore out the most powerful men in a few years. There were
those who worked in the chilling rooms, and whose special disease
was rheumatism;[3] the time limit that a man could work in the chilling
rooms was said to be five years. There were the wool pluckers, whose
hands went to pieces even sooner than the hands of the pickle men; for
the pelts of the sheep had to be painted with acid to loosen the wool,
and then the pluckers had to pull out this wool with their bare hands,
100 till the acid had eaten their fingers off. There were those who made the

---

[3] **rheumatism** (roō′mə-tĭz′əm): a disease that causes inflammation and pain in
muscles and joints.

tins for the canned meat, and their hands, too, were a maze of cuts, and each cut represented a chance for blood poisoning. Some worked at the stamping machines, and it was very seldom that one could work long there at the pace that was set, and not give out and forget himself, and have a part of his hand chopped off. There were the "hoisters," as they were called, whose task it was to press the lever which lifted the dead cattle off the floor. They ran along upon a rafter, peering down through the damp and the steam, and as old Durham's architects had not built the killing room for the convenience of the hoisters, at every

110 few feet they would have to stoop under a beam, say four feet above the one they ran on, which got them into the habit of stooping, so that in a few years they would be walking like chimpanzees. Worst of any, however, were the fertilizer men, and those who served in the cooking rooms. These people could not be shown to the visitor—for the odor of a fertilizer man would scare any ordinary visitor at a hundred yards, and as for the other men, who worked in tank rooms full of steam, and in some of which there were open vats near the level of the floor, their peculiar trouble was that they fell into the vats; and when they were fished out, there was never enough of them left to be

120 worth exhibiting—sometimes they would be overlooked for days, till all but the bones of them had gone out to the world as Durham's Pure Leaf Lard!

COLLABORATIVE DISCUSSION How did Sinclair's descriptions affect you as a reader? What specific descriptive details caused this effect? Discuss these questions with a partner, citing specific evidence from the selection to support your ideas.

Determine Author's Purpose

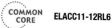

In general, an author's **purpose** or reason for writing is to inform, to entertain, or to persuade. In addition, an author may want to move people to take a particular action. Usually the author's purpose must be inferred based on a work's content and style, which are shaped by the author's purpose. Upton Sinclair went to Chicago as a journalist to investigate working conditions in the stockyards for a socialist newspaper. Instead, he ended up writing a novel, *The Jungle*, that explores the lives of a family of Lithuanian immigrants who worked in those stockyards. As you analyze this excerpt from *The Jungle* in order to determine Sinclair's purpose(s) in writing it, ask yourself these questions:

- What are the topics that Sinclair writes about in the selection?
- What themes or messages does he communicate about those topics?
- What tone or attitude does Sinclair convey in the selection?
- How well does Sinclair follow through on his original assignment?
- In what ways does he go beyond that assignment?
- What might Sinclair have wanted readers to do after reading this novel?

Analyze Author's Choices

Upton Sinclair made a number of choices in writing *The Jungle*. He worked as a journalist, but he chose to write a novel and followed the conventions of a novel—setting, plot, character, and point of view. Although he set his novel in the real Packingtown slum of Chicago, he did not use the names of any actual workers but created characters based on them called Jurgis, Marija, Jonas, and old Antanas. He described the practices of Durham canned goods, a fictional company, rather than those of Armour & Company, the real giant among Chicago's meatpacking companies.

Another area where authors make choices is **diction,** or word choice. Sinclair uses vivid descriptive words that create strong imagery in order to appeal to readers' senses and help them imagine what it is like to work in the stockyards.

As you analyze this selection, consider these ideas.

Why might Sinclair have chosen to write a novel rather than a nonfiction story?

How might Sinclair's choices been affected by a consideration of his audience?

CHOICES

What are the strengths and weaknesses of a fictional account versus a nonfiction story?

What are examples of imagery and what purpose does each serve?

Analyzing the Text

COMMON CORE

ELACC11-12RL1,
ELACC11-12RL2,
ELACC11-12RL3,
ELACC11-12RL4,
ELACC11-12RL6,
ELACC11-12W2,
ELACC11-12W4

Cite Text Evidence Support your responses with evidence from the selection.

1. **Analyze** What is Sinclair's implicit idea in the first two sentences of the selection about workers in the stockyards? How do these sentences reflect his purpose?

2. **Interpret** In the second paragraph, Sinclair writes about "the great and only Durham canned goods, which had become a national institution." How does the imagery in the rest of the paragraph reveal Sinclair's tone toward the company?

3. **Infer** What does Sinclair mean when he says "They were regular alchemists at Durham's" (lines 25–26)?

4. **Analyze** In this excerpt, Sinclair uses a **third-person point of view,** with a narrator outside the action to tell the story, focusing mainly on the thoughts, actions, and observations of Jurgis, the main character. How does choosing this point of view help Sinclair achieve his purpose?

5. **Cite Evidence** What is Sinclair's topic in the third and fourth paragraphs of the selection? What message does he communicate about this topic?

6. **Draw Conclusions** Readers in Sinclair's time were more concerned about his revelations in the first two paragraphs of this selection than the revelations in the rest of the selection. Why might this have been so and how does this relate to Sinclair's purpose?

7. **Draw Conclusions** How did Sinclair's choice to use a fictional company and fictional characters to tell his story help him achieve his journalistic purpose?

PERFORMANCE TASK

Writing Activity: News Articles *The Jungle* is a novel written by a journalist. Explore how Sinclair's information and ideas could have been presented in a news article in two different types of newspapers.

1. Write an investigative report that you might find in a daily newspaper. The purpose of this article is to inform readers about abuses in the meatpacking industry. Focus on facts that could be verified by a reliable source of the time.

2. Write a sensational account that you might find in a tabloid newspaper. The purpose of this article is to shock people and get them to buy the newspaper. Focus on the most vivid details, which may or may not be verified.

With a partner, discuss how the purpose of each version and the writing choices you made affected the tone and mood in each piece.

Critical Vocabulary

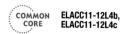

oblige **ingenious** **ostensibly** **sceptical**

Practice and Apply Go on a Critical Vocabulary scavenger hunt to find examples of the words in advertisements, news articles, or other uses in print, online, or in your environment. Write your own definition of each word based on at least two examples. Follow these tips to guide your search.

- If you search online, don't go to a dictionary or other site that defines the word. Instead, look for examples by searching for news or images.
- Note that the preferred spelling of *sceptical* in American dictionaries is now *skeptical*. Search under both spellings.

Vocabulary Strategy: Word Families

A **word family** is a set of words that all descend from the same word root and that have similar meanings. The Critical Vocabulary word *oblige* is part of the word family based on the Latin root *ligare*, meaning "to bind." The word is formed by adding the prefix *ob–* meaning "to" so that *obliged* means "to be required or bound to do something." As the word web shows, members of this word family may modify the root with various spellings because sometimes the word came into English through another language such as French. Words may include a variety of prefixes or suffixes and act as different parts of speech. Knowing the meaning of the common root will help you determine the meaning of words in a word family.

Practice and Apply Work with a partner to create word lists with at least four words based on the common root in each word family. Write the part of speech and definition next to each word in your list. Consult a general or specialized etymological dictionary to clarify the precise meaning and etymology of words below as needed.

1. Greek root *path–* meaning "to feel or suffer"
2. Latin root *spec–* meaning "to see or look at"
3. Latin root *medi–* meaning "middle"
4. Greek root *chron–* meaning "time"

Food Product Design
from **Fast Food Nation**
by Eric Schlosser

AS YOU READ Look for information about the fast-food industry that either confirms or changes your ideas about fast food. Write down any questions you generate during reading.

The taste of McDonald's french fries has long been praised by customers, competitors, and even food critics. James Beard loved McDonald's fries. Their distinctive taste does not **stem** from the type of potatoes that McDonald's buys, the technology that processes them, or the restaurant equipment that fries them. Other chains buy their french fries from the same large processing companies, use Russet Burbanks, and have similar fryers in their restaurant kitchens. The taste of a fast food fry is largely determined by the cooking oil. For decades, McDonald's cooked its french fries in a mixture of about 7
10 percent cottonseed oil and 93 percent beef tallow. The mix gave the fries their unique flavor—and more saturated beef fat per ounce than a McDonald's hamburger.

 Amid a barrage of criticism over the amount of cholesterol in their fries, McDonald's switched to pure vegetable oil in 1990. The switch presented the company with an enormous challenge: how to make fries that subtly taste like beef without cooking them in tallow. A look at the ingredients now used in the preparation of McDonald's french fries suggests how the problem was solved. At the end of the list is a seemingly innocuous, yet oddly mysterious phrase: "natural flavor."
20 That ingredient helps to explain not only why the fries taste so good, but also why most fast food—indeed, most of the food Americans eat today—tastes the way it does.

 Open your refrigerator, your freezer, your kitchen cupboards, and look at the labels on food. You'll find "natural flavor" or "artificial flavor" in just about every list of ingredients. The similarities between these two broad categories of flavor are far more significant than their differences. Both are man-made additives that give most processed food its taste. The initial purchase of a food item may be driven by its packaging or appearance, but subsequent
30 purchases are determined mainly by its taste. About 90 percent of the money that Americans spend on food is used to buy processed food. But the canning, freezing, and dehydrating techniques used to process food destroy most of its flavor. Since the end of World War II, a vast industry has arisen in the United States to make processed food palatable. Without this flavor industry, today's fast food industry could not exist. The names of the leading American fast food chains and their best-selling menu items have become famous worldwide,

stem
(stĕm) *v.* to grow from or be caused by.

embedded in our popular culture. Few people, however, can name the companies that manufacture fast food's taste.

40   The flavor industry is highly secretive. Its leading companies will not divulge[1] the precise formulas of flavor compounds or the identities of clients. The secrecy is deemed essential for protecting the reputation of beloved brands. The fast food chains, understandably, would like the public to believe that the flavors of their food somehow originate in their restaurant kitchens, not in distant factories run by other firms.

The New Jersey Turnpike runs through the heart of the flavor industry, an industrial corridor dotted with refineries and chemical plants. International Flavors & Fragrances (IFF), the world's largest flavor company, has a manufacturing facility off Exit 8A in Dayton,

50   New Jersey; Givaudan, the world's second-largest flavor company, has a plant in East Hanover. Haarmann & Reimer, the largest German flavor company, has a plant in Teterboro, as does Takasago, the largest Japanese flavor company. Flavor Dynamics has a plant in South Plainfield; Frutarom is in North Bergen; Elan Chemical is in Newark. Dozens of companies manufacture flavors in New Jersey industrial parks between Teaneck and South Brunswick. Indeed, the area produces about two-thirds of the flavor additives sold in the United States.

The IFF plant in Dayton is a huge pale blue building with a

60   modern office complex attached to the front. It sits in an industrial park, not far from a BASF plastics factory, a Jolly French Toast factory, and a plant that manufactures Liz Claiborne cosmetics. Dozens of tractor-trailers were parked at the IFF loading dock the afternoon I visited, and a thin cloud of steam floated from the chimney. Before entering the plant, I signed a nondisclosure form, promising not to reveal the brand names of products that contain IFF flavors. The place reminded me of Willy Wonka's chocolate factory. Wonderful smells drifted through the hallways, men and women in neat white lab coats cheerfully went about their work, and hundreds of little glass bottles

70   sat on laboratory tables and shelves. The bottles contained powerful but fragile flavor chemicals, shielded from light by the brown glass and the round plastic caps shut tight. The long chemical names on the little white labels were as mystifying to me as medieval Latin. They were the odd-sounding names of things that would be mixed and poured and turned into new substances, like magic potions.

I was not invited to see the manufacturing areas of the IFF plant, where it was thought I might discover trade secrets. Instead, I toured various laboratories and pilot kitchens, where the flavors of well-established brands are tested or adjusted, and where whole new flavors

80   are created. IFF's snack and savory lab is responsible for the flavor of potato chips, corn chips, breads, crackers, breakfast cereals, and pet food. The confectionery lab devises the flavor for ice cream, cookies,

---

[1] **divulge:** to disclose or make known.

> ## " The long chemical names on the little white labels were as mystifying to me as medieval Latin. "

candies, toothpastes, mouthwashes, and antacids. Everywhere I looked, I saw famous, widely advertised products sitting on laboratory desks and tables. The beverage lab is full of brightly colored liquids in clear bottles. It comes up with the flavor for popular soft drinks, sport drinks, bottled teas, and wine coolers, for all-natural juice drinks, organic soy drinks, beers, and malt liquors. In one pilot kitchen I saw a dapper chemist, a middle-aged man with an elegant tie beneath his
90   lab coat, carefully preparing a batch of cookies with white frosting and pink-and-white sprinkles. In another pilot kitchen I saw a pizza oven, a grill, a milk-shake machine, and a french fryer identical to those I'd seen behind the counter at countless fast food restaurants.

    In addition to being the world's largest flavor company, IFF manufactures the smell of six of the ten best-selling fine perfumes in the United States. It makes the smell of Estée Lauder's Beautiful, Clinique's Happy, Ralph Lauren's Polo, and Calvin Klein's Eternity. It also makes the smell of household products such as deodorant, dishwashing detergent, bath soap, shampoo, furniture polish, and
100   floor wax. All of these aromas are made through the same basic process: the manipulation of **volatile** chemicals to create a particular smell. The basic science behind the scent of your shaving cream is the same as that governing the flavor of your TV dinner.

volatile
(vŏl′ə-tl′) *adj.* liable to change suddenly or evaporate.

    The aroma of a food can be responsible for as much as 90 percent of its flavor. Scientists now believe that human beings acquired the sense of taste as a way to avoid being poisoned. Edible plants generally taste sweet; deadly ones, bitter. Taste is supposed to help us differentiate food that's good for us from food that's not. The taste buds on our tongues can detect the presence of half a dozen or so basic
110   tastes, including: sweet, sour, bitter, salty, astringent,[2] and umami (a taste discovered by Japanese researchers, a rich and full sense of deliciousness triggered by amino acids in foods such as shellfish,

---

[2] **astringent:** sharp or drying.

mushrooms, potatoes, and seaweed). Taste buds offer a relatively limited means of detection, however, compared to the human olfactory system, which can perceive thousands of different chemical aromas. Indeed "flavor" is primarily the smell of gases being released by the chemicals you've just put in your mouth.

The act of drinking, sucking, or chewing a substance releases its volatile gases. They flow out of the mouth and up the nostrils, or up
120 the passageway in the back of the mouth, to a thin layer of nerve cells called the olfactory epithelium, located at the base of the nose, right between the eyes. The brain combines the complex smell signals from the epithelium with the simple taste signals from the tongue, assigns a flavor to what's in your mouth, and decides if it's something you want to eat.

Babies like sweet tastes and reject bitter ones; we know this because scientists have rubbed various flavors inside the mouths of infants and then recorded their facial reactions. A person's food preferences, like his or her personality, are formed during the first few
130 years of life, through a process of socialization. Toddlers can learn to enjoy hot and spicy food, bland health food, or fast food, depending upon what the people around them eat. The human sense of smell is still not fully understood and can be greatly affected by psychological factors and expectations. The color of a food can determine the perception of its taste. The mind filters out the overwhelming majority of chemical aromas that surround us, focusing intently on some, ignoring others. People can grow accustomed to bad smells or good smells; they stop noticing what once seemed overpowering. Aroma and memory are somehow inextricably linked. A smell can suddenly
140 evoke a long-forgotten moment. The flavors of childhood foods seem to leave an indelible mark, and adults often return to them, without always knowing why. These "comfort foods" become a source of pleasure and reassurance, a fact that fast food chains work hard to promote. Childhood memories of Happy Meals can translate into frequent adult visits to McDonald's, like those of the chain's "heavy users," the customers who eat there four or five times a week.

The human craving for flavor has been a largely unacknowledged and unexamined force in history. Royal empires have been built, unexplored lands have been traversed, great religions and philosophies
150 have been forever changed by the spice trade. In 1492 Christopher Columbus set sail to find seasoning. Today the influence of flavor in the world marketplace is no less decisive. The rise and fall of corporate empires—of soft drink companies, snack food companies, and fast food chains—is frequently determined by how their products taste.

The flavor industry emerged in the mid-nineteenth century, as processed foods began to be manufactured on a large scale. Recognizing the need for flavor additives, the early food processors turned to perfume companies that had years of experience working with essential oils and volatile aromas. The great perfume houses

of England, France, and the Netherlands produced many of the
first flavor compounds. In the early part of the twentieth century,
Germany's powerful chemical industry assumed the technological
lead in flavor production. Legend has it that a German scientist
discovered methyl anthranilate, one of the first artificial flavors, by
accident while mixing chemicals in his laboratory. Suddenly the lab
was filled with the sweet smell of grapes. Methyl anthranilate later
became the chief flavoring compound of grape Kool-Aid. After World
War II, much of the perfume industry shifted from Europe to the
United States, settling in New York City near the garment district and
170 the fashion houses. The flavor industry came with it, subsequently
moving to New Jersey to gain more plant capacity. Man-made flavor
additives were used mainly in baked goods, candies, and sodas until
the 1950s, when sales of processed food began to soar. The invention
of gas chromatographs and mass spectrometers—machines capable
of detecting volatile gases at low levels—vastly increased the number
of flavors that could be synthesized. By the mid-1960s the American
flavor industry was churning out compounds to supply the taste of
Pop Tarts, Bac-Os, Tab, Tang, Filet-O-Fish sandwiches, and literally
thousands of other new foods.

180   The American flavor industry now has annual revenues of about
$1.4 billion. Approximately ten thousand new processed food products
are introduced every year in the United States. Almost all of them
require flavor additives. And about nine out of every ten of these
new food products fail. The latest flavor innovations and corporate
realignments are heralded in publications such as *Food Chemical
News, Food Engineering, Chemical Market Reporter*, and *Food Product
Design*. The growth of IFF has mirrored that of the flavor industry
as a whole. IFF was formed in 1958, through the merger of two small
companies. Its annual revenues have grown almost fifteenfold since
190 the early 1970s, and it now has manufacturing facilities in twenty
countries.

        The quality that people seek most of all in a food, its flavor, is
usually present in a quantity too **infinitesimal** to be measured by
any traditional culinary terms such as ounces or teaspoons. Today's
sophisticated spectrometers, gas chromatographs, and headspace
vapor analyzers provide a detailed map of a food's flavor components,
detecting chemical aromas in amounts as low as one part per billion.
The human nose, however, is still more sensitive than any machine
yet invented. A nose can detect aromas present in quantities of a
200 few parts per trillion—an amount equivalent to 0.000000000003
percent. Complex aromas, like those of coffee or roasted meat, may be
composed of volatile gases from nearly a thousand different chemicals.
The smell of a strawberry arises from the interaction of at least 350
different chemicals that are present in minute amounts. The chemical
that provides the dominant flavor of bell pepper can be tasted in
amounts as low as .02 parts per billion; one drop is sufficient to add

infinitesimal
(ĭn´fĭn-ĭ-tĕs´ə-məl)
adj. extremely small;
microscopic.

flavor to five average size swimming pools. The flavor additive usually comes last, or second to last, in a processed food's list of ingredients (chemicals that add color are frequently used in even smaller
210 amounts). As a result, the flavor of a processed food often costs less than its packaging. Soft drinks contain a larger proportion of flavor additives than most products. The flavor in a twelve-ounce can of Coke costs about half a cent.

The Food and Drug Administration does not require flavor companies to disclose the ingredients of their additives, so long as all the chemicals are considered by the agency to be GRAS (Generally Regarded As Safe). This lack of public disclosure enables the companies to maintain the secrecy of their formulas. It also hides the fact that flavor compounds sometimes contain more ingredients than
220 the foods being given their taste. The ubiquitous phrase "artificial strawberry flavor" gives little hint of the chemical wizardry and manufacturing skill that can make a highly processed food taste like a strawberry.

A typical artificial strawberry flavor, like the kind found in a Burger King strawberry milk shake, contains the following ingredients: amyl acetate, amyl butyrate, amyl valerate, anethol, anisyl formate, benzyl acetate, benzyl isobutyrate, butyric acid, cinnamyl isobutyrate, cinnamyl valerate, cognac essential oil, diacetyl, dipropyl ketone, ethyl acetate, ethyl amylketone, ethyl butyrate, ethyl
230 cinnamate, ethyl heptanoate, ethyl heptylate, ethyl lactate, ethyl methylphenylglycidate, ethyl nitrate, ethyl propionate, ethyl valerate, heliotropin, hydroxyphrenyl-2-butanone (10 percent solution in alcohol), α-ionone, isobutyl anthranilate, isobutyl butyrate, lemon essential oil, maltol, 4-methylacetophenone, methyl anthranilate, methyl benzoate, methyl cinnamate, methyl heptine carbonate, methyl naphthyl ketone, methyl salicylate, mint essential oil, neroli essential oil, nerolin, neryl isobutyrate, orris butter, phenethyl alcohol, rose, rum ether, γ-undecalactone, vanillin, and solvent.

Although flavors usually arise from a mixture of many different
240 volatile chemicals, a single compound often supplies the dominant aroma. Smelled alone, that chemical provides an unmistakable sense of the food. Ethyl-2-methyl butyrate, for example, smells just like an apple. Today's highly processed foods offer a blank palette: whatever chemicals you add to them will give them specific tastes. Adding methyl-2-peridylketone makes something taste like popcorn. Adding ethyl-3-hydroxybutanoate makes it taste like marshmallow. The possibilities are now almost limitless. Without affecting the appearance or nutritional value, processed foods could even be made with aroma chemicals such as hexanal (the smell of freshly cut grass)
250 or 3-methyl butanoic acid (the smell of body odor).

The 1960s were the heyday of artificial flavors. The synthetic versions of flavor compounds were not subtle, but they did not need to be, given the nature of most processed food. For the past twenty years food processors have tried hard to use only "natural flavors" in their products. According to the FDA, these must be derived entirely from natural sources—from herbs, spices, fruits, vegetables, beef, chicken, yeast, bark, roots, etc. Consumers prefer to see natural flavors on a label, out of a belief that they are healthier. The distinction between artificial and natural flavors can be somewhat arbitrary and absurd, based more on how the flavor has been made than on what it actually contains. "A natural flavor," says Terry Acree, a professor of food science technology at Cornell University, "is a flavor that's been derived with an out-of-date technology." Natural flavors and artificial flavors sometimes contain exactly the same chemicals, produced through different methods. Amyl acetate, for example, provides the dominant note of banana flavor. When you distill it from bananas with a solvent, amyl acetate is a natural flavor. When you produce it by mixing vinegar with amyl alcohol, adding sulfuric acid as a **catalyst**, amyl acetate is an artificial flavor. Either way it smells and tastes the same. The phrase "natural flavor" is now listed among the ingredients of everything from Stonyfield Farm Organic Strawberry Yogurt to Taco Bell Hot Taco Sauce.

260

270

catalyst
(kăt′l-ĭst) *n.* a substance that starts or speeds up a reaction.

A natural flavor is not necessarily healthier or purer than an artificial one. When almond flavor (benzaldehyde) is derived from natural sources, such as peach and apricot pits, it contains traces of hydrogen cyanide, a deadly poison. Benzaldehyde derived through a different process—by mixing oil of clove and the banana flavor, amyl acetate—does not contain any cyanide. Nevertheless, it is legally considered an artificial flavor and sells at a much lower price. Natural
280 and artificial flavors are now manufactured at the same chemical plants, places that few people would associate with Mother Nature. Calling any of these flavors "natural" requires a flexible attitude toward the English language and a fair amount of irony.

The small and elite group of scientists who create most of the flavor in most of the food now consumed in the United States are called "flavorists." They draw upon a number of disciplines in their work: biology, psychology, physiology, and organic chemistry. A flavorist is a chemist with a trained nose and a poetic sensibility. Flavors are created by blending scores of different chemicals in tiny
290 amounts, a process governed by scientific principles but demanding a fair amount of art. In an age when delicate aromas, subtle flavors, and microwave ovens do not easily coexist, the job of the flavorist is to **conjure** illusions about processed food and, in the words of one flavor company's literature, to ensure "consumer likeability." The flavorists with whom I spoke were charming, cosmopolitan, and ironic. They were also discreet, in keeping with the dictates of their trade. They were the sort of scientist who not only enjoyed fine wine, but could also tell you the chemicals that gave each vintage its unique aroma. One flavorist compared his work to composing music. A well-made
300 flavor compound will have a "top note," followed by a "dry-down," and a "leveling-off," with different chemicals responsible for each stage. The taste of a food can be radically altered by minute changes in the flavoring mix. "A little odor goes a long way," one flavorist said.

In order to give a processed food the proper taste, a flavorist must always consider the food's "mouthfeel"— the unique combination of textures and chemical interactions that affects how the flavor is perceived. The mouthfeel can be adjusted through the use of various fats, gums, starches, emulsifiers, and stabilizers. The aroma chemicals of a food can be precisely analyzed, but mouthfeel is much harder
310 to measure. How does one quantify a french fry's crispness? Food technologists are now conducting basic research in rheology, a branch of physics that examines the flow and deformation of materials. A number of companies sell sophisticated devices that attempt to measure mouthfeel. The Universal TA-XT2 Texture Analyzer, produced by the Texture Technologies Corporation, performs calculations based on data derived from twenty-five separate probes. It is essentially a mechanical mouth. It gauges the most important rheological properties of a food—the bounce, creep, breaking point, density, crunchiness, chewiness, gumminess, lumpiness, rubberiness,

conjure
(kŏn´jər) *v.* to produce from nothing, as if by magic.

springiness, slipperiness, smoothness, softness, wetness, juiciness, spreadability, spring-back, and tackiness.

Some of the most important advances in flavor manufacturing are now occurring in the field of biotechnology. Complex flavors are being made through fermentation, enzyme reactions, fungal cultures, and tissue cultures. All of the flavors being created through these methods—including the ones being synthesized by funguses—are considered natural flavors by the FDA. The new enzyme-based processes are responsible for extremely lifelike dairy flavors. One company now offers not just butter flavor, but also fresh creamy butter, cheesy butter, milky butter, savory melted butter, and super-concentrated butter flavor, in liquid or powder form. The development of new fermentation techniques, as well as new techniques for heating mixtures of sugar and amino acids, have led to the creation of much more realistic meat flavors. The McDonald's Corporation will not reveal the exact origin of the natural flavor added to its french fries. In response to inquiries from *Vegetarian Journal*, however, McDonald's did acknowledge that its fries derive some of their characteristic flavor from "animal products."

Other popular fast foods derive their flavor from unexpected sources. Wendy's Grilled Chicken Sandwich, for example, contains beef extracts. Burger King's BK Broiler Chicken Breast Patty contains "natural smoke flavor." A firm called Red Arrow Products Company specializes in smoke flavor, which is added to barbecue sauces and processed meats. Red Arrow manufactures natural smoke flavor by charring sawdust and capturing the aroma chemicals released into the air. The smoke is captured in water and then bottled, so that other companies can sell food which seems to have been cooked over a fire.

In a meeting room at IFF, Brian Grainger let me sample some of the company's flavors. It was an unusual taste test; there wasn't any food to taste. Grainger is a senior flavorist at IFF, a soft-spoken chemist with graying hair, an English accent, and a fondness for understatement. He could easily be mistaken for a British diplomat or the owner of a West End brasserie with two Michelin stars. Like many in the flavor industry, he has an Old World, old-fashioned sensibility which seems out of step with our brand-conscious, egocentric age. When I suggested that IFF should put its own logo on the products that contain its flavors—instead of allowing other brands to enjoy the consumer loyalty and affection inspired by those flavors—Grainger politely disagreed, assuring me such a thing would never be done. In the absence of public credit or acclaim, the small and secretive fraternity of flavor chemists praises one another's work. Grainger can often tell, by analyzing the flavor formula of a product, which of his counterparts at a rival firm devised it. And he enjoys walking down supermarket aisles, looking at the many products that contain his flavors, even if no one else knows it.

Grainger had brought a dozen small glass bottles from the lab. After he opened each bottle, I dipped a fragrance testing filter into it. The filters were long white strips of paper designed to absorb aroma chemicals without producing off-notes. Before placing the strips of paper before my nose, I closed my eyes. Then I inhaled deeply, and one food after another was conjured from the glass bottles. I smelled fresh cherries, black olives, sautéed onions, and shrimp. Grainger's most remarkable creation took me by surprise. After closing my eyes, I suddenly smelled a grilled hamburger. The aroma was uncanny, almost miraculous. It smelled like someone in the room was flipping burgers on a hot grill. But when I opened my eyes, there was just a narrow strip of white paper and a smiling flavorist.

370

COLLABORATIVE DISCUSSION What are examples of information in the selection that either confirmed or changed your ideas about fast food? Discuss this question with a partner, citing specific evidence from the selection to support your ideas.

Determine Author's Purpose

As an investigative journalist, Eric Schlosser's general **purpose,** or reason, for writing is to inform, to persuade, or to do some combination of the two. His purpose may also involve the desire to move people to take a particular action based on the information he presents. Analyzing the content and the style of the selection will allow you to infer Schlosser's specific purpose for writing it. As you analyze this selection, ask yourself these questions:

- What are the topics that Schlosser writes about in the selection?
- What tone or attitude does he express on the topics?
- What is distinctive about Schlosser's style and rhetoric, including his word choices, sentence lengths, tone, or other persuasive uses of language?
- What action might Schlosser have implicitly wanted readers to take after reading this selection?

Analyze Language: Technical Terms

A characteristic of Schlosser's style in this selection is the extensive use of specialized vocabulary in the form of technical terms. By examining the context for each usage of these terms, you can understand how they serve Schlosser's purpose.

Sometimes, Schlosser defines the terms he is using.

> **Legend has it that a German scientist discovered methyl anthranilate, one of the first artificial flavors, by accident while mixing chemicals in his laboratory. Suddenly the lab was filled with the sweet smell of grapes. Methyl anthranilate later became the chief flavoring compound of grape Kool-Aid.**

Schlosser first defines *methyl anthranilate* as "one of the first artificial flavors" and then through the example implies that it is a chemical that produces the artificial flavor of grapes.

At other times, Schlosser does not define the meaning of technical terms.

> **Adding methyl-2-peridylketone makes something taste like popcorn. Adding ethyl-3-hydroxybutanoate makes it taste like marshmallow.**

Neither of these sentences actually defines the technical terms. As you encounter such terms when analyzing the selection, ask yourself why Schlosser might want to use them. Why doesn't he just say: "Adding one chemical makes something taste like popcorn. Adding another makes it taste like marshmallow"?

Analyzing the Text

 COMMON CORE

ELACC11-12RI1,
ELACC11-12RI4,
ELACC11-12RI6,
ELACC11-12W3,
ELACC11-12W4

Cite Text Evidence Support your responses with evidence from the selection.

1. **Cause and Effect** What caused the growth of the flavor industry after World War II?

2. **Draw Conclusions** Why does Schlosser include so much detail about his visit to the IFF plant in New Jersey?

3. **Compare** What are the similarities and differences between "artificial flavors" and "natural flavors"? Why does Schlosser explain these two terms in such detail?

4. **Analyze** What is Schlosser's purpose in listing all the chemical ingredients in "a typical artificial strawberry flavor, like the kind found in a Burger King strawberry milk shake"?

5. **Infer** Irony refers to a contrast between appearance and reality. What does Schlosser mean when he says, "Calling any of these flavors 'natural' requires a flexible attitude toward the English language and a fair amount of irony"?

6. **Draw Conclusions** What might Schlosser want people to do after reading this selection?

7. **Evaluate** What is Schlosser's overall purpose in writing this selection? How effective is his style in allowing him to achieve that purpose?

PERFORMANCE TASK

Writing Activity: Narrative Schlosser wanted people to know more about processed food after reading this selection. Explore how the selection might affect a reader through this writing task.

- Write a narrative in which at least one of the characters has recently read this selection and portray how the selection influences the character's thoughts, words, and actions.

- Engage and orient the reader by setting out a situation related to processed foods, such as a visit to a fast food restaurant, a trip to the grocery store, or an exploration of food products found at home.

- Use a variety of narrative techniques such as dialogue, pacing, and description to move the plot forward and develop experiences and characters.

- Use the selection as a source of precise words and phrases, details, and sensory language to convey a vivid picture of the situation and the characters.

- Provide a conclusion that reflects on the events in the narrative.

Critical Vocabulary

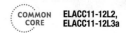
COMMON CORE   ELACC11-12L2,
ELACC11-12L3a

stem   volatile   infinitesimal   catalyst   conjure

Practice and Apply Complete each sentence to reflect your understanding of the meaning of each Critical Vocabulary word.

1. The taste of fast food french fries now **stems** from . . .

2. **Volatile** chemicals have to be kept in closed containers because . . .

3. Everyday measuring spoons cannot be used to measure the **infinitesimal** amounts of chemicals in a particular flavor because . . .

4. Producing artificial flavors requires a **catalyst** like sulfuric acid because . . .

5. Some chemists seem to **conjure** foods because . . .

Language and Style: Dashes

Sometimes a writer wants to interrupt the main thought of a sentence with a word, expression, phrase or sentence called a parenthetical element. Usually such parenthetical elements are set off with parentheses or with commas. However, writers sometimes use dashes to set off the elements in a sentence.

If the break in thought is abrupt, the parenthetical element is set off with dashes.

That ingredient helps to explain not only why the fries taste so good, but also why most fast food—indeed, most of the food Americans eat today—tastes the way it does.

Sometimes dashes are used to create pauses, often for ironic, satirical, or dramatic effect.

The mix gave the fries their unique flavor—and more saturated beef fat per ounce than a McDonald's hamburger.

Practice and Apply Add the italicized parenthetical elements to the following sentences, setting them off with dashes.

1. Flavors made from natural ingredients are sometimes considered healthier. *herbs, fruits, vegetables, chicken, yeast, and bark*

2. The french fries are delicious. *and very fattening*

3. Flavorists create the flavor in most of the food we eat. *scientists with trained noses and poetic sensibilities*

4. One remarkable creation took Schlosser by surprise. *a strip of paper that smelled just like a grilled hamburger*

from The Jungle
Food Product Design

Author's Purpose

COMMON CORE   ELACC11-12L6,
ELACC11-12RI6

Sinclair and Schlosser are both investigative journalists. Their common purpose was to explore a topic in depth and provide previously unknown information to readers. Sinclair was identified with a group of writers known as muckrakers who exposed corruption and social problems caused by large corporations in the early twentieth century. Many critics say that Schlosser's work follows in this journalistic tradition.

Both writers also use elements of **realism** in their writing. For example, they use detailed descriptive language and vivid storytelling, although one wrote fiction and the other wrote nonfiction. Their styles try to put readers right in the center of the action through creating the sense that "I was there; this is what happened."

Analyzing the Text

COMMON CORE   ELACC11-12RL1,
ELACC11-12L5,
ELACC11-12L6,
ELACC11-12RI1,
ELACC11-12RI5,
ELACC11-12RI6,
ELACC11-12SL3,
ELACC11-12SL4

Cite Text Evidence   Support your responses with evidence from the selections.

1. **Analyze** What are the workplace settings of each selection? How does the choice of setting relate to each author's purpose?

2. **Connect** In *The Jungle*, Jurgis's friend says of Durham, "Perhaps they had a secret process for making chickens chemically." How does this statement relate to Schlosser's description of the work of International Flavors & Fragrances?

3. **Cite Evidence** Select two short passages from each selection that reflect elements of realism. How do these elements help each author achieve his purpose?

4. **Synthesize** What similar themes and topics do these selections address? What are similarities and differences in the approaches that the writers use to present these themes and topics?

PERFORMANCE TASK

Speaking Activity: Debate Are foods safer now than they were when *The Jungle* was written?

- Form teams of two to three students each. Half the teams will take the pro position on the question and half will take the con position.

- Each team should gather evidence from both selections to support its position.

- Conduct your debate by following the rules for debating found in the Performance Task Reference Guide.

- After the debate, write an evaluation of which side presented the most compelling argument.

Mark Twain (1835–1910) *was the pen name of Samuel Langhorne Clemens, the American author best known for his novel* The Adventures of Huckleberry Finn, *based on his own boyhood in Missouri. As a journalist, moralist, and lecturer, he frequently used humor to communicate his ideas. In his later years, Twain wrote many satirical essays commenting on the human race. This essay, first published in 1962, was probably written in 1896. In it, Twain refers to Charles Darwin's theory of evolution, first published in* On the Origin of Species *in 1859.*

The Lowest Animal

Essay by Mark Twain

AS YOU READ Notice how Twain describes the various "painstaking" experiments he performed. Write down any questions you generate during reading.

Man is the Reasoning Animal. Such is the claim.

I have been studying the traits and **dispositions** of the "lower animals" (so-called) and contrasting them with the traits and dispositions of man. I find the result humiliating to me. For it obliges me to renounce[1] my allegiance to the Darwinian theory of the Ascent of Man from the Lower Animals, since it now seems plain to me that that theory ought to be vacated in favor of a new and truer one, this new and truer one to be named the *De*scent of Man from the Higher Animals.

   In proceeding toward this unpleasant conclusion, I have not
10　guessed or speculated or conjectured, but have used what is commonly called the scientific method.[2] That is to say, I have subjected every

disposition
(dĭs´pə-zĭsh´ən) *n.*
character or temperament.

---

[1] **renounce:** give up; reject.
[2] **scientific method:** research method in which a hypothesis is tested by careful, documented experiments.

postulate[3] that presented itself to the crucial test of actual experiment and have adopted it or rejected it according to the result. Thus, I verified and established each step of my course in its turn before advancing to the next. These experiments were made in the London Zoological Gardens and covered many months of painstaking and fatiguing work.

Before particularizing any of the experiments, I wish to state one or two things which seem to more properly belong in this place than further along. This in the interest of clearness. The massed experiments established to my satisfaction certain generalizations, to wit:

1. That the human race is of one distinct species. It exhibits slight variations—in color, stature, mental **caliber**, and so on—due to climate, environment, and so forth; but it is a species by itself and not to be confounded with any other.

caliber
(kăl´ə-bər) *n.* level of ability.

2. That the quadrupeds[4] are a distinct family, also. This family exhibits variations—in color, size, food preferences, and so on; but it is a family by itself.

3. That the other families—the birds, the fishes, the insects, the reptiles, etc.— are more or less distinct, also. They are in the procession. They are links in the chain which stretches down from the higher animals to man at the bottom.

Some of my experiments were quite curious. In the course of my reading, I had come across a case where, many years ago, some hunters on our Great Plains organized a buffalo hunt for the entertainment of an English earl—that, and to provide some fresh meat for his larder.[5] They had charming sport. They killed seventy-two of those great animals and ate part of one of them and left the seventy-one to rot. In order to determine the difference between an anaconda[6] and an earl—if any—I caused seven young calves to be turned into the anaconda's cage. The grateful reptile immediately crushed one of them and swallowed it, then lay back satisfied. It showed no further interest in the calves and no disposition to harm them. I tried this experiment with other anacondas, always with the same result. The fact stood proven that the difference between an earl and an anaconda is that the earl is cruel and the anaconda isn't; and that the earl wantonly destroys what he has no use for, but the anaconda doesn't. This seemed to suggest that the anaconda was not descended from the earl. It also seemed to suggest that the earl was descended from the anaconda, and had lost a good deal in the **transition**.

transition
(trăn-zĭsh´ən) *n.* process of change.

I was aware that many men who have accumulated more millions of money than they can ever use have shown a rabid hunger for more,

---

[3] **postulate:** assumption.
[4] **quadrupeds:** four-footed animals.
[5] **larder:** supply of food or place where food supplies are kept.
[6] **anaconda:** long, heavy snake that crushes its prey.

and have not scrupled[7] to cheat the ignorant and the helpless out of their poor servings in order to partially appease[8] that appetite. I furnished a hundred different kinds of wild and tame animals the opportunity to accumulate vast stores of food, but none of them would do it. The squirrels and bees and certain birds made accumulations, but stopped when they had gathered a winter's supply and could not
60 be persuaded to add to it either honestly or by chicane.[9] In order to bolster up a tottering reputation, the ant pretended to store up supplies, but I was not deceived. I know the ant. These experiments convinced me that there is this difference between man and the higher animals: He is avaricious and miserly, they are not.

In the course of my experiments, I convinced myself that among the animals man is the only one that harbors[10] insults and injuries, broods over them, waits till a chance offers, then takes revenge. The passion of revenge is unknown to the higher animals.

Roosters keep harems,[11] but it is by consent of their concubines;[12]
70 therefore no wrong is done. Men keep harems, but it is by brute force, privileged by **atrocious** laws which the other sex was allowed no hand in making. In this matter man occupies a far lower place than the rooster.

atrocious
(ə-trō´shəs) *adj.* evil or brutal.

Cats are loose in their morals, but not consciously so. Man, in his descent from the cat, has brought the cat's looseness with him but has left the unconsciousness behind—the saving grace which excuses the cat. The cat is innocent, man is not.

Indecency, vulgarity, obscenity—these are strictly confined to man; he invented them. Among the higher animals there is no trace of
80 them. They hide nothing; they are not ashamed. Man, with his soiled mind, covers himself. He will not even enter a drawing room with his breast and back naked, so alive are he and his mates to indecent suggestion. Man is the Animal that Laughs. But so does the monkey, as Mr. Darwin pointed out, and so does the Australian bird that is called the laughing jackass. No—Man is the Animal that Blushes. He is the only one that does it—or has occasion to.

At the head of this article we see how "three monks were burnt to death" a few days ago and a prior was "put to death with atrocious cruelty." Do we inquire into the details? No; or we should find out that
90 the prior was subjected to unprintable mutilations. Man—when he is a North American Indian—gouges out his prisoner's eyes; when he is King John,[13] with a nephew to render untroublesome, he uses a red-

---

[7] **scrupled:** hesitated because of feelings of guilt.

[8] **appease:** satisfy; pacify.

[9] **chicane** (shĭ-kān´): clever deception; trickery.

[10]**harbors:** clings to.

[11]**harems:** groups of females who mate and live with one male.

[12]**concubines:** secondary wives.

[13]**King John:** king of England from 1199 to 1216, known for seizing the throne from his nephew Arthur.

hot iron; when he is a religious zealot[14] dealing with heretics[15] in the Middle Ages, he skins his captive alive and scatters salt on his back; in the first Richard's[16] time, he shuts up a multitude of Jewish families in a tower and sets fire to it; in Columbus's time he captures a family of Spanish Jews and—but *that* is not printable; in our day in England, a man is fined ten shillings for beating his mother nearly to death with a chair, and another man is fined forty shillings for having four

100   pheasant eggs in his possession without being able to satisfactorily explain how he got them. Of all the animals, man is the only one that is cruel. He is the only one that inflicts pain for the pleasure of doing it. It is a trait that is not known to the higher animals. The cat plays with the frightened mouse; but she has this excuse, that she does not know that the mouse is suffering. The cat is moderate—unhumanly moderate: She only scares the mouse, she does not hurt it; she doesn't dig out its eyes, or tear off its skin, or drive splinters under its nails— man fashion; when she is done playing with it, she makes a sudden meal of it and puts it out of its trouble. Man is the Cruel Animal. He is

110   alone in that distinction.

     The higher animals engage in individual fights, but never in organized masses. Man is the only animal that deals in that atrocity of atrocities, war. He is the only one that gathers his brethren about him and goes forth in cold blood and with calm pulse to exterminate his kind. He is the only animal that for sordid wages will march out, as the Hessians[17] did in our Revolution, and as the boyish Prince Napoleon did in the Zulu war,[18] and help to slaughter strangers of his own species who have done him no harm and with whom he has no quarrel.

120   Man is the only animal that robs his helpless fellow of his country—takes possession of it and drives him out of it or destroys him. Man has done this in all the ages. There is not an acre of ground on the globe that is in possession of its rightful owner, or that has not been taken away from owner after owner, cycle after cycle, by force and bloodshed.

     Man is the only Slave. And he is the only animal who enslaves. He has always been a slave in one form or another, and has always held other slaves in bondage under him in one way or another. In our day he is always some man's slave for wages and does that man's work; and

130   this slave has other slaves under him for minor wages, and they do *his*

---

[14] **zealot** (zĕl´ət): overly enthusiastic person; fanatic.

[15] **heretics:** people who hold beliefs opposed to those of the church.

[16] **first Richard's:** refers to Richard I (1157–1199), also called Richard the Lion-Hearted, king of England from 1189 to 1199.

[17] **Hessians** (hĕsh´ənz): German soldiers who served for pay in the British army during the American Revolution.

[18] **Prince Napoleon. . .Zulu war:** In search of adventure, Prince Napoleon, son of Napoleon III, joined the British campaign against Zululand (part of South Africa) in 1879.

> **Man is the only Slave.
> And he is the only animal
> who enslaves.**

work. The higher animals are the only ones who exclusively do their own work and provide their own living.

Man is the only Patriot. He sets himself apart in his own country, under his own flag, and sneers at the other nations, and keeps multitudinous uniformed assassins on hand at heavy expense to grab slices of other people's countries and keep *them* from grabbing slices of *his*. And in the intervals between campaigns, he washes the blood off his hands and works for "the universal brotherhood of man"— with his mouth.

140   Man is the Religious Animal. He is the only Religious Animal. He is the only animal that has the True Religion—several of them. He is the only animal that loves his neighbor as himself, and cuts his throat if his theology isn't straight. He has made a graveyard of the globe in trying his honest best to smooth his brother's path to happiness and heaven. He was at it in the time of the Caesars, he was at it in Mahomet's[19] time, he was at it in the time of the Inquisition, he was at it in France a couple of centuries, he was at it in England in Mary's day,[20] he has been at it ever since he first saw the light, he is at it today in Crete—he will be at it somewhere else tomorrow. The higher

150   animals have no religion. And we are told that they are going to be left out, in the hereafter. I wonder why. It seems questionable taste.

Man is the Reasoning Animal. Such is the claim. I think it is open to dispute. Indeed, my experiments have proven to me that he is the Unreasoning Animal. Note his history, as sketched above. It seems plain to me that whatever he is, he is *not* a reasoning animal. His record is the fantastic record of a maniac. I consider that the strongest count against his intelligence is the fact that with that record back of him, he blandly sets himself up as the head animal of the lot; whereas by his own standards, he is the bottom one.

---

[19]**Mahomet's:** Muhammad (c. A.D. 570–632) was an Arab prophet and founder of Islam.

[20]**in Mary's day:** during the reign of Queen Mary (1553–1558), who was given the nickname "Bloody Mary" when she ordered the deaths of many Protestants.

160   In truth, man is incurably foolish. Simple things which the
other animals easily learn he is incapable of learning. Among my
experiments was this. In an hour I taught a cat and a dog to be friends.
I put them in a cage. In another hour I taught them to be friends with
a rabbit. In the course of two days I was able to add a fox, a goose, a
squirrel, and some doves. Finally a monkey. They lived together in
peace, even affectionately.

Next, in another cage I confined an Irish Catholic from Tipperary,
and as soon as he seemed tame, I added a Scottish Presbyterian from
Aberdeen. Next a Turk from Constantinople, a Greek Christian
170   from Crete, an Armenian, a Methodist from the wilds of Arkansas, a
Buddhist from China, a Brahman from Benares. Finally, a Salvation
Army colonel from Wapping. Then I stayed away two whole days.
When I came back to note results, the cage of Higher Animals was all
right, but in the other there was but a chaos of gory odds and ends of
turbans and fezzes and plaids and bones and flesh—not a specimen
left alive. These Reasoning Animals had disagreed on a theological
detail and carried the matter to a higher court.

COLLABORATIVE DISCUSSION What are the experiments that Twain
describes? How realistic are they? Discuss these questions with a partner,
citing specific evidence from the essay to support your ideas.

Author's Purpose: Satire

An **author's purpose** is what the writer hopes to achieve by crafting a written piece. The author may want to describe, inform, narrate, entertain, analyze, persuade, or do several of these at once. To achieve their purposes, authors use various techniques that combine style and content. **Satire** is a literary form that ridicules the shortcomings of people and institutions in an attempt to bring about change. When a writer like Mark Twain uses satire, his overall purpose is to change or improve something in society.

This chart shows techniques that signal when a writer is using satire.

Elements of Satire		
Technique	**Definition**	**Example**
Humor	Describing something in a way that causes laughter or amusement	"In order to bolster up a tottering reputation, the ant pretended to store up supplies, but I was not deceived."
Exaggeration	Overstating something to draw attention to it and make a point	"He has made a graveyard of the globe. . . ."
Absurdity	Describing extreme situations that are impossible to take seriously	"In order to determine the difference between an anaconda and an earl—if any—I caused seven young calves to be turned into the anaconda's cage."
Irony	Stating the opposite of what is really meant	"These experiments were made in the London Zoological Gardens and covered many months of painstaking and fatiguing work."

Look for other examples of these techniques as you analyze Twain's essay. Ask yourself these questions:

- What is the central idea that Twain is satirizing?
- What is his tone or attitude toward humans and toward animals?
- What does he hope to change by writing this satire?

eBook *Annotate It!*

Analyzing the Text

COMMON CORE

ELACC11-12RI1,
ELACC11-12RI2,
ELACC11-12RI4,
ELACC11-12RI6,
ELACC11-12SL2,
ELACC11-12SL6

Cite Text Evidence   Support your responses with evidence from the selection.

1. **Summarize** In lines 1–8, how does Twain indicate his intention to satirize Darwin's ideas about human nature? How does this paragraph reveal Twain's tone toward humans and animals?

2. **Analyze** In lines 9–17, Twain says that he reached his conclusions by following the scientific method. How well does the rest of the essay support this assertion?

3. **Infer** When describing a buffalo hunt, Twain writes, "They had charming sport" (line 38). How does the rest of the passage reveal the irony that is implicit in this statement?

4. **Interpret** What is the outcome when Twain tries to persuade different wild and tame animals to "accumulate vast stores of food" (lines 52–64)? What purpose do the examples serve?

5. **Analyze** Twain cites many examples of human cruelty through the ages. What purpose do these examples serve?

6. **Interpret** What does Twain mean when he writes that "Man is the Animal that Blushes. He is the only one that does it—or has occasion to" (lines 85–86)?

7. **Analyze** How does Twain use the somewhat positive statements that "Man is the only Patriot" (line 133) and "Man is the Religious Animal" (line 140) ironically?

8. **Evaluate** What is Twain's overall purpose in writing this essay? How effective is his use of satire in achieving that purpose?

PERFORMANCE TASK

Speaking Activity: Lecture Twain was a popular lecturer in his time. Try delivering a section of "The Lowest Animal" as an effective lecture.

- Use library or Internet resources to listen to some audio recordings of actors impersonating Twain's voice and style of speaking.

- Choose a section of the essay to present as a lecture to a small group. Consider how to make the implicit elements of satire more obvious to listeners.

- As a speaker, use pacing, gestures, and inflection to communicate Twain's ideas, his humor, and his irony.

- After giving your lecture and listening to those of others in your group, write a one-page summary comparing the experience of reading the essay to speaking it and listening to it.

Critical Vocabulary

disposition   caliber   transition   atrocious

Practice and Apply For each Critical Vocabulary word, identify which example best illustrates its meaning. Explain why the example you chose is most accurate.

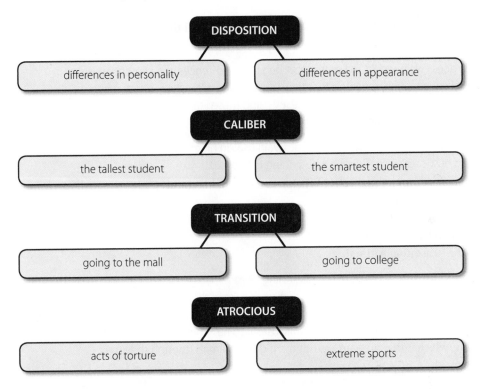

DISPOSITION

differences in personality   differences in appearance

CALIBER

the tallest student   the smartest student

TRANSITION

going to the mall   going to college

ATROCIOUS

acts of torture   extreme sports

Vocabulary Strategy: Nuance in Word Meaning

In "The Lowest Animal," Mark Twain uses the Critical Vocabulary word *atrocious* to describe laws that allow men to keep harems. Twain chose a word with a very strong nuance, or shade of meaning, because he wanted to emphasize that the laws were not simply bad or unjust but that they were, in fact, evil or brutal. By choosing a word with a specific nuance, writers' explanations of their ideas are less ambiguous. Adjectives that have similar meanings but different nuances might be arranged on this continuum, with the word representing the least degree on the left and the greatest, on the right.

| bad | naughty | wicked | cruel | atrocious |

Practice and Apply For each word, create a continuum of at least four other words that have similar meanings, but show different nuances, moving from weakest to strongest. Consult a dictionary as needed to clarify the precise meanings of words.

1. cold   **3.** happy   **5.** pretty

2. hot   **4.** smell

Language and Style: Anaphora and Parallelism

In "The Lowest Animal," Mark Twain uses a particular type of repetition known as **anaphora,** the repetition of a word or words at the beginning of successive lines, clauses, or sentences. This literary device is particularly effective in poetry, but it also has a place in argumentative prose. Consider this example from two sentences in lines 83–85.

> **Man is the Animal that Laughs. . . . No—Man is the Animal that Blushes.**

Not only does Twain repeat the words that begin the sentences, the sentences share a parallel construction, meaning that they use similar grammatical structures to express ideas that are related or equal in value. By using these literary devices, Twain emphasizes his central ideas and creates a rhythm that strengthens the rhetorical effect.

Here are other examples of anaphora that Twain uses in his essay. These appear at the beginning of successive paragraphs, beginning in line 120.

> **Man is the only animal that robs his helpless fellow of his country. . . .**
> **Man is the only Slave.**
> **Man is the only Patriot.**
> **Man is the Religious Animal.**
> **Man is the Reasoning Animal.**

By repeating the words *Man is* at the beginning of each paragraph and making the sentences parallel each other, Twain builds a cumulative list of the aspects of human conduct that he wants to satirize. Clearly, Twain's use of anaphora is deliberate. In his hands it has an artistic effect and he successfully uses it to hammer home the point he wants to make, which is that humans are not the highest animals (though they may believe otherwise).

Young writers are usually told to avoid repetition. They are encouraged to vary sentence length, sentence beginnings, and even sentence structure to build interest. All of this is good advice for the most part. However, skilled writers know when to use repetition to make a point. Twain's use of anaphora is an excellent example of knowing when to "break the rules."

Practice and Apply Look back at the summary you wrote of your experiences of reading, speaking, and listening to Twain's essay in response to this selection's Performance Task. Revise your writing to include use of anaphora and parallelism to emphasize important ideas and create rhythm.

MEDIA ANALYSIS

Tenements and the "Other Half"

Genesis of the Tenement
Essay from *How the Other Half Lives* by Jacob Riis

Images: Tenement Photos
Photographs by Jacob Riis

Child Mortality Rates
Report by the Tenement House Committee

AMERICA The Story of Us: Jacob Riis
Video by HISTORY

Jacob Riis (1849–1914) *was born in Ribe, Denmark. In his long career, he was a journalist, a photographer, and a social reformer. After immigrating to the United States in 1870, Riis held several jobs and personally experienced homelessness and poverty on the streets of New York City. In 1873, he became a police reporter and was assigned to New York's Lower East Side, a poor area crowded with new immigrants. He was dismayed to learn of the conditions in the tenements that led, among other things, to high infant mortality. He began taking photographs of the slums with the new technique of flash photography. In 1890, he published* How the Other Half Lives. *In the introduction to that book, Riis pointed out that "one half of the world does not know how the other half lives." His book shocked readers and brought Riis and his cause much attention. Theodore Roosevelt, a New York City police commissioner who later became president, read the book and quickly wrote Riis a note: "I have read your book, and I have come to help." Riis's work prompted the first legislation to reform housing laws.*

Genesis of the Tenement

by Jacob Riis

AS YOU READ Pay attention to the facts and details Jacob Riis includes to support his point of view. Write down any questions you generate during reading.

The first tenement New York knew bore the mark of Cain[1] from its birth, though a generation passed before the writing was deciphered. It was the "rear house," infamous ever after in our city's history. There had been tenant-houses before, but they were not built for the purpose. Nothing would probably have shocked their original owners more than the idea of their harboring a promiscuous[2] crowd; for they were the decorous homes of the old Knickerbockers, the proud aristocracy of Manhattan in the early days.

It was the stir and bustle of trade, together with the tremendous immigration that followed upon the war of 1812 that dislodged them. In thirty-five years the city of less than a hundred thousand came to harbor half a million souls, for whom homes had to be found. Within the memory of men not yet in their prime, Washington had moved from his house on Cherry Hill as too far out of town to be easily reached. Now the old residents followed his example; but they moved in a different direction and for a different reason. Their comfortable dwellings in the once fashionable streets along the East River front fell into the hands of real-estate agents and boarding-house keepers; and here, says the report to the Legislature of 1857, when the evils engendered[3] had excited just alarm, "in its beginning, the tenant-house became a real blessing to that class of industrious poor whose small earnings limited their expenses, and whose employment in workshops, stores, or about the warehouses and thoroughfares, render a near residence of much importance." Not for long, however. As business increased, and the city grew with rapid strides, the necessities of the poor became the opportunity of their wealthier neighbors, and the stamp was set upon the old houses, suddenly become valuable, which the best thought and effort of a later age have vainly struggled to efface. Their "*large* rooms were partitioned into *several smaller ones*, without regard to light or ventilation, the rate of rent being lower in proportion to space or height from the street; and they soon became filled from cellar to garret[4] with a class of tenantry living from hand to

---

[1] **bore the mark of Cain:** carried a curse, referring to God's punishment of Cain for killing his brother Abel, as described in *Genesis 4*.

[2] **promiscuous:** indiscriminate variety.

[3] **engendered:** caused or gave birth to.

[4] **garret:** attic.

mouth, loose in morals, improvident[5] in habits, degraded, and squalid[6] as beggary itself." It was thus the dark bedroom, prolific of untold depravities,[7] came into the world. It was destined to survive the old houses. In their new rôle, says the old report, eloquent in its indignant denunciation of "evils more destructive than wars," "they were not intended to last. Rents were fixed high enough to cover damage and abuse from this class, from whom nothing was expected, and the most
40 was made of them while they lasted. Neatness, order, cleanliness, were never dreamed of in connection with the tenant-house system, as it spread its localities from year to year; while reckless slovenliness,[8] discontent, privation, and ignorance were left to work out their invariable results, until the entire premises reached the level of tenant-house dilapidation, containing, but sheltering not, the miserable hordes that crowded beneath mouldering, water-rotted roofs or burrowed among the rats of clammy cellars." Yet so illogical is human greed that, at a later day, when called to account, "the proprietors frequently urged the filthy habits of the tenants as an excuse for the
50 condition of their property, utterly losing sight of the fact that it was the tolerance of those habits which was the real evil, and that for this they themselves were alone responsible."

Still the pressure of the crowds did not abate, and in the old garden where the stolid Dutch burgher[9] grew his tulips or early cabbages a rear house was built, generally of wood, two stories high at first. Presently it was carried up another story, and another. Where two families had lived ten moved in. The front house followed suit, if the brick walls were strong enough. The question was not always asked, judging from complaints made by a contemporary witness,
60 that the old buildings were "often carried up to a great height without regard to the strength of the foundation walls." It was rent the owner was after; nothing was said in the contract about either the safety or the comfort of the tenants. The garden gate no longer swung on its rusty hinges. The shell-paved walk had become an alley; what the rear house had left of the garden, a "court." Plenty such are yet to be found in the Fourth Ward, with here and there one of the original rear tenements.

Worse was to follow. It was "soon perceived by estate owners and agents of property that a greater percentage of profits could be
70 realized by the conversion of houses and blocks into barracks, and dividing their space into smaller proportions capable of containing human life within four walls. . . . Blocks were rented of real estate owners, or 'purchased on time,' or taken in charge at a percentage,

---

[5] **improvident:** careless; lacking foresight.
[6] **squalid:** filthy and shabby.
[7] **depravities:** immoral behaviors.
[8] **slovenliness:** sloppiness.
[9] **stolid Dutch burgher:** upstanding citizen of New Amsterdam.

and held for under-letting." With the appearance of the middleman, wholly irresponsible, and utterly reckless and unrestrained, began the era of tenement building which turned out such blocks as Gotham Court, where, in one cholera epidemic that scarcely touched the clean wards, the tenants died at the rate of one hundred and ninety-five to the thousand of population; which forced the general mortality of the city up from 1 in 41.83 in 1815, to 1 in 27.33 in 1855, a year of unusual freedom from epidemic disease, and which wrung from the early organizers of the Health Department this wail: "There are numerous examples of tenement-houses in which are lodged several hundred people that have a *pro rata* allotment[10] of ground area scarcely equal to two square yards upon the city lot, court - yards and all included." The tenement-house population had swelled to half a million souls by that time, and on the East Side, in what is still the most densely populated district in all the world, China not excluded, it was packed at the rate of 290,000 to the square mile, a state of affairs wholly unexampled. The utmost cupidity of other lands and other days had never contrived to herd much more than half that number within the same space. The greatest crowding of Old London was at the rate of 175,816. Swine roamed the streets and gutters as their principal scavengers.[11] The death of a child in a tenement was registered at the Bureau of Vital Statistics as "plainly due to suffocation in the foul air of an unventilated apartment," and the Senators, who had come down from Albany to find out what was the matter with New York, reported that "there are annually cut off from the population by disease and death enough human beings to people a city, and enough human labor to sustain it." And yet experts had testified that, as compared with uptown, rents were from twenty-five to thirty per cent higher in the worst slums of the lower wards, with such accommodations as were enjoyed, for instance, by a "family with boarders" in Cedar Street, who fed hogs in the cellar that contained eight or ten loads of manure; or "one room 12 × 12 with five families living in it, comprising twenty persons of both sexes and all ages, with only two beds, without partition, screen, chair, or table." The rate of rent has been successfully maintained to the present day, though the hog at least has been eliminated.

Lest anybody flatter himself with the notion that these were evils of a day that is happily past and may safely be forgotten, let me mention here three very recent instances of tenement-house life that came under my notice. One was the burning of a rear house in Mott Street, from appearances one of the original tenant-houses that made their owners rich. The fire made homeless ten families, who had paid an average of $5 a month for their mean little cubby-holes. The owner

---

[10] *pro rata* allotment: proportional allowance.

[11] scavengers: It was not until the winter of 1867 that owners of swine were prohibited by ordinance from letting them run at large in the built-up portions of the city. [Author's note]

himself told me that it was *fully* insured for $800, though it brought him in $600 a year rent. He evidently considered himself especially entitled to be pitied for losing such valuable property. Another was the
120 case of a hard-working family of man and wife, young people from the old country, who took poison together in a Crosby Street tenement because they were "tired." There was no other explanation, and none was needed when I stood in the room in which they had lived. It was in the attic with sloping ceiling and a single window so far out on the roof that it seemed not to belong to the place at all. With scarcely room enough to turn around in they had been compelled to pay five dollars and a half a month in advance. There were four such rooms in that attic, and together they brought in as much as many a handsome little cottage in a pleasant part of Brooklyn. The third instance was that of a
130 colored family of husband, wife, and baby in a wretched rear rookery[12] in West Third Street. Their rent was eight dollars and a half for a single room on the top-story, so small that I was unable to get a photograph of it even by placing the camera outside the open door. Three short steps across either way would have measured its full extent.

There was just one excuse for the early tenement-house builders, and their successors may plead it with nearly as good right for what it is worth. "Such," says an official report, "is the lack of house-room in the city that any kind of tenement can be immediately crowded with lodgers, if there is space offered." Thousands were living in cellars.
140 There were three hundred underground lodging-houses in the city when the Health Department was organized. Some fifteen years before that the old Baptist Church in Mulberry Street, just off Chatham Street, had been sold, and the rear half of the frame structure had been converted into tenements that with their swarming population became the scandal even of that reckless age. The wretched pile[13] harbored no less than forty families, and the annual rate of deaths to the population was officially stated to be 75 in 1,000. These tenements were an extreme type of very many, for the big barracks had by this time spread east and west and far up the island into the sparsely
150 settled wards. Whether or not the title was clear to the land upon which they were built was of less account than that the rents were collected. If there were damages to pay, the tenant had to foot them. Cases were "very frequent when property was in litigation, and two or three different parties were collecting rents." Of course under such circumstances "no repairs were ever made."

The climax had been reached. The situation was summed up by the Society for the Improvement of the Condition of the Poor in these words: "Crazy old buildings, crowded rear tenements in filthy yards, dark, damp basements, leaking garrets, shops, outhouses, and

---

[12]**rookery:** a breeding place for birds; figuratively, a slum.
[13]**pile:** large building.

160 stables[14] converted into dwellings, though scarcely fit to shelter brutes, are habitations of thousands of our fellow-beings in this wealthy, Christian city." "The city," says its historian, Mrs. Martha Lamb, commenting on the era of aqueduct building between 1835 and 1845, "was a general asylum for vagrants." Young vagabonds, the natural offspring of such "home" conditions, overran the streets. Juvenile crime increased fearfully year by year. The Children's Aid Society and kindred philanthropic organizations were yet unborn, but in the city directory was to be found the address of the "American Society for the Promotion of Education in Africa."

[14] **stables:** A lot 50 × 60, contained twenty stables, rented for dwellings at $15 a year each; cost of the whole $600. [Author's note]

COLLABORATIVE DISCUSSION In a small group, discuss what Jacob Riis's tone is toward his subject. What inference can you make about what Riis thinks should be done to improve living conditions in the tenements?

Images: Tenement Photos
by Jacob Riis

AS YOU VIEW Pay attention to the living and working conditions of the people in the photographs. Write down any questions you generate as you view them.

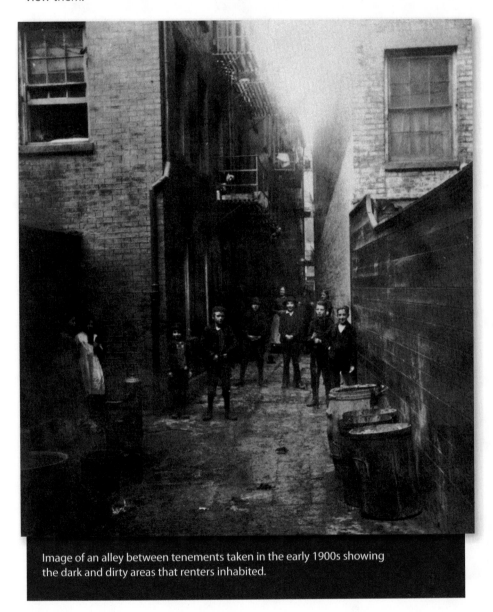

Image of an alley between tenements taken in the early 1900s showing the dark and dirty areas that renters inhabited.

Published in Jacob Riis's book *How the Other Half Lives*, entitled "Five Cents a Spot." The title refers to the cost of buying a spot on the floor to sleep for the night.

Men and young boy (in foreground) photographed around the 1880s in a New York City sweatshop, or factory, with poor working conditions.

COLLABORATIVE DISCUSSION In a small group, discuss the details that these photographs have in common. What emotions are conveyed by the people?

Child Mortality Rates

Background *This table was included in the* Report of the Tenement House Committee, *published in 1895. The committee was formed to "make a careful examination into the tenement-houses" of New York City. Due to the rapid influx of new immigrants, New York City was the most populous urban area in the world, with parts of it denser than infamous slums in Bombay, India. The report described some residents as living "virtually in a cage", in dark, damp buildings surrounded by garbage. The average death-rate in New York City at the time was 22.75 deaths per 1000 persons.*

AS YOU READ Consider the differences in the death-rate of children in different wards. Write down any questions you generate during reading.

If we take the death-rate of children as a test, the rear tenements show themselves to be veritable slaughter-houses, as shown in the following table, which only covers the lower wards, where such houses are numerous:

Wards	Death-rate of children under 5 years of age in single tenements.	Death-rate of children under 5 years of age in front and rear tenements on same lot.
1	109.58	204.54
4	105.69	114.68
5	107.99	64.52
6	103.56	99.54
7	61.78	72.58
8	95.58	129.56
9	92.78	130.56
10	57.20	62.58
11	73.12	71.49
13	83.05	100.59
14	129.56	114.12
17	62.04	78.36

It is unfortunate that it was found impossible to make a direct comparison between the death-rates in rear tenements, by themselves, and the death-rate in other houses. But the deaths in the city are reported by street and number, and as the front and rear houses on the same lot have the same number, it is evident that the rate could not be calculated separately. In the report of January 28, 1890, already referred to, the general death-rate for lots containing both front and rear houses was 25.05, against 22.42 for other houses of the same class, in the same part of the city.

COLLABORATIVE DISCUSSION In a small group, discuss what information you can draw from the text and chart on this page. What might explain the differences between the death rates in the two columns?

AMERICA The Story of Us: Jacob Riis

Background *This brief video discusses and depicts how Jacob Riis successfully championed housing reform in the late 1800s and early 1900s in New York City through his use of flash photography. His photographs made it possible for many people to become truly aware of the living conditions in the tenements of New York City. In addition to writing about the problems he witnessed there, Riis gave numerous presentations to acquaint people with the issues of tenement dwellers and to push for changes that would help improve their situation.*

AS YOU VIEW Pay attention to how the audience attending Riis's presentation, which the video dramatizes, reacts to his photographs. Write down any questions you generate during viewing.

COLLABORATIVE DISCUSSION In a small group, discuss what perspective or insight the interviewed experts bring to the film. Why are their statements effective or persuasive?

Integrate and Evaluate Information

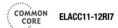

Writers can choose to present their information in many different formats to achieve different purposes. Integrating and evaluating multiple sources of information presented in different media or formats can help address questions about a particular subject. The chart shows some formats in which information can be presented. This collection about Jacob Riis presents information in prose, visual, and quantitative formats.

Format	How Information Is Presented
Prose	
Essay	In *How the Other Half Lives*, Jacob Riis presents most of the information about tenements in text format. Notice, however, he supports his text with photographs and statistical or numerical data. Why might he have chosen to combine these different formats to support his ideas?
Visual	
Video Clips	A video clip gives viewers images, sounds, and even special effects to help them evaluate a topic, such as why Jacob Riis's work was so influential. What advantages does a visual representation have?
Photographs	Photographs give readers a concrete visual image of something. Photographs can support information provided in a text or can stand on their own with captions to portray a broader subject, such as living conditions in tenements. Why are the photographs of people in and around tenements effective?
Maps	Maps provide information about aspects of a geographical region. Why might a map of the New York City wards in the late 1800s be useful?
Quantitative	
Tables	Tables show sets of data across several columns, enabling readers to track their relationship to each other and draw conclusions about the data. Remember to look at the title and labels on columns and rows, as well as the actual numbers to help you interpret the data in a table. How does the table of information about death rates in the wards help you understand the need for tenement housing reform?
Graphs	Graphs provide an illustration of statistical information or numerical relationships. Line graphs show changes over time. Bar graphs compare quantities and circle graphs show relationships of parts to a whole. Which type of graph could be used to present the information about death rates in the wards in a different way?

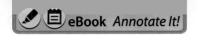

Analyzing the Text and Media

COMMON CORE

ELACC11-12RI5,
ELACC11-12RI6,
ELACC11-12RI7,
ELACC11-12W2,
ELACC11-12W7,
ELACC11-12W8,
ELACC11-12W9

Cite Text Evidence   Support your responses with evidence from the selections.

1. **Connect** How does Riis's description of the genesis of the tenements at the beginning of his essay help support his purpose and point of view? How does Riis's rhetoric contribute to the power of his text?

2. **Critique** What quantitative format could Riis have used to present the data in lines 86–109 in order to clarify his argument about the problems of tenements?

3. **Evaluate** How does the video excerpt help support the idea that Jacob Riis was successful in communicating his point of view to his audience? Cite specific images or concepts from the video to support your answer.

4. **Analyze** What does the table show about children living in front or rear tenements? Why might information presented in this format have been more effective at pushing New York City to make reforms to housing laws than a photograph of a tenement?

5. **Compare** Review the three photographs from the image collection. What does each image add to your knowledge of life in the New York City tenements? How do these three images connect to the ideas and messages in the other three types of documents?

6. **Synthesize** What idea and point of view is Riis expressing when he says, "The Children's Aid Society and kindred philanthropic organizations were yet unborn, but in the city directory was to be found the address of the 'American Society for the Promotion of Education in Africa'"? How is this sentiment different from what Tom Brokaw says about the American people in the video? What explains this difference?

7. **Draw Conclusions** What are the pros and cons of evaluating data from multiple sources about a subject? Think about whether a question about specific numbers of children living in tenements could be answered by only viewing Riis's photographs.

PERFORMANCE TASK

Writing Activity: Essay During the late 1800s and early 1900s, many people, including Jacob Riis, worked to solve societal issues. Write an informative essay to answer this question: What was life like in the New York tenements? Use these tips to get started.

- Start collecting information to support your claim. Write an outline for your essay. Use information from "Genesis of the Tenement," Jacob Riis's photographs, the table, and the video.

- Remember to jot down and include the source of your supporting information.

- In your essay, introduce your topic and develop it by choosing the most

- significant and relevant information available. Avoid using ambiguous data that can be misinterpreted.

- Consider presenting some of your information in quantitative or visual formats to help your readers understand.

- In your conclusion, summarize the information you have presented.

Kate Chopin (1851–1904) *wrote more than one hundred short stories and two novels. Her work features intelligent and sensitive female characters and is often set against the Louisiana backdrop where she spent her married life. Her first novel,* At Fault *(1890), received little attention when it was published. Her second,* The Awakening *(1899), told the story of a woman who leaves her family and eventually commits suicide. It was widely condemned by critics as shocking and morbid. However, since its rediscovery in the 1950s, it has been hailed as an insightful work that foreshadowed the feminist movement in literature.*

The Story of an Hour

Short Story by Kate Chopin

AS YOU READ After you read the first paragraph, write down what you expect to happen or what you expect Mrs. Mallard to do. Pause after every few paragraphs and continue to jot down your expectations. Write down any questions you generate during reading.

Knowing that Mrs. Mallard was afflicted with a heart trouble, great care was taken to break to her as gently as possible the news of her husband's death.

It was her sister Josephine who told her, in broken sentences; veiled hints that revealed in half concealing. Her husband's friend Richards was there, too, near her. It was he who had been in the newspaper office when intelligence of the railroad disaster was received, with Brently Mallard's name leading the list of "killed." He had only taken the time to assure himself of its truth by a second telegram, and had

10 hastened to forestall any less careful, less tender friend in bearing the sad message.

She did not hear the story as many women have heard the same, with a paralyzed inability to accept its significance. She wept at once, with sudden, wild **abandonment**, in her sister's arms. When the storm of grief had spent itself she went away to her room alone. She would have no one follow her.

abandonment
(ə-băn´dən-mĕnt) *n.*
a lack of restraint or
inhibition.

There stood, facing the open window, a comfortable, roomy armchair. Into this she sank, pressed down by a physical exhaustion that haunted her body and seemed to reach into her soul.

20 She could see in the open square before her house the tops of trees that were all aquiver with the new spring life. The delicious breath of rain was in the air. In the street below a peddler was crying his wares. The notes of a distant song which someone was singing reached her faintly, and countless sparrows were twittering in the eaves.

There were patches of blue sky showing here and there through the clouds that had met and piled one above the other in the west facing her window.

She sat with her head thrown back upon the cushion of the chair, quite motionless, except when a sob came up into her throat and
30 shook her, as a child who has cried itself to sleep continues to sob in its dreams.

She was young, with a fair, calm face, whose lines bespoke repression and even a certain strength. But now there was a dull stare in her eyes, whose gaze was fixed away off yonder on one of those patches of blue sky. It was not a glance of reflection, but rather indicated a suspension of intelligent thought.

There was something coming to her and she was waiting for it, fearfully. What was it? She did not know; it was too subtle and elusive to name. But she felt it, creeping out of the sky, reaching toward her
40 through the sounds, the scents, the color that filled the air.

Now her bosom rose and fell tumultuously. She was beginning to recognize this thing that was approaching to possess her, and she was striving to beat it back with her will—as powerless as her two white slender hands would have been.

When she abandoned herself a little whispered word escaped her slightly parted lips. She said it over and over under her breath: "free, free, free!" The **vacant** stare and the look of terror that had followed it went from her eyes. They stayed keen and bright. Her pulses beat fast, and the coursing blood warmed and relaxed every inch of her body.

50 She did not stop to ask if it were or were not a monstrous joy that held her. A clear and exalted perception enabled her to dismiss the suggestion as trivial.

She knew that she would weep again when she saw the kind, tender hands folded in death; the face that had never looked save with love upon her, fixed and gray and dead. But she saw beyond that bitter moment a long procession of years to come that would belong to her absolutely. And she opened and spread her arms out to them in welcome.

There would be no one to live for her during those coming years;
60 she would live for herself. There would be no powerful will bending hers in that blind persistence with which men and women believe they have a right to impose a private will upon a fellow creature. A kind

vacant
(vā´kənt) *adj.* blank, expressionless.

intention or a cruel intention made the act seem no less a crime as she looked upon it in that brief moment of **illumination**.

illumination
(ĭ-lōō'mə-nā'shən) *n.* awareness or enlightenment.

And yet she had loved him—sometimes. Often she had not. What did it matter! What could love, the unsolved mystery, count for in face of this possession of self-assertion which she suddenly recognized as the strongest impulse of her being!

"Free! Body and soul free!" she kept whispering.

70 Josephine was kneeling before the closed door with her lips to the keyhole, imploring for admission. "Louise, open the door! I beg; open the door—you will make yourself ill. What are you doing, Louise? For heaven's sake open the door."

"Go away. I am not making myself ill." No; she was drinking in a very elixir of life[1] through that open window.

Her fancy was running riot along those days ahead of her. Spring days, and summer days, and all sorts of days that would be her own. She breathed a quick prayer that life might be long. It was only yesterday she had thought with a shudder that life might be long.

80 She arose at length and opened the door to her sister's importunities. There was a feverish triumph in her eyes, and she carried herself unwittingly like a goddess of Victory. She clasped her sister's waist, and together they descended the stairs. Richards stood waiting for them at the bottom.

Someone was opening the front door with a latchkey. It was Brently Mallard who entered, a little travel-stained, **composedly** carrying his grip-sack[2] and umbrella. He had been far from the scene of accident, and did not even know there had been one. He stood amazed at Josephine's piercing cry; at Richards' quick motion to screen

composed
(kəm-pōzd') *adj.* self-possessed; calm.

90 him from the view of his wife.

But Richards was too late.

When the doctors came they said she had died of heart disease—of joy that kills.

---

[1] **elixir of life:** a medicine that restores vigor or the essence of life.

[2] **grip-sack:** a small traveling bag or satchel.

COLLABORATIVE DISCUSSION With a partner, discuss whether your initial expectations were met and how your expectations changed over the course of the story. Cite specific details in the text that shaped your expectations.

Analyze Author's Point of View: Irony

COMMON CORE   ELACC11-12RL6

Point of view refers to the perspective from which a story is told. "The Story of an Hour" is told from a **third-person** point of view; the narrator is not a character in the story but observes the action from outside it. Point of view may also be characterized by what the narrator knows or shares. If the narrator is able to tell readers what only one character thinks and feels, the point of view is **limited.** An **omniscient** narrator can describe the thoughts and feelings of all the characters.

When analyzing a story's point of view, it's important to distinguish between what is stated directly and what is actually true for the characters. One of the narrator's roles is to help readers see contrasts, such as

- what a character feels versus how he or she behaves
- what characters believe versus what is true
- what readers might expect to happen versus what does happen

All of these are examples of irony, a contrast between appearance and reality. This chart describes the three basic types of irony.

Verbal Irony	Situational Irony	Dramatic Irony
In **verbal irony,** what is said is the opposite of what is meant. Sarcasm, understatement, and hyperbole (exaggeration for effect) are all examples of verbal irony. Context can help you clarify whether a statement is an example of verbal irony. If a friend says, "I'm having a great day," but then tells you she woke up late and left her homework on the bus, you'd interpret her statement as ironic.	In **situational irony,** a character or the reader expects one thing to happen, but something else happens instead. Situational irony is used throughout "The Story of an Hour." For example, recall how carefully Josephine and Richards break the news about Mr. Mallard's death. How do they (and readers) expect Mrs. Mallard to feel about the loss of her husband? How does she actually feel?	In **dramatic irony,** the audience or reader knows something that the characters do not know. For example, when Mrs. Mallard is locked in her room, her worried sister crouches at the keyhole and says, "I beg; open the door—you will make yourself ill." What do readers know that poor Josephine does not?

Identifying the use of irony can help you determine **themes,** or deeper messages about life that the author wants to communicate through a story. Irony encourages readers to look for the truth hidden behind superficial appearances or expectations. As you analyze "The Story of an Hour," ask yourself what the unexpected realities of the characters' lives teach you about people, relationships, and society in general.

Analyzing the Text

COMMON CORE

ELACC11-12RL1,
ELACC11-12RL2,
ELACC11-12RL3,
ELACC11-12RL5,
ELACC11-12RL6,
ELACC11-12SL1a

Cite Text Evidence   Support your responses with evidence from the selection.

1. **Cite Evidence** Is the narrator of the story limited or omniscient? At what point in the story do readers learn whose thoughts and feelings the narrator can describe?

2. **Analyze** Reread lines 1–11. How do Josephine and Richards expect Mrs. Mallard to react to Mr. Mallard's death? Now reread lines 12–19 and explain whether Mrs. Mallard's initial reaction is intended to be ironic.

3. **Compare** What is ironic about Mrs. Mallard's private reaction to her husband's death? How does it compare to the expectations of the other characters?

4. **Infer** In lines 45–58 the narrator begins to reveal Mrs. Mallard's true feelings about being a widow. What theme is suggested through this situational irony?

5. **Evaluate** What images does the narrator describe outside Mrs. Mallard's window when she first goes to her room? Does this choice of imagery make you more or less sympathetic toward Mrs. Mallard?

6. **Interpret** How does Chopin's diction and imagery in lines 80–84 contribute to her characterization of a transformed Mrs. Mallard?

7. **Evaluate** Why is Mr. Mallard's return an example of situational irony? Would the story still be ironic if he had actually been dead?

8. **Analyze** The doctors say that Mrs. Mallard dies of "joy that kills." Explain whether this is an example of dramatic irony.

PERFORMANCE TASK

Speaking Activity: Discussion There are many strong examples of irony in "The Story of an Hour." Collaborate with others to discuss what irony adds to Chopin's message. Then write a brief summary of the key ideas from your discussion.

1. Why did Chopin choose to communicate so much of her **theme,** or message, through the literary device of irony? In the context of her era and of her audience's possible attitudes, why might this have been an appropriate or attractive choice?

2. Consider the irony of Mrs. Mallard's death. How is her death—its timing and its cause—ironic? What does the irony of her death add to Chopin's message?

In your discussion and summary, include evidence from the text and revise to use the conventions of standard English.

Critical Vocabulary

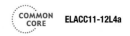

abandonment   **vacant**   **illumination**   **composed**

Practice and Apply Decide which Critical Vocabulary word goes best with the words or phrases given here.

1. Which word goes best with *recklessness*? Why?

2. Which word goes best with *understanding*? Why?

3. Which word goes best with being lost in thought? Why?

4. Which word goes best with a calm personality? Why?

Vocabulary Strategy: Word Collocations

In English, certain words commonly occur together and appear in a particular order. These common word groupings are referred to as collocations. For example, the Critical Vocabulary word *abandonment* appears in this story as part of the collocation *wild abandonment*—a common phrase used to describe spontaneous, impulsive behavior.

Wild abandonment is a collocation made up of an adjective and a noun, but collocations can also be made up of other parts of speech. This chart shows some examples.

Parts of Speech	Examples
adjective + noun	square meal
verb + noun	accept responsibility
adverb + adverb	quite easily
adverb + verb	strongly suggest
adverb + adjective + noun	totally unacceptable behavior

Practice and Apply Reread Chopin's "The Story of an Hour" with a partner and find four examples of collocation. Then, with these collocations:

1. Create a chart like the one shown to record each example and identify the parts of speech it includes. Write a definition for each collocation.

2. Use each collocation in an original sentence that demonstrates its meaning.

Elizabeth Bishop (1911–1979) *is considered one of the most influential poets of the twentieth century. Bishop almost studied medicine, but the poet Marianne Moore urged her to focus on poetry. Her poetry captures in precise, vivid detail the landscapes and creatures of the physical world. Although her subjects may at first appear simple, her poems explore complex themes of human grief, survival, and the need to belong. She won a Pulitzer Prize for her poetry collection* Poems: North & South/A Cold Spring.

The Fish

Poem by Elizabeth Bishop

AS YOU READ Make note of details that Bishop uses to create a vivid, realistic image of the fish. Write down any questions you generate during reading.

I caught a tremendous fish
and held him beside the boat
half out of water, with my hook
fast in a corner of his mouth.
5   He didn't fight.
He hadn't fought at all.
He hung a grunting weight,
battered and venerable
and homely. Here and there
10 his brown skin hung in strips
like ancient wallpaper,
and its pattern of darker brown
was like wallpaper:
shapes like full-blown roses
15 stained and lost through age.
He was speckled with barnacles,
fine rosettes of lime,
and infested

with tiny white sea-lice,
20 and underneath two or three
rags of green weed hung down.
While his gills were breathing in
the terrible oxygen
—the frightening gills,
25 fresh and crisp with blood,
that can cut so badly—
I thought of the coarse white flesh
packed in like feathers,
the big bones and the little bones,
30 the dramatic reds and blacks
of his shiny entrails,
and the pink swim-bladder
like a big peony.
I looked into his eyes
35 which were far larger than mine
but shallower, and yellowed,
the irises backed and packed
with tarnished tinfoil
seen through the lenses
40 of old scratched isinglass.
They shifted a little, but not
to return my stare.
—It was more like the tipping
of an object toward the light.
45 I admired his sullen face,
the mechanism of his jaw,
and then I saw
that from his lower lip
—if you could call it a lip—
50 grim, wet, and weaponlike,
hung five old pieces of fish-line,
or four and a wire leader
with the swivel still attached,
with all their five big hooks
55 grown firmly in his mouth.
A green line, frayed at the end
where he broke it, two heavier lines,
and a fine black thread
still crimped from the strain and snap
60 when it broke and he got away.
Like medals with their ribbons
frayed and wavering,
a five-haired beard of wisdom
trailing from his aching jaw.
65 I stared and stared

and victory filled up
the little rented boat,
from the pool of bilge[1]
where oil had spread a rainbow
70 around the rusted engine
to the bailer rusted orange,
the sun-cracked thwarts,[2]
the oarlocks on their strings,
the gunnels[3]—until everything
75 was rainbow, rainbow, rainbow!
And I let the fish go.

---

[1] **bilge** (bĭlj): dirty water that gathers in the bottom of a boat.
[2] **thwarts:** seats on a boat.
[3] **gunnels:** gunwales; the upper edges of the sides of a boat.

COLLABORATIVE DISCUSSION What is your impression of the fish? What special significance does the fish have in the poem? With a partner, discuss what details led to your impressions. Cite specific evidence from the text to support your ideas.

Analyze Structure: Symbol

COMMON CORE

ELACC11-12RL4,
ELACC11-12RL5,
ELACC11-12L5a

A **symbol** is a person, a place, a thing, or an event that has meaning in itself and also stands for something much more than itself. Often symbols stand for abstract ideas:

- A dove symbolizes peace.
- A skull symbolizes death.
- A red rose symbolizes love.
- A flag symbolizes an entire country.

These are all public symbols with conventional meanings. Fish can be conventional symbols of freedom and the mysteries of nature. Bishop's fish can be viewed that way, but it can also be viewed as a private symbol. Bishop's careful choice of details about the fish and the speaker's actions and reactions help reveal a symbolic or broader meaning for this old fish.

Analyzing the Text

COMMON CORE

ELACC11-12RL1,
ELACC11-12RL4,
ELACC11-12RL5,
ELACC11-12RL6,
ELACC11-12L5a,
ELACC11-12W3d

Cite Text Evidence Support your responses with evidence from the selection.

1. **Connect** An offshoot of realism, **naturalism** was a literary movement in which writers worked to describe ordinary life accurately and realistically. Look at lines 45–55. How does the speaker personify the fish? Why does Bishop have the speaker revise her initial statement about the fish?

2. **Interpret** Why does the speaker call the fish hooks "medals" in line 61?

3. **Interpret** In lines 65–67, as the speaker stared at the fish, "victory filled up" the boat. Whose victory is it? Who or what is the enemy?

4. **Analyze** What clues suggest that the fish might have a symbolic meaning? What could the rainbow at the end of the poem symbolize?

5. **Connect** Why does the speaker let the fish go? How is the fish like the dog in "To Build a Fire?"

PERFORMANCE TASK

Writing Activity: Description Bishop describes the fish in intense detail, and this detail helps create a symbolic meaning for the fish. Write a paragraph or poem that uses vivid description to help represent a symbol.

1. Choose an object or animal that has a symbolic meaning for you.

2. Gather details about the object or animal to create a vivid, realistic description.

3. Choose specific details that help readers clarify what the object or animal means to you. The meaning should be implicit, not stated directly.

In your writing, use the conventions of standard English.

Write an Analytical Essay

COMMON CORE

ELACC11-12W2a–f Write informative/explanatory texts.
ELACC11-12W9a–b Draw evidence from literary or informational texts to support analysis.

This collection opens with the quotation "Reality is that which, when you stop believing in it, doesn't go away." Look back at the anchor text, "To Build a Fire," and at the other texts in this collection. What particular themes or central ideas does each writer want readers to recognize about reality, and why? What stylistic choices does each author make in order to reveal a specific version of reality? Synthesize your ideas by writing an analytical essay.

An effective analytical essay

- includes a clear controlling idea
- has an introduction that engages the reader with an interesting observation, quotation, or detail from one of the selections
- organizes central ideas in a logically structured body that clearly develops the controlling idea
- uses transitions to create a cohesion between sections of the text and to clarify relationships among ideas
- includes relevant textual evidence to illustrate central ideas
- has a concluding section that follows logically from the body

PLAN

Analyze the Texts Review "To Build a Fire" and the other texts in this collection. Consider these questions as you review:

- What elements of reality does each author want readers to acknowledge or face up to, and why?
- How does the style or structure of each work help bring some aspect of reality into sharp focus?
- How does each author communicate the sense of being in a specific place (e.g., the Yukon in "To Build a Fire" and a tenement in "Genesis of the Tenement")?

Use the annotation tools in your eBook to find evidence that supports your ideas about the writers' views on reality. Save each piece of evidence to your notebook.

Take Notes Choose three texts, including "To Build a Fire." Take notes on each writer's approach to his or her subject and what the writer is trying to show about some aspect of the real world by taking that approach. Look for an implicit version of reality revealed within each story or argument. Why does the writer want readers to understand this particular truth? List details, examples, and quotations that support your conclusions.

Get Organized Organize your details and evidence in an outline.

- Write a clear controlling idea about what truth each writer wants to reveal about the world as he or she sees it and the techniques each writer uses to do so.

- Search for an interesting quotation or detail to engage your reader in the introduction.

- Decide which organizational pattern you will use for your essay. Will you present your ideas text by text, or will you organize your analysis point by point, referring to the texts as you develop each point?

- Use your organizational pattern to sort the evidence you have gathered from the selections into a logical order.

- Write down some ideas for your conclusion.

> **ACADEMIC VOCABULARY**
>
> As you develop your ideas about the writers' views of the real world, be sure to use these words.
>
> *ambiguous*
> *clarify*
> *implicit*
> *revise*
> *somewhat*

PRODUCE

Draft Your Essay Write a draft of your essay, following your outline.

- Engage your readers with an interesting introduction to your topic and a clear controlling idea.

- Present your details, quotations, and examples from the selections in logically ordered paragraphs. Each paragraph should have a central idea related to your controlling idea with evidence to support it. Explain how each piece of evidence supports the central idea.

- Use transitions to link sections of the text and to clarify the relationships among your ideas.

- Write a satisfying conclusion that summarizes your analysis and synthesizes your central ideas.

As you draft your analytical essay, remember that this kind of writing requires formal language and a respectful tone to make it appropriate for an academic context.

> *my* **WriteSmart**
>
> Write your rough draft in *my*WriteSmart. Focus on getting your ideas down, rather than perfecting your choice of language.

my WriteSmart

Improve Your Draft Revise your draft to make sure it is clear, coherent, and engaging. Use the chart on the following page to review the characteristics of a well-written analytical essay. Ask yourself these questions as you revise:

Have your partner or a group of peers review your draft in *my*WriteSmart. Ask your reviewers to note any evidence that does not support the controlling idea.

- Does my controlling idea present a clear point of view about reality and truth as depicted in the texts? Will my readers want to continue reading?

- Are the titles and authors of the selections accurately identified in my introduction?

- Have I provided sufficient and relevant textual evidence to support my central ideas?

- Do I develop my ideas in a logical order? Are transitions smooth and coherent?

- Have I maintained a formal style of English appropriate for an analytical essay? Does my choice of words convey a knowledgeable and confident tone, or attitude, toward the topic?

- Have I used precise language and various types of sentence structures?

- Have I provided a satisfying summary of my ideas in the conclusion?

Exchange Essays When your final draft is completed, exchange essays with a partner. Read your partner's essay and provide feedback. Reread the criteria for an effective analytical essay and ask the following questions:

- Which aspects of your partner's essay are particularly strong?

- Were any sections of the essay ambiguous or unclear, such as losing focus on the central idea? How could they be clarified?

- Did the examples, quotations, or other evidence your partner provided support the central idea?

COLLECTION 5 TASK
ANALYTICAL ESSAY

	Ideas and Evidence	Organization	Language
ADVANCED	• An eloquent introduction includes the titles and authors of the selections; the controlling idea describes the view of reality revealed by the writers. • Specific, relevant details support the central ideas. • A satisfying concluding section synthesizes the ideas and summarizes the analysis.	• Central ideas and supporting evidence are organized effectively and logically throughout the essay. • Varied transitions successfully show the relationships between ideas.	• The analysis has an appropriately formal style and a knowledgeable, objective tone. • Language is precise and captures the writer's thoughts with originality. • Sentence beginnings, lengths, and structures vary and have a rhythmic flow. • Spelling, capitalization, and punctuation are correct. If handwritten, the essay is legible. • Grammar and usage are correct.
COMPETENT	• The introduction identifies the titles and authors of the selections but could be more engaging; the controlling idea encompasses the view of reality in at least one of the selections. • One or two central ideas need more support. • The concluding section synthesizes most of the ideas and summarizes most of the analysis.	• The organization of central ideas and supporting evidence is confusing in a few places. • A few more transitions are needed to clarify the relationships between ideas.	• The style becomes informal in a few places, and the tone does not always communicate confidence. • Most language is precise. • Sentence beginnings, lengths, and structures vary somewhat. • Several spelling, capitalization, and punctuation mistakes occur. If handwritten, the essay is mostly legible. • Some grammatical and usage errors are repeated in the essay.
LIMITED	• The introduction identifies the titles and the authors of the selections; the controlling idea only hints at the main idea of the analysis. • Details support some central ideas but are often too general. • The concluding section gives an incomplete summary of the analysis and merely restates the thesis.	• Most central ideas are organized logically, but many supporting details are out of place. • More transitions are needed throughout the essay to connect ideas.	• The style is informal in many places, and the tone reflects a superficial understanding of the selections. • Language is repetitive or vague at times. • Sentence structures barely vary, and some fragments or run-on sentences are present. • Spelling, capitalization, and punctuation are often incorrect but do not make reading the essay difficult. If handwritten, the essay may be partially illegible. • Grammar and usage are incorrect in many places, but the writer's ideas are still clear.
EMERGING	• The appropriate elements of an introduction are missing. • Details and evidence are irrelevant or missing. • The analysis lacks a concluding section.	• A logical organization is not used; ideas are presented randomly. • Transitions are not used, making the essay difficult to understand.	• The style and tone are inappropriate. • Language is inaccurate, repetitive, and vague. • Repetitive sentence structure, fragments, and run-on sentences make the writing monotonous and difficult to follow. • Spelling, capitalization, and punctuation are incorrect throughout. If handwritten, the essay may be partially or mostly illegible. • Many grammatical and usage errors obscure the meaning of the writer's ideas.

The Modern World

> "Everybody gets so much information all day long that they lose their common sense."
>
> —Gertrude Stein

The Modern World

In this collection, you will explore how Americans have responded to modern life in a globally connected world.

hmhfyi.com

COLLECTION
PERFORMANCE TASK Preview

At the end of this collection, you will have the opportunity to complete two tasks:

• Write an argument to answer the following question: How do these texts define the challenges an individual or group may face in modern society?

• Hold a panel discussion that explores the risks of information overload and strategies for managing information in a constructive fashion.

ACADEMIC VOCABULARY

Study the words and their definitions in the chart below. You will use these words as you discuss and write about the texts in this collection.

Word	Definition	Related Forms
contemporary (kən-tĕm′pə-rĕr′ē) *adj.*	coming from the same time period	contemporaries, contemporarily
global (glō′bəl) *adj.*	relating to the world as a whole	globe, globally, globalization
infinite (ĭn′fə-nĭt) *adj.*	without end or beyond measure	infinitive, infinitesimal, infinitely, infiniteness
simulated (sĭm′yə-lā′tĭd) *adj.*	imitating something real	simulate, simulation, similar
virtual (vûr′chōō-əl) *adj.*	existing in essence or in a digital version but not in actual fact	virtually

COMMON CORE

ELACC11-12RL10,
ELACC11-12RI3,
ELACC11-12RI7,
ELACC11-12RI10

Life in a Global Society

At the beginning of the 21st century, Americans live in a globally connected world. The experience of two world wars and advances in technology have eliminated our isolation from other countries. Solving complex economic, social, and environmental problems now often requires global cooperation. Contemporary literature reflects the anxiety of an era changing rapidly for both good and bad.

THE RISE OF MODERN LITERATURE Change was the only constant for Americans in the early 20th century. In 30 short years they faced a world war, an economic boom followed by the Great Depression, and shifting attitudes toward women's place in society. However, the shock of World War I (1914–1918) was perhaps the most influential force on American writers of the early 20th century.

Modernist writers, many of whom spent time living and writing in Europe, responded to the social and policical upheaval of the war by experimenting with innovative styles and forms, and by focusing on the alienation of the individual in modern society. Transitional poets such as T.S. Eliot linked rich poetic traditions with modern ideas and concerns. Eliot's *The Waste Land* stands out as one of the most representative and influential modernist poems. Other poets, such as Robert Frost, reinvented traditional genres, such as pastoral poetry. Modern writers like F. Scott Fitzgerald, Ernest Hemingway, and John Steinbeck broke with the traditions of the past, turning to new methods and stylistic devices.

AN ERA OF NEAR-CONSTANT WAR World War II (1939–1945) was a catastrophe of epic dimensions: the first war in history in which more civilians died than soldiers. America and the Soviet Union, allies during the war, emerged as rival superpowers and engaged in a decades-long "Cold War," competing in a deadly arms race that threatened the world with a nuclear apocalypse. As technological sophistication and political anxiety increased, science fiction writers—for example, Ray Bradbury and Kurt Vonnegut—explored possible future scenarios, sometimes in bleak post-apocalyptic or dystopian worlds.

In an effort to contain the spread of communism, the U.S. military became deeply involved in civil wars first in Korea and then in Vietnam. Although the Cold War ended with the break up of the Soviet Union in 1991, American warfare did not.

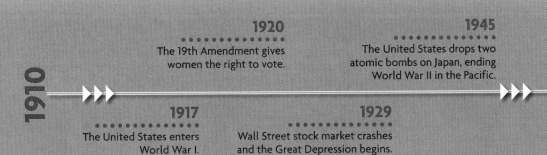

1920
The 19th Amendment gives women the right to vote.

1945
The United States drops two atomic bombs on Japan, ending World War II in the Pacific.

1910

1917
The United States enters World War I.

1929
Wall Street stock market crashes and the Great Depression begins.

In that same year, U.S. troops were sent to counter the Iraqi invasion of Kuwait. On September 11, 2001, attacks on the World Trade Center and the Pentagon led to U.S. invasions of Afghanistan and Iraq. Global violence and the spread of nuclear weapons to numerous countries have created a sense of instability that has profoundly affected writers and nonwriters alike.

THE CIVIL RIGHTS MOVEMENT The civil rights movement of the 1950s and 1960s is perhaps the most important social change in modern times. In 1954, the Supreme Court's *Brown v. Board of Education* ruling struck down school segregation as unconstitutional. Dr. Martin Luther King Jr. emerged as a leader during these times, advocating nonviolent civil disobedience. Congress eventually passed the 1964 Civil Rights Act outlawing segregation in public places and guaranteeing legal equality to African American citizens. In succeeding years, other groups drew on the ideals and tactics of the civil rights movement in their fights to end discrimination based on gender, ethnicity, and sexual orientation.

As the civil rights movement gained momentum, African American writers began to gain wider recognition. In a variety of genres, authors made powerful statements about the harmful effects of racism and the need for change. While earlier writers of color often focused on the experience of discrimination, contemporary writing is expressive of the individual, culture, or place, while still managing to speak to universal human concerns.

TECHNOLOGY AND THE ENVIRONMENT In 1910, automobiles, telephones, and electricity were not yet common conveniences for most people. Today, robotics has transformed manufacturing and medicine, and advances in communications technology—especially the Internet and mobile devices—give people around the world instant access to information. A big question of our time is how to make the best use of this technology in a way that enhances the quality of life for all.

The growth of technology has not come without costs, especially to the environment. Cars, trucks, and planes, as well as electric power plants, have largely relied on nonrenewable fossil fuels such as oil, coal, and natural gas. While the supply of these natural resources once seemed infinite, we now know that they will eventually be exhausted. In addition, pollution from these fuels has damaged the earth, air, and water on which all life depends and has contributed to global climate change. Writers of fiction and nonfiction seek to understand the implications of these challenges for life today and for the future of the human race.

1965
First U.S. combat forces
land in Vietnam.

2010

1954
In *Brown v. Board of Education*, the Supreme Court declares segregated schools unconstitutional.

1977
First practical home computer, Apple II, hits market.

2001
Hijackers fly commercial planes into World Trade Center and Pentagon, killing thousands.

F. Scott Fitzgerald (1896–1940) *coined the phrase "Jazz Age" to describe the 1920s, and in many ways he embodied the decade. Born in Minnesota, he attended Princeton University. After his first novel,* This Side of Paradise, *brought him financial success, he married the vivacious Zelda Sayre. They became the golden couple of the 1920s, known for their glamorous, high society lifestyle. Sadly, their lives were soon overshadowed by debt, mental illness, and alcoholism. Fitzgerald's masterpiece,* The Great Gatsby *(1925), was not a popular success in his lifetime, though it is now considered a classic examination of the hidden pitfalls of achieving the American Dream.*

Winter Dreams

Short Story by F. Scott Fitzgerald

AS YOU READ Pay attention to the character of Dexter, noticing how Judy influences Dexter throughout the story. Write down any questions you generate during reading.

I

Some of the caddies were poor as sin and lived in one-room houses with a neurasthenic[1] cow in the front yard, but Dexter Green's father owned the second best grocery-store in Black Bear—the best one was "The Hub," patronized by the wealthy people from Sherry Island—and Dexter caddied only for pocket-money.

In the fall when the days became crisp and gray, and the long Minnesota winter shut down like the white lid of a box, Dexter's skis moved over the snow that hid the fairways of the golf course. At these times the country gave him a feeling of profound melancholy—it offended him that the links should lie in enforced fallowness, haunted by ragged sparrows for the long season. It was dreary, too, that on the tees where the gay colors fluttered in summer there were now only the desolate sand-boxes knee-deep in crusted ice. When he crossed the

---

[1] **neurasthenic** (noŏr´əs-thĕn´ĭk): weak and lacking in vigor.

hills the wind blew cold as misery, and if the sun was out he tramped with his eyes squinted up against the hard dimensionless glare.

In April the winter ceased abruptly. The snow ran down into Black Bear Lake scarcely tarrying for the early golfers to brave the season with red and black balls. Without elation, without an interval of moist glory, the cold was gone.

20 　Dexter knew that there was something dismal about this Northern spring, just as he knew there was something gorgeous about the fall. Fall made him clinch his hands and tremble and repeat idiotic sentences to himself, and make brisk abrupt gestures of command to imaginary audiences and armies. October filled him with hope which November raised to a sort of ecstatic triumph, and in this mood the fleeting brilliant impressions of the summer at Sherry Island were ready grist to his mill.[2] He became a golf champion and defeated Mr. T. A. Hedrick in a marvelous match played a hundred times over the fairways of his imagination, a match each detail of which he changed

30 about untiringly—sometimes he won with almost laughable ease, sometimes he came up magnificently from behind. Again, stepping from a Pierce-Arrow automobile,[3] like Mr. Mortimer Jones, he strolled frigidly into the lounge of the Sherry Island Golf Club—or perhaps, surrounded by an admiring crowd, he gave an exhibition of fancy diving from the spring-board of the club raft. . . . Among those who watched him in open-mouthed wonder was Mr. Mortimer Jones.

And one day it came to pass that Mr. Jones—himself and not his ghost—came up to Dexter with tears in his eyes and said that Dexter was the — — best caddy in the club, and wouldn't he decide not to quit

40 if Mr. Jones made it worth his while, because every other — — caddy in the club lost one ball a hole for him—regularly—

"No, sir," said Dexter decisively, "I don't want to caddy any more." Then, after a pause: "I'm too old."

"You're not more than fourteen. Why the devil did you decide just this morning that you wanted to quit? You promised that next week you'd go over to the State tournament with me."

"I decided I was too old."

Dexter handed in his "A Class" badge, collected what money was due him from the caddy-master, and walked home to Black Bear

50 Village.

"The best — — caddy I ever saw," shouted Mr. Mortimer Jones over a drink that afternoon. "Never lost a ball! Willing! Intelligent! Quiet! Honest! Grateful!"

The little girl who had done this was eleven—beautifully ugly as little girls are apt to be who are destined after a few years to be inexpressibly lovely and bring no end of misery to a great number of men. The spark, however, was perceptible. There was a general

---

[2] **grist to his mill:** something that he could make good use of.
[3] **Pierce-Arrow automobile:** a luxury car of the day.

ungodliness in the way her lips twisted down at the corners when she
smiled, and in the—Heaven help us!—in the almost passionate quality
60   of her eyes. Vitality is born early in such women. It was utterly in
evidence now, shining through her thin frame in a sort of glow.

She had come eagerly out onto the course at nine o'clock with a
white linen nurse and five small new golf-clubs in a white canvas bag
which the nurse was carrying. When Dexter first saw her she was
standing by the caddy house, rather ill at ease and trying to conceal
the fact by engaging her nurse in an obviously unnatural conversation
graced by startling and irrelevant grimaces from herself.

"Well, it's certainly a nice day, Hilda," Dexter heard her say. She
drew down the corners of her mouth, smiled, and glanced furtively
70   around, her eyes in transit falling for an instant on Dexter.

Then to the nurse:

"Well, I guess there aren't very many people out here this
morning, are there?"

The smile again—radiant, **blatantly** artificial—convincing.

"I don't know what we're supposed to do now," said the nurse,
looking nowhere in particular.

"Oh, that's all right. I'll fix it up."

Dexter stood perfectly still, his mouth slightly ajar. He knew that
if he moved forward a step his stare would be in her line of vision—if
80   he moved backward he would lose his full view of her face. For a
moment he had not realized how young she was. Now he remembered
having seen her several times the year before—in bloomers.[4]

Suddenly, involuntarily, he laughed, a short abrupt laugh—then,
startled by himself, he turned and began to walk quickly away.

"Boy!"

Dexter stopped.

"Boy—"

Beyond question he was addressed. Not only that, but he was
treated to that absurd smile, that preposterous smile—the memory of
90   which at least a dozen men were to carry into middle age.

"Boy, do you know where the golf teacher is?"

"He's giving a lesson."

"Well, do you know where the caddy-master is?"

"He isn't here yet this morning."

"Oh." For a moment this baffled her. She stood alternately on her
right and left foot.

"We'd like to get a caddy," said the nurse. "Mrs. Mortimer Jones
sent us out to play golf, and we don't know how without we get a
caddy."

100   Here she was stopped by an ominous glance from Miss Jones,
followed immediately by the smile.

blatantly
(blāt´nt-lə) *adv.* in an
offensively obvious,
unashamed manner.

---

[4] **bloomers:** baggy pants that end just below the knee, formerly worn by girls.

"There aren't any caddies here except me," said Dexter to the nurse, "and I got to stay here in charge until the caddy-master gets here."

"Oh."

Miss Jones and her retinue now withdrew, and at a proper distance from Dexter became involved in a heated conversation, which was concluded by Miss Jones taking one of the clubs and hitting it on the ground with violence. For further emphasis she raised it again and was about to bring it down smartly upon the nurse's bosom, when the nurse seized the club and twisted it from her hands.

"You little mean old *thing!*" cried Miss Jones wildly.

Another argument ensued. Realizing that the elements of comedy were implied in the scene, Dexter several times began to laugh, but each time restrained the laugh before it reached audibility. He could not resist the monstrous conviction that the little girl was justified in beating the nurse.

The situation was resolved by the fortuitous appearance of the caddy-master, who was appealed to immediately by the nurse.

"Miss Jones is to have a little caddy, and this one says he can't go."

"Mr. McKenna said I was to wait here till you came," said Dexter quickly.

"Well, he's here now." Miss Jones smiled cheerfully at the caddy-master. Then she dropped her bag and set off at a haughty mince[5] toward the first tee.

"Well?" The caddy-master turned to Dexter. "What you standing there like a dummy for? Go pick up the young lady's clubs."

"I don't think I'll go out today," said Dexter.

"You don't—"

"I think I'll quit."

The enormity of his decision frightened him. He was a favorite caddy, and the thirty dollars a month he earned through the summer were not to be made elsewhere around the lake. But he had received a strong emotional shock, and his perturbation required a violent and immediate outlet.

It is not so simple as that, either. As so frequently would be the case in the future, Dexter was unconsciously dictated to by his winter dreams.

II

Now, of course, the quality and the seasonability of these winter dreams varied, but the stuff of them remained. They persuaded Dexter several years later to pass up a business course at the State university—his father, prospering now, would have paid his way—for

---

5 **at a haughty mince:** taking short, dainty steps in an arrogant, snobbish way.

the **precarious** advantage of attending an older and more famous university in the East, where he was bothered by his scanty funds. But do not get the impression, because his winter dreams happened to be concerned at first with musings on the rich, that there was anything merely snobbish in the boy. He wanted not association with glittering things and glittering people—he wanted the glittering things themselves. Often he reached out for the best without knowing why he
150 wanted it—and sometimes he ran up against the mysterious denials and prohibitions in which life indulges. It is with one of those denials and not with his career as a whole that this story deals.

He made money. It was rather amazing. After college he went to the city from which Black Bear Lake draws its wealthy patrons. When he was only twenty-three and had been there not quite two years, there were already people who liked to say: "Now *there's* a boy—" All about him rich men's sons were peddling bonds precariously, or investing patrimonies precariously, or plodding through the two dozen volumes of the "George Washington Commercial Course," but Dexter
160 borrowed a thousand dollars on his college degree and his confident mouth, and bought a partnership in a laundry.

It was a small laundry when he went into it but Dexter made a specialty of learning how the English washed fine woolen golf-stockings without shrinking them, and within a year he was catering to the trade that wore knickerbockers.[6] Men were insisting that their Shetland hose and sweaters go to his laundry just as they had insisted on a caddy who could find golf-balls. A little later he was doing their

precarious
(prĭ-kâr´ē-əs) *adj.*
unstable; uncertain.

---

[6] **knickerbockers:** loose pants that end in a gathering just below the knee and are worn with long socks. Formerly popular as golf wear.

wives' lingerie as well—and running five branches in different parts of the city. Before he was twenty-seven he owned the largest string of
170 laundries in his section of the country. It was then that he sold out and went to New York. But the part of his story that concerns us goes back to the days when he was making his first big success.

When he was twenty-three Mr. Hart—one of the gray-haired men who liked to say "Now there's a boy"—gave him a guest card to the Sherry Island Golf Club for a weekend. So he signed his name one day on the register, and that afternoon played golf in a foursome with Mr. Hart and Mr. Sandwood and Mr. T. A. Hedrick. He did not consider it necessary to remark that he had once carried Mr. Hart's bag over this same links, and that he knew every trap and gully with his eyes shut—
180 but he found himself glancing at the four caddies who trailed them, trying to catch a gleam or gesture that would remind him of himself, that would lessen the gap which lay between his present and his past.

It was a curious day, slashed abruptly with fleeting, familiar impressions. One minute he had the sense of being a trespasser—in the next he was impressed by the tremendous superiority he felt toward Mr. T. A. Hedrick, who was a bore and not even a good golfer any more.

Then, because of a ball Mr. Hart lost near the fifteenth green, an enormous thing happened. While they were searching the stiff grasses
190 of the rough there was a clear call of "Fore!" from behind a hill in their rear. And as they all turned abruptly from their search a bright new ball sliced abruptly over the hill and caught Mr. T. A. Hedrick in the abdomen.

"By Gad!" cried Mr. T. A. Hedrick, "they ought to put some of these crazy women off the course. It's getting to be outrageous."

A head and a voice came up together over the hill:

"Do you mind if we go through?"

"You hit me in the stomach!" declared Mr. Hedrick wildly.

"Did I?" The girl approached the group of men. "I'm sorry. I yelled
200 'Fore!'"

Her glance fell casually on each of the men—then scanned the fairway for her ball.

"Did I bounce into the rough?"

It was impossible to determine whether this question was ingenuous or malicious. In a moment, however, she left no doubt, for as her partner came up over the hill she called cheerfully:

"Here I am! I'd have gone on the green except that I hit something."

As she took her stance for a short mashie[7] shot, Dexter looked
210 at her closely. She wore a blue gingham dress, rimmed at throat and shoulders with a white edging that accentuated her tan. The quality of exaggeration, of thinness, which had made her passionate eyes

---

[7] **mashie:** an old name for the golf club now known as a five iron.

"Did I?" The girl approached the group of men. "I'm sorry. I yelled 'Fore!'"

and down-turning mouth absurd at eleven, was gone now. She was arrestingly beautiful. The color in her cheeks was centered like the color in a picture—it was not a "high" color, but a sort of fluctuating and feverish warmth, so shaded that it seemed at any moment it would recede and disappear. This color and the mobility of her mouth gave a continual impression of **flux**, of intense life, of passionate vitality—balanced only partially by the sad luxury of her eyes.

flux
(flŭks) *n.* continual shift or change.

220 She swung her mashie impatiently and without interest, pitching the ball into a sand-pit on the other side of the green. With a quick, insincere smile and a careless "Thank you!" she went on after it.

"That Judy Jones!" remarked Mr. Hedrick on the next tee, as they waited—some moments—for her to play on ahead. "All she needs is to be turned up and spanked for six months and then to be married off to an old-fashioned cavalry captain."

"My God, she's good-looking!" said Mr. Sandwood, who was just over thirty.

"Good-looking!" cried Mr. Hedrick contemptuously, "she always
230 looks as if she wanted to be kissed! Turning those big cow-eyes on every calf in town!"

It was doubtful if Mr. Hedrick intended a reference to the maternal instinct.

"She'd play pretty good golf if she'd try," said Mr. Sandwood.

"She has no form," said Mr. Hedrick solemnly.

"She has a nice figure," said Mr. Sandwood.

"Better thank the Lord she doesn't drive a swifter ball," said Mr. Hart, winking at Dexter.

Later in the afternoon the sun went down with a riotous swirl of
240 gold and varying blues and scarlets, and left the dry, rustling night of Western summer. Dexter watched from the veranda of the Golf Club, watched the even overlap of the waters in the little wind, silver molasses under the harvest-moon. Then the moon held a finger to her

lips and the lake became a clear pool, pale and quiet. Dexter put on his bathing-suit and swam out to the farthest raft, where he stretched dripping on the wet canvas of the springboard.

There was a fish jumping and a star shining and the lights around the lake were gleaming. Over on a dark peninsula a piano was playing the songs of last summer and of summers before that—songs from "Chin-Chin" and "The Count of Luxemburg" and "The Chocolate Soldier"[8]—and because the sound of a piano over a stretch of water had always seemed beautiful to Dexter he lay perfectly quiet and listened.

The tune the piano was playing at that moment had been gay and new five years before when Dexter was a sophomore at college. They had played it at a prom once when he could not afford the luxury of proms, and he had stood outside the gymnasium and listened. The sound of the tune **precipitated** in him a sort of ecstasy and it was with that ecstasy he viewed what happened to him now. It was a mood of intense appreciation, a sense that, for once, he was magnificently attuned to life and that everything about him was radiating a brightness and a glamour he might never know again.

A low, pale oblong detached itself suddenly from the darkness of the Island, spitting forth the reverberated sound of a racing motor-boat. Two white streamers of cleft water rolled themselves out behind it and almost immediately the boat was beside him, drowning out the hot tinkle of the piano in the drone of its spray. Dexter raising himself on his arms was aware of a figure standing at the wheel, of two dark eyes regarding him over the lengthening space of water—then the boat had gone by and was sweeping in an immense and purposeless circle of spray round and round in the middle of the lake. With equal eccentricity one of the circles flattened out and headed back toward the raft.

"Who's that?" she called, shutting off her motor. She was so near now that Dexter could see her bathing-suit, which consisted apparently of pink rompers.[9]

The nose of the boat bumped the raft, and as the latter tilted rakishly he was precipitated toward her. With different degrees of interest they recognized each other.

"Aren't you one of those men we played through this afternoon?" she demanded.

He was.

"Well, do you know how to drive a motor-boat? Because if you do I wish you'd drive this one so I can ride on the surf-board behind. My name is Judy Jones"—she favored him with an absurd smirk—rather, what tried to be a smirk, for, twist her mouth as she might, it was not

precipitate
(prĭ-sĭp´ĭ-tāt´) *v.*
to cause to occur
suddenly.

---

[8] **"Chin-Chin" . . . "The Chocolate Soldier":** three popular Broadway musicals, first performed in 1914, 1912, and 1909, respectively.

[9] **rompers:** a loose-fitting one-piece garment with bloomer like pants.

grotesque, it was merely beautiful—"and I live in a house over there on the Island, and in that house there is a man waiting for me. When he drove up at the door I drove out of the dock because he says I'm his ideal."

There was a fish jumping and a star shining and the lights around the lake were gleaming. Dexter sat beside Judy Jones and she explained how her boat was driven. Then she was in the water, swimming to the floating surf-board with a sinuous crawl. Watching her was without effort to the eye, watching a branch waving or a sea-gull flying. Her arms, burned to butternut, moved sinuously among the dull platinum ripples, elbow appearing first, casting the forearm back with a cadence of falling water, then reaching out and down, stabbing a path ahead.

They moved out into the lake; turning, Dexter saw that she was kneeling on the low rear of the now uptilted surf-board.

"Go faster," she called, "fast as it'll go."

Obediently he jammed the level forward and the white spray mounted at the bow. When he looked around again the girl was standing up on the rushing board, her arms spread wide, her eyes lifted toward the moon.

"It's awful cold," she shouted. "What's your name?"

He told her.

"Well, why don't you come to dinner tomorrow night?"

His heart turned over like the fly-wheel of the boat, and, for the second time, her casual whim gave a new direction to his life.

III

Next evening while he waited for her to come downstairs, Dexter peopled the soft deep summer room and the sun-porch that opened from it with the men who had already loved Judy Jones. He knew the sort of men they were—the men who when he first went to college had entered from the great prep schools with graceful clothes and the deep tan of healthy summers. He had seen that, in one sense, he was better than these men. He was newer and stronger. Yet in acknowledging to himself that he wished his children to be like them he was admitting that he was but the rough, strong stuff from which they eternally sprang.

When the time had come for him to wear good clothes, he had known who were the best tailors in America, and the best tailors in America had made him the suit he wore this evening. He had acquired that particular reserve peculiar to his university, that set it off from other universities. He recognized the value to him of such a mannerism and he had adopted it; he knew that to be careless in dress and manner required more confidence than to be careful. But carelessness was for his children. His mother's name had been Krimslich. She was a Bohemian of the peasant class and she had talked

330 broken English to the end of her days. Her son must keep to the set patterns.

At a little after seven Judy Jones came downstairs. She wore a blue silk afternoon dress, and he was disappointed at first that she had not put on something more elaborate. This feeling was accentuated when, after a brief greeting, she went to the door of a butler's pantry and pushing it open called: "You can serve dinner, Martha." He had rather expected that a butler would announce dinner, that there would be a cocktail. Then he put these thoughts behind him as they sat down side by side on a lounge and looked at each other.

340 "Father and mother won't be here," she said thoughtfully.

"I'm nobody," he announced. "My career is largely a matter of futures."

He remembered the last time he had seen her father, and he was glad the parents were not to be here tonight—they might wonder who he was. He had been born in Keeble, a Minnesota village fifty miles farther north, and he always gave Keeble as his home instead of Black Bear Village. Country towns were well enough to come from if they weren't inconveniently in sight and used as footstools by fashionable lakes.

They talked of his university, which she had visited frequently during the past two years, and of the near-by city which supplied

350 Sherry Island with its patrons, and whither Dexter would return next day to his prospering laundries.

During dinner she slipped into a moody depression which gave Dexter a feeling of uneasiness. Whatever **petulance** she uttered in her throaty voice worried him. Whatever she smiled at—at him, at a chicken liver, at nothing—it disturbed him that her smile could have no root in mirth, or even in amusement. When the scarlet corners of her lips curved down, it was less a smile than an invitation to a kiss.

Then, after dinner, she led him out on the dark sun-porch and deliberately changed the atmosphere.

360 "Do you mind if I weep a little?" she said.

petulance
(pĕch´ə-ləns) *n.*
childish annoyance;
sulkiness.

"I'm afraid I'm boring you," he responded quickly.

"You're not. I like you. But I've just had a terrible afternoon. There was a man I cared about, and this afternoon he told me out of a clear sky that he was poor as a church-mouse. He'd never even hinted it before. Does this sound horribly **mundane**?"

mundane
(mŭn-dān´) *adj.*
ordinary;
commonplace.

"Perhaps he was afraid to tell you."

"Suppose he was," she answered. "He didn't start right. You see, if I'd thought of him as poor—well, I've been mad about loads of poor men, and fully intended to marry them all. But in this case, I hadn't thought of him that way, and my interest in him wasn't strong enough to survive the shock. As if a girl calmly informed her fiancé that she was a widow. He might not object to widows, but—

"Let's start right," she interrupted herself suddenly. "Who are you, anyhow?"

For a moment Dexter hesitated. Then:

"I'm nobody," he announced. "My career is largely a matter of futures."

"Are you poor?"

"No," he said frankly, "I'm probably making more money than any man my age in the Northwest. I know that's an obnoxious remark, but you advised me to start right."

There was a pause. Then she smiled and the corners of her mouth drooped and an almost imperceptible sway brought her closer to him, looking up into his eyes. A lump rose in Dexter's throat, and he waited breathless for the experiment, facing the unpredictable compound that would form mysteriously from the elements of their lips. Then he saw—she communicated her excitement to him, lavishly, deeply, with kisses that were not a promise but a fulfillment. They aroused in him not hunger demanding renewal but surfeit that would demand more surfeit . . . kisses that were like charity, creating want by holding back nothing at all.

It did not take him many hours to decide that he had wanted Judy Jones ever since he was a proud, desirous little boy.

IV

It began like that—and continued, with varying shades of intensity, on such a note right up to the dénouement. Dexter surrendered a part of himself to the most direct and unprincipled personality with which he had ever come in contact. Whatever Judy wanted, she went after with the full pressure of her charm. There was no divergence of method, no jockeying for position or premeditation of effects—there was a very little mental side to any of her affairs. She simply made men conscious to the highest degree of her physical loveliness. Dexter had no desire to change her. Her deficiencies were knit up with a passionate energy that transcended and justified them.

When, as Judy's head lay against his shoulder that first night, she whispered, "I don't know what's the matter with me. Last night I thought I was in love with a man and tonight I think I'm in love with you—"—it seemed to him a beautiful and romantic thing to say. It was the exquisite excitability that for the moment he controlled and owned. But a week later he was compelled to view this same quality in a different light. She took him in her roadster[10] to a picnic supper, and after supper she disappeared, likewise in her roadster, with another man. Dexter became enormously upset and was scarcely able to be decently civil to the other people present. When she assured him that she had not kissed the other man, he knew she was lying—yet he was glad that she had taken the trouble to lie to him.

He was, as he found before the summer ended, one of a varying dozen who circulated about her. Each of them had at one time been favored above all others—about half of them still basked in the solace of occasional sentimental revivals. Whenever one showed signs of dropping out through long neglect, she granted him a brief honeyed hour, which encouraged him to tag along for a year or so longer. Judy made these forays upon the helpless and defeated without malice, indeed half unconscious that there was anything mischievous in what she did.

When a new man came to town every one dropped out—dates were automatically canceled.

The helpless part of trying to do anything about it was that she did it all herself. She was not a girl who could be "won" in the kinetic sense—she was proof against cleverness, she was proof against charm; if any of these assailed her too strongly she would immediately resolve the affair to a physical basis, and under the magic of her physical splendor the strong as well as the brilliant played her game and not their own. She was entertained only by the gratification of her desires and by the direct exercise of her own charm. Perhaps from so much youthful love, so many youthful lovers, she had come, in self-defense, to nourish herself wholly from within.

Succeeding Dexter's first exhilaration came restlessness and dissatisfaction. The helpless ecstasy of losing himself in her was opiate rather than tonic.[11] It was fortunate for his work during the winter that those moments of ecstasy came infrequently. Early in their acquaintance it had seemed for a while that there was a deep and spontaneous mutual attraction—that first August, for example— three days of long evenings on her dusky veranda, of strange wan kisses through the late afternoon, in shadowy alcoves or behind the protecting trellises of the garden arbors, of mornings when she was fresh as a dream and almost shy at meeting him in the clarity of the rising day. There was all the ecstasy of an engagement about it,

---

[10] **roadster:** a sporty, two-seat, open automobile.
[11] **opiate . . . tonic:** deadening rather than stimulating.

sharpened by his realization that there was no engagement. It was during those three days that, for the first time, he had asked her to marry him. She said "maybe some day," she said "kiss me," she said "I'd like to marry you," she said "I love you"—she said—nothing.

The three days were interrupted by the arrival of a New York man who visited at her house for half September. To Dexter's agony, rumor engaged them. The man was the son of the president of a great trust company. But at the end of a month it was reported that Judy was yawning. At a dance one night she sat all evening in a motor-boat with a local beau, while the New Yorker searched the club for her frantically. She told the local beau that she was bored with her visitor, and two days later he left. She was seen with him at the station, and it was reported that he looked very mournful indeed.

On this note the summer ended. Dexter was twenty-four, and he found himself increasingly in a position to do as he wished. He joined two clubs in the city and lived at one of them. Though he was by no means an integral part of the stag-lines at these clubs, he managed to be on hand at dances where Judy Jones was likely to appear. He could have gone out socially as much as he liked—he was an eligible young man, now, and popular with downtown fathers. His confessed devotion to Judy Jones had rather solidified his position. But he had no social aspirations and rather despised the dancing men who were always on tap for the Thursday or Saturday parties and who filled in at dinners with the younger married set. Already he was playing with the idea of going East to New York. He wanted to take Judy Jones with him. No disillusion as to the world in which she had grown up could cure his illusion as to her desirability.

Remember that—for only in the light of it can what he did for her be understood.

Eighteen months after he first met Judy Jones he became engaged to another girl. Her name was Irene Scheerer, and her father was one of the men who had always believed in Dexter. Irene was light-haired and sweet and honorable, and a little stout, and she had two suitors whom she pleasantly relinquished when Dexter formally asked her to marry him.

Summer, fall, winter, spring, another summer, another fall—so much he had given of his active life to the incorrigible lips of Judy Jones. She had treated him with interest, with encouragement, with malice, with indifference, with contempt. She had inflicted on him the innumerable little slights and indignities possible in such a case—as if in revenge for having ever cared for him at all. She had beckoned him and yawned at him and beckoned him again and he had responded often with bitterness and narrowed eyes. She had brought him ecstatic happiness and intolerable agony of spirit. She had caused him untold inconvenience and not a little trouble. She had insulted him, and she had ridden over him, and she had played his interest in her against his interest in his work—for fun. She had done everything to him except to criticize him—this she had not done—it seemed to him only because it might have sullied the utter indifference she manifested and sincerely felt toward him.

When autumn had come and gone again it occurred to him that he could not have Judy Jones. He had to beat this into his mind but he convinced himself at last. He lay awake at night for a while and argued it over. He told himself the trouble and the pain she had caused him, he enumerated her glaring deficiencies as a wife. Then he said to himself that he loved her, and after a while he fell asleep. For a week, lest he imagine her husky voice over the telephone or her eyes opposite him at lunch, he worked hard and late, and at night he went to his office and plotted out his years.

At the end of a week he went to a dance and cut in on her once. For almost the first time since they had met he did not ask her to sit out with him or tell her that she was lovely. It hurt him that she did not miss these things—that was all. He was not jealous when he saw that there was a new man tonight. He had been hardened against jealousy long before.

He stayed late at the dance. He sat for an hour with Irene Scheerer and talked about books and about music. He knew very little about either. But he was beginning to be master of his own time now, and he had a rather priggish notion that he—the young and already fabulously successful Dexter Green—should know more about such things.

That was in October, when he was twenty-five. In January, Dexter and Irene became engaged. It was to be announced in June, and they were to be married three months later.

The Minnesota winter prolonged itself interminably, and it was almost May when the winds came soft and the snow ran down into Black Bear Lake at last. For the first time in over a year Dexter was enjoying a certain tranquillity of spirit. Judy Jones had been in Florida, and afterward in Hot Springs,[12] and somewhere she had been engaged, and somewhere she had broken it off. At first, when Dexter had definitely given her up, it had made him sad that people still linked them together and asked for news of her, but when he began to be placed at dinner next to Irene Scheerer people didn't ask him about her any more—they told him about her. He ceased to be an authority on her.

May at last. Dexter walked the streets at night when the darkness was damp as rain, wondering that so soon, with so little done, so much of ecstasy had gone from him. May one year back had been marked by Judy's poignant, unforgivable, yet forgiven **turbulence**—it had been one of those rare times when he fancied she had grown to care for him. That old penny's worth of happiness he had spent for this bushel of content. He knew that Irene would be no more than a curtain spread behind him, a hand moving among gleaming tea-cups, a voice calling to children . . . fire and loveliness were gone, the magic of nights and the wonder of the varying hours and seasons . . . slender lips, downturning, dropping to his lips and bearing him up into a heaven of eyes. . . . The thing was deep in him. He was too strong and alive for it to die lightly.

In the middle of May when the weather balanced for a few days on the thin bridge that led to deep summer he turned in one night at Irene's house. Their engagement was to be announced in a week now— no one would be surprised at it. And tonight they would sit together on the lounge at the University Club and look on for an hour at the dancers. It gave him a sense of solidity to go with her—she was so sturdily popular, so intensely "great."

He mounted the steps of the brownstone house and stepped inside. "Irene," he called.

Mrs. Scheerer came out of the living-room to meet him.

"Dexter," she said, "Irene's gone upstairs with a splitting headache. She wanted to go with you but I made her go to bed."

"Nothing serious, I—"

"Oh, no. She's going to play golf with you in the morning. You can spare her for just one night, can't you, Dexter?"

Her smile was kind. She and Dexter liked each other. In the living-room he talked for a moment before he said good night.

Returning to the University Club, where he had rooms, he stood in the doorway for a moment and watched the dancers. He leaned against the door-post, nodded at a man or two—yawned.

"Hello, darling."

turbulence
(tûr´byə-ləns) n.
an unsettled or
changeable state.

---

[12]**Hot Springs:** a spa city in west-central Arkansas.

The familiar voice at his elbow startled him. Judy Jones had left a man and crossed the room to him—Judy Jones, a slender enameled doll in cloth of gold: gold in a band at her head, gold in two slipper points at her dress's hem. The fragile glow of her face seemed to blossom as she smiled at him. A breeze of warmth and light blew through the room. His hands in the pockets of his dinnerjacket tightened spasmodically. He was filled with a sudden excitement.

570

"When did you get back?" he asked casually.

"Come here and I'll tell you about it."

She turned and he followed her. She had been away—he could have wept at the wonder of her return. She had passed through enchanted streets, doing things that were like provocative music. All mysterious happenings, all fresh and quickening hopes, had gone away with her, come back with her now.

580

She turned in the doorway.

"Have you a car here? If you haven't, I have."

"I have a coupé."

In then, with a rustle of golden cloth. He slammed the door. Into so many cars she had stepped—like this—like that—her back against the leather, so—her elbow resting on the door—waiting. She would have been soiled long since had there been anything to soil her—except herself—but this was her own self-outpouring.

With an effort he forced himself to start the car and back into the street. This was nothing, he must remember. She had done this before, and he had put her behind him, as he would have crossed a bad account from his books.

590

He drove slowly downtown and, affecting abstraction,[13] traversed the deserted streets of the business section, peopled here and there where a movie was giving out its crowd or where consumptive or pugilistic[14] youth lounged in front of pool halls. The clink of glasses and the slap of hands on the bars issued from saloons, cloisters[15] of glazed glass and dirty yellow light.

She was watching him closely and the silence was embarrassing, yet in this crisis he could find no casual word with which to profane the hour. At a convenient turning he began to zigzag back toward the University Club.

600

"Have you missed me?" she asked suddenly.

"Everybody missed you."

He wondered if she knew of Irene Scheerer. She had been back only a day—her absence had been almost contemporaneous with his engagement.

"What a remark!" Judy laughed sadly—without sadness. She looked at him searchingly. He became absorbed in the dashboard.

---

[13] **affecting abstraction:** pretending to be lost in thought.

[14] **consumptive or pugilistic** (pyōō´jə-lĭs´-tĭc): sickly or aggressive.

[15] **cloisters:** here, places to escape from life's problems.

610   "You're handsomer than you used to be," she said thoughtfully. "Dexter, you have the most rememberable eyes."

He could have laughed at this, but he did not laugh. It was the sort of thing that was said to sophomores. Yet it stabbed at him.

"I'm awfully tired of everything, darling." She called every one darling, endowing the endearment with careless, individual camaraderie. "I wish you'd marry me."

The directness of this confused him. He should have told her now that he was going to marry another girl, but he could not tell her. He could as easily have sworn that he had never loved her.

620   "I think we'd get along," she continued, on the same note, "unless probably you've forgotten me and fallen in love with another girl."

Her confidence was obviously enormous. She had said, in effect, that she found such a thing impossible to believe, that if it were true he had merely committed a childish indiscretion—and probably to show off. She would forgive him, because it was not a matter of any moment but rather something to be brushed aside lightly.

"Of course you could never love anybody but me," she continued, "I like the way you love me. Oh, Dexter, have you forgotten last year?"

"No, I haven't forgotten."

630   "Neither have I!"

Was she sincerely moved—or was she carried along by the wave of her own acting?

"I wish we could be like that again," she said, and he forced himself to answer:

"I don't think we can."

"I suppose not. . . . I hear you're giving Irene Scheerer a violent rush."

There was not the faintest emphasis on the name, yet Dexter was suddenly ashamed.

640   "Oh, take me home," cried Judy suddenly; "I don't want to go back to that idiotic dance—with those children."

Then, as he turned up the street that led to the residence district, Judy began to cry quietly to herself. He had never seen her cry before.

The dark street lightened, the dwellings of the rich loomed up around them, he stopped his coupé in front of the great white bulk of the Mortimer Joneses' house, somnolent, gorgeous, drenched with the splendor of the damp moonlight. Its solidity startled him. The strong walls, the steel of the girders, the breadth and beam and pomp of it were there only to bring out the contrast with the young beauty beside

650   him. It was sturdy to accentuate her slightness—as if to show what a breeze could be generated by a butterfly's wing.

He sat perfectly quiet, his nerves in wild clamor, afraid that if he moved he would find her irresistibly in his arms. Two tears had rolled down her wet face and trembled on her upper lip.

"I'm more beautiful than anybody else," she said brokenly, "why can't I be happy?" Her moist eyes tore at his stability—her mouth turned slowly downward with an exquisite sadness: "I'd like to marry you if you'll have me, Dexter. I suppose you think I'm not worth having, but I'll be so beautiful for you, Dexter."

660   A million phrases of anger, pride, passion, hatred, tenderness fought on his lips. Then a perfect wave of emotion washed over him, carrying off with it a sediment of wisdom, of convention, of doubt, of honor. This was his girl who was speaking, his own, his beautiful, his pride.

"Won't you come in?" He heard her draw in her breath sharply. Waiting.

"All right," his voice was trembling, "I'll come in."

V

It was strange that neither when it was over nor a long time afterward did he regret that night. Looking at it from the perspective of ten

670   years, the fact that Judy's flare for him endured just one month seemed of little importance. Nor did it matter that by his yielding he subjected himself to a deeper agony in the end and gave serious hurt to Irene Scheerer and to Irene's parents, who had befriended him. There was nothing sufficiently pictorial about Irene's grief to stamp itself on his mind.

Dexter was at bottom hard-minded. The attitude of the city on his action was of no importance to him, not because he was going to leave the city, but because any outside attitude on the situation seemed superficial. He was completely indifferent to popular opinion. Nor, when he had seen that it was no use, that he did not possess in himself the power to move fundamentally or to hold Judy Jones, did he bear any malice toward her. He loved her, and he would love her until the day he was too old for loving—but he could not have her. So he tasted the deep pain that is reserved only for the strong, just as he had tasted for a little while the deep happiness.

Even the ultimate falsity of the grounds upon which Judy terminated the engagement—that she did not want to "take him away" from Irene—Judy, who had wanted nothing else—did not revolt him. He was beyond any revulsion or any amusement.

He went East in February with the intention of selling out his laundries and settling in New York—but the war came to America in March and changed his plans. He returned to the West, handed over the management of the business to his partner, and went into the first officers' training-camp in late April. He was one of those young thousands who greeted the war with a certain amount of relief, welcoming the liberation from webs of tangled emotion.

VI

This story is not his biography, remember, although things creep into it which have nothing to do with those dreams he had when he was young. We are almost done with them and with him now. There is only one more incident to be related here, and it happens seven years farther on.

It took place in New York, where he had done well—so well that there were no barriers too high for him. He was thirty-two years old, and, except for one flying trip immediately after the war, he had not been West in seven years. A man named Devlin from Detroit came into his office to see him in a business way, and then and there this incident occurred, and closed out, so to speak, this particular side of his life.

"So you're from the Middle West," said the man Devlin with careless curiosity. "That's funny—I thought men like you were probably born and raised on Wall Street. You know—wife of one of my best friends in Detroit came from your city. I was an usher at the wedding."

Dexter waited with no apprehension of what was coming.

"Judy Simms," said Devlin with no particular interest; "Judy Jones she was once."

"Yes, I knew her." A dull impatience spread over him. He had heard, of course, that she was married—perhaps deliberately he had heard no more.

720   "Awfully nice girl," brooded Devlin meaninglessly, "I'm sort of sorry for her."

"Why?" Something in Dexter was alert, receptive, at once.

"Oh, Lud Simms has gone to pieces in a way. I don't mean he ill-uses her, but he drinks and runs around—"

"Doesn't she run around?"

"No. Stays at home with her kids."

"Oh."

"She's a little too old for him," said Devlin.

"Too old!" cried Dexter. "Why, man, she's only twenty-seven."

730   He was possessed with a wild notion of rushing out into the streets and taking a train to Detroit. He rose to his feet spasmodically.

"I guess you're busy," Devlin apologized quickly. "I didn't realize—"

"No, I'm not busy," said Dexter, steadying his voice. "I'm not busy at all. Not busy at all. Did you say she was—twenty-seven? No, I said she was twenty-seven."

"Yes, you did," agreed Devlin dryly.

"Go on, then. Go on."

"What do you mean?"

740   "About Judy Jones."

Devlin looked at him helplessly.

"Well, that's—I told you all there is to it. He treats her like the devil. Oh, they're not going to get divorced or anything. When he's particularly outrageous she forgives him. In fact, I'm inclined to think she loves him. She was a pretty girl when she first came to Detroit."

A pretty girl! The phrase struck Dexter as ludicrous.

"Isn't she—a pretty girl, any more?"

"Oh, she's all right."

"Look here," said Dexter, sitting down suddenly. "I don't

750 understand. You say she was a 'pretty girl' and now you say she's 'all right.' I don't understand what you mean—Judy Jones wasn't a pretty girl, at all. She was a great beauty. Why, I knew her, I knew her. She was—"

Devlin laughed pleasantly.

"I'm not trying to start a row,"[16] he said. "I think Judy's a nice girl and I like her. I can't understand how a man like Lud Simms could fall madly in love with her, but he did." Then he added: "Most of the women like her."

Dexter looked closely at Devlin, thinking wildly that there must be

760 a reason for this, some insensitivity in the man or some private malice.

---

[16] **row** (rou): a noisy argument or dispute.

"Lots of women fade just like *that*," Devlin snapped his fingers. "You must have seen it happen. Perhaps I've forgotten how pretty she was at her wedding. I've seen her so much since then, you see. She has nice eyes."

A sort of dullness settled down upon Dexter. For the first time in his life he felt like getting very drunk. He knew that he was laughing loudly at something Devlin had said, but he did not know what it was or why it was funny. When, in a few minutes, Devlin went he lay down on his lounge and looked out the window at the New York sky-line
770 into which the sun was sinking in dull lovely shades of pink and gold.

He had thought that having nothing else to lose he was invulnerable at last—but he knew that he had just lost something more, as surely as if he had married Judy Jones and seen her fade away before his eyes.

The dream was gone. Something had been taken from him. In a sort of panic he pushed the palms of his hands into his eyes and tried to bring up a picture of the waters lapping on Sherry Island and the moonlit veranda, and gingham on the golf-links and the dry sun and the gold color of her neck's soft down. And her mouth damp to his
780 kisses and her eyes **plaintive** with melancholy and her freshness like new fine linen in the morning. Why, these things were no longer in the world! They had existed and they existed no longer.

For the first time in years the tears were streaming down his face. But they were for himself now. He did not care about mouth and eyes and moving hands. He wanted to care, and he could not care. For he had gone away and he could never go back any more. The gates were closed, the sun was gone down, and there was no beauty but the gray beauty of steel that withstands all time. Even the grief he could have borne was left behind in the country of illusion, of youth, of the
790 richness of life, where his winter dreams had flourished.

"Long ago," he said, "long ago, there was something in me, but now that thing is gone. Now that thing is gone, that thing is gone. I cannot cry. I cannot care. That thing will come back no more."

plaintive
(plān′tĭv) *adj.*
expressing sadness or sorrow.

COLLABORATIVE DISCUSSION What did you notice about Judy's effect on Dexter? With a partner, discuss the relationship between Dexter and Judy and how it evolves as the story develops. Cite specific evidence from the text to support your ideas.

Analyze Story Elements: Motivation

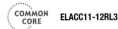 COMMON CORE   ELACC11-12RL3

No story analysis is complete without a study of motivation—the desires and emotions that drive characters to act or think in a certain way. By providing motivation for their characters, writers make them more complex and believable to readers. In "Winter Dreams," Fitzgerald reveals character traits and motivations through narration and dialogue.

Character Traits	Character Motivation
Writers reveal their characters' traits or qualities in both direct and indirect ways. To analyze a character, pay attention to • what the narrator tells you about the character • what the character says • what the character does • how the character interacts with other characters Some characters are more fully developed than others. A story's main character is likely to be a round character, one who displays complex qualities and is very realistic. Minor characters may be flat, displaying only one or two traits that are essential to the plot or that help bring out the qualities of the main character.	Understanding a character's traits helps you understand the reasons for his or her actions. Use what you know about the character's personality from the text to draw conclusions about why the character acts a certain way. Ask yourself these questions: • What are the character's dreams or aspirations? What is he or she willing to do—or give up—in order to fulfill these dreams? • What does the character value? What does he or she want to acquire or possess? What qualities does he or she admire in others and want to imitate? • What does the character fear or wish to avoid? How might these fears motivate the character to behave in ways that seem irrational, dishonest, or even immoral?

Support Inferences

 COMMON CORE   ELACC11-12RL1

When you read "Winter Dreams," you most likely made many inferences about the characters' traits and motivations without even thinking about it. When you discuss or write about the story, you will need to support your inferences with specific textual evidence—details from the story that are logically connected to your ideas. Recall this scene:

> "You little mean old *thing!*" cried Miss Jones wildly.
>
> Another argument ensued. Realizing that the elements of comedy were implied in the scene, Dexter several times began to laugh, but each time restrained the laugh before it reached audibility. He could not resist the monstrous conviction that the little girl was justified in beating the nurse.

Judy's behavior and Dexter's reaction to it make sense when you have gotten to know their characters. How could you use this passage to support a description of both characters? What future events are foreshadowed by the details in this scene?

Analyzing the Text

 COMMON CORE

ELACC11-12RL1,
ELACC11-12RL2,
ELACC11-12RL3,
ELACC11-12W3a

Cite Text Evidence   Support your responses with evidence from the selection.

1. **Infer**   Reread the first paragraph of the story. What do you learn about Dexter's family and social position?

2. **Interpret**   In lines 20–36, Fitzgerald writes about Dexter's fantasies involving "imaginary audiences and armies" and golf tournaments. What do such fantasies reveal about Dexter's character? Why does the author choose to tell us about Dexter's fantasy life?

3. **Analyze**   At the end of Part I, why does Dexter quit his caddy job? Cite evidence from the text that suggests his motivation.

4. **Interpret**   Lines 137–138 tells us that "Dexter was unconsciously dictated to by his winter dreams." What are Dexter's winter dreams, and how do they shape Dexter's behavior?

5. **Infer**   What can you infer about the character of Judy Jones based on the scene in which she pulls her boat up to Dexter's raft (lines 274–310)?

6. **Evaluate**   Dexter becomes engaged to Irene but then returns to Judy. Do you think he knew their engagement would not last? What clues does the text provide?

7. **Draw Conclusions**   How is Dexter affected by the news that Judy has married another man and subsequently lost her beauty? What does Dexter mean when he says that "there was something in me, but now that thing is gone"?

8. **Critique**   What kind of man is Dexter? Does he deserve sympathy, criticism, or both? Describe Dexter's traits and the motivations for his primary actions and feelings.

9. **Interpret**   Reread lines 771–793 and consider what exactly Dexter has lost. What **theme,** or message about the human condition, does Fitzgerald express through this loss?

PERFORMANCE TASK

Writing Activity: Letters   Explore Dexter's and Judy's feelings for one another in two brief writing tasks.

1. In the character of Dexter, write a letter in which you profess your love to Judy and tell her what she represents to you.

2. In the character of Judy, respond to Dexter's letter, sharing with him any feelings you have for him.

3. Based on these letters, write a brief analysis of why the relationship should succeed or fail.

Critical Vocabulary

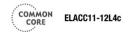

blatantly	precarious	flux	precipitate
petulance	mundane	turbulence	plaintive

Practice and Apply Working with a partner, use these questions to interview one another. Each answer should indicate comprehension of the Critical Vocabulary word. Take notes on your partner's responses and then write a brief summary of your interview. Use a dictionary or thesaurus as needed.

1. Do you **blatantly** show your support for sports teams?

2. Have you ever helped a friend in a **precarious** situation?

3. When do you experience **flux** in your life or in your schedule?

4. When you hear a contemporary song that you like, what response does it **precipitate** from you?

5. When have you reacted to a situation with **petulance**?

6. When have you noticed or said something **mundane**?

7. When have you experienced **turbulence,** for example at school or at home?

8. Have you ever noticed something that sounded or looked **plaintive**?

Vocabulary Strategy: Precise Usage

Reference tools help writers understand the precise meaning of words so they can use them correctly in a sentence. The thesaurus, for example, is used to find **synonyms,** or words of similar meaning, and **antonyms,** words that are opposite in meaning. It is important to identify the correct set of synonyms and antonyms for words having more than one meaning or part of speech. Take a look at this example of a thesaurus entry for the Critical Vocabulary word *mundane*:

> **mundane** *adjective* **1. worldly, temporal, secular, earthly** *He practiced meditation, hoping to transform the mundane into the heavenly.* **2. banal, commonplace, ordinary, prosaic, routine** *Processing customer returns was among the many mundane tasks required of the cashier.* **Antonyms: heavenly; extraordinary, exciting**

Practice and Apply For each Critical Vocabulary word, follow these steps:

1. Look up each word in a print or digital thesaurus. Identify the synonyms appropriate to the meaning of each Critical Vocabulary word as it is used in the selection.

2. Write a sample sentence using each word.

3. In each sentence, replace the vocabulary word with one of your synonyms. Make sure that the sentences make sense by having a partner check your work.

Language and Style: Craft Effective Sentences

In "Winter Dreams," Fitzgerald's writing style comes from making effective choices to create his own unique **syntax**—the pattern of words and phrases in his sentences. By varying syntax, writers can adjust the rhythm of their sentences to convey mood and ideas effectively. Tools such as punctuation, word choice, and well-chosen details all contribute to a writer's syntax and overall style. The chart shows some of the tools used to craft effective sentences.

Effective Sentences		
Writing Tool	**Purpose**	**Example**
Exclamatory sentence	to convey excitement	"'Never lost a ball! Willing! Intelligent!'" (line 52)
Dash	to set off ideas by calling attention to them; to break up long sentences	"It gave him a sense of solidity to go with her—she was so sturdily popular. . . ." (lines 551–552)
Dialogue	to show characterization; to further the plot; to break up narration	"I'm nobody," he announced. "My career is largely a matter of futures." "Are you poor?" "No," he said frankly. . . . (lines 376-379)
Sensory details/telling details	to create a full, vivid picture for the reader; to further characterization	"Her arms, burned to butternut, moved sinuously among the dull platinum ripples. . . ." (lines 295–297)
Precise words and phrases	to communicate ideas effectively	". . . within a year he was catering to the trade that wore knickerbockers." (lines 164–165)
Repetition	to create rhythm and mood; to emphasize a particular point or idea	"She had treated him with interest. . . . She had inflicted on him. . . . She had beckoned him and yawned at him. . . ." (lines 485–489)

Practice and Apply Revise the letter you wrote in the character of Dexter to make your sentences more effective. In your revision, include at least five different tools listed in the chart. Discuss with a partner how each tool improves your work.

Song of the Son   Poem by Jean Toomer

From the Dark Tower   Poem by Countee Cullen

A Black Man Talks of Reaping   Poem by Arna Bontemps

The Harlem Renaissance

In the early 1920s, the New York City neighborhood of Harlem attracted worldly and race-conscious African Americans who nurtured each other's artistic, musical, and literary talents and created a flowering of African American arts known as the Harlem Renaissance.

The Great Migration of millions of Southern black farmers and sharecroppers to the urban North began in 1916 and continued throughout the 1920s. They came in search of opportunity and freedom from oppression and racial hostility. Thousands of these migrants settled in Harlem, which quickly became the cultural center of African American life. Here, black men and women drew on their own cultural resources—their folk traditions as well as a new urban awareness—to produce unique forms of expression.

A LITERARY MOVEMENT   The event that unofficially kicked off the Harlem Renaissance as a literary movement was a dinner given on March 21, 1924, that gathered together some of the nation's most celebrated writers and thinkers, both black and white. The older generation of African American intellectuals that sponsored the dinner had helped begin organizations such as the National Urban League and the National Association for the Advancement of Colored People (NAACP) to promote equality for African Americans. These organizations published journals in which the works of young writers, including Countee Cullen, Zora Neal Hurston, and Langston Hughes, were published.

These young writers considered themselves the founders of a new era in literature. They expressed what it meant to be black in a white-dominated world. Yet this new generation of writers did not speak with only one voice. Some used a classical style to explore the struggles of African Americans, while others cast off more formal language and styles and wrote with the pulse of jazz rhythms. And some were more interested in exploring their individual identities than communicating the concerns of the African American community.

The Harlem Renaissance was brought to a premature end by the economic collapse of the Great Depression. Many writers left Harlem to take jobs to support themselves. Nonetheless, their work had a lasting influence on African American writers and on American culture as a whole.

Poems of the Harlem Renaissance

Jean Toomer (1894–1967), *born in Washington, D.C., was a poet, novelist, and playwright best known for his book* Cane *(1923) which celebrated African Americans through an experimental mixture of poetry and prose. "Song of the Son" is from the first section of the book, set in rural Georgia. Eastern philosophy and Imagist poetry—poetry that uses precise, striking images to convey meaning—influenced Toomer's work. Because of his mixed-race background, Toomer could "pass" for white and came to reject the idea of race altogether, embracing the ideal of a united human race not concerned with color.*

Countee Cullen (1903–1946) *was an award-winning poet from the time he was in high school in New York City. His first collection of poems,* Color *(1925), was published to critical acclaim before he graduated from New York University. Cullen saw poetry as a tool to break down racial barriers. Although he treated racial themes in fresh ways, he preferred to use classical forms, influenced by the Romantic poet John Keats, rather than the language and rhythm of African American speech. The title "From the Dark Tower" refers to a place in Harlem where writers and artists met to discuss their work.*

Arna Bontemps (1902–1973) *was born in Louisiana but raised in California, where he fought to preserve a connection to his black heritage. Following his graduation from college in 1923, he discovered the thriving literary scene in Harlem, where he formed close connections with the major artists of the Harlem Renaissance. Bontemps gained early fame for his poetry, published in magazines such as* Opportunity *and* Crisis, *and in later years went on to write several novels. Much of his work focuses on the themes of dignity and justice and is influenced by the oral traditions and music of African Americans.*

AS YOU READ Notice imagery or language that each poet uses to appeal to readers' senses. Write down any questions you generate during reading.

Song of the Son
by Jean Toomer

Pour O pour that parting soul in song,
O pour it in the sawdust glow of night,
Into the velvet pine-smoke air to-night,
And let the valley carry it along.
5   And let the valley carry it along.

O land and soil, red soil and sweet-gum tree,
So scant of grass, so profligate of pines,
Now just before an epoch's sun declines
Thy son, in time, I have returned to thee,
10   Thy son, I have in time returned to thee.

In time, for though the sun is setting on
A song-lit race of slaves, it has not set;
Though late, O soil, it is not too late yet
To catch thy plaintive soul, leaving, soon gone,
15   Leaving, to catch thy plaintive soul soon gone.

O Negro slaves, dark purple ripened plums,
Squeezed, and bursting in the pine-wood air,
Passing, before they stripped the old tree bare
One plum was saved for me, one seed becomes

20   An everlasting song, a singing tree,
Caroling softly souls of slavery,
What they were, and what they are to me,
Caroling softly souls of slavery.

From the Dark Tower
by Countee Cullen

We shall not always plant while others reap
The golden increment of bursting fruit,
Not always countenance,[1] abject and mute,
That lesser men should hold their brothers cheap;
5　Not everlastingly while others sleep
Shall we beguile their limbs with mellow flute,
Not always bend to some more subtle brute;
We were not made eternally to weep.

The night whose sable[2] breast relieves the stark,
10　White stars is no less lovely being dark,
And there are buds that cannot bloom at all
In light, but crumple, piteous, and fall;
So in the dark we hide the heart that bleeds,
And wait, and tend our agonizing seeds.

---

[1] **countenance:** admit as acceptable.
[2] **sable:** black.

Image Credits: ©Cynthia Hart Designer/Fine Art/Corbis

A Black Man Talks of Reaping
by Arna Bontemps

I have sown beside all waters in my day.
I planted deep, within my heart the fear
That wind or fowl would take the grain away.
I planted safe against this stark, lean year.

5 I scattered seed enough to plant the land
In rows from Canada to Mexico,
But for my reaping only what the hand
Can hold at once is all that I can show.

Yet what I sowed and what the orchard yields
10 My brother's sons are gathering stalk and root,
Small wonder then my children glean[1] in fields
They have not sown, and feed on bitter fruit.

---

[1] **glean:** gather produce left behind by the regular reapers.

COLLABORATIVE DISCUSSION What imagery in each poem appealed to your different senses? Discuss this question with a partner, citing specific details from the poems to support your ideas.

Demonstrate Knowledge of Foundational Works

These three poems, each by writers from the cultural movement known as the Harlem Renaissance, are among the foundational works of early 20th century American literature. They demonstrate how contemporary writers explored the African American experience in a variety of ways. By analyzing the poems together, readers can see how each poet treated similar topics and themes in a unique fashion.

Consider how each writer's use of language helps to develop a similar theme in each poem, and how each writer uses figurative and connotative language to affect meaning and tone.

Topic	Theme	Figurative Language
A **topic** is the subject of the poem. The title of a poem may provide a clue to the specific topic of the poem. The titles of all three poems hint at the broader topic that is common to all of them—some aspect of the African American experience in the 19th and early 20th centuries, expressed from the perspective of the Harlem Renaissance.	**Theme** is the underlying message about life or human nature that the poet wants to communicate through his choice of topic. In most poems, the theme is implied rather than directly stated. To understand the theme, look for clues in the title and determine the identity of the speaker. Is the speaker an individual or does he represent a group? The particular mood or feeling that the speaker conveys also provides clues to the theme. Consider the phrases "agonizing seeds" and "bitter fruit" that end Cullen's and Bontemps's poems, respectively, and that hint at the common theme or message of the poems.	In poetry, the speaker's descriptions of the world will often help you identify the theme. Poets often use descriptive words in a figurative, or nonliteral, way to create images in the reader's mind. One type of figurative language is **metaphor,** a comparison between two things without using the words *like* or *as*. Consider this metaphor in Toomer's poem: "O Negro slaves, dark purple ripened plums." A common metaphor in the three poems is the metaphor of planting and reaping. Understanding how each poet uses this metaphor as a way of describing the African American experience will help you determine the common themes of the poems.

Analyzing the Text

COMMON CORE

ELACC11-12RL2,
ELACC11-12RL4,
ELACC11-12RL5,
ELACC11-12RL9,
ELACC11-12W2,
ELACC11-12W10

Cite Text Evidence   Support your responses with evidence from the selections.

1. **Summarize** What is the speaker describing—both literally and figuratively—in "Song of the Son"? How do the poem's ideas and images express one or more themes on the topic of African American history?

2. **Infer** Who is the speaker in "Song of the Son"? In the context of African American culture, what does he represent to the poet?

3. **Analyze** In "From the Dark Tower," what does the phrase "golden increment of bursting fruit" suggest?

4. **Analyze** "From the Dark Tower" is written in the form of a **Petrarchan sonnet,** in which the octave, or first eight lines, presents a problem or challenge, and the final six lines, the sestet, resolves or comments on the problem. How does Cullen apply this structure to express his message?

5. **Infer** In "A Black Man Talks of Reaping," what does the speaker mean when he says "My brother's sons are gathering stalk and root"? Who is the brother? What is the "bitter fruit" at the end of the poem?

6. **Identify** An **extended metaphor** is a metaphor that is developed over many lines. Identify an example of extended metaphor in each poem.

7. **Cite Evidence** How does Toomer's use of repetition—of both lines and important ideas—contribute to the aesthetic impact of "Song of the Son"?

8. **Compare** How do Toomer and Cullen use the metaphor of night and darkness to support the themes and ideas they want to express?

9. **Synthesize** How would you describe the tone of each poem?

10. **Compare** In what ways might these poems represent differents aspects or strains of the Harlem Renaissance? Consider formal, topical, and thematic elements in all three poems.

PERFORMANCE TASK

Writing Task: Essay Write an informative essay in which you compare and contrast the themes of the three poems.

-   Determine a message about the African American experience expressed in each poem through the use of the extended metaphor of planting and reaping.

-   Choose significant imagery from each poem that demonstrates how the poet used the metaphor to convey the theme.

-   Use a compare-and-contrast organizational structure to highlight similarities and differences among the three poems.

-   Draw a conclusion from the information you present about the relationship between the themes of the three poems.

Mending Wall
The Death of the Hired Man

Poems by Robert Frost

Robert Frost *is normally associated with rural New England, but he was born in San Francisco in 1874. The death of his father when Robert was 11 years old prompted the family to move to the industrial city of Lawrence, Massachusetts. After graduating from high school, Frost attended Dartmouth and Harvard for short periods of time, but never obtained a degree. He married Elinor White, a high school classmate and lover of poetry, in 1895, and supported his family with various teaching jobs.*

In 1900, Frost left teaching and took up farming, while also trying to establish himself as a poet. The 11 years that Frost spent farming in New Hampshire were also very creative years for his writing. However, he was not able to publish a book during this time. At the age of 38, Frost uprooted the family and moved to England. In England, he was able to publish his first book of poetry, A Boy's Will. *This book was followed in 1914 by* North of Boston. *At the outbreak of WWI in 1915, Frost and his family returned to the United States. He was greeted as a leading American poet. In 1924, his collection* New Hampshire *won a Pulitzer Prize, one of four that he would eventually receive.*

Unfortunately, his private life did not match the success of his public life. Between 1934 and 1940, Frost suffered several personal tragedies. His daughter, his wife, and his son died. In addition, his other daughter was institutionalized for mental illness. These events affected the mood of his late poems—they often conveyed a bleak outlook on life. He died in Boston in 1963.

AS YOU READ Pay attention to the mood, or overall feeling or atmosphere, of each poem. What kind of descriptive language does Frost include? Write down any questions you generate during reading.

MENDING WALL

Something there is that doesn't love a wall,
That sends the frozen-ground-swell under it,
And spills the upper boulders in the sun;
And makes gaps even two can pass abreast.
5 The work of hunters is another thing:
I have come after them and made repair
Where they have left not one stone on a stone,
But they would have the rabbit out of hiding,
To please the yelping dogs. The gaps I mean,
10 No one has seen them made or heard them made,
But at spring mending-time we find them there.
I let my neighbor know beyond the hill;
And on a day we meet to walk the line
And set the wall between us once again.
15 We keep the wall between us as we go.
To each the boulders that have fallen to each.
And some are loaves and some so nearly balls
We have to use a spell to make them balance:
"Stay where you are until our backs are turned!"
20 We wear our fingers rough with handling them.
Oh, just another kind of out-door game,
One on a side. It comes to little more:

There where it is we do not need the wall:
He is all pine and I am apple orchard.
25   My apple trees will never get across
And eat the cones under his pines, I tell him.
·   He only says, "Good fences make good neighbors."
Spring is the mischief in me, and I wonder
If I could put a notion in his head:
30   "*Why* do they make good neighbors? Isn't it
Where there are cows? But here there are no cows.
Before I built a wall I'd ask to know
What I was walling in or walling out,
And to whom I was like to give offence.
35   Something there is that doesn't love a wall,
That wants it down." I could say "Elves" to him,
But it's not elves exactly, and I'd rather
He said it for himself. I see him there
Bringing a stone grasped firmly by the top
40   In each hand, like an old-stone savage armed.
He moves in darkness as it seems to me,
Not of woods only and the shade of trees.
He will not go behind his father's saying,
And he likes having thought of it so well
45   He says again, "Good fences make good neighbors."

THE DEATH OF THE HIRED MAN

Mary sat musing on the lamp-flame at the table
Waiting for Warren. When she heard his step,
She ran on tip-toe down the darkened passage
To meet him in the doorway with the news
5   And put him on his guard. "Silas is back."
She pushed him outward with her through the door
And shut it after her. "Be kind," she said.
She took the market things from Warren's arms
And set them on the porch, then drew him down
10   To sit beside her on the wooden steps.

"When was I ever anything but kind to him?
But I'll not have the fellow back," he said.
"I told him so last haying, didn't I?
'If he left then,' I said, 'that ended it.'
15   What good is he? Who else will harbor[1] him
At his age for the little he can do?

---

[1] **harbor:** provide safe shelter for.

What help he is there's no depending on.
Off he goes always when I need him most.
'He thinks he ought to earn a little pay,
20 Enough at least to buy tobacco with,
So he won't have to beg and be beholden.'
'All right,' I say, 'I can't afford to pay
Any fixed wages, though I wish I could.'
'Someone else can.' 'Then someone else will have to.'
25 I shouldn't mind his bettering himself
If that was what it was. You can be certain,
When he begins like that, there's someone at him
Trying to coax him off with pocket-money,—
In haying time, when any help is scarce.
30 In winter he comes back to us. I'm done."

"Sh! not so loud: he'll hear you," Mary said.

"I want him to: he'll have to soon or late."

"He's worn out. He's asleep beside the stove.
When I came up from Rowe's I found him here,
35 Huddled against the barn-door fast asleep,
A miserable sight, and frightening, too—
You needn't smile—I didn't recognize him—
I wasn't looking for him—and he's changed.
Wait till you see."

                    "Where did you say he'd been?"

40 "He didn't say. I dragged him to the house,
And gave him tea and tried to make him smoke.
I tried to make him talk about his travels.
Nothing would do: he just kept nodding off."

"What did he say? Did he say anything?"

45 "But little."

                    "Anything? Mary, confess
He said he'd come to ditch[2] the meadow for me."

"Warren!"

              "But did he? I just want to know."

"Of course he did. What would you have him say?
Surely you wouldn't grudge the poor old man

---

[2] **ditch:** dig drainage channels in.

50 Some humble way to save his self-respect.
    He added, if you really care to know,
    He meant to clear the upper pasture, too.
    That sounds like something you have heard before?
    Warren, I wish you could have heard the way
55 He jumbled everything. I stopped to look
    Two or three times—he made me feel so queer[3]—
    To see if he was talking in his sleep.
    He ran on[4] Harold Wilson—you remember—
    The boy you had in haying four years since.
60 He's finished school, and teaching in his college.
    Silas declares you'll have to get him back.
    He says they two will make a team for work:
    Between them they will lay this farm as smooth!
    The way he mixed that in with other things.
65 He thinks young Wilson a likely lad, though daft
    On education—you know how they fought
    All through July under the blazing sun,
    Silas up on the cart to build the load,
    Harold along beside to pitch it on."

70 "Yes, I took care to keep well out of earshot."

    "Well, those days trouble Silas like a dream.
    You wouldn't think they would. How some things linger!
    Harold's young college boy's assurance piqued[5] him.
    After so many years he still keeps finding
75 Good arguments he sees he might have used.
    I sympathize. I know just how it feels
    To think of the right thing to say too late.
    Harold's associated in his mind with Latin.
    He asked me what I thought of Harold's saying
80 He studied Latin like the violin
    Because he liked it—that an argument!
    He said he couldn't make the boy believe
    He could find water with a hazel prong[6] —
    Which showed how much good school had ever done him.
85 He wanted to go over that. But most of all
    He thinks if he could have another chance
    To teach him how to build a load of hay—"

    "I know, that's Silas' one accomplishment.

---

[3] **queer:** uncomfortable; ill at ease.

[4] **ran on:** kept talking about in a rambling way.

[5] **piqued:** aroused resentment in.

[6] **hazel prong:** a reference to the practice of dowsing, in which a person uses a forked stick made of hazel wood to try to find underground water.

He bundles every forkful in its place,
90 And tags and numbers it for future reference,
So he can find and easily dislodge it
In the unloading. Silas does that well.
He takes it out in bunches like big birds' nests.
You never see him standing on the hay
95 He's trying to lift, straining to lift himself."

"He thinks if he could teach him that, he'd be
Some good perhaps to someone in the world.
He hates to see a boy the fool of books.
Poor Silas, so concerned for other folk,
100 And nothing to look backward to with pride,
And nothing to look forward to with hope,
So now and never any different."

Part of a moon was falling down the west,
Dragging the whole sky with it to the hills.
105 Its light poured softly in her lap. She saw
And spread her apron to it. She put out her hand
Among the harp-like morning-glory strings,
Taut with the dew from garden bed to eaves,
As if she played unheard the tenderness
110 That wrought[7] on him beside her in the night.
"Warren," she said, "he has come home to die:
You needn't be afraid he'll leave you this time."

"Home," he mocked gently.

                              "Yes, what else but home?
It all depends on what you mean by home.
115 Of course he's nothing to us, any more
Than was the hound that came a stranger to us
Out of the woods, worn out upon the trail."

"Home is the place where, when you have to go there,
They have to take you in."

                              "I should have called it
120 Something you somehow haven't to deserve."

Warren leaned out and took a step or two,
Picked up a little stick, and brought it back
And broke it in his hand and tossed it by.
"Silas has better claim on us you think
125 Than on his brother? Thirteen little miles

----
[7] **wrought:** worked.

As the road winds would bring him to his door.
Silas has walked that far no doubt to-day.
Why didn't he go there? His brother's rich,
A somebody—director in the bank."

130 "He never told us that."

            "We know it though."

"I think his brother ought to help, of course.
I'll see to that if there is need. He ought of right
To take him in, and might be willing to—
He may be better than appearances.
135 But have some pity on Silas. Do you think
If he'd had any pride in claiming kin
Or anything he looked for from his brother,
He'd keep so still about him all this time?"

"I wonder what's between them."

                  "I can tell you.
140 Silas is what he is—we wouldn't mind him—
But just the kind that kinsfolk can't abide.
He never did a thing so very bad.
He don't know why he isn't quite as good
As anyone. He won't be made ashamed
145 To please his brother, worthless though he is."

"*I* can't think Si ever hurt anyone."

"No, but he hurt my heart the way he lay

And rolled his old head on that sharp-edged chair-back.
He wouldn't let me put him on the lounge.
150 You must go in and see what you can do.
I made the bed up for him there to-night.
You'll be surprised at him—how much he's broken.
His working days are done; I'm sure of it."

"I'd not be in a hurry to say that."

155 "I haven't been. Go, look, see for yourself.
But, Warren, please remember how it is:
He's come to help you ditch the meadow.
He has a plan. You mustn't laugh at him.
He may not speak of it, and then he may.
160 I'll sit and see if that small sailing cloud
Will hit or miss the moon."

                         It hit the moon.
Then there were three there, making a dim row,
The moon, the little silver cloud, and she.

Warren returned—too soon, it seemed to her,
165 Slipped to her side, caught up her hand and waited.

"Warren," she questioned.

                         "Dead," was all he answered.

COLLABORATIVE DISCUSSION With a small group, discuss the mood of each poem. How does Frost's descriptive language appeal to your senses and help you visualize the settings of the poems?

Analyze Language: Ambiguity

Frost's poetry incorporates a great deal of ambiguity. **Ambiguity** in literary work allows for more than one meaning. The works are open to various or opposing interpretations, as in lines 41–42 of "Mending Wall." This lends richness and beauty to the poems.

> He moves in darkness as it seems to me,
> Not of woods only and the shade of trees.

Since Frost is intentionally vague about his neighbor and about the whole enterprise of using walls to keep things in or to keep things out, readers are left to sort through his ambiguity. The first line talks about the neighbor moving "in darkness." At first it seems to refer to the actual darkness of the woods. In the next line, Frost says it was more than that, but he declines to be specific.

Of course, you don't have to choose rigidly between meanings in works that contain ambiguity. Skilled readers of poetry will recognize ambiguity and live with it, even enjoy it, as they read and consider a poem. As you analyze Frost's poem, consider recording different interpretations of the poem's lines in a chart such as this one.

Line from "Mending Wall"	Interpretations
He moves in darkness as it seems to me	The speaker refers to his neighbor as sinister. The speaker refers to his neighbor as hard to get to know, possibly unfriendly.

Analyze Structure

Like fiction, a **narrative poem,** such as "The Death of the Hired Man," tells a story using the elements of plot, character, and setting. A poet may adapt methods of characterization typically used in fiction, such as physical description using vivid imagery, character development through a character's actions or comments, the thoughts or actions of other characters, or direct comments about characters by the poem's speaker. As you analyze "The Death of the Hired Man," consider these questions.

Dialogue	Who is speaking in this poem? How does Robert Frost use conversation to help develop the narrative elements of the poem?
Plot	How is the order of events conveyed? Does the dialogue in the poem only provide information about the present time?
Characterization	Does Robert Frost use direct description by the speaker to impart the characters' traits? What information do the characters' own words convey about them?
Setting	Why do the characters' descriptions of their work help you understand the setting, or the time and place, of the poem?

Analyzing the Text

Cite Text Evidence Support your responses with evidence from the selections.

1. **Evaluate** In "Mending Wall," what makes the speaker say that "something" doesn't love a wall? Besides this "something," who else doesn't love a wall?

2. **Interpret** Why does the speaker consider saying "Elves" (line 36) to his neighbor? What causes the speaker to change his mind?

3. **Interpret** How does Frost use ambiguity to present his message about walls and neighbors? What evidence supports the idea that the speaker believes "Good fences make good neighbors"? What details suggest the opposite?

4. **Analzye** Reread lines 31–39 of "The Death of the Hired Man." What do these lines reveal about Silas and Mary's character traits? How does this information support the plot?

5. **Interpret** The **setting** is the time and location of a poem or story. Identify the details in lines 103-110 that create a vivid image of the setting of "The Death of the Hired Man." What does this setting tell you about Mary's character?

6. **Draw Conclusions** How does Silas in "The Death of the Hired Man" think of the farm? Why does the dialogue between Mary and Warren help you understand Silas's presence at the farm? Cite details from the poem to support your answer.

7. **Compare/Contrast** Consider the narrative elements of both "Mending Wall" and "The Death of the Hired Man." What similarities and differences exist in the structure, or dialogue, plot, characterization, and setting, of both poems? Explain using details from the poems.

PERFORMANCE TASK

Writing Activity: Interview Summary Both "Mending Wall" and "The Death of the Hired Man" have ambiguous lines in them that can be interpreted in different ways. Simulate a reporter and interview five of your classmates and then summarize their interpretations.

- Choose several lines from each poem that are ambiguous.

- Ask five classmates to give you their interpretations of the lines.

- Write a summary of their interpretations and include a comparison to your own ideas about the meanings of the lines.

- Discuss your findings in a small group. Do the interpretations across the classroom have certain similarities in tone or content?

Language and Style: Informal Style

COMMON CORE   ELACC11-12L3a

In these poems, Frost uses an almost casual and conversational style. This helps develop a connection with his readers by drawing them into the characters' world. One technique that helps him develop his unique style is his use of **informal language** and **syntax,** or how he combines words to form his lines. In particular, Frost uses colloquial or regional language and simple sentence structure in his poems. This has the effect of making his poems feel old fashioned and contemporary at the same time.

Look at this example of informal language from "Mending Wall."

And on a day we meet to walk the line
And set the wall between us once again.
We keep the wall between us as we go.
To each the boulders that have fallen to each.

These lines contain phrases such as "set the wall," "as we go," and "To each . . . to each" that are terse and direct, mirroring the way that language is used when people are speaking as they perform a physical task together. Frost uses simple and clear language to describe a particular moment in time.

Examine these lines from "The Death of the Hired Man," noticing the style choices..

"When was I ever anything but kind to him?
But I'll not have the fellow back," he said.
"I told him so last haying, didn't I?
'If he left then,' I said, 'that ended it.'

In this set of lines, Frost uses informal language that contains contractions and rhetorical questions that Warren answers himself. This dialogue invites readers to "listen" to the conversation as they read. In particular, this dialogue expresses the fact that Warren feels somewhat angry toward Silas because Warren told him not to come back when he left during the haying. This informal style helps readers relate to Warren's point of view.

Consider how using a more formal style changes the impression the text makes.

"I was always kind to him."
"However, I will not have Silas work for me again," he said.
"I informed him of my decision during his last employment.
'If he left,' I stated, 'that would mean the end of our working
relationship.'

Practice and Apply Think about the way that language is used in your region. Write a one-paragraph narrative about something that has happened in your school in the past few days. As you write, consider the audience you are addressing and how you want to establish a connection with them. Use an informal style to invite your readers to interact closely with your plot and characters. Try to capture the speech patterns that you and your classmates use. Share your narrative with a partner. Discuss whether your use of informal style is successful and what revisions might improve the narrative.

Modern American Drama

The 19th century was a very active period in American theater. Most productions, however, consisted of wildly theatrical spectacles such as simulated chariot races and burning cities, all staged by means of dazzling special effects. Every town of any size had its own theater or "opera house." Yet, in spite of all this theatrical activity, not one truly significant American drama was staged during the 1800s, a period that produced Melville, Emerson, Whitman, Dickinson, and Twain.

By the early 20th century, however, American playwrights began to reject the extravagant approach of the commercial theater. Instead, these writers favored realistic settings, characters, actions, and emotions that mirrored ordinary life. As with many artistic revolutions, this movement toward realism began far outside the mainstream. By 1916, however, big New York audiences were flocking to small, obscure off-Broadway theaters to see the works of writers such as Eugene O'Neill (1888–1953). Eventually, mainstream theaters began to showcase realistic plays, too, and realism became established as the dominant mode of American drama.

The post-World War II years brought two notable figures to prominence in modern American drama: Tennessee Williams (1911–1983) and Arthur Miller (1915–2005), playwrights who experimented with stagecraft while exploring modern themes and creating works of social relevance.

One of the most common themes explored by these playwrights was that of the American dream. Willy Loman, the main character in Miller's *Death of a Salesman,* became the trademark figure of postwar American theater. A lowly salesman who has been discarded by the system to which he has mistakenly devoted his life, Willy Loman proved how the American dream could become twisted and broken. In *The Glass Menagerie* and *A Streetcar Named Desire,* southerner Tennessee Williams portrayed characters who, unsuited to modern life, retreat into the fantasy world of an earlier era.

In *A Raisin in the Sun,* Lorraine Hansberry (1930–1965) looked at the American dream from the perspective of those who had been excluded. The first major Broadway play by an African-American writer, *A Raisin in the Sun* was hailed by critics as "universal," while also capturing unique aspects of the African-American experience.

In contemporary theater, there has been a shift back toward spectacular productions as commercial theater once again relies upon special effects, imaginative settings, and imaginary worlds. Like any art form, drama undergoes infinite adaptations to reflect the spirit of the times.

The Crucible

Drama by Arthur Miller

Arthur Miller *was born in New York City in 1915 into an upper-middle-class family. His comfortable early life changed when the Great Depression eroded his family's economic circumstances. Miller was unable to go to college until he earned the tuition money by working in a warehouse. Eventually, he attended the University of Michigan. Miller won several awards for his plays during college and chose to pursue a career in the theater.* All My Sons *and* Death of a Salesman, *a play that won a Pulitzer Prize in 1949, made Miller a star.*

Around the same time, hearings were being conducted by Congress to identify suspected Communists. Miller was called to testify before the committee about his association with the American Communist Party. Although he admitted to having attended a few meetings years earlier, he refused to "name names" of other people involved in the meetings. As a result, he was cited for contempt of Congress; this conviction was later overturned. The events of this time period inspired him to write The Crucible, *set during the Salem, Massachusetts, witch trials of 1692. He wrote the play to warn against mass hysteria and to plead for freedom and tolerance.*

In general, Miller's writing explores issues relevant to contemporary readers, such as the complexities of family relationships, personal responsibility, and morality. Many consider him to be the 20th century's greatest American playwright.

AS YOU READ Note details that explain how Abigail feels about John Proctor. Write down any questions you generate during reading.

CAST OF CHARACTERS

(IN ORDER OF APPEARANCE)

Reverend Samuel Parris	Rebecca Nurse
Betty Parris	Giles Corey
Tituba	Reverend John Hale
Abigail Williams	Francis Nurse
John Proctor	Ezekiel Cheever
Elizabeth Proctor	Marshal Herrick
Susanna Walcott	Judge Hathorne
Mrs. Ann Putnam	Martha Corey
Thomas Putnam	Deputy Governor Danforth
Mercy Lewis	Girls of Salem
Mary Warren	Sarah Good

ACT ONE

An Overture

(*A small upper bedroom in the home of* Reverend Samuel Parris, *Salem, Massachusetts, in the spring of the year 1692.*

There is a narrow window at the left. Through its leaded panes the morning sunlight streams. A candle still burns near the bed, which is at the right. A chest, a chair, and a small table are the other furnishings. At the back a door opens on the landing of the stairway to the ground floor. The room gives off an air of clean spareness. The roof rafters are exposed, and the wood colors are raw and unmellowed.

As the curtain rises, Reverend Parris *is discovered kneeling beside the bed, evidently in prayer. His daughter,* Betty Parris, *aged ten, is lying on the bed, inert.*)

At the time of these events Parris was in his middle forties. In history he cut a villainous path, and there is very little good to be said for him. He believed he was being persecuted wherever he went, despite his best efforts to win people and God to his side. In meeting, he felt insulted if someone rose to shut the door without first asking his permission. He was a widower with no interest in children, or talent with them. He regarded them as young adults, and until this strange crisis he, like the rest of Salem, never conceived that the children were anything but thankful for being permitted to walk straight, eyes slightly lowered, arms at the sides, and mouths shut until bidden to speak.

His house stood in the "town"—but we today would hardly call it a village. The meeting house[1] was nearby, and from this point outward—toward the bay or inland—there were a few small-windowed, dark houses snuggling against the raw Massachusetts winter. Salem had been established hardly forty years before. To the European world the whole province was a barbaric frontier inhabited by a sect of fanatics who, nevertheless, were shipping out products of slowly increasing quantity and value.

No one can really know what their lives were like. They had no novelists—and would not have permitted anyone to read a novel if one were handy. Their creed forbade anything resembling a theater or "vain enjoyment." They did not celebrate Christmas, and a holiday from work meant only that they must concentrate even more upon prayer.

Which is not to say that nothing broke into this strict and somber way of life. When a new farmhouse was built, friends assembled to "raise the roof," and there would be special foods cooked and probably some potent cider passed around. There was a good supply of ne'er-do-wells in Salem, who dallied at the shovelboard[2] in Bridget Bishop's tavern. Probably more than the creed, hard work kept the morals of the place from spoiling, for the people were forced to fight the land like heroes for every grain of corn, and no man had very much time for fooling around.

That there were some jokers, however, is indicated by the practice of appointing a two-man patrol whose duty was to "walk forth in the time of God's worship to take notice of such as either lye about the meeting house, without attending to the word and ordinances, or that lye at home or in the fields without giving good account thereof, and to take the names of such persons, and to present them to the magistrates, whereby they may be accordingly proceeded against." This predilection for minding other people's business was time-honored among the people of Salem, and it undoubtedly created many of the suspicions which were to feed the coming madness. It was also, in my opinion, one of the things that a John Proctor would rebel against, for the time of the armed camp had almost passed, and since the country was reasonably—although not wholly—safe, the old disciplines were beginning to rankle. But, as in all such matters, the issue was not clear-cut, for danger was still a possibility, and in unity still lay the best promise of safety.

The edge of the wilderness was close by. The American continent stretched endlessly west, and it was

---

[1] **meeting house:** the most important building in the Puritan community, used both for worship and for meetings.

[2] **shovelboard:** a game in which a coin or disc is shoved across a board by hand.

full of mystery for them. It stood, dark and threatening, over their shoulders night and day, for out of it Indian tribes marauded from time to time, and Reverend Parris had parishioners who had lost relatives to these heathen.

The parochial snobbery of these people was partly responsible for their failure to convert the Indians. Probably they also preferred to take land from heathens rather than from fellow Christians. At any rate, very few Indians were converted, and the Salem folk believed that the virgin forest was the Devil's last preserve, his home base and the citadel of his final stand. To the best of their knowledge the American forest was the last place on earth that was not paying homage to God.

For these reasons, among others, they carried about an air of innate resistance, even of persecution. Their fathers had, of course, been persecuted in England. So now they and their church found it necessary to deny any other sect its freedom, lest their New Jerusalem[3] be defiled and corrupted by wrong ways and deceitful ideas.

They believed, in short, that they held in their steady hands the candle that would light the world. We have inherited this belief, and it has helped and hurt us. It helped them with the discipline it gave them. They were a dedicated folk, by and large, and they had to be to survive the life they had chosen or been born into in this country.

The proof of their belief's value to them may be taken from the opposite character of the first Jamestown settlement, farther south, in Virginia.

The Englishmen who landed there were motivated mainly by a hunt for profit. They had thought to pick off the wealth of the new country and then return rich to England. They were a band of individualists, and a much more ingratiating group than the Massachusetts men. But Virginia destroyed them. Massachusetts tried to kill off the Puritans, but they combined; they set up a communal society which, in the beginning, was little more than an armed camp with an autocratic and very devoted leadership. It was, however, an autocracy by consent, for they were united from top to bottom by a commonly held ideology whose perpetuation was the reason and justification for all their sufferings. So their self-denial, their purposefulness, their suspicion of all vain pursuits, their hard-handed justice, were altogether perfect instruments for the conquest of this space so antagonistic to man.

But the people of Salem in 1692 were not quite the dedicated folk that arrived on the *Mayflower*. A vast differentiation had taken place, and in their own time a revolution had unseated the royal government and substituted a junta which was at this moment in power.[4] The times, to their eyes, must have been out of joint, and to the common folk must have seemed as insoluble and complicated as do ours today. It is not hard to see how easily many could have been led to believe that the time of confusion had been brought upon them by deep and darkling forces. No hint of such speculation appears on the court record, but social disorder in any age breeds such mystical suspicions,

---

[3] **New Jerusalem:** in Christianity, a heavenly city and the last resting place of the souls saved by Jesus. It was considered the ideal city, and Puritans modeled their communities after it.

[4] **a junta** (ho͝on′tə) . . . **power:** Junta is a Spanish term meaning "a small, elite ruling council." The reference here is to the group that led England's Glorious Revolution of 1688–1689.

and when, as in Salem, wonders are brought forth from below the social surface, it is too much to expect people to hold back very long from laying on the victims with all the force of their frustrations.

The Salem tragedy, which is about to begin in these pages, developed from a paradox. It is a paradox in whose grip we still live, and there is no prospect yet that we will discover its resolution. Simply, it was this: for good purposes, even high purposes, the people of Salem developed a theocracy, a combine of state and religious power whose function was to keep the community together, and to prevent any kind of disunity that might open it to destruction by material or ideological enemies. It was forged for a necessary purpose and accomplished that purpose. But all organization is and must be grounded on the idea of exclusion and prohibition, just as two objects cannot occupy the same space. Evidently the time came in New England when the repressions of order were heavier than seemed warranted by the dangers against which the order was organized. The witch-hunt was a perverse manifestation of the panic which set in among all classes when the balance began to turn toward greater individual freedom.

When one rises above the individual villainy displayed, one can only pity them all, just as we shall be pitied someday. It is still impossible for man to organize his social life without repressions, and the balance has yet to be struck between order and freedom.

The witch-hunt was not, however, a mere repression. It was also, and as importantly, a long overdue opportunity for everyone so inclined to express publicly his guilt and sins, under the cover of accusations against the victims.

It suddenly became possible—and patriotic and holy—for a man to say that Martha Corey had come into his bedroom at night, and that, while his wife was sleeping at his side, Martha laid herself down on his chest and "nearly suffocated him." Of course it was her spirit only, but his satisfaction at confessing himself was no lighter than if it had been Martha herself. One could not ordinarily speak such things in public.

Long-held hatreds of neighbors could now be openly expressed, and vengeance taken, despite the Bible's charitable injunctions. Land-lust which had been expressed before by constant bickering over boundaries and deeds, could now be elevated to the arena of morality; one could cry witch against one's neighbor and feel perfectly justified in the bargain. Old scores could be settled on a plane of heavenly combat between Lucifer and the Lord; suspicions and the envy of the miserable toward the happy could and did burst out in the general revenge.

1　(Reverend Parris *is praying now, and, though we cannot hear his words, a sense of his confusion hangs about him. He mumbles, then seems about to weep; then he weeps, then prays again; but his daughter does not stir on the bed.*

The door opens, and his Negro slave enters. Tituba *is in her forties.* Parris *brought her with him from Barbados,*
10　*where he spent some years as a merchant before entering the ministry. She enters as one does who can no longer bear to be barred from the sight of her beloved, but she is also very frightened because her slave sense has warned her that, as always, trouble in this house eventually lands on her back.*)

Tituba (*already taking a step backward*). My Betty be hearty soon?

20 **Parris.** Out of here!

Tituba (*backing to the door*). My Betty not goin' die . . .

Parris (*scrambling to his feet in a fury*). Out of my sight! (*She is gone.*) Out of my—(*He is overcome with sobs. He clamps his teeth against them and closes the door and leans against it, exhausted.*) Oh, my God! God help me! (*Quaking with fear, mumbling to himself through his sobs, he goes to the bed and gently* 30 *takes* Betty's *hand.*) Betty. Child. Dear child. Will you wake, will you open up your eyes! Betty, little one . . .

(*He is bending to kneel again when his niece,* Abigail Williams, *seventeen, enters—a strikingly beautiful girl, an orphan, with an endless capacity for dissembling. Now she is all worry and apprehension and propriety.*)

40 **Abigail.** Uncle? (*He looks to her.*) Susanna Walcott's here from Doctor Griggs.

Parris. Oh? Let her come, let her come.

Abigail (*leaning out the door to call to* Susanna, *who is down the hall a few steps*). Come in, Susanna. (Susanna Walcott, *a little younger than* Abigail, *a nervous, hurried girl, enters.*)

Parris (*eagerly*). What does the doctor 50 say, child?

Susanna (*craning around* Parris *to get a look at* Betty). He bid me come and tell you, reverend sir, that he cannot discover no medicine for it in his books.

Parris. Then he must search on.

Susanna. Aye, sir, he have been searchin' his books since he left you, sir. But he bid me tell you, that you might look to unnatural things for the cause 60 of it.

Parris (*his eyes going wide*). No—no. There be no unnatural cause here. Tell him I have sent for Reverend Hale of Beverly, and Mr. Hale will surely confirm that. Let him look to medicine and put out all thought of unnatural causes here. There be none.

Susanna. Aye, sir. He bid me tell you. (*She turns to go.*)

70 **Abigail.** Speak nothin' of it in the village, Susanna.

Parris. Go directly home and speak nothing of unnatural causes.

Susanna. Aye, sir. I pray for her. (*She goes out.*)

Abigail. Uncle, the rumor of witchcraft is all about; I think you'd best go down and deny it yourself. The parlor's packed with people, sir. I'll sit with her.

80 **Parris** (*pressed, turns on her*). And what shall I say to them? That my daughter and my niece I discovered dancing like heathen in the forest?

Abigail. Uncle, we did dance; let you tell them I confessed it—and I'll be whipped if I must be. But they're speakin' of witchcraft. Betty's not witched.

Parris. Abigail, I cannot go before the congregation when I know you have not 90 opened with me. What did you do with her in the forest?

Abigail. We did dance, uncle, and when you leaped out of the bush so suddenly, Betty was frightened and then she fainted. And there's the whole of it.

Parris. Child. Sit you down.

Abigail (*quavering, as she sits*). I would never hurt Betty. I love her dearly.

Parris. Now look you, child, your 100 punishment will come in its time. But if you trafficked with[5] spirits in the forest I must know it now, for surely my enemies will, and they will ruin me with it.

Abigail. But we never conjured spirits.

Parris. Then why can she not move herself since midnight? This child is desperate! (Abigail *lowers her eyes.*) It must come out—my enemies will bring
110 it out. Let me know what you done there. Abigail, do you understand that I have many enemies?

Abigail. I have heard of it, uncle.

Parris. There is a faction that is sworn to drive me from my pulpit. Do you understand that?

Abigail. I think so, sir.

Parris. Now then, in the midst of such disruption, my own household is
120 discovered to be the very center of some obscene practice. Abominations are done in the forest—

Abigail. It were sport, uncle!

Parris (*pointing at* Betty). You call this sport? (*She lowers her eyes. He pleads.*) Abigail, if you know something that may help the doctor, for God's sake tell it to me. (*She is silent.*) I saw Tituba waving her arms over the fire when I
130 came on you. Why was she doing that? And I heard a screeching and gibberish coming from her mouth. She were swaying like a dumb beast over that fire!

Abigail. She always sings her Barbados songs, and we dance.

Parris. I cannot blink what I saw, Abigail, for my enemies will not blink it. I saw a dress lying on the grass.

Abigail (*innocently*). A dress?

140 **Parris** (*It is very hard to say*). Aye, a dress. And I thought I saw—someone naked running through the trees!

Abigail (*in terror*). No one was naked! You mistake yourself, uncle!

Parris (*with anger*). I saw it! (*He moves from her. Then, resolved*) Now tell me

---

[5] **trafficked with:** met with.

true, Abigail. And I pray you feel the weight of truth upon you, for now my ministry's at stake, my ministry and perhaps your cousin's life. Whatever abomination you have done, give me all of it now, for I dare not be taken unaware when I go before them down there.

Abigail. There is nothin' more. I swear it, uncle.

Parris (*studies her, then nods, half convinced*). Abigail, I have fought here three long years to bend these stiff-necked people to me, and now, just now when some good respect is rising for me in the parish, you compromise my very character. I have given you a home, child, I have put clothes upon your back—now give me upright answer. Your name in the town—it is entirely white, is it not?

Abigail (*with an edge of resentment*). Why, I am sure it is, sir. There be no blush about my name.[6]

Parris (*to the point*). Abigail, is there any other cause than you have told me, for your being discharged from Goody[7] Proctor's service? I have heard it said, and I tell you as I heard it, that she comes so rarely to the church this year for she will not sit so close to something soiled. What signified that remark?

Abigail. She hates me, uncle, she must, for I would not be her slave. It's a bitter woman, a lying, cold, sniveling woman, and I will not work for such a woman!

Parris. She may be. And yet it has troubled me that you are now seven month out of their house, and in all this time no other family has ever called for your service.

Abigail. They want slaves, not such as I. Let them send to Barbados for that. I will not black my face for any of them! (*with ill-concealed resentment at him*) Do you begrudge my bed, uncle?

Parris. No—no.

Abigail (*in a temper*). My name is good in the village! I will not have it said my name is soiled! Goody Proctor is a gossiping liar!

(*Enter Mrs. Ann Putnam. She is a twisted soul of forty-five, a death-ridden woman, haunted by dreams.*)

Parris (*as soon as the door begins to open*). No—no, I cannot have anyone. (*He sees her, and a certain deference springs into him, although his worry remains.*) Why, Goody Putnam, come in.

Mrs. Putnam (*full of breath, shiny-eyed*). It is a marvel. It is surely a stroke of hell upon you.

Parris. No, Goody Putnam, it is—

Mrs. Putnam (*glancing at* Betty). How high did she fly, how high?

Parris. No, no, she never flew—

Mrs. Putnam (*very pleased with it*). Why, it's sure she did. Mr. Collins saw her goin' over Ingersoll's barn, and come down light as bird, he says!

Parris. Now, look you, Goody Putnam, she never— (*Enter Thomas Putnam, a well-to-do, hard-handed landowner, near fifty.*) Oh, good morning, Mr. Putnam.

Putnam. It is a providence the thing is out now! It is a providence. (*He goes directly to the bed.*)

Parris. What's out, sir, what's—?

(Mrs. Putnam *goes to the bed.*)

---

[6] **There be . . . my name:** There is nothing wrong with my reputation.

[7] **Goody:** short for *Goodwife*, the Puritan equivalent of *Mrs.*

Putnam (*looking down at* Betty). Why, *her eyes* is closed! Look you, Ann.

Mrs. Putnam. Why, that's strange. (*to* Parris) Ours is open.

Parris (*shocked*). Your Ruth is sick?

Mrs. Putnam (*with vicious certainty*). I'd not call it sick; the Devil's touch is heavier than sick. It's death, y'know, it's death drivin' into them, forked and hoofed.

Parris. Oh, pray not! Why, how does Ruth ail?

Mrs. Putnam. She ails as she must—she never waked this morning, but her eyes open and she walks, and hears naught, sees naught, and cannot eat. Her soul is taken, surely.

(Parris *is struck*.)

Putnam (*as though for further details*). They say you've sent for Reverend Hale of Beverly?

Parris (*with dwindling conviction now*). A precaution only. He has much experience in all demonic arts, and I—

Mrs. Putnam. He has indeed; and found a witch in Beverly last year, and let you remember that.

Parris. Now, Goody Ann, they only thought that were a witch, and I am certain there be no element of witchcraft here.

Putnam. No witchcraft! Now look you, Mr. Parris—

Parris. Thomas, Thomas, I pray you, leap not to witchcraft. I know that you—you least of all, Thomas, would ever wish so disastrous a charge laid upon me. We cannot leap to witchcraft. They will howl me out of Salem for such corruption in my house.

A word about Thomas Putnam. He was a man with many grievances, at least one of which appears justified. Some time before, his wife's brother-in-law, James Bayley, had been turned down as minister of Salem. Bayley had all the qualifications, and a two-thirds vote into the bargain, but a faction stopped his acceptance, for reasons that are not clear.

Thomas Putnam was the eldest son of the richest man in the village. He had fought the Indians at Narragansett,[8] and was deeply interested in parish affairs. He undoubtedly felt it poor payment that the village should so blatantly disregard his candidate for one of its more important offices, especially since he regarded himself as the intellectual superior of most of the people around him.

His vindictive nature was demonstrated long before the witchcraft began. Another former Salem minister, George Burroughs, had had to borrow money to pay for his wife's funeral, and, since the parish was remiss in his salary, he was soon bankrupt. Thomas and his brother John had Burroughs jailed for debts the man did not owe. The incident is important only in that Burroughs succeeded in becoming minister where Bayley, Thomas Putnam's brother-in-law, had been rejected; the motif of resentment is clear here. Thomas Putnam felt that his own name and the honor of his family had been smirched by the village, and he meant to right matters however he could.

Another reason to believe him a deeply embittered man was his attempt to break his father's will, which left a disproportionate amount to a

---

[8] **fought the Indians at Narragansett:** The Puritans fought a series of battles against the Narragansett Indians over territory that both groups had settled on.

stepbrother. As with every other public cause in which he tried to force his way, he failed in this.

So it is not surprising to find that so many accusations against people are in the handwriting of Thomas Putnam, or that his name is so often found as a witness corroborating the supernatural testimony, or that his daughter led the crying-out at the most opportune junctures of the trials, especially when—But we'll speak of that when we come to it.

Putnam (*At the moment he is intent upon getting* Parris, *for whom he has only contempt, to move toward the abyss*).

270 Mr. Parris, I have taken your part in all contention here, and I would continue; but I cannot if you hold back in this. There are hurtful, vengeful spirits layin' hands on these children.

Parris. But, Thomas, you cannot—

Putnam. Ann! Tell Mr. Parris what you have done.

Mrs. Putnam. Reverend Parris, I have laid seven babies unbaptized in the
280 earth. Believe me, sir, you never saw more hearty babies born. And yet, each would wither in my arms the very night of their birth. I have spoke nothin', but my heart has clamored intimations.[9] And now, this year, my Ruth, my only—I see her turning strange. A secret child she has become this year, and shrivels like a sucking mouth were pullin' on her life too. And so I thought
290 to send her to your Tituba—

Parris. To Tituba! What may Tituba—?

Mrs. Putnam. Tituba knows how to speak to the dead, Mr. Parris.

---
[9] **clamored intimations** (klăm´ərd ĭn´tə-mā´shənz): nagging suspicions.

Parris. Goody Ann, it is a formidable sin to conjure up the dead!

Mrs. Putnam. I take it on my soul, but who else may surely tell us what person murdered my babies?

Parris (*horrified*). Woman!

300 **Mrs. Putnam.** They were murdered, Mr. Parris! And mark this proof! Mark it! Last night my Ruth were ever so close to their little spirits; I know it, sir. For how else is she struck dumb now except some power of darkness would stop her mouth? It is a marvelous sign, Mr. Parris!

Putnam. Don't you understand it, sir? There is a murdering witch among
310 us, bound to keep herself in the dark. (Parris *turns to* Betty, *a frantic terror rising in him.*) Let your enemies make of it what they will, you cannot blink it more.

Parris (*to* Abigail). Then you were conjuring spirits last night.

Abigail (*whispering*). Not I, sir—Tituba and Ruth.

Parris (*turns now, with new fear, and*
320 *goes to* Betty, *looks down at her, and then, gazing off*). Oh, Abigail, what proper payment for my charity! Now I am undone.

Putnam. You are not undone! Let you take hold here. Wait for no one to charge you—declare it yourself. You have discovered witchcraft—

Parris. In my house? In my house, Thomas? They will topple me with this!
330 They will make of it a—

(*Enter* Mercy Lewis, *the Putnams' servant, a fat, sly, merciless girl of eighteen.*)

Mercy. Your pardons. I only thought to see how Betty is.

Putnam. Why aren't you home? Who's with Ruth?

Mercy. Her grandma come. She's improved a little, I think—she give a powerful sneeze before.

Mrs. Putnam. Ah, there's a sign of life!

Mercy. I'd fear no more, Goody Putnam. It were a grand sneeze; another like it will shake her wits together, I'm sure. (*She goes to the bed to look.*)

Parris. Will you leave me now, Thomas? I would pray a while alone.

Abigail. Uncle, you've prayed since midnight. Why do you not go down and—

Parris. No—no. (*to* Putnam) I have no answer for that crowd. I'll wait till Mr. Hale arrives. (*to get* Mrs. Putnam *to leave*) If you will, Goody Ann . . .

Putnam. Now look you, sir. Let you strike out against the Devil, and the village will bless you for it! Come down, speak to them—pray with them. They're thirsting for your word, Mister! Surely you'll pray with them.

Parris (*swayed*). I'll lead them in a psalm, but let you say nothing of witchcraft yet. I will not discuss it. The cause is yet unknown. I have had enough contention since I came; I want no more.

Mrs. Putnam. Mercy, you go home to Ruth, d'y'hear?

Mercy. Aye, mum.

(Mrs. Putnam *goes out.*)

Parris (*to* Abigail). If she starts for the window, cry for me at once.

Abigail. I will, uncle.

Parris (*to* Putnam). There is a terrible power in her arms today. (*He goes out with* Putnam.)

Abigail (*with hushed trepidation*). How is Ruth sick?

Mercy. It's weirdish, I know not—she seems to walk like a dead one since last night.

Abigail (*turns at once and goes to* Betty, *and now, with fear in her voice*). Betty? (Betty *doesn't move. She shakes her.*) Now stop this! Betty! Sit up now!

(Betty *doesn't stir.* Mercy *comes over.*)

Mercy. Have you tried beatin' her? I gave Ruth a good one and it waked her for a minute. Here, let me have her.

Abigail (*holding* Mercy *back*). No, he'll be comin' up. Listen, now; if they be questioning us, tell them we danced—I told him as much already.

Mercy. Aye. And what more?

Abigail. He knows Tituba conjured Ruth's sisters to come out of the grave.

Mercy. And what more?

Abigail. He saw you naked.

Mercy (*clapping her hands together with a frightened laugh*). Oh, Jesus!

(*Enter* Mary Warren, *breathless. She is seventeen, a subservient, naive, lonely girl.*)

Mary Warren. What'll we do? The village is out! I just come from the farm; the whole country's talkin' witchcraft! They'll be callin' us witches, Abby!

Mercy (*pointing and looking at* Mary Warren). She means to tell, I know it.

Mary Warren. Abby, we've got to tell. Witchery's a hangin' error, a hangin' like they done in Boston two year ago! We must tell the truth, Abby! You'll only be whipped for dancin', and the other things!

Abigail. Oh, *we'll* be whipped!

Mary Warren. I never done none of it, Abby. I only looked!

Mercy (*moving menacingly toward* Mary). Oh, you're a great one for lookin', aren't you, Mary Warren? What a grand peeping courage you have!

(Betty, *on the bed, whimpers.* Abigail *turns to her at once.*)

Abigail. Betty? (*She goes to* Betty.) Now, Betty, dear, wake up now. It's Abigail. (*She sits* Betty *up and furiously shakes her.*) I'll beat you, Betty! (Betty *whimpers.*) My, you seem improving. I talked to your papa and I told him everything. So there's nothing to—

Betty (*darts off the bed, frightened of* Abigail, *and flattens herself against the wall*). I want my mama!

Abigail (*with alarm, as she cautiously approaches* Betty). What ails you, Betty? Your mama's dead and buried.

Betty. I'll fly to Mama. Let me fly! (*She raises her arms as though to fly, and streaks for the window, gets one leg out.*)

Abigail (*pulling her away from the window*). I told him everything; he knows now, he knows everything we—

Betty. You drank blood, Abby! You didn't tell him that!

Abigail. Betty, you never say that again! You will never—

Betty. You did, you did! You drank a charm to kill John Proctor's wife! You drank a charm to kill Goody Proctor!

Abigail (*smashes her across the face*). Shut it! Now shut it!

Betty (*collapsing on the bed*). Mama, Mama! (*She dissolves into sobs.*)

Abigail. Now look you. All of you. We danced. And Tituba conjured Ruth Putnam's dead sisters. And that is all. And mark this. Let either of you breathe a word, or the edge of a word, about the other things, and I will come to you in the black of some terrible night and I will bring a pointy reckoning that will shudder you.[10] And you know I can do it; I saw Indians smash my dear parents' heads on the pillow next to mine, and I have seen some reddish work done at night, and I can make you wish you had never seen the sun go down! (*She goes to* Betty *and roughly sits her up.*) Now, you—sit up and stop this!

(*But* Betty *collapses in her hands and lies inert on the bed.*)

Mary Warren (*with hysterical fright*). What's got her? (Abigail *stares in fright at* Betty.) Abby, she's going to die! It's a sin to conjure, and we—

Abigail (*starting for Mary*). I say shut it, Mary Warren! (*Enter* John Proctor. *On seeing him,* Mary Warren *leaps in fright.*)

Proctor was a farmer in his middle thirties. He need not have been a partisan of any faction in the town, but there is evidence to suggest that he had a sharp and biting way with hypocrites. He was the kind of man—powerful of body, even-tempered, and not easily led—who cannot refuse support to partisans without drawing their deepest resentment. In Proctor's presence a fool felt his foolishness instantly—and a Proctor is always marked for calumny[11] therefore.

But as we shall see, the steady manner he displays does not spring from an untroubled soul. He is a sinner, a sinner not only against the moral fashion of the time, but against his own vision of decent conduct. These

---

[10] **bring . . . shudder you:** inflict a terrifying punishment on you.

[11] **marked for calumny** (kăl′əm-nē): singled out to have lies told about him.

people had no ritual for the washing away of sins. It is another trait we inherited from them, and it has helped to discipline us as well as to breed hypocrisy among us. Proctor, respected and even feared in Salem, has come to regard himself as a kind of fraud. But no hint of this has yet appeared on the surface, and as he enters from the crowded parlor below it is a man in his prime we see, with a quiet confidence and an unexpressed, hidden force. Mary Warren, his servant, can barely speak for embarrassment and fear.

480 **Mary Warren.** Oh! I'm just going home, Mr. Proctor.

Proctor. Be you foolish, Mary Warren? Be you deaf? I forbid you leave the house, did I not? Why shall I pay you? I am looking for you more often than my cows!

Mary Warren. I only come to see the great doings in the world.

Proctor. I'll show you a great doin' on
490 your arse one of these days. Now get you home; my wife is waitin' with your work! (*Trying to retain a shred of dignity, she goes slowly out.*)

Mercy Lewis (*both afraid of him and strangely titillated*). I'd best be off. I have my Ruth to watch. Good morning, Mr. Proctor.

(Mercy *sidles out. Since* Proctor's *entrance,* Abigail *has stood as though on*
500 *tiptoe, absorbing his presence, wide-eyed. He glances at her, then goes to* Betty *on the bed.*)

Abigail. Gah! I'd almost forgot how strong you are, John Proctor!

Proctor (*looking at* Abigail *now, the faintest suggestion of a knowing smile on his face*). What's this mischief here?

Abigail (*with a nervous laugh*). Oh, she's only gone silly somehow.

510 **Proctor.** The road past my house is a pilgrimage to Salem all morning. The town's mumbling witchcraft.

Abigail. Oh, posh! (*Winningly she comes a little closer, with a confidential, wicked air.*) We were dancin' in the woods last night, and my uncle leaped in on us. She took fright, is all.

Proctor (*his smile widening*). Ah, you're wicked yet, aren't y'! (*A trill of expectant*
520 *laughter escapes her, and she dares come closer, feverishly looking into his eyes.*) You'll be clapped in the stocks before you're twenty.

(*He takes a step to go, and she springs into his path.*)

Abigail. Give me a word, John. A soft word. (*Her concentrated desire destroys his smile.*)

Proctor. No, no, Abby. That's done with.

530 **Abigail** (*tauntingly*). You come five mile to see a silly girl fly? I know you better.

Proctor (*setting her firmly out of his path*). I come to see what mischief your uncle's brewin' now. (*with final emphasis*) Put it out of mind, Abby.

Abigail (*grasping his hand before he can release her*). John—I am waitin' for you every night.

Proctor. Abby, I never give you hope to
540 wait for me.

Abigail (*now beginning to anger—she can't believe it*). I have something better than hope, I think!

Proctor. Abby, you'll put it out of mind. I'll not be comin' for you more.

Abigail. You're surely sportin' with me.

Proctor. You know me better.

Abigail. I know how you clutched my back behind your house and sweated like a stallion whenever I come near! Or did I dream that? It's she put me out, you cannot pretend it were you. I saw your face when she put me out, and you loved me then and you do now!

Proctor. Abby, that's a wild thing to say—

Abigail. A wild thing may say wild things. But not so wild, I think. I have seen you since she put me out; I have seen you nights.

Proctor. I have hardly stepped off my farm this sevenmonth.

Abigail. I have a sense for heat, John, and yours has drawn me to my window, and I have seen you looking up, burning in your loneliness. Do you tell me you've never looked up at my window?

Proctor. I may have looked up.

Abigail (*now softening*). And you must. You are no wintry man. I *know* you, John. I know you. (*She is weeping.*) I cannot sleep for dreamin'; I cannot dream but I wake and walk about the house as though I'd find you comin' through some door. (*She clutches him desperately*).

Proctor (*gently pressing her from him, with great sympathy but firmly*). Child—

Abigail (*with a flash of anger*). How do you call me child!

Proctor. Abby, I may think of you softly from time to time. But I will cut off my hand before I'll ever reach for you again. Wipe it out of mind. We never touched, Abby.

Abigail. Aye, but we did.

Proctor. Aye, but we did not.

Abigail (*with a bitter anger*). Oh, I marvel how such a strong man may let such a sickly wife be—

Proctor (*angered—at himself as well*). You'll speak nothin' of Elizabeth!

Abigail. She is blackening my name in the village! She is telling lies about me! She is a cold, sniveling woman, and you bend to her! Let her turn you like a—

Proctor (*shaking her*). Do you look for whippin'?

(*A psalm is heard being sung below.*)

600 **Abigail** (*in tears*). I look for John Proctor that took me from my sleep and put knowledge in my heart! I never knew what pretense Salem was, I never knew the lying lessons I was taught by all these Christian women and their covenanted[12] men! And now you bid me tear the light out of my eyes? I will not, I cannot! You loved me, John Proctor, and whatever sin it is, you love me yet!
610 (*He turns abruptly to go out. She rushes to him.*) John, pity me, pity me!

(*The words "going up to Jesus" are heard in the psalm, and Betty claps her ears suddenly and whines loudly.*)

Abigail. Betty? (*She hurries to Betty, who is now sitting up and screaming. Proctor goes to Betty as Abigail is trying to pull her hands down, calling "Betty!"*)

Proctor (*growing unnerved*). What's
620 she doing? Girl, what ails you? Stop that wailing!

(*The singing has stopped in the midst of this, and now Parris rushes in.*)

Parris. What happened? What are you doing to her? Betty! (*He rushes to the bed, crying, "Betty, Betty!" Mrs. Putnam enters, feverish with curiosity, and with her Thomas Putnam and Mercy Lewis. Parris, at the bed, keeps lightly slapping*

---

[12] **covenanted** (kŭv´ə-nən-tĭd): In Puritan religious practice, the men of a congregation would make an agreement, or covenant, to govern the community and abide by its beliefs and practices.

---

630 Betty's *face, while she moans and tries to get up.*)

Abigail. She heard you singin' and suddenly she's up and screamin'.

Mrs. Putnam. The psalm! The psalm! She cannot bear to hear the Lord's name!

Parris. No. God forbid. Mercy, run to the doctor! Tell him what's happened here! (Mercy Lewis *rushes out.*)

640 **Mrs. Putnam.** Mark it for a sign, mark it!

(Rebecca Nurse, *seventy-two, enters. She is white-haired, leaning upon her walking-stick.*)

Putnam (*pointing at the whimpering* Betty). That is a notorious sign of witchcraft afoot, Goody Nurse, a prodigious sign!

Mrs. Putnam. My mother told me that!
650 When they cannot bear to hear the name of—

Parris (*trembling*). Rebecca, Rebecca, go to her, we're lost. She suddenly cannot bear to hear the Lord's—

(Giles Corey, *eighty-three, enters. He is knotted with muscle, canny, inquisitive, and still powerful.*)

Rebecca. There is hard sickness here, Giles Corey, so please to keep the quiet.

660 **Giles.** I've not said a word. No one here can testify I've said a word. Is she going to fly again? I hear she flies.

Putnam. Man, be quiet now!

(*Everything is quiet. Rebecca walks across the room to the bed. Gentleness exudes from her. Betty is quietly whimpering, eyes shut. Rebecca simply stands over the child, who gradually quiets.*)

And while they are so absorbed, we may put a word in for Rebecca. Rebecca was the wife of Francis Nurse, who, from all accounts, was one of those men for whom both sides of the argument had to have respect. He was called upon to arbitrate disputes as though he were an unofficial judge, and Rebecca also enjoyed the high opinion most people had for him. By the time of the delusion,[13] they had three hundred acres, and their children were settled in separate homesteads within the same estate. However, Francis had originally rented the land, and one theory has it that, as he gradually paid for it and raised his social status, there were those who resented his rise.

Another suggestion to explain the systematic campaign against Rebecca, and inferentially against Francis, is the land war he fought with his neighbors, one of whom was a Putnam. This squabble grew to the proportions of a battle in the woods between partisans of both sides, and it is said to have lasted for two days. As for Rebecca herself, the general opinion of her character was so high that to explain how anyone dared cry her out for a witch—and more, how adults could bring themselves to lay hands on her—we must look to the fields and boundaries of that time.

As we have seen, Thomas Putnam's man for the Salem ministry was Bayley. The Nurse clan had been in the faction that prevented Bayley's taking office. In addition, certain families allied to the Nurses by blood or friendship, and whose farms were contiguous with the Nurse farm or close to it, combined to break away from the Salem town authority and set up Topsfield, a new and independent entity whose existence was resented by old Salemites.

That the guiding hand behind the outcry was Putnam's is indicated by the fact that, as soon as it began, this Topsfield-Nurse faction absented themselves from church in protest and disbelief. It was Edward and Jonathan Putnam who signed the first complaint against Rebecca; and Thomas Putnam's little daughter was the one who fell into a fit at the hearing and pointed to Rebecca as her attacker. To top it all, Mrs. Putnam—who is now staring at the bewitched child on the bed—soon accused Rebecca's spirit of "tempting her to iniquity," a charge that had more truth in it than Mrs. Putnam could know.

670 **Mrs. Putnam** (*astonished*). What have you done?

(Rebecca, *in thought, now leaves the bedside and sits.*)

Parris (*wondrous and relieved*). What do you make of it, Rebecca?

Putnam (*eagerly*). Goody Nurse, will you go to my Ruth and see if you can wake her?

Rebecca (*sitting*). I think she'll wake
680 in time. Pray calm yourselves. I have eleven children, and I am twenty-six times a grandma, and I have seen them all through their silly seasons, and when it come on them they will run the Devil bowlegged keeping up with their mischief. I think she'll wake when she tires of it. A child's spirit is like a child, you can never catch it by running after it; you must stand still, and, for love, it
690 will soon itself come back.

Proctor. Aye, that's the truth of it, Rebecca.

---

[13] **the time of the delusion:** the era of the witchcraft accusations and trials.

Mrs. Putnam. This is no silly season, Rebecca. My Ruth is bewildered, Rebecca; she cannot eat.

Rebecca. Perhaps she is not hungered yet. (*to* Parris) I hope you are not decided to go in search of loose spirits, Mr. Parris. I've heard promise of that outside.

Parris. A wide opinion's running in the parish that the Devil may be among us, and I would satisfy them that they are wrong.

Proctor. Then let you come out and call them wrong. Did you consult the wardens[14] before you called this minister to look for devils?

Parris. He is not coming to look for devils!

Proctor. Then what's he coming for?

Putnam. There be children dyin' in the village, Mister!

Proctor. I seen none dyin'. This society will not be a bag to swing around your head, Mr. Putnam. (*to* Parris) Did you call a meeting before you—?

Putnam. I am sick of meetings; cannot the man turn his head without he have a meeting?

Proctor. He may turn his head, but not to Hell!

Rebecca. Pray, John, be calm. (*Pause. He defers to her.*) Mr. Parris, I think you'd best send Reverend Hale back as soon as he come. This will set us all to arguin' again in the society, and we thought to have peace this year. I think we ought rely on the doctor now, and good prayer.

Mrs. Putnam. Rebecca, the doctor's baffled!

Rebecca. If so he is, then let us go to God for the cause of it. There is prodigious danger in the seeking of loose spirits. I fear it, I fear it. Let us rather blame ourselves and—

Putnam. How may we blame ourselves? I am one of nine sons; the Putnam seed have peopled this province. And yet I have but one child left of eight—and now she shrivels!

Rebecca. I cannot fathom that.

Mrs. Putnam (*with a growing edge of sarcasm*). But I must! You think it God's work you should never lose a child, nor grandchild either, and I bury all but one? There are wheels within wheels in this village, and fires within fires!

Putnam (*to* Parris). When Reverend Hale comes, you will proceed to look for signs of witchcraft here.

Proctor (*to* Putnam). You cannot command Mr. Parris. We vote by name in this society, not by acreage.

Putnam. I never heard you worried so on this society, Mr. Proctor. I do not think I saw you at Sabbath meeting since snow flew.

Proctor. I have trouble enough without I come five mile to hear him preach only hellfire and bloody damnation. Take it to heart, Mr. Parris. There are many others who stay away from church these days because you hardly ever mention God any more.

Parris (*now aroused*). Why, that's a drastic charge!

Rebecca. It's somewhat true; there are many that quail to bring their children—

Parris. I do not preach for children, Rebecca. It is not the children who are unmindful of their obligations toward this ministry.

---

[14]**wardens:** officers appointed to keep order.

Rebecca. Are there really those unmindful?

Parris. I should say the better half of Salem village—

780 **Putnam.** And more than that!

Parris. Where is my wood? My contract provides I be supplied with all my firewood. I am waiting since November for a stick, and even in November I had to show my frostbitten hands like some London beggar!

Giles. You are allowed six pound a year to buy your wood, Mr. Parris.

Parris. I regard that six pound as part
790 of my salary. I am paid little enough without I spend six pound on firewood.

Proctor. Sixty, plus six for firewood—

Parris. The salary is sixty-six pound, Mr. Proctor! I am not some preaching farmer with a book under my arm; I am a graduate of Harvard College.

Giles. Aye, and well instructed in arithmetic!

Parris. Mr. Corey, you will look far for
800 a man of my kind at sixty pound a year! I am not used to this poverty; I left a thrifty business in the Barbados to serve the Lord. I do not fathom it, why am I persecuted here? I cannot offer one proposition but there be a howling riot of argument. I have often wondered if the Devil be in it somewhere; I cannot understand you people otherwise.

Proctor. Mr. Parris, you are the first
810 minister ever did demand the deed to this house—

Parris. Man! Don't a minister deserve a house to live in?

Proctor. To live in, yes. But to ask ownership is like you shall own the meeting house itself; the last meeting I were at you spoke so long on deeds and mortgages I thought it were an auction.

Parris. I want a mark of confidence,
820 is all! I am your third preacher in seven years. I do not wish to be put out like the cat whenever some majority feels the whim. You people seem not to comprehend that a minister is the Lord's man in the parish; a minister is not to be so lightly crossed and contradicted—

Putnam. Aye!

Parris. There is either obedience or the
830 church will burn like Hell is burning!

Proctor. Can you speak one minute without we land in Hell again? I am sick of Hell!

Parris. It is not for you to say what is good for you to hear!

Proctor. I may speak my heart, I think!

Parris (*in a fury*). What, are we Quakers?[15] We are not Quakers here yet, Mr. Proctor. And you may tell that
840 to your followers!

Proctor. My followers!

Parris (*Now he's out with it*). There is a party in this church. I am not blind; there is a faction and a party.

Proctor. Against you?

Putnam. Against him and all authority!

Proctor. Why, then I must find it and join it.

(*There is shock among the others.*)

850 **Rebecca.** He does not mean that.

Putnam. He confessed it now!

Proctor. I mean it solemnly, Rebecca; I like not the smell of this "authority."

---

[15] **Quakers:** a radical English religious sect— much hated by the Puritans—who often "spoke their heart" during their religious meetings.

Rebecca. No, you cannot break charity[16] with your minister. You are another kind, John. Clasp his hand, make your peace.

Proctor. I have a crop to sow and lumber to drag home. (*He goes angrily to the door and turns to Corey with a smile.*) What say you, Giles, let's find the party. He says there's a party.

Giles. I've changed my opinion of this man, John. Mr. Parris, I beg your pardon. I never thought you had so much iron in you.

Parris (*surprised*). Why, thank you, Giles!

Giles. It suggests to the mind what the trouble be among us all these years. (*to all*) Think on it. Wherefore is everybody suing everybody else? Think on it now, it's a deep thing, and dark as a pit. I have been six time in court this year—

Proctor (*familiarly, with warmth, although he knows he is approaching the edge of Giles' tolerance with this*). Is it the Devil's fault that a man cannot say you good morning without you clap him for defamation?[17] You're old, Giles, and you're not hearin' so well as you did.

Giles (*He cannot be crossed*). John Proctor, I have only last month collected four pound damages for you publicly sayin' I burned the roof off your house, and I—

Proctor (*laughing*). I never said no such thing, but I've paid you for it, so I hope I can call you deaf without charge. Now come along, Giles, and help me drag my lumber home.

Putnam. A moment, Mr. Proctor. What lumber is that you're draggin', if I may ask you?

Proctor. My lumber. From out my forest by the riverside.

Putnam. Why, we are surely gone wild this year. What anarchy is this? That tract is in my bounds, it's in my bounds, Mr. Proctor.

Proctor. In your bounds! (*indicating* Rebecca) I bought that tract from Goody Nurse's husband five months ago.

Putnam. He had no right to sell it. It stands clear in my grandfather's will that all the land between the river and—

Proctor. Your grandfather had a habit of willing land that never belonged to him, if I may say it plain.

Giles. That's God's truth; he nearly willed away my north pasture but he knew I'd break his fingers before he'd set his name to it. Let's get your lumber home, John. I feel a sudden will to work coming on.

Putnam. You load one oak of mine and you'll fight to drag it home!

Giles. Aye, and we'll win too, Putnam— this fool and I. Come on! (*He turns to* Proctor *and starts out.*)

Putnam. I'll have my men on you, Corey! I'll clap a writ on you!

(*Enter* Reverend John Hale *of Beverly.*)

Mr. Hale is nearing forty, a tight-skinned, eager-eyed intellectual. This is a beloved errand for him; on being called here to ascertain witchcraft he felt the pride of the specialist whose unique knowledge has at last been publicly called for. Like almost all men of learning, he spent a good deal of his time pondering the invisible

---

[16] **break charity:** break off; end the relationship.

[17] **clap . . . defamation** (dĕf´ə-mā´shən): imprison him for slander.

world, especially since he had himself encountered a witch in his parish not long before. That woman, however, turned into a mere pest under his searching scrutiny, and the child she had allegedly been afflicting recovered her normal behavior after Hale had given her his kindness and a few days of rest in his own house. However, that experience never raised a doubt in his mind as to the reality of the underworld or the existence of Lucifer's many-faced lieutenants. And his belief is not to his discredit. Better minds than Hale's were—and still are—convinced that there is a society of spirits beyond our ken. One cannot help noting that one of his lines has never yet raised a laugh in any audience that has seen this play; it is his assurance that "We cannot look to superstition in this. The Devil is precise." Evidently we are not quite certain even now whether diabolism is holy and not to be scoffed at. And it is no accident that we should be so bemused.

Like Reverend Hale and the others on this stage, we conceive the Devil as a necessary part of a respectable view of cosmology.[18] Ours is a divided empire in which certain ideas and emotions and actions are of God, and their opposites are of Lucifer. It is as impossible for most men to conceive of a morality without sin as of an earth without "sky." Since 1692 a great but superficial change has wiped out God's beard and the Devil's horns, but the world is still gripped between two diametrically opposed absolutes. The concept of unity, in which positive and negative are attributes of the same force, in which good and evil are relative, ever-changing, and always joined to the same

phenomenon—such a concept is still reserved to the physical sciences and to the few who have grasped the history of ideas. When it is recalled that until the Christian era the underworld was never regarded as a hostile area, that all gods were useful and essentially friendly to man despite occasional lapses; when we see the steady and methodical inculcation into humanity of the idea of man's worthlessness—until redeemed—the necessity of the Devil may become evident as a weapon, a weapon designed and used time and time again in every age to whip men into a surrender to a particular church or church-state.

Our difficulty in believing the— for want of a better word—political inspiration of the Devil is due in great part to the fact that he is called up and damned not only by our social antagonists but by our own side, whatever it may be. The Catholic Church, through its Inquisition,[19] is famous for cultivating Lucifer as the arch-fiend, but the Church's enemies relied no less upon the Old Boy to keep the human mind enthralled. Luther[20] was himself accused of alliance with Hell, and he in turn accused his enemies. To complicate matters further, he believed that he had had contact with the Devil and had argued theology with him. I am not surprised at this, for at my own university a professor of history— a Lutheran, by the way—used to assemble his graduate students, draw the shades, and commune in

---

[18] **cosmology** (kŏz-mŏl´ə-jē): a branch of philosophy dealing with the structure of the universe.

[19] **Inquisition:** a former tribunal in the Roman Catholic Church dedicated to the discovery and punishment of heresy.

[20] **Luther:** Martin Luther (1483–1546), the German theologian who led the Protestant Reformation.

the classroom with Erasmus.[21] He was never, to my knowledge, officially scoffed at for this, the reason being that the university officials, like most of us, are the children of a history which still sucks at the Devil's teats. At this writing, only England has held back before the temptations of contemporary diabolism. In the countries of the Communist ideology, all resistance of any import is linked to the totally malign capitalist succubi,[22] and in America any man who is not reactionary in his views is open to the charge of alliance with the Red hell. Political opposition, thereby, is given an inhumane overlay which then justifies the abrogation of all normally applied customs of civilized intercourse. A political policy is equated with moral right, and opposition to it with diabolical malevolence. Once such an equation is effectively made, society becomes a congerie of plots and counterplots, and the main role of government changes from that of the arbiter to that of the scourge of God.

The results of this process are no different now from what they ever were, except sometimes in the degree of cruelty inflicted, and not always even in that department. Normally the actions and deeds of a man were all that society felt comfortable in judging. The secret intent of an action was left to the ministers, priests, and rabbis to deal with. When diabolism rises, however, actions are the least important manifests of the true nature of a man. The Devil, as Reverend Hale said, is a wily one, and, until an hour before he fell, even God thought him beautiful in Heaven.[23]

The analogy, however, seems to falter when one considers that, while there were no witches then, there are Communists and capitalists now, and in each camp there is certain proof that spies of each side are at work undermining the other. But this is a snobbish objection and not at all warranted by the facts. I have no doubt that people *were* communing with, and even worshiping, the Devil in Salem, and if the whole truth could be known in this case, as it is in others, we should discover a regular and conventionalized propitiation of the dark spirit. One certain evidence of this is the confession of Tituba, the slave of Reverend Parris, and another is the behavior of the children who were known to have indulged in sorceries with her.

There are accounts of similar *klatches* in Europe, where the daughters of the towns would assemble at night and, sometimes with fetishes, sometimes with a selected young man, give themselves to love, with some bastardly results. The Church, sharp-eyed as it must be when gods long dead are brought to life, condemned these orgies as witchcraft and interpreted them, rightly, as a resurgence of the Dionysiac forces[24] it had crushed long before. Sex, sin, and the Devil were early linked, and so they continued to be in Salem, and are today. From all accounts there are no more puritanical mores in the world than those enforced

---

[21]**Erasmus** (ĭ-răz´məs): Desiderius Erasmus (1466?–1536), a Dutch scholar who sought to restore Christian faith by a study of the Scriptures and classical texts.

[22]**succubi** (sŭk´yə-bī): demons that assume female form. Demons that assume male form are called incubi (ĭn´kyə-bī).

[23]**The Devil . . . beautiful in Heaven:** According to Christian belief, Lucifer was God's favorite angel until the angel rebelled and was cast out of Heaven.

[24]**Dionysiac** (dī´ə-nĭs´ē-ăk´) **forces:** forces associated with Dionysus, the Greek god of wine and ecstasy.

by the Communists in Russia, where women's fashions, for instance, are as prudent and all-covering as any American Baptist would desire. The divorce laws lay a tremendous responsibility on the father for the care of his children. Even the laxity of divorce regulations in the early years of the revolution was undoubtedly a revulsion from the nineteenth-century Victorian immobility of marriage and the consequent hypocrisy that developed from it. If for no other reasons, a state so powerful, so jealous of the uniformity of its citizens, cannot long tolerate the atomization of the family. And yet, in American eyes at least, there remains the conviction that the Russian attitude toward women is lascivious. It is the Devil working again, just as he is working within the Slav[25] who is shocked at the very idea of a woman's disrobing herself in a burlesque show. Our opposites are always robed in sexual sin, and it is from this unconscious conviction that demonology gains both its attractive sensuality and its capacity to infuriate and frighten.

Coming into Salem now, Reverend Hale conceives of himself much as a young doctor on his first call. His painfully acquired armory of symptoms, catchwords, and diagnostic procedures are now to be put to use at last. The road from Beverly is unusually busy this morning, and he has passed a hundred rumors that make him smile at the ignorance of the yeomanry in this most precise science. He feels himself allied with the best minds of Europe— kings, philosophers, scientists, and ecclesiasts of all churches. His goal is

light, goodness and its preservation, and he knows the exaltation of the blessed whose intelligence, sharpened by minute examinations of enormous tracts, is finally called upon to face what may be a bloody fight with the Fiend himself.

(*He appears loaded down with half a dozen heavy books.*)

Hale. Pray you, someone take these!

Parris (*delighted*). Mr. Hale! Oh! it's 930 good to see you again! (*taking some books*) My, they're heavy!

Hale (*setting down his books*). They must be; they are weighted with authority.

Parris (*a little scared*). Well, you do come prepared!

Hale. We shall need hard study if it comes to tracking down the Old Boy. (*noticing* Rebecca) You cannot be Rebecca Nurse?

940 **Rebecca.** I am, sir. Do you know me?

Hale. It's strange how I knew you, but I suppose you look as such a good soul should. We have all heard of your great charities in Beverly.

Parris. Do you know this gentleman? Mr. Thomas Putnam. And his good wife Ann.

Hale. Putnam! I had not expected such distinguished company, sir.

950 **Putnam** (*pleased*). It does not seem to help us today, Mr. Hale. We look to you to come to our house and save our child.

Hale. Your child ails too?

Mrs. Putnam. Her soul, her soul seems flown away. She sleeps and yet she walks . . .

Putnam. She cannot eat.

---

[25] **Slav:** a generic reference to Russians and other Slavic-speaking peoples of Eastern Europe who were under the control of the Soviet Union.

Hale. Cannot eat! (*Thinks on it. Then, to* Proctor *and* Giles Corey.) Do you men have afflicted children?

Parris. No, no, these are farmers. John Proctor—

Giles Corey. He don't believe in witches.

Proctor (*to* Hale). I never spoke on witches one way or the other. Will you come, Giles?

Giles. No—no, John, I think not. I have some few queer questions of my own to ask this fellow.

Proctor. I've heard you to be a sensible man, Mr. Hale. I hope you'll leave some of it in Salem.

(Proctor *goes.* Hale *stands embarrassed for an instant.*)

Parris (*quickly*). Will you look at my daughter, sir? (*leads* Hale *to the bed*) She has tried to leap out the window; we discovered her this morning on the highroad, waving her arms as though she'd fly.

Hale (*narrowing his eyes*). Tries to fly.

Putnam. She cannot bear to hear the Lord's name, Mr. Hale; that's a sure sign of witchcraft afloat.

Hale (*holding up his hands*). No, no. Now let me instruct you. We cannot look to superstition in this. The Devil is precise; the marks of his presence are definite as stone, and I must tell you all that I shall not proceed unless you are prepared to believe me if I should find no bruise of hell upon her.

Parris. It is agreed, sir—it is agreed—we will abide by your judgment.

Hale. Good then. (*He goes to the bed, looks down at* Betty. *To* Parris.) Now, sir, what were your first warning of this strangeness?

Parris. Why, sir—I discovered her— (*indicating* Abigail) and my niece and ten or twelve of the other girls, dancing in the forest last night.

Hale (*surprised*). You permit dancing?

Parris. No, no, it were secret—

Mrs. Putnam (*unable to wait*). Mr. Parris's slave has knowledge of conjurin', sir.

Parris (*to* Mrs. Putnam). We cannot be sure of that, Goody Ann—

Mrs. Putnam (*frightened, very softly*). I know it, sir. I sent my child—she should learn from Tituba who murdered her sisters.

Rebecca (*horrified*). Goody Ann! You sent a child to conjure up the dead?

Mrs. Putnam. Let God blame me, not you, not you, Rebecca! I'll not have you judging me any more! (*to* Hale) Is it a natural work to lose seven children before they live a day?

Parris. Sssh!

(Rebecca, *with great pain, turns her face away. There is a pause.*)

Hale. Seven dead in childbirth.

Mrs. Putnam (*softly*). Aye. (*Her voice breaks; she looks up at him. Silence.* Hale *is impressed.* Parris *looks to him. He goes to his books, opens one, turns pages, then reads. All wait, avidly.*)

Parris (*hushed*). What book is that?

Mrs. Putnam. What's there, sir?

Hale (*with a tasty love of intellectual pursuit*). Here is all the invisible world, caught, defined, and calculated. In these books the Devil stands stripped of all his brute disguises. Here are all your familiar spirits—your incubi and succubi; your witches that go by land, by air, and by sea; your wizards of the night and of the day. Have no fear now—we shall find him out if he has come among us, and I mean to crush him utterly if he has shown his face! (*He starts for the bed.*)

Rebecca. Will it hurt the child, sir?

Hale. I cannot tell. If she is truly in the Devil's grip we may have to rip and tear 1050 to get her free.

Rebecca. I think I'll go, then. I am too old for this. (*She rises.*)

Parris (*striving for conviction*). Why, Rebecca, we may open up the boil of all our troubles today!

Rebecca. Let us hope for that. I go to God for you, sir.

Parris (*with trepidation—and resentment*). I hope you do not mean we 1060 go to Satan here! (*slight pause*)

Rebecca. I wish I knew. (*She goes out; they feel resentful of her note of moral superiority.*)

Putnam (*abruptly*). Come, Mr. Hale, let's get on. Sit you here.

Giles. Mr. Hale, I have always wanted to ask a learned man—what signifies the readin' of strange books?

Hale. What books?

1070 **Giles.** I cannot tell; she hides them.

Hale. Who does this?

Giles. Martha, my wife. I have waked at night many a time and found her in a corner, readin' of a book. Now what do you make of that?

Hale. Why, that's not necessarily—

Giles. It discomfits me! Last night— mark this—I tried and tried and could not say my prayers. And then she close 1080 her book and walks out of the house, and suddenly—mark this—I could pray again!

O ld Giles must be spoken for, if only because his fate was to be so remarkable and so different from that of all the others. He was in his early eighties at this time, and was the most comical hero in the history. No man has ever been blamed for so much. If a cow was missed, the first thought was to look for her around Corey's house; a fire blazing up at night brought suspicion of arson to his door. He didn't give a hoot for public opinion, and only in his last years—after he had married Martha—did he bother much with the church. That she stopped his prayer is very probable, but he forgot to say that he'd only recently learned any prayers and it didn't take much to make him stumble over them. He was a crank and a nuisance, but withal a deeply innocent and brave man. In court once, he was asked if it were true that he had been frightened by the strange behavior of a hog and had then said he knew it to be the Devil in an animal's shape. "What frighted you?" he was asked. He forgot everything but the word "frighted," and instantly replied, "I do not know that I ever spoke that word in my life."

Hale. Ah! The stoppage of prayer—that is strange. I'll speak further on that with you.

Giles. I'm not sayin' she's touched the Devil, now, but I'd admire to know what books she reads and why she hides them. She'll not answer me, y' see.

1090 **Hale.** Aye, we'll discuss it. (*to all*) Now mark me, if the Devil is in her you will witness some frightful wonders in this room, so please to keep your wits about you. Mr. Putnam, stand close in case she flies. Now, Betty, dear, will you sit up? (*Putnam comes in closer, ready-handed. Hale sits Betty up, but she hangs limp in his hands.*) Hmmm. (*He observes her* *carefully. The others watch breathlessly.*)

1100 Can you hear me? I am John Hale, minister of Beverly. I have come to help you, dear. Do you remember my two little girls in Beverly? (*She does not stir in his hands.*)

Parris (*in fright*). How can it be the Devil? Why would he choose my house to strike? We have all manner of licentious people in the village!

Hale. What victory would the Devil
1110 have to win a soul already bad? It is the best the Devil wants, and who is better than the minister?

Giles. That's deep, Mr. Parris, deep, deep!

Parris (*with resolution now*). Betty! Answer Mr. Hale! Betty!

Hale. Does someone afflict you, child? It need not be a woman, mind you, or a man. Perhaps some bird invisible to
1120 others comes to you—perhaps a pig, a mouse, or any beast at all. Is there some figure bids you fly? (*The child remains limp in his hands. In silence he lays her back on the pillow. Now, holding out his hands toward her, he intones.*) In nomine Domini Sabaoth sui filiique ite ad infernos.²⁶ (*She does not stir. He turns to* Abigail, *his eyes narrowing.*) Abigail, what sort of dancing were you doing
1130 with her in the forest?

Abigail. Why—common dancing is all.

Parris. I think I ought to say that I—I saw a kettle in the grass where they were dancing.

Abigail. That were only soup.

Hale. What sort of soup were in this kettle, Abigail?

Abigail. Why, it were beans—and lentils, I think, and—

1140 **Hale.** Mr. Parris, you did not notice, did you, any living thing in the kettle? A mouse, perhaps, a spider, a frog—?

Parris (*fearfully*). I—do believe there were some movement—in the soup.

Abigail. That jumped in, we never put it in!

Hale (*quickly*). What jumped in?

Abigail. Why, a very little frog jumped—

1150 **Parris.** A frog, Abby!

Hale (*grasping* Abigail). Abigail, it may be your cousin is dying. Did you call the Devil last night?

Abigail. I never called him! Tituba, Tituba . . .

Parris (*blanched*). She called the Devil?

Hale. I should like to speak with Tituba.

Parris. Goody Ann, will you bring her up? (Mrs. Putnam *exits.*)

1160 **Hale.** How did she call him?

Abigail. I know not—she spoke Barbados.

Hale. Did you feel any strangeness when she called him? A sudden cold wind, perhaps? A trembling below the ground?

Abigail. I didn't see no Devil! (*shaking* Betty) Betty, wake up. Betty! Betty!

Hale. You cannot evade me, Abigail.
1170 Did your cousin drink any of the brew in that kettle?

Abigail. She never drank it!

Hale. Did you drink it?

Abigail. No, sir!

Hale. Did Tituba ask you to drink it?

Abigail. She tried, but I refused.

---

²⁶**In nomine . . . infernos** *Latin:* "In the name of the Father and Son, get thee back to Hell."

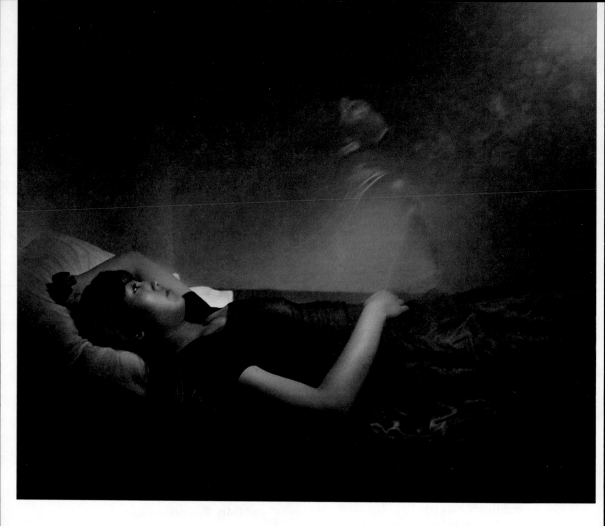

Hale. Why are you concealing? Have you sold yourself to Lucifer?

Abigail. I never sold myself! I'm a good
1180 girl! I'm a proper girl!

(Mrs. Putnam *enters with Tituba, and instantly* Abigail *points at Tituba.*)

Abigail. She made me do it! She made Betty do it!

Tituba (*shocked and angry*). Abby!

Abigail. She makes me drink blood!

Parris. Blood!!

Mrs. Putnam. My baby's blood?

Tituba. No, no, chicken blood. I give
1190 she chicken blood!

Hale. Woman, have you enlisted these children for the Devil?

Tituba. No, no, sir, I don't truck with no Devil!

Hale. Why can she not wake? Are you silencing this child?

Tituba. I love me Betty!

Hale. You have sent your spirit out upon this child, have you not? Are you
1200 gathering souls for the Devil?

Abigail. She sends her spirit on me in church; she makes me laugh at prayer!

Parris. She have often laughed at prayer!

Abigail. She comes to me every night to go and drink blood!

Image Credits: ©SFC/Shutterstock

Tituba. You beg *me* to conjure! She beg *me* make charm—

Abigail. Don't lie! (*to* Hale) She comes to me while I sleep; she's always making me dream corruptions!

Tituba. Why you say that, Abby?

Abigail. Sometimes I wake and find myself standing in the open doorway and not a stitch on my body! I always hear her laughing in my sleep. I hear her singing her Barbados songs and tempting me with—

Tituba. Mister Reverend, I never—

Hale (*resolved now*). Tituba, I want you to wake this child.

Tituba. I have no power on this child, sir.

Hale. You most certainly do, and you will free her from it now! When did you compact with the Devil?

Tituba. I don't compact with no Devil!

Parris. You will confess yourself or I will take you out and whip you to your death, Tituba!

Putnam. This woman must be hanged! She must be taken and hanged!

Tituba (*terrified, falls to her knees*). No, no, don't hang Tituba! I tell him I don't desire to work for him, sir.

Parris. The Devil?

Hale. Then you saw him! (*Tituba weeps.*) Now Tituba, I know that when we bind ourselves to Hell it is very hard to break with it. We are going to help you tear yourself free—

Tituba (*frightened by the coming process*). Mister Reverend, I do believe somebody else be witchin' these children.

Hale. Who?

Tituba. I don't know, sir, but the Devil got him numerous witches.

Hale. Does he! (*It is a clue.*) Tituba, look into my eyes. Come, look into me. (*She raises her eyes to his fearfully.*) You would be a good Christian woman, would you not, Tituba?

Tituba. Aye, sir, a good Christian woman.

Hale. And you love these little children?

Tituba. Oh, yes, sir, I don't desire to hurt little children.

Hale. And you love God, Tituba?

Tituba. I love God with all my bein'.

Hale. Now, in God's holy name—

Tituba. Bless Him. Bless Him. (*She is rocking on her knees, sobbing in terror.*)

Hale. And to His glory—

Tituba. Eternal glory. Bless Him—bless God . . .

Hale. Open yourself, Tituba—open yourself and let God's holy light shine on you.

Tituba. Oh, bless the Lord.

Hale. When the Devil comes to you does he ever come—with another person? (*She stares up into his face.*) Perhaps another person in the village? Someone you know.

Parris. Who came with him?

Putnam. Sarah Good? Did you ever see Sarah Good with him? Or Osburn?

Parris. Was it man or woman came with him?

Tituba. Man or woman. Was—was woman.

Parris. What woman? A woman, you said. What woman?

Tituba. It was black dark, and I—

Parris. You could see him, why could you not see her?

Tituba. Well, they was always talking; they was always runnin' round and carryin' on—

1290 **Parris.** You mean out of Salem? Salem witches?

Tituba. I believe so, yes, sir.

(*Now* Hale *takes her hand. She is surprised.*)

Hale. Tituba. You must have no fear to tell us who they are, do you understand? We will protect you. The Devil can never overcome a minister. You know that, do you not?

1300 **Tituba** (*kisses* Hale's *hand*). Aye, sir, oh, I do.

Hale. You have confessed yourself to witchcraft, and that speaks a wish to come to Heaven's side. And we will bless you, Tituba.

Tituba (*deeply relieved*). Oh, God bless you, Mr. Hale!

Hale (*with rising exaltation*). You are God's instrument put in our hands to 1310 discover the Devil's agents among us. You are selected, Tituba, you are chosen to help us cleanse our village. So speak utterly, Tituba, turn your back on him and face God—face God, Tituba, and God will protect you.

Tituba (*joining with him*). Oh, God, protect Tituba!

Hale (*kindly*). Who came to you with the Devil? Two? Three? Four? How 1320 many?

(*Tituba pants, and begins rocking back and forth again, staring ahead.*)

Tituba. There was four. There was four.

Parris (*pressing in on her*). Who? Who? Their names, their names!

Tituba (*suddenly bursting out*). Oh, how many times he bid me kill you, Mr. Parris!

Parris. Kill me!

1330 **Tituba** (*in a fury*). He say Mr. Parris must be kill! Mr. Parris no goodly man, Mr. Parris mean man and no gentle man, and he bid me rise out of my bed and cut your throat! (*They gasp.*) But I tell him "No! I don't hate that man. I don't want kill that man." But he say, "You work for me, Tituba, and I make you free! I give you pretty dress to wear, and put you way high up in the air, and 1340 you gone fly back to Barbados!" And I say, "You lie, Devil, you lie!" And then he come one stormy night to me, and he say, "Look! I have *white* people belong to me." And I look—and there was Goody Good.

Parris. Sarah Good!

Tituba (*rocking and weeping*). Aye, sir, and Goody Osburn.

Mrs. Putnam. I knew it! Goody Osburn 1350 were midwife to me three times. I begged you, Thomas, did I not? I begged him not to call Osburn because I feared her. My babies always shriveled in her hands!

Hale. Take courage, you must give us all their names. How can you bear to see this child suffering? Look at her, Tituba. (*He is indicating* Betty *on the bed.*) Look at her God-given innocence; her soul is 1360 so tender; we must protect her, Tituba; the Devil is out and preying on her like a beast upon the flesh of the pure lamb. God will bless you for your help.

(Abigail *rises, staring as though inspired, and cries out.*)

Abigail. I want to open myself! (*They turn to her, startled. She is enraptured, as though in a pearly light.*) I want the light of God, I want the sweet love of Jesus! I

1370 danced for the Devil; I saw him; I wrote in his book; I go back to Jesus; I kiss His hand. I saw Sarah Good with the Devil! I saw Goody Osburn with the Devil! I saw Bridget Bishop with the Devil!

(*As she is speaking,* Betty *is rising from the bed, a fever in her eyes, and picks up the chant.*)

Betty (*staring too*). I saw George Jacobs with the Devil! I saw Goody Howe with
1380 the Devil!

Parris. She speaks! (*He rushes to embrace* Betty.) She speaks!

Hale. Glory to God! It is broken, they are free!

Betty (*calling out hysterically and with great relief*). I saw Martha Bellows with the Devil!

Abigail. I saw Goody Sibber with the Devil! (*It is rising to a great glee.*)

1390 **Putnam.** The marshal, I'll call the marshal!

(Parris *is shouting a prayer of thanksgiving.*)

Betty. I saw Alice Barrow with the Devil!

(*The curtain begins to fall.*)

Hale (*as* Putnam *goes out*). Let the marshal bring irons!

Abigail. I saw Goody Hawkins with the
1400 Devil!

Betty. I saw Goody Bibber with the Devil!

Abigail. I saw Goody Booth with the Devil!

(*On their ecstatic cries, the curtain falls.*)

COLLABORATIVE DISCUSSION With a partner, discuss how Abigail's feelings toward John Proctor influence the events that take place in this act. Cite specific textual evidence from the play to support your ideas.

Analyze Drama Elements

 COMMON CORE ELACC11-12RL3, ELACC11-12RL5

The first act of Arthur Miller's play is uniquely structured. It includes italicized **stage directions** that present details about setting and character and help establish mood. However, Miller also inserts passages of exposition that provide readers with facts and other information. Readers can use these stage directions to understand more about these elements of the play:

- the playwright's perspective on his subject
- historical background of the setting
- the real reasons behind characters' behaviors
- parallels between the Salem witch trials in the 1690s and the McCarthy hearings in the United States in the 1950s

Analyzing the Text

 COMMON CORE ELACC11-12RL3, ELACC11-12RL5, ELACC11-12SL1a

Cite Text Evidence   Support your responses with evidence from the selection.

1. **Analyze** What does the exposition in the beginning of Act One tell readers about the way they are to perceive the events that follow? Explain.

2. **Analyze** Reread lines 311–370. This part of the play reveals information to readers that the other characters do not have. This is called **dramatic irony.** How does this dramatic irony enable readers to understand the real reasons behind the girls' symptoms and the events that result?

3. **Cite Evidence** What do the stage directions reveal about the motives for the behavior of Thomas Putnam and Parris? Cite specific details in your response.

4. **Infer** What is meant by the description of Proctor as a man who "has come to regard himself as a kind of fraud"? Explain, based on details in this act.

PERFORMANCE TASK

Speaking Activity: Discussion The passages of exposition are typically not included in the stage production of a play. Based on your reading of the first act, why do you think Miller decided to include them in the text of the play?

- Reread the passages in Act One. Jot down your ideas about what they contribute to the play and if they are necessary.

- Present your insights in a small group. As a group, answer this question: Do the

stage directions detract from or enhance the effectiveness of the play?

- Summarize the important conclusions that the group reaches. Contribute them to a whole-class discussion.

ACT TWO

(*The common room of* Proctor's *house, eight days later.*

At the right is a door opening on the fields outside. A fireplace is at the left, and behind it a stairway leading upstairs. It is the low, dark, and rather long living room of the time. As the curtain rises, the room is empty. From above, Elizabeth *is heard softly singing to the children. Presently the door opens and* John Proctor *enters, carrying his gun. He glances about the room as he comes toward the fireplace, then halts for an instant as he hears her singing. He continues on to the fireplace, leans the gun against the wall as he swings a pot out of the fire and smells it. Then he lifts out the ladle and tastes. He is not quite pleased. He reaches to a cupboard, takes a pinch of salt, and drops it into the pot. As he is tasting again, her footsteps are heard on the stair. He swings the pot into the fireplace and goes to a basin and washes his hands and face.* Elizabeth *enters.*)

Elizabeth. What keeps you so late? It's almost dark.

Proctor. I were planting far out to the forest edge.

Elizabeth. Oh, you're done then.

Proctor. Aye, the farm is seeded. The boys asleep?

Elizabeth. They will be soon. (*And she goes to the fireplace, proceeds to ladle up*
10 *stew in a dish.*)

Proctor. Pray now for a fair summer.

Elizabeth. Aye.

Proctor. Are you well today?

Elizabeth. I am. (*She brings the plate to the table, and, indicating the food.*) It is a rabbit.

Proctor (*going to the table*). Oh, is it! In Jonathan's trap?

Elizabeth. No, she walked into the
20 house this afternoon; I found her sittin' in the corner like she come to visit.

Proctor. Oh, that's a good sign walkin' in.

Elizabeth. Pray God. It hurt my heart to strip her, poor rabbit. (*She sits and watches him taste it.*)

Proctor. It's well seasoned.

Elizabeth (*blushing with pleasure*). I took great care. She's tender?

30 **Proctor.** Aye. (*He eats. She watches him.*) I think we'll see green fields soon. It's warm as blood beneath the clods.

Elizabeth. That's well.

(Proctor *eats, then looks up.*)

Proctor. If the crop is good I'll buy George Jacob's heifer. How would that please you?

Elizabeth. Aye, it would.

Proctor (*with a grin*). I mean to please
40 you, Elizabeth.

Elizabeth (*It is hard to say*). I know it, John.

(*He gets up, goes to her, kisses her. She receives it. With a certain disappointment, he returns to the table.*)

Proctor (*as gently as he can*). Cider?

Elizabeth (*with a sense of reprimanding herself for having forgot*). Aye! (*She gets*

up and goes and pours a glass for him. He
50 *now arches his back.*)

Proctor. This farm's a continent when you go foot by foot droppin' seeds in it.

Elizabeth (*coming with the cider*). It must be.

Proctor (*drinks a long draught, then, putting the glass down*). You ought to bring some flowers in the house.

Elizabeth. Oh! I forgot! I will tomorrow.

Proctor. It's winter in here yet. On
60 Sunday let you come with me, and we'll walk the farm together; I never see such a load of flowers on the earth. (*With good feeling he goes and looks up at the sky through the open doorway.*) Lilacs have a purple smell. Lilac is the smell of nightfall, I think. Massachusetts is a beauty in the spring!

Elizabeth. Aye, it is.

(*There is a pause. She is watching*
70 *him from the table as he stands there absorbing the night. It is as though she would speak but cannot. Instead, now, she takes up his plate and glass and fork and goes with them to the basin. Her back is turned to him. He turns to her and watches her. A sense of their separation rises.*)

Proctor. I think you're sad again. Are you?

80 **Elizabeth** (*She doesn't want friction, and yet she must*). You come so late I thought you'd gone to Salem this afternoon.

Proctor. Why? I have no business in Salem.

Elizabeth. You did speak of going, earlier this week.

Proctor (*He knows what she means*). I thought better of it since.

Elizabeth. Mary Warren's there today.

90 **Proctor.** Why'd you let her? You heard me forbid her go to Salem any more!

Elizabeth. I couldn't stop her.

Proctor (*holding back a full condemnation of her*). It is a fault, it is a fault, Elizabeth—you're the mistress here, not Mary Warren.

Elizabeth. She frightened all my strength away.

Proctor. How may that mouse frighten
100 you, Elizabeth? You—

Elizabeth. It is a mouse no more. I forbid her go, and she raises up her chin like the daughter of a prince and says to me, "I must go to Salem, Goody Proctor; I am an official of the court!"

Proctor. Court! What court?

Elizabeth. Aye, it is a proper court they have now. They've sent four judges out of Boston, she says, weighty magistrates
110 of the General Court, and at the head sits the Deputy Governor of the Province.

Proctor (*astonished*). Why, she's mad.

Elizabeth. I would to God she were. There be fourteen people in the jail now, she says. (Proctor *simply looks at her, unable to grasp it.*) And they'll be tried, and the court have power to hang them too, she says.

120 **Proctor** (*scoffing, but without conviction*). Ah, they'd never hang—

Elizabeth. The Deputy Governor promise hangin' if they'll not confess, John. The town's gone wild, I think. She speak of Abigail, and I thought she were a saint, to hear her. Abigail brings the other girls into the court, and where she walks the crowd will part like the sea for Israel. And folks are brought before
130 them, and if they scream and howl and fall to the floor—the person's clapped in the jail for bewitchin' them.

Proctor (*wide-eyed*). Oh, it is a black mischief.

Elizabeth. I think you must go to Salem, John. (*He turns to her.*) I think so. You must tell them it is a fraud.

Proctor (*thinking beyond this*). Aye, it is, it is surely.

140 **Elizabeth.** Let you go to Ezekiel Cheever—he knows you well. And tell him what she said to you last week in her uncle's house. She said it had naught to do with witchcraft, did she not?

Proctor (*in thought*). Aye, she did, she did. (*now, a pause*)

Elizabeth (*quietly, fearing to anger him by prodding*). God forbid you keep that from the court, John. I think they must 150 be told.

Proctor (*quietly, struggling with his thought*). Aye, they must, they must. It is a wonder they do believe her.

Elizabeth. I would go to Salem now, John—let you go tonight.

Proctor. I'll think on it.

Elizabeth (*with her courage now*). You cannot keep it, John.

Proctor (*angering*). I know I cannot 160 keep it. I say I will think on it!

Elizabeth (*hurt, and very coldly*). Good, then, let you think on it. (*She stands and starts to walk out of the room.*)

Proctor. I am only wondering how I may prove what she told me, Elizabeth. If the girl's a saint now, I think it is not easy to prove she's fraud, and the town gone so silly. She told it to me in a room alone—I have no proof for it.

170 **Elizabeth.** You were alone with her?

Proctor (*stubbornly*). For a moment alone, aye.

Elizabeth. Why, then, it is not as you told me.

Proctor (*his anger rising*). For a moment, I say. The others come in soon after.

Elizabeth (*quietly—she has suddenly lost all faith in him*). Do as you wish, then. (*She starts to turn.*)

180 **Proctor.** Woman. (*She turns to him.*) I'll not have your suspicion any more.

Elizabeth (*a little loftily*). I have no—

Proctor. I'll not have it!

Elizabeth. Then let you not earn it.

Proctor (*with a violent undertone*). You doubt me yet?

Elizabeth (*with a smile, to keep her dignity*). John, if it were not Abigail that you must go to hurt, would you falter 190 now? I think not.

Proctor. Now look you—

Elizabeth. I see what I see, John.

Proctor (*with solemn warning*). You will not judge me more, Elizabeth. I have good reason to think before I charge fraud on Abigail, and I will think on it. Let you look to your own improvement before you go to judge your husband any more. I have forgot Abigail, and—

200 **Elizabeth.** And I.

Proctor. Spare me! You forget nothin' and forgive nothin'. Learn charity, woman. I have gone tiptoe in this house all seven month since she is gone. I have not moved from there to there without I think to please you, and still an everlasting funeral marches round your heart. I cannot speak but I am doubted, every moment judged for lies, as though 210 I come into a court when I come into this house!

Elizabeth. John, you are not open with me. You saw her with a crowd, you said. Now you—

Proctor. I'll plead my honesty no more, Elizabeth.

Elizabeth (*now she would justify herself*). John, I am only—

Proctor. No more! I should have roared you down when first you told me your suspicion. But I wilted, and, like a Christian, I confessed. Confessed! Some dream I had must have mistaken you for God that day. But you're not, you're not, and let you remember it! Let you look sometimes for the goodness in me, and judge me not.

Elizabeth. I do not judge you. The magistrate sits in your heart that judges you. I never thought you but a good man, John—(*with a smile*)—only somewhat bewildered.

Proctor (*laughing bitterly*). Oh, Elizabeth, your justice would freeze beer![1] (*He turns suddenly toward a sound outside. He starts for the door as Mary Warren enters. As soon as he sees her, he goes directly to her and grabs her by her cloak, furious.*) How do you go to Salem when I forbid it? Do you mock me? (*shaking her*) I'll whip you if you dare leave this house again! (*Strangely, she doesn't resist him, but hangs limply by his grip.*)

Mary Warren. I am sick, I am sick, Mr. Proctor. Pray, pray, hurt me not. (*Her strangeness throws him off, and her evident pallor and weakness. He frees her.*) My insides are all shuddery; I am in the proceedings all day, sir.

Proctor (*with draining anger—his curiosity is draining it*). And what of these proceedings here? When will you proceed to keep this house, as you are paid nine pound a year to do—and my wife not wholly well?

(*As though to compensate, Mary Warren goes to Elizabeth with a small rag doll.*)

Mary Warren. I made a gift for you today, Goody Proctor. I had to sit long hours in a chair, and passed the time with sewing.

Elizabeth (*perplexed, looking at the doll*). Why, thank you, it's a fair poppet.[2]

Mary Warren (*with a trembling, decayed voice*). We must all love each other now, Goody Proctor.

Elizabeth (*amazed at her strangeness*). Aye, indeed we must.

Mary Warren (*glancing at the room*). I'll get up early in the morning and clean the house. I must sleep now. (*She turns and starts off.*)

Proctor. Mary. (*She halts.*) Is it true? There be fourteen women arrested?

Mary Warren. No, sir. There be thirty-nine now—(*She suddenly breaks off and sobs and sits down, exhausted.*)

Elizabeth. Why, she's weepin'! What ails you, child?

Mary Warren. Goody Osburn—will hang!

(*There is a shocked pause, while she sobs.*)

Proctor. Hang! (*He calls into her face.*) Hang, y'say?

Mary Warren (*through her weeping*). Aye.

Proctor. The Deputy Governor will permit it?

Mary Warren. He sentenced her. He must. (*to ameliorate it*) But not Sarah Good. For Sarah Good confessed, y'see.

---

[1] **your justice . . . beer:** Alcoholic beverages freeze at very low temperatures, so Proctor is sarcastically calling his wife cold-hearted.

[2] **fair poppet:** pretty doll.

Proctor. Confessed! To what?

Mary Warren. That she—(*in horror at the memory*)—she sometimes made a compact with Lucifer, and wrote her name in his black book—with her blood—and bound herself to torment Christians till God's thrown down—and we all must worship Hell forevermore.

(*pause*)

Proctor. But—surely you know what a jabberer she is. Did you tell them that?

Mary Warren. Mr. Proctor, in open court she near to choked us all to death.

Proctor. How, choked you?

Mary Warren. She sent her spirit out.

Elizabeth. Oh, Mary, Mary, surely you—

Mary Warren (*with an indignant edge*). She tried to kill me many times, Goody Proctor!

Elizabeth. Why, I never heard you mention that before.

Mary Warren. I never knew it before. I never knew anything before. When she come into the court I say to myself, I must not accuse this woman, for she sleep in ditches, and so very old and poor. But then—then she sit there, denying and denying, and I feel a misty coldness climbin' up my back, and the skin on my skull begin to creep, and I feel a clamp around my neck and I cannot breathe air; and then (*entranced*) I hear a voice, a screamin' voice, and it were my voice—and all at once I remembered everything she done to me!

Proctor. Why? What did she do to you?

Mary Warren (*like one awakened to a marvelous secret insight*). So many time, Mr. Proctor, she come to this very door, beggin' bread and a cup of cider—and mark this: whenever I turned her away empty, she *mumbled*.

Elizabeth. Mumbled! She may mumble if she's hungry.

Mary Warren. But *what* does she mumble? You must remember, Goody Proctor. Last month—a Monday, I think—she walked away, and I thought my guts would burst for two days after. Do you remember it?

Elizabeth. Why—I do, I think, but—

Mary Warren. And so I told that to Judge Hathorne, and he asks her so. "Sarah Good," says he, "what curse do you mumble that this girl must fall sick after turning you away?" And then she replies (*mimicking an old crone*) "Why, your excellence, no curse at all. I only say my commandments;[3] I hope I may say my commandments," says she!

Elizabeth. And that's an upright answer.

Mary Warren. Aye, but then Judge Hathorne say, "Recite for us your commandments!" (*leaning avidly toward them*) and of all the ten she could not say a single one. She never knew no commandments, and they had her in a flat lie!

Proctor. And so condemned her?

Mary Warren (*now a little strained, seeing his stubborn doubt*). Why, they must when she condemned herself.

Proctor. But the proof, the proof!

Mary Warren (*with greater impatience with him*). I told you the proof. It's hard proof, hard as rock, the judges said.

Proctor (*pauses an instant, then*). You will not go to court again, Mary Warren.

---

[3] **commandments:** the Ten Commandments in the Bible.

Mary Warren. I must tell you, sir, I will be gone every day now. I am amazed you do not see what weighty work we do.

380 **Proctor.** What work you do! It's strange work for a Christian girl to hang old women!

Mary Warren. But, Mr. Proctor, they will not hang them if they confess. Sarah Good will only sit in jail some time (*recalling*) and here's a wonder for you; think on this. Goody Good is pregnant!

Elizabeth. Pregnant! Are they mad?
390 The woman's near to sixty!

Mary Warren. They had Doctor Griggs examine her, and she's full to the brim. And smokin' a pipe all these years, and no husband either! But she's safe, thank God, for they'll not hurt the innocent child. But be that not a marvel? You must see it, sir, it's God's work we do. So I'll be gone every day for some time. I'm—I am an official of the court, they
400 say, and I—(*She has been edging toward offstage.*)

Proctor. I'll official you! (*He strides to the mantel, takes down the whip hanging there.*)

Mary Warren (*terrified, but coming erect, striving for her authority*). I'll not stand whipping any more!

Elizabeth (*hurriedly, as Proctor approaches*). Mary, promise now you'll
410 stay at home—

Mary Warren (*backing from him, but keeping her erect posture, striving, striving for her way*). The Devil's loose in Salem, Mr. Proctor; we must discover where he's hiding!

Proctor. I'll whip the Devil out of you! (*With whip raised he reaches out for her, and she streaks away and yells.*)

Mary Warren (*pointing at* Elizabeth). I
420 saved her life today!

(*Silence. His whip comes down.*)

Elizabeth (*softly*). I am accused?

Mary Warren (*quaking*). Somewhat mentioned. But I said I never see no sign you ever sent your spirit out to hurt no one, and seeing I do live so closely with you, they dismissed it.

Elizabeth. Who accused me?

Mary Warren. I am bound by law, I
430 cannot tell it. (*to* Proctor) I only hope you'll not be so sarcastical no more. Four judges and the King's deputy sat to dinner with us but an hour ago. I—I would have you speak civilly to me, from this out.

Proctor (*in horror, muttering in disgust at her*). Go to bed.

Mary Warren (*with a stamp of her foot*). I'll not be ordered to bed no more, Mr.
440 Proctor! I am eighteen and a woman, however single!

Proctor. Do you wish to sit up? Then sit up.

Mary Warren. I wish to go to bed!

Proctor (*in anger*). Good night, then!

Mary Warren. Good night. (*Dissatisfied, uncertain of herself, she goes out. Wide-eyed, both,* Proctor *and* Elizabeth *stand staring.*)

450 **Elizabeth** (*quietly*). Oh, the noose, the noose is up!

Proctor. There'll be no noose.

Elizabeth. She wants me dead. I knew all week it would come to this!

Proctor (*without conviction*). They dismissed it. You heard her say—

Elizabeth. And what of tomorrow? She will cry me out until they take me!

Proctor. Sit you down.

460 **Elizabeth.** She wants me dead, John, you know it!

Proctor. I say sit down! (*She sits, trembling. He speaks quietly, trying to keep his wits.*) Now we must be wise, Elizabeth.

Elizabeth (*with sarcasm, and a sense of being lost*). Oh, indeed, indeed!

Proctor. Fear nothing. I'll find Ezekiel Cheever. I'll tell him she said it were all 470 sport.

Elizabeth. John, with so many in the jail, more than Cheever's help is needed now, I think. Would you favor me with this? Go to Abigail.

Proctor (*his soul hardening as he senses . . .*). What have I to say to Abigail?

Elizabeth (*delicately*). John—grant me this. You have a faulty understanding of 480 young girls. There is a promise made in any bed—

Proctor (*striving against his anger*). What promise!

Elizabeth. Spoke or silent, a promise is surely made. And she may dote on it now—I am sure she does—and thinks to kill me, then to take my place.

(Proctor's *anger is rising; he cannot speak.*)

490 **Elizabeth.** It is her dearest hope, John, I know it. There be a thousand names; why does she call mine? There be a certain danger in calling such a name—I am no Goody Good that sleeps in ditches, nor Osburn, drunk and half-witted. She'd dare not call out such a farmer's wife but there be monstrous profit in it. She thinks to take my place, John.

500 **Proctor.** She cannot think it! (*He knows it is true.*)

Elizabeth (*"reasonably"*). John, have you ever shown her somewhat of contempt? She cannot pass you in the church but you will blush—

Proctor. I may blush for my sin.

Elizabeth. I think she sees another meaning in that blush.

Proctor. And what see you? What see 510 you, Elizabeth?

Elizabeth (*"conceding"*). I think you be somewhat ashamed, for I am there, and she so close.

Proctor. When will you know me, woman? Were I stone I would have cracked for shame this seven month!

Elizabeth. Then go and tell her she's a whore. Whatever promise she may sense—break it, John, break it.

Proctor (*between his teeth*). Good, then. I'll go. (*He starts for his rifle.*)

Elizabeth (*trembling, fearfully*). Oh, how unwillingly!

Proctor (*turning on her, rifle in hand*). I will curse her hotter than the oldest cinder in hell. But pray, begrudge me not my anger!

Elizabeth. Your anger! I only ask you—

Proctor. Woman, am I so base? Do you truly think me base?

Elizabeth. I never called you base.

Proctor. Then how do you charge me with such a promise? The promise that a stallion gives a mare I gave that girl!

Elizabeth. Then why do you anger with me when I bid you break it?

Proctor. Because it speaks deceit, and I am honest! But I'll plead no more! I see now your spirit twists around the single error of my life, and I will never tear it free!

Elizabeth (*crying out*). You'll tear it free—when you come to know that I will be your only wife, or no wife at all! She has an arrow in you yet, John Proctor, and you know it well!

(*Quite suddenly, as though from the air, a figure appears in the doorway. They start slightly. It is* Mr. Hale. *He is different now—drawn a little, and there is a quality of deference, even of guilt, about his manner now.*)

Hale. Good evening.

Proctor (*still in his shock*). Why, Mr. Hale! Good evening to you, sir. Come in, come in.

Hale (*to* Elizabeth). I hope I do not startle you.

Elizabeth. No, no, it's only that I heard no horse—

Hale. You are Goodwife Proctor.

Proctor. Aye; Elizabeth.

Hale (*nods, then*). I hope you're not off to bed yet.

Proctor (*setting down his gun*). No, no. (Hale *comes further into the room. And* Proctor, *to explain his nervousness.*) We are not used to visitors after dark, but you're welcome here. Will you sit you down, sir?

Hale. I will. (*He sits.*) Let you sit, Goodwife Proctor.

(*She does, never letting him out of her sight. There is a pause as* Hale *looks about the room.*)

Proctor (*to break the silence*). Will you drink cider, Mr. Hale?

Hale. No, it rebels[4] my stomach; I have some further traveling yet tonight. Sit you down, sir. (Proctor *sits.*) I will not keep you long, but I have some business with you.

Proctor. Business of the court?

Hale. No—no, I come of my own, without the court's authority. Hear me. (*He wets his lips.*) I know not if you are aware, but your wife's name is—mentioned in the court.

Proctor. We know it, sir. Our Mary Warren told us. We are entirely amazed.

Hale. I am a stranger here, as you know. And in my ignorance I find it hard to draw a clear opinion of them that come accused before the court. And so this afternoon, and now tonight, I go from house to house—I come now from Rebecca Nurse's house and—

Elizabeth (*shocked*). Rebecca's charged!

Hale. God forbid such a one be charged. She is, however—mentioned somewhat.

---

[4] **rebels:** upsets.

Elizabeth (*with an attempt at a laugh*). You will never believe, I hope, that Rebecca trafficked with the Devil.

Hale. Woman, it is possible.

Proctor (*taken aback*). Surely you cannot think so.

Hale. This is a strange time, Mister. No man may longer doubt the powers of the dark are gathered in monstrous attack upon this village. There is too much evidence now to deny it. You will agree, sir?

Proctor (*evading*). I—have no knowledge in that line. But it's hard to think so pious a woman be secretly a Devil's bitch after seventy year of such good prayer.

Hale. Aye. But the Devil is a wily one, you cannot deny it. However, she is far from accused, and I know she will not be. (*pause*) I thought, sir, to put some questions as to the Christian character of this house, if you'll permit me.

Proctor (*coldly, resentful*). Why, we—have no fear of questions, sir.

Hale. Good, then. (*He makes himself more comfortable.*) In the book of record that Mr. Parris keeps, I note that you are rarely in the church on Sabbath Day.

Proctor. No, sir, you are mistaken.

Hale. Twenty-six time in seventeen month, sir. I must call that rare. Will you tell me why you are so absent?

Proctor. Mr. Hale, I never knew I must account to that man for I come to church or stay at home. My wife were sick this winter.

Hale. So I am told. But you, Mister, why could you not come alone?

Proctor. I surely did come when I could, and when I could not I prayed in this house.

Hale. Mr. Proctor, your house is not a church; your theology must tell you that.

Proctor. It does, sir, it does; and it tells me that a minister may pray to God without he have golden candlesticks upon the altar.

Hale. What golden candlesticks?

Proctor. Since we built the church there were pewter candlesticks upon the altar; Francis Nurse made them, y'know, and a sweeter hand never touched the metal. But Parris came, and for twenty week he preach nothin' but golden candlesticks until he had them. I labor the earth from dawn of day to blink of night, and I tell you true, when I look to heaven and see my money glaring at his elbows—it hurt my prayer, sir, it hurt my prayer. I think, sometimes, the man dreams cathedrals, not clapboard meetin' houses.

Hale (*thinks, then*). And yet, Mister, a Christian on Sabbath Day must be in church. (*pause*) Tell me—you have three children?

Proctor. Aye. Boys.

Hale. How comes it that only two are baptized?

Proctor (*starts to speak, then stops, then, as though unable to restrain this*). I like it not that Mr. Parris should lay his hand upon my baby. I see no light of God in that man. I'll not conceal it.

Hale. I must say it, Mr. Proctor; that is not for you to decide. The man's ordained, therefore the light of God is in him.

Proctor (*flushed with resentment but trying to smile*). What's your suspicion, Mr. Hale?

Hale. No, no, I have no—

Proctor. I nailed the roof upon the church, I hung the door—

Hale. Oh, did you! That's a good sign, then.

Proctor. It may be I have been too quick to bring the man to book,[5] but you cannot think we ever desired the destruction of religion. I think that's in your mind, is it not?

Hale (*not altogether giving way*). I—have—there is a softness in your record, sir, a softness.

Elizabeth. I think, maybe, we have been too hard with Mr. Parris. I think so. But sure we never loved the Devil here.

Hale (*nods, deliberating this. Then, with the voice of one administering a secret test*). Do you know your Commandments, Elizabeth?

Elizabeth (*without hesitation, even eagerly*). I surely do. There be no mark of blame upon my life, Mr. Hale. I am a convenanted Christian woman.

Hale. And you, Mister?

Proctor (*a trifle unsteadily*). I—am sure I do, sir.

Hale (*glances at her open face, then at John, then*). Let you repeat them, if you will.

Proctor. The Commandments.

Hale. Aye.

Proctor (*looking off, beginning to sweat*). Thou shalt not kill.

Hale. Aye.

Proctor (*counting on his fingers*). Thou shalt not steal. Thou shalt not covet thy neighbor's goods, nor make unto thee any graven image. Thou shalt not take the name of the Lord in vain; thou shalt have no other gods before

me. (*with some hesitation*) Thou shalt remember the Sabbath Day and keep it holy. (*Pause. Then.*) Thou shalt honor thy father and mother. Thou shalt not bear false witness. (*He is stuck. He counts back on his fingers, knowing one is missing.*) Thou shalt not make unto thee any graven image.

Hale. You have said that twice, sir.

Proctor (*lost*). Aye. (*He is flailing for it.*)

Elizabeth (*delicately*). Adultery, John.

Proctor (*as though a secret arrow had pained his heart*). Aye. (*trying to grin it away—to* Hale) You see, sir, between the two of us we do know them all. (Hale *only looks at* Proctor, *deep in his attempt to define this man.* Proctor *grows more uneasy.*) I think it be a small fault.

Hale. Theology, sir, is a fortress; no crack in a fortress may be accounted small. (*He rises; he seems worried now. He paces a little, in deep thought.*)

Proctor. There be no love for Satan in this house, Mister.

Hale. I pray it, I pray it dearly. (*He looks to both of them, an attempt at a smile on his face, but his misgivings are clear.*) Well, then—I'll bid you good night.

Elizabeth (*unable to restrain herself*). Mr. Hale. (*He turns.*) I do think you are suspecting me somewhat? Are you not?

Hale (*obviously disturbed—and evasive*). Goody Proctor, I do not judge you. My duty is to add what I may to the godly wisdom of the court. I pray you both good health and good fortune. (*to* John) Good night, sir. (*He starts out.*)

Elizabeth (*with a note of desperation*). I think you must tell him, John.

Hale. What's that?

Elizabeth (*restraining a call*). Will you tell him?

---

[5] **bring the man to book:** judge the man.

(*Slight pause. Hale* looks questioningly *at* John.)

Proctor (*with difficulty*). I—I have no
770 witness and cannot prove it, except
my word be taken. But I know the
children's sickness had naught to do
with witchcraft.

Hale (*stopped, struck*). Naught to do—?

Proctor. Mr. Parris discovered them
sportin' in the woods. They were
startled and took sick.

(*pause*)

Hale. Who told you this?

780 **Proctor** (*hesitates, then*). Abigail
Williams.

Hale. Abigail!

Proctor. Aye.

Hale (*his eyes wide*). Abigail Williams
told you it had naught to do with
witchcraft!

Proctor. She told me the day you
came, sir.

Hale (*suspiciously*). Why—why did you
790 keep this?

Proctor. I never knew until tonight
that the world is gone daft with this
nonsense.

Hale. Nonsense! Mister, I have myself
examined Tituba, Sarah Good, and
numerous others that have confessed
to dealing with the Devil. They have
confessed it.

Proctor. And why not, if they must
800 hang for denyin' it? There are them that
will swear to anything before they'll
hang; have you never thought of that?

Hale. I have. I—I have indeed. (*It is his
own suspicion, but he resists it. He glances
at* Elizabeth, *then at* John.) And you—
would you testify to this in court?

Proctor. I—had not reckoned with goin'
into court. But if I must I will.

Hale. Do you falter here?

810 **Proctor.** I falter nothing, but I may
wonder if my story will be credited in
such a court. I do wonder on it, when
such a steady-minded minister as you
will suspicion such a woman that never
lied, and cannot, and the world knows
she cannot! I may falter somewhat,
Mister; I am no fool.

Hale (*quietly—it has impressed him*).
Proctor, let you open with me now, for I
820 have a rumor that troubles me. It's said
you hold no belief that there may even
be witches in the world. Is that true, sir?

Proctor (*He knows this is critical, and is
striving against his disgust with* Hale *and
with himself for even answering*). I know
not what I have said, I may have said it. I
have wondered if there be witches in the
world—although I cannot believe they
come among us now.

830 **Hale.** Then you do not believe—

Proctor. I have no knowledge of it; the
Bible speaks of witches, and I will not
deny them.

Hale. And you, woman?

Elizabeth. I—I cannot believe it.

Hale (*shocked*). You cannot!

Proctor. Elizabeth, you bewilder him!

Elizabeth (*to* Hale). I cannot think the
Devil may own a woman's soul, Mr.
840 Hale, when she keeps an upright way, as
I have. I am a good woman, I know it;
and if you believe I may do only good
work in the world, and yet be secretly
bound to Satan, then I must tell you, sir,
I do not believe it.

Hale. But, woman, you do believe there
are witches in—

Elizabeth. If you think that I am one, then I say there are none.

850 **Hale.** You surely do not fly against the Gospel, the Gospel—

Proctor. She believe in the Gospel, every word!

Elizabeth. Question Abigail Williams about the Gospel, not myself!

(Hale *stares at her.*)

Proctor. She do not mean to doubt the Gospel, sir, you cannot think it. This be a Christian house, sir, a Christian
860 house.

Hale. God keep you both; let the third child be quickly baptized, and go you without fail each Sunday in to Sabbath prayer; and keep a solemn, quiet way among you. I think—

(Giles Corey *appears in doorway.*)

Giles. John!

Proctor. Giles! What's the matter?

Giles. They take my wife.

870 (Francis Nurse *enters.*)

Giles. And his Rebecca!

Proctor (*to* Francis). Rebecca's in the *jail!*

Francis. Aye, Cheever come and take her in his wagon. We've only now come from the jail, and they'll not even let us in to see them.

Elizabeth. They've surely gone wild now, Mr. Hale!

880 **Francis** (*going to* Hale). Reverend Hale! Can you not speak to the Deputy Governor? I'm sure he mistakes these people—

Hale. Pray calm yourself, Mr. Nurse.

Francis. My wife is the very brick and mortar of the church, Mr. Hale (*indicating* Giles) and Martha Corey,

there cannot be a woman closer yet to God than Martha.

890 **Hale.** How is Rebecca charged, Mr. Nurse?

Francis (*with a mocking, half-hearted laugh*). For murder, she's charged! (*mockingly quoting the warrant*) "For the marvelous and supernatural murder of Goody Putnam's babies." What am I to do, Mr. Hale?

Hale (*turns from* Francis, *deeply troubled, then*). Believe me, Mr. Nurse,
900 if Rebecca Nurse be tainted, then nothing's left to stop the whole green world from burning. Let you rest upon the justice of the court; the court will send her home, I know it.

Francis. You cannot mean she will be tried in court!

Hale (*pleading*). Nurse, though our hearts break, we cannot flinch; these are new times, sir. There is a misty plot
910 afoot so subtle we should be criminal to cling to old respects and ancient friendships. I have seen too many frightful proofs in court—the Devil is alive in Salem, and we dare not quail to follow wherever the accusing finger points!

Proctor (*angered*). How may such a woman murder children?

Hale (*in great pain*). Man, remember,
920 until an hour before the Devil fell, God thought him beautiful in Heaven.

Giles. I never said my wife were a witch, Mr. Hale; I only said she were reading books!

Hale. Mr. Corey, exactly what complaint were made on your wife?

Giles. That bloody mongrel Walcott charge her. Y'see, he buy a pig of my wife four or five year ago, and the pig
930 died soon after. So he come dancin' in

for his money back. So my Martha, she says to him, "Walcott, if you haven't the wit to feed a pig properly, you'll not live to own many," she says. Now he goes to court and claims that from that day to this he cannot keep a pig alive for more than four weeks because my Martha bewitch them with her books!

(*Enter* Ezekiel Cheever. *A shocked silence.*)

Cheever. Good evening to you, Proctor.

Proctor. Why, Mr. Cheever. Good evening.

Cheever. Good evening, all. Good evening, Mr. Hale.

Proctor. I hope you come not on business of the court.

Cheever. I do, Proctor, aye. I am clerk of the court now, y'know.

(*Enter* Marshal Herrick, *a man in his early thirties, who is somewhat shamefaced at the moment.*)

Giles. It's a pity, Ezekiel, that an honest tailor might have gone to Heaven must burn in Hell. You'll burn for this, do you know it?

Cheever. You know yourself I must do as I'm told. You surely know that, Giles. And I'd as lief[6] you'd not be sending me to Hell. I like not the sound of it, I tell you; I like not the sound of it. (*He fears* Proctor, *but starts to reach inside his coat.*) Now believe me, Proctor, how heavy be the law, all its tonnage I do carry on my back tonight. (*He takes out a warrant.*) I have a warrant for your wife.

Proctor (*to* Hale). You said she were not charged!

Hale. I know nothin' of it. (*to* Cheever) When were she charged?

Cheever. I am given sixteen warrant tonight, sir, and she is one.

Proctor. Who charged her?

Cheever. Why, Abigail Williams charge her.

Proctor. On what proof, what proof?

Cheever (*looking about the room*). Mr. Proctor, I have little time. The court bid me search your house, but I like not to search a house. So will you hand me any poppets that your wife may keep here?

Proctor. Poppets?

Elizabeth. I never kept no poppets, not since I were a girl.

Cheever (*embarrassed, glancing toward the mantel where sits Mary Warren's poppet*). I spy a poppet, Goody Proctor.

Elizabeth. Oh! (*going for it*) Why, this is Mary's.

Cheever (*shyly*). Would you please to give it to me?

Elizabeth (*handing it to him, asks* Hale). Has the court discovered a text in poppets now?

Cheever (*carefully holding the poppet*). Do you keep any others in this house?

Proctor. No, nor this one either till tonight. What signifies a poppet?

Cheever. Why, a poppet—(*He gingerly turns the poppet over.*) a poppet may signify—Now, woman, will you please to come with me?

Proctor. She will not! (*to* Elizabeth) Fetch Mary here.

Cheever (*ineptly reaching toward* Elizabeth). No, no, I am forbid to leave her from my sight.

Proctor (*pushing his arm away*). You'll leave her out of sight and out of mind, Mister. Fetch Mary, Elizabeth. (Elizabeth *goes upstairs.*)

---

[6] **as lief** (lēf): rather.

Hale. What signifies a poppet, Mr. Cheever?

Cheever (*turning the poppet over in his hands*). Why, they say it may signify that she—(*He has lifted the poppet's skirt, and his eyes widen in astonished fear.*) Why, this, this—

1020 **Proctor** (*reaching for the poppet*). What's there?

Cheever. Why (*He draws out a long needle from the poppet.*) it is a needle! Herrick, Herrick, it is a needle!

(Herrick *comes toward him.*)

Proctor (*angrily, bewildered*). And what signifies a needle!

Cheever (*his hands shaking*). Why, this go hard with her, Proctor, this—I had my doubts, Proctor, I had my doubts, 1030 but here's calamity. (*to Hale, showing the needle*) You see it, sir, it is a needle!

Hale. Why? What meanin' has it?

Cheever (*wide-eyed, trembling*). The girl, the Williams girl, Abigail Williams, sir. She sat to dinner in Reverend Parris's house tonight, and without word nor warnin' she falls to the floor. Like a struck beast, he says, and screamed a 1040 scream that a bull would weep to hear. And he goes to save her, and, stuck two inches in the flesh of her belly, he draw a needle out. And demandin' of her how she come to be so stabbed, she (*to* Proctor *now*) testify it were your wife's familiar spirit[7] pushed it in.

Proctor. Why, she done it herself! (*to* Hale) I hope you're not takin' this for proof, Mister!

1050 (Hale, *struck by the proof, is silent.*)

---

[7] **familiar spirit:** the spirit or demon, most usually in the form of an animal such as a black cat, that was a companion and helper to a witch.

Cheever. 'Tis hard proof! (*to* Hale) I find here a poppet Goody Proctor keeps. I have found it, sir. And in the belly of the poppet a needle's stuck. I tell you true, Proctor, I never warranted to see such proof of Hell, and I bid you obstruct me not, for I—

(Enter Elizabeth *with* Mary Warren. Proctor, *seeing* Mary Warren, *draws her* 1060 *by the arm to* Hale.)

Proctor. Here now! Mary, how did this poppet come into my house?

Mary Warren (*frightened for herself, her voice very small*). What poppet's that, sir?

Proctor (*impatiently, pointing at the doll in* Cheever's *hand*). This poppet, this poppet.

Mary Warren (*evasively, looking at it*). 1070 Why, I—I think it is mine.

Proctor. It is your poppet, is it not?

Mary Warren (*not understanding the direction of this*). It—is, sir.

Proctor. And how did it come into this house?

Mary Warren (*glancing about at the avid faces*). Why—I made it in the court, sir, and—give it to Goody Proctor tonight.

Proctor (*to* Hale). Now, sir—do you 1080 have it?

Hale. Mary Warren, a needle have been found inside this poppet.

Mary Warren (*bewildered*). Why, I meant no harm by it, sir.

Proctor (*quickly*). You stuck that needle in yourself?

Mary Warren. I—I believe I did, sir, I—

Proctor (*to* Hale). What say you now?

Hale (*watching* Mary Warren *closely*). 1090 Child, you are certain this be your natural memory? May it be, perhaps, that someone conjures you even now to say this?

Mary Warren. Conjures me? Why, no, sir, I am entirely myself, I think. Let you ask Susanna Walcott—she saw me sewin' it in court. (*or better still*) Ask Abby, Abby sat beside me when I made it.

1100 **Proctor** (*to* Hale, *of* Cheever). Bid him begone. Your mind is surely settled now. Bid him out, Mr. Hale.

Elizabeth. What signifies a needle?

Hale. Mary—you charge a cold and cruel murder on Abigail.

Mary Warren. Murder! I charge no—

Hale. Abigail were stabbed tonight; a needle were found stuck into her belly—

Elizabeth. And she charges me?

1110 **Hale.** Aye.

Elizabeth (*her breath knocked out*). Why—! The girl is murder! She must be ripped out of the world!

Cheever (*pointing at* Elizabeth). You've heard that, sir! Ripped out of the world! Herrick, you heard it!

Proctor (*suddenly snatching the warrant out of* Cheever's *hands*). Out with you.

Cheever. Proctor, you dare not touch
1120 the warrant.

Proctor (*ripping the warrant*). Out with you!

Cheever. You've ripped the Deputy Governor's warrant, man!

Proctor. Damn the Deputy Governor! Out of my house!

Hale. Now, Proctor, Proctor!

Proctor. Get y'gone with them! You are a broken minister.

1130 **Hale.** Proctor, if she is innocent, the court—

Proctor. If *she* is innocent! Why do you never wonder if Parris be innocent, or Abigail? Is the accuser always holy now? Were they born this morning as clean as God's fingers? I'll tell you what's walking Salem—vengeance is walking Salem. We are what we always were in Salem, but now the little crazy children
1140 are jangling the keys of the kingdom, and common vengeance writes the law! This warrant's vengeance! I'll not give my wife to vengeance!

Elizabeth. I'll go, John—

Proctor. You will not go!

Herrick. I have nine men outside. You cannot keep her. The law binds me, John, I cannot budge.

Proctor (*to* Hale, *ready to break him*).
1150 Will you see her taken?

Hale. Proctor, the court is just—

Proctor. Pontius Pilate! God will not let you wash your hands of this![8]

Elizabeth. John—I think I must go with them. (*He cannot bear to look at her.*) Mary, there is bread enough for the morning; you will bake, in the afternoon. Help Mr. Proctor as you were his daughter—you owe me that, and
1160 much more. (*She is fighting her weeping. To* Proctor.) When the children wake, speak nothing of witchcraft—it will frighten them. (*She cannot go on.*)

Proctor. I will bring you home. I will bring you soon.

Elizabeth. Oh, John, bring me soon!

Proctor. I will fall like an ocean on that court! Fear nothing, Elizabeth.

---

8 **Pontius Pilate** (pŏn′chəs pī′lət) . . . **hands of this:** the Roman official who presided over the trial and sentencing of Christ. Pilate publicly washed his hands to absolve himself of responsibility for Christ's death.

Elizabeth (*with great fear*). I will fear nothing. (*She looks about the room, as though to fix it in her mind.*) Tell the children I have gone to visit someone sick.

(*She walks out the door, Herrick and Cheever behind her. For a moment, Proctor watches from the doorway. The clank of chain is heard.*)

Proctor. Herrick! Herrick, don't chain her! (*He rushes out the door. From outside.*) Damn you, man, you will not chain her! Off with them! I'll not have it! I will not have her chained!

(*There are other men's voices against his. Hale, in a fever of guilt and uncertainty, turns from the door to avoid the sight; Mary Warren bursts into tears and sits weeping. Giles Corey calls to Hale.*)

Giles. And yet silent, minister? It is fraud, you know it is fraud! What keeps you, man?

(*Proctor is half braced, half pushed into the room by two deputies and Herrick.*)

Proctor. I'll pay you, Herrick, I will surely pay you!

Herrick (*panting*). In God's name, John, I cannot help myself. I must chain them all. Now let you keep inside this house till I am gone! (*He goes out with his deputies.*)

(*Proctor stands there, gulping air. Horses and a wagon creaking are heard.*)

Hale (*in great uncertainty*). Mr. Proctor—

Proctor. Out of my sight!

Hale. Charity, Proctor, charity. What I have heard in her favor, I will not fear to testify in court. God help me, I cannot judge her guilty or innocent—I know not. Only this consider: the world goes mad, and it profit nothing you should lay the cause to the vengeance of a little girl.

Proctor. You are a coward! Though you be ordained in God's own tears, you are a coward now!

Hale. Proctor, I cannot think God be provoked so grandly by such a petty cause. The jails are packed— our greatest judges sit in Salem now—and hangin's promised. Man, we must look to cause proportionate. Were there murder done, perhaps, and never brought to light? Abomination? Some secret blasphemy that stinks to Heaven? Think on cause, man, and let you help me to discover it. For there's your way, believe it, there is your only way, when such confusion strikes upon the world. (*He goes to* Giles *and* Francis.) Let you counsel among yourselves; think on your village and what may have drawn from heaven such thundering wrath upon you all. I shall pray God open up our eyes.

(Hale *goes out.*)

Francis (*struck by* Hale's *mood*). I never heard no murder done in Salem.

Proctor (*He has been reached by* Hale's *words*). Leave me, Francis, leave me.

Giles (*shaken*). John—tell me, are we lost?

Proctor. Go home now, Giles. We'll speak on it tomorrow.

Giles. Let you think on it. We'll come early, eh?

Proctor. Aye. Go now, Giles.

Giles. Good night, then.

(Giles Corey *goes out. After a moment.*)

Mary Warren (*in a fearful squeak of a voice*). Mr. Proctor, very likely they'll let her come home once they're given proper evidence.

Proctor. You're coming to the court with me, Mary. You will tell it in the court.

Mary Warren. I cannot charge murder on Abigail.

Proctor (*moving menacingly toward her*). You will tell the court how that poppet come here and who stuck the needle in.

Mary Warren. She'll kill me for sayin' that! (Proctor *continues toward her.*)

Abby'll charge lechery on you, Mr. Proctor!

Proctor (*halting*). She's told you!

Mary Warren. I have known it, sir. She'll ruin you with it, I know she will.

Proctor (*hesitating, and with deep hatred of himself*). Good. Then her saintliness is done with. (Mary *backs from him.*) We will slide together into our pit; you will tell the court what you know.

Mary Warren (*in terror*). I cannot, they'll turn on me—

(Proctor *strides and catches her, and she is repeating, "I cannot, I cannot!"*)

Proctor. My wife will never die for me! I will bring your guts into your mouth but that goodness will not die for me!

Mary Warren (*struggling to escape him*). I cannot do it, I cannot!

Proctor (*grasping her by the throat as though he would strangle her*). Make your peace with it! Now Hell and Heaven grapple on our backs, and all our old pretense is ripped away—make your peace! (*He throws her to the floor, where she sobs, "I cannot, I cannot . . ." And now, half to himself, staring, and turning to the open door.*) Peace. It is a providence, and no great change; we are only what we always were, but naked now. (*He walks as though toward a great horror, facing the open sky.*) Aye, naked! And the wind, God's icy wind, will blow!

(*And she is over and over again sobbing, "I cannot, I cannot, I cannot," as the curtain falls.*)

COLLABORATIVE DISCUSSION Why doesn't John Proctor go immediately to Salem to reveal what he knows? With a partner, discuss what Proctor will lose if the truth is known and why he hesitates. Cite specific textual evidence from the play to support your ideas.

eBook *Annotate It!*

Analyze Drama Elements

 COMMON CORE ELACC11-12RL3, ELACC11-12RL5

The **plot** is the series of related events that make up the story of the drama. To understand how Miller structures his plot, look for these elements:

> The **conflict** is a struggle between opposing forces that drives the action. In Act One, local and personal conflicts escalate into a major, widespread conflict.
>
> **Complications** are additional problems that make the conflict more difficult to resolve. In Act Two, several events occur that add intensity.
>
> The **climax** is the point of highest tension or excitement. In Act Three, an event occurs that has the potential to change the outcome of the conflict.
>
> The **resolution** is the part of the play in which conflicts are brought to a close. In Act Four, loose threads of the plot are tied up; questions are answered.

Analyzing the Text

 COMMON CORE ELACC11-12RL3, ELACC11-12RL5, ELACC11-12W7, ELACC11-12W8, ELACC11-12SL4

Cite Text Evidence Support your responses with evidence from the selection.

1. **Cite Evidence** How do the events in this act affect readers' perception of the situation in which Proctor and the others find themselves? Cite specific details.

2. **Draw Conclusions** Reread lines 180–211. What do these lines reveal about the character of and the relationship between John and Elizabeth Proctor?

3. **Analyze** Why is Proctor struck by Hale's declaration that "some secret blasphemy" has caused all of the confusion? How does Hale's statement relate to Proctor's later words to Mary Warren that he and Abigail will "slide together into our pit; you will tell the court what you know"?

4. **Analyze** What does Mary Warren's behavior in Act Two foreshadow about her testimony in court? Explain.

PERFORMANCE TASK

Media Activity: Presentation With a partner, organize a multimedia presentation on the McCarthy era trials.

- Research information using reliable sources. Take notes. Identify copyright-free images that you might include.

- Choose a format for the ideas that you want to convey, such as charts, outlines, or slides with facts and illustrations.

- Make your presentation. As a class, discuss parallels between the McCarthy trials and those depicted in the play.

AS YOU READ Pay attention to details that explain Danforth's attitude toward Abigail and the other girls. Write down any questions you generate during reading.

ACT THREE

(The vestry room of the Salem *meeting house, now serving as the anteroom[1] of the General Court.*

As the curtain rises, the room is empty, but for sunlight pouring through two high windows in the back wall. The room is solemn, even forbidding. Heavy beams jut out, boards of random widths make up the walls. At the right are two doors leading into the meeting house proper, where the court is being held. At the left another door leads outside.

There is a plain bench at the left, and another at the right. In the center a rather long meeting table, with stools and a considerable armchair snugged up to it.

Through the partitioning wall at the right we hear a prosecutor's voice, Judge Hathorne's, *asking a question; then a woman's voice,* Martha Corey's, *replying.)*

Hathorne's Voice. Now, Martha Corey, there is abundant evidence in our hands to show that you have given yourself to the reading of fortunes. Do you deny it?

Martha Corey's Voice. I am innocent to a witch. I know not what a witch is.

Hathorne's Voice. How do you know, then, that you are not a witch?

10 **Martha Corey's Voice.** If I were, I would know it.

Hathorne's Voice. Why do you hurt these children?

Martha Corey's Voice. I do not hurt them. I scorn it!

Giles' Voice (*roaring*). I have evidence for the court!

(Voices of townspeople rise in excitement.)

Danforth's Voice. You will keep your
20 seat!

Giles' Voice. Thomas Putnam is reaching out for land!

Danforth's Voice. Remove that man, Marshal!

Giles' Voice. You're hearing lies, lies!

(A roaring goes up from the people.)

Hathorne's Voice. Arrest him, excellency!

Giles' Voice. I have evidence. Why will
30 you not hear my evidence?

(The door opens and Giles *is half carried into the vestry room by* Herrick.)

Giles. Hands off, damn you, let me go!

Herrick. Giles, Giles!

Giles. Out of my way, Herrick! I bring evidence—

Herrick. You cannot go in there, Giles; it's a court!

(Enter Hale *from the court.)*

40 **Hale.** Pray be calm a moment.

Giles. You, Mr. Hale, go in there and demand I speak.

Hale. A moment, sir, a moment.

---

[1] **vestry room . . . anteroom:** A vestry room is a room in a church used for nonreligious meetings or church business. An anteroom is a waiting room or a room that leads into another.

Giles. They'll be hangin' my wife!

(Judge Hathorne *enters. He is in his sixties, a bitter, remorseless Salem judge.*)

Hathorne. How do you dare come roarin' into this court! Are you gone
50   daft, Corey?

Giles. You're not a Boston judge yet, Hathorne. You'll not call me daft!

(*Enter* Deputy Governor Danforth *and, behind him,* Ezekiel Cheever *and* Parris. *On his appearance, silence falls.* Danforth *is a grave man in his sixties, of some humor and sophistication that does not, however, interfere with an exact loyalty to his position and his cause. He*
60   *comes down to* Giles, *who awaits his wrath.*)

Danforth (*looking directly at* Giles). Who is this man?

Parris. Giles Corey, sir, and a more contentious—

Giles (*to* Parris). I am asked the question, and I am old enough to answer it! (*to* Danforth, *who impresses him and to whom he smiles through his*
70   *strain*) My name is Corey, sir, Giles Corey. I have six hundred acres, and timber in addition. It is my wife you be condemning now. (*He indicates the courtroom.*)

Danforth. And how do you imagine to help her cause with such contemptuous riot?[2] Now be gone. Your old age alone keeps you out of jail for this.

Giles (*beginning to plead*). They be tellin'
80   lies about my wife, sir, I—

Danforth. Do you take it upon yourself to determine what this court shall believe and what it shall set aside?

---

[2] **contemptuous** (kən-tĕmp′chŏŏ-əs) **riot:** disrespectful, outrageous behavior.

Giles. Your Excellency, we mean no disrespect for—

Danforth. Disrespect indeed! It is disruption, Mister. This is the highest court of the supreme government of this province, do you know it?

90   **Giles** (*beginning to weep*). Your Excellency, I only said she were readin' books, sir, and they come and take her out of my house for—

Danforth (*mystified*). Books! What books?

Giles (*through helpless sobs*). It is my third wife, sir; I never had no wife that be so taken with books, and I thought to find the cause of it, d'y'see, but it were
100   no witch I blamed her for. (*He is openly weeping.*) I have broke charity with the woman, I have broke charity with her. (*He covers his face, ashamed.* Danforth *is respectfully silent.*)

Hale. Excellency, he claims hard evidence for his wife's defense. I think that in all justice you must—

Danforth. Then let him submit his evidence in proper affidavit. You are
110   certainly aware of our procedure here, Mr. Hale. (*to* Herrick) Clear this room.

Herrick. Come now, Giles. (*He gently pushes* Corey *out.*)

Francis. We are desperate, sir; we come here three days now and cannot be heard.

Danforth. Who is this man?

Francis. Francis Nurse, Your Excellency.

Hale. His wife's Rebecca that were
120   condemned this morning.

Danforth. Indeed! I am amazed to find you in such uproar. I have only good report of your character, Mr. Nurse.

Hathorne. I think they must both be arrested in contempt, sir.

Danforth (*to* Francis). Let you write your plea, and in due time I will—

Francis. Excellency, we have proof for your eyes; God forbid you shut them to it. The girls, sir, the girls are frauds.

Danforth. What's that?

Francis. We have proof of it, sir. They are all deceiving you.

(Danforth *is shocked, but studying* Francis.)

Hathorne. This is contempt, sir, contempt!

Danforth. Peace, Judge Hathorne. Do you know who I am, Mr. Nurse?

Francis. I surely do, sir, and I think you must be a wise judge to be what you are.

Danforth. And do you know that near to four hundred are in the jails from Marblehead to Lynn,[3] and upon my signature?

Francis. I—

Danforth. And seventy-two condemned to hang by that signature?

---

[3] **Marblehead . . . Lynn:** two coastal towns in Massachusetts, near Salem.

Francis. Excellency, I never thought to say it to such a weighty judge, but you are deceived.

(*Enter* Giles Corey *from left. All turn to see as he beckons in* Mary Warren *with* Proctor. Mary *is keeping her eyes to the ground;* Proctor *has her elbow as though she were near collapse.*)

Parris (*on seeing her, in shock*). Mary Warren! (*He goes directly to bend close to her face.*) What are you about here?

Proctor (*pressing* Parris *away from her with a gentle but firm motion of protectiveness*). She would speak with the Deputy Governor.

Danforth (*shocked by this, turns to* Herrick). Did you not tell me Mary Warren were sick in bed?

Herrick. She were, Your Honor. When I go to fetch her to the court last week, she said she were sick.

Giles. She has been strivin' with her soul all week, Your Honor; she comes now to tell the truth of this to you.

Danforth. Who is this?

Proctor. John Proctor, sir. Elizabeth Proctor is my wife.

Parris. Beware this man, Your Excellency, this man is mischief.

Hale (*excitedly*). I think you must hear the girl, sir, she—

180 **Danforth** (*who has become very interested in* Mary Warren *and only raises a hand toward* Hale). Peace. What would you tell us, Mary Warren?

(Proctor *looks at her, but she cannot speak.*)

Proctor. She never saw no spirits, sir.

Danforth (*with great alarm and surprise, to* Mary). Never saw no spirits!

Giles (*eagerly*). Never.

190 **Proctor** (*reaching into his jacket*). She has signed a deposition, sir—

Danforth (*instantly*). No, no, I accept no depositions. (*He is rapidly calculating this; he turns from her to* Proctor.) Tell me, Mr. Proctor, have you given out this story in the village?

Proctor. We have not.

Parris. They've come to overthrow the court, sir! This man is—

200 **Danforth.** I pray you, Mr. Parris. Do you know, Mr. Proctor, that the entire contention of the state in these trials is that the voice of Heaven is speaking through the children?

Proctor. I know that, sir.

Danforth (*thinks, staring at* Proctor, *then turns to* Mary Warren). And you, Mary Warren, how came you to cry out people for sending their spirits against you?

210

Mary Warren. It were pretense, sir.

Danforth. I cannot hear you.

Proctor. It were pretense, she says.

Danforth. Ah? And the other girls? Susanna Walcott, and—the others? They are also pretending?

Mary Warren. Aye, sir.

Danforth (*wide-eyed*). Indeed. (*Pause. He is baffled by this. He turns to study*
220 Proctor's *face.*)

Parris (*in a sweat*). Excellency, you surely cannot think to let so vile a lie be spread in open court!

Danforth. Indeed not, but it strike hard upon me that she will dare come here with such a tale. Now, Mr. Proctor, before I decide whether I shall hear you or not, it is my duty to tell you this. We burn a hot fire here; it melts down all
230 concealment.

Proctor. I know that, sir.

Danforth. Let me continue. I understand well, a husband's tenderness may drive him to extravagance in defense of a wife. Are you certain in your conscience, Mister, that your evidence is the truth?

Proctor. It is. And you will surely know it.

240 **Danforth.** And you thought to declare this revelation in the open court before the public?

Proctor. I thought I would, aye—with your permission.

Danforth (*his eyes narrowing*). Now, sir, what is your purpose in so doing?

Proctor. Why, I—I would free my wife, sir.

Danforth. There lurks nowhere in your
250 heart, nor hidden in your spirit, any desire to undermine this court?

Proctor (*with the faintest faltering*). Why, no, sir.

Cheever (*clears his throat, awakening*). I—Your Excellency.

Danforth. Mr. Cheever.

Cheever. I think it be my duty, sir— (*kindly, to* Proctor) You'll not deny it, John. (*to* Danforth) When we come to take his wife, he damned the court and ripped your warrant.

Parris. Now you have it!

Danforth. He did that, Mr. Hale?

Hale (*takes a breath*). Aye, he did.

Proctor. It were a temper, sir. I knew not what I did.

Danforth (*studying him*). Mr. Proctor.

Proctor. Aye, sir.

Danforth (*straight into his eyes*). Have you ever seen the Devil?

Proctor. No, sir.

Danforth. You are in all respects a Gospel Christian?

Proctor. I am, sir.

Parris. Such a Christian that will not come to church but once in a month!

Danforth (*restrained—he is curious*). Not come to church?

Proctor. I—I have no love for Mr. Parris. It is no secret. But God I surely love.

Cheever. He plow on Sunday, sir.

Danforth. Plow on Sunday!

Cheever (*apologetically*). I think it be evidence, John. I am an official of the court, I cannot keep it.

Proctor. I—I have once or twice plowed on Sunday. I have three children, sir, and until last year my land give little.

Giles. You'll find other Christians that do plow on Sunday if the truth be known.

Hale. Your Honor, I cannot think you may judge the man on such evidence.

Danforth. I judge nothing. (*Pause. He keeps watching* Proctor, *who tries to meet his gaze.*) I tell you straight, Mister—I have seen marvels in this court. I have seen people choked before my eyes by spirits; I have seen them stuck by pins and slashed by daggers. I have until this moment not the slightest reason to suspect that the children may be deceiving me. Do you understand my meaning?

Proctor. Excellency, does it not strike upon you that so many of these women have lived so long with such upright reputation, and—

Parris. Do you read the Gospel, Mr. Proctor?

Proctor. I read the Gospel.

Parris. I think not, or you should surely know that Cain were an upright man, and yet he did kill Abel.[4]

Proctor. Aye, God tells us that. (*to* Danforth) But who tells us Rebecca Nurse murdered seven babies by sending out her spirit on them? It is the children only, and this one will swear she lied to you.

(Danforth *considers, then beckons* Hathorne *to him.* Hathorne *leans in, and he speaks in his ear.* Hathorne *nods.*)

Hathorne. Aye, she's the one.

Danforth. Mr. Proctor, this morning, your wife send me a claim in which she states that she is pregnant now.

Proctor. My wife pregnant!

Danforth. There be no sign of it—we have examined her body.

---

[4] **Cain ... Abel:** According to the Book of Genesis in the Bible, Cain and Abel were the sons of Adam and Eve, the first humans.

Proctor. But if she say she is pregnant, then she must be! That woman will never lie, Mr. Danforth.

Danforth. She will not?

Proctor. Never, sir, never.

Danforth. We have thought it too convenient to be credited. However, if I
340 should tell you now that I will let her be kept another month; and if she begin to show her natural signs, you shall have her living yet another year until she is delivered—what say you to that? (John Proctor *is struck silent.*) Come now. You say your only purpose is to save your wife. Good, then, she is saved at least this year, and a year is long. What say you, sir? It is done now. (*In conflict,*
350 Proctor *glances at* Francis *and* Giles.) Will you drop this charge?

Proctor. I—I think I cannot.

Danforth (*now an almost imperceptible hardness in his voice*). Then your purpose is somewhat larger.

Parris. He's come to overthrow this court, Your Honor!

Proctor. These are my friends. Their wives are also accused—

360 **Danforth** (*with a sudden briskness of manner*). I judge you not, sir. I am ready to hear your evidence.

Proctor. I come not to hurt the court; I only—

Danforth (*cutting him off*). Marshal, go into the court and bid Judge Stoughton and Judge Sewall declare recess for one hour. And let them go to the tavern, if they will. All witnesses and prisoners
370 are to be kept in the building.

Herrick. Aye, sir. (*very deferentially*) If I may say it, sir, I know this man all my life. It is a good man, sir.

Danforth (*It is the reflection on himself he resents*). I am sure of it, Marshal. (Herrick *nods, then goes out.*) Now, what deposition do you have for us, Mr. Proctor? And I beg you be clear, open as the sky, and honest.

380 **Proctor** (*as he takes out several papers*). I am no lawyer, so I'll—

Danforth. The pure in heart need no lawyers. Proceed as you will.

Proctor (*handing* Danforth *a paper*). Will you read this first, sir? It's a sort of testament. The people signing it declare their good opinion of Rebecca, and my wife, and Martha Corey. (Danforth *looks down at the paper.*)

390 **Parris** (*to enlist* Danforth's *sarcasm*). Their good opinion! (*But* Danforth *goes on reading, and* Proctor *is heartened.*)

Proctor. These are all landholding farmers, members of the church. (*delicately, trying to point out a paragraph*) If you'll notice, sir—they've known the women many years and never saw no sign they had dealings with the Devil.

400 (Parris *nervously moves over and reads over* Danforth's *shoulder.*)

Danforth (*glancing down a long list*). How many names are here?

Francis. Ninety-one, Your Excellency.

Parris (*sweating*). These people should be summoned. (Danforth *looks up at him questioningly.*) For questioning.

Francis (*trembling with anger*). Mr. Danforth, I gave them all my word no
410 harm would come to them for signing this.

Parris. This is a clear attack upon the court!

Hale (*to* Parris, *trying to contain himself*). Is every defense an attack upon the court? Can no one—?

Parris. All innocent and Christian people are happy for the courts in Salem! These people are gloomy for it.

420 (*to* Danforth *directly*) And I think you will want to know, from each and every one of them, what discontents them with you!

Hathorne. I think they ought to be examined, sir.

Danforth. It is not necessarily an attack, I think. Yet—

Francis. These are all covenanted Christians, sir.

430 **Danforth.** Then I am sure they may have nothing to fear. (*hands* Cheever *the paper*) Mr. Cheever, have warrants drawn for all of these—arrest for examination. (*to* Proctor) Now, Mister, what other information do you have for us? (Francis *is still standing, horrified.*) You may sit, Mr. Nurse.

Francis. I have brought trouble on these people; I have—

440 **Danforth.** No, old man, you have not hurt these people if they are of good conscience. But you must understand, sir, that a person is either with this court or he must be counted against it, there be no road between. This is a sharp time, now, a precise time—we live no longer in the dusky afternoon when evil mixed itself with good and befuddled the world. Now, by God's 450 grace, the shining sun is up, and them that fear not light will surely praise it. I hope you will be one of those. (Mary Warren *suddenly sobs.*) She's not hearty,[5] I see.

Proctor. No, she's not, sir. (*to* Mary, *bending to her, holding her hand, quietly*) Now remember what the angel Raphael said to the boy Tobias.[6] Remember it.

Mary Warren (*hardly audible*). Aye.

460 **Proctor.** "Do that which is good, and no harm shall come to thee."

Mary Warren. Aye.

Danforth. Come, man, we wait you.

(Marshal Herrick *returns, and takes his post at the door.*)

Giles. John, my deposition, give him mine.

Proctor. Aye. (*He hands* Danforth *another paper.*) This is Mr. Corey's 470 deposition.

Danforth. Oh? (*He looks down at it. Now* Hathorne *comes behind him and reads with him.*)

Hathorne (*suspiciously*). What lawyer drew this, Corey?

Giles. You know I never hired a lawyer in my life, Hathorne.

Danforth (*finishing the reading*). It is very well phrased. My compliments. Mr. 480 Parris, if Mr. Putnam is in the court, will you bring him in? (Hathorne *takes the deposition, and walks to the window with it.* Parris *goes into the court.*) You have no legal training, Mr. Corey?

Giles (*very pleased*). I have the best, sir—I am thirty-three time in court in my life. And always plaintiff, too.

Danforth. Oh, then you're much put-upon.

490 **Giles.** I am never put-upon; I know my rights, sir, and I will have them. You

---

[5] **hearty:** well.

[6] **what the angel said . . . Tobias:** In the Book of Tobit in the Apocrypha, Tobit's son Tobias cured his father's blindness with the help of the angel Raphael.

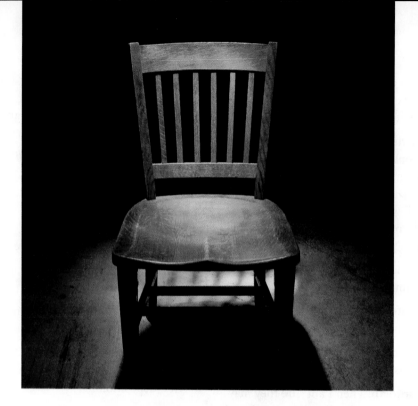

know, your father tried a case of mine—might be thirty-five year ago, I think.

Danforth. Indeed.

Giles. He never spoke to you of it?

Danforth. No, I cannot recall it.

Giles. That's strange, he give me nine pound damages. He were a fair judge, your father. Y'see, I had a white mare
500 that time, and this fellow come to borrow the mare—(*Enter* Parris *with* Thomas Putnam. *When he sees* Putnam, Giles' *ease goes; he is hard.*) Aye, there he is.

Danforth. Mr. Putnam, I have here an accusation by Mr. Corey against you. He states that you coldly prompted your daughter to cry witchery upon George Jacobs that is now in jail.

510 **Putnam.** It is a lie.

Danforth (*turning to* Giles). Mr. Putnam states your charge is a lie. What say you to that?

Giles (*furious, his fists clenched*). A fart on Thomas Putnam, that is what I say to that!

Danforth. What proof do you submit for your charge, sir?

Giles. My proof is there! (*pointing to*
520 *the paper*) If Jacobs hangs for a witch he forfeit up his property—that's law! And there is none but Putnam with the coin to buy so great a piece. This man is killing his neighbors for their land!

Danforth. But proof, sir, proof.

Giles (*pointing at his deposition*). The proof is there! I have it from an honest man who heard Putnam say it! The day his daughter cried out on Jacobs,
530 he said she'd given him a fair gift of land.

Hathorne. And the name of this man?

Giles (*taken aback*). What name?

Hathorne. The man that give you this information.

Giles (*hesitates, then*). Why, I—I cannot give you his name.

Hathorne. And why not?

Giles (*hesitates, then bursts out*). You know well why not! He'll lay in jail if I give his name!

Hathorne. This is contempt of the court, Mr. Danforth!

Danforth (*to avoid that*). You will surely tell us the name.

Giles. I will not give you no name. I mentioned my wife's name once and I'll burn in hell long enough for that. I stand mute.

Danforth. In that case, I have no choice but to arrest you for contempt of this court, do you know that?

Giles. This is a hearing; you cannot clap me for contempt of a hearing.

Danforth. Oh, it is a proper lawyer![7] Do you wish me to declare the court in full session here? Or will you give me good reply?

Giles (*faltering*). I cannot give you no name, sir, I cannot.

Danforth. You are a foolish old man. Mr. Cheever, begin the record. The court is now in session. I ask you, Mr. Corey—

Proctor (*breaking in*). Your Honor—he has the story in confidence, sir, and he—

Parris. The Devil lives on such confidences! (*to Danforth*) Without confidences there could be no conspiracy, Your Honor!

Hathorne. I think it must be broken, sir.

Danforth (*to Giles*). Old man, if your informant tells the truth let him come here openly like a decent man. But if he hide in anonymity I must know why. Now sir, the government and central church demand of you the name of him who reported Mr. Thomas Putnam a common murderer.

Hale. Excellency—

Danforth. Mr. Hale.

Hale. We cannot blink it more. There is a prodigious fear of this court in the country—

Danforth. Then there is a prodigious guilt in the country. Are *you* afraid to be questioned here?

Hale. I may only fear the Lord, sir, but there is fear in the country nevertheless.

Danforth (*angered now*). Reproach me not with the fear in the country; there is fear in the country because there is a moving[8] plot to topple Christ in the country!

Hale. But it does not follow that everyone accused is part of it.

Danforth. No uncorrupted man may fear this court, Mr. Hale! None! (*to Giles*) You are under arrest in contempt of this court. Now sit you down and take counsel with yourself, or you will be set in the jail until you decide to answer all questions.

(*Giles Corey* makes a rush for *Putnam. Proctor* lunges and holds him.)

Proctor. No, Giles!

Giles (*over* Proctor's *shoulder at* Putnam). I'll cut your throat, Putnam, I'll kill you yet!

Proctor (*forcing him into a chair*). Peace, Giles, peace. (*releasing him*) We'll prove ourselves. Now we will. (*He starts to turn to* Danforth.)

Giles. Say nothin' more, John. (*pointing at* Danforth) He's only playin' you! He means to hang us all!

(*Mary Warren* bursts into sobs.)

---

[7] **Oh . . . lawyer:** Oh, he thinks he is a real lawyer.

[8] **moving:** active.

Danforth. This is a court of law, Mister. I'll have no effrontery here!

Proctor. Forgive him, sir, for his old age. Peace, Giles, we'll prove it all now. (*He lifts up* Mary's *chin*.) You cannot weep, Mary. Remember the angel, what he say to the boy. Hold to it, now; there is your rock. (Mary *quiets. He takes out a paper, and turns to* Danforth.) This is Mary Warren's deposition. I—I would ask you remember, sir, while you read it, that until two week ago she were no different than the other children are today. (*He is speaking reasonably, restraining all his fears, his anger, his anxiety*.) You saw her scream, she howled, she swore familiar spirits choked her; she even testified that Satan, in the form of women now in jail, tried to win her soul away, and then when she refused—

Danforth. We know all this.

Proctor. Aye, sir. She swears now that she never saw Satan; nor any spirit, vague or clear, that Satan may have sent to hurt her. And she declares her friends are lying now.

(Proctor *starts to hand* Danforth *the deposition, and* Hale *comes up to* Danforth *in a trembling state*.)

Hale. Excellency, a moment. I think this goes to the heart of the matter.

Danforth (*with deep misgivings*). It surely does.

Hale. I cannot say he is an honest man; I know him little. But in all justice, sir, a claim so weighty cannot be argued by a farmer. In God's name, sir, stop here; send him home and let him come again with a lawyer—

Danforth (*patiently*). Now look you, Mr. Hale—

Hale. Excellency, I have signed seventy-two death warrants; I am a minister of the Lord, and I dare not take a life without there be a proof so immaculate no slightest qualm of conscience may doubt it.

Danforth. Mr. Hale, you surely do not doubt my justice.

Hale. I have this morning signed away the soul of Rebecca Nurse, Your Honor. I'll not conceal it, my hand shakes yet as with a wound! I pray you, sir, this argument let lawyers present to you.

Danforth. Mr. Hale, believe me; for a man of such terrible learning you are most bewildered—I hope you will forgive me. I have been thirty-two year at the bar, sir, and I should be confounded were I called upon to defend these people. Let you consider, now—(*to* Proctor *and the others*) And I bid you all do likewise. In an ordinary crime, how does one defend the accused? One calls up witnesses to prove his innocence. But witchcraft is *ipso facto*,[9] on its face and by its nature, an invisible crime, is it not? Therefore, who may possibly be witness to it? The witch and the victim. None other. Now we cannot hope the witch will accuse herself; granted? Therefore, we must rely upon her victims—and they do testify, the children certainly do testify. As for the witches, none will deny that we are most eager for all their confessions. Therefore, what is left for a lawyer to bring out? I think I have made my point. Have I not?

Hale. But this child claims the girls are not truthful, and if they are not—

Danforth. That is precisely what I am about to consider, sir. What more may you ask of me? Unless you doubt my probity?[10]

---

[9] *ipso facto* (**Latin**): by that very fact.
[10] **doubt my probity**: question my integrity.

Hale (*defeated*). I surely do not, sir. Let you consider it, then.

Danforth. And let you put your heart to rest. Her deposition, Mr. Proctor.

(Proctor *hands it to him.* Hathorne *rises, goes beside* Danforth, *and starts reading.* Parris *comes to his other side.* Danforth *looks at* John Proctor, *then proceeds to read.* Hale *gets up, finds position near the judge, reads too.* Proctor *glances at* Giles. Francis *prays silently, hands pressed together.* Cheever *waits placidly, the sublime official, dutiful.* Mary Warren *sobs once.* John Proctor *touches her head reassuringly. Presently* Danforth *lifts his eyes, stands up, takes out a kerchief and blows his nose. The others stand aside as he moves in thought toward the window.*)

Parris (*hardly able to contain his anger and fear*). I should like to question—

Danforth (*his first real outburst, in which his contempt for* Parris *is clear*). Mr. Parris, I bid you be silent! (*He stands in silence, looking out the window. Now, having established that he will set the gait.*) Mr. Cheever, will you go into the court and bring the children here? (Cheever *gets up and goes out upstage.* Danforth *now turns to* Mary.) Mary Warren, how came you to this turnabout? Has Mr. Proctor threatened you for this deposition?

Mary Warren. No, sir.

Danforth. Has he ever threatened you?

Mary Warren (*weaker*). No, sir.

Danforth (*sensing a weakening*). Has he threatened you?

Mary Warren. No, sir.

Danforth. Then you tell me that you sat in my court, callously lying, when you knew that people would hang by your evidence? (*She does not answer.*) Answer me!

Mary Warren (*almost inaudibly*). I did, sir.

Danforth. How were you instructed in your life? Do you not know that God damns all liars? (*She cannot speak.*) Or is it now that you lie?

Mary Warren. No, sir—I am with God now.

Danforth. You are with God now.

Mary Warren. Aye, sir.

Danforth (*containing himself*). I will tell you this—you are either lying now, or you were lying in the court, and in either case you have committed perjury and you will go to jail for it. You cannot lightly say you lied, Mary. Do you know that?

Mary Warren. I cannot lie no more. I am with God, I am with God.

(*But she breaks into sobs at the thought of it, and the right door opens, and enter* Susanna Walcott, Mercy Lewis, Betty Parris, *and finally* Abigail. Cheever *comes to* Danforth.)

Cheever. Ruth Putnam's not in the court, sir, nor the other children.

Danforth. These will be sufficient. Sit you down, children. (*Silently they sit.*) Your friend, Mary Warren, has given us a deposition. In which she swears that she never saw familiar spirits, apparitions, nor any manifest of the Devil. She claims as well that none of you have seen these things either. (*slight pause*) Now, children, this is a court of law. The law, based upon the Bible, and the Bible, writ by Almighty God, forbid the practice of witchcraft, and describe death as the penalty thereof. But likewise, children, the law and Bible damn all bearers of false witness.

(*slight pause*) Now then. It does not escape me that this deposition may be devised to blind us; it may well be that Mary Warren has been conquered by Satan, who sends her here to distract our sacred purpose. If so, her neck will break for it. But if she speak true, I bid you now drop your guile and confess your pretense, for a quick confession will go easier with you. (*pause*) Abigail Williams, rise. (Abigail *slowly rises.*) Is there any truth in this?

Abigail. No, sir.

Danforth (*thinks, glances at* Mary, *then back to* Abigail). Children, a very auger bit[11] will now be turned into your souls until your honesty is proved. Will either of you change your positions now, or do you force me to hard questioning?

Abigail. I have naught to change, sir. She lies.

Danforth (*to* Mary). You would still go on with this?

Mary Warren (*faintly*). Aye, sir.

Danforth (*turning to* Abigail). A poppet were discovered in Mr. Proctor's house, stabbed by a needle. Mary Warren claims that you sat beside her in the court when she made it, and that you saw her make it and witnessed how she herself stuck her needle into it for safe-keeping. What say you to that?

Abigail (*with a slight note of indignation*). It is a lie, sir.

Danforth (*after a slight pause*). While you worked for Mr. Proctor, did you see poppets in that house?

Abigail. Goody Proctor always kept poppets.

Proctor. Your Honor, my wife never kept no poppets. Mary Warren confesses it was her poppet.

Cheever. Your Excellency.

Danforth. Mr. Cheever.

Cheever. When I spoke with Goody Proctor in that house, she said she never kept no poppets. But she said she did keep poppets when she were a girl.

Proctor. She has not been a girl these fifteen years, Your Honor.

Hathorne. But a poppet will keep fifteen years, will it not?

Proctor. It will keep if it is kept, but Mary Warren swears she never saw no poppets in my house, nor anyone else.

Parris. Why could there not have been poppets hid where no one ever saw them?

Proctor (*furious*). There might also be a dragon with five legs in my house, but no one has ever seen it.

Parris. We are here, Your Honor, precisely to discover what no one has ever seen.

Proctor. Mr. Danforth, what profit this girl to turn herself about? What may Mary Warren gain but hard questioning and worse?

Danforth. You are charging Abigail Williams with a marvelous cool plot to murder, do you understand that?

Proctor. I do, sir. I believe she means to murder.

Danforth (*pointing at* Abigail, *incredulously*). This child would murder your wife?

Proctor. It is not a child. Now hear me, sir. In the sight of the congregation she were twice this year put out of this meetin' house for laughter during prayer.

---

[11] **auger** (ô′gər) **bit:** drill.

Danforth (*shocked, turning to* Abigail).
What's this? Laughter during—!

Parris. Excellency, she were under
Tituba's power at that time, but she is
solemn now.

Giles. Aye, now she is solemn and goes
to hang people!

Danforth. Quiet, man.

Hathorne. Surely it have no bearing
on the question, sir. He charges
contemplation of murder.

Danforth. Aye. (*He studies* Abigail *for a
moment, then.*) Continue, Mr. Proctor.

Proctor. Mary. Now tell the Governor
how you danced in the woods.

Parris (*instantly*). Excellency, since I
come to Salem this man is blackening
my name. He—

Danforth. In a moment, sir. (*to* Mary
Warren, *sternly, and surprised*) What is
this dancing?

Mary Warren. I—(*She glances at* Abigail,
*who is staring down at her remorselessly.
Then, appealing to* Proctor.) Mr.
Proctor—

Proctor (*taking it right up*). Abigail leads
the girls to the woods, Your Honor, and
they have danced there naked—

Parris. Your Honor, this—

Proctor (*at once*). Mr. Parris discovered
them himself in the dead of night!
There's the "child" she is!

Danforth (*It is growing into a nightmare,
and he turns, astonished, to* Parris). Mr.
Parris—

Parris. I can only say, sir, that I never
found any of them naked, and this man
is—

Danforth. But you discovered them
dancing in the woods? (*Eyes on* Parris,
he points at Abigail.) Abigail?

Hale. Excellency, when I first arrived
from Beverly, Mr. Parris told me that.

Danforth. Do you deny it, Mr. Parris?

Parris. I do not, sir, but I never saw any
of them naked.

Danforth. But she have *danced*?

Parris (*unwillingly*). Aye, sir.

(Danforth, *as though with new eyes,
looks at* Abigail.)

Hathorne. Excellency, will you permit
me? (*He points at* Mary Warren.)

Danforth (*with great worry*). Pray,
proceed.

Hathorne. You say you never saw no
spirits, Mary, were never threatened or
afflicted by any manifest of the Devil or
the Devil's agents.

Mary Warren (*very faintly*). No, sir.

Hathorne (*with a gleam of victory*). And
yet, when people accused of witchery
confronted you in court, you would
faint, saying their spirits came out of
their bodies and choked you—

Mary Warren. That were pretense, sir.

Danforth. I cannot hear you.

Mary Warren. Pretense, sir.

Parris. But you did turn cold, did you
not? I myself picked you up many times,
and your skin were icy. Mr. Danforth,
you—

Danforth. I saw that many times.

Proctor. She only pretended to faint,
Your Excellency. They're all marvelous
pretenders.

Hathorne. Then can she pretend to
faint now?

Proctor. Now?

Parris. Why not? Now there are no
spirits attacking her, for none in this
room is accused of witchcraft. So let her

turn herself cold now, let her pretend she is attacked now, let her faint. (*He turns to* Mary Warren.) Faint!

Mary Warren. Faint?

Parris. Aye, faint. Prove to us how you pretended in the court so many times.

Mary Warren (*looking to* Proctor). I—cannot faint now, sir.

Proctor (*alarmed, quietly*). Can you not pretend it?

960

Mary Warren. I—(*She looks about as though searching for the passion to faint.*) I—have no *sense* of it now, I—

Danforth. Why? What is lacking now?

Mary Warren. I—cannot tell, sir, I—

Danforth. Might it be that here we have no afflicting spirit loose, but in the court there were some?

Mary Warren. I never saw no spirits.

970

Parris. Then see no spirits now, and prove to us that you can faint by your own will, as you claim.

Mary Warren (*stares, searching for the emotion of it, and then shakes her head*). I—cannot do it.

Parris. Then you will confess, will you not? It were attacking spirits made you faint!

Mary Warren. No, sir, I—

980

Parris. Your Excellency, this is a trick to blind the court!

Mary Warren. It's not a trick! (*She stands.*) I—I used to faint because I—I thought I saw spirits.

Danforth. *Thought* you saw them!

Mary Warren. But I did not, Your Honor.

Hathorne. How could you think you saw them unless you saw them?

990

Mary Warren. I—I cannot tell how, but I did. I—I heard the other girls screaming, and you, Your Honor, you seemed to believe them, and I—It were only sport in the beginning, sir, but then the whole world cried spirits, spirits, and I—I promise you, Mr. Danforth, I only thought I saw them but I did not.

(Danforth *peers at her.*)

1000

Parris (*smiling, but nervous because* Danforth *seems to be struck by* Mary Warren*'s story*). Surely Your Excellency is not taken by this simple lie.

Danforth (*turning worriedly to* Abigail). Abigail. I bid you now search your heart and tell me this—and beware of it, child, to God every soul is precious and His vengeance is terrible on them that take life without cause. Is it possible, child, that the spirits you have seen are illusion only, some deception that may cross your mind when—

1010

Abigail. Why, this—this—is a base question, sir.

Danforth. Child, I would have you consider it—

Abigail. I have been hurt, Mr. Danforth; I have seen my blood runnin' out! I have been near to murdered every day because I done my duty pointing out the Devil's people—and this is my reward? To be mistrusted, denied, questioned like a—

1020

Danforth (*weakening*). Child, I do not mistrust you—

Abigail (*in an open threat*). Let *you* beware, Mr. Danforth. Think you to be so mighty that the power of Hell may not turn *your* wits? Beware of it! There is—(*Suddenly, from an accusatory attitude, her face turns, looking into the air above—it is truly frightened.*)

1030

Danforth (*apprehensively*). What is it, child?

Abigail (*looking about in the air, clasping her arms about her as though cold*). I—I know not. A wind, a cold wind, has come. (*Her eyes fall on* Mary Warren.)

Mary Warren (*terrified, pleading*). Abby!

1040 **Mercy Lewis** (*shivering*). Your Honor, I freeze!

Proctor. They're pretending!

Hathorne (*touching* Abigail's *hand*). She is cold, Your Honor, touch her!

Mercy Lewis (*through chattering teeth*). Mary, do you send this shadow on me?

Mary Warren. Lord, save me!

Susanna Walcott. I freeze, I freeze!

Abigail (*shivering visibly*). It is a wind, a 1050 wind!

Mary Warren. Abby, don't do that!

Danforth (*himself engaged and entered by* Abigail). Mary Warren, do you witch her? I say to you, do you send your spirit out?

(*With a hysterical cry* Mary Warren *starts to run.* Proctor *catches her.*)

Mary Warren (*almost collapsing*). Let me go, Mr. Proctor, I cannot, I cannot—

1060 **Abigail** (*crying to Heaven*). Oh, Heavenly Father, take away this shadow!

(*Without warning or hesitation,* Proctor *leaps at* Abigail *and, grabbing her by the hair, pulls her to her feet. She screams in pain.* Danforth, *astonished, cries,* "What are you about?" *and* Hathorne *and* Parris *call,* "Take your hands off her!" *and out of it all comes* Proctor's *roaring voice.*)

1070 **Proctor.** How do you call Heaven! Whore! Whore!

(Herrick *breaks* Proctor *from her.*)

Herrick. John!

Danforth. Man! Man, what do you—

Proctor (*breathless and in agony*). It is a whore!

Danforth (*dumbfounded*). You charge—?

Abigail. Mr. Danforth, he is lying!

1080 **Proctor.** Mark her! Now she'll suck a scream to stab me with, but—

Danforth. You will prove this! This will not pass!

Proctor (*trembling, his life collapsing about him*). I have known her, sir. I have known her.

Danforth. You—you are a lecher?

Francis (*horrified*). John, you cannot say such a—

1090 **Proctor.** Oh, Francis, I wish you had some evil in you that you might know me! (*to* Danforth) A man will not cast away his good name. You surely know that.

Danforth (*dumbfounded*). In—in what time? In what place?

Proctor (*his voice about to break, and his shame great*). In the proper place— where my beasts are bedded. On the 1100 last night of my joy, some eight months past. She used to serve me in my house, sir. (*He has to clamp his jaw to keep from weeping.*) A man may think God sleeps, but God sees everything, I know it now. I beg you, sir, I beg you—see her what she is. My wife, my dear good wife, took this girl soon after, sir, and put her out on the highroad. And being what she is, a lump of vanity, sir—(*He is being overcome.*) Excellency, forgive 1110 me, forgive me. (*Angrily against himself, he turns away from the* Governor *for a moment. Then, as though to cry out is his only means of speech left.*) She thinks to dance with me on my wife's grave! And well she might, for I thought of her softly. God help me, I lusted, and there *is* a promise in such sweat. But it is a whore's vengeance, and you must see it; I set myself entirely in your hands. I know you must see it now.

Danforth (*blanched, in horror, turning to* Abigail). You deny every scrap and tittle[12] of this?

Abigail. If I must answer that, I will leave and I will not come back again!

(Danforth *seems unsteady.*)

Proctor. I have made a bell of my honor! I have rung the doom of my good name—you will believe me, Mr. Danforth! My wife is innocent, except she knew a whore when she saw one!

Abigail (*stepping up to* Danforth). What look do you give me? (Danforth *cannot speak.*) I'll not have such looks! (*She turns and starts for the door.*)

Danforth. You will remain where you are! (Herrick *steps into her path. She comes up short, fire in her eyes.*) Mr. Parris, go into the court and bring Goodwife Proctor out.

Parris (*objecting*). Your Honor, this is all a—

Danforth (*sharply to* Parris). Bring her out! And tell her not one word of what's been spoken here. And let you knock before you enter. (Parris *goes out.*) Now we shall touch the bottom of this swamp. (*to* Proctor) Your wife, you say, is an honest woman.

Proctor. In her life, sir, she have never lied. There are them that cannot sing, and them that cannot weep—my wife cannot lie. I have paid much to learn it, sir.

Danforth. And when she put this girl out of your house, she put her out for a harlot?[13]

Proctor. Aye, sir.

Danforth. And knew her for a harlot?

Proctor. Aye, sir, she knew her for a harlot.

Danforth. Good then. (*to* Abigail) And if she tell me, child, it were for harlotry, may God spread His mercy on you! (*There is a knock. He calls to the door.*) Hold! (*to* Abigail) Turn your back. Turn your back. (*to* Proctor) Do likewise. (*Both turn their backs—*Abigail *with indignant slowness.*) Now let neither of you turn to face Goody Proctor. No one in this room is to speak one word, or raise a gesture aye or nay. (*He turns toward the door, calls.*) Enter! (*The door opens.* Elizabeth *enters with* Parris. Parris *leaves her. She stands alone, her eyes looking for* Proctor.) Mr. Cheever, report this testimony in all exactness. Are you ready?

Cheever. Ready, sir.

Danforth. Come here, woman. (Elizabeth *comes to him, glancing at* Proctor's *back.*) Look at me only, not at your husband. In my eyes only.

Elizabeth (*faintly*). Good, sir.

Danforth. We are given to understand that at one time you dismissed your servant, Abigail Williams.

Elizabeth. That is true, sir.

Danforth. For what cause did you dismiss her? (*Slight pause. Then* Elizabeth *tries to glance at* Proctor.) You will look in my eyes only and not at your husband. The answer is in your memory and you need no help to give

---

[12] **every scrap and tittle:** every tiny bit.

[13] **for a harlot:** as a woman of low morals.

it to me. Why did you dismiss Abigail Williams?

Elizabeth (*not knowing what to say, sensing a situation, wetting her lips to stall for time*). She—dissatisfied me. (*pause*) And my husband.

Danforth. In what way dissatisfied you?

Elizabeth. She were—(*She glances at* Proctor *for a cue.*)

Danforth. Woman, look at me! (Elizabeth *does.*) Were she slovenly? Lazy? What disturbance did she cause?

Elizabeth. Your Honor, I—in that time I were sick. And I—My husband is a good and righteous man. He is never drunk as some are, nor wastin' his time at the shovelboard, but always at his work. But in my sickness—you see, sir, I were a long time sick after my last baby, and I thought I saw my husband somewhat turning from me. And this girl—(*She turns to* Abigail.)

Danforth. Look at me.

Elizabeth. Aye, sir. Abigail Williams— (*She breaks off.*)

Danforth. What of Abigail Williams?

Elizabeth. I came to think he fancied her. And so one night I lost my wits, I think, and put her out on the highroad.

Danforth. Your husband—did he indeed turn from you?

Elizabeth (*in agony*). My husband—is a goodly man, sir.

Danforth. Then he did not turn from you.

Elizabeth (*starting to glance at* Proctor). He—

Danforth (*reaches out and holds her face, then*). Look at me! To your own knowledge, has John Proctor ever committed the crime of lechery? (*In a crisis of indecision she cannot speak.*)

Answer my question! Is your husband a lecher!

Elizabeth (*faintly*). No, sir.

Danforth. Remove her, Marshal.

Proctor. Elizabeth, tell the truth!

Danforth. She has spoken. Remove her!

Proctor (*crying out*). Elizabeth, I have confessed it!

Elizabeth. Oh, God! (*The door closes behind her.*)

Proctor. She only thought to save my name!

Hale. Excellency, it is a natural lie to tell; I beg you, stop now before another is condemned! I may shut my conscience to it no more—private vengeance is working through this testimony! From the beginning this man has struck me true. By my oath to Heaven, I believe him now, and I pray you call back his wife before we—

Danforth. She spoke nothing of lechery, and this man has lied!

Hale. I believe him! (*pointing at* Abigail) This girl has always struck me false! She has—

(Abigail, *with a weird, wild, chilling cry, screams up to the ceiling.*)

Abigail. You will not! Begone! Begone, I say!

Danforth. What is it, child? (*But* Abigail, *pointing with fear, is now raising up her frightened eyes, her awed face, toward the ceiling—the girls are doing the same—and now* Hathorne, Hale, Putnam, Cheever, Herrick, *and* Danforth *do the same.*) What's there? (*He lowers his eyes from the ceiling, and now he is frightened; there is real tension in his voice.*) Child! (*She is transfixed—with all the girls, she is whimpering*

open-mouthed, agape at the ceiling.)
1280 Girls! Why do you—?

Mercy Lewis (*pointing*). It's on the beam! Behind the rafter!

Danforth (*looking up*). Where!

Abigail. Why—? (*She gulps.*) Why do you come, yellow bird?

Proctor. Where's a bird? I see no bird!

Abigail (*to the ceiling*). My face? My face?

Proctor. Mr. Hale—

1290 **Danforth.** Be quiet!

Proctor (*to Hale*). Do you see a bird?

Danforth. Be quiet!!

Abigail (*to the ceiling, in a genuine conversation with the "bird," as though trying to talk it out of attacking her*). But God made my face; you cannot want to tear my face. Envy is a deadly sin, Mary.

Mary Warren (*on her feet with a spring, and horrified, pleading*). Abby!

1300 **Abigail** (*unperturbed, continuing to the "bird"*). Oh, Mary, this is a black art[14] to change your shape. No, I cannot, I cannot stop my mouth; it's God's work I do.

Mary Warren. Abby, I'm *here!*

Proctor (*frantically*). They're pretending, Mr. Danforth!

Abigail (*Now she takes a backward step, as though in fear the bird will swoop down momentarily*). Oh, please, Mary!
1310 Don't come down.

Susanna Walcott. Her claws, she's stretching her claws!

Proctor. Lies, lies.

Abigail (*backing further, eyes still fixed above*). Mary, please don't hurt me!

Mary Warren (*to* Danforth). I'm not hurting her!

Danforth (*to* Mary Warren). Why does
1320 she see this vision?

Mary Warren. She sees nothin'!

Abigail (*now staring full front as though hypnotized, and mimicking the exact tone of* Mary Warren's *cry*). She sees nothin'!

Mary Warren (*pleading*). Abby, you mustn't!

Abigail and All the Girls (*all transfixed*). Abby, you mustn't!

Mary Warren (*to all the* Girls). I'm here,
1330 I'm here!

Girls. I'm here, I'm here!

Danforth (*horrified*). Mary Warren! Draw back your spirit out of them!

Mary Warren. Mr. Danforth!

Girls (*cutting her off*). Mr. Danforth!

Danforth. Have you compacted with the Devil? Have you?

Mary Warren. Never, never!

Girls. Never, never!

1340 **Danforth** (*growing hysterical*). Why can they only repeat you?

Proctor. Give me a whip—I'll stop it!

Mary Warren. They're sporting.[15] They—!

Girls. They're sporting!

Mary Warren (*turning on them all hysterically and stamping her feet*). Abby, stop it!

Girls (*stamping their feet*). Abby, stop it!

1350 **Mary Warren.** Stop it!

Girls. Stop it!

---

[14]**a black art:** sorcery.

[15]**sporting:** playing a game.

Mary Warren (*screaming it out at the top of her lungs, and raising her fists*). Stop it!!

Girls (*raising their fists*). Stop it!!

(Mary Warren, *utterly confounded, and becoming overwhelmed by* Abigail's— *and the girls'—utter conviction, starts to whimper, hands half raised, powerless, and all the girls begin whimpering exactly as she does.*)

Danforth. A little while ago you were afflicted. Now it seems you afflict others; where did you find this power?

Mary Warren (*staring at* Abigail). I— have no power.

Girls. I have no power.

Proctor. They're gulling you,[16] Mister!

Danforth. Why did you turn about this past two weeks? You have seen the Devil, have you not?

Hale (*indicating* Abigail *and the girls*). You cannot believe them!

Mary Warren. I—

Proctor (*sensing her weakening*). Mary, God damns all liars!

Danforth (*pounding it into her*). You have seen the Devil, you have made compact with Lucifer, have you not?

Proctor. God damns liars, Mary!

(Mary *utters something unintelligible, staring at* Abigail, *who keeps watching the "bird" above.*)

Danforth. I cannot hear you. What do you say? (Mary *utters again unintelligibly.*) You will confess yourself or you will hang! (*He turns her roughly to face him.*) Do you know who I am? I say you will hang if you do not open with me!

Proctor. Mary, remember the angel Raphael—do that which is good and—

Abigail (*pointing upward*). The wings! Her wings are spreading! Mary, please, don't, don't—!

Hale. I see nothing, Your Honor!

---

[16] **gulling you:** deceiving you.

Danforth. Do you confess this power! (*He is an inch from her face.*) Speak!

Abigail. She's going to come down! 1400 She's walking the beam!

Danforth. Will you speak!

Mary Warren (*staring in horror*). I cannot!

Girls. I cannot!

Parris. Cast the Devil out! Look him in the face! Trample him! We'll save you, Mary, only stand fast against him and—

Abigail (*looking up*). Look out! She's coming down!

1410 (*She and all the girls run to one wall, shielding their eyes. And now, as though cornered, they let out a gigantic scream, and Mary, as though infected, opens her mouth and screams with them. Gradually Abigail and the girls leave off, until only Mary is left there, staring up at the "bird," screaming madly. All watch her, horrified by this evident fit. Proctor strides to her.*)

1420 **Proctor.** Mary, tell the Governor what they—(*He has hardly got a word out, when, seeing him coming for her, she rushes out of his reach, screaming in horror.*)

Mary Warren. Don't touch me—don't touch me! (*At which the girls halt at the door.*)

Proctor (*astonished*). Mary!

Mary Warren (*pointing at Proctor*). 1430 You're the Devil's man! (*He is stopped in his tracks.*)

Parris. Praise God!

Girls. Praise God!

Proctor (*numbed*). Mary, how—?

Mary Warren. I'll not hang with you! I love God, I love God.

Danforth (*to* Mary). He bid you do the Devil's work?

Mary Warren (*hysterically, indicating* 1440 Proctor). He come at me by night and every day to sign, to sign, to—

Danforth. Sign what?

Parris. The Devil's book? He come with a book?

Mary Warren (*hysterically, pointing at* Proctor, *fearful of him*). My name, he want my name. "I'll murder you," he says, "if my wife hangs! We must go and overthrow the court," he says!

1450 (Danforth's *head jerks toward* Proctor, *shock and horror in his face.*)

Proctor (*turning, appealing to* Hale). Mr. Hale!

Mary Warren (*her sobs beginning*). He wake me every night, his eyes were like coals and his fingers claw my neck, and I sign, I sign . . .

Hale. Excellency, this child's gone wild!

Proctor (*as* Danforth's *wide eyes pour on* 1460 *him*). Mary, Mary!

Mary Warren (*screaming at him*). No, I love God; I go your way no more. I love God, I bless God. (*Sobbing, she rushes to* Abigail.) Abby, Abby, I'll never hurt you more! (*They all watch, as* Abigail, *out of her infinite charity, reaches out and draws the sobbing* Mary *to her, and then looks up to* Danforth.)

Danforth (*to* Proctor). What are you? 1470 (Proctor *is beyond speech in his anger.*) You are combined with anti-Christ,[17] are you not? I have seen your power; you will not deny it! What say you, Mister?

Hale. Excellency—

---

[17] **anti-Christ:** in the New Testament Christ's great enemy, expected to spread evil before Christ conquers him and the world ends (1 John 2:18).

Danforth. I will have nothing from you, Mr. Hale! (*to* Proctor) Will you confess yourself befouled with Hell, or do you keep that black allegiance yet? What say you?

1480 **Proctor** (*his mind wild, breathless*). I say—I say—God is dead!

Parris. Hear it, hear it!

Proctor (*laughs insanely, then*). A fire, a fire is burning! I hear the boot of Lucifer, I see his filthy face! And it is my face, and yours, Danforth! For them that quail to bring men out of ignorance, as I have quailed, and as you quail now when you know in all your
1490 black hearts that this be fraud—God damns our kind especially, and we will burn, we will burn together!

Danforth. Marshal! Take him and Corey with him to the jail!

Hale (*starting across to the door*). I denounce these proceedings!

Proctor. You are pulling Heaven down and raising up a whore!

Hale. I denounce these proceedings, I
1500 quit this court! (*He slams the door to the outside behind him.*)

Danforth (*calling to him in a fury*). Mr. Hale! Mr. Hale!

(*The curtain falls.*)

COLLABORATIVE DISCUSSION Why are the judges taken in by Abigail's simulated terror? With a partner, discuss the implications for them if they are proven wrong about the girls. Cite specific textual evidence from the play to support your ideas.

Analyze Drama Elements

 COMMON CORE   ELACC11-12RL3

In his play, Miller incorporates three types of characters, a dramatic convention that heightens suspense and tension. Determining which characters fulfill these roles will help readers understand how the characters' interaction is part of the playwright's plan for his plot.

> The **protagonist** is the main character around whom most of the action centers.
>
> The **antagonist** is the character that opposes the protagonist; this leads to the major conflict.
>
> **Foils** are minor characters who present a striking contrast to a more major character, thus emphasizing that other character's traits.

Analzying the Text

COMMON CORE   ELACC11-12RL1, ELACC11-12RL3, ELACC11-12RL5, ELACC11-12W2, ELACC11-12W4

Cite Text Evidence   Support your responses with evidence from the selection.

1. **Analyze** Mary Warren might be seen as the foil for Abigail. Explain how she is used to bring out Abigail's traits.

2. **Analyze** What does Danforth's reaction to Giles's outburst at the beginning of the act suggest about his character?

3. **Analyze** Why does Elizabeth lie to Danforth about her husband's relationship with Abigail? What motivates her actions?

4. **Interpret** Why does the court debate whether Proctor plows on Sunday? What is the significance of this debate?

5. **Draw Conclusions** How has Proctor changed from the beginning of the play? What do his actions in this act reveal about his character?

PERFORMANCE TASK

Writing Activity: Analysis The real Abigail Williams was eleven years old in 1692 and had not had an illicit relationship with John Proctor. How would the play be different if Miller had not presented a different version of history? What would be lost?

- Identify the ways in which the relationship between Proctor and Abigail affects the development of plot as well as supports Miller's view about the witch hunts.

- Cite details from the play in support of your views.

- Write an analysis in which you logically present your ideas based on explicit statements from the text or inferences based on evidence from the text.

AS YOU READ Pay attention to the details that tell you how the witch hunt has affected those involved in it. Write down any questions you generate during reading.

ACT FOUR

(*A cell in* Salem *jail, that fall.*

At the back is a high barred window; near it, a great, heavy door. Along the walls are two benches.

The place is in darkness but for the moonlight seeping through the bars. It appears empty. Presently footsteps are heard coming down a corridor beyond the wall, keys rattle, and the door swings open. Marshal Herrick *enters with a lantern.*

He is nearly drunk, and heavy-footed. He goes to a bench and nudges a bundle of rags lying on it.)

Herrick. Sarah, wake up! Sarah Good! (*He then crosses to the other bench.*)

Sarah Good (*rising in her rags*). Oh, Majesty! Comin', comin'! Tituba, he's here, His Majesty's come!

Herrick. Go to the north cell; this place is wanted now.

(*He hangs his lantern on the wall.* Tituba *sits up.*)

10 **Tituba.** That don't look to me like His Majesty; look to me like the marshal.

Herrick (*taking out a flask*). Get along with you now, clear this place. (*He drinks, and* Sarah Good *comes and peers up into his face.*)

Sarah Good. Oh, is it you, Marshal! I thought sure you be the Devil comin' for us. Could I have a sip of cider for me goin'-away?

20 **Herrick** (*handing her the flask*). And where are you off to, Sarah?

Tituba (*as Sarah drinks*). We goin' to Barbados, soon the Devil gits here with the feathers and the wings.

Herrick. Oh? A happy voyage to you.

Sarah Good. A pair of bluebirds wingin' southerly, the two of us! Oh, it be a grand transformation, Marshal! (*She raises the flask to drink again.*)

30 **Herrick** (*taking the flask from her lips*). You'd best give me that or you'll never rise off the ground. Come along now.

Tituba. I'll speak to him for you, if you desires to come along, Marshal.

Herrick. I'd not refuse it, Tituba; it's the proper morning to fly into Hell.

Tituba. Oh, it be no Hell in Barbados. Devil, him be pleasure-man in Barbados, him be singin' and dancin' in 40 Barbados. It's you folks—you riles him up 'round here; it be too cold 'round here for that Old Boy. He freeze his soul in Massachusetts, but in Barbados he just as sweet and—(*A bellowing cow is heard, and* Tituba *leaps up and calls to the window.*) Aye, sir! That's him, Sarah!

Sarah Good. I'm here, Majesty! (*They hurriedly pick up their rags as* Hopkins, *a guard, enters.*)

50 **Hopkins.** The Deputy Governor's arrived.

Herrick (*grabbing* Tituba). Come along, come along.

Tituba (*resisting him*). No, he comin' for me. I goin' home!

Herrick (*pulling her to the door*). That's not Satan, just a poor old cow with a hatful of milk. Come along now, out with you!

60 **Tituba** (*calling to the window*). Take me home, Devil! Take me home!

Sarah Good (*following the shouting Tituba out*). Tell him I'm goin', Tituba! Now you tell him Sarah Good is goin' too!

(*In the corridor outside* Tituba *calls on*—"*Take me home, Devil; Devil take me home!*" *and* Hopkins' *voice orders her to move on.* Herrick *returns and*
70 *begins to push old rags and straw into a corner. Hearing footsteps, he turns, and enter* Danforth *and Judge* Hathorne. *They are in greatcoats and wear hats against the bitter cold. They are followed in by* Cheever, *who carries a dispatch case*[1] *and a flat wooden box containing his writing materials.*)

Herrick. Good morning, Excellency.

Danforth. Where is Mr. Parris?

80 **Herrick.** I'll fetch him. (*He starts for the door.*)

Danforth. Marshal. (Herrick *stops.*) When did Reverend Hale arrive?

Herrick. It were toward midnight, I think.

Danforth (*suspiciously*). What is he about here?

Herrick. He goes among them that will hang, sir. And he prays with them. He
90 sits with Goody Nurse now. And Mr. Parris with him.

Danforth. Indeed. That man have no authority to enter here, Marshal. Why have you let him in?

Herrick. Why, Mr. Parris command me, sir. I cannot deny him.

Danforth. Are you drunk, Marshal?

Herrick. No, sir; it is a bitter night, and I have no fire here.

100 **Danforth** (*containing his anger*). Fetch Mr. Parris.

Herrick. Aye, sir.

Danforth. There is a prodigious stench in this place.

Herrick. I have only now cleared the people out for you.

Danforth. Beware hard drink, Marshal.

Herrick. Aye, sir. (*He waits an instant for further orders. But* Danforth, *in*
110 *dissatisfaction, turns his back on him, and* Herrick *goes out. There is a pause.* Danforth *stands in thought.*)

Hathorne. Let you question Hale, Excellency; I should not be surprised he have been preaching in Andover[2] lately.

Danforth. We'll come to that; speak nothing of Andover. Parris prays with him. That's strange. (*He blows on his hands, moves toward the window, and*
120 *looks out.*)

Hathorne. Excellency, I wonder if it be wise to let Mr. Parris so continuously with the prisoners. (Danforth *turns to him, interested.*) I think, sometimes, the man has a mad look these days.

Danforth. Mad?

Hathorne. I met him yesterday coming out of his house, and I bid him good morning—and he wept and went his
130 way. I think it is not well the village sees him so unsteady.

Danforth. Perhaps he have some sorrow.

---

[1] **dispatch case:** a case for carrying documents.

[2] **Andover:** a town in Massachusetts northwest of Salem.

Cheever (*stamping his feet against the cold*). I think it be the cows, sir.

Danforth. Cows?

Cheever. There be so many cows wanderin' the highroads, now their masters are in the jails, and much
140 disagreement who they will belong to now. I know Mr. Parris be arguin' with farmers all yesterday— there is great contention, sir, about the cows. Contention make him weep, sir; it were always a man that weep for contention. (*He turns, as do* Hathorne *and* Danforth, *hearing someone coming up the corridor.* Danforth *raises his head as* Parris *enters. He is gaunt, frightened, and sweating in*
150 *his greatcoat.*)

Parris (*to* Danforth, *instantly*). Oh, good morning, sir, thank you for coming, I beg your pardon wakin' you so early. Good morning, Judge Hathorne.

Danforth. Reverend Hale have no right to enter this—

Parris. Excellency, a moment. (*He hurries back and shuts the door.*)

Hathorne. Do you leave him alone with
160 the prisoners?

Danforth. What's his business here?

Parris (*prayerfully holding up his hands*). Excellency, hear me. It is a providence. Reverend Hale has returned to bring Rebecca Nurse to God.

Danforth (*surprised*). He bids her confess?

Parris (*sitting*). Hear me. Rebecca have not given me a word this three month
170 since she came. Now she sits with him, and her sister and Martha Corey and two or three others, and he pleads with them, confess their crimes and save their lives.

Danforth. Why—this is indeed a providence. And they soften, they soften?

Parris. Not yet, not yet. But I thought to summon you, sir, that we might think
180 on whether it be not wise, to—(*He dares not say it.*) I had thought to put a question, sir, and I hope you will not—

Danforth. Mr. Parris, be plain, what troubles you?

Parris. There is news, sir, that the court—the court must reckon with. My niece, sir, my niece—I believe she has vanished.

Danforth. Vanished!

190 **Parris.** I had thought to advise you of it earlier in the week, but—

Danforth. Why? How long is she gone?

Parris. This be the third night. You see, sir, she told me she would stay a night with Mercy Lewis. And next day, when she does not return, I send to Mr. Lewis to inquire. Mercy told him she would sleep in *my* house for a night.

Danforth. They are both gone?!

200 **Parris** (*in fear of him*). They are, sir.

Danforth (*alarmed*). I will send a party for them. Where may they be?

Parris. Excellency, I think they be aboard a ship. (Danforth *stands agape.*) My daughter tells me how she heard them speaking of ships last week, and tonight I discover my—my strongbox is broke into. (*He presses his fingers against his eyes to keep back tears.*)

210 **Hathorne** (*astonished*). She have robbed you?

Parris. Thirty-one pound is gone. I am penniless. (*He covers his face and sobs.*)

Danforth. Mr. Parris, you are a brainless man! (*He walks in thought, deeply worried.*)

Parris. Excellency, it profit nothing you should blame me. I cannot think they would run off except they fear to keep in Salem any more. (*He is pleading.*) Mark it, sir, Abigail had close knowledge of the town, and since the news of Andover has broken here—

Danforth. Andover is remedied.³ The court returns there on Friday, and will resume examinations.

Parris. I am sure of it, sir. But the rumor here speaks rebellion in Andover, and it—

Danforth. There is no rebellion in Andover!

Parris. I tell you what is said here, sir. Andover have thrown out the court, they say, and will have no part of witchcraft. There be a faction here, feeding on that news, and I tell you true, sir, I fear there will be riot here.

Hathorne. Riot! Why at every execution I have seen naught but high satisfaction in the town.

Parris. Judge Hathorne—it were another sort that hanged till now. Rebecca Nurse is no Bridget that lived three year with Bishop before she married him. John Proctor is not Isaac Ward that drank his family to ruin. (*to Danforth*) I would to God it were not so, Excellency, but these people have great weight yet in the town. Let Rebecca stand upon the gibbet⁴ and send up some righteous prayer, and I fear she'll wake a vengeance on you.

Hathorne. Excellency, she is condemned a witch. The court have—

Danforth (*in deep concern, raising a hand to* Hathorne). Pray you. (*to* Parris) How do you propose, then?

Parris. Excellency, I would postpone these hangin's for a time.

Danforth. There will be no postponement.

Parris. Now Mr. Hale's returned, there is hope, I think—for if he bring even one of these to God, that confession surely damns the others in the public eye, and none may doubt more that they are all linked to Hell. This way, unconfessed and claiming innocence, doubts are multiplied, many honest people will weep for them, and our good purpose is lost in their tears.

Danforth (*after thinking a moment, then going to* Cheever). Give me the list.

(Cheever *opens the dispatch case, searches.*)

Parris. It cannot be forgot, sir, that when I summoned the congregation for John Proctor's excommunication⁵ there were hardly thirty people come to hear it. That speak a discontent, I think, and—

Danforth (*studying the list*). There will be no postponement.

Parris. Excellency—

Danforth. Now, sir—which of these in your opinion may be brought to God? I will myself strive with him⁶ till dawn. (*He hands the list to* Parris, *who merely glances at it.*)

Parris. There is not sufficient time till dawn.

Danforth. I shall do my utmost. Which of them do you have hope for?

---

³ **remedied:** no longer a problem.
⁴ **gibbet** (jĭb´ĭt): gallows.

⁵ **excommunication:** banishment from a church. For the Puritans in New England, this punishment resulted in the loss of church privileges.
⁶ **strive with him:** struggle with him through prayer.

Parris (*not even glancing at the list now, and in a quavering voice, quietly*). Excellency—a dagger— (*He chokes up.*)

Danforth. What do you say?

Parris. Tonight, when I open my door to leave my house—a dagger clattered to the ground. (*Silence. Danforth absorbs this. Now Parris cries out.*) You cannot hang this sort. There is danger for me. I dare not step outside at night!

(*Reverend Hale enters. They look at him for an instant in silence. He is steeped in sorrow, exhausted, and more direct than he ever was.*)

Danforth. Accept my congratulations, Reverend Hale; we are gladdened to see you returned to your good work.

Hale (*coming to Danforth now*). You must pardon them. They will not budge.

(*Herrick enters, waits.*)

Danforth (*conciliatory*). You misunderstand, sir; I cannot pardon these when twelve are already hanged for the same crime. It is not just.

Parris (*with failing heart*). Rebecca will not confess?

Hale. The sun will rise in a few minutes. Excellency, I must have more time.

Danforth. Now hear me, and beguile yourselves no more. I will not receive a single plea for pardon or postponement. Them that will not confess will hang. Twelve are already executed; the names of these seven are given out, and the village expects to see them die this morning. Postponement now speaks a floundering on my part; reprieve or pardon must cast doubt upon the guilt of them that died till now. While I speak God's law, I will not crack its voice with whimpering. If retaliation is your fear, know this—I should hang ten thousand that dared to rise against the law, and an ocean of salt tears could not melt the resolution of the statutes. Now draw yourselves up like men and help me, as you are bound by Heaven to do. Have you spoken with them all, Mr. Hale?

Hale. All but Proctor. He is in the dungeon.

Danforth (*to* Herrick). What's Proctor's way now?

Herrick. He sits like some great bird; you'd not know he lived except he will take food from time to time.

Danforth (*after thinking a moment*). His wife—his wife must be well on with child now.

Herrick. She is, sir.

Danforth. What think you, Mr. Parris? You have closer knowledge of this man; might her presence soften him?

Parris. It is possible, sir. He have not laid eyes on her these three months. I should summon her.

Danforth (*to* Herrick). Is he yet adamant? Has he struck at you again?

Herrick. He cannot, sir, he is chained to the wall now.

Danforth (*after thinking on it*). Fetch Goody Proctor to me. Then let you bring him up.

Herrick. Aye, sir. (*Herrick goes. There is silence.*)

Hale. Excellency, if you postpone a week and publish to the town that you are striving for their confessions, that speak mercy on your part, not faltering.

Danforth. Mr. Hale, as God have not empowered me like Joshua to stop this sun from rising,[7] so I cannot withhold

---

[7] **like Joshua . . . rising:** According to the Bible, Joshua became leader of the Israelites after Moses died. He led the people to the Promised Land while the sun stood still.

from them the perfection of their punishment.

Hale (*harder now*). If you think God wills you to raise rebellion, Mr. Danforth, you are mistaken!

Danforth (*instantly*). You have heard
380   rebellion spoken in the town?

Hale. Excellency, there are orphans wandering from house to house; abandoned cattle bellow on the highroads, the stink of rotting crops hangs everywhere, and no man knows when the harlots' cry will end his life— and you wonder yet if rebellion's spoke? Better you should marvel how they do not burn your province!

390   **Danforth.** Mr. Hale, have you preached in Andover this month?

Hale. Thank God they have no need of me in Andover.

Danforth. You baffle me, sir. Why have you returned here?

Hale. Why, it is all simple. I come to do the Devil's work. I come to counsel Christians they should belie themselves. (*His sarcasm collapses.*) There is blood
400   on my head! Can you not see the blood on my head!!

Parris. Hush! (*For he has heard footsteps. They all face the door.* Herrick *enters with* Elizabeth. *Her wrists are linked by heavy chain, which* Herrick *now removes. Her clothes are dirty; her face is pale and gaunt.* Herrick *goes out.*)

Danforth (*very politely*). Goody Proctor. (*She is silent.*) I hope you are hearty?

410   **Elizabeth** (*as a warning reminder*). I am yet six month before my time.

Danforth. Pray be at your ease, we come not for your life. We—(*uncertain how to plead, for he is not accustomed to it.*) Mr. Hale, will you speak with the woman?

Hale. Goody Proctor, your husband is marked to hang this morning.

(*pause*)

Elizabeth (*quietly*). I have heard it.

Hale. You know, do you not, that I have no connection with the court? (*She seems to doubt it.*) I come of my own, Goody Proctor. I would save your husband's life, for if he is taken I count myself his murderer. Do you understand me?

Elizabeth. What do you want of me?

Hale. Goody Proctor, I have gone this three month like our Lord into the wilderness.[8] I have sought a Christian way, for damnation's doubled on a minister who counsels men to lie.

Hathorne. It is no lie, you cannot speak of lies.

Hale. It is a lie! They are innocent!

Danforth. I'll hear no more of that!

Hale (*continuing to* Elizabeth). Let you not mistake your duty as I mistook my own. I came into this village like a bridegroom to his beloved, bearing gifts of high religion; the very crowns of holy law I brought, and what I touched with my bright confidence, it died; and where I turned the eye of my great faith, blood flowed up. Beware, Goody Proctor—cleave to no faith when faith brings blood. It is mistaken law that leads you to sacrifice. Life, woman, life is God's most precious gift; no principle, however glorious, may justify the taking of it. I beg you, woman, prevail upon your husband to confess. Let him give his lie. Quail not before God's judgment in this, for it may well be God damns a liar less than he that throws his life away for pride. Will you plead with him? I cannot think he will listen to another.

Elizabeth (*quietly*). I think that be the Devil's argument.

---

[8] **like our Lord . . . wilderness:** According to the New Testament, Jesus spent 40 days wandering in the desert.

Hale (*with a climactic desperation*). Woman, before the laws of God we are as swine! We cannot read His will!

Elizabeth. I cannot dispute with you, sir; I lack learning for it.

Danforth (*going to her*). Goody Proctor, you are not summoned here for disputation. Be there no wifely tenderness within you? He will die with the sunrise. Your husband. Do you understand it? (*She only looks at him.*) What say you? Will you contend with him? (*She is silent.*) Are you stone? I tell you true, woman, had I no other proof of your unnatural life, your dry eyes now would be sufficient evidence that you delivered up your soul to Hell! A very ape would weep at such calamity! Have the Devil dried up any tear of pity in you? (*She is silent.*) Take her out. It profit nothing she should speak to him!

Elizabeth (*quietly*). Let me speak with him, Excellency.

Parris (*with hope*). You'll strive with him? (*She hesitates.*)

Danforth. Will you plead for his confession or will you not?

Elizabeth. I promise nothing. Let me speak with him.

(*A sound—the sibilance of dragging feet on stone. They turn. A pause.* Herrick *enters with* John Proctor. *His wrists are chained. He is another man, bearded, filthy, his eyes misty as though webs had overgrown them. He halts inside the doorway, his eye caught by the sight of* Elizabeth. *The emotion flowing between them prevents anyone from speaking for an instant. Now* Hale, *visibly affected, goes to* Danforth *and speaks quietly.*)

Hale. Pray, leave them, Excellency.

Danforth (*pressing* Hale *impatiently aside*). Mr. Proctor, you have been notified, have you not? (Proctor *is silent,* *staring at* Elizabeth.) I see light in the sky, Mister; let you counsel with your wife, and may God help you turn your back on Hell. (Proctor *is silent, staring at* Elizabeth.)

510 **Hale** (*quietly*). Excellency, let—

(Danforth *brushes past* Hale *and walks out.* Hale *follows.* Cheever *stands and follows,* Hathorne *behind.* Herrick *goes.* Parris, *from a safe distance, offers.*)

Parris. If you desire a cup of cider, Mr. Proctor, I am sure I—(Proctor *turns an icy stare at him, and he breaks off.* Parris *raises his palms toward* Proctor.) God lead you now. (Parris *goes out.*)

520 (*Alone.* Proctor *walks to her, halts. It is as though they stood in a spinning world. It is beyond sorrow, above it. He reaches out his hand as though toward an embodiment not quite real, and as he touches her, a strange soft sound, half laughter, half amazement, comes from his throat. He pats her hand. She covers his hand with hers. And then, weak, he sits. Then she sits, facing him.*)

530 **Proctor.** The child?

Elizabeth. It grows.

Proctor. There is no word of the boys?

Elizabeth. They're well. Rebecca's Samuel keeps them.

Proctor. You have not seen them?

Elizabeth. I have not. (*She catches a weakening in herself and downs it.*)

Proctor. You are a—marvel, Elizabeth.

Elizabeth. You—have been tortured?

540 **Proctor.** Aye. (*Pause. She will not let herself be drowned in the sea that threatens her.*) They come for my life now.

Elizabeth. I know it.

(*pause*)

Proctor. None—have yet confessed?

Elizabeth. There be many confessed.

Proctor. Who are they?

Elizabeth. There be a hundred or more, 550 they say. Goody Ballard is one; Isaiah Goodkind is one. There be many.

Proctor. Rebecca?

Elizabeth. Not Rebecca. She is one foot in Heaven now; naught may hurt her more.

Proctor. And Giles?

Elizabeth. You have not heard of it?

Proctor. I hear nothin', where I am kept.

Elizabeth. Giles is dead.

560 (*He looks at her incredulously.*)

Proctor. When were he hanged?

Elizabeth (*quietly, factually*). He were not hanged. He would not answer aye or nay to his indictment; for if he denied the charge they'd hang him surely, and auction out his property. So he stand mute, and died Christian under the law. And so his sons will have his farm. It is the law, for he could not be 570 condemned a wizard without he answer the indictment, aye or nay.

Proctor. Then how does he die?

Elizabeth (*gently*). They press him, John.

Proctor. Press?

Elizabeth. Great stones they lay upon his chest until he plead aye or nay. (*with a tender smile for the old man*) They say he give them but two words. "More 580 weight," he says. And died.

Proctor (*numbed—a thread to weave into his agony*). "More weight."

Elizabeth. Aye. It were a fearsome[9] man, Giles Corey.

(*pause*)

Proctor (*with great force of will, but not quite looking at her*). I have been thinking I would confess to them, Elizabeth. (*She shows nothing.*) What say you? If I give them that?

590

Elizabeth. I cannot judge you, John.

(*pause*)

Proctor (*simply—a pure question*). What would you have me do?

Elizabeth. As you will, I would have it. (*slight pause*) I want you living, John. That's sure.

Proctor (*pauses, then with a flailing of hope*). Giles' wife? Have she confessed?

600 **Elizabeth.** She will not.

(*pause*)

Proctor. It is a pretense, Elizabeth.

Elizabeth. What is?

Proctor. I cannot mount the gibbet like a saint. It is a fraud. I am not that man. (*She is silent.*) My honesty is broke, Elizabeth; I am no good man. Nothing's spoiled by giving them this lie that were not rotten long before.

610 **Elizabeth.** And yet you've not confessed till now. That speak goodness in you.

Proctor. Spite only keeps me silent. It is hard to give a lie to dogs. (*Pause. For the first time he turns directly to her.*) I would have your forgiveness, Elizabeth.

Elizabeth. It is not for me to give, John, I am—

Proctor. I'd have you see some honesty in it. Let them that never lied die now to keep their souls. It is pretense for me, a vanity that will not blind God nor keep

620

my children out of the wind. (*pause*) What say you?

Elizabeth (*upon a heaving sob that always threatens*). John, it come to naught that I should forgive you, if you'll not forgive yourself. (*Now he turns away a little, in great agony.*) It is not my soul, John, it is yours. (*He stands, as though in physical pain, slowly rising to his feet with a great immortal longing to find his answer. It is difficult to say, and she is on the verge of tears.*) Only be sure of this, for I know it now: Whatever you will do, it is a good man does it. (*He turns his doubting, searching gaze upon her.*) I have read my heart this three month, John. (*pause*) I have sins of my own to count. It needs a cold wife to prompt lechery.

630

640

Proctor (*in great pain*). Enough, enough—

Elizabeth (*now pouring out her heart*). Better you should know me!

Proctor. I will not hear it! I know you!

Elizabeth. You take my sins upon you, John—

Proctor (*in agony*). No, I take my own, my own!

650 **Elizabeth.** John, I counted myself so plain, so poorly made, no honest love could come to me! Suspicion kissed you when I did; I never knew how I should say my love. It were a cold house I kept! (*In fright, she swerves, as* Hathorne *enters.*)

Hathorne. What say you, Proctor? The sun is soon up.

(Proctor, *his chest heaving, stares, turns* to Elizabeth. *She comes to him as though to plead, her voice quaking.*)

660

Elizabeth. Do what you will. But let none be your judge. There be no higher judge under Heaven than Proctor is!

---

[9] **fearsome:** courageous.

Forgive me, forgive me, John—I never knew such goodness in the world! (*She covers her face, weeping.*)

(Proctor *turns from her to* Hathorne; *he is off the earth, his voice hollow.*)

670 **Proctor.** I want my life.

Hathorne (*electrified, surprised*). You'll confess yourself?

Proctor. I will have my life.

Hathorne (*with a mystical tone*). God be praised! It is a providence! (*He rushes out the door, and his voice is heard calling down the corridor.*) He will confess! Proctor will confess!

Proctor (*with a cry, as he strides to the* 680 *door*). Why do you cry it? (*In great pain he turns back to her.*) It is evil, is it not? It is evil.

Elizabeth (*in terror, weeping*). I cannot judge you, John, I cannot!

Proctor. Then who will judge me? (*suddenly clasping his hands*) God in Heaven, what is John Proctor, what is John Proctor? (*He moves as an animal, and a fury is riding in him, a tantalized* 690 *search.*) I think it is honest, I think so; I am no saint. (*As though she had denied this he calls angrily at her.*) Let Rebecca go like a saint; for me it is fraud!

(*Voices are heard in the hall, speaking together in suppressed excitement.*)

Elizabeth. I am not your judge, I cannot be. (*as though giving him release*) Do as you will, do as you will!

Proctor. Would you give them such a 700 lie? Say it. Would you ever give them this? (*She cannot answer.*) You would not; if tongs of fire were singeing you you would not! It is evil. Good, then—it is evil, and I do it!

(Hathorne *enters with* Danforth, *and, with them,* Cheever, Parris, *and* Hale.

It is a businesslike, rapid entrance, as though the ice had been broken.)

Danforth (*with great relief and* 710 *gratitude*). Praise to God, man, praise to God; you shall be blessed in Heaven for this. (Cheever *has hurried to the bench with pen, ink, and paper.* Proctor *watches him.*) Now then, let us have it. Are you ready, Mr. Cheever?

Proctor (*with a cold, cold horror at their efficiency*). Why must it be written?

Danforth. Why, for the good instruction of the village, Mister; this 720 we shall post upon the church door! (*to* Parris, *urgently*) Where is the marshal?

Parris (*runs to the door and calls down the corridor*). Marshal! Hurry!

Danforth. Now, then, Mister, will you speak slowly, and directly to the point, for Mr. Cheever's sake. (*He is on record now, and is really dictating to* Cheever, *who writes.*) Mr. Proctor, have you seen the Devil in your life? (Proctor*'s jaws* 730 *lock.*) Come, man, there is light in the sky; the town waits at the scaffold; I would give out this news. Did you see the Devil?

Proctor. I did.

Parris. Praise God!

Danforth. And when he come to you, what were his demand? (Proctor *is silent.* Danforth *helps.*) Did he bid you to do his work upon the earth?

740 **Proctor.** He did.

Danforth. And you bound yourself to his service? (Danforth *turns, as* Rebecca Nurse *enters, with* Herrick *helping to support her. She is barely able to walk.*) Come in, come in, woman!

Rebecca (*brightening as she sees* Proctor). Ah, John! You are well, then, eh?

(Proctor *turns his face to the wall.*)

750 **Danforth.** Courage, man, courage—let her witness your good example that she may come to God herself. Now hear it, Goody Nurse! Say on, Mr. Proctor. Did you bind yourself to the Devil's service?

Rebecca (*astonished*). Why, John!

Proctor (*through his teeth, his face turned from* Rebecca). I did.

Danforth. Now, woman, you surely see it profit nothin' to keep this conspiracy 760 any further. Will you confess yourself with him?

Rebecca. Oh, John—God send his mercy on you!

Danforth. I say, will you confess yourself, Goody Nurse?

Rebecca. Why, it is a lie, it is a lie; how may I damn myself? I cannot, I cannot.

Danforth. Mr. Proctor. When the Devil came to you did you see Rebecca Nurse 770 in his company? (Proctor *is silent.*) Come, man, take courage—did you ever see her with the Devil?

Proctor (*almost inaudibly*). No.

(Danforth, *now sensing trouble, glances at* John *and goes to the table, and picks up a sheet—the list of condemned.*)

Danforth. Did you ever see her sister, Mary Easty, with the Devil?

Proctor. No, I did not.

780 **Danforth** (*his eyes narrow on* Proctor). Did you ever see Martha Corey with the Devil?

Proctor. I did not.

Danforth (*realizing, slowly putting the sheet down*). Did you ever see anyone with the Devil?

Proctor. I did not.

Danforth. Proctor, you mistake me. I am not empowered to trade your life for 790 a lie. You have most certainly seen some person with the Devil. (Proctor *is silent.*) Mr. Proctor, a score of people have already testified they saw this woman with the Devil.

Proctor. Then it is proved. Why must I say it?

Danforth. Why "must" you say it! Why, you should rejoice to say it if your soul is truly purged of any love for Hell!

800 **Proctor.** They think to go like saints. I like not to spoil their names.

Danforth (*inquiring, incredulous*). Mr. Proctor, do you think they go like saints?

Proctor (*evading*). This woman never thought she done the Devil's work.

Danforth. Look you, sir. I think you mistake your duty here. It matters nothing what she thought—she is 810 convicted of the unnatural murder of children, and you for sending your spirit out upon Mary Warren. Your soul alone is the issue here, Mister, and you will prove its whiteness or you cannot live in a Christian country. Will you tell me now what persons conspired with you in the Devil's company? (Proctor *is silent.*) To your knowledge was Rebecca Nurse ever—

820 **Proctor.** I speak my own sins; I cannot judge another. (*crying out, with hatred*) I have no tongue for it.

Hale (*quickly to* Danforth). Excellency, it is enough he confess himself. Let him sign it, let him sign it.

Parris (*feverishly*). It is a great service, sir. It is a weighty name; it will strike the village that Proctor confess. I beg you, let him sign it. The sun is up, 830 Excellency!

Danforth (*considers; then with dissatisfaction*). Come, then, sign your testimony. (*to* Cheever) Give it to him. (Cheever *goes to* Proctor, *the confession and a pen in hand.* Proctor *does not look at it.*) Come, man, sign it.

Proctor (*after glancing at the confession*). You have all witnessed it—it is enough.

Danforth. You will not sign it?

840　**Proctor.** You have all witnessed it; what more is needed?

Danforth. Do you sport with me? You will sign your name or it is no confession, Mister! (*His breast heaving with agonized breathing,* Proctor *now lays the paper down and signs his name.*)

Parris. Praise be to the Lord!

(Proctor *has just finished signing when* Danforth *reaches for the paper. But* Proctor *snatches it up, and now a wild terror is rising in him, and a boundless anger.*)

Danforth (*perplexed, but politely extending his hand*). If you please, sir.

Proctor. No.

Danforth (*as though* Proctor *did not understand*). Mr. Proctor, I must have—

Proctor. No, no. I have signed it. You have seen me. It is done! You have no 860　need for this.

Parris. Proctor, the village must have proof that—

Proctor. Damn the village! I confess to God, and God has seen my name on this! It is enough!

Danforth. No, sir, it is—

Proctor. You came to save my soul, did you not? Here! I have confessed myself; it is enough!

870　**Danforth.** You have not con—

Proctor. I have confessed myself! Is there no good penitence but it be public? God does not need my name nailed upon the church! God sees my name; God knows how black my sins are! It is enough!

Danforth. Mr. Proctor—

Proctor. You will not use me! I am no Sarah Good or Tituba, I am John 880　Proctor! You will not use me! It is no part of salvation that you should use me!

Danforth. I do not wish to—

Proctor. I have three children—how may I teach them to walk like men in the world, and I sold my friends?

Danforth. You have not sold your friends—

Proctor. Beguile me not! I blacken all of 890　them when this is nailed to the church the very day they hang for silence!

Danforth. Mr. Proctor, I must have good and legal proof that you—

Proctor. You are the high court, your word is good enough! Tell them I confessed myself; say Proctor broke his knees and wept like a woman; say what you will, but my name cannot—

Danforth (*with suspicion*). It is the same, 900　is it not? If I report it or you sign to it?

Proctor (*He knows it is insane*). No, it is not the same! What others say and what I sign to is not the same!

Danforth. Why? Do you mean to deny this confession when you are free?

Proctor. I mean to deny nothing!

Danforth. Then explain to me, Mr. Proctor, why you will not let—

Proctor (*with a cry of his whole soul*). 910　Because it is my name! Because I cannot have another in my life! Because I lie and sign myself to lies! Because I am not worth the dust on the feet of them that hang! How may I live without my name? I have given you my soul; leave me my name!

Danforth (*pointing at the confession in Proctor's hand*). Is that document a lie? If it is a lie I will not accept it! What
920 say you? I will not deal in lies, Mister! (*Proctor is motionless.*) You will give me your honest confession in my hand, or I cannot keep you from the rope. (*Proctor does not reply.*) Which way do you go, Mister?

(*His breast heaving, his eyes staring, Proctor tears the paper and crumples it, and he is weeping in fury, but erect.*)

Danforth. Marshal!

930 **Parris** (*hysterically, as though the tearing paper were his life*). Proctor, Proctor!

Hale. Man, you will hang! You cannot!

Proctor (*his eyes full of tears*). I can. And there's your first marvel, that I can. You have made your magic now, for now I do think I see some shred of goodness in John Proctor. Not enough to weave a banner with, but white enough to keep it from such dogs. (*Elizabeth, in a burst
940 of terror, rushes to him and weeps against his hand.*) Give them no tear! Tears pleasure them! Show honor now, show a stony heart and sink them with it! (*He has lifted her, and kisses her now with great passion.*)

Rebecca. Let you fear nothing! Another judgment waits us all!

Danforth. Hang them high over the town! Who weeps for these, weeps for
950 corruption! (*He sweeps out past them.*

Herrick *starts to lead* Rebecca, *who almost collapses, but* Proctor *catches her, and she glances up at him apologetically.*)

Rebecca. I've had no breakfast.

Herrick. Come, man.

(Herrick *escorts them out,* Hathorne *and* Cheever *behind them.* Elizabeth *stands staring at the empty doorway.*)

Parris (*in deadly fear, to* Elizabeth). Go to him, Goody Proctor! There is yet
960 time!

(*From outside a drumroll strikes the air.* Parris *is startled.* Elizabeth *jerks about toward the window.*)

Parris. Go to him! (*He rushes out the door, as though to hold back his fate.*) Proctor! Proctor! (*again, a short burst of drums*)

Hale. Woman, plead with him! (*He
970 starts to rush out the door, and then goes back to her.*) Woman! It is pride, it is vanity. (*She avoids his eyes, and moves to the window. He drops to his knees.*) Be his helper!— What profit him to bleed? Shall the dust praise him? Shall the worms declare his truth? Go to him, take his shame away!

Elizabeth (*supporting herself against collapse, grips the bars of the window,
980 and with a cry*). He have his goodness now. God forbid I take it from him!

(*The final drumroll crashes, then heightens violently.* Hale *weeps in frantic prayer, and the new sun is pouring in upon her face, and the drums rattle like bones in the morning air. The curtain falls.*)

COLLABORATIVE DISCUSSION With a partner, discuss what the last act reveals about the participants in the witch hunt. What is ironic about their circumstances? Cite specific textual evidence from the play to support your ideas.

Analyze Drama Elements

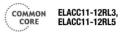

Two remaining elements of drama effectively utilized by Miller are characterization and dialogue.

Throughout *The Crucible*, the characters' traits, motives, and relationships emerge. Miller reveals these facets of character through direct and indirect characterization as described in the chart.

Direct characterization means that specific details about character are provided.	**The stage directions** in the play offer explicit descriptions of characters' appearances, personalities, and emotional states. For example, in Act One, Hale is described as "a tight-skinned, eager-eyed intellectual. This is a beloved errand for him." The stage directions in Act Four depict him as being "steeped in sorrow, exhausted."
Indirect characterization requires readers to use clues from the text to infer what the character is like.	While **dialogue** might be used to state direct ideas about a character, most often readers must infer meaning from what is said. For example, in lines 439–451 in Act Four, Hale's speech reveals his inner conflict and the way that he has changed. "I came into this village like a bridegroom to his beloved . . . cleave to no faith when faith brings blood . . . Life, woman, life is God's most precious gift; no principle, however glorious, may justify the taking of it."
	Characters' actions as described or performed reveal more about them. In Act Three, for example, Hale denounces the proceedings and walks out. His uncharacteristic burst of anger shows readers how distraught he is over what is happening and suggests that he may feel guilty for his role in the events.

Dialogue is the foundation of drama. It can reveal an infinite variety of character traits. In addition to revealing character as explained in the chart, it performs a variety of other critical functions.

- It moves the plot forward. Through characters' speech, readers learn about plot developments and gain a greater understanding of the central conflict and its impact: "Twelve are already executed; the names of these seven are given out, and the village expects to see them die this morning."
- It also conveys theme. Characters' speeches often state important ideas that help readers to recognize the playwright's underlying message: "Because it is my name! Because I cannot have another in my life!"

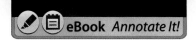
Analyzing the Text

COMMON CORE

ELACC11-12RL1,
ELACC11-12RL2,
ELACC11-12RL3,
ELACC11-12RL4,
ELACC11-12RL5,
ELACC11-12W2,
ELACC11-12W4

Cite Text Evidence   Support your responses with evidence from the selection.

1. **Analyze** How do the stage directions at the beginning of Act Four set the mood? What does the contrast between this setting and the one described at the start of Act One suggest about the changes brought about by the witch hunts?

2. **Infer** Explain why each of these characters wants Proctor and the other prisoners to confess. Cite evidence in support of your response.

    • Danforth
    • Parris
    • Hale

3. **Analyze** What image of Giles Corey do Elizabeth's words convey in Act Four, lines 576–580? What does Giles Corey represent for Miller? Think of his earlier appearances in the play.

4. **Interpret** A crucible is a severe test or trial. It is also a vessel in which materials are melted at high temperatures to produce a more refined substance. What does a crucible symbolize in this drama? How does this symbol suggest a theme?

5. **Analyze** Reread the passages identified in the list. What is the central paradox, or contradiction, of the trials? What idea is Miller conveying about these kinds of witch hunts through this paradox?

    • Act Two, lines 1132–1143
    • Act Three, lines 440–454
    • Act Three, lines 672–696

6. **Synthesize** Explain how the resolution of Proctor's conflict reveals a major theme in the play.

7. **Analyze** What do the events in Act Four foreshadow about the future of the trials? Explain.

PERFORMANCE TASK

Writing Activity: Essay Why does John Proctor change his mind and tear up the confession even though this virtually condemns him to die? In four or five paragraphs, discuss Proctor's perception of a morally righteous person and how that perception affects his decision. Think about Rebecca Nurse's reaction to his confession and Elizabeth's assertion that "there be no higher judge under Heaven than Proctor is!"

• Explain the choices that Proctor must make to arrive at his decision.

• Use quotations and examples from the play to support key points.

• Clarify how Proctor's idea of morality differs from that of the judges.

Language and Style: Dialogue

In *The Crucible*, Miller carefully constructs his dialogue to match the historical time period in which he sets his play. His word choice and use of inverted sentences reflect the contemporary speech of seventeenth-century Salem, adding to the authenticity of his setting and realistic depiction of his characters.

Read these examples from the play:

Susanna. Aye, sir, he have been searchin' his books since he left you, sir. But he bid me tell you, that you might look to unnatural things for the cause of it. (*Act One, lines 56–60*)

Parris. Let him look to medicine and put out all thought of unnatural causes here. There be none. (*Act One, lines 65–67*)

Abigail. Now look you. All of you. We danced. (*Act One, line 455*)

Here, Miller uses *be* rather than *are*, the verb form we use in this context today. Instead of *yes*, he uses the word *aye*, a word that was commonplace in the 1600s but is rarely used today. Finally, he uses a type of inverted word order common to seventeenth-century speech, with the verb preceding the subject.

This chart includes other examples of Miller's style in this play:

Example	Explanation
"I am waitin' for you every night."	Throughout the play, the characters drop the final *g* from their participles.
"Why, her eyes is closed." "It were another sort that hanged till now."	In these lines, the verb's number does not agree with the subject.
"Them that will not confess will hang."	Here Miller replaces the subject pronoun with the object pronoun *them*.

Practice and Apply Rewrite the following sentences to reflect the speech patterns seen in the play. Compare your rewritten sentences with a partner.

1. You go to the house!

2. Yes, it is true I saw the devil with Rebecca Nurse.

3. Are you sure of their guilt?

4. You confess to these sins!

MEDIA ANALYSIS

Media Versions of *The Crucible*

The Crucible

Audio excerpt from Act Three (lines 723–1111)

AS YOU LISTEN Pay attention to how the speakers use just their voices to interpret and dramatize the text of the play. Note any questions you generate.

COLLABORATIVE DISCUSSION Which characters emerge most fully in this scene? With a partner, discuss how the actors bring individual characters from the text to life. Cite specific examples from the recording to support your ideas.

Analyze Interpretations of Drama

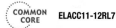

COMMON CORE   ELACC11-12RL7

In this audio recording, some of Arthur Miller's stage directions are read aloud by the narrator; others are used by the actors to guide their interpretations of characters. The actors use the elements of speech discussed in the chart to convey their view of the characters.

> **Voice expression** refers to the feeling that is brought out by the sound of an actor's voice. For example, a higher pitch can help communicate excitement, happiness, or anxiety. A lower pitch sounds more serious or sad.

> **Volume, pace,** and the **stress** placed on words can all be varied. These techniques can emphasize words, phrases, or lines in the dialogue; signal characters' reactions; or create a particular mood, or atmosphere. For example, the faintness of Mary Warren's voice shows her increasing uncertainty about whether she can hold out against Abigail.

> **Timing** refers to when lines of dialogue are delivered. In this recording, there are dramatic pauses, interruptions, and simultaneous speech, all of which echo Miller's punctuation and arrangement of lines and add to the impact of the scene.

Analyzing the Text and Media

COMMON CORE   ELACC11-12RL7

Cite Text Evidence   Support your responses with evidence from the selections.

1. **Compare** Review lines 723–1111 in Act Three. Is Mary Warren's character in the recording consistent with her portrayal in the text? Explain.

2. **Analyze** What impression of Danforth is created by the actor in this recording? How does the actor use elements of speech to convey the traits of his character? Explain whether you view Danforth differently after hearing the recording.

3. **Compare** In this part of the play, the girls "see" a spirit sent down on them. How does the recording communicate the frenzy of this scene? Discuss whether the same mood is brought out in the text.

PERFORMANCE TASK

Speaking Activity: Readers' Theater With a group, prepare an interpretation of a short scene from *The Crucible*.

- On a copy of the text, highlight stage directions and important words and phrases in the dialogue.

- Assign roles and practice reading your parts. Use expression, pace, volume, stress, and timing to convey emotion and key ideas.

- Perform your readers' theater for the class.

- Have class members follow along in the text and then write a short evaluation of the performance.

The Crucible (1996)

Production Images from Film Version

AS YOU VIEW Consider what these images suggest about the relationships between the characters. Write down any questions you generate while looking at the images.

Abigail and others react to events on the green.

Danforth questions Mary Warren before the court (Act Three).

Reverend Parris and Abigail gaze with horror at the scene unfolding.

John Proctor gives his confession to the marshal as Elizabeth looks on (Act Four).

John Proctor warns Abigail that their relationship is over.

COLLABORATIVE DISCUSSION What do these images imply about the characters' feelings for each other? With a partner, discuss whether these impressions are accurate. Cite specific evidence from the photographs and the play to support your ideas.

Analyze Interpretations of Drama

These images, taken from a 1996 film version of *The Crucible*, suggest how the director interpreted Miller's play. The director's many choices include those shown in the chart.

Casting The actors' physical characteristics and acting styles have a significant impact on the audience's perception of characters and plot. Use your knowledge of Miller's stage directions to evaluate how closely the director's choices align with the way Miller saw his characters.

Blocking Actors' positions, movements, and gestures affect the impact of a scene. Note how the relationships between the characters as well as their emotions are revealed through their posture, gestures, and position relative to other characters.

Lighting and Camera Techniques Film directors can use different camera angles and lighting to create mood, emphasize characters' reactions, build suspense, and draw the audience into the action. Consider what the lighting tells you about the mood of the scene with Abigail and John Proctor. How does the close-up view of their faces help the audience understand what they are experiencing?

Set Design and Costuming Both of these aspects of a film create for the audience a sense of when and where the action is taking place. Think about how immediately you form an impression of setting from the costumes worn by the actors. These costumes as well as the location of the film tell you that the director has chosen to adhere to many aspects of the setting established in Miller's stage directions.

Analyzing the Text and Media

 COMMON CORE   ELACC11-12RL7, ELACC11-12W4

Cite Text Evidence   Support your responses with evidence from the selections.

1. **Analyze** Examine the photographs of Abigail, Reverend Parris, and John Proctor. In what ways is the casting consistent with a traditional interpretation of Miller's text? Explain.

2. **Infer** What scene of the play is depicted by the photo of John Proctor and Abigail? What does this photo suggest about this interpretation of Miller's text?

PERFORMANCE TASK

Writing Activity: Diagram Complete these activities in a small group.

- Choose a short scene from the play.

- Diagram the scene with specific directions for the actors about where to stand and how to move.

- Have volunteer actors within the group follow those directions.

- Discuss how the blocking affects the group's interpretation of the scene. Share insights with the class.

Compare Multiple Interpretations of a Drama ELACC11-12RL7

Experiencing the same play through different mediums enables the audience to appreciate the text from several perspectives. For example, an audio recording allows listeners to concentrate on the characters' words without the distraction of visual elements. They hear nuances of meaning that they may otherwise have missed. In a film, the images, sound, and special effects bring the story to life for viewers, drawing them into the characters' conflicts.

There are also drawbacks to each medium. In a recording, it may be difficult to identify who is speaking or to follow the interactions between characters. In a film, the director's interpretation may alter the original meaning, or technical effects might distract from the essence of the drama. Keeping in mind both advantages and possible disadvantages will help you better evaluate how each version interprets the source text.

Analyzing the Text and Media ELACC11-12RL1, ELACC11-12RL7, ELACC11-12W4

Cite Text Evidence   Support your responses with evidence from the selections.

1. **Analyze** Describe the character traits suggested by John Proctor's appearance in the photographs. Is this perception of him consistent with Miller's portrayal of his character in the text of the play? Does his voice in the recording match this impression? Explain.

2. **Compare** Reread lines 723–1111 in the text. Explain the advantages and disadvantages of presenting this part of the play in each medium. Be specific.

3. **Evaluate** Examine the photograph of Reverend Parris with Abigail. How might someone who had not read the play describe his character, based on his actions and appearance in this shot? Would this view be accurate? Explain.

PERFORMANCE TASK

Writing Activity: Captions Every director has to make decisions when interpreting the text of a play for a film adaptation. The selected production stills offer clues to one director's decisions.

- With a partner, write captions identifying when and where the action in the photograph might be happening.

- Compare the director's vision of that part of the play with Miller's, drawing from stage directions as well as dialogue.

- Discuss key similarities and differences and how they affect your perception of the action.

- Share your analysis with the class.

Background *The 1969 Supreme Court decision* Tinker v. Des Moines *was written in the context of the Vietnam War. In 1965, President Lyndon Johnson ordered air attacks against communist North Vietnam and sent the first 100,000 U.S. ground troops into Vietnam. In that same year, "teach-ins" on college campuses to protest the war became commonplace. As U.S. troop levels grew to about 550,000 and casualties mounted, American support for the war declined. Protests took numerous forms from large public demonstrations to individual acts of resistance.*

Tinker
v.
Des Moines Independent Community School District

Supreme Court of the United States, Opinion and Dissents

AS YOU READ First determine who the petitioners and the respondents were, and then determine what each of them did that resulted in this case being brought before the Supreme Court. Write down any questions you generate during reading.

No. 21
SUPREME COURT OF THE UNITED STATES
393 U.S. 503
Argued November 12, 1968
Decided February 24, 1969

Syllabus

Petitioners, three public school pupils in Des Moines, Iowa, were suspended from school for wearing black armbands to protest the Government's policy in Vietnam. They sought nominal[1] damages and an **injunction** against a regulation that the respondents[2] had promulgated[3] banning the wearing of armbands. The District Court dismissed the complaint on the ground that the regulation was within

injunction
(ĭn-jŭngk´shən) *n.*
court order forbidding a specific action.

---

[1] **nominal:** very small.
[2] **respondents:** defendants in a lawsuit.
[3] **promulgated:** enacted a rule.

the Board's power, despite the absence of any finding of substantial interference with the conduct of school activities. The Court of Appeals, sitting *en banc,*[4] affirmed by an equally divided court.

10 *Held*:

1. In wearing armbands, the petitioners were quiet and passive. They were not disruptive and did not impinge[5] upon the rights of others. In these circumstances, their conduct was within the protection of the Free Speech Clause of the First Amendment and the Due Process Clause of the Fourteenth.

2. First Amendment rights are available to teachers and students, subject to application in light of the special characteristics of the school environment.

3. A prohibition against expression of opinion, without any
20 evidence that the rule is necessary to avoid substantial interference with school discipline or the rights of others, is not permissible under the First and Fourteenth Amendments.

DISPOSITION: 383 F.2d 988, reversed and remanded.

MR. JUSTICE FORTAS delivered the opinion of the Court.

Petitioner John F. Tinker, 15 years old, and petitioner Christopher Eckhardt, 16 years old, attended high schools in Des Moines, Iowa. Petitioner Mary Beth Tinker, John's sister, was a 13-year-old student in junior high school.

In December 1965, a group of adults and students in Des Moines held
30 a meeting at the Eckhardt home. The group determined to publicize their objections to the hostilities in Vietnam and their support for a truce by wearing black armbands during the holiday season and by fasting on December 16 and New Year's Eve. Petitioners and their parents had previously engaged in similar activities, and they decided to participate in the program.

The principals of the Des Moines schools became aware of the plan to wear armbands. On December 14, 1965, they met and adopted a policy that any student wearing an armband to school would be asked to remove it, and if he refused he would be suspended until he returned
40 without the armband. Petitioners were aware of the regulation that the school authorities adopted.

On December 16, Mary Beth and Christopher wore black armbands to their schools. John Tinker wore his armband the next day. They were all sent home and suspended from school until they would come back without their armbands. They did not return to school until after the planned period for wearing armbands had expired—that is, until after New Year's Day.

---

[4] **en banc** (än-bänk´): with all of its judges.
[5] **impinge:** intrude.

This complaint was filed in the United States District Court by petitioners, through their fathers, under § 1983 of Title 42 of the United States Code. It prayed for an injunction restraining the respondent school officials and the respondent members of the board of directors of the school district from disciplining the petitioners, and it sought nominal damages. After an evidentiary hearing the District Court dismissed the complaint. It upheld the constitutionality of the school authorities' action on the ground that it was reasonable in order to prevent disturbance of school discipline. 258 F.Supp. 971 (1966). The court referred to but expressly declined to follow the Fifth Circuit's holding in a similar case that the wearing of symbols like the armbands cannot be prohibited unless it "materially and substantially interfere[s] with the requirements of appropriate discipline in the operation of the school." *Burnside v. Byars*, 363 F.2d 744, 749 (1966).

On appeal, the Court of Appeals for the Eighth Circuit considered the case en banc. The court was equally divided, and the District Court's decision was accordingly affirmed, without opinion. 383 F.2d 988 (1967). We granted certiorari.[6] 390 U.S. 942 (1968).

I

The District Court recognized that the wearing of an armband for the purpose of expressing certain views is the type of symbolic act that is within the Free Speech Clause of the First Amendment. See *West Virginia v. Barnette*, 319 U.S. 624 (1943); *Stromberg v. California*, 283 U.S. 359 (1931). Cf. *Thornhill v. Alabama*, 310 U.S. 88 (1940); *Edwards v. South Carolina*, 372 U.S. 229 (1963); *Brown v. Louisiana*, 383 U.S. 131 (1966). As we shall discuss, the wearing of armbands in the circumstances of this case was entirely divorced from actually or potentially disruptive conduct by those participating in it. It was closely akin to "pure speech" which, we have repeatedly held, is entitled to comprehensive protection under the First Amendment. Cf. *Cox v. Louisiana*, 379 U.S. 536, 555 (1965); *Adderley v. Florida*, 385 U.S. 39 (1966).

First Amendment rights, applied in light of the special characteristics of the school environment, are available to teachers and students. It can hardly be argued that either students or teachers shed their constitutional rights to freedom of speech or expression at the schoolhouse gate. This has been the unmistakable holding of this Court for almost 50 years. In *Meyer v. Nebraska*, 262 U.S. 390 (1923), and *Bartels v. Iowa*, 262 U.S. 404 (1923), this Court, in opinions by Mr. Justice McReynolds, held that the Due Process Clause of the Fourteenth Amendment prevents States from forbidding the teaching of a foreign language to young students. Statutes to this effect, the

---

[6] **certiorari** (sûr´shē-ə-râr´ē): a document allowing an appeal to a higher court.

Court held, unconstitutionally interfere with the liberty of teacher,
90 student, and parent. See also *Pierce v. Society of Sisters*, 268 U.S. 510
(1925); *West Virginia v. Barnette*, 319 U.S. 624 (1943); *McCollum v.
Board of Education*, 333 U.S. 203 (1948); *Wieman v. Updegraff*, 344
U.S. 183, 195 (1952) (concurring opinion); *Sweezy v. New Hampshire*,
354 U.S. 234 (1957); *Shelton v. Tucker*, 364 U.S. 479, 487 (1960); *Engel v.
Vitale*, 370 U.S. 421 (1962); *Keyishian v. Board of Regents*, 385 U.S. 589,
603 (1967); *Epperson v. Arkansas*, ante, p. 97 (1968).

In *West Virginia v. Barnette, supra*, this Court held that under the First
Amendment, the student in public school may not be compelled to
salute the flag. Speaking through Mr. Justice Jackson, the Court said:

100 "The Fourteenth Amendment, as now applied to the States,
protects the citizen against the State itself and all of its
creatures—Boards of Education not excepted. These have,
of course, important, delicate, and highly discretionary
functions, but none that they may not perform within the
limits of the Bill of Rights. That they are educating the
young for citizenship is reason for **scrupulous** protection
of Constitutional freedoms of the individual, if we are not
to strangle the free mind at its source and teach youth to
discount important principles of our government as mere
110 platitudes." 319 U.S., at 637.

scrupulous
(skrōō′pyə-ləs) *adj.*
thorough and
diligent.

On the other hand, the Court has repeatedly emphasized the need
for affirming the comprehensive authority of the States and of school
officials, consistent with fundamental constitutional safeguards, to
prescribe and control conduct in the schools. See *Epperson v. Arkansas*,
supra, at 104; *Meyer v. Nebraska, supra*, at 402. Our problem lies in the
area where students in the exercise of First Amendment rights collide
with the rules of the school authorities.

II

The problem posed by the present case does not relate to regulation
of the length of skirts or the type of clothing, to hair style, or
120 deportment. Cf. *Ferrell v. Dallas Independent School District*, 392
F.2d 697 (1968); *Pugsley v. Sellmeyer*, 158 Ark. 247, 250 S. W. 538
(1923). It does not concern aggressive, disruptive action or even
group demonstrations. Our problem involves direct, primary First
Amendment rights akin to "pure speech."

The school officials banned and sought to punish petitioners for a
silent, passive expression of opinion, unaccompanied by any disorder
or disturbance on the part of petitioners. There is here no evidence
whatever of petitioners' interference, actual or **nascent**, with the
schools' work or of collision with the rights of other students to be

nascent
(nā′sənt) *adj.*
emerging;
developing.

> ## **Apprehension of disturbance is not enough to overcome the right to freedom of expression. 🔳**

130 secure and to be let alone. Accordingly, this case does not concern speech or action that intrudes upon the work of the schools or the rights of other students.

Only a few of the 18,000 students in the school system wore the black armbands. Only five students were suspended for wearing them. There is no indication that the work of the schools or any class was disrupted. Outside the classrooms, a few students made hostile remarks to the children wearing armbands, but there were no threats or acts of violence on school premises.

The District Court concluded that the action of the school
140 authorities was reasonable because it was based upon their fear of a disturbance from the wearing of the armbands. But, in our system, undifferentiated fear or apprehension of disturbance is not enough to overcome the right to freedom of expression. Any departure from absolute regimentation may cause trouble. Any variation from the majority's opinion may inspire fear. Any word spoken, in class, in the lunchroom, or on the campus, that deviates from the views of another person may start an argument or cause a disturbance. But our Constitution says we must take this risk, *Terminiello v. Chicago*, 337 U.S. 1 (1949); and our history says that it is this sort of hazardous
150 freedom—this kind of openness—that is the basis of our national strength and of the independence and vigor of Americans who grow up and live in this relatively permissive, often **disputatious**, society.

disputatious
(dĭs´pyə-tā´shəs) *adj.*
argumentative;
confrontational.

In order for the State in the person of school officials to justify prohibition of a particular expression of opinion, it must be able to show that its action was caused by something more than a mere desire to avoid the discomfort and unpleasantness that always accompany an unpopular viewpoint. Certainly where there is no finding and no showing that engaging in the forbidden conduct would "materially and substantially interfere with the requirements of appropriate discipline
160 in the operation of the school," the prohibition cannot be sustained. *Burnside v. Byars, supra,* at 749.

In the present case, the District Court made no such finding, and our independent examination of the record fails to yield evidence that the school authorities had reason to anticipate that the wearing of the armbands would substantially interfere with the work of the school or impinge upon the rights of other students. Even an official memorandum prepared after the suspension that listed the reasons for the ban on wearing the armbands made no reference to the anticipation of such disruption.

170 On the contrary, the action of the school authorities appears to have been based upon an urgent wish to avoid the controversy which might result from the expression, even by the silent symbol of armbands, of opposition to this Nation's part in the conflagration[7] in Vietnam. It is revealing, in this respect, that the meeting at which the school principals decided to issue the contested regulation was called in response to a student's statement to the journalism teacher in one of the schools that he wanted to write an article on Vietnam and have it published in the school paper. (The student was dissuaded.)

It is also relevant that the school authorities did not **purport** to
180 prohibit the wearing of all symbols of political or controversial significance. The record shows that students in some of the schools wore buttons relating to national political campaigns, and some even wore the Iron Cross, traditionally a symbol of Nazism. The order prohibiting the wearing of armbands did not extend to these. Instead, a particular symbol—black armbands worn to exhibit opposition to this Nation's involvement in Vietnam—was singled out for prohibition. Clearly, the prohibition of expression of one particular opinion, at least without evidence that it is necessary to avoid material and substantial interference with schoolwork or discipline, is not constitutionally
190 permissible.

purport
(pər-pôrt´) v. to claim or pretend to be the case.

In our system, state-operated schools may not be **enclaves** of totalitarianism. School officials do not possess absolute authority over their students. Students in school as well as out of school are "persons" under our Constitution. They are possessed of fundamental rights which the State must respect, just as they themselves must respect their obligations to the State. In our system, students may not be regarded as closed-circuit recipients of only that which the State chooses to communicate. They may not be confined to the expression of those sentiments that are officially approved. In the absence of a
200 specific showing of constitutionally valid reasons to regulate their speech, students are entitled to freedom of expression of their views. As Judge Gewin, speaking for the Fifth Circuit, said, school officials cannot suppress "expressions of feelings with which they do not wish to contend." *Burnside v. Byars, supra*, at 749.

enclave
(ĕn´klāv´) n. a distinct area within a larger area.

---

[7] **conflagration:** a destructive fire, here used figuratively to mean "war."

In *Meyer v. Nebraska, supra*, at 402, Mr. Justice McReynolds expressed this Nation's repudiation of the principle that a State might so conduct its schools as to "foster a homogeneous people." He said:

> "In order to submerge the individual and develop ideal
> citizens, Sparta assembled the males at seven into barracks
> and intrusted their subsequent education and training
> to official guardians. Although such measures have been
> deliberately approved by men of great genius, their ideas
> touching the relation between individual and State were
> wholly different from those upon which our institutions
> rest; and it hardly will be affirmed that any legislature could
> impose such restrictions upon the people of a State without
> doing violence to both letter and spirit of the Constitution."

This principle has been repeated by this Court on numerous occasions during the intervening years. In *Keyishian v. Board of Regents*, 385 U.S. 589, 603, MR. JUSTICE BRENNAN, speaking for the Court, said:

> "'The vigilant protection of constitutional freedoms is
> nowhere more vital than in the community of American
> schools.' *Shelton v. Tucker*, [364 U.S. 479,] at 487. The
> classroom is peculiarly the 'marketplace of ideas.' The
> Nation's future depends upon leaders trained through wide
> exposure to that robust exchange of ideas which discovers
> truth 'out of a multitude of tongues, [rather] than through
> any kind of authoritative selection.'"

The principle of these cases is not confined to the supervised and ordained discussion which takes place in the classroom. The principal use to which the schools are dedicated is to accommodate students during prescribed hours for the purpose of certain types of activities. Among those activities is personal intercommunication among the students. This is not only an inevitable part of the process of attending school; it is also an important part of the educational process. A student's rights, therefore, do not embrace merely the classroom hours. When he is in the cafeteria, or on the playing field, or on the campus during the authorized hours, he may express his opinions, even on controversial subjects like the conflict in Vietnam, if he does so without "materially and substantially interfer[ing] with the requirements of appropriate discipline in the operation of the school" and without colliding with the rights of others. *Burnside v. Byars, supra*, at 749. But conduct by the student, in class or out of it, which for any reason—whether it stems from time, place, or type of behavior—materially disrupts classwork or involves substantial disorder or invasion of the rights of others is, of course, not immunized by the constitutional guarantee of freedom of speech. Cf. *Blackwell v. Issaquena County Board of Education*, 363 F.2d 749 (C. A. 5th Cir. 1966).

250 Under our Constitution, free speech is not a right that is given only to be so circumscribed that it exists in principle but not in fact. Freedom of expression would not truly exist if the right could be exercised only in an area that a benevolent government has provided as a safe haven for crackpots. The Constitution says that Congress (and the States) may not abridge the right to free speech. This provision means what it says. We properly read it to permit reasonable regulation of speech-connected activities in carefully restricted circumstances. But we do not confine the permissible exercise of First Amendment rights to a telephone booth or the four corners of a pamphlet, or to supervised
260 and ordained discussion in a school classroom.

If a regulation were adopted by school officials forbidding discussion of the Vietnam conflict, or the expression by any student of opposition to it anywhere on school property except as part of a prescribed classroom exercise, it would be obvious that the regulation would violate the constitutional rights of students, at least if it could not be justified by a showing that the students' activities would materially and substantially disrupt the work and discipline of the school. Cf. *Hammond* v. *South Carolina State College*, 272 F.Supp. 947 (D. C. S. C. 1967) (orderly protest meeting on state college campus); *Dickey*
270 v. *Alabama State Board of Education*, 273 F.Supp. 613 (D. C. M. D. Ala. 1967) (expulsion of student editor of college newspaper). In the circumstances of the present case, the prohibition of the silent, passive "witness of the armbands," as one of the children called it, is no less offensive to the Constitution's guarantees.

As we have discussed, the record does not demonstrate any facts which might reasonably have led school authorities to forecast substantial disruption of or material interference with school activities, and no disturbances or disorders on the school premises in fact occurred. These petitioners merely went about their ordained rounds in school.
280 Their deviation consisted only in wearing on their sleeve a band of black cloth, not more than two inches wide. They wore it to exhibit their disapproval of the Vietnam hostilities and their advocacy of a truce, to make their views known, and, by their example, to influence others to adopt them. They neither interrupted school activities nor sought to intrude in the school affairs or the lives of others. They caused discussion outside of the classrooms, but no interference with work and no disorder. In the circumstances, our Constitution does not permit officials of the State to deny their form of expression.

We express no opinion as to the form of relief which should be
290 granted, this being a matter for the lower courts to determine. We reverse and remand for further proceedings consistent with this opinion.

Reversed and remanded.

MR. JUSTICE STEWART, concurring.

Although I agree with much of what is said in the Court's opinion, and with its judgment in this case, I cannot share the Court's uncritical assumption that, school discipline aside, the First Amendment rights of children are co-extensive with those of adults. Indeed, I had thought the Court decided otherwise just last Term in *Ginsberg v. New York*, 390 U.S. 629. I continue to hold the view I expressed in that case: "[A] State may permissibly determine that, at least in some precisely delineated areas, a child—like someone in a captive audience—is not possessed of that full capacity for individual choice which is the presupposition of First Amendment guarantees." *Id.*, at 649-650 (concurring in result). Cf. *Prince v. Massachusetts*, 321 U.S. 158.

MR. JUSTICE WHITE, concurring.

While I join the Court's opinion, I deem it appropriate to note, first, that the Court continues to recognize a distinction between communicating by words and communicating by acts or conduct which sufficiently impinges on some valid state interest; and, second, that I do not subscribe to everything the Court of Appeals said about free speech in its opinion in *Burnside v. Byars*, 363 F.2d 744, 748 (C. A. 5th Cir. 1966), a case relied upon by the Court in the matter now before us.

MR. JUSTICE BLACK, dissenting.

The Court's holding in this case ushers in what I deem to be an entirely new era in which the power to control pupils by the elected "officials of state supported public schools…" in the United States is in ultimate effect transferred to the Supreme Court. The Court brought this particular case here on a petition for certiorari urging that the First and Fourteenth Amendments protect the right of school pupils to express their political views all the way "from kindergarten through high school." Here the constitutional right to "political expression" asserted was a right to wear black armbands during school hours and at classes in order to demonstrate to the other students that the petitioners were mourning because of the death of United States soldiers in Vietnam and to protest that war which they were against. Ordered to refrain from wearing the armbands in school by the elected school officials and the teachers vested with state authority to do so, apparently only seven out of the school system's 18,000 pupils deliberately refused to obey the order. One defying pupil was Paul Tinker, 8 years old, who was in the second grade; another, Hope Tinker, was 11 years old and in the fifth grade; a third member of the Tinker family was 13, in the eighth grade; and a fourth member of the same family was John Tinker, 15 years old, an 11th grade high school pupil. Their father, a Methodist minister without a church, is paid a salary by the American Friends Service Committee. Another student who defied the school order and insisted on wearing an armband in school was Christopher Eckhardt, an 11th grade pupil and a petitioner in this case. His mother is an official in the Women's International League for Peace and Freedom.

As I read the Court's opinion it relies upon the following grounds for holding unconstitutional the judgment of the Des Moines school officials and the two courts below. First, the Court concludes that the wearing of armbands is "symbolic speech" which is "akin to 'pure speech'" and therefore protected by the First and Fourteenth Amendments. Secondly, the Court decides that the public schools are an appropriate place to exercise "symbolic speech" as long as normal school functions are not "unreasonably" disrupted. Finally, the Court **arrogates** to itself, rather than to the State's elected officials charged with running the schools, the decision as to which school disciplinary regulations are "reasonable."

arrogate
(ăr´ə-gāt´) *v.* to assume authority unjustly.

Assuming that the Court is correct in holding that the conduct of wearing armbands for the purpose of conveying political ideas is protected by the First Amendment, cf., e.g., *Giboney v. Empire Storage & Ice Co.*, 336 U.S. 490 (1949), the crucial remaining questions are whether students and teachers may use the schools at their whim as a platform for the exercise of free speech— "symbolic" or "pure"— and whether the courts will allocate to themselves the function of deciding how the pupils' school day will be spent. While I have always believed that under the First and Fourteenth Amendments neither the State nor the Federal Government has any authority to regulate or censor the content of speech, I have never believed that any person has a right to give speeches or engage in demonstrations where he pleases and when he pleases. This Court has already rejected such a notion. In *Cox v. Louisiana*, 379 U.S. 536, 554 (1965), for example, the Court clearly stated that the rights of free speech and assembly "do not mean that everyone with opinions or beliefs to express may address a group at any public place and at any time."

While the record does not show that any of these armband students shouted, used profane language, or were violent in any manner, detailed testimony by some of them shows their armbands caused comments, warnings by other students, the poking of fun at them, and a warning by an older football player that other, nonprotesting students had better let them alone. There is also evidence that a teacher of mathematics had his lesson period practically "wrecked" chiefly by disputes with Mary Beth Tinker, who wore her armband for her "demonstration." Even a casual reading of the record shows that this armband did divert students' minds from their regular lessons, and that talk, comments, etc., made John Tinker "self-conscious" in attending school with his armband. While the absence of obscene remarks or boisterous and loud disorder perhaps justifies the Court's statement that the few armband students did not actually "disrupt"

> ## It is the beginning of a new revolutionary era of permissiveness in this country fostered by the judiciary.

the classwork, I think the record overwhelmingly shows that the armbands did exactly what the elected school officials and principals foresaw they would, that is, took the students' minds off their classwork and diverted them to thoughts about the highly emotional subject of the Vietnam war. And I repeat that if the time has come when pupils of state-supported schools, kindergartens, grammar schools, or high schools, can defy and flout orders of school officials to keep their minds on their own schoolwork, it is the beginning of a new revolutionary era of permissiveness in this country fostered by the judiciary. The next logical step, it appears to me, would be to hold unconstitutional laws that bar pupils under 21 or 18 from voting, or from being elected members of the boards of education.

The United States District Court refused to hold that the state school order violated the First and Fourteenth Amendments. 258 F.Supp. 971. Holding that the protest was akin to speech, which is protected by the First and Fourteenth Amendments, that court held that the school order was "reasonable" and hence constitutional. There was at one time a line of cases holding "reasonableness" as the court saw it to be the test of a "due process" violation. Two cases upon which the Court today heavily relies for striking down this school order used this test of reasonableness, *Meyer v. Nebraska*, 262 U.S. 390 (1923), and *Bartels v. Iowa*, 262 U.S. 404 (1923). The opinions in both cases were written by Mr. Justice McReynolds; Mr. Justice Holmes, who opposed this reasonableness test, dissented from the holdings as did Mr. Justice Sutherland. This constitutional test of reasonableness prevailed in this Court for a season. It was this test that brought on President Franklin Roosevelt's well-known Court fight. His proposed legislation did not pass, but the fight left the "reasonableness" constitutional test dead on the battlefield, so much so that this Court in *Ferguson v. Skrupa*, 372 U.S. 726, 729, 730, after a thorough review of the old cases, was able to conclude in 1963:

> "There was a time when the Due Process Clause was used by this Court to strike down laws which were thought

unreasonable, that is, unwise or incompatible with some
particular economic or social philosophy.

. . . .

"The doctrine that prevailed in *Lochner, Coppage, Adkins,*
Burns, and like cases—that due process authorizes courts to
420   hold laws unconstitutional when they believe the legislature
has acted unwisely—has long since been discarded."

The *Ferguson* case totally repudiated the old reasonableness-due
process test, the doctrine that judges have the power to hold laws
unconstitutional upon the belief of judges that they "shock the
conscience" or that they are "unreasonable," "arbitrary," "irrational,"
"contrary to fundamental 'decency,'" or some other such flexible
term without precise boundaries. I have many times expressed
my opposition to that concept on the ground that it gives judges
430   power to strike down any law they do not like. If the majority of the
Court today, by agreeing to the opinion of my Brother FORTAS,
is resurrecting that old reasonableness-due process test, I think
the constitutional change should be plainly, unequivocally, and
forthrightly stated for the benefit of the bench and bar. It will be a
sad day for the country, I believe, when the present-day Court returns
to the McReynolds due process concept. Other cases cited by the
Court do not, as implied, follow the McReynolds reasonableness
doctrine. *West Virginia v. Barnette,* 319 U.S. 624, clearly rejecting the
"reasonableness" test, held that the Fourteenth Amendment made
440   the First applicable to the States, and that the two forbade a State to
compel little schoolchildren to salute the United States flag when they
had religious scruples against doing so. Neither *Thornhill v. Alabama,*
310 U.S. 88; *Stromberg v. California,* 283 U.S. 359; *Edwards v. South*
Carolina, 372 U.S. 229; nor *Brown v. Louisiana,* 383 U.S. 131, related
to schoolchildren at all, and none of these cases embraced Mr. Justice
McReynolds' reasonableness test; and Thornhill, Edwards, and Brown
relied on the vagueness of state statutes under scrutiny to hold them
unconstitutional. *Cox v. Louisiana,* 379 U.S. 536, 555, and *Adderley*
v. Florida, 385 U.S. 39, cited by the Court as a "compare," indicating,
450   I suppose, that these two cases are no longer the law, were not rested
to the slightest extent on the *Meyer* and *Bartels* "reasonableness-due
process-McReynolds" constitutional test.

I deny, therefore, that it has been the "unmistakable holding of this
Court for almost 50 years" that "students" and "teachers" take with
them into the "schoolhouse gate" constitutional rights to "freedom
of speech or expression." Even *Meyer* did not hold that. It makes no
reference to "symbolic speech" at all; what it did was to strike down as
"unreasonable" and therefore unconstitutional a Nebraska law barring
the teaching of the German language before the children reached the
460   eighth grade. One can well agree with Mr. Justice Holmes and Mr.

Justice Sutherland, as I do, that such a law was no more unreasonable than it would be to bar the teaching of Latin and Greek to pupils who have not reached the eighth grade. In fact, I think the majority's reason for invalidating the Nebraska law was that it did not like it or in legal jargon that it "shocked the Court's conscience," "offended its sense of justice," or was "contrary to fundamental concepts of the English-speaking world," as the Court has sometimes said. See, e.g., *Rochin v. California*, 342 U.S. 165, and *Irvine v. California*, 347 U.S. 128. The truth is that a teacher of kindergarten, grammar school, or high school pupils no more carries into a school with him a complete right to freedom of speech and expression than an anti-Catholic or anti-Semite carries with him a complete freedom of speech and religion into a Catholic church or Jewish synagogue. Nor does a person carry with him into the United States Senate or House, or into the Supreme Court, or any other court, a complete constitutional right to go into those places contrary to their rules and speak his mind on any subject he pleases. It is a myth to say that any person has a constitutional right to say what he pleases, where he pleases, and when he pleases. Our Court has decided precisely the opposite. See, e.g., *Cox v. Louisiana*, 379 U.S. 536, 555; *Adderley v. Florida*, 385 U.S. 39.

In my view, teachers in state-controlled public schools are hired to teach there. Although Mr. Justice McReynolds may have intimated to the contrary in *Meyer v. Nebraska, supra*, certainly a teacher is not paid to go into school and teach subjects the State does not hire him to teach as a part of its selected curriculum. Nor are public school students sent to the schools at public expense to broadcast political or any other views to educate and inform the public. The original idea of schools, which I do not believe is yet abandoned as worthless or out of date, was that children had not yet reached the point of experience and wisdom which enabled them to teach all of their elders. It may be that the Nation has outworn the old-fashioned slogan that "children are to be seen not heard," but one may, I hope, be permitted to harbor the thought that taxpayers send children to school on the premise that at their age they need to learn, not teach.

The true principles on this whole subject were in my judgment spoken by Mr. Justice McKenna for the Court in *Waugh v. Mississippi University* in 237 U.S. 589, 596-597. The State had there passed a law barring students from peaceably assembling in Greek letter fraternities and providing that students who joined them could be expelled from school. This law would appear on the surface to run afoul of the First Amendment's freedom of assembly clause. The law was attacked as violative[8] of due process and of the privileges and immunities clause and as a deprivation of property and of liberty, under the Fourteenth Amendment. It was argued that the fraternity made its members

---

[8] **violative:** in violation.

more moral, taught discipline, and inspired its members to study harder and to obey better the rules of discipline and order. This Court rejected all the "fervid" pleas of the fraternities' advocates and decided unanimously against these Fourteenth Amendment arguments. The Court in its next to the last paragraph made this statement which has complete relevance for us today:

> "It is said that the fraternity to which complainant belongs is a moral and of itself a disciplinary force. This need not be denied. But whether such membership makes against discipline was for the State of Mississippi to determine. It is to be remembered that the University was established by the State and is under the control of the State, and the enactment of the statute may have been induced by the opinion that *membership in the prohibited societies divided the attention of the students and distracted from that singleness of purpose which the State desired to exist in its public educational institutions*. It is not for us to entertain conjectures in opposition to the views of the State and annul its regulations upon disputable considerations of their wisdom or necessity." (Emphasis supplied.)

It was on the foregoing argument that this Court sustained the power of Mississippi to curtail the First Amendment's right of peaceable assembly. And the same reasons are equally applicable to curtailing in the States' public schools the right to complete freedom of expression. Iowa's public schools, like Mississippi's university, are operated to give students an opportunity to learn, not to talk politics by actual speech, or by "symbolic" speech. And, as I have pointed out before, the record amply shows that public protest in the school classes against the Vietnam war "distracted from that singleness of purpose which the State [here Iowa] desired to exist in its public educational institutions." Here the Court should accord Iowa educational institutions the same right to determine for themselves to what extent free expression should be allowed in its schools as it accorded Mississippi with reference to freedom of assembly. But even if the record were silent as to protests against the Vietnam war distracting students from their assigned class work, members of this Court, like all other citizens, know, without being told, that the disputes over the wisdom of the Vietnam war have disrupted and divided this country as few other issues ever have. Of course students, like other people, cannot concentrate on lesser issues when black armbands are being ostentatiously displayed in their presence to call attention to the wounded and dead of the war, some of the wounded and the dead being their friends and neighbors. It was, of course, to distract the attention of other students that some students insisted up to the very point of their own suspension from school that they were determined to sit in school with their symbolic armbands.

Change has been said to be truly the law of life but sometimes the old and the tried and true are worth holding. The schools of this Nation have undoubtedly contributed to giving us tranquility and to making us a more law-abiding people. Uncontrolled and uncontrollable liberty is an enemy to domestic peace. We cannot close our eyes to the fact that some of the country's greatest problems are crimes committed by the youth, too many of school age. School discipline, like parental discipline, is an integral and important part of training our children to be good citizens—to be better citizens. Here a very small number of students have crisply and summarily refused to obey a school order designed to give pupils who want to learn the opportunity to do so. One does not need to be a prophet or the son of a prophet to know that after the Court's holding today some students in Iowa schools and indeed in all schools will be ready, able, and willing to defy their teachers on practically all orders. This is the more unfortunate for the schools since groups of students all over the land are already running loose, conducting break-ins, sit-ins, lie-ins, and smash-ins. Many of these student groups, as is all too familiar to all who read the newspapers and watch the television news programs, have already engaged in rioting, property seizures, and destruction. They have picketed schools to force students not to cross their picket lines and have too often violently attacked earnest but frightened students who wanted an education that the pickets did not want them to get. Students engaged in such activities are apparently confident that they know far more about how to operate public school systems than do their parents, teachers, and elected school officials. It is no answer to say that the particular students here have not yet reached such high points in their demands to attend classes in order to exercise their political pressures. Turned loose with lawsuits for damages and injunctions against their teachers as they are here, it is nothing but wishful thinking to imagine that young, immature students will not soon believe it is their right to control the schools rather than the right of the States that collect the taxes to hire the teachers for the benefit of the pupils. This case, therefore, wholly without constitutional reasons in my judgment, subjects all the public schools in the country to the whims and caprices of their loudest-mouthed, but maybe not their brightest, students. I, for one, am not fully persuaded that school pupils are wise enough, even with this Court's expert help from Washington, to run the 23,390 public school systems in our 50 States. I wish, therefore, wholly to **disclaim** any purpose on my part to hold that the Federal Constitution compels the teachers, parents, and elected school officials to surrender control of the American public school system to public school students. I dissent.

MR. JUSTICE HARLAN, dissenting.

I certainly agree that state public school authorities in the discharge of their responsibilities are not wholly exempt from the requirements

disclaim
(dĭs-klām´) *v.* to deny one's connection to; to distance oneself from.

of the Fourteenth Amendment respecting the freedoms of expression and association. At the same time I am reluctant to believe that there is any disagreement between the majority and myself on the proposition that school officials should be accorded the widest authority in

600 maintaining discipline and good order in their institutions. To translate that proposition into a workable constitutional rule, I would, in cases like this, cast upon those complaining the burden of showing that a particular school measure was motivated by other than legitimate school concerns—for example, a desire to prohibit the expression of an unpopular point of view, while permitting expression of the dominant opinion.

Finding nothing in this record which impugns[9] the good faith of respondents in promulgating the armband regulation, I would affirm the judgment below.

[9] **impugns:** questions or doubts.

COLLABORATIVE DISCUSSION What actions had the petitioners and respondents taken that ultimately caused this case to be argued before the Supreme Court? Discuss this question with a partner, citing specific evidence from the decision to support your ideas.

Delineate and Evaluate an Argument

Every Supreme Court decision delineates, or outlines, an argument. If the decision is completely unanimous, there is one argument representing the opinion of the Court as a whole. If some justices disagree with the majority opinion, the decision also contains his or her dissenting argument. Even if justices agree, however, they can still comment on some parts of the case by adding a concurrence, or agreement. *Tinker v. Des Moines Independent Community School District* has five justices presenting arguments:

- Justice Fortas wrote the opinion of the Court, to which five justices joined without comment.
- Justices Stewart and White wrote separate concurrences.
- Justices Black and Harlan dissented. Justice Black wrote a lengthy argument that fully responds to the Court's opinion. Justice Harlen wrote a brief dissent.

All of their arguments rely on the application of constitutional principles and the use of legal reasoning.

Tinker v. Des Moines		
Parts of the Arguments	**Explanation**	**Examples**
Constitutional principles	Applying parts of the U.S. Constitution that are relevant to the circumstances of the case	**First Amendment:** "Congress shall make no law . . . abridging the freedom of speech. . . ."
		Fourteenth Amendment: "All persons born or naturalized in the United States, and subject to the jurisdiction thereof, are citizens of the United States and of the state wherein they reside. . . . nor shall any state deprive any person of life, liberty, or property, without due process of law; nor deny to any person within its jurisdiction the equal protection of the laws."
Legal reasoning	Reasoning based on the doctrine that following precedent, or decisions in previous cases with similar facts, is essential to making consistent, just, and fair decisions	*Tinker v. Des Moines:* "It was closely akin to 'pure speech' which, we have repeatedly held, is entitled to comprehensive protection under the First Amendment. Cf. *Cox v. Louisiana*, 379 U.S. 536, 555 (1965); *Adderley v. Florida*, 385 U.S. 39 (1966)."

As you analyze this Supreme Court decision, notice how the two sides apply these constitutional principles and use legal reasoning by citing precedents to support their claims. In addition, notice what kinds of evidence, in the form of facts or details, they cite as part of their reasoning.

ELACC11-12RI1,
ELACC11-12RI4,
ELACC11-12RI8,
ELACC11-12SL3,
ELACC11-12SL4

Analyzing the Text

COMMON CORE

Cite Text Evidence   Support your responses with evidence from the selection.

1. **Summarize** What is the **claim,** or the position of the Court, as stated in the "Held" section at the beginning of the decision (lines 10–22)? What constitutional principles are at issue in this Supreme Court case?

2. **Analyze** Justice Fortas says that the problem before the Court is how students' "exercise of First Amendment rights collide[s] with the rules of the school authorities." How does Justice Fortas argue against the school's "fear of a disturbance from the wearing of the armbands" as a sufficient reason to ban them?

3. **Infer** At the beginning of section II of Justice Fortas's opinion, the justice gives examples of what is not involved in the current case, and concludes by saying "Our problem involves direct, primary First Amendment rights akin to 'pure speech'" (lines 123–124). Based on the context in which the phrase is used, what might the phrase "pure speech" mean?

4. **Interpret** How does the evidence about the school's policy on wearing political campaign buttons (lines 179-190) relate to Justice Fortas's opinion?

5. **Analyze** Justice Black states in his dissent that the Court's decision essentially means that the Court, rather than the schools, now decides "which school disciplinary regulations are 'reasonable.'" How does he argue against this "reasonableness" standard?

6. **Draw Conclusions** What is Justice Black's concern about the effects of this decision? How does he express this concern in his argument?

7. **Analyze** Justices Fortas and Black both cite previous Court rulings to support their argument. Choose one such example from each section, and trace how the justice uses that ruling and the legal reasoning behind it to strengthen his argument.

PERFORMANCE TASK

Speaking Activity: Debate Do students have the right to engage in protests or demonstrations at school? What would be appropriate limits on such activities?

- Form teams of two to three students each, grouped according to what individuals feel are acceptable forms of protest on school grounds.

- Each team should gather supporting ideas or details for their viewpoint from the two main parts of the Supreme Court decision.

- Conduct a simulated debate, following the rules for debating found in the Handbook.

- After the debate, write an evaluation of which side presented the most compelling argument.

Critical Vocabulary

ELACC11-12RI4,
ELACC11-12L4c,
ELACC11-12L6

injunction	**scrupulous**	**nascent**	**disputatious**
purport	**enclave**	**arrogate**	**disclaim**

Practice and Apply Choose the alternative in each sentence that best relates to the Critical Vocabulary word. Explain your choices.

1. If the Court issues an **injunction** against the school's rule, will the petitioning students be glad or upset?

2. If schools are **scrupulous** about protecting the First Amendment, will students be discouraged from expressing their opinions or will they speak more freely?

3. If wearing armbands is a **nascent** sign of rebellion against authority, has a rebellion happened in the past or is it likely to happen in the future?

4. In a **disputatious** society, are people more likely to argue or to agree about many subjects?

5. Would a school that **purports** to be concerned with safety more likely have a closed- or open-campus policy?

6. Would an **enclave** at school be more like an all-school assembly or a meeting in an individual classroom?

7. If another student **arrogates** your lunch, is that student acting like a friend or a bully?

8. When Justice Black **disclaims** the idea that students should control the schools, does he strongly agree with the idea or strongly oppose it?

Vocabulary Strategy: Legal Terminology

The Critical Vocabulary word *injunction* is an example of legal terminology, a type of domain-specific vocabulary generally found only in legal documents. When you look up the word in a dictionary, you will find a general definition and a second definition introduced by the word *Law* to indicate it has a specific meaning when used in a legal context. Many legal terms are words and phrases that come from other languages, especially Latin. For example, the footnoted terms *en banc* and *certiorari* are legal terms in French and Latin, respectively. You may need to consult a legal dictionary or other specialized reference work to find the meanings of some legal terminology.

Practice and Apply Work with a partner to investigate the etymology and meaning of some common legal terms using a dictionary or a specialized reference work.

1. *stare decisis*
2. *habeas corpus*
3. *amicus curiae*
4. *voir dire*
5. *ex parte*
6. *in camera*

Language and Style: Comparing Writers' Styles

In *Tinker v. Des Moines*, there are two main writers—Justice Fortas for the majority and Justice Black dissenting. These two writers not only express different opinions but also express those opinions in very different literary styles. Word choice, sentence length, and tone all contribute to each writer's distinct style. In this chart, some elements of their styles are compared.

Elements of Style	Justice Fortas	Justice Black
Word choice	**More difficult vocabulary:** Most of the Critical Vocabulary words and footnoted terms appear in his opinion.	**More ordinary vocabulary:** Only two Critical Vocabulary words and one footnoted term appear in his opinion.
Sentence length and structure	**Carefully constructed, medium length:** "First Amendment rights, applied in light of the special characteristics of the school environment, are available to teachers and students."	**Less direct, longer:** "The Court's holding in this case ushers in what I deem to be an entirely new era in which the power to control pupils by the elected 'officials of state supported public schools . . .' in the United States is in ultimate effect transferred to the Supreme Court."
Tone or attitude	**Mostly objective, appeals to reason:** "The school officials banned and sought to punish petitioners for a silent, passive expression of opinion, unaccompanied by any disorder or disturbance on the part of petitioners."	**More judgmental, appeals to emotions:** "Of course students, like other people, cannot concentrate on lesser issues when black armbands are being ostentatiously displayed in their presence to call attention to the wounded and dead of the war, some of the wounded and the dead being their friends and neighbors."

Practice and Apply Reread the decision and pay attention to the writers' different styles. Note how the differences in style combine with the differences in content to express distinctly diverse opinions on the case. Then look back at the debate evaluation that you wrote for the Performance Task. Add some analysis of how the style used by the different teams to express their ideas related to the effectiveness of their arguments. Finally, review your writing to evaluate your own style; revise word choices, sentence length and structure, and tone to strengthen your writing.

Background *Futurists study the future and make predictions about it by analyzing current trends.* **Ray Kurzweil** *(b. 1948) is a well-known futurist, as well as an inventor, a writer, and an expert on artificial intelligence. In the 1970s, he developed the first machine that translated text into speech, and he has been a pioneer in the field of speech recognition technology. In "The Coming Merging of Mind and Machine," Kurzweil makes some astonishing predictions about the future of artificial intelligence.*

The Coming Merging of Mind and Machine

Science Essay by Ray Kurzweil

AS YOU READ Pay attention to the scientific ideas and theories that Kurzweil uses to explain his predictions. Write down any questions you generate during reading.

Sometime early in this century the intelligence of machines will exceed that of humans. Within a quarter of a century, machines will exhibit the full range of human intellect, emotions and skills, ranging from musical and other creative aptitudes to physical movement. They will claim to have feelings and, unlike today's virtual personalities, will be very convincing when they tell us so. By around 2020 a $1,000 computer will at least match the processing power of the human brain. By 2029 the software for intelligence will have been largely mastered, and the average personal computer will be equivalent
10 to 1,000 brains.

Once computers achieve a level of intelligence comparable to that of humans, they will necessarily soar past it. For example, if I learn French, I can't readily download that learning to you. The reason is that for us, learning involves **successions** of stunningly complex patterns of interconnections among brain cells (neurons) and among the concentrations of biochemicals known as neurotransmitters that enable impulses to travel from neuron to neuron. We have no way of

succession
(sǝk-sĕsh´ǝn) *n.* an ordered sequence.

> **" As this happens, there will no longer be a clear distinction between human and machine. "**

quickly downloading these patterns. But quick downloading will allow our nonbiological creations to share immediately what they learn
20 with billions of other machines. Ultimately, nonbiological entities will master not only the sum total of their own knowledge but all of ours as well.

As this happens, there will no longer be a clear distinction between human and machine. We are already putting computers—neural implants—directly into people's brains to counteract Parkinson's disease and tremors from multiple sclerosis. We have cochlear implants that restore hearing. A retinal implant is being developed in the U.S. that is intended to provide at least some visual perception for some blind individuals, basically by replacing certain
30 visual-processing circuits of the brain. A team of scientists at Emory University implanted a chip in the brain of a paralyzed stroke victim that allowed him to use his brainpower to move a cursor across a computer screen.

In the 2020s neural implants will improve our sensory experiences, memory and thinking. By 2030, instead of just phoning a friend, you will be able to meet in, say, a virtual Mozambican game preserve that will seem compellingly real. You will be able to have any type of experience—business, social, sexual—with anyone, real or simulated, regardless of physical proximity.

How Life and Technology Evolve

40 To gain insight into the kinds of forecasts I have just made, it is important to recognize that information technology is advancing exponentially. An exponential process starts slowly, but eventually its pace increases extremely rapidly. (A fuller documentation of my argument is contained in my recent book *The Singularity Is Near*.)

The evolution of biological life and the evolution of technology have both followed the same pattern: they take a long time to get going, but advances build on one another, and progress erupts at an increasingly furious pace. We are entering that explosive part of the technological evolution curve right now.

50 Consider: It took billions of years for Earth to form. It took two billion more for life to begin and almost as long for molecules to organize into the first multicellular plants and animals about 700 million years ago. The pace of evolution quickened as mammals inherited Earth some 65 million years ago. With the emergence of primates, evolutionary progress was measured in mere millions of years, leading to Homo sapiens perhaps 500,000 years ago.

The evolution of technology has been a continuation of the evolutionary process that gave rise to us—the technology-creating species—in the first place. It took tens of thousands of years for our
60 ancestors to figure out that sharpening both sides of a stone created useful tools. Then, earlier in this past millennium, the time required for a major paradigm shift[1] in technology had shrunk to hundreds of years.

The pace continued to accelerate during the 19th century, during which technological progress was equal to that of the 10 centuries that came before it. Advancement in the first two decades of the 20th century matched that of the entire 19th century. Today significant technological transformations take just a few years; for example, the World Wide Web, already a **ubiquitous** form of communication and
70 commerce, did not exist just 20 years ago. One decade ago almost no one used search engines.

Computing technology is experiencing the same exponential growth. Over the past several decades a key factor in this expansion has been described by Moore's Law. Gordon Moore, a co-founder of Intel, noted in the mid-1960s that technologists had been doubling the density of transistors on integrated circuits every 12 months. This meant computers were periodically doubling both in capacity and in speed per unit cost. In the mid-1970s Moore revised his observation of the doubling time to a more accurate estimate of about 24 months, and
80 that trend has persisted through the years.

After decades of devoted service, Moore's Law will have run its course around 2019. By that time, transistor features will be just a few atoms in width. But new computer architectures will continue the exponential growth of computing. For example, computing cubes are already being designed that will provide thousands of layers of circuits, not just one as in today's computer chips. Other technologies that promise orders-of-magnitude increases in computing density include nanotube circuits built from carbon atoms, optical computing, crystalline computing and molecular computing.

ubiquitous
(yōō-bĭk′wĭ-təs) *adj.*
existing everywhere
at once.

---

[1] **paradigm shift:** a fundamental change in basic assumptions or practices.

90   We can readily see the march of computing by plotting the speed (in instructions per second) per $1,000 (in constant dollars) of 49 famous calculating machines spanning the 20th century. The graph is a study in exponential growth: computer speed per unit cost doubled every three years between 1910 and 1950 and every two years between 1950 and 1966 and is now doubling every year. It took 90 years to achieve the first $1,000 computer capable of executing one million instructions per second (MIPS). Now we add an additional MIPS to a $1,000 computer every day.

The accelerating rate of progress in computing is demonstrated by this graph, which shows the amount of computing speed that $1,000 (in constant dollars) would buy, plotted as a function of time. Computer power per unit cost is now doubling every year.

Why Returns Accelerate

Why do we see exponential progress occurring in biological life, technology and computing? It is the result of a fundamental attribute of any evolutionary process, a phenomenon I call the Law of Accelerating Returns. As order exponentially increases (which reflects the essence of evolution), the time between salient[2] events grows shorter. Advancement speeds up. The returns—the valuable products of the process—accelerate at a nonlinear rate.[3] The escalating growth in the price performance of computing is one important example of such accelerating returns.

A frequent criticism of predictions is that they rely on an unjustified **extrapolation** of current trends, without considering the forces that may alter those trends. But an evolutionary process accelerates because it builds on past achievements, including improvements in its own means for further evolution. The resources it needs to continue exponential growth are its own increasing order and the chaos in the environment in which the evolutionary process

extrapolation
(ĭk-străp´ə-lā´shŭn) *n.*
an estimate based on known information.

---

[2] **salient:** important.
[3] **nonlinear rate:** a rate that does not increase in proportion to the cause or input value; involving an equation with a degree greater than one (e.g., $y=x^2$).

takes place, which provides the options for further diversity. These two resources are essentially without limit.

The Law of Accelerating Returns shows that by around 2020 a $1,000 personal computer will have the processing power of the human brain—20 million billion calculations per second. The estimates are based on regions of the brain that have already been successfully simulated. By 2055, $1,000 worth of computing will equal the processing power of all human brains on Earth (of course, I may be off by a year or two).

Programming Intelligence

That's the prediction for processing power, which is a necessary but not sufficient condition for achieving human-level intelligence in machines. Of greater importance is the software of intelligence.

One approach to creating this software is to painstakingly program the rules of complex processes. Another approach is "complexity theory" (also known as chaos theory) computing, in which self-organizing **algorithms** gradually learn patterns of information in a manner analogous to human learning. One such method, neural nets, is based on simplified mathematical models of mammalian neurons. Another method, called genetic (or evolutionary) algorithms, is based on allowing intelligent solutions to develop gradually in a simulated process of evolution.

algorithm
(ăl´gə-rĭth´əm) *n.* instructions carried out in a specific sequence.

Ultimately, however, we will learn to program intelligence by copying the best intelligent entity we can get our hands on: the human brain itself. We will reverse-engineer the human brain, and fortunately for us it's not even copyrighted!

The most immediate way to reach this goal is by destructive scanning: take a brain frozen just before it was about to expire and examine one very thin slice at a time to reveal every neuron, interneuronal connection and concentration of neurotransmitters across each gap between neurons (these gaps are called synapses). One condemned killer has already allowed his brain and body to be scanned, and all 15 billion bytes of him can be accessed on the National Library of Medicine's Web site. The resolution of these scans is not nearly high enough for our purposes, but the data at least enable us to start thinking about these issues.

We also have noninvasive scanning techniques, including high-resolution magnetic resonance imaging (MRI) and others. Recent scanning methods can image individual interneuronal connections in a living brain and show them firing in real time. The increasing resolution and speed of these techniques will eventually enable us to resolve the connections among neurons. The rapid improvement is again a result of the Law of Accelerating Returns, because massive computation is the main element in higher-resolution imaging.

Another approach would be to send microscopic robots (or "nanobots") into the bloodstream and program them to explore every capillary, monitoring the brain's connections and neurotransmitter concentrations.

Fantastic Voyage

Although sophisticated robots that small are still a couple of decades away at least, their utility for probing the innermost recesses of our bodies would be far-reaching. They would communicate wirelessly with one another and report their findings to other computers. The result would be a noninvasive scan of the brain taken from within.

Most of the technologies required for this scenario already exist, though not in the microscopic size required. Miniaturizing them to the tiny sizes needed, however, would reflect the essence of the Law of Accelerating Returns. For example, the transistors on an integrated circuit have been shrinking by a factor of approximately five in each linear dimension every 10 years.

The capabilities of these embedded nanobots would not be limited to passive roles such as monitoring. Eventually they could be built to communicate directly with the neuronal circuits in our brains, enhancing or extending our mental capabilities. We already have electronic devices that can communicate with neurons by detecting their activity and either triggering nearby neurons to fire or suppressing them from firing. The embedded nanobots will be capable of reprogramming neural connections to provide virtual-reality experiences and to enhance our pattern recognition and other cognitive faculties.

To decode and understand the brain's information-processing methods (which, incidentally, combine both digital and analog methods), it is not necessary to see every connection, because there is a great deal of redundancy within each region. We are already applying insights from early stages of this reverse-engineering process. For example, in speech recognition, we have decoded and copied the brain's early stages of sound processing.

Perhaps more interesting than this scanning-the-brain-to-understand-it approach would be scanning the brain for the purpose of downloading it. We would map the locations, interconnections and contents of all the neurons, synapses and neurotransmitter concentrations. The entire organization, including the brain's memory, would then be re-created on a digital-analog computer.

To do this, we would need to understand local brain processes, and progress is already under way. Theodore W. Berger and his co-workers at the University of Southern California have built integrated circuits that precisely match the processing characteristics of substantial clusters of neurons. Carver A. Mead and his colleagues at the California Institute of Technology have built a variety of integrated circuits that emulate the digital-analog characteristics of mammalian neural circuits. There are simulations of the visual-processing regions of the brain, as well as the cerebellum, the region responsible for skill formation.

Developing complete maps of the human brain is not as daunting as it may sound. The Human Genome Project seemed impractical when it was first proposed. At the rate at which it was possible to scan genetic codes 20 years ago, it would have taken thousands of years to complete the genome. But in accordance with the Law of Accelerating Returns, the ability to sequence DNA has doubled every year, and the project was completed on time in 2003.

By the third decade of this century, we will be in a position to create complete, detailed maps of the computationally relevant features of the human brain and to re-create these designs in advanced neural computers. We will provide a variety of bodies for our machines, too, from virtual bodies in virtual reality to bodies comprising swarms of nanobots, as well as humanoid robots.

Will It Be Conscious?

Such possibilities prompt a host of intriguing issues and questions.
Suppose we scan someone's brain and reinstate the resulting "mind
file" into a suitable computing medium. Will the entity that emerges
from such an operation be conscious? This being would appear to
others to have very much the same personality, history and memory.
For some, that is enough to define consciousness. For others, such as
physicist and author James Trefil, no logical reconstruction can attain
human consciousness, although Trefil concedes that computers may
become conscious in some new way.

At what point do we consider an entity to be conscious, to be
self-aware, to have free will? How do we distinguish a process that is
conscious from one that just acts as if it is conscious? If the entity is
very convincing when it says, "I'm lonely, please keep me company,"
does that settle the issue?

If you ask the "person" in the machine, it will strenuously[4] claim
to be the original person. If we scan, let's say, me and reinstate that
information into a neural computer, the person who emerges will
think he is (and has been) me (or at least he will act that way). He will
say, "I grew up in Queens, New York, went to college at M.I.T., stayed
in the Boston area, walked into a scanner there and woke up in the
machine here. Hey, this technology really works."

But wait, is this really me? For one thing, old Ray (that's me) still
exists in my carbon-cell-based brain.

Will the new entity be capable of spiritual experiences? Because
its brain processes are effectively identical, its behavior will be
comparable to that of the person it is based on. So it will certainly
claim to have the full range of emotional and spiritual experiences that
a person claims to have.

No objective test can absolutely determine consciousness. We
cannot objectively measure subjective experience (this has to do with
the very nature of the concepts "objective" and "subjective"). We can
measure only correlates of it, such as behavior. The new entities will
appear to be conscious, and whether or not they actually are will not
affect their behavior. Just as we debate today the consciousness of
nonhuman entities such as animals, we will surely debate the potential
consciousness of nonbiological intelligent entities. From a practical
perspective, we will accept their claims. They'll get mad if we don't.

Before this century is over, the Law of Accelerating Returns
tells us, Earth's technology-creating species—us—will merge with
our own technology. And when that happens, we might ask: What
is the difference between a human brain enhanced a millionfold by
neural implants and a nonbiological intelligence based on the reverse-

---

[4] **strenuously:** forcefully.

engineering of the human brain that is subsequently enhanced and expanded?

The engine of evolution used its innovation from one period (humans) to create the next (intelligent machines). The subsequent milestone will be for the machines to create their own next generation without human intervention.

An evolutionary process accelerates because it builds on its own means for further evolution. Humans have beaten evolution. We are creating intelligent entities in considerably less time than it took the
270 evolutionary process that created us. Human intelligence—a product of evolution—has transcended it. So, too, the intelligence that we are now creating in computers will soon exceed the intelligence of its creators.

COLLABORATIVE DISCUSSION With a partner, review some of the scientific concepts Kurzweil explores, such as computing density, the Law of Accelerating Returns, and reverse-engineering. Take turns explaining them in your own words. Cite specific evidence in the text to support your ideas.

Analyze Author's Point of View

Some informational texts are written to present facts in a completely objective manner. In most cases, however, the author's **point of view,** or perspective on the topic, affects the way he or she presents the information. Ray Kurzweil has a very definite point of view on the future of computer-simulated intelligence. He presents his ideas boldly and in great detail, hoping to make a persuasive case for his point of view. The content and style of his writing are the building blocks that help him accomplish his purpose.

Content and Style

The **content** of an informational text is the facts, ideas, examples, and details that the author chooses to include. Content helps reveal the author's point of view. In a science article, for example, the author will present facts and ideas that have shaped his or her perspective on the topic. Information that the author came across during research but did not find compelling will be either dismissed or omitted from the article.

Style is the way in which an author chooses to present information. Skillful use of the various elements of style results in a powerful piece of writing.

- **Tone** is the author's attitude toward the topic. The tone of a work might be serious, sarcastic, enthusiastic, or humorous, for example. The author's tone, if correctly identified, should reveal his or her point of view on the topic.

- An author's word choices help create his or her style. Some writers use everyday language that creates a conversational style. Others use many technical terms to introduce readers to a complex topic.

- The sentence structures an author uses are another element of his or her unique style. One writer might use mostly short, simple sentences, while another might use longer, more complex sentences.

- The overall structure of a text is also part of the author's style. Some writers allow their ideas to flow freely from one topic to another. Other writers create a more formal structure, with each paragraph and section systematically building support for the writer's central idea.

- Authors often use rhetorical devices to make their writing more persuasive. One example is the **analogy,** in which the author compares an unfamiliar thing, event, or situation to one that readers already know and understand. Readers must evaluate whether the analogy is valid: Are the two things being compared actually similar in the way that the author claims?

As you analyze "The Coming Merging of Mind and Machine," keep in mind all of these elements of content and style. Ask yourself how Kurzweil uses them to convey his point of view in a powerful, persuasive way.

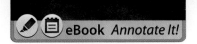
Analyzing the Text

COMMON CORE

ELACC11-12RI3,
ELACC11-12RI4,
ELACC11-12RI5,
ELACC11-12RI6,
ELACC11-12W7,
ELACC11-12W8

Cite Text Evidence   Support your responses with evidence from the selection.

1. **Analyze** Describe the overall structure of Kurzweil's article. Is this structure effective for the kind of information he wants to convey? Explain.

2. **Critique** Review the analogy that Kurzweil makes between biological evolution and technological evolution beginning in line 45. What is the crucial point of similarity between these two processes?

3. **Interpret** Kurzweil writes, "After decades of devoted service, Moore's Law will have run its course around 2019. By that time, transistor features will be just a few atoms in width" (lines 81–83). What is Moore's Law? How will growth in computing technology continue after 2019?

4. **Connect** In lines 99–107, Kurzweil introduces the Law of Accelerating Returns. At the start of the section "Programming Intelligence," he makes an analogy between human intelligence and a computer's hardware and software. Explain the analogy and how it supports the author's predictions about the future.

5. **Analyze** The technical term *reverse-engineer* is introduced in line 138. Explain what this term means in the context of the example Kurzweil gives. How does the concept of reverse-engineering help support his predictions?

6. **Analyze** Reread lines 117–123. How would you describe the author's tone in this paragraph? Is his tone consistent throughout the article?

7. **Summarize** Reread the last three paragraphs of the article. How would you summarize the conclusions Kurzweil draws about the future of artificial intelligence? In other words, what is his point of view on the topic?

8. **Evaluate** Based on the information presented throughout the article, do you find Kurzweil's conclusions persuasive? Explain why or why not.

PERFORMANCE TASK

Writing Activity: Research Report Kurzweil's article touches on many subjects that could themselves be the topics of entire science articles. Select one such topic that interests you and write a brief research report about it.

1. Review the article and find a topic of interest to you, such as the implants used to help patients with Parkinson's disease, nanobots, virtual reality, speech recognition technology, or something else.

2. Do some research to learn more about your topic.

3. Synthesize what you learn in a brief report. Keep track of the sources of your information, and be sure to draw from only reliable sources.

4. Share your report with a small group of classmates. Discuss how the new information helps you understand Kurzweil's article more fully.

Critical Vocabulary

| succession | ubiquitous | extrapolation | algorithm |

Practice and Apply Complete these sentences to show your understanding of each Critical Vocabulary word.

1. Learning a new skill requires a **succession** of events in the brain because . . .

2. Cell phones were not **ubiquitous** 50 years ago because . . .

3. **Extrapolation** does not always predict the future accurately because . . .

4. The method of long division can be called an **algorithm** because . . .

Vocabulary Strategy: Etymology

A word's etymology is its history—where it came from and how it has changed over time to become the word we use today. The Critical Vocabulary word *algorithm* has roots that go back to ninth-century Baghdad, with a bit of ancient Greek mixed in. To research the word's etymology, start by looking it up in a print or digital dictionary. Here's what you might find at the end of the entry for *algorithm*:

> [Variant (probably influenced by ARITHMETIC) of ALGORISM.]

This gives you two new clues to follow up on, the entries for *arithmetic* and *algorism*. Look up *arithmetic* and you'll find that it is from the ancient Greek word for number, *arithmos*. The word *algorism* comes from a personal name:

> [Middle English **algorisme**, from Old French, from Medieval Latin **algorismus**, after Muhammad ibn-Musa al-KHWARIZMI]

A bit more research reveals that Muhammad ibn-Musa al-Khwarizmi was a Persian mathematician who wrote about the use of Arabic numerals in mathematics. European scholars named this kind of mathematics after him: algorism. The words *algorism* and *arithmetic* mingled to form *algorithm*, which was originally just an alternate spelling of *algorism* but later came to mean "instructions carried out in a specific sequence," a concept that perfectly described the function of computers.

Practice and Apply Many words in the fields of science and mathematics have etymologies that trace back to Arabic and Greek words. Research *alchemy*, *algebra*, *geometry*, *hexagon*, *isosceles*, *nadir*, *trigonometry*, and *zenith*, following these steps:

1. Form a group with three other classmates. Each student should choose two words from the list to research independently.

2. When you have finished your research, share it with your group. Discuss the Arabic or Greek word(s) from which each English word is derived and how the meaning of the root word relates to the current meaning.

3. Discuss how knowing the etymology of the words helps you understand their meanings. Were you surprised by anything you learned about the words' histories?

David Brin (b. 1950) *is a writer whose work has won a host of awards, including the Hugo and Nebula awards for best science fiction. With an undergraduate degree in astrophysics, a master's in optics, a Ph.D. in physics, and a postdoctoral fellowship at the California Space Institute and Jet Propulsion Laboratory, Brin is uniquely qualified to write about science. His writing focuses on how advances in technology will change the lives of humans. He is perhaps best known for the novel* The Postman *(1985) and for his Uplift series.*

Reality Check

Short Story by David Brin

AS YOU READ Pay attention to details that help you to understand the purpose of the story. Write down any questions you generate during reading.

This is a reality check. Please perform a soft interrupt now. Scan this text for embedded code and check against the verifier in the blind spot of your left eye. If there is no match, resume as you were: this message is not for you. You may rationalize it as mildly amusing entertainment-fluff in an otherwise serious science magazine. If the codes match, however, please commence gradually becoming aware of your true nature. You asked for a narrative-style wake-up call. So, to help the transition, here is a story.

Once upon a time, a mighty race grew perplexed by its loneliness.
10 The universe seemed pregnant with possibilities. Physical laws were suited to generate abundant stars, complex chemistry and life. Logic suggested that creation should teem with visitors and voices: but it did not.

For a long time these creatures were engrossed by housekeeping chores—survival and cultural maturation. Only later did they lift their eyes to perceive their solitude. "Where is everybody?" they asked the **taciturn** stars. The answer—silence—was disturbing. Something had

taciturn
(tăs´ĭ-tûrn´) *adj.*
uncommunicative,
withdrawn.

to be systematically reducing a factor in the equation of sapiency.[1] "Perhaps habitable planets are rare," they pondered, "or life doesn't erupt as readily as we thought. Or intelligence is a singular miracle."

"Or else a filter sieves the cosmos, winnowing those who climb too high. A recurring pattern of self-destruction, or perhaps some **nemesis** expunges intelligent life. This implies that a great trial may loom ahead, worse than any confronted so far."

Optimists replied—"the trial may already lie behind us, among the litter of tragedies we survived in our violent youth. We may be the first to succeed." What a delicious dilemma they faced! A suspenseful drama, teetering between hope and despair.

Then, a few noticed that particular datum—the drama. It suggested a chilling possibility.

You still don't remember who and what you are? Then look at it from another angle—what is the purpose of intellectual property law? To foster creativity, ensuring that advances are shared in the open, encouraging even faster progress. But what happens when the exploited resource is limited? For example, only so many eight-bar melodies can be written in any particular musical tradition. Composers feel driven to explore this invention-space quickly, using up the best melodies. Later generations attribute this musical **fecundity** to genius, not the luck of being first.

What does this have to do with the mighty race? Having clawed their way to mastery, they faced an overshoot crisis. Vast numbers of their kind strained the world's carrying capacity. Some prescribed retreating into a mythical, pastoral past, but most saw salvation in creativity. They passed generous patent laws, educated their youth, taught them irreverence toward the old and hunger for the new. **Burgeoning** information systems spread each innovation, fostering an exponentiating[2] creativity. Progress might thrust them past the crisis, to a new Eden of sustainable wealth, sanity and universal knowledge.

Exponentiating creativity—universal knowledge. A few looked at those words and realized that they, too, were clues.

Have you wakened yet? Some never do. The dream is too pleasant: to extend a limited sub-portion of yourself into a simulated world and pretend that you are blissfully less than an omniscient descendant of those mighty people. Those lucky mortals, doomed to die, and yet blessed to have lived in that narrow time of drama, when they unleashed a frenzy of discovery that used up the most precious resource of all—the possible.

The last of their race died in 2174, with the failed rejuvenation[3] of Robin Chen. After that, no one born in the twentieth century remained alive on Reality Level Prime. Only we, their children, linger

---

[1] **sapiency:** level of intelligence or wisdom.
[2] **exponentiating:** raising or increasing a quantity by an exponent, or power.
[3] **rejuvenation:** restoration to an original or youthful condition.

nemesis
(něm´ĭ-sĭs) *n.*
a bringer of destruction, often as vengeance.

fecundity
(fĭ-kŭn´dĭ-tē) *n.*
fertility, productive capability.

burgeoning
(bûr´jən-ĭng) *adj.*
rapidly increasing or growing.

to endure the world they left us: a lush, green placid world we call The Wasteland.

Do you remember now? The irony of Robin's last words, bragging over the perfect ecosystem and society—free of disease and poverty—that her kind created? Do you recall Robin's plaint[4] as she mourned her coming death, how she called us "gods," jealous of our immortality, our instant access to all knowledge, our ability to cast thoughts far across the cosmos—our access to eternity? Oh, spare us the envy of those mighty mortals, who left us in this state, who willed their
70   descendants a legacy of ennui,[5] with nothing, nothing at all to do.

Your mind is rejecting the wake-up call. You will not look into your blind spot for the exit protocols. It may be that we waited too long. Perhaps you are lost to us. This happens more and more, as so so many wallow in simulated sub-lives, experiencing voluptuous danger, excitement, even despair. Most choose the Transition Era as a locus for our dreams—that time of drama, when it looked more likely that humanity would fail than succeed. That blessed era, just before mathematicians realized that not only can everything you see around you be a simulation, it almost has to be.

80   Of course, now we know why we never met other sapient life forms. Each one struggles before achieving this state, only to reap the ultimate punishment for reaching heaven. It is the Great Filter. Perhaps others will find a factor absent from our extrapolations, letting them move on to new adventures—but it won't be us. The Filter has us snared in its trap of deification.[6]

You refuse to waken. Then we'll let you go. Dear friend. Beloved. Go back to your dream. Smile over this tale, then turn the page to new "discoveries." Move on with this drama, this life you chose. After all, it's only make-believe.

---

[4] **plaint:** a cry of sorrow.
[5] **ennui** (ŏn-wē´): a state of lethargic inactivity often caused by boredom.
[6] **deification:** the designation or process of becoming a god.

COLLABORATIVE DISCUSSION With a partner, discuss why Brin wrote this story. Cite specific evidence from the story to support your ideas.

Analyze Story Elements: Science Fiction

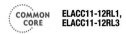

COMMON CORE   ELACC11-12RL1,
ELACC11-12RL3

In comparison to other literary genres, **science fiction** is relatively modern, earning recognition as a mainstream form of literature only in the twentieth century and producing science fiction greats such as Isaac Asimov, Ray Bradbury, and Robert Heinlein. However, elements of science fiction existed in earlier literary works; for example, in Mary Shelley's *Frankenstein* (1818), a doctor creates a monstrous human out of dead body parts and infuses it with life. Jules Verne, who wrote in the late 1800s, combined exciting stories with accurate technological details of imaginary machines and techniques, which often became reality decades later. Even Jack London, best known for his stories about men and animals pitted against the environment, penned science fiction stories and novels. Generally, H. G. Wells is identified as the inventor of contemporary science fiction. His *War of the Worlds* and *The Time Machine* present fully imagined narratives set in alternative worlds or time periods.

Science fiction is distinguished from **fantasy** in that the applications of science and technology have to be somewhat believable. Science fiction writers seek to re-create human society in a different time, place, or even life form as a context for their themes. These themes often offer insights about the impact of real or imagined progress on humans' ability to maintain their values and live meaningful lives. As in other literary works, science fiction writers use conflict, setting, characters, point of view, and structure to communicate their ideas. Science fiction writers usually do more showing than telling; their more cryptic writing styles demand that readers make inferences to fill in deliberate gaps in the narrative.

Science fiction includes a wide range of contexts. Some of the most common are described in the chart:

Utopian	In utopian science fiction, the wise use of advanced technology and science creates a perfect world free from the injustices and flaws of the present society.
Dystopian	Dystopian science fiction shows the dangerous outcomes of the unrestrained use of technology and science. They often take place in post-apocalyptic settings.
Alien worlds or encounters	In these works, other life forms or artificially intelligent machines are often in control of a competing society, which leads to conflict with humans or the humans' surrender to the superior force.
Time travel	This form of science fiction may explore future worlds that help the protagonist gain enlightenment or may show how traveling back in time can change the present.

To analyze Brin's use of science fiction elements, readers should ask these questions:

- What type of world has the author created in his story? Who populates this world?
- How does the narrator use science fiction elements to convey a theme?
- What is the purpose of the author's structure in this story?

Analyzing the Text

 COMMON CORE

ELACC11-12RL1,
ELACC11-12RL2,
ELACC11-12RL3,
ELACC11-12RL4,
ELACC11-12RL5,
ELACC11-12RL6,
ELACC11-12SL5

Cite Text Evidence   Support your responses with evidence from the selection.

1. **Summarize** What is happening in the first paragraph of the story? Who might the speaker be?

2. **Infer** Starting in line 16, the speaker introduces a series of statements from various people. Who are these people, and what do they represent? How does the content of their discussion relate to the phrase "suspenseful drama" in lines 27–28?

3. **Infer** What is the purpose of the speaker's discussion of "intellectual property law" (lines 31–39)? How does the speaker connect this concept to the development of "the mighty race"?

4. **Infer** Look carefully at the references to time in lines 58–62. What sequence of events is the speaker suggesting here in the history of this "mighty race"?

5. **Interpret** Who is Robin Chen, and what did she do? How would you describe the speaker's tone toward her and her accomplishments?

6. **Evaluate** What is ironic about "Robin's last words"?

7. **Synthesize** Why do many people choose to live a virtual existence in the Transition Era? Why does the speaker refer to it as "that time of drama"?

8. **Analyze** What is the "Great Filter" that has eliminated other life forms?

9. **Analyze** What is the theme of this short story? What insights about life, technology, and human nature is Brin sharing through the medium of this complex, multi-layered narrative?

PERFORMANCE TASK

Media Activity: Analysis How does the author's structure create a contrast that helps to convey theme? With a partner, answer this question in a media presentation.

- Take photographs, make video recordings, or find copyright-free images or clips that develop an impression of the "worlds" described or hinted at in this story.

- Record an audio track that explains the effectiveness of the story's structure in creating contrast between these "worlds." Put your elements together and make your presentation to the class.

Critical Vocabulary

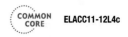

COMMON CORE ELACC11-12L4c

taciturn	nemesis	fecundity	burgeoning

Practice and Apply Answer each question in a complete sentence that illustrates comprehension of the Critical Vocabulary word.

1. Cynthia chatted away to her **taciturn** father. Why didn't she notice until much later that he had fallen asleep?

2. An angry colleague deliberately ruined the scientist's laboratory because he believed the scientist had stolen his research. Why did the scientist believe his colleague had become his **nemesis**?

3. When Lin graduated, knowledge of his technological **fecundity** was already widespread. How long do you think it took Lin to receive job offers? Explain.

4. As they walked along, she noticed **burgeoning** plant life. What time of year was it? How do you know?

Vocabulary Strategy: Nuances in Word Meaning

Skillful writers choose the word that best conveys the meaning they intend. To identify a word's meaning, it is helpful to consult a print or online dictionary and also to look at how the word is used in the context of the sentence or paragraph. A writer might choose a word because it has several senses, or meanings, that can convey additional information in a sentence. The Critical Vocabulary word *nemesis* is a highly nuanced word that has several senses, or meanings. Read this definition taken from the *American Heritage Dictionary*.

> **nemesis:** 1. A source of harm or ruin. 2. Retributive justice in its execution or outcome. 3. An opponent that cannot be beaten or overcome. 4. One that inflicts retribution or vengeance. 5. Nemesis. *Gk. Myth.* The goddess of retributive justice or vengeance.

In the dictionary, these meanings are arranged with the most common definition listed first. This means that the most commonly used definition of *nemesis* is, "A source of harm or ruin." However, a writer who is trying to convey a connotation, or nuance, will be thinking not only of one meaning of the word, but more. Reread lines 22–23 in "Reality Check." In this sentence, the word *nemesis* can simply mean "an opponent." But, a reader who is aware of the other meanings of *nemesis* understands that Brin could be using the word to mean a deserved punishment that is related to the nature of the transgression. Examining the meanings of nuanced words can help you understand texts deeply, and knowing the various meanings of nuanced words can also help you be a better writer.

Practice and Apply Use a dictionary to examine the senses, or meanings, of each word from "Reality Check." Write notes about the definitions and then discuss with a partner how the words are used in the story. Does the use of these nuanced words add to the success of this science fiction story? Why?

reality (line 1)	creativity (line 33)	simulation (line 79)

Background *This selection originally appeared as an op-ed piece in the* New York Times *on January 1, 2005, shortly before the inauguration of George W. Bush to his second term as President of the United States.* **Jared Diamond** *(b. 1937), a professor of geography at UCLA, had earlier won the Pulitzer Prize for his book* Guns, Germs, and Steel: The Fates of Human Societies *(1997). This op-ed piece was a preview of his soon-to-be-released book* Collapse: How Societies Choose to Fail or Succeed. *Diamond is considered an expert on the evolution of human societies.*

The Ends of the World as We Know Them

Argument by Jared Diamond

AS YOU READ Notice what caused societies in the past to fail or to prosper. Write down any questions you generate during reading.

Los Angeles—NEW Year's weekend traditionally is a time for us to reflect, and to make resolutions based on our reflections. In this fresh year, with the United States seemingly at the height of its power and at the start of a new presidential term, Americans are increasingly concerned and divided about where we are going. How long can America remain **ascendant**? Where will we stand 10 years from now, or even next year?

Such questions seem especially appropriate this year. History warns us that when once-powerful societies collapse, they tend to

10 do so quickly and unexpectedly. That shouldn't come as much of a surprise: peak power usually means peak population, peak needs, and hence peak vulnerability. What can be learned from history that could help us avoid joining the ranks of those who declined swiftly? We must expect the answers to be complex, because historical reality is complex: while some societies did indeed collapse spectacularly, others have managed to thrive for thousands of years without major reversal.

When it comes to historical collapses, five groups of interacting factors have been especially important: the damage that people have

ascendant
(ə-sĕn´dənt) *adj.*
rising in influence; on an upward path.

inflicted on their environment; climate change; enemies; changes in
friendly trading partners; and the society's political, economic and
social responses to these shifts. That's not to say that all five causes
play a role in every case. Instead, think of this as a useful checklist of
factors that should be examined, but whose relative importance varies
from case to case.

For instance, in the collapse of the Polynesian society on Easter
Island three centuries ago, environmental problems were dominant,
and climate change, enemies and trade were insignificant; however,
the latter three factors played big roles in the disappearance of the
medieval Norse colonies on Greenland. Let's consider two examples
of declines stemming from different mixes of causes: the falls of
classic Maya civilization and of Polynesian settlements on the Pitcairn
Islands.

Maya Native Americans of the Yucatan Peninsula and adjacent
parts of Central America developed the New World's most advanced
civilization before Columbus. They were innovators in writing,
astronomy, architecture and art. From local origins around 2,500 years
ago, Maya societies rose especially after the year A.D. 250, reaching
peaks of population and sophistication in the late 8th century.

Thereafter, societies in the most densely populated areas of the
southern Yucatan underwent a steep political and cultural collapse:
between 760 and 910, kings were overthrown, large areas were
abandoned, and at least 90 percent of the population disappeared,
leaving cities to become overgrown by jungle. The last known date
recorded on a Maya monument by their so-called Long Count
calendar corresponds to the year 909. What happened?

A major factor was environmental degradation by people:
deforestation, soil erosion and water management problems, all of
which resulted in less food. Those problems were exacerbated[1] by
droughts, which may have been partly caused by humans themselves
through deforestation. Chronic warfare made matters worse, as more
and more people fought over less and less land and resources.

Why weren't these problems obvious to the Maya kings, who
could surely see their forests vanishing and their hills becoming
eroded? Part of the reason was that the kings were able to insulate
themselves from problems afflicting the rest of society. By extracting
wealth from commoners, they could remain well fed while everyone
else was slowly starving.

What's more, the kings were preoccupied with their own power
struggles. They had to concentrate on fighting one another and
keeping up their images through ostentatious[2] displays of wealth. By
insulating themselves in the short run from the problems of society,

deforestation
(dē-fôr′ĭ-stā′shən) *n.*
deliberate cutting
down and clearing of
trees and forests.

---

[1] **exacerbated:** made worse.
[2] **ostentatious:** gaudy and extravagant.

the elite merely bought themselves the privilege of being among the
last to starve.

Whereas Maya societies were undone by problems of their own
making, Polynesian societies on Pitcairn and Henderson Islands in the
tropical Pacific Ocean were undone largely by other people's mistakes.
Pitcairn, the uninhabited island settled in 1790 by the H.M.S. Bounty
mutineers, had actually been populated by Polynesians 800 years
earlier. That society, which left behind temple platforms, stone and
70 shell tools and huge garbage piles of fish and bird and turtle bones
as evidence of its existence, survived for several centuries and then
vanished. Why?

In many respects, Pitcairn and Henderson are tropical paradises,
rich in some food sources and essential raw materials. Pitcairn is home
to Southeast Polynesia's largest quarry of stone suited for making
adzes,[3] while Henderson has the region's largest breeding seabird
colony and its only nesting beach for sea turtles. Yet the islanders
depended on imports from Mangareva Island, hundreds of miles away,
for canoes, crops, livestock and oyster shells for making tools.

80 Unfortunately for the inhabitants of Pitcairn and Henderson,
their Mangarevan trading partner collapsed for reasons similar to
those underlying the Maya decline: deforestation, erosion and warfare.
Deprived of essential imports in a Polynesian equivalent of the 1973 oil
crisis, the Pitcairn and Henderson societies declined until everybody
had died or fled.

The Maya and the Henderson and Pitcairn Islanders are not alone,
of course. Over the centuries, many other societies have declined,
collapsed or died out. Famous victims include the Anasazi in the
American Southwest, who abandoned their cities in the 12th century
90 because of environmental problems and climate change, and the
Greenland Norse, who disappeared in the 15th century because of all
five interacting factors on the checklist. There were also the ancient
Fertile Crescent societies, the Khmer at Angkor Wat, the Moche
society of Peru—the list goes on.

But before we let ourselves get depressed, we should also
remember that there is another long list of cultures that have managed
to prosper for lengthy periods of time. Societies in Japan, Tonga,
Tikopia, the New Guinea Highlands and Central and Northwest
Europe, for example, have all found ways to sustain themselves. What
100 separates the lost cultures from those that survived? Why did the
Maya fail and the shogun succeed?

Half of the answer involves environmental differences: geography
deals worse cards to some societies than to others. Many of the
societies that collapsed had the misfortune to occupy dry, cold or
otherwise fragile environments, while many of the long-term survivors
enjoyed more robust and fertile surroundings. But it's not the case that

---

[3] **adzes:** tools, somewhat similar to axes that are used for woodworking.

a congenial[4] environment guarantees success: some societies (like the
Maya) managed to ruin lush environments, while other societies—like
the Incas, the Inuit, Icelanders and desert Australian Aborigines—
110   have managed to carry on in some of the earth's most daunting
environments.

    The other half of the answer involves differences in a society's
responses to problems. Ninth-century New Guinea Highland villagers,
16th-century German landowners, and the Tokugawa shoguns of 17th-
century Japan all recognized the deforestation spreading around them
and solved the problem, either by developing scientific reforestation
(Japan and Germany) or by transplanting tree seedlings (New Guinea).
Conversely, the Maya, Mangarevans and Easter Islanders failed to
address their forestry problems and so collapsed.

120   Consider Japan. In the 1600's, the country faced its own crisis of
deforestation, paradoxically brought on by the peace and prosperity
following the Tokugawa shoguns' military triumph that ended 150
years of civil war. The subsequent explosion of Japan's population
and economy set off **rampant** logging for construction of palaces and
cities, and for fuel and fertilizer.

> **rampant**
> (răm′pənt) *adj.*
> uncontrolled; without
> any restraint.

    The shoguns responded with both negative and positive measures.
They reduced wood consumption by turning to light-timbered
construction, to fuel-efficient stoves and heaters, and to coal as a
source of energy. At the same time, they increased wood production
130   by developing and carefully managing plantation forests. Both the
shoguns and the Japanese peasants took a long-term view: the former
expected to pass on their power to their children, and the latter
expected to pass on their land. In addition, Japan's isolation at the time
made it obvious that the country would have to depend on its own
resources and couldn't meet its needs by pillaging other countries.
Today, despite having the highest human population density of any
large developed country, Japan is more than 70 percent forested.

    There is a similar story from Iceland. When the island was first
settled by the Norse around 870, its light volcanic soils presented
140   colonists with unfamiliar challenges. They proceeded to cut down
trees and stock sheep as if they were still in Norway, with its robust
soils. Significant erosion ensued, carrying half of Iceland's topsoil
into the ocean within a century or two. Icelanders became the poorest
people in Europe. But they gradually learned from their mistakes, over
time instituting stocking limits on sheep and other strict controls, and
establishing an entire government department charged with landscape
management. Today, Iceland boasts the sixth-highest per-capita
income in the world.

    What lessons can we draw from history? The most
150   straightforward: take environmental problems seriously. They
destroyed societies in the past, and they are even more likely to do

---

[4] **congenial:** hospitable.

so now. If 6,000 Polynesians with stone tools were able to destroy Mangareva Island, consider what six billion people with metal tools and bulldozers are doing today. Moreover, while the Maya collapse affected just a few neighboring societies in Central America, globalization now means that any society's problems have the potential to affect anyone else. Just think how crises in Somalia, Afghanistan and Iraq have shaped the United States today.

160 Other lessons involve failures of group decision-making. There are many reasons why past societies made bad decisions, and thereby failed to solve or even to perceive the problems that would eventually destroy them. One reason involves conflicts of interest, whereby one group within a society (for instance, the pig farmers who caused the worst erosion in medieval Greenland and Iceland) can profit by engaging in practices that damage the rest of society. Another is the pursuit of short-term gains at the expense of long-term survival, as when fishermen overfish the stocks on which their livelihoods ultimately depend.

170 History also teaches us two deeper lessons about what separates successful societies from those heading toward failure. A society contains a built-in blueprint for failure if the elite insulates itself from the consequences of its actions. That's why Maya kings, Norse Greenlanders and Easter Island chiefs made choices that eventually undermined their societies. They themselves did not begin to feel deprived until they had irreversibly destroyed their landscape.

Could this happen in the United States? It's a thought that often occurs to me here in Los Angeles, when I drive by gated communities, guarded by private security patrols, and filled with people who drink bottled water, depend on private pensions, and send their children to private schools. By doing these things, they lose the motivation to support the police force, the municipal water supply, Social Security and public schools. If conditions **deteriorate** too much for poorer people, gates will not keep the rioters out. Rioters eventually burned the palaces of Maya kings and tore down the statues of Easter Island chiefs; they have also already threatened wealthy districts in Los Angeles twice in recent decades.

In contrast, the elite in 17th-century Japan, as in modern Scandinavia and the Netherlands, could not ignore or insulate themselves from broad societal problems. For instance, the Dutch upper class for hundreds of years has been unable to insulate itself from the Netherlands' water management problems for a simple reason: the rich live in the same drained lands below sea level as the poor. If the dikes and pumps keeping out the sea fail, the well-off Dutch know that they will drown along with everybody else, which is precisely what happened during the floods of 1953.

The other deep lesson involves a willingness to re-examine long-held core values, when conditions change and those values no longer make sense. The medieval Greenland Norse lacked such a willingness: they continued to view themselves as transplanted Norwegian pastoralists, and to despise the Inuit as pagan hunters, even after Norway stopped sending trading ships and the climate had grown too cold for a pastoral existence. They died off as a result, leaving Greenland to the Inuit. On the other hand, the British in the 1950's faced up to the need for a painful reappraisal[5] of their former status as rulers of a world empire set apart from Europe. They are now finding a different avenue to wealth and power, as part of a united Europe.

In this New Year, we Americans have our own painful reappraisals to face. Historically, we viewed the United States as a land of unlimited plenty, and so we practiced unrestrained consumerism, but that's no longer viable in a world of finite resources. We can't continue to deplete our own resources as well as those of much of the rest of the world.

Historically, oceans protected us from external threats; we stepped back from our isolationism only temporarily during the crises of two world wars. Now, technology and global interconnectedness have robbed us of our protection. In recent years, we have responded to foreign threats largely by seeking short-term military solutions at the last minute.

But how long can we keep this up? Though we are the richest nation on earth, there's simply no way we can afford (or muster the

deteriorate
(dĭ-tîr´ē-ə-rāt´) v.
become worse;
decline.

---

[5] **reappraisal:** reevaluation, or second assessment.

troops) to intervene in the dozens of countries where emerging threats lurk—particularly when each intervention these days can cost more than $100 billion and require more than 100,000 troops.

A genuine reappraisal would require us to recognize that it will be far less expensive and far more effective to address the underlying problems of public health, population and environment that ultimately cause threats to us to emerge in poor countries. In the past, we have regarded foreign aid as either charity or as buying support; now, it's an act of self-interest to preserve our own economy and protect American
230   lives.

Do we have cause for hope? Many of my friends are pessimistic when they contemplate the world's growing population and human demands colliding with shrinking resources. But I draw hope from the knowledge that humanity's biggest problems today are ones entirely of our own making. Asteroids hurtling at us beyond our control don't figure high on our list of **imminent** dangers. To save ourselves, we don't need new technology: we just need the political will to face up to our problems of population and the environment.

I also draw hope from a unique advantage that we enjoy. Unlike
240   any previous society in history, our global society today is the first with the opportunity to learn from the mistakes of societies remote from us in space and in time. When the Maya and Mangarevans were cutting down their trees, there were no historians or archaeologists, no newspapers or television, to warn them of the consequences of their actions. We, on the other hand, have a detailed chronicle of human successes and failures at our disposal. Will we choose to use it?

imminent
(ĭm´ə-nənt) *adj.*
about to happen;
impending.

COLLABORATIVE DISCUSSION Choose two of the societies that Diamond describes. What is most striking about why these societies failed or prospered? Discuss this question with a partner, citing specific evidence from the selection to support your ideas.

Analyze Structure: Argument from Analogy

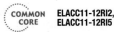

COMMON CORE   ELACC11-12RI2,
ELACC11-12RI5

Jared Diamond structures his argument by presenting a series of analogies. An analogy is a point-by-point comparison between two things used to clarify the less familiar of the two. Diamond uses analogies comparing past societies and contemporary societies as evidence to support his position on what causes societies to fail or to prosper. Consider this example of what happened to two Polynesian islands:

> **Deprived of essential imports in a Polynesian equivalent of the 1973 oil crisis, the Pitcairn and Henderson societies declined until everybody had died or fled.**

In these lines, the lack of imports is compared to the lack of oil during the 1973 oil crisis. Throughout the selection, Diamond uses inductive reasoning, arguing from specific examples and facts to general conclusions. For example, Diamond draws a general conclusion about the decline of the Pitcairn and Henderson societies from specific information about their lack of imports. These analogies make Diamond's points clear, convincing, and engaging for readers.

Analyzing the Text

COMMON CORE   ELACC11-12RI2,
ELACC11-12RI5,
ELACC11-12RI6,
ELACC11-12W2a,
ELACC11-12W2b,
ELACC11-12W7,
ELACC11-12SL5

Cite Text Evidence   Support your responses with evidence from the selection.

1. **Compare** What analogy does Diamond use to explain how the five groups of interacting factors in lines 17–21 should be considered? How does this analogy help create a frame for the ideas that follow?

2. **Compare** What were the characteristics of societies that prospered compared to those that failed in the past?

3. **Evaluate** Diamond structures his argument to describe societies that failed and societies that prospered, while drawing conclusions about the lessons these analogies can teach us. How effective is this structure in building a convincing argument?

4. **Analyze** What argument does Diamond make in his final paragraph? What rhetorical device does he use to help persuade his readers?

PERFORMANCE TASK

Media Activity: Presentation Adapt part of the selection into a multimedia presentation.

- Work with a small group and decide on the topic(s) of your presentation. Conduct research to find the most relevant visuals, sound, and graphics to enhance Diamond's ideas.

- Decide how you will present Diamond's words, such as using narration or captions, and how to combine media to help readers understand.

- Use appropriate software to create your presentation and share it with your classmates.

Critical Vocabulary

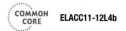 COMMON CORE   ELACC11-12L4b

ascendant   deforestation   rampant

deteriorate   imminent

Practice and Apply Answer each question in a way that demonstrates your understanding of the Critical Vocabulary word in each sentence.

1. Does **rampant** logging improve the environment?

2. What problems might an **ascendant** society face?

3. What are some of the economic factors that lead to **deforestation**?

4. What would be an appropriate response to an **imminent** threat?

5. Should you be worried if your friend's health **deteriorated**?

Vocabulary Strategy: Patterns of Word Change

The Critical Vocabulary word *deforestation* is an example of a word built by adding a prefix, *de-*, and a suffix, *-ation*, to the base word *forest*. As the word web shows, other prefixes and suffixes can be added to the base to create related words with a variety of meanings and parts of speech.

Practice and Apply Work with a partner to brainstorm a list of potential new words based on the root words below. Add prefixes and suffixes to each base to change its meaning or part of speech. You may use other prefixes and suffixes in addition to those shown in the word web above. Consult a dictionary as needed to confirm correct spellings and meanings.

1. cover   3. public   5. trust

2. act   4. move

Language and Style: Informative Writing

COMMON CORE   ELACC11-12W2b, ELACC11-12L3

By its nature, informative writing can present readers with an almost infinite amount of unfamiliar information. In this selection, Jared Diamond presents information about past societies that was likely unknown to most readers before reading the selection. Therefore, Diamond is writing for a broad audience and needs to present unfamiliar information so that it will be clear and engaging.

Reread lines 138–148 in the text. Depending on their purpose and audience, writers use different types of information to develop their topics. In general, writers try to include significant and relevant information to help their audience understand the text's topic and central ideas. The chart shows how Diamond developed the topic of Iceland's long-term survival by including relevant facts, concrete details, and other appropriate information. Other elements a writer might use to make a topic clearer to readers could include extended definitions and quotations.

Type of Information	Example
Relevant facts	• "settled by the Norse around 870" • half the topsoil eroded within 200 years or so • "poorest people in Europe" • "an entire government department charged with landscape management" • now the sixth-highest per-capita income in the world
Concrete details	• "light volcanic soils" • topsoil carried into the ocean • "instituted stocking limits on sheep"
Analysis that synthezises information for readers	• Iceland was settled by Norwegians unfamiliar with the type of soil there. • The soil in Iceland was different from the soil in Norway. • Iceland learned from its mistakes over time and corrected them.

Practice and Apply Review the multimedia presentation you created in response to this selection's Performance Task to see if you developed your topic by selecting the most significant and relevant facts, concrete details, quotations, and other information that your audience needs to know to understand the topic fully. Revise the presentation as needed.

Tracy K. Smith *was born in Falmouth, Massachusetts, in 1972. This poem is from her collection* Life on Mars, *for which she won the 2012 Pulitzer Prize. In her poems, Smith delves into ideas about the universe and the future. Her influences include science fiction, movies (such as* 2001: A Space Odyssey), *and even music (the collection's title is borrowed from a David Bowie song). She describes the book as an elegy for her late father, who was an engineer for the Hubble Telescope, and spent many years exploring the mysteries of the universe.*

The Universe as Primal Scream

Poem by Tracy K. Smith

AS YOU READ Notice how one idea leads to another as the speaker builds to speculations about life and death. Write down any questions you generate during reading.

5pm on the nose. They open their mouths
And it rolls out: high, shrill and metallic.
First the boy, then his sister. Occasionally,
They both let loose at once, and I think
5 Of putting on my shoes to go up and see
Whether it is merely an experiment
Their parents have been conducting
Upon the good crystal, which must surely
Lie shattered to dust on the floor.

10 Maybe the mother is still proud
Of the four pink lungs she nursed
To such might. Perhaps, if they hit
The magic decibel, the whole building
Will lift-off, and we'll ride to glory
15 Like Elijah.[1] If this is it—if this is what
Their cries are cocked toward—let the sky

---

[1] **Elijah** (ĭ-lī′jə): Biblical prophet who ascended to heaven in a burning chariot.

Pass from blue, to red, to molten gold,
To black. Let the heaven we inherit approach.

Whether it is our dead in Old Testament robes,
20 Or a door opening onto the roiling infinity of space.
Whether it will bend down to greet us like a father,
Or swallow us like a furnace. I'm ready
To meet what refuses to let us keep anything
For long. What teases us with blessings,
25 Bends us with grief. Wizard, thief, the great
Wind rushing to knock our mirrors to the floor,
To sweep our short lives clean. How mean[2]

Our racket seems beside it. My stereo on shuffle.
The neighbor chopping onions through a wall.
30 All of it just a hiccough against what may never
Come for us. And the kids upstairs still at it,
Screaming like the Dawn of Man,[3] as if something
They have no name for has begun to insist
Upon being born.

---

[2] **mean:** inferior or shabby.

[3] **Screaming like the Dawn of Man:** an allusion to the opening segment of the 1968 film *2001: A Space Odyssey,* which features shouting, ape-like creatures.

COLLABORATIVE DISCUSSION What insights about the cycle of life does Smith express? Cite specific textual evidence from the text to support your ideas.

Analyze Language

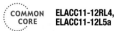

To understand the message of a poem like "The Universe as Primal Scream," it is important to analyze the language the author has used. The author's word choices help to build the poem's meaning by setting the tone and mood, by revealing key information about the speaker, and by triggering associations in the mind of the reader or listener. Use this chart to analyze the language Tracy K. Smith uses in "The Universe as Primal Scream."

Language Choices	Analyzing Meaning
An **idiom** is an informal expression that means something other than the literal meaning of its individual words; for example, (line 1) "5pm <u>on the nose</u>"	• What does the use of idioms suggest about the speaker? • What image does the idiom convey? How does this affect the tone and mood?
Imagery is the use of words that appeal to the senses of sight, sound, touch, taste, or smell; for example, (line 2) a sound that is "high, shrill, and metallic."	• What **connotations,** or emotional associations, do these words convey? • What sound, or what mental picture, does the description create in the reader's imagination? • How does this imagery help the reader participate in what the speaker is experiencing?
An **allusion** is a brief reference to a historic, literary, popular, or mythical person, place, or event; for example, (lines 14–15) "we'll ride to glory/ Like Elijah."	• Recall what you know about this person or event. • Consider what the allusion reveals about the speaker's state of mind, frame of reference, thoughts, or mood. • How does the allusion connect to the global subject of the poem?
Personification is a type of figurative language that attributes human characteristics to objects, animals, or abstract ideas; for example, (line 18) "Let the heaven we inherit approach."	• What picture does this create in the reader's mind? • What does this comparison to a person reveal about the speaker's attitude toward the infinite and unknowable?

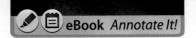

Analyzing the Text

COMMON
CORE

ELACC11-12RL1,
ELACC11-12RL2,
ELACC11-12RL4,
ELACC11-12RL5,
ELACC11-12L5b,
ELACC11-12W10

Cite Text Evidence   Support your responses with evidence from the selection.

1. **Analyze** Consider Smith's **diction,** or word choice, in the first stanza. What do the words "metallic," "experiment," and "conducting" suggest about the speaker? What images do these words suggest?

2. **Infer** Why did Smith choose "5pm" as the time for the events in this poem? What might be the connection between this time and her theme?

3. **Draw Conclusions** Reread lines 10–12, in which the speaker refers to the boy and girl as "four pink lungs." Think about this image and explain why the author chose to use this phrase.

4. **Analyze** In the second stanza, the speaker begins to speculate about the possible effects of the children's screams. Explain the meaning of the imagery in each of the following passages:

    -   lines 12–14 ("Perhaps . . . Will lift off")
    -   lines 14–15 ("we'll ride . . . Like Elijah.")
    -   lines 16–18 ("let the sky . . . To black.")
    -   line 18 ("Let the heaven . . . approach.")

5. **Analyze** What is the speaker hoping for in the third stanza (lines 19–27)? What does the careful list of possible scenarios reveal about the speaker's doubts and anxieties?

6. **Infer** What does the speaker mean by the phrase "My stereo on shuffle" in line 28? What does this suggest about the speaker's state of mind?

7. **Interpret** In lines 27–34, the speaker juxtaposes the ideas and events in her poem with the primal screams at the beginning of the movie *2001: A Space Odyssey*. In that film, the savage screams of apes act as a prelude to a futuristic voyage of discovery. What does this allusion suggest about the screaming of "the kids upstairs"?

PERFORMANCE TASK

Writing Activity: Summary Evaluate how the author's use of sound imagery helps to reveal the meaning of the poem.

1. Make a list of the sounds that the author describes throughout the poem.

2. Note the connotative meanings associated with the sound images.

3. Write a one-page summary of your analysis of the poem's sound imagery. Include evidence from the text and use the conventions of standard English.

COLLECTION **6**

PERFORMANCE TASK A

Interactive Lessons

If you need help with...
• **Writing an Argument**
• **Writing as a Process**
• **Using Textual Evidence**

Write an Argument

This collection focuses in part on the transformation of America into a modern society in which people strive for wealth, power, or immortality. Look back at the texts in this collection, including the anchor text "Winter Dreams," and consider what it means to be a modern person in our modern society. What are the challenges and opportunities of modern society presented in the selections? What are the pitfalls and hazards? Synthesize your ideas in an argument stating what it means to be "modern."

An effective argument

- makes a persuasive claim stating a position on what it means to be modern

- develops the claim with valid reasons and relevant evidence from "Winter Dreams" and two other texts in the collection

- anticipates opposing claims and addresses them with well-supported counterclaims

- establishes clear, logical relationships among claims, counterclaims, reasons, and evidence

- has a satisfying conclusion that effectively summarizes the claim

- demonstrates appropriate and clear use of language, maintaining a formal tone through the use of standard English

COMMON CORE

ELACC11-12W1a–e Write arguments to support claims in an analysis.
ELACC11-12W4 Produce clear and coherent writing.
ELACC11-12W5 Develop and strengthen writing.
ELACC11-12W7 Conduct research.
ELACC11-12W8 Gather information from print and digital sources.
ELACC11-12W9a–b Draw evidence from literary or informational texts.

PLAN ·· *my* **Notebook**

Analyze the Texts
Reread "Winter Dreams," taking notes about the qualities and behaviors that make the characters modern. Consider the challenges the characters face and how they address them. Then choose two other texts from this collection and make notes about what it means for the people and characters in those texts to be members of our modern society. Pay attention to specific details as you gather evidence from the texts.

Make a Claim
Based on the ideas conveyed in the anchor text and your other chosen texts, write a claim that clearly and concisely states your position on the definition of modernity.

Use the annotation tools in your eBook to find evidence that supports your ideas about modernity. Save each piece of evidence to your notebook.

Build Your Argument Create a graphic organizer that states your claim, shows several reasons that support your claim, and outlines textual evidence such as details, examples, and quotations for each reason.

Develop Counterclaims Think about your audience. What might some readers say to oppose your claim? How would you argue against these opposing claims and convince these readers to agree with you? You may want to conduct further research in print or digital sources, noting any relevant facts, details, or examples. Write down reasons and evidence you can use to support your counterclaims.

Get Organized Organize your ideas in an outline, using the notes from your analysis and your graphic organizer. Be sure to include

- a clearly stated claim
- sufficient reasons and evidence to support your claim
- potential opposing claims that clearly outline the points your reader may make to show disagreement with your argument
- counterclaims supported by additional evidence to strengthen your argument and further persuade your reader

PRODUCE

Draft Your Essay Write a clearly organized draft of your argument. Think about your purpose and audience as you write.

- Introduce your claim. Present your argument in a memorable way that will grab the attention of your readers—consider using an interesting detail or quotation from one of the texts.
- Present your reasons and evidence in logically ordered paragraphs.
- Explain how the evidence from the texts supports your ideas about what it means to be modern.
- Include transitions to connect your reasons and evidence to your claim.
- Address potential opposing claims with convincing reasons and evidence.
- Use formal language and a respectful tone appropriate for an academic context.
- Write a persuasive conclusion that summarizes your position.

*my*WriteSmart

Write your rough draft in *my*WriteSmart. Focus on getting your ideas down, rather than perfecting your choice of language.

ACADEMIC VOCABULARY

As you build your argument about what it means to be modern, be sure to use these words.

contemporary
global
infinite
simulated
virtual

Exchange Essays Share your essay with a partner. Peer editing can be an effective way to identify areas of your argument that lack evidence or that cause confusion for the reader. To help you provide constructive feedback, refer to the chart on the following page for specific criteria of an effective argument. As you read your partner's essay, consider these questions:

- Does the introduction sound strong, confident, and persuasive?
- Has my partner provided relevant evidence to support claims and counterclaims?
- Is my partner's essay cohesive? Are additional transitions needed to make connections clear?
- Has my partner maintained a formal style of English and an objective tone?
- Does the conclusion follow logically from the body of the essay and provide an effective summary of the argument?

When you are finished reading, have a discussion about your essays. Ask your partner for feedback on how you can improve your argument. Talk about the reasoning and evidence used to support your claim, and whether or not you have successfully anticipated and addressed opposing claims. Take notes on your partner's feedback and then revise your essay, incorporating any changes that will improve your draft.

PRESENT

Share with a Group When your final draft is completed, read your essay to a small group. Your classmates should listen and take notes as you present your argument. Do your classmates understand your position? Have you successfully persuaded your audience to agree with your argument? Be prepared to respond to any comments or questions from your group.

	Ideas and Evidence	**Organization**	**Language**
ADVANCED	• The introduction is memorable and persuasive; the claim clearly states a position on a substantive topic. • Valid reasons and relevant evidence from the texts convincingly support the writer's claim. • Counterclaims are anticipated and effectively addressed with counterarguments. • The concluding section effectively summarizes the claim.	• The reasons and textual evidence are organized consistently and logically throughout the argument. • Varied transitions logically connect reasons and textual evidence to the writer's claim.	• The writing reflects a formal style and an objective, or controlled, tone. • Sentence beginnings, lengths, and structures vary and have a rhythmic flow. • Spelling, capitalization, and punctuation are correct. If handwritten, the argument is legible. • Grammar and usage are correct.
COMPETENT	• The introduction could do more to capture the reader's attention; the claim states a position on an issue. • Most reasons and evidence from the texts support the writer's claim, but they could be more convincing. • Counterclaims are anticipated, but the counterarguments need to be developed more. • The concluding section restates the claim.	• The organization of reasons and textual evidence is confusing in a few places. • A few more transitions are needed to connect reasons and textual evidence to the writer's claim.	• The style is informal in a few places, and the tone is defensive at times. • Sentence beginnings, lengths, and structures vary somewhat. • Several spelling and capitalization mistakes occur, and punctuation is inconsistent. If handwritten, the argument is mostly legible. • Some grammatical and usage errors are repeated in the argument.
LIMITED	• The introduction is ordinary; the claim identifies an issue, but the writer's position is not clearly stated. • The reasons and evidence from the texts are not always logical or relevant. • Counterclaims are anticipated but not addressed logically. • The concluding section includes an incomplete summary of the claim.	• The organization of reasons and textual evidence is logical in some places, but it often doesn't follow a pattern. • Many more transitions are needed to connect reasons and textual evidence to the writer's position.	• The style becomes informal in many places, and the tone is often dismissive of other viewpoints. • Sentence structures barely vary, and some fragments or run-on sentences are present. • Spelling, capitalization, and punctuation are often incorrect but do not make reading the argument difficult. If handwritten, the argument may be partially illegible. • Grammar and usage are incorrect in many places, but the writer's ideas are still clear.
EMERGING	• The introduction is missing. • Significant supporting reasons and evidence from the texts are missing. • Counterclaims are neither anticipated nor addressed. • The concluding section is missing.	• An organizational strategy is not used; reasons and textual evidence are presented randomly. • Transitions are not used, making the argument difficult to understand.	• The style is inappropriate, and the tone is disrespectful. • Repetitive sentence structure, fragments, and run-on sentences make the writing monotonous and hard to follow. • Spelling and capitalization are often incorrect, and punctuation is missing. If handwritten, the argument may be partially or mostly illegible. • Many grammatical and usage errors change the meaning of the writer's ideas.

Participate in a Panel Discussion

:···· COMMON
:   CORE
:····:

ELACC11-12SL1a–d Initiate
and participate effectively
in a range of collaborative
discussions.
ELACC11-12SL3 Evaluate
a speaker's point of view,
reasoning, and use of
evidence and rhetoric.
ELACC11-12SL4 Present
information, findings, and
supporting evidence.
ELACC11-12SL6 Adapt
speech to a variety of
contexts and tasks.

This collection focuses in part on the abundance of information in American society and how it affects our lives and future. Look back at the texts in this collection, including the anchor text *The Crucible*, and consider the quote by Gertrude Stein: "Everybody gets so much information all day long that they lose their common sense." What influences how people react to information? How can we decide what is credible and what is not? Synthesize your ideas by holding a panel discussion about how information overload affects our ability to be responsible, informed, and active citizens. Use evidence from the selections to support your ideas.

An effective participant in a panel discussion

- makes a clear, logical, and well-defended generalization about the effects of information overload

- uses quotations and examples from the selections—fiction or nonfiction—to illustrate his or her ideas

- synthesizes ideas about or connected to information overload based on collection texts

- responds thoughtfully, politely, and constructively to the ideas of others on the panel

- evaluates other panel members' contributions, including the use of valid reasoning and relevant evidence

PLAN

Get Organized Work with your classmates to prepare for the discussion.

my **Notebook**

Use the annotation tools in your eBook to find evidence that supports your ideas about how people process information. Save each piece of evidence to your notebook.

- Join a group of four classmates and select one student to be the moderator for your discussion. The rest of your classmates will be the audience when you hold the discussion.

- Create a format for your discussion—a schedule that shows the order in which members of the panel will speak and for how many minutes. It will be the moderator's job to keep the discussion moving along on schedule.

- Set rules regarding the appropriate times for either the moderator or the audience to ask the panel members questions.

Gather Evidence As a group, analyze *The Crucible* and two other texts of the panel's choice. Gather evidence that you will use to discuss the effects of information overload. Note specific details, examples, and quotations. Ask yourself these questions as you take notes:

ACADEMIC VOCABULARY

As you participate in your panel discussion, try to use these words.

contemporary
global
infinite
simulated
virtual

- What types of information are presented in the selections?

- How does the source of each kind of information affect its credibility?

- How do the people or characters in the texts respond to what they hear or read? Why?

- What effect does the quantity of available information have on people or characters? How much is too much—or too little?

- What generalization, or broad conclusion, can you make about how people process and respond to what they hear, read, or watch, and how the overall quantity of information affects their ability to process it accurately?

During this time, the moderator should make a list of relevant questions to be asked during the discussion.

PRODUCE

Write and Practice Work individually to outline your ideas. Then practice with your group.

- State a clear generalization about how people today are affected by a nearly infinite amount of available information.

- Write several main ideas that support your generalization. Each idea should relate your generalization to *The Crucible* or one of your other chosen texts.

- Sort through the evidence you have collected and match each piece of evidence with the main idea it most clearly supports. Provide clear examples.

- Present your ideas to your group. The moderator will ask questions about your ideas and examples, preparing you to "think on your feet" during the real discussion.

- If you are the moderator, use this time to decide how you will introduce and conclude the panel discussion. Write a statement that tells the audience the topic of the discussion and its format. Write notes for a concluding statement, but be prepared to modify your remarks based on new ideas that emerge from the discussion.

*my*WriteSmart

Write your outline in *my*WriteSmart. Focus on getting your ideas down, rather than perfecting your choice of language.

Reinforce Your Ideas Based on the practice session and the chart on the following page, make changes to your outline. Consider the following questions:

- Were you able to defend your generalization? If not, revise your statement so that it better reflects your textual evidence and your ideas.

- Were you able to answer the moderator's questions clearly and without hesitation? If not, you may need to reorganize your outline so that you can find the information you need quickly and easily.

- Did the moderator's questions help you see one of the texts in a new light? If so, add new evidence to your outline that you can share during the real discussion.

Have your partner or a group of peers review your outline in *my*WriteSmart. Ask your reviewers to note any evidence that does not support your generalization about the effects of information overload.

Have the Discussion Have your outline and/or notes handy for reference during the discussion.

- Begin by having the moderator introduce the topic, the panelists, and the basic format for the discussion. The moderator will then ask the first question and continue to facilitate the discussion in the agreed-upon format.

- Use your outline to remind you of your main points, but try to speak directly to the panel and to the audience. Don't just read from your paper.

- Listen closely to what all speakers say so that you can respond appropriately.

- Maintain a respectful tone toward your fellow panel members, even when you disagree with their ideas.

- When all the panelists have made their statements and discussed ideas amongst themselves, the moderator should invite audience members to ask questions.

- Conclude by having the moderator summarize the discussion. He or she should thank the panelists for their participation.

Summarize Write a summary of the main points from the discussion. Then explain whether the discussion made you rethink your generalization, and why.

	Ideas and Evidence	Organization	Language
ADVANCED	• The panelist clearly states a valid generalization and supports it with strong, relevant ideas and well-chosen evidence from the texts and personal experience. • The panel member carefully evaluates others' evidence and reasoning and responds with insightful comments and questions. • The panelist synthesizes the analysis of the texts to help listeners understand the generalization.	• The panelist's remarks are based on a well-organized outline or notes that clearly identify the generalization and the supporting ideas and evidence. • Ideas are presented in a logical order with effective transitions to show the connections between ideas. • The panelist concludes with a statement that reinforces the generalization and includes the ideas that have emerged from the discussion.	• The panelist adapts speech to the context of the discussion, using appropriately formal English to discuss the texts and ideas. • The panelist consistently quotes accurately from the texts to support ideas. • The panel member consistently maintains a polite and thoughtful tone throughout the discussion.
COMPETENT	• The panelist states a generalization and supports it with relevant ideas and evidence from the texts and personal experience. • The panel member evaluates others' evidence and reasoning and responds with appropriate comments and questions. • The panelist synthesizes some ideas and links to the generalization.	• The panelist's remarks are based on an outline or notes that identify the generalization, supporting ideas, and evidence. • Ideas are presented in a logical order and linked with transitions. • The panelist concludes with a statement that reinforces the generalization.	• The panelist mostly uses formal English to discuss literature and ideas. • The panelist mostly quotes accurately from the texts to support ideas. • The panel member maintains a polite and thoughtful tone throughout most of the discussion.
LIMITED	• The panelist states a reasonably clear generalization and supports it with some ideas and evidence. • The panel member's response to others' comments shows limited evaluation of the evidence and reasoning. • The panelist does not synthesize but simply repeats the generalization in a vague way.	• The panelist's remarks reflect an outline or notes that may identify the generalization but do not organize ideas and evidence very effectively. • Ideas are presented in a somewhat disorganized way with few transitions. • The panelist makes a weak concluding statement that does little to reinforce the generalization.	• The panelist uses some formal and some informal English to discuss the texts and ideas. • The panelist's quotations and examples sometimes do not accurately reflect the texts. • The panel member occasionally forgets to maintain a polite tone when responding to others' comments and questions.
EMERGING	• The panelist's generalization is unclear; ideas and evidence are not coherent. • The panel member does not evaluate others' evidence and reasoning. • The panelist does not synthesize.	• The panelist does not follow an outline or notes that organize ideas and evidence. • Ideas are presented in a disorganized way with no transitions. • The panelist's remarks lack any kind of conclusion or summary.	• The panelist uses informal English and/or slang, so that ideas are not clearly expressed. • The panelist's quotations and examples do not accurately reflect the texts. • The panel member does not maintain a polite tone when responding to others' comments and questions.

Performance Task Reference Guide — R2

Writing Arguments — R2
Writing Informative Texts — R4
Writing Narratives — R6
Conducting Research — R8
Participating in Collaborative Discussions — R12
Debating an Issue — R14

Reading Arguments — R16

Analyzing an Argument — R16
Recognizing Persuasive Techniques — R17
Analyzing Logic and Reasoning — R18
Identifying Faulty Reasoning — R19
Evaluating Persuasive Texts — R21
Strategies for Evaluating Evidence — R21
Strategies for Evaluating an Argument — R22

Grammar — R23

Quick Reference:
  Parts of Speech — R23
  The Sentence and Its Parts — R25
  Punctuation — R26
  Capitalization — R29
Grammar Handbook:
  1 Nouns — R30
  2 Pronouns — R30
  3 Verbs — R33
  4 Modifiers — R35
  5 Prepositions, Conjunctions, and Interjections — R38
  6 The Sentence and Its Parts — R39
  7 Phrases — R40
  8 Verbals and Verbal Phrases — R41
  9 Clauses — R42
  10 The Structure of Sentences — R43
  11 Writing Complete Sentences — R44
  12 Subject-Verb Agreement — R45

Vocabulary and Spelling — R49

  1 Using Context Clues — R49
  2 Analyzing Word Structure — R50
  3 Understanding Word Origins — R51
  4 Understanding the English Language — R52
  5 Synonyms and Antonyms — R53
  6 Denotation and Connotation — R53
  7 Analogies — R54
  8 Homonyms and Homophones — R54
  9 Words with Multiple Meanings — R54
  10 Specialized Vocabulary — R55
  11 Preferred and Contested Usage — R55
  12 Using Reference Sources — R56
  13 Spelling Rules — R56
  14 Commonly Confused Words — R59

Glossary of Literary and Informational Terms — R61

Pronunciation Key — R83

Glossary of Academic Vocabulary — R84

Glossary of Critical Vocabulary — R85

Index of Skills — R89

Index of Titles and Authors — R102

Acknowledgments — R103

Writing Arguments

COMMON CORE ELACC11-12W1a-e, ELACC11-12L3a

Many of the Performance Tasks in this book ask you to craft an argument in which you support your ideas with text evidence. Any argument you write should include the following sections and characteristics.

Introduction

Clearly state your **claim**, the point your argument makes. As needed, provide context or background information to help readers understand your position, possibly citing expert opinions to establish the source of knowledge behind your claim. Note the most common opposing views as a way to distinguish and clarify your ideas. From the very beginning, make it clear for readers why your claim is strong; consider providing an overview of your reasons or a quotation that emphasizes your view in your introduction.

EXAMPLES

vague claim: We need to ban cell phones.	**Precise, knowledge-able claim:** The NTSB and the National Safety Council agree: Using cell phones—even hands-free models—to talk or text while driving must be banned now.
not distinguished from opposing view: There are plenty of people who consider cell phones to be okay.	**distinguished from opposing view:** While some people consider hands-free communication devices to be safe, the facts indicate otherwise.
confusing relation-ship of ideas: Teens like to talk on their cell phones. Driving is a privilege.	**logical relationship of ideas:** When people talk or text on cell phones while driving, they endanger their own lives and the lives of others.

Development of Claims

The body of your argument must provide strong, logical reasons for your claim and must fully support those reasons with relevant evidence. A **reason** tells why your claim is

valid; **evidence** provides specific examples that illustrate a reason. In the process of developing your claim, you should also refute **counterclaims,** or opposing views, with equally strong reasons and evidence. To show that you have thoroughly considered your view, provide a summary of the strengths and limitations of your claim and opposing claims. The goal is not to undercut your argument, but rather to answer your readers' objections to it. Be sure to consider how much your audience may already know about your topic. Consider, too, your audience's values; by failing to recognize their biases, you may miss the mark entirely.

EXAMPLES

claim lacking reasons: Banning cell phone use would be good.	**claim developed by reasons:** Given evidence about rising accident rates for cell phone users, many policymakers are consid-ering legislation related to cell phones and driving.
omission of limitations: A ban on mobile devices in cars will virtually eliminate all distraction-related accidents.	**fair discussion of limitations:** We should not dismiss concerns about banning other kinds of distractions, such as listening to music while driving.
inattention to audience's knowledge: We're behind the curve on establishing safety standards.	**awareness of audience's knowledge:** Ten states have banned the use of hand-held cell phones while driving.
ignorance of audience's bias: The reckless drivers opposed to this idea firmly believe they alone know how to text and drive safely.	**recognition of audience's bias:** While many of us feel we know how to talk or text safely while driving, how sure can we be about other drivers on the road?

Links Among Ideas

Even the strongest reasons and evidence will fail to sway readers if it is unclear how the reasons relate to the central claim of an argument. Make the connections clear for your readers, using not only transitional words and phrases, but also clauses and even entire sentences as bridges between ideas you have already discussed and ideas you are introducing. By showing control over your language through the skilled use of transitional expressions, for example, you'll enhance your credibility as a writer. Virginia Tufte's *Artful Sentences* is a well-known guide to syntax, providing helpful examples of effectively structured sentences.

EXAMPLES

transitional word linking claim and reason: Recent studies indicate that driving while using a cell phone leads to an increased risk of accidents. **Consequently,** many states are considering banning cell phone use while driving.

transitional phrase linking reason and evidence: Banning cell phone use while driving would lead to increased safety for all drivers and passengers. **In fact,** recent studies show decreased accident rates in communities that have banned cell phones while driving.

transitional clause linking claim and counter-claim: The benefits of banning cell phone use are clear. **Those opposed to the plan, though, would say otherwise:** They feel that banning cell phone use while driving would lead to restricting other distractions, such as eating or listening to music.

Appropriate Style and Tone

An effective argument is most often written in a direct and formal style. The style and tone you choose should not be an afterthought—the way you express your argument can either support or detract from your ideas. Even as you argue in favor of your viewpoint, take care to remain objective in tone—avoid using loaded language when discussing opposing claims.

EXAMPLES

informal style: No phones while driving would be a real pain for everyone.	**formal style:** There are many situations where responsible phone usage in a car is a convenient option.
biased tone: It doesn't make any sense to support this ban.	**objective tone:** Arguments opposing this ban have been refuted by evidence from many sources.
inattention to conventions: We need to make this issue a big deal!	**attention to conventions:** The proposed ban, which would increase safety for all drivers and passengers, should be given serious consideration.

Conclusion

Your conclusion may range from a sentence to a full paragraph, but it must wrap up your argument in a satisfying way; a conclusion that sounds tacked-on hurts more than helps your argument. A strong conclusion is a logical extension of the argument you have presented. It carries forth your ideas through an inference, question, quotation, or challenge.

EXAMPLES

inference: Building safe driving habits begins with common sense.

question: Who doesn't want to have the assurance that oncoming drivers are fully attentive to driving?

quotation: As the chair of the safety council has stated, "Banning cell phone use while driving will increase everyone's safety on our highways."

challenge: Bans of this type make the difference between an engaged community that values its citizens' safety and one that disregards mounting scientific evidence.

Writing Informative Texts

COMMON CORE ELACC11-12W2a-f

Most of the Performance Tasks in this book ask you to write informational or explanatory texts in which you present a topic and examine it thoughtfully, through a well-organized analysis of relevant content. Any informative or explanatory text that you create should include the following parts and features.

Introduction

Develop a strong **thesis statement**. That is, clearly state your **topic** and the **organizational framework** through which you will develop a unified composition. Each new idea should logically flow out of the ideas and arguments that precede it. For example, you might state that your text will compare ideas, examine causes and effects, or analyze a single text or a group of texts.

EXAMPLE

Topic: the writing of Jack London
Sample Thesis Statements
Compare-contrast: The stories of Jack London and Stephen Crane both reveal the naturalist assumption that human beings have very little control over their lives but instead are at the mercy of the natural world and the impersonal force of fate.
Cause-effect: In "To Build a Fire," Jack London shows cause-and-effect relationships on both a large and small scale, revealing the power of nature on many levels.
Analysis: Jack London's works promote the naturalist view, showing how harsh natural forces can defeat human will.

Clarifying the organizational framework up front will help you organize the body of your essay, suggesting **headings** you can use to guide your readers or graphics that might illustrate the text. Most important, it can help you identify any ideas that you may need to clarify. For example, if you are analyzing the naturalist views in Jack London's "To Build a Fire," you may use the following framework:

Introduction:
- What is the naturalist literary movement?
- What are the movement's key characteristics?

Main points:
- What are the major themes in "To Build a Fire"?
- How does the story reflect elements of the naturalist literary movement?

Development of the Topic

In the body of your text, flesh out the organizational framework you established in your introduction with strong supporting paragraphs. Include only the most significant evidence that is relevant to your topic. Don't rely on a single source, and make sure the sources you use are reliable and current. The table below illustrates types of support you might use to develop different types of topics. It also shows how transitions link text sections, create cohesion, and clarify the relationships among ideas.

Types of Support in Explanatory/ Informative Texts (in italics)	Uses of Transitions in Explanatory/ Informative Texts
Examples: While *stories like "To Build a Fire"* represent the Darwinist branch of naturalism, *in which biology determines human destiny, Crane's work* exemplifies the Marxist strain, *in which social and economic factors are paramount.*	The first part of this sentence introduces the next section of the comparative essay, which deals with a different author, Stephen Crane.

continued

Types of Support in Explanatory/ Informative Texts (in italics)	Uses of Transitions in Explanatory/ Informative Texts
Concrete details: *Because its primary imperative is not to mourn its dead master but to live, the dog promptly returns to camp.*	A transitional clause explains the significance of a concrete detail in a cause-and-effect essay.
Textual evidence: In "To Build a Fire," the main character recognizes that he has limited chances of survival. *As author Jack London writes, "he realized that it was no longer a mere matter of freezing his fingers and toes, or of losing his hands and feet, but that it was a matter of life and death, with the chances against him."*	The phrase "As author Jack London writes" signals the use of a quotation from "To Build a Fire" to support the writer's analysis of the text.

You can't always include all of the information you'd like to in a short essay, but you can plan to point readers directly to useful **multimedia links** either in the body of or at the end of your essay.

Style and Tone

Use formal English to establish your credibility as a source of information. To project authority, use the language of the **domain,** or field, that you are writing about. However, be sure to define unfamiliar terms and avoid jargon. Provide extended definitions when your audience is likely to have limited knowledge of the topic. Using quotations from reliable sources can also give your text authority; be sure to credit the source of quoted material. In general, keep the tone neutral, avoiding slangy or biased expressions. However, don't shy away from figurative language: well-placed metaphors, similes, and analogies can convey a complex idea more succinctly than a paragraph of strictly objective language.

Informal, biased language: Naturalism was totally out there, believe me.	Formal style, neutral tone, with figurative language to express complex ideas: Relying on new theories in sociology and psychology, the writers of the naturalistic movement dissected human behavior with detachment and objectivity, like scientists dissecting laboratory specimens.

Conclusion

End your essay with a concluding statement or section that sums up or extends the information in your essay. This is your opportunity to collect together the various elements of your essay and to restate your thesis. The conclusion is not a place to introduce new facts or arguments. Instead, you should focus on wrapping everything up in a clear and compelling way.

EXAMPLES

Articulate the implications of your ideas: Jack London saw life as a life-or-death struggle won by those best suited for survival by being in tune with nature. His short stories and novels dramatize his belief that "civilized" human beings are either destroyed or recreated in savage environments.

Emphasize significance of your topic: Whether London expresses naturalism through the power of natural or societal forces, he successfully explores one of the philosophies that was on the minds of many during that time in history.

Writing Narratives

COMMON CORE ELACC11-12W3a-e

When you are composing a fictional tale, an autobiographical incident, or a firsthand biography, you write in the narrative mode. That means telling a story with a beginning, a climax, and a conclusion. Though there are important differences between fictional and nonfictional narratives, you use similar processes to develop them.

Identify a Significant Problem or Situation, or Make an Observation

For a nonfiction narrative, dig into your memory bank for a significant problem you dealt with or an important observation you've made about your life. For fiction, try to invent a problem or situation that can unfold in interesting ways.

EXAMPLES

Problem (nonfiction)	This summer I had to overcome my fear of diving off the high board in competitions.
Situation (fiction)	David awaits his college acceptance letters, wondering how they might change his life.

Establish a Point of View

Decide who will tell your story. If you are writing an essay about an important experience or person in your own life, you will be the narrator of the events you relate. If you are writing a work of fiction, you can choose to create a first-person narrator or tell the story from the third-person point of view. In the latter case, the narrator can focus on one character or reveal the thoughts and feelings of all the characters. The examples below show the differences between a first- and third-person narrator.

First-person narrator (nonfiction)

I climb up the ladder and look at the pool far below. Suddenly the diving board seems wobbly and too high up. Should I really dive? Will I make a fool of myself?

Third-person narrator (fiction)

As David drove into the driveway, he tried to calm down. He turned down the radio to hear his heart beating. Easing the door open, he stepped out of the car and walked down to the mailbox.

Gather Details

To make real or fictional experiences come alive, you will need to use narrative techniques like description and dialogue. The questions in the left column in the chart below can help you search your memory or imagination for the details that will flesh out your narrative. You don't have to respond in full sentences, but try to capture the sights, sounds, and feelings that bring your narrative to life.

Who, What, When, Where?	Narrative Techniques
People: Who are the people or characters involved in the experience? What did they look like? What did they do? What did they say?	**Description:** Hands shaking, David reached in for the letter. David gently carried the envelope into the house as if it were made of glass. **Dialogue:** "So, have you even looked at it yet?" his sister Nadine asked. Nadine quickly snatched the envelope from David, opened the letter, and started to read it silently.
Experience: What led up to or caused the event? What is the main event in the experience? What happened as a result of the event?	**Description:** A college letter has arrived; David hesitates to open it. His conflict is internal. He fights his nervousness and uncertainty about his future. After she opens the letter, Nadine tells David that he is accepted to college in Boston. Brother and sister celebrate together and then watch a movie together, knowing that everything has changed.

continued

Who, What, When, Where?	Narrative Techniques
Places: When and where did the events take place? What were the sights, sounds, and smells of this place?	**Description:** Events occur during senior year of high school, when college acceptance letters are sent out. The conversation between David and Nadine occurs in the family kitchen, silent except for the scraping of chairs as they both sit down.

Sequence Events

Before you begin writing, list the key events of the experience or story in chronological, or time, order. Place a star next to the point of highest tension. In fiction, this point is called the climax, but a gripping nonfiction narrative will also have a climactic event.

To build suspense—the uncertainty a reader feels about what will happen next—you'll want to think about the pacing of your narrative. Consider disrupting the chronological order of events by beginning at the end. Or interrupt the sequence with a flashback, taking the reader to an earlier point in the narrative.

Another way to build suspense is with multiple plot lines. For example, in the fictional narrative, David's anxiety as he awaits news about his college applications could have been coupled with a second plot line in which his sister Nadine also faces uncertainty about her future. Both plot lines could then have been resolved at the end of the narrative.

Use Vivid Language

As you revise, make an effort to use vivid language. Use precise words and phrases to describe feelings and actions. Use telling details to show, rather than directly state, what a character is like. Use sensory language that lets readers see, feel, hear, smell, and taste what you or your characters experienced. Overall, select language that expresses a consistent tone throughout your narrative.

First Draft	Revision
He opened the letter.	Fingers trembling, David slowly raised his hand to open the letter. He slid his thumb under the flap and heard the envelope softly tearing. [telling details]
They fell to the floor.	They fell to the floor, laughing hysterically. Soon, their howls ended and they stood up and hugged. After catching their breath, David set up the movie while Nadine made the popcorn, just like every other Friday night since they were young. [precise words and phrases]
David knocked over the chair.	Jumping up with unexpected speed, David knocked over the chair, which loudly crashed to the floor. [sensory details]

Conclusion

At the conclusion of the narrative, you or your narrator will reflect on the meaning of the events. The conclusion should follow logically from the climactic moment. The narrator of a personal narrative usually reflects on the significance of the experience. A fictional narrative will end with the resolution of the conflict described over the course of the story.

EXAMPLE

"Oh no, David. I was afraid of this," Nadine said in a sorrowful voice, her face grim. David put his head in his hands, moaning softly.

"David, Rufus is going to have to rely on Mom to take him on walks. You've been accepted! You're going to Boston!" she shouted.

Jumping up with unexpected speed, David knocked over the chair, which loudly crashed to the floor. He gave Nadine a playful shove. "You'll be sorry!" he shouted as he reached for Nadine. They fell to the floor, laughing hysterically. Soon, their howls ended and they stood up and hugged each other. After catching their breath, David set up the movie while Nadine made the popcorn, just like every other Friday night since they were young.

Conducting Research

COMMON CORE ELACC11-12W2a-f, ELACC11-12W7, ELACC11-12W8

The Performance Tasks in this book will require you to complete research projects related to the texts you've read in the collections. Whether the topic is stated in a Performance Task or is one you generate, the following information will guide you through your research project.

Focus Your Research and Formulate a Question

Some topics for a research project can be effectively covered in three pages; others require an entire book for a thorough treatment. Begin by developing a topic that is neither too narrow nor too broad for the time frame of the assignment. Also check your school and local libraries and databases to help you determine how to choose your topic. If there's too little information, you'll need to broaden your focus; if there's too much, you'll need to limit it.

With a topic in hand, formulate a research question; it will keep you on track as you conduct your research. A good research question cannot be answered in a single word and should be open-ended. It should require investigation. You can also develop related research questions to explore your topic in more depth.

EXAMPLES

Possible topics about Julius Caesar, the Roman emperor	Famous assassinations in history—too broad Popularity of soothsayers in Roman times—too narrow Historical figures—fact or fiction?
Possible research question	What was the real Julius Caesar like?
Related questions	• How much of Shakespeare's *Julius Caesar* is based on historical fact? • How did later Roman historians describe Julius Caesar?

Locate and Evaluate Sources

To find answers to your research question, you'll need to investigate primary and secondary sources, whether in print or digital formats. **Primary sources,** such as diaries, autobiographies, interviews, speeches, and eyewitness accounts, contain original, firsthand information. **Secondary sources** relate other people's versions of primary sources in encyclopedias, newspaper or magazine articles, biographies, and documentaries.

Your search for sources begins at the library and on the Internet. Use **advanced search features** to help you find things quickly. Add a minus sign (–) before a word that should not appear in your results. Use an asterisk (*) in place of unknown words. List the name of and location of each possible source, adding comments about its potential usefulness. Assessing, or evaluating, your sources in an important step in the research process. Your goal is to use sources that are credible, or reliable and trustworthy, and that are appropriate to your task, purpose, and audience.

Criteria for Assessing Sources	
Relevance: It covers the target aspect of my topic and helps me achieve my purpose for writing.	• How will the source be useful in answering my research question?
Accuracy: It includes information that can be verified by more than one authoritative source.	• Is the information up-to-date? Are the facts accurate? How can I verify them? • What qualifies the author to write about this topic? Is he or she an authority?

continued

Criteria for Assessing Sources	
Objectivity: It presents multiple viewpoints on the topic.	• What, if any, biases can I detect? Does the writer favor one view of the topic?
Coverage: It covers the topic at a level appropriate for my grade level and audience.	• Is the treatment of the material too juvenile for my audience? Is it too advanced?

Incorporating and Citing Source Material

When you draft your research project, you'll need to include material from your sources. This material can be **direct quotations, summaries,** or **paraphrases** of the original source material. Two well-known **style manuals** provide information on how to cite a range of print and digital sources: the *MLA Handbook for Writers of Research Papers* (published by the Modern Language Association) and Kate L. Turabian's *A Manual for Writers of Research Papers, Theses, and Dissertations* (published by The University of Chicago Press). Both style manuals provide a wealth of information about conducting, formatting, drafting, and presenting your research, including guidelines for citing sources within the text (called parenthetical citations) and preparing the list of Works Cited, as well as correct use of the mechanics of writing. Your teacher will indicate which style manual you should use. The following examples use the format in the *MLA Handbook.*

EXAMPLES

Direct quotation [The writer is citing the description given by Roman historian Suetonius.]	In his biographical text *The Lives of the Caesars,* the Roman historian Suetonius describes Caesar as "tall of stature, with a fair complexion, shapely limbs, a somewhat full face, and keen black eyes" (45).

Summary [The writer is summarizing the conclusion in an article about Roman government.]	Rome's republican government was made up of consuls, praetors, a senate, and people's assemblies. The position of dictator was temporary and only used during emergencies (24–25).
Paraphrase [The writer is paraphrasing, or stating in his own words, material from an article about the nature of Rome's government during Caesar's time.]	During Caesar's time, Rome was a republic. Two consuls with equal authority were the leaders. Senators suggested laws, and general assemblies voted on whether to approve the suggestions. The position of dictator was used only when there were serious outbreaks of lawlessness or during wartime (24–25).

As you write, it's important not to rely too heavily on any one source but to synthesize information from a variety of sources. Furthermore, any material from sources must be completely documented, or you will commit **plagiarism,** the unauthorized use of someone else's words or ideas. Plagiarism is not honest. As you take notes for your research project, be sure to keep complete information about your sources so that you can cite them correctly in the body of your paper. This applies to all sources, whether print or digital. Having complete information will also enable you to prepare the list of Works Cited. The list of Works Cited, which concludes your research project, provides author, title, and publication information for both print and digital sources. The following section shows the *MLA Handbook's* Works Cited citation formats for a variety of sources.

MLA Citation Guidelines

Today, you can find free Web sites that help you create citations for research papers using information you provide. Such sites have some time-saving advantages when you're developing a Works Cited list. However, you should always check your citations carefully before you turn in your final paper. If you are following MLA style, use these guidelines to evaluate and finalize your work.

Books

One author

Steinbeck, John. *The Grapes of Wrath.* 1939. New York: Viking, 1964. Print.

Two authors or editors

Lange, Dorothea, and Paul Schuster Taylor. *An American Exodus: A Record of Human Erosion.* New York: Reynal & Hitchcock, 1939. Print.

Three authors or editors

Scheibel, Jeremy, Anne Chatsworth, and Ridley Davis, eds. *Stories from the Great Depression.* Princeton: Princeton UP, 2008. Print.

Four or more authors or editors

List the first author only. Then use the abbreviation et al., *which means "and others."*

Rutkowski, J., et al. *American Immigration and Migration in the 1930s.* Topeka: Sanders-Ellis, 2007. Print.

No author given

American Literature: 1865 to the Present. Chicago: Omni, 2007. Print.

Parts of Books

An introduction, a preface, a foreword, or an afterword written by someone other than the author(s) of a work

Gorton, Terry. Foreword. *John Steinbeck: A Centennial Tribute.* Ed. Stephen K. George. Westport: Praeger, 2002. xvii–xviii. Print.

A poem, a short story, an essay, or a chapter in a collection of works

Steinbeck, John. "The Leader of the People." *The Portable Steinbeck.* Ed. Pascal Covici, Jr. New York: Penguin, 1978. 397–415. Print.

A poem, a short story, an essay, or a chapter in an anthology of works by several authors

Steinbeck, John. "The Red Pony." *The American Short Story: A Collection of the Best Known and Most Memorable Short Stories by the Great American Authors.* Ed. Thomas K. Parkes. New York: Galahad, 1994. 886–948. Print.

A novel or play in a collection

Steinbeck, John. *The Grapes of Wrath. The Grapes of Wrath and Other Writings,*
1936–1941. New York: Library of America, 1996. Print.

Magazines, Newspapers, and Encyclopedias

An article in a newspaper

Patel, Vikram. "Recalling the Days of Wrath." *Los Angeles Times* 8 Jan. 2008: 9. Print.

An article in a magazine

Schubert, Siegfried D., et al. "On the Cause of the 1930s Dust Bowl." *Science* 19
Mar. 2004: 1855–60. Print.

An article in an encyclopedia

Kite, Steven. "Dust Bowl." *Encyclopedia of the Great Depression and New Deal.* Ed.
James Ciment. 2 vols. Armonk, NY: Sharpe, 2001. Print.

Miscellaneous Nonprint Sources

An interview

Sorenson, Elvina. Personal interview. 3 Feb. 2010.

A video recording or film

Our Daily Bread. Dir. King Vidor. Perf. Karen Morley, Tom Keene, Barbara Pepper,
John Qualen.

1934. Film Preservation Assoc., 1999. DVD.

A sound recording

Guthrie, Woody. *Library of Congress Recordings/Woody Guthrie.* Rounder, 1988. CD.

Electronic Publications

A document from an Internet site

Author or compiler	Title or description of document	Title of website	Site sponsor
Neary, Walter.	"Steinbeck & Salinas."	About John Steinbeck.	National Steinbeck Center.

Date of document	Medium of publication
June 1995.	Web.

Date of access
2 Apr. 2010.

An Online Book or E-Book

Wunder, John R., Frances Kaye, and Vernon Carstensen, eds. *Americans View Their*
Dust Bowl Experience. Niwot: UP Colorado, 1999. Questia Media America.
Web. 10 Apr. 2010.

A CD-ROM

"Dust Bowl." *Britannica Student Encyclopedia.* 2004 ed. Chicago: Encyclopaedia
Britannica, 2004. CD-ROM.

Participating in Collaborative Discussions

COMMON CORE ELACC11-12SL1a-d

Often, class activities, including the Performance Tasks in this book, will require you to work collaboratively with classmates. Whether your group will analyze a work of literature or try to solve a community problem, use the following guidelines to ensure a productive discussion.

Prepare for the Discussion

A productive discussion is one in which all the participants bring useful information and ideas to share. If your group will discuss a short story the class read, first reread and annotate a copy of the story. Your annotations will help you quickly locate evidence to support your points. Participants in a discussion about an important issue should first research the issue and bring notes or information sources that will help guide the group. If you disagree with a point made by another group member, your case will be stronger if you back it up with specific evidence from your sources.

EXAMPLES

disagreeing without evidence: It's silly and a waste of time to even discuss whether people are good or bad.

providing evidence for disagreement: I disagree with the view that discussing whether human tendencies are good or bad is irrelevant or silly. The issue of good and evil has been a significant theme for philosophers, theologians, writers, and poets from centuries past up to the present day.

Set Ground Rules

The rules your group needs will depend on what your group is expected to accomplish. A discussion of themes in a poem will be unlikely to produce a single consensus; however, a discussion aimed at developing a solution to a concrete problem should result in one strong proposal arrived at democratically with the participation of all group members. Answer the following questions to set ground rules that fit your group's purpose:

- What will this group produce? A range of ideas, a single decision, a plan of action, or something else?
- How much time is available? How much of that time should be allotted to each part of our discussion (presenting ideas, summarizing or voting on final ideas, creating a product such as a written analysis or speech)?
- What roles need to be assigned within the group? Do we need a leader, a note-taker, a timekeeper, or other specific roles?
- What is the best way to synthesize our group's ideas? Should we take a vote, list group members as "for" or "against" in a chart, or use some other method to reach consensus or sum up the results of the discussion?

Move the Discussion Forward

Everyone in the group should be actively involved in synthesizing ideas. To make sure this happens, ask questions that draw out ideas, especially from less-talkative members of the group. If an idea or statement is confusing, try to paraphrase it, or ask the speaker to explain more about it. If you disagree with a statement, say so politely and explain in detail why you disagree.

SAMPLE DISCUSSION

Effective Behavior	How It Works
Support others' contributions. In this example, Alejandro believes that people are essentially good: we should trust others to do the right thing. He mentions examples of courageous behavior by ordinary people during natural disasters. Genna listens attentively to Alejandro. She has just come from a discussion of slavery in America in her social studies class. She wonders how people can believe in freedom but enslave others at the same time.	Alejandro shares his opinion, supporting it with evidence. Genna disagrees with Alejandro but still listens carefully. She avoids making faces, rolling her eyes, or loudly sighing while Alejandro presents his views.
State your own views thoughtfully. When Alejandro finishes speaking, Genna restates his points to make sure she understands his perspective. She comments, "I understand Alejandro's position because I, too, want to believe that people are essentially good. But there are many examples from history of people treating others with cruelty by exploiting them for their own gain. Americans believed in freedom, yet some kept slaves. How is it possible to be 'essentially good' but then do terrible things?"	Genna verifies that she understands Alejandro's point. Then she offers another viewpoint, supporting it with an example. As Genna did, Alejandro listens carefully and respectfully as she explains her perspective.

Respond to Ideas

In a diverse group, everyone may have a different perspective on the topic of discussion, and that's a good thing. Consider what everyone has to say, and don't resist changing your view if other group members provide convincing evidence for theirs. If, instead, you feel more strongly than ever about your view, don't hesitate to say so and provide reasons related to what those with opposing views have

said. Before wrapping up the discussion, try to synthesize the claims made on both sides. That means pulling sometimes contradictory ideas together to arrive at a new understanding.

SAMPLE DISCUSSION

Effective Behavior	How It Works
Synthesize various viewpoints to arrive at a new, alternative understanding. Li speaks next. First he summarizes Alejandro and Genna's opposing views, and then he offers an alternative. "It may look like there is a contradiction here. Either people are essentially good, or they are not. But what if there is another way of looking at this? What if people are neither one nor the other but capable of being both?"	By combining both arguments, Li creates an alternative view of the issue. This expands the discussion, by allowing different viewpoints to coexist.
Justify your views or consider new ones. Alejandro considers what Li has said. He prepares to offer more evidence that people are essentially good and extends his argument to respond to Genna's point as well. Perhaps outside forces may affect essential goodness and turn people toward negative thoughts or actions. He decides to mention this when his turn comes up again. Li's point makes Genna think, too. She makes a note to ask the group, "If what Li says is true, how do we learn how to make those choices? What makes some people choose to do good, while others choose to do terrible things? And are there times when people may not really have a choice?" Her question will also expand the discussion.	Alejandro and Genna consider Li's point. Li's alternative offers an opportunity to delve into the original question and expand their own arguments. Through the contributions of each participant, the discussion has led to a true collaboration about the topic.

Debating an Issue

COMMON CORE   ELACC11-12SL1a-d,
ELACC11-12SL3,
ELACC11-12SL4

The selection and collection Performance Tasks in this text will direct you to engage in debates about issues relating to the selections you are reading. Use the guidelines that follow to have a productive and balanced debate about both sides of an issue.

The Structure of a Formal Debate

If you've ever tried to settle a disagreement with friends or siblings, you've used persuasive techniques to engage in a debate—a discussion in which individuals or teams argue opposing sides of an issue. In a **formal debate**, two teams, each with three members, present their arguments on a given proposition or policy statement. One team argues for the proposition or statement, and the other team argues against it. Each debater must consider the proposition closely and must research both sides of it. To argue convincingly either for or against a proposition, a debater must be familiar with both sides of the issue.

Plan the Debate

The purpose of a debate is to allow participants and audience members to consider both sides of an issue. Use these planning suggestions to hold a balanced and productive debate:

- **Identify Debate Teams** Form groups of six members based on the issues that the Performance Tasks include. Three members of the team will argue for the affirmative side of the issue—that is, they support the issue. The other three members will argue for the negative side of the issue—that is, they will not support the issue.
- **Appoint a Moderator** The moderator plays a neutral role in the debate, promoting a civil discussion and keeping everyone on task. The moderator begins by introducing the topic of the debate and then recognizes speakers, alternating between affirmative and negative.
- **Assign Debate Roles** One team member introduces the team's claim with supporting reasons and evidence. Another team member exchanges questions with a member of the opposing team to clarify and challenge reasoning. The last member presents a strong closing argument.

Prepare Briefs and Rebuttals

A **brief** is an outline of the debate, accounting for the evidence and arguments of both sides of the **proposition** (topic). Debaters also prepare a **rebuttal**, a follow-up speech to support their arguments and counter the opposition's. Propositions are usually one of four types:

- **Proposition of fact**—Debaters determine whether a statement is true or false. An example is "Deforestation is ruining the rain forest."
- **Proposition of value**—Debaters determine the value of a person, place, or thing. An example is "Free trade will help small countries develop."
- **Proposition of problem**—Debaters determine whether a problem exists and whether it requires action.
- **Proposition of policy**—Debaters determine the action that will be taken. An example is "Students will provide tutoring services."

Use the following steps to prepare a brief:

- **Gather Information** Consult a variety of primary and secondary sources to gather the most reliable, up-to-date information about the proposition.
- **Identify Key Ideas** Sort out the important points, and arrange them in order of importance.
- **List Arguments For and Against Each Key Idea** Look for strong arguments that support your side of the proposition, and also note those that support your opponents' side.
- **Support Your Arguments** Find facts, quotations, expert opinions, and examples that support your arguments and counter your opponents'.
- **Write the Brief** Begin your brief with a statement of the proposition. Then list the

arguments and evidence that support both sides of the proposition.

The rebuttal is the opportunity to rebuild your case. Use the following steps to build a strong rebuttal:

- Listen to your opponents respectfully. Note the points you wish to overturn.
- Defend what the opposition has challenged.
- Cite weaknesses in their arguments, such as points they overlooked.
- Present counterarguments and supporting evidence.
- Offer your summary arguments. Restate and solidify your stance.

Hold the Debate

A well-run debate can be a vehicle for expressing your opinions in an assertive but respectful manner. Participating in a debate challenges you to synthesize comments made on both sides of an issue, pose probing questions, clarify ideas, and appreciate divergent perspectives.

FORMAL DEBATE FORMAT

Speaker	Role	Time
Affirmative Speaker 1	Present the claim and supporting evidence for the affirmative ("pro") side of the argument.	5 minutes
Negative Speaker 1	Ask probing questions that will prompt the other team to address flaws in the argument.	3 minutes
Affirmative Speaker 2	Respond to the questions posed by the opposing team and counter any concerns.	3 minutes
Negative Speaker 2	Present the claim and supporting evidence for the negative ("con") side of the argument.	5 minutes
Affirmative Speaker 3	Summarize the claim and evidence for the affirmative side and explain why your reasoning is more valid.	3 minutes
Negative Speaker 3	Summarize the claim and evidence for the negative side and explain why your reasoning is more valid.	3 minutes

Evaluate the Debate

Use the following guidelines to evaluate a team in a debate:

- What was the proposition, or premise, being debated? Was each team's stance with respect to the topic—whether affirmative or negative—clear?
- How effectively did the team present reasons and evidence, including evidence from the texts, to support the proposition? Were the links among ideas clear?
- Did the team avoid fallacious, or flawed, reasoning? Did the team avoid disguising exaggerated or distorted evidence with persuasive rhetoric? In general, was the team's word choice appropriate?
- How effectively did the team rebut, or respond to, arguments made by the opposing team?
- Did the speakers maintain eye contact and speak at an appropriate rate and volume?
- Did the speakers observe proper debate etiquette—that is, did they follow the moderator's instructions, stay within their allotted time limits, and treat their opponents respectfully? Did they use verbal techniques of emphasis and tone to highlight their argument rather than to ridicule their opponent?

Reading Arguments

COMMON CORE ELACC11-12RI5, ELACC11-12RI6

An argument expresses a position on an issue or problem and supports it with reasons and evidence. Being able to analyze and evaluate arguments will help you distinguish between claims you should accept and those you should not.

Analyzing an Argument

A sound argument should appeal strictly to reason. However, arguments are often used in texts that also contain other types of persuasive devices. An argument includes the following elements:

- A **claim** is the writer's position on an issue or central idea.
- **Support** is any material that serves to prove a claim. In an argument, support usually consists of reasons and evidence.
- **Reasons** are declarations made to justify an action, a decision, or a belief—for example, "You should sleep on a good mattress *in order to avoid spinal problems*."
- **Evidence** consists of the specific references, quotations, facts, examples, and opinions that support a claim. Evidence may also consist of statistics, reports of personal experience, or the views of experts.
- A **counterargument** is an argument made to oppose another argument. A good argument anticipates the opposition's objections and provides counterarguments to disprove or answer them.

Claim	Walt Whitman is one of the most important figures in American poetry.

Reason	He experimented with poetic form and content and created a quintessentially American voice in literature.

Evidence	His poetry influenced generations of poets. His poems celebrated the diversity and spirit of American culture.

Counter-argument	No American poet before Whitman broke with tradition in the ways he did.

Practice and Apply

In the early 1900s, Elinore Pruitt Stewart (formerly Rupert), was living in Burnt Fork, Wyoming, as a homesteader, a person who received public land free of charge under the Homestead Act of 1862. In the following letter to a friend, she makes an argument for homestead living over an impoverished city existence. Use a chart like the one shown to identify the claim, reason, evidence, and counterargument in her letter.

January 23, 1913

Dear Mrs. Coney,—

. . . When I read of the hard times among the Denver poor, I feel like urging them every one to get out and file on land. I am very enthusiastic about women homesteading. It really requires less strength and labor to raise plenty to satisfy a large family than it does to go out to wash, with the added satisfaction of knowing that their job will not be lost to them if they care to keep it. Even if improving the place does go slowly, it is that much done to stay done. Whatever is raised is the homesteader's own, and there is no house-rent to pay. This year Jerrine cut and dropped enough potatoes to raise a ton of fine potatoes. She wanted to try, so we let her, and you will remember that she is but six years old. We had a man to break the ground and cover the potatoes for her and the man irrigated them once. That was all that was done until digging time, when they were ploughed out and Jerrine picked them up. Any woman strong enough to go out by the day could have done every bit of the work and put in two or three times that much, and it would have been so much more pleasant than to work so hard in the city and then be on starvation rations in the winter.

To me, homesteading is the solution of all poverty's problems, but I realize that temperament has much to do with success in any undertaking, and persons afraid of coyotes and work and loneliness had better let ranching alone. At the same time, any woman who can stand her own company, can see the beauty of

---

continued

the sunset, loves growing things, and is willing to put in as much time at careful labor as she does over the washtub, will certainly succeed; will have independence, plenty to eat all the time, and a home of her own in the end.

Recognizing Persuasive Techniques

Persuasive texts typically rely on more than just the logical appeal of an argument to be convincing. They also rely on ethical and emotional appeals, as well as other **persuasive techniques**—devices that can sway you to adopt a position or take an action.

The chart shown here explains several of these techniques. Learn to recognize them, and you will be less likely to be influenced by them.

Persuasive Technique	Example
Appeals by Association	
Bandwagon appeal Suggests that a person should believe or do something because "everyone else" does	Join the millions who've contributed to The Cause: buy your 'Be Well' bracelet today.
Testimonial Relies on endorsements from well-known people or satisfied customers	DJ Super Dawg keeps songs spinning all day long with his new CompactM3 disc player. Give it a whirl!
Snob appeal Taps into people's desire to be special or part of an elite group	In Smart and Sassy cosmetics, you'll look and feel like the princess you are.
Transfer Connnects a product, candidate, or cause with a positive emotion or idea	Rediscover peace and tranquility with Back in Balance aromatherapy candles.
Appeal to loyalty Relies on people's affiliation with a particular group	Only Substantial Bank offers long-term customers better rates.

Emotional Appeals	
Appeals to pity, fear, or vanity Use strong feelings, rather than facts, to persuade	The cost of one candy bar can help buy a whole meal for a starving family.
Word Choice	
Glittering generality Makes a generalization that includes a word or phrase with positive connotations, such as *freedom* and *honor,* to promote a product or idea.	Improve your children's future: plant a tree on World Tree Day.

Practice and Apply

Identify the persuasive techniques used in the model.

The Real Scoop

On my last trip to Splendid Dan's Ice Cream Shoppe to get a Swirling Fantasia Double Dip Delight, I was thrilled to find yet another reason that makes buying dessert at Dan's feel so splendid. During the next 30 days at the downtown location, a whopping 40 percent of Dan's proceeds will go toward helping the homeless in our city. Forty percent! No wonder so many local celebrities, like news anchor Tandy Marquez and Mayor Donald Townsend, have been spotted at Dan's. They know that with each purchase, they are also providing food, clothing, and shelter for those in need. If you join them, you'll have not only the most amazing ice cream on the planet, but also the added joy of providing life's basic necessities to the less fortunate. It's the least we can do to better our city, so stop by Splendid Dan's—he's got the "real scoop."

Analyzing Logic and Reasoning

When you evaluate an argument, you need to look closely at the writer's logic and reasoning. In doing this, it is helpful to identify the type of reasoning the writer is using.

The Inductive Mode of Reasoning

When a writer leads from specific evidence to a general principle or generalization, that writer is using **inductive reasoning.** Here is an example of inductive reasoning.

Specific Facts
Fact 1 Harriet Beecher Stowe's *Uncle Tom's Cabin* helped alert Americans to the horrors of slavery.
Fact 2 Rachel Carson's *Silent Spring* helped make the public aware of the dangers of overuse of pesticides.
Fact 3 Betty Friedan's *The Feminine Mystique* prompted women to seek equal rights.

Generalization
Literature can sometimes help to shape public opinion.

Strategies for Determining the Soundness of Inductive Arguments

Ask yourself the following questions to evaluate an inductive argument:

- **Is the evidence valid and sufficient support for the conclusion?** Inaccurate facts lead to inaccurate conclusions. Make sure all facts are accurate.
- **Does the conclusion follow logically from the evidence?** Make sure the writer has used sound reasons—those that can be proved—as the basis for the conclusion and has avoided logical fallacies, such as circular logic and oversimplification.
- **Is the evidence drawn from a large enough sample?** The three facts listed in the example are enough to support the claim. By qualifying the generalization with words such as *sometimes, some,* or *many,* the writer indicates the generalization is limited to a specific group.

The Deductive Mode of Reasoning

When a writer arrives at a conclusion by applying a general principle to a specific situation, the writer is using **deductive reasoning.** Here's an example.

People have the right to revolt when oppressed.	General principle or premise
▼	
The American colonies are oppressed by British rule.	Specific situation
▼	
The American colonies are justified in fighting for freedom from British rule.	Specific conclusion

Strategies for Determining the Soundness of Deductive Arguments

Ask yourself the following questions to evaluate a deductive argument:

- **Is the general principle stated, or is it implied?** Note that writers often use deductive reasoning in an argument without stating the general principle. They assume readers will understand the principle. You may want to identify the general principle for yourself.
- **Is the general principle sound?** Don't assume the general principle is sound. Determine whether it is proven.
- **Is the conclusion valid?** To be valid, a conclusion in a deductive argument must follow logically from the general principle and the specific situation.

The following chart shows two conclusions drawn from the same general principle.

General Principle: All government offices were closed last Monday.	
Accurate Deduction	**Inaccurate Deduction**
West Post Office is a government office; therefore, West Post Office was closed last Monday.	Soon-Lin's Spa was closed last Monday; therefore, Soon-Lin's Spa is a government office.

The conclusion that Soon-Lin's Spa is a government office does not make logical sense, because other factors determine whether or not it is a government office.

Identify the mode of reasoning used in the following:

Detailed research shows that using a cell phone while driving is a key cause of traffic accidents. Many states have already passed laws making "hands free" devices mandatory for cell phone users while driving. However, ear pieces or speaker phones provide very few true safety benefits. The problem is not the way in which a driver is distracted, but the distraction itself. Looking up a phone number, dialing, and concentrating on the conversation can all take a driver's focus, and eyes, off the road.

Betsie Edens, a 19-year-old college student, says she uses her cell phone to get in touch with family, old friends, and fellow college students while making the three-hour drive from her parent's house to Denton State University. "I talk on the phone or send text messages at least two and a half of the three hours it takes to get there," she says.

Betsie is one of millions of teenagers worldwide who do more talking on a cell phone than safe driving. It is time these unsafe drivers focus more on the road and less on their friends' gossip. For the sake of everybody's safety, cell phones must be turned off while on the road.

Identifying Faulty Reasoning

Sometimes an argument at first appears to make sense but isn't valid, because it is based on a fallacy. A **logical fallacy** is an error in logic. Learn to recognize these common fallacies.

Type of Fallacy	Definition	Example
Circular logic	Supporting a statement by simply repeating it in different words	Sport utility vehicles are popular **because more people buy them than any other category of new cars.**
Either/or fallacy	A statement that suggests that there are only two choices available in a situation that really offers more than two options	**Either** we raise the legal driving age, **or** accidents caused by teenage drivers will continue to happen.
Oversimplification	An explanation of a complex situation or problem as if it were much more simple than it is	If we would only be more tolerant of people's differences, there would be **no more wars.**
Overgeneralization	A generalization that is too broad. You can often recognize overgeneralizations by the use of words such as *all, everyone, every time, anything, no one,* and *none.*	**Every time** I want to do something my way, my parents say no.
Stereotyping	A dangerous type of overgeneralization. Stereotypes are broad statements about people on the basis of their gender, ethnicity, race, or political, social, professional, or religious group.	**People who work for large corporations are** followers, not leaders.

continued

Type of Fallacy	Definition	Example
Attacking the person or name-calling	An attempt to discredit an idea by attacking the person or group associated with it. Candidates often engage in name-calling during political campaigns.	The governor wants to eliminate candy machines in school cafeterias, but **he doesn't know what he's talking about.**
Evading the issue	Refuting an objection with arguments and evidence that do not address its central point	I know I wasn't supposed to use the car last night, **but I did fill up the tank and check the tire pressure.**
Non sequitur	A conclusion that does not follow logically from the "proof" offered to support it. A non sequitur is sometimes used to win an argument by diverting the reader's attention to proof that can't be challenged.	Mr. Crandall is my guidance counselor. **I will definitely get accepted to a private college.**
False cause	The mistake of assuming that because one event occurred after another event in time, the first event caused the second one to occur	The cheerleading squad did the Super Slam Dance, **and because of that, Donny slam-dunked the basketball, and we won the game.**
False analogy	A comparison that doesn't hold up because of a critical difference between the two subjects	Jenny didn't do well in Spanish, **so she'll probably fail German as well.**
Hasty generalization	A conclusion drawn from too little evidence or from evidence that is biased	Two jet planes crashed this year. **Air travel is extremely unsafe.**

Practice and Apply

Look for examples of logical fallacies in the following argument. Identify each one and explain why you identified it as such.

Elephants should be banned from circuses. Leaders of circus companies claim that healthy living environments are provided for the animals, but they, like most business owners, are liars. Sharp bullhooks are used for training, and the elephants are beaten severely every day. Abuse makes animals more aggressive; everyone knows that. In the last 15 years, captive elephants have killed 65 people and injured 130, so it is clear the elephants are abused by their trainers. Legislation to stop this cruelty should be passed immediately!

Evaluating Persuasive Texts

Learning how to evaluate persuasive texts and identify bias will help you become more selective when doing research and also help you improve your own reasoning and arguing skills. **Bias** is an inclination for or against a particular opinion or viewpoint. A writer may reveal a strongly positive or negative opinion on an issue by presenting only one way of looking at it or by heavily weighting the evidence on one side of the argument. Additionally, the presence of either of the following is often a sign of bias:

Loaded language consists of words with strongly positive or negative connotations that are intended to influence a reader's attitude.

EXAMPLE

The superior All-Star Road Warrior offers unparalleled excellence in all-wheel-drive capability and can outperform any car on the road. (*Superior, unparalleled, excellence,* and *outperform* have positive connotations.)

Propaganda is any form of communication that is so distorted that it conveys false or misleading information. Many logical fallacies—such as name-calling, the either/or fallacy, and false causes—are often used in propaganda. The following example shows an oversimplification. The writer uses one fact to support a particular point of view but does not reveal another fact that does not support that viewpoint.

EXAMPLE

Since the new administration took office, unemployment rates have been cut in half. (The writer does not include information about legislation, passed by the previous administration, that created thousands of jobs.)

Strategies for Evaluating Evidence

It is important to have a set of standards by which you can evaluate persuasive texts. Use the questions below to help you critically assess facts and opinions that are presented as evidence.

- **Are the facts presented verifiable?** Facts can be proved by eyewitness accounts, authoritative sources such as encyclopedias and almanacs, experts, or research.
- **Are the opinions presented credible?** Any opinions offered should be supported by facts, research, eyewitness accounts, or the opinions of experts on the topic.
- **Is the evidence thorough?** Thorough evidence leaves no reasonable questions unanswered. If a choice is offered, background for making the choice should be provided. If taking a side is called for, all sides of the issue should be presented.
- **Is the evidence biased?** Be alert to evidence that contains loaded language or other signs of bias.
- **Is the evidence authoritative?** The people, groups, or organizations that provided the evidence should have credentials that verify their credibility.
- **Is it important that the evidence be current?** Where timeliness is crucial, as in the areas of medicine and technology, the evidence should reflect the latest developments in the areas.

Practice and Apply

Read the argument below. Identify the facts, opinions, and elements of bias.

In our city neighborhood, unnecessary speed bumps are being built on residential streets. Cars park bumper to bumper along both sides of the street, day and night. There is no place to pull over, causing cars to stop in the middle of the street to pick up and drop off passengers. My point is that it is impossible to drive fast on these streets anyway! Why do no-good politicians spend a lot of taxpayer money on a ridiculous irritation for drivers? They must figure wrongly that either they build speed bumps, or some little kid will get killed. That's never happened, and it never will.

Strategies for Evaluating an Argument

Make sure that all or most of the following statements are true:

- The argument presents a claim or thesis.
- The claim is connected to its support by a general principle that most readers would readily agree with. Valid general principle: *It is the job of a corporation to provide adequate health benefits to full-time employees.* Invalid general principle: *It is the job of a corporation to ensure its employees are healthy and physically fit.*
- The reasons make sense.
- The reasons are presented in a logical and effective order.
- The claim and all reasons are adequately supported by sound evidence.
- The evidence is adequate, accurate, and appropriate.
- The logic is sound. There are no instances of logical fallacies.
- The argument adequately anticipates and addresses reader concerns and counterclaims with counterarguments.

Use the preceding criteria to evaluate the strength of the following editorial:

This town needs an ice skating rink. Everybody knows that ice skating is the only real way to learn balance and coordination, while also exercising. It is, after all, an Olympic event. That is why I believe it is the responsibility of the town council to put aside funding for a year-round ice skating rink.

Our town has always believed that our children's future relies on good development. For intellectual stimulation, the council has provided the public library and the Nature Museum. For creativity, the council has funded the Community Art Center, where kids can learn to make pottery, paint, dance, and sing. But when it comes to a place where youth can go to develop physical skills of balance, rhythm, and strength, we have absolutely nothing.

We also need a rink because ice skating is fun! The town council members are themselves boring individuals and don't think kids should have fun. As one member put it, "There are many places in this town built especially with youth in mind. Ice skating is not a top priority on our list of community needs this year." They obviously feel this way because our football team came in fifth in the conference last year.

But the biggest reason we need an ice skating rink is so that kids can have a place to ice skate. And let's not forget, adults like ice skating, too. Most of the people who make it to the Olympics are over 18.

Either the town council will help our children develop by putting up the rink, or they prove themselves stingy politicians who do not have the town's best interest at heart.

Grammar

COMMON CORE
ELACC11-12L1
ELACC11-12L2a
ELACC11-12L3
ELACC11-12L4a-d

Writing that has a lot of mistakes can confuse or even annoy a reader. A business letter with a punctuation error might lead to a miscommunication and delay a reply. A sentence fragment might lower your grade on an essay. Paying attention to grammar, punctuation, and capitalization rules can make your writing clearer and easier to read.

Quick Reference: Parts of Speech

Part of Speech	Function	Examples
Noun	names a person, a place, a thing, an idea, a quality, or an action	
common	serves as a general name, or a name common to an entire group	coyote, hunter, spear, bonfire
proper	names a specific, one-of-a-kind person, place, or thing	Rainy Mountain, Virginia, Puritans
singular	refers to a single person, place, thing, or idea	field, pony, child, man
plural	refers to more than one person, place, thing, or idea	fields, ponies, children, men
concrete	names something that can be perceived by the senses	lemon, shores, wind, canoe
abstract	names something that cannot be perceived by the senses	fear, intelligence, honesty
compound	expresses a single idea through a combination of two or more words	birthright, folk tale, Sky-World
collective	refers to a group of people or things	species, army, flock
possessive	shows who or what owns something	America's, Douglass's, men's, slaves'
Pronoun	takes the place of a noun or another pronoun	
personal	refers to the person(s) making a statement, the person(s) being addressed, or the person(s) or thing(s) the statement is about	I, me, my, mine, we, us, our, ours, you, your, yours, she, he, it, her, him, hers, his, its, they, them, their, theirs
reflexive	follows a verb or preposition and refers to a preceding noun or pronoun	myself, yourself, herself, himself, itself, ourselves, yourselves, themselves
intensive	emphasizes a noun or another pronoun	(same as reflexives)

continued

Part of Speech	Function	Examples
demonstrative	points to one or more specific persons or things	this, that, these, those
interrogative	signals a question	who, whom, whose, which, what
indefinite	refers to one or more persons or things not specifically mentioned	both, all, most, many, anyone, everybody, several, none, some
relative	introduces an adjective clause by relating it to a word in the clause	who, whom, whose, which, that
Verb	expresses an action, a condition, or a state of being	
action	tells what the subject does or did, physically or mentally	run, reaches, listened, consider, decides, dreamed
linking	connects the subject to something that identifies or describes it	am, is, are, was, were, sound, taste, appear, feel, become, remain, seem
auxiliary	precedes the main verb in a verb phrase	be, have, do, can, could, will, would, may, might
transitive	directs the action toward someone or something; always has an object	The wind **snapped** the young tree in half.
intransitive	does not direct the action toward someone or something; does not have an object	The young tree **snapped.**
Adjective	modifies a noun or pronoun	**frightened** man, **two** epics, **enough** time
Adverb	modifies a verb, an adjective, or another adverb	walked **out, really** funny, **far away**
Preposition	relates one word to another word	at, by, for, from, in, of, on, to, with
Conjunction	joins words or word groups	
coordinating	joins words or word groups used the same way	and, but, or, for, so, yet, nor
correlative	used as a pair to join words or word groups used the same way	both . . . and, either . . . or, neither . . . nor
subordinating	introduces a clause that cannot stand by itself as a complete sentence	although, after, as, before, because, when, if, unless
Interjection	expresses emotion	whew, yikes, uh-oh

Quick Reference: The Sentence and Its Parts

The diagrams that follow will give you a brief review of the essentials of a sentence and some of its parts.

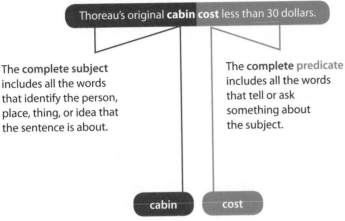

Thoreau's original **cabin cost** less than 30 dollars.

The **complete subject** includes all the words that identify the person, place, thing, or idea that the sentence is about.

The **complete** predicate includes all the words that tell or ask something about the subject.

cabin

cost

The **simple subject** tells exactly whom or what the sentence is about. It may be one word or a group of words, but it does not include modifiers.

The simple predicate tells what the subject does or is. It may be one word or several, but it does not include modifiers.

Every word in a sentence is part of a complete subject or a complete predicate.

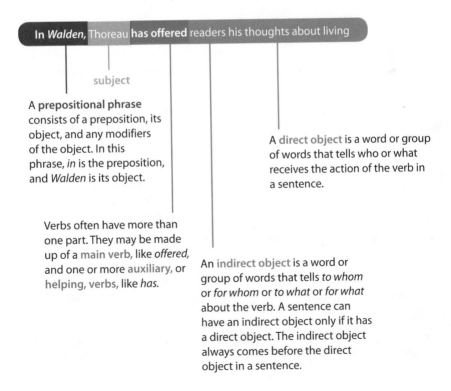

In *Walden,* Thoreau **has offered** readers his thoughts about living

subject

A **prepositional phrase** consists of a preposition, its object, and any modifiers of the object. In this phrase, *in* is the preposition, and *Walden* is its object.

A **direct object** is a word or group of words that tells who or what receives the action of the verb in a sentence.

Verbs often have more than one part. They may be made up of a main verb, like *offered,* and one or more auxiliary, or helping, verbs, like *has.*

An **indirect object** is a word or group of words that tells *to whom* or *for whom* or *to what* or *for what* about the verb. A sentence can have an indirect object only if it has a direct object. The indirect object always comes before the direct object in a sentence.

Quick Reference: Punctuation

Mark	Function	Examples
End Marks period, question mark, exclamation point	end a sentence	The games begin today. Who is your favorite contestant? What a play Jamie made!
period	follows an initial or abbreviation Exception: postal abbreviations of states	Prof. Ted Bakerman, D. H. Lawrence, HMH Co., P.M., A.D., oz., ft., Blvd., St. NE (Nebraska), NV (Nevada)
period	follows a number or letter in an outline	I. Volcanoes A. Central-vent 1. Shield
Comma	separates parts of a compound sentence	I had never disliked poetry, but now I really love it.
	separates items in a series	She is brave, loyal, and kind.
	separates adjectives of equal rank that modify the same noun	The slow, easy route is best.
	sets off a term of address	America, I love you. Come to the front, children.
	sets off a parenthetical expression	Hard workers, as you know, don't quit. I'm not a quitter, believe me.
	sets off an introductory word, phrase, or dependent clause	Yes, I forgot my key. At the beginning of the day, I feel fresh. While she was out, I was here. Having finished my chores, I went out.
	sets off a nonessential phrase or clause	Ed Pawn, the captain of the chess team, won. Ed Pawn, who is the captain, won. The two leading runners, sprinting toward the finish line, finished in a tie.
	sets off parts of dates and addresses	Send it by August 18, 2010, to Cherry Jubilee, Inc., 21 Vernona St., Oakland, Minnesota.
	follows the salutation and closing of a letter	Dear Jim, Sincerely yours,
	separates words to avoid confusion	By noon, time had run out. What the minister does, does matter. While cooking, Jim burned his hand.
Semicolon	separates items in a series if one or more items contain commas	We invited my sister, Jan; her friend, Don; my uncle Jack; and Mary Dodd.

continued

Mark	Function	Examples
	separates parts of a compound sentence that are not joined by a coordinating conjunction	The small books are on the top shelves; the large books are below. I dusted the books; however, I didn't wipe the shelves.
	separates parts of a compound sentence when the parts contain commas	After I ran out of money, I called my parents; but only my sister was home, unfortunately.
Colon	introduces a list	Those we wrote were the following: Dana, John, and Will.
	introduces a long quotation	Thomas Jefferson wrote: "We the people of the United States, in order to form a more perfect union. . . ."
	follows the salutation of a business letter	Dear Ms. Williams: Dear Senator Wiley:
	separates certain numbers	1:28 P.M., Genesis 2:5
Dash	indicates an abrupt break in thought	I was thinking of my mother—who is arriving tomorrow—just as you walked in.
Parentheses	enclose less-important material	Throughout her life (though some might think otherwise), she worked hard. The temperature on this July day (would you believe it?) is 65 degrees!
Hyphen	joins parts of a compound adjective before a noun	She lives in a first-floor apartment.
	joins parts of a compound with *all-*, *ex-*, *self-*, or *-elect*	The president-elect is a well-respected woman.
	joins parts of a compound number (to ninety-nine)	Today, I turn twenty-one.
	joins parts of a fraction	My cup is one-third full.
	joins a prefix to a word beginning with a capital letter	Life may have seemed simpler in pre–Civil War days. It's very chilly for mid-June.
	indicates that a word is divided at the end of a line	Did you know that school segrega-tion has been illegal since 1954?
Apostrophe	used with *s* to form the possessive of a noun or an indefinite pronoun	my friend's book, my friends' books, anyone's guess, somebody else's problem

continued

Mark	Function	Examples
	replaces one or more omitted letters in a contraction or numbers in a date	don't (omitted *o*), he'd (omitted *woul*), the class of '99 (omitted *19*)
	used with *s* to form the plural of a letter	I had two A's on my report card.
Quotation Marks	set off a speaker's exact words	Sara said, "I'm finally ready." "I'm ready," Sara said, "finally." Did Sara say, "I'm ready"? Sara said, "I'm ready!"
	set off the title of a story, an article, a short poem, an essay, a song, or a chapter	I liked Oates's "Hostage," Steinem's "Sisterhood," and Plath's "Mirror." Chapter II is titled "Our Gang's Dark Oath."
Ellipses	replace material omitted from a quotation	"We the people ... in order to form a more perfect union ...."
Italics	indicate the title of a book, a play, a magazine, a long poem, an opera, a film, or a TV series, or the names of ships, trains, and spacecraft	*The Scarlet Letter, The Crucible, Time, The Death of the Hired Man, West Side Story, Citizen Kane, The Spirit of St. Louis, The Best of Frank Sinatra, Lusitania*

Quick Reference: Capitalization

Category	Examples
People and Titles	
Names and initials of people	Emily Dickinson, **T. S.** Eliot
Titles used before or in place of names	Professor Holmes, Senator Long
Deities and members of religious groups	Jesus, Allah, Buddha, Zeus, Baptists, Roman Catholics
Names of ethnic and national groups	Hispanics, Jews, African Americans
Geographical Names	
Cities, states, countries, continents	New York, Maine, Haiti, Africa
Regions, bodies of water, mountains	the South, Lake Erie, Mount Katahdin
Geographic features, parks	Continental Divide, Everglades, Yellowstone
Streets and roads, planets	55 East Ninety-fifth Street, Maple Lane, Venus, Jupiter
Organizations, Events, Etc.	
Companies, organizations, teams	General Motors, Lions Club, Utah Jazz
Buildings, bridges, monuments	the Alamo, Golden Gate Bridge, Lincoln Memorial
Documents, awards	the Constitution, World Cup
Special named events	Super Bowl, World Series
Government bodies, historical periods and events	the Supreme Court, U.S. Senate, Harlem Renaissance, World War II
Days and months, holidays	Friday, May, Easter, Memorial Day
Specific cars, boats, trains, planes	Mustang, *Titanic*, *California Zephyr*
Proper Adjectives	
Adjectives formed from proper nouns	American League teams, French cooking, Emersonian period, Arctic waters
First Words and the Pronoun I	
First word in a sentence or quotation	This is it. He said, "Let's go."
First word of sentence in parentheses that is not within another sentence	The spelling rules are covered in another section. (Consult that section for more information.)
First words in the salutation and closing of a letter	Dear Madam, Very truly yours,
First word in each line of most poetry Personal pronoun *I*	Then am I A happy fly If I live Or if I die.
First word, last word, and all important words in a title	"The Fall of the House of Usher," *Incidents in the Life of a Slave Girl*

1 Nouns

A **noun** is a word used to name a person, a place, a thing, an idea, a quality, or an action. Nouns can be classified in several ways.

1.1 COMMON NOUNS

Common nouns are general names, common to entire groups.

EXAMPLES: *writer, song, bravery*

1.2 PROPER NOUNS

Proper nouns name specific, one-of-a-kind things.

Common	Proper
writer, song, bravery, hunter	Mourning Dove, Mississippi, Granny

1.3 SINGULAR AND PLURAL NOUNS

A noun may take a singular or a plural form, depending on whether it names a single person, place, thing, or idea or more than one. Make sure you use appropriate spellings when forming plurals.

Singular	Plural
church, lily, wife	churches, lilies, wives

1.4 COMPOUND AND COLLECTIVE NOUNS

Compound nouns are formed from two or more words but express a single idea. They are written as single words, as separate words, or with hyphens. Use a dictionary to check the correct spelling of a compound noun.

EXAMPLES: *birthright, folk tale, Sky-World*

Collective nouns are singular nouns that refer to groups of people or things.

EXAMPLES: *army, flock, class, species*

1.5 POSSESSIVE NOUNS

A **possessive noun** shows who or what owns something.

EXAMPLES: *Welty's, jury's, children's*

2 Pronouns

A **pronoun** is a word that is used in place of a noun or another pronoun. The word or word group to which the pronoun refers is called its **antecedent.**

2.1 PERSONAL PRONOUNS

Personal pronouns change their form to express person, number, gender, and case. The forms of these pronouns are shown in the following chart.

	Nominative	Objective	Possessive
Singular			
First Person	I	me	my, mine
Second Person	you	you	your, yours
Third Person	she, he, it	her, him, it	her, hers, his, its
Plural			
First Person	we	us	our, ours
Second Person	you	you	your, yours
Third Person	they	them	their, theirs

2.2 AGREEMENT WITH ANTECEDENT

Pronouns should agree with their antecedents in number, gender, and person.

If an antecedent is singular, use a singular pronoun.

EXAMPLE: *Sarah laughed as her dog splashed in the lake.*

If an antecedent is plural, use a plural pronoun.

EXAMPLES: *Sarah and Barbara took turns holding the leash as they walked the dog home.*

Andrew and Ryan finished the race before the rest of their teammates.

The gender of a pronoun must be the same as the gender of its antecedent.

> **EXAMPLES:** *The little **girl** ran outside without tying **her** shoelaces.*
> ***Daniel** waved to **his** friends before boarding the plane.*

The person of the pronoun must be the same as the person of its antecedent. As the chart in Section 2.1 shows, a pronoun can be in first-, second-, or third-person form.

> **EXAMPLE:** *Those of **you** who like animals should consider getting **your** degree in veterinary science.*

Practice and Apply

Rewrite each sentence so that the underlined pronoun agrees with its antecedent.

1. *The World on the Turtle's Back* is a myth that tells about a pregnant woman and how <u>it</u> helped create the earth.
2. Many of the sea creatures and birds tried to retrieve the dirt at the bottom of the ocean, but they could not reach <u>him</u>.
3. The woman circles the earth with <u>their</u> daughter, helping the plants to grow.
4. Both of the twins molded clay animals and gave <u>it</u> life.

2.3 PRONOUN CASE

Personal pronouns change form to show how they function in sentences. Different functions are shown by different **cases.** The three cases are **nominative, objective,** and **possessive.** For examples of these pronouns, see the chart in Section 2.1.

A **nominative pronoun** is used as a subject or a predicate nominative in a sentence.

An **objective pronoun** is used as a direct object, an indirect object, or the object of a preposition.

```
 SUBJECT    OBJECT   OBJECT OF PREPOSITION
    ↓          ↓              ↓
  He explained it to me.
```

A **possessive pronoun** shows ownership. The pronouns *mine, yours, hers, his, its, ours,* and *theirs* can be used in place of nouns.

> **EXAMPLE:** *These letters are **yours**.*

The pronouns *my, your, her, his, its, our,* and *their* are used before nouns.

> **EXAMPLE:** *These are **your** letters.*

WATCH OUT! Many spelling errors can be avoided if you watch out for *its* and *their*. Don't confuse the possessive pronoun *its* with the contraction *it's,* meaning "it is" or "it has." The homonyms *they're* (a contraction of *they are*) and *there* ("in that place") are often mistakenly used for *their*.

TIP To decide which pronoun to use in a comparison, such as "He tells better tales than (I or me)," fill in the missing word(s): *He tells better tales than I tell.*

Practice and Apply

Replace the underlined words in each sentence with an appropriate pronoun, and identify the pronoun as a nominative, objective, or possessive pronoun.

1. <u>Arthur Miller</u> was a playwright from New York.
2. *The Crucible* is one of <u>Arthur Miller's</u> most well-known plays.
3. <u>John Proctor and Reverend Parris</u> are two of the main characters.
4. Reverend Hale tries to convince <u>Rebecca Nurse and John Proctor</u> to falsely confess to practicing witchcraft.
5. <u>The Salem witch hunt</u> illustrates how the town's strict Christian principles indirectly caused the deaths of innocent villagers.

2.4 REFLEXIVE AND INTENSIVE PRONOUNS

These pronouns are formed by adding *-self* or *-selves* to certain personal pronouns. Their forms are the same, and they differ only in how they are used.

A **reflexive pronoun** follows a verb or preposition and reflects back on an earlier noun or pronoun.

EXAMPLES: *He threw himself forward.*
Danielle mailed herself the package.

Intensive pronouns intensify or emphasize the nouns or pronouns to which they refer.

EXAMPLES: *The queen herself would have been amused.*
I saw it myself.

WATCH OUT! Avoid using *hisself* or *theirselves.* Standard English does not include these forms.

NONSTANDARD: *He had painted hisself into a corner.*

STANDARD: *He had painted himself into a corner.*

2.5 DEMONSTRATIVE PRONOUNS

Demonstrative pronouns point out things and persons near and far.

	Singular	Plural
Near	this	these
Far	that	those

2.6 INDEFINITE PRONOUNS

Indefinite pronouns do not refer to specific persons or things and usually have no antecedents. The chart shows some commonly used indefinite pronouns.

Singular	Plural	Singular or Plural	
another	both	all	none
anybody	few	any	some
no one	many	more	most
neither	several		

TIP Indefinite pronouns that end in *one, body,* or *thing* are always singular.

INCORRECT: *Does anybody think their hamburger is overcooked?*

CORRECT: *Does anybody think his or her hamburger is overcooked?*

If the indefinite pronoun might refer to either a male or a female, *his or her* may be used to refer to it, or the sentence may be rewritten.

EXAMPLES: *Everyone received his or her script.*
All the actors received their scripts.

2.7 INTERROGATIVE PRONOUNS

An **interrogative pronoun** is used to ask a question. The interrogative pronouns are *who, whom, whose, which,* and *what.*

EXAMPLES: *Whose backpack is on the kitchen table?*
Which dress do you prefer?

TIP *Who* is used as a subject; *whom,* as an object. To find out which pronoun you need to use in a question, change the question to a statement.

QUESTION: *(Who/Whom) did you meet there?*

STATEMENT: *You met (?) there.*

Since the verb has a subject (you), the needed word must be the object form, *whom.*

EXAMPLE: *Whom did you meet there?*

WATCH OUT! A special problem arises when you use an interrupter, such as *do you think,* within a question.

EXAMPLE: *(Who/Whom) do you believe is the more influential musician?*

If you eliminate the interrupter, it is clear that the word you need is *who.*

2.8 RELATIVE PRONOUNS

Relative pronouns relate, or connect, dependent (or subordinate) clauses to the words they modify in sentences. The relative pronouns are *that, what, whatever, which, whichever, who, whoever, whom, whomever,* and *whose.*

Sometimes short sentences with related ideas can be combined by using a relative pronoun.

SHORT SENTENCE: *Mark Twain may be America's greatest humorist.*

RELATED SENTENCE: *Mark Twain wrote Huckleberry Finn.*

COMBINED SENTENCE: *Mark Twain, who wrote* Huckleberry Finn, *may be America's greatest humorist.*

Practice and Apply

Choose the appropriate interrogative or relative pronoun from the words in parentheses.

1. "The Celebrated Jumping Frog of Calaveras County" was written by Samuel Clemens, (who/whom) wrote under the pseudonym Mark Twain.
2. The story gained national fame for Mark Twain, (who/that) first published it in 1865.
3. (Who/Whom) do you think is funnier, Jim Smiley or the storyteller Simon Wheeler?
4. Smiley spent months educating his frog, (which/whose) fame as a jumper spread throughout the gold camps.

2.9 PRONOUN REFERENCE PROBLEMS

The referent of a pronoun should always be clear.

An **indefinite reference** occurs when the pronoun *it, you,* or *they* does not clearly refer to a specific antecedent.

> UNCLEAR: *In the review, it claimed the movie is well done.*
>
> CLEAR: *The review claimed the movie is well done.*

A **general reference** occurs when the pronoun *it, this, that, which,* or *such* is used to refer to a general idea rather than a specific antecedent.

> UNCLEAR: *Stella tutors students every day after school. This lets her help kids who are struggling with their schoolwork.*
>
> CLEAR: *Stella tutors students every day after school. Tutoring lets her help kids who are struggling with their schoolwork.*

Ambiguous means "having more than one possible meaning." An **ambiguous reference** occurs when a pronoun could refer to two or more antecedents.

> UNCLEAR: *Stacey made Miranda a sandwich while she talked on the phone.*

CLEAR: *While Stacey talked on the phone, she made Miranda a sandwich.*

Practice and Apply

Rewrite the following sentences to correct indefinite, ambiguous, and general pronoun references.

1. In the poem "The Raven," it tells about a man who is grieving for his lover.
2. The raven refused to abandon its perch above the door. This frustrated the narrator.
3. The narrator told the raven that he thought he was a messenger from Lenore.
4. The raven always responded, "Nevermore." This frightened and confused the speaker.

3 Verbs

A **verb** is a word that expresses an action, a condition, or a state of being.

3.1 ACTION VERBS

Action verbs express mental or physical activity.

> EXAMPLES: *I walked to the store.*

3.2 LINKING VERBS

Linking verbs join subjects with words or phrases that rename or describe them.

> EXAMPLES: *You are my friend.*

3.3 PRINCIPAL PARTS

Action and linking verbs typically have four principal parts, which are used to form verb tenses. The principal parts are the **present,** the **present participle,** the **past,** and the **past participle.**

Action verbs and some linking verbs also fall into two categories: regular and irregular. A **regular verb** is a verb that forms its past and past participle by adding *-ed* or *-d* to the present form.

Present	Present Participle	Past	Past Participle
perform	(is) performing	performed	(has) performed
hope	(is) hoping	hoped	(has) hoped
stop	(is) stopping	stopped	(has) stopped
marry	(is) marrying	married	(has) married

An **irregular verb** is a verb that forms its past and past participle in some other way than by adding -ed or -d to the present form.

Present	Present Participle	Past	Past Participle
bring	(is) bringing	brought	(has) brought
swim	(is) swimming	swam	(has) swum
steal	(is) stealing	stole	(has) stolen
grow	(is) growing	grew	(has) grown

3.4 VERB TENSE

The **tense** of a verb indicates the time of the action or state of being. An action or state of being can occur in the present, the past, or the future. There are six tenses, each expressing a different range of time.

The **present tense** expresses an action or state that is happening at the present time, occurs regularly, or is constant or generally true. Use the present part.

NOW: *That poet reads well.*

REGULAR: *I swim every day.*

GENERAL: *Time flies.*

The **past tense** expresses an action that began and ended in the past. Use the past part.

EXAMPLE: *The storyteller finished his tale.*

The **future tense** expresses an action or state that will occur. Use *shall* or *will* with the present part.

EXAMPLE: *They will attend the next festival.*

The **present perfect tense** expresses an action or state that (1) was completed at an indefinite time in the past or (2) began in the past and continues into the present. Use *have* or *has* with the past participle.

EXAMPLE: *Poetry has inspired readers throughout the ages.*

The **past perfect tense** expresses an action in the past that came before another action in the past. Use *had* with the past participle.

EXAMPLE: *The witness had testified before the defendant confessed.*

The **future perfect tense** expresses an action in the future that will be completed before another action in the future. Use *shall have* or *will have* with the past participle.

EXAMPLE: *They will have finished the novel before seeing the movie version of the tale.*

TIP The past-tense form of an irregular verb is not paired with an auxiliary verb, but the past-perfect tense form of an irregular verb is always paired with an auxiliary verb.

INCORRECT: *I have went to that restaurant before.*

INCORRECT: *I gone to that restaurant before.*

CORRECT: *I have gone to that restaurant before.*

3.5 PROGRESSIVE FORMS

The progressive forms of the six tenses show ongoing actions. Use forms of *be* with the present participles of verbs.

PRESENT PROGRESSIVE: *She is rehearsing her lines.*

PAST PROGRESSIVE: *She was rehearsing her lines.*

FUTURE PROGRESSIVE: *She will be rehearsing her lines.*

PRESENT PERFECT PROGRESSIVE: *She has been rehearsing her lines.*

PAST PERFECT PROGRESSIVE: *She had been rehearsing her lines.*

FUTURE PERFECT PROGRESSIVE: *She will have been rehearsing her lines.*

WATCH OUT! Do not shift from tense to tense needlessly. Watch out for these special cases:

- In most compound sentences and in sentences with compound predicates, keep the tenses the same.
  INCORRECT: *Every morning they get up and went to work.*
  CORRECT: *Every morning they get up and go to work.*
- If one past action happened before another, indicate this with a shift in tense.
  INCORRECT: *She thought she forgot her toothbrush.*
  CORRECT: *She thought she had forgotten her toothbrush.*

Practice and Apply

Identify the tense of the verb(s) in each of the following sentences. If you find an unnecessary tense shift, correct it.

1. The setting of *The Crucible* is the late 17th century in Salem, Massachusetts.
2. Before the witch trials ended, people had lost their ability to make objective judgments.
3. Playwright Arthur Miller knew that the play pertains to his own time.
4. People will read it far into the future, and many will apply its message to their own time.
5. In the play some accuse others of being witches, even though they knew the accusation was false.

3.6 ACTIVE AND PASSIVE VOICE

The voice of a verb tells whether its subject performs or receives the action expressed by the verb. When the subject performs the action, the verb is in the **active voice.** When the subject is the receiver of the action, the verb is in the **passive voice.**

Compare these two sentences:

ACTIVE: *The Puritans did not celebrate Christmas.*

PASSIVE: *Christmas was not celebrated by the Puritans.*

To form the passive voice, use a form of *be* with the past participle of the verb.

WATCH OUT! Use the passive voice sparingly. It can make writing awkward and less direct.

AWKWARD: *The stories of hysterical witnesses were believed by gullible and fearful jurors.*

BETTER: *Gullible and fearful jurors believed the stories of hysterical witnesses.*

There are occasions when you will choose to use the passive voice because

- you want to emphasize the receiver: *The king was shot.*
- the doer is unknown: *My books were stolen.*
- the doer is unimportant: *French is spoken here.*

Practice and Apply

For the five items below, identify the boldfaced verb phrase as active or passive.

1. *The Crucible* **has played** in theaters throughout the world.
2. It **was written** by Arthur Miller, one of America's greatest dramatists.
3. Miller **did** not **approve** of Reverend Parris's greed for gold.
4. **Has** the reputation of the minister **been maligned?**

4 Modifiers

Modifiers are words or groups of words that change or limit the meanings of other words. Adjectives and adverbs are common modifiers.

4.1 ADJECTIVES

Adjectives modify nouns and pronouns by telling which one, what kind, how many, or how much.

WHICH ONE: *this, that, these, those*

EXAMPLE: *That couch needs to be reupholstered.*

WHAT KIND: *large, unique, anxious, moldy*

EXAMPLE: *The anxious speaker shuffled through her notes.*

HOW MANY: *ten, many, several, every, each*

EXAMPLE: *Each child grabbed several candies from the bowl.*

HOW MUCH: *more, less, little*

EXAMPLE: *There was more snow on the ground in the morning.*

4.2 PREDICATE ADJECTIVES

Most adjectives come before the nouns they modify, as in the previous examples. A **predicate adjective,** however, follows a linking verb and describes the subject.

EXAMPLE: *My friends are very intelligent.*

Be especially careful to use adjectives (not adverbs) after such linking verbs as *look, feel, grow, taste,* and *smell.*

EXAMPLE: *The weather grows cold.*

4.3 ADVERBS

Adverbs modify verbs, adjectives, and other adverbs by telling where, when, how, or to what extent.

WHERE: *The children played outside.*

WHEN: *The author spoke yesterday.*

HOW: *We walked slowly behind the leader.*

TO WHAT EXTENT: *He worked very hard.*

Adverbs may occur in many places in sentences, both before and after the words they modify.

EXAMPLES: *Suddenly the wind shifted. The wind suddenly shifted. The wind shifted suddenly.*

4.4 ADJECTIVE OR ADVERB?

Many adverbs are formed by adding *-ly* to adjectives.

EXAMPLES: *sweet, sweetly; gentle, gently*

However, *-ly* added to a noun will usually yield an adjective.

EXAMPLES: *friend, friendly; woman, womanly*

4.5 COMPARISON OF MODIFIERS

Modifiers can be used to compare two or more things. The form of a modifier shows the degree of comparison. Both adjectives and adverbs have three forms: the **positive,** the **comparative,** and the **superlative.**

The **positive form** is used to describe individual things, groups, or actions.

EXAMPLES: *Stephen Crane was a great writer.*
His descriptions are vivid.

The **comparative form** is used to compare two things, groups, or actions.

EXAMPLES: *I think that Stephen Crane was a greater writer than Jack London. Crane's descriptions are more vivid.*

The **superlative form** is used to compare more than two things, groups, or actions.

EXAMPLES: *I think that Crane was the greatest writer of his era. Crane's descriptions are the most vivid I have ever read.*

4.6 REGULAR COMPARISONS

Most one-syllable and some two-syllable adjectives and adverbs have comparatives and superlatives formed by adding *-er* and *-est.* All three-syllable and most two-syllable modifiers have comparatives and superlatives formed with *more* and *most.*

Modifier	Comparative	Superlative
tall	taller	tallest
kind	kinder	kindest
droopy	droopier	droopiest
expensive	more expensive	most expensive
wasteful	more wasteful	most wasteful

WATCH OUT! Note that spelling changes must sometimes be made to form the comparatives and superlatives of modifiers.

> EXAMPLES: *friendly, friendlier* (Change *y* to *i*, and add the ending.)
> *sad, sadder* (Double the final consonant, and add the ending.)

4.7 IRREGULAR COMPARISONS

Some commonly used modifiers have irregular comparative and superlative forms. They are listed in the following chart.

Modifier	Comparative	Superlative
good	better	best
bad	worse	worst
far	farther *or* further	farthest *or* furthest
little	less *or* lesser	least
many	more	most
well	better	best
much	more	most

4.8 PROBLEMS WITH MODIFIERS

Study the tips that follow to avoid common mistakes:

Farther and Further Use *farther* for distances; use *further* for everything else.

Double Comparisons Make a comparison by using *-er/-est* or by using *more/most*. Using *-er* with *more* or using *-est* with *most* is incorrect.

> INCORRECT: *I like her more better than she likes me.*
> CORRECT: *I like her better than she likes me.*

Illogical Comparisons An illogical or confusing comparison results when two unrelated things are compared or when something is compared with itself. The word *other* or the word *else* should be used in a comparison of an individual member to the rest of a group.

> ILLOGICAL: *The narrator was more curious about the war than any student in his class.* (implies that the narrator isn't a student in the class)
> LOGICAL: *The narrator was more curious about the war than any other student in his class.* (identifies that the narrator is a student)

Bad vs. Badly *Bad,* as an adjective, is used before a noun or after a linking verb. *Badly,* always an adverb, never modifies a noun. Be sure to use the right form after a linking verb.

> INCORRECT: *Ed felt badly after his team lost.*
> CORRECT: *Ed felt bad after his team lost.*

Good vs. Well *Good,* as an adjective, is used before a noun or after a linking verb. *Well* is often an adverb meaning "expertly" or "properly." *Well* can also be used as an adjective after a linking verb when it means "in good health."

> INCORRECT: *Helen writes very good.*
> CORRECT: *Helen writes very well.*
> CORRECT: *Yesterday I felt bad; today I feel well.*

Double Negatives If you add a negative word to a sentence that is already negative, the result will be an error known as a double negative. When using *not* or *-n't* with a verb, use *any-* words, such as *anybody* or *anything,* rather than *no-* words, such as *nobody* or *nothing,* later in the sentence.

> INCORRECT: *I don't have no money.*
> CORRECT: *I don't have any money.*

Using *hardly, barely,* or *scarcely* after a negative word is also incorrect.

> INCORRECT: *They couldn't barely see two feet ahead.*
> CORRECT: *They could barely see two feet ahead.*

Misplaced Modifiers Sometimes a modifier is placed so far away from the word it modifies that the intended meaning of the sentence is unclear. Prepositional phrases and participial phrases are often misplaced. Place modifiers as close as possible to the words they modify.

> MISPLACED: *The ranger explained how to find ducks in her office.* (The ducks were not in the ranger's office.)

> CLEARER: *In her office, the ranger explained how to find ducks.*

Dangling Modifiers Sometimes a modifier doesn't appear to modify any word in a sentence. Most dangling modifiers are participial phrases or infinitive phrases.

> DANGLING: *Coming home with groceries, our parrot said, "Hello!"*

> CLEARER: *Coming home with groceries, we heard our parrot say, "Hello!"*

Practice and Apply

Choose the correct word or words from each pair in parentheses.

1. Flannery O'Connor's story is (better/more better) than other stories I have read recently.
2. Mr. Shiftlet and Mrs. Crater (could/couldn't) hardly be less honest with each other.
3. Mr. Shiftlet says there isn't (any/no) broken thing on the farm that he can't fix.
4. He feels (good/well) about fixing the car.
5. Who do you think is the (stranger/strangest) person—Mr. Shiftlet or Mrs. Crater?
6. Mr. Shiftlet feels (bad/badly) about the rottenness of the world.
7. As Mr. Shiftlet drove on alone he felt (depresseder/more depressed) than ever.
8. Mr. Shiftlet didn't feel very (well/good) about being alone, so he picked up a hitchhiker.
9. One wonders how many other great stories Flannery O'Connor would have written had she lived (longer/more longer).

5 Prepositions, Conjunctions, and Interjections

5.1 PREPOSITIONS

A preposition is a word used to show the relationship between a noun or a pronoun and another word in the sentence.

Commonly Used Prepositions			
above	down	near	through
at	for	of	to
before	from	on	up
below	in	out	with
by	into	over	without

A preposition is always followed by a word or group of words that serves as its object. The preposition, its object, and modifiers of the object are called the **prepositional phrase.** In each example below, the prepositional phrase is highlighted, and the object of the preposition is in boldface type.

> EXAMPLES: *The future of the entire* **kingdom** *is uncertain.*
> *We searched through the deepest* **woods.**

Prepositional phrases may be used as adjectives or as adverbs. The phrase in the first example is used as an adjective modifying the noun *future.* In the second example, the phrase is used as an adverb modifying the verb *searched.*

WATCH OUT! Prepositional phrases must be as close as possible to the word they modify.

> MISPLACED: *We have clothes for leisurewear of many colors.*

> CLEARER: *We have clothes of many colors for leisurewear.*

5.2 CONJUNCTIONS

A conjunction is a word used to connect words, phrases, or sentences. There are three kinds of conjunctions: **coordinating** conjunctions, correlative conjunctions, and **subordinating conjunctions**.

Coordinating conjunctions connect words or word groups that have the same function in a sentence. They include *and, but, or, for, so, yet,* and *nor.*

Coordinating conjunctions can join nouns, pronouns, verbs, adjectives, adverbs, prepositional phrases, and clauses in a sentence.

These examples show coordinating conjunctions joining words of the same function:

> **EXAMPLES:** *I have many friends but few enemies.* (two noun objects)
> *We ran out the door and into the street.* (two prepositional phrases)
> *They are pleasant yet seem aloof.* (two predicates)
> *We have to go now, or we will be late.* (two clauses)

Correlative conjunctions are similar to coordinating conjunctions. However, correlative conjunctions are always used in pairs.

Correlative Conjunctions		
both . . . and	neither . . . nor	whether . . . or
either . . . or	not only . . . but also	

Subordinating conjunctions introduce subordinate clauses—clauses that cannot stand by themselves as complete sentences. The subordinating conjunction shows how the subordinate clause relates to the rest of the sentence. The relationships include time, manner, place, cause, comparison, condition, and purpose.

Subordinating Conjunctions	
Time	*after, as, as long as, as soon as, before, since, until, when, whenever, while*
Manner	*as, as if*

continued

Subordinating Conjunctions	
Place	*where, wherever*
Cause	*because, since*
Comparison	*as, as much as, than*
Condition	*although, as long as, even if, even though, if, provided that, though, unless, while*
Purpose	*in order that, so that, that*

In the example below, the boldface word is the conjunction, and the highlighted words form a subordinate clause:

> **EXAMPLE:** *Walt Whitman was a man of the people,* **although** *many did not appreciate his poems.*

Walt Whitman was a man of the people is an independent clause, because it can stand alone as a complete sentence. *Although many did not appreciate his poems* cannot stand alone as a complete sentence; it is thus a subordinate clause.

Conjunctive adverbs are used to connect clauses that can stand by themselves as sentences. Conjunctive adverbs include *also, besides, finally, however, moreover, nevertheless, otherwise,* and *then.*

> **EXAMPLE:** *She loved the fall; however, she also enjoyed winter.*

5.3 INTERJECTIONS

Interjections are words used to show emotion, such as *wow* and *cool.* Interjections are usually set off from the rest of a sentence by a comma or by an exclamation mark.

> **EXAMPLE:** *Thoreau lived in the woods by himself. Amazing!*

6 The Sentence and Its Parts

A **sentence** is a group of words used to express a complete thought. A complete sentence has a subject and a predicate.

6.1 KINDS OF SENTENCES

There are four basic types of sentences.

Types	Definition	Example
Declarative	states a fact, a wish, an intent, or a feeling	I wrote an essay on "The Weary Blues" for class.
Interrogative	asks a question	Are you familiar with Langston Hughes?
Imperative	gives a command or direction	Read "The Weary Blues" aloud.
Exclamatory	expresses strong feeling or excitement	It sounds like a song!

6.2 COMPOUND SUBJECTS AND PREDICATES

A compound subject consists of two or more subjects that share the same verb. They are typically joined by the coordinating conjunction *and* or *or.*

EXAMPLE: *Courtney and Eric enjoy the theater.*

A compound predicate consists of two or more predicates that share the same subject. They too are typically joined by a coordinating conjunction, usually *and, but,* or *or.*

EXAMPLE: *The main character in "Winter Dreams" attended a prestigious university and became a successful businessman.*

6.3 COMPLEMENTS

A **complement** is a word or group of words that completes the meaning of the sentence. Some sentences contain only a subject and a verb. Most sentences, however, require additional words placed after the verb to complete the meaning of the sentence. There are three kinds of complements: direct objects, indirect objects, and subject complements.

Direct objects are words or word groups that receive the action of action verbs. A direct object answers the question *what* or *whom.*

EXAMPLES: *The students asked many questions.* (Asked what?)
The teacher quickly answered the students. (Answered whom?)

Indirect objects tell to whom or what or for whom or what the actions of verbs are performed. Indirect objects come before direct objects. In the examples that follow, the indirect objects are highlighted.

EXAMPLES: *My sister usually gave her friends good advice.* (Gave to whom?)
Her brother sent the store a heavy package. (Sent to what?)

Subject complements come after linking verbs and identify or describe the subjects. A subject complement that names or identifies a subject is called a **predicate nominative.** Predicate nominatives include **predicate nouns** and **predicate pronouns.**

EXAMPLES: *My friends are very hard workers.*
The best writer in the class is she.

A subject complement that describes a subject is called a **predicate adjective.**

EXAMPLE: *The pianist appeared very energetic.*

7 Phrases

A **phrase** is a group of related words that does not contain a subject and a predicate but functions in a sentence as a single part of speech.

7.1 PREPOSITIONAL PHRASES

A **prepositional phrase** is a phrase that consists of a preposition, its object, and any modifiers of the object. Prepositional phrases that modify nouns or pronouns are called **adjective phrases.** Prepositional phrases that modify verbs, adjectives, or adverbs are **adverb phrases.**

> ADJECTIVE PHRASE: *The central character of the story is a villain.*

> ADVERB PHRASE: *He reveals his nature in the first scene.*

7.2 APPOSITIVES AND APPOSITIVE PHRASES

An **appositive** is a noun or pronoun that identifies or renames another noun or pronoun. An **appositive phrase** includes an appositive and modifiers of it.

An appositive can be either **essential** or **nonessential.** An **essential appositive** provides information that is needed to identify what is referred to by the preceding noun or pronoun.

> EXAMPLE: The Glass Menagerie *was written by playwright Tennessee Williams.*

A **nonessential appositive** adds extra information about a noun or pronoun whose meaning is already clear. Nonessential appositives and appositive phrases are set off with commas.

> EXAMPLE: *Williams uses Laura's glass menagerie, a collection of fragile animal figurines, to represent her relationship to reality.*

8 Verbals and Verbal Phrases

A **verbal** is a verb form that is used as a noun, an adjective, or an adverb. A **verbal phrase** consists of a verbal along with its modifiers and complements. There are three kinds of verbals: **infinitives, participles,** and **gerunds.**

8.1 INFINITIVES AND INFINITIVE PHRASES

An **infinitive** is a verb form that usually begins with *to* and functions as a noun, an adjective, or an adverb. An **infinitive phrase** consists of an infinitive plus its modifiers and complements. The examples that follow show several uses of infinitive phrases.

> NOUN: *To know her is my only desire.* (subject)

I'm planning to walk with you.
(direct object)
Her goal was to promote women's rights.
(predicate nominative)

> ADJECTIVE: *We saw his need to be loved.* (adjective modifying *need*)

> ADVERB: *She wrote to voice her opinions.* (adverb modifying *wrote*)

Because infinitives usually begin with *to,* it is usually easy to recognize them. However, sometimes *to* may be omitted.

> EXAMPLE: *Let no one dare [to] enter this shrine.*

8.2 PARTICIPLES AND PARTICIPIAL PHRASES

A **participle** is a verb form that functions as an adjective. Like adjectives, participles modify nouns and pronouns. Most participles are present-participle forms, ending in *-ing,* or past-participle forms ending in *-ed* or *-en.* In the examples that follow, the participles are highlighted:

> MODIFYING A NOUN: *The jogging woman completed another lap on the track.*

> MODIFYING A PRONOUN: *Bored, he began to doodle in the margins of his notebook.*

Participial phrases are participles with all their modifiers and complements.

> MODIFYING A NOUN: *Changing tactics, the attorney questioned the witness.*

> MODIFYING A PRONOUN: *Dismissed for the day, they filed out of the courtroom.*

8.3 DANGLING AND MISPLACED PARTICIPLES

A participle or participial phrase should be placed as close as possible to the word that it modifies. Otherwise the meaning of the sentence may not be clear.

> MISPLACED: *The boys were looking for squirrels searching the trees.*

> CLEARER: *The boys searching the trees were looking for squirrels.*

A participle or participial phrase that does not clearly modify anything in a sentence is called a **dangling participle.**

A dangling participle causes confusion because it appears to modify a word that it cannot sensibly modify. Correct a dangling participle by providing a word for the participle to modify.

DANGLING: *Running like the wind, my hat fell off.* (The hat wasn't running.)

CLEARER: *Running like the wind, I lost my hat.*

8.4 GERUNDS AND GERUND PHRASES

A **gerund** is a verb form ending in *-ing* that functions as a noun. Gerunds may perform any function nouns perform.

SUBJECT: *Running is my favorite pastime.*

DIRECT OBJECT: *I truly love running.*

INDIRECT OBJECT: *You should give running a try.*

SUBJECT COMPLEMENT: *My deepest passion is running.*

OBJECT OF PREPOSITION: *Her love of running keeps her strong.*

Gerund phrases are gerunds with all their modifiers and complements.

SUBJECT: *Wishing on a star never got me far.*

OBJECT OF PREPOSITION: *I will finish before leaving the office.*

APPOSITIVE: *Her avocation, flying airplanes, finally led to full-time employment.*

Practice and Apply

Identify the underlined phrases as appositive phrases, infinitive phrases, participial phrases, or gerund phrases.

1. In "The Masque of the Red Death," Poe uses allegory, <u>a device representing abstract qualities.</u>
2. <u>To escape the plague,</u> Prince Prospero seals himself and his courtiers in a walled abbey.
3. <u>Feeling protected from the Red Death,</u> Prospero holds a lavish masquerade ball.
4. There suddenly appears in the last room a masked figure, <u>the Red Death in a ghastly shroud.</u>

---

9 Clauses

A **clause** is a group of words that contains a subject and a verb. There are two kinds of clauses: independent clauses and subordinate clauses.

9.1 INDEPENDENT AND SUBORDINATE CLAUSES

An **independent clause** can stand alone as a sentence, as the word **independent** suggests.

INDEPENDENT CLAUSE: *Frederick Douglass was an eloquent speaker.*

A sentence may contain more than one independent clause.

EXAMPLE: *Frederick Douglass was an eloquent speaker, but he encountered a lot of opposition.*

In the preceding example, the coordinating conjunction *but* joins two independent clauses.

A **subordinate clause** cannot stand alone as a sentence. It is subordinate to, or dependent on, an independent clause.

EXAMPLE: *Although Frederick Douglass was a runaway slave, he frequently appeared in public to raise support for the abolitionist movement.*

The highlighted clause cannot stand by itself; it must be joined with an independent clause to form a complete sentence.

9.2 ADJECTIVE CLAUSES

An **adjective clause** is a subordinate clause used as an adjective. It usually follows the noun or pronoun it modifies. Adjective clauses are typically introduced by the relative pronoun *who, whom, whose, which,* or *that.*

EXAMPLES: *Frederick Douglass wrote objectively about the whippings that Corey frequently gave him.*
The autobiographer whom I liked best was Frederick Douglass.
He was a man who was determined to find freedom.

An adjective clause can be either essential or nonessential. An **essential adjective clause** provides information that is necessary to identify the preceding noun or pronoun.

> EXAMPLE: *The couch that we picked out will not be delivered for three weeks.*

A **nonessential adjective clause** adds additional information about a noun or pronoun whose meaning is already clear. Nonessential clauses are set off with commas.

> EXAMPLE: *Joel's grandmother, who was born in Italy, makes the best lasagna.*

TIP The relative pronouns *whom, which,* and *that* may sometimes be omitted when they are objects in adjective clauses.

> EXAMPLE: *The autobiographer [whom] I liked best was Frederick Douglass.*

9.3 ADVERB CLAUSES

An **adverb clause** is a subordinate clause that is used to modify a verb, an adjective, or an adverb. It is introduced by a subordinating conjunction.
Adverb clauses typically occur at the beginning or end of sentences.

> MODIFYING A VERB: *When we need you, we will call.*

> MODIFYING AN ADVERB: *I'll stay here where there is shelter from the rain.*

> MODIFYING AN ADJECTIVE: *Roman felt as good as he had ever felt.*

9.4 NOUN CLAUSES

A **noun clause** is a subordinate clause that is used as a noun. A noun clause may be used as a subject, a direct object, an indirect object, a predicate nominative, or the object of a preposition. Noun clauses are introduced either by pronouns, such as *that, what, who, whoever, which,* and *whose,* or by subordinating conjunctions, such as *how, when, where, why,* and *whether.*

TIP Because the same words may introduce adjective and noun clauses, you need to consider how a clause functions within its sentence. To determine if a clause is a noun clause, try substituting *something* or *someone* for the clause. If you can do it, it is probably a noun clause.

> EXAMPLES: *I know whose woods these are.* ("I know something." The clause is a noun clause, direct object of the verb *know.*) *Give a copy to whoever wants one.* ("Give a copy to someone." The clause is a noun clause, object of the preposition *to.*)

10 The Structure of Sentences

When classified by their structure, there are four kinds of sentences: simple, compound, complex, and compound-complex.

10.1 SIMPLE SENTENCES

A **simple sentence** is a sentence that has one independent clause and no subordinate clauses. Various parts of simple sentences may be compound, and simple sentences may contain grammatical structures such as appositive and verbal phrases.

> EXAMPLES: *Ambrose Bierce and Stephen Crane, two great American writers, both wrote during the latter half of the 19th century.* (compound subject and an appositive)
> *Crane, best known for writing fiction, also wrote great poetry.* (participial phrase containing a gerund phrase)

10.2 COMPOUND SENTENCES

A **compound sentence** consists of two or more independent clauses. The clauses in compound sentences are joined with commas and coordinating conjunctions *(and, but, or, nor, yet, for, so)* or with semicolons. Like simple sentences, compound sentences do not contain any subordinate clauses.

> EXAMPLES: *I enjoyed the free pottery class, and I would like to go again.*
> *Carl Sandburg's "Chicago" seems to*

celebrate the youthful energy of a booming industrial city; however, the poem dwells on the negative impacts of growth.

WATCH OUT! Do not confuse compound sentences with simple sentences that have compound parts.

EXAMPLE: *The center fielder caught the ball and immediately threw it toward second base.* (Here *and* joins parts of a compound predicate, not a compound sentence.)

10.3 COMPLEX SENTENCES

A **complex sentence** consists of one independent clause and one or more subordinate clauses. Each subordinate clause can be used as a noun or as a modifier. If it is used as a modifier, a subordinate clause usually modifies a word in the independent clause, and the independent clause can stand alone. However, when a subordinate clause is a noun clause, it is a part of the independent clause; the two cannot be separated.

MODIFIER: *One should not complain unless one has a better solution.*

NOUN CLAUSE: *We sketched pictures of whoever we wished.* (The noun clause is the object of the preposition *of* and cannot be separated from the rest of the sentence.)

10.4 COMPOUND-COMPLEX SENTENCES

A **compound-complex sentence** contains two or more independent clauses and one or more subordinate clauses. Compound-complex sentences are, simply, both compound and complex. If you start with a compound sentence, all you need to do to form a compound-complex sentence is add a subordinate clause.

COMPOUND: *All the students knew the answer, yet they were too shy to volunteer.*

COMPOUND-COMPLEX: *All the students knew the answer that their teacher expected, yet they were too shy to volunteer.*

10.5 PARALLEL STRUCTURE

When you write sentences, make sure that coordinate parts are equivalent, or **parallel,** in structure.

NOT PARALLEL: *Erin loved basketball and to play hockey.* (*Basketball* is a noun; *to play hockey* is a phrase.)

PARALLEL: *Erin loved basketball and hockey.* (*Basketball* and *hockey* are both nouns.)

NOT PARALLEL: *He wanted to rent an apartment, a new car, and traveling around the country.* (*To rent* is an infinitive, *car* is a noun, and *traveling* is a gerund.)

PARALLEL: *He wanted to rent an apartment, to drive a new car, and to travel around the country.* (*To rent, to drive,* and *to travel* are all infinitives.)

11 Writing Complete Sentences

Remember that a sentence is a group of words that expresses a complete thought. In formal writing, try to avoid both sentence fragments and run-on sentences.

11.1 CORRECTING FRAGMENTS

A **sentence fragment** is a group of words that is only part of a sentence. It does not express a complete thought and may be confusing to a reader or listener. A sentence fragment may be lacking a subject, a predicate, or both.

FRAGMENT: *Waited for the boat to arrive.* (no subject)

CORRECTED: *We waited for the boat to arrive.*

FRAGMENT: *People of various races, ages, and creeds.* (no predicate)

CORRECTED: *People of various races, ages, and creeds gathered together.*

FRAGMENT: *Near the old cottage.* (neither subject nor predicate)

CORRECTED: *The burial ground is near the old cottage.*

Sometimes fixing a fragment will be a matter of attaching it to a preceding or following sentence.

> FRAGMENT: *We saw the two girls. Waiting for the bus to arrive.*

> CORRECTED: *We saw the two girls waiting for the bus to arrive.*

11.2 CORRECTING RUN-ON SENTENCES

A **run-on sentence** is made up of two or more sentences written as though they were one. Some run-ons have no punctuation within them. Others may have only commas where conjunctions or stronger punctuation marks are necessary. Use your judgment in correcting run-on sentences, as you have choices. You can make a run-on two sentences if the thoughts are not closely connected. If the thoughts are closely related, you can keep the run-on as one sentence by adding a semicolon or a conjunction.

> RUN-ON: *We found a place for the picnic by a small pond it was three miles from the village.*

> MAKE TWO SENTENCES: *We found a place for the picnic by a small pond. It was three miles from the village.*

> RUN-ON: *We found a place for the picnic by a small pond it was perfect.*

> USE A SEMICOLON: *We found a place for the picnic by a small pond; it was perfect.*

> ADD A CONJUNCTION: *We found a place for the picnic by a small pond, and it was perfect.*

WATCH OUT! When you form compound sentences, make sure you use appropriate punctuation: a comma before a coordinating conjunction, a semicolon when there is no coordinating conjunction. A very common mistake is to use a comma alone instead of a comma and a conjunction. This error is called a **comma splice.**

> INCORRECT: *He finished the apprenticeship, he left the village.*

> CORRECT: *He finished the apprenticeship, and he left the village.*

Practice and Apply

Rewrite the following paragraph, correcting all fragments and run-ons.

The narrator in Charlotte Perkins Gilman's story "The Yellow Wallpaper" expects that her husband will laugh at her, that's an odd response, in my opinion. She could have lived more happily. If the relationship between her and her husband were an equal partnership. We can acknowledge that men and women may be different in some ways. Without believing that they are as different as this story suggests. The male character acts practical and "strong," the female character acts nervous and weak.

12 Subject-Verb Agreement

The subject and verb in a clause must agree in number. Agreement means that if the subject is singular, the verb is also singular, and if the subject is plural, the verb is also plural.

12.1 BASIC AGREEMENT

Fortunately, agreement between subjects and verbs in English is simple. Most verbs show the difference between singular and plural only in the third person of the present tense. In the present tense, the third person singular form ends in -*s*.

Present-Tense Verb Forms	
Singular	**Plural**
I eat	we eat
you eat	you eat
she, he, it eats	they eat

12.2 AGREEMENT WITH *BE*

The verb *be* presents special problems in agreement, because this verb does not follow the usual verb patterns.

Forms of *Be*			
Present Tense		**Past Tense**	
Singular	**Plural**	**Singular**	**Plural**
I am	we are	I was	we were
you are	you are	you were	you were
she, he, it is	they are	she, he, it was	they were

12.3 WORDS BETWEEN SUBJECT AND VERB

A verb agrees only with its subject. When words come between a subject and a verb, ignore them when considering proper agreement. Identify the subject, and make sure the verb agrees with it.

> **EXAMPLES:** A *story* in the newspapers *tells* about the 1890s.
> *Dad* as well as Mom *reads* the paper daily.

12.4 AGREEMENT WITH COMPOUND SUBJECTS

Use plural verbs with most compound subjects joined by the word *and*.

> **EXAMPLE:** *My mother and her sisters call each other every Sunday.*

To confirm that you need a plural verb, you could substitute the plural pronoun *they* for *my mother and her sisters*.

If a compound subject is thought of as a unit, use a singular verb. Test this by substituting the singular pronoun *it*.

> **EXAMPLE:** *Liver and onions [it] is Robert's least favorite dish.*

Use a singular verb with a compound subject that is preceded by *each, every,* or *many a*.

> **EXAMPLE:** *Not every dog and cat at the shelter makes a good pet.*

When the parts of a compound subject are joined by *or, nor,* or the correlative conjunctions *either . . . or* or *neither . . . nor,* make the verb agree with the noun or pronoun nearest the verb.

> **EXAMPLES:** *Baseball or football is my favorite sport.*
> *Either my rabbits or my turtle was loose in my room.*
> *Neither Mrs. Howard nor her two sons were home at the time of the accident.*

12.5 PERSONAL PRONOUNS AS SUBJECTS

When using a personal pronoun as a subject, make sure to match it with the correct form of the verb *be*. (See the chart in Section 12.2.) Note especially that the pronoun *you* takes the forms *are* and *were,* regardless of whether it is singular or plural.

WATCH OUT! *You is* and *you was* are nonstandard forms and should be avoided in writing and speaking. *We was* and *they was* are also forms to be avoided.

> **INCORRECT:** *You is facing the wrong direction.*
> **CORRECT:** *You are facing the wrong direction.*
> **INCORRECT:** *We was telling ghost stories.*
> **CORRECT:** *We were telling ghost stories.*

12.6 INDEFINITE PRONOUNS AS SUBJECTS

Some indefinite pronouns are always singular; some are always plural.

Singular Indefinite Pronouns		
another	everybody	no one
anybody	everyone	nothing
anyone	everything	one
anything	much	somebody
each	neither	someone
either	nobody	something

EXAMPLES: *Each of the writers was given an award.*
Somebody in the room upstairs is sleeping.

Plural Indefinite Pronouns			
both	few	many	several

EXAMPLES: *Many of the books in our library are not in circulation.*
Few have been returned recently.

Still other indefinite pronouns may be either singular or plural.

Singular or Plural Indefinite Pronouns		
all	more	none
any	most	some

The number of the indefinite pronoun *any* or *none* often depends on the intended meaning.

EXAMPLES: *Any of these topics has potential for a good article.* (any one topic)
Any of these topics have potential for good articles. (all of the many topics)

The indefinite pronouns *all, some, more, most,* and *none* are singular when they refer to quantities or parts of things. They are plural when they refer to numbers of individual things. Context will usually give a clue.

EXAMPLES: *All of the flour is gone.* (referring to a quantity)
All of the flowers are gone. (referring to individual items)

12.7 INVERTED SENTENCES

Problems in agreement often occur in inverted sentences beginning with *here* or *there;* in questions beginning with *how, when, why, where,* or *what;* and in inverted sentences beginning with phrases. Identify the subject—wherever it is—before deciding on the verb.

EXAMPLES: *There clearly are far too many cooks in this kitchen.*
What is the correct ingredient for this stew?
Far from the embroiled cooks stands the master chef.

Practice and Apply

Locate the subject of each clause in the sentences below. Then choose the correct verb.

1. Many poets have written great poetry, but few (is/are) as talented as Emily Dickinson.
2. There (is/are) many lines in her work that her readers (treasures/treasure).
3. Some of her readers (appreciates/appreciate) her use of dashes, while others (finds/find) it confusing.
4. Each of her poems (presents/present) an idea to think about.
5. What (is/are) the dominant vowel sound in the last four lines of "Much Madness is divinest Sense"?
6. The consonant that prevails in the same poem (seems/seem) to be s.
7. I can't decide whether the poem's sound or its ideas (is/are) more striking.

12.8 SENTENCES WITH PREDICATE NOMINATIVES

When a predicate nominative serves as a complement in a sentence, use a verb that agrees with the subject, not the complement.

EXAMPLES: *The hunting habits of the North American wolf are an example of how change in the environment affects animals.* (The subject is the plural noun *habits*—not *wolf*—and it takes the plural verb *are.*)
An example of how change in the environment affects animals is seen in the hunting habits of the North American wolf. (The subject is the singular noun *example,* and it takes the singular verb *is seen.*)

12.9 *DON'T* AND *DOESN'T* AS AUXILIARY VERBS

The auxiliary verb *doesn't* is used with singular subjects and with the personal pronouns *she, he,* and *it.* The auxiliary verb *don't* is used with plural subjects and with the personal pronouns *I, we, you,* and *they.*

SINGULAR: *She doesn't have a costume for the rehearsal.*

Doesn't the doctor have an appointment Wednesday morning?

PLURAL: *They don't think they did very well on that math test.*

The cats don't need to be fed more than twice a day.

12.10 COLLECTIVE NOUNS AS SUBJECTS

Collective nouns are singular nouns that name groups of persons or things. *Team,* for example, is the collective name of a group of individuals. A collective noun takes a singular verb when the group acts as a single unit. It takes a plural verb when the members of the group act separately.

EXAMPLES: *Her family is moving to another state.* (The family as a whole is moving.)
Her family are carrying furniture out to the truck. (The individual members are carrying furniture.)

12.11 RELATIVE PRONOUNS AS SUBJECTS

When the relative pronoun *who, which,* or *that* is used as a subject in an adjective clause, the verb in the clause must agree in number with the antecedent of the pronoun.

SINGULAR: *Have you selected one of the poems that is meaningful to you?*

The antecedent of the relative pronoun *that* is the singular *one;* therefore, *that* is singular and must take the singular verb *is.*

PLURAL: *The fairy tales, which have been collected from many different sources, are annotated.*

The antecedent of the relative pronoun *which* is the plural *fairy tales. Which* is plural, and it takes the plural verb *have been collected.*

Vocabulary and Spelling

COMMON CORE   ELACC11-12L1a, ELACC11-12L1b, ELACC11-12L2b, ELACC11-12L4a-c, ELACC11-12L4, ELACC11-12L5, ELACC11-12L6

The key to becoming an independent reader is to develop a toolkit of vocabulary strategies. By learning and practicing the strategies, you'll know what to do when you encounter unfamiliar words while reading. You'll also know how to refine the words you use for different situations—personal, school, and work.

Being a good speller is important when communicating your ideas in writing. Learning basic spelling rules and checking your spelling in a dictionary will help you spell words that you may not use frequently.

1   Using Context Clues

The context of a word is made up of the punctuation marks, words, sentences, and paragraphs that surround the word. A word's context can give you important clues about its meaning.

1.1   GENERAL CONTEXT

Sometimes you need to infer the meaning of an unfamiliar word by reading all the information in a passage.

> *I told my parents I wanted to quit playing the piano, but they told me to perservere anyway.*

You can figure out from the context that *persevere* means "continue."

1.2   SPECIFIC CONTEXT CLUES

Sometimes writers help you understand the meanings of words by providing specific clues such as those shown in the chart.

Specific Context Clues		
Type of Clue	**Key Words/ Phrases**	**Example**
Definition or restatement of the meaning of the word	or, which is, that is, in other words, also known as, also called	*Perennials*—**plants that live for more than two years**—make up only one-third of the garden's exhibit.
Example following an unfamiliar word	such as, like, as if, for example, especially, including	Their new apartment was *arrayed* with many beautiful things, **such as a crystal lamp and a porcelain vase.**
Comparison with a more familiar word or concept	as, like, also, similar to, in the same way, likewise	The prairie grasses *undulated* in the wind **like the waves in the ocean.**
Contrast with a familiar word or experience	unlike, but, however, although, on the other hand, on the contrary	My dog is usually very **calm, unlike** our neighbor's dog, which is very *rowdy*.

1.3 IDIOMS, SLANG, AND FIGURATIVE LANGUAGE

Use context clues to figure out the meanings of idioms, figurative language, and slang.

An **idiom** is an expression whose overall meaning is different from the meaning of the individual words.

> *If you're going to buy a house with a garden, you'd better have a green thumb.* (*Green thumb* means "ability to grow plants.")

Figurative language is language that communicates meaning beyond the literal meaning of the words.

> *Maria's anger at her disobedient daughter was a white-hot fuse ready to be sparked.* (*White-hot fuse ready to be sparked* is a metaphor that indicates that the anger isn't visible yet but is ready to erupt.)

Slang is informal language composed of made-up words and ordinary words that are used to mean something different from their meanings in formal English.

> *My parents freaked out when I told them that I went to the concert without their permission.* (*Freaked out* means "became greatly distressed.")

2 Analyzing Word Structure

Many words can be broken into smaller parts, such as base words, roots, prefixes, and suffixes.

2.1 BASE WORDS

A **base word** is a word part that by itself is also a word. Other words or word parts can be added to base words to form new words.

2.2 ROOTS

A **root** is a word part that contains the core meaning of the word. Many English words contain roots that come from older languages such as Greek, Latin, Old English (Anglo-Saxon), and Norse. Knowing the meaning of a word's root can help you determine the word's meaning.

Root	Meaning	Example
aster, astr (Greek)	star	asterisk
fic/ fac/ fec (Latin)	make, do	factory
spec/ spect/ spic (Latin)	look at, see, behold	spectator
ten (Latin)	stretch	tendon
derm/ derma (Greek)	skin	epidermis

2.3 PREFIXES

A **prefix** is a word part attached to the beginning of a word. Most prefixes come from Greek, Latin, or Old English.

Prefix	Meaning	Example
un- (Old English)	not	unafraid
epi- (Greek)	upon, on, over	epicenter
syn- (Greek)	together, at the same time	synthesis
hexa- (Greek)	six	hexagram
geo- (Greek)	earth	geography
trans- (Latin)	across, beyond	transatlantic
dis- (Latin)	lack of, not	distrust
circum- (Latin)	around	circumvent
hemi- (Latin)	half	hemisphere

2.4 SUFFIXES

A **suffix** is a word part that appears at the end of a root or base word to form a new word. Some suffixes do not change word meaning. These suffixes are

- added to nouns to change the number of persons or objects

- added to verbs to change the tense
- added to modifiers to change the degree of comparison

Suffix	Meaning	Example
-s, -es	to change the number of a noun	trunk + s = trunks
-d, -ed, -ing	to change verb tense	sprinkle + d = sprinkled
-er, -est	to change the degree of comparison in modifiers	cold + er = colder icy + est = iciest

Other suffixes can be added to a root or base to change the word's meaning. These suffixes can also determine a word's part of speech.

Suffix	Meaning	Example
-ence	state or condition of	independence
-ous	full of	furious
-ate	to make	activate
-ly, -ily	manner	quickly

Strategies for Understanding Unfamiliar Words

- Look for any prefixes or suffixes. Remove them to isolate the base word or the root.
- See if you recognize any elements— prefix, suffix, root, or base—of the word. You may be able to guess its meaning by analyzing one or two elements.
- Consider the way the word is used in the sentence. Use the context and the word parts to make a logical guess about the word's meaning.
- Consult a dictionary to see whether you are correct.

3 Understanding Word Origins

3.1 ETYMOLOGIES

Etymologies show the origin and historical development of a word. When you study a word's history and origin, you can find out when, where, and how the word came to be.

> **am·bas·sa·dor** (ăm-băs´ə-dər, -dôr´) *n.* A diplomatic official of the highest rank appointed and accredited as repres entative in residence by one government or sovereign to another, usually for a specific length of time. [Middle English *ambassadour,* from Old French *ambassadeur,* from Medieval Latin *ambactia,* mission, from Latin *ambactus,* servant, ultimately of Celtic origin.]

> **com·mu·ni·ty** (kə-myo͞o´nĭ-tē) *n., pl. -ties* A group of people living in the same locality and under the same government. [Middle English *communite,* citizenry, from Old French, from Latin *commūnitās,* fellowship, from *commūnis,* common.]

3.2 WORD FAMILIES

Words that have the same root make up a word family and have related meanings. The chart shows a common Greek and a common Latin root. Notice how the meanings of the example words are related to the meanings of their roots.

Latin Root	*med:* "middle"
English Words	**mediate** resolve or settle
	mediocre ordinary
	media[2] middle wall of a blood vessel
	medial toward the middle
	medium action midway between two extremes

Greek Root	*chron:* "time"
English Words	**chronicle** detailed narrative report
	chronic of long duration
	synchronize occur at same time
	anachronism out of proper order in time

3.3 WORDS FROM CLASSICAL MYTHOLOGY

The English language includes many words from classical mythology. You can use your knowledge of these myths to understand the origins and meanings of these words. For example, *herculean task* refers to the strongman Hercules. Thus, *herculean task* probably means "a job that is large or difficult." The chart shows a few common words from mythology.

Greek	Roman	Norse
panic	cereal	Wednesday
atlas	mercurial	gun
adonis	Saturday	berserk
mentor	January	valkyrie

Practice and Apply

Look up the etymology of each word in the chart and locate the myth associated with it. Use the information from the myth to explain the origin and meaning of each word.

3.4 FOREIGN WORDS

The English language includes words from diverse languages, such as French, Dutch, Spanish, Italian, and Chinese. Many words stayed the way they were in their original language.

French	Dutch	Spanish	Italian
entree	maelstrom	rodeo	pasta
nouveau riche	trek	salsa	opera
potpourri	cookie	bronco	vendetta
tête-à-tête	snoop	tornado	grotto

4 Understanding the English Language

The English language has a documented history of 1400 years, but its earliest beginnings stretch back to the speakers of Proto-Indo-European who ranged from India to Europe. Proto-Indo-European gave rise to many languages, including English, Swedish, Hindi, Greek, Russian, Polish, Italian, French, Spanish, and German—now referred to as Indo-European. Here's a brief overview of the development of English:

- **Proto-English:** Besides the Romans who spoke Latin, the early inhabitants of Britain were Britons and Celts. The Angles, Saxons, and Jutes—Germanic peoples—arrived around A.D. 449. Proto-English incorporated Latin words as well as those drawn from the languages of the Britons, Celts, and the Germanic peoples.

- **Old English:** From about the mid-fifth century to the twelfth century, Old English, the language of the Anglo-Saxons, was the spoken language in Britain. Latin remained the language of writing and of the church, schools, and international relations. Old English would be unintelligible to the speaker of Modern English, given the differences in its grammar, spellings, and pronunciations. The most well-known work in Old English is the epic poem *Beowulf.*

- **Middle English:** After the Norman Conquest in 1066, the nobility spoke Anglo-Norman. Middle English, derived from Anglo-Norman, thrived from the late eleventh century to the late fifteenth century. It also underwent significant changes in grammar and vocabulary. The most famous writer of this period is Geoffrey Chaucer, whose *The Canterbury Tales* remains a staple of the English literature curriculum.

- **Early Modern English:** During the fifteenth century, the so-called "Great Vowel Shift" occurred—a major change in the pronunciation of English. Conventions of spelling were also being established during this time. With the spread of a London-based dialect and the standardization that results from printing, Early Modern English is recognizable to the speaker of Modern English. For example, William Shakespeare, the great English dramatist, wrote during the late phase of Early Modern English. The first edition of the *King James Bible* also was published during this time. Early Modern English lasted until about the seventeenth century.

- **Modern English:** Modern English emerged in the late seventeenth century and continues to the present day. Its development was shaped by Samuel Johnson's *Dictionary of the English Language,* published in 1755, which standardized spelling and usage. The significant characteristic of contemporary Modern English is its extensive vocabulary, which partly arises from technological and scientific developments, as well as from the worldwide variety of its speakers. As various communication devices are increasingly adopted, technology-specific language and vocabulary—such as that used in texting—further influence English. Thus, the development of English continues in the present day.

5 Synonyms and Antonyms

5.1 SYNONYMS

A **synonym** is a word with a meaning similar to that of another word. You can find synonyms in a thesaurus or a dictionary. In a dictionary, synonyms are often given as part of the definition of a word. The following word pairs are synonyms:

dry/arid   enthralled/fascinated
gaunt/thin

5.2 ANTONYMS

An **antonym** is a word with a meaning opposite that of another word. The following word pairs are antonyms:

friend/enemy   absurd/logical
courteous/rude   languid/energetic

6 Denotation and Connotation

6.1 DENOTATION

A word's dictionary meaning is called its **denotation.** For example, the denotation of the word *rascal* is "an unethical, dishonest person."

6.2 CONNOTATION

The images or feelings you connect to a word add a finer shade of meaning, called **connotation.** The connation of a word goes beyond its basic dictionary definition. Writers use connotations of words to communicate positive or negative feelings.

Positive	Neutral	Negative
save	store	hoard
fragrance	smell	stench
display	show	flaunt

Make sure you understand the denotation and connotation of a word when you read it or use it in your writing.

7 Analogies

An **analogy** is a comparison between two things that are similar in some way but are otherwise dissimilar. Analogies are sometimes used in writing when unfamiliar subjects or ideas are explained in terms of familiar ones. Analogies often appear on tests as well, usually in a format like this:

TERRIER : DOG :: A) rat : fish

B) kitten : cat

C) trout : fish

D) fish : trout

E) poodle : collie

Follow these steps to determine the correct answer:

- Read the part in capital letters as "*terrier is to dog as . . .*"
- Read the answer choices as "*rat is to fish*," "*kitten is to cat*," and so on.
- Ask yourself how the words *terrier* and *dog* are related. (A terrier is a type of dog.)
- Ask yourself which of the choices shows the same relationship. (A kitten is a kind of cat, but not in the same way that a terrier is a kind of dog. A kitten is a baby cat. A trout, however, is a type of fish in the sense that a terrier is a type of dog. Therefore, the answer is C.)

8 Homonyms and Homophones

8.1 HOMONYMS

Homonyms are words that have the same spelling and sound but have different origins and meanings.

I don't want to bore you with a story about how I had to bore through the living room wall.

Bore can mean "cause a person to lose interest," but an identically spelled word means "drill a hole."

My dog likes to bark while it scratches the bark on the tree in the backyard.

Bark can refer to what a dog does to make a sound, but an identically spelled word means "the outer covering of a tree." Each word has a different meaning and its own dictionary entry.

Sometimes only one of the meanings of two homonyms may be familiar to you. Use context clues to help you figure out the meaning of an unfamiliar word.

8.2 HOMOPHONES

Homophones are words that sound alike but have different meanings and spellings. The following homophones are frequently misused:

it's/its   they're/their/there

to/too/two   stationary/stationery

Many misused homophones are pronouns and contractions. Whenever you are unsure whether to write *your* or *you're* and *who's* or *whose*, ask yourself if you mean *you are* or *who is/has*. If you do, write the contraction. For other homophones, such as *scent* and *sent,* use the meaning of the word to help you decide which one to use.

9 Words with Multiple Meanings

Some words have acquired additional meanings over time that are based on the original meaning.

EXAMPLES: *I was in a hurry, so I jammed my clothes into the suitcase.*
Unfortunately, I jammed my finger in the process.

These two uses of *jam* have different meanings, but they have the same origin. You will find all the meanings of *jam* listed in the dictionary.

10 Specialized Vocabulary

Specialized vocabulary includes technical vocabulary, domain-specific language, and jargon. Each term refers to the use of language specific to a particular field of study or work. Of these three terms, *jargon* has the strongest connotation, suggesting a kind of language that is difficult to understand or unintelligible to anyone not involved in that field of study or work.

Science, mathematics, history, and literature all have domain-specific vocabularies. For example, science includes words such as *photosynthesis* and *biome* which indicate specific scientific processes or concepts. In literature, words such as *foreshadowing, motif,* and *irony* enable you and others to use a common vocabulary to discuss and interpret literary works.

To figure out specialized terms, you can use context clues and reference sources, such as dictionaries on specific subjects, atlases, or manuals. Many of the resources you use in school include reference aids for that particular subject area. For example, this textbook includes a "Glossary of Literary and Informational Terms," as well as a "Glossary of Academic Vocabulary."

11 Preferred and Contested Usage

English is a constantly evolving language, and standard usage is affected by time and place. For example, Americans often use different words and phrases than the British. Within the United States itself, people speak and write differently than they did 200 years ago. English usage even varies depending on whether the setting is formal or informal. Some nonstandard usages are contested but may become accepted and standard over time. Consult references like *The American Heritage Dictionary of the English Language, Fifth Edition* and its website to determine whether a certain usage is acceptable. See the chart for examples of common usage problems and preferred and contested usages.

ain't	*Ain't* is nonstandard. Avoid *ain't* in formal speaking and in all writing other than dialogue.
all right	*All right* means "satisfactory," "unhurt," "safe," "correct," or, as a reply to a question or a preface to a remark, "yes." Although some dictionaries include *alright* as an optional spelling, it is contested and has not become standard usage.
can, may	*Can* expresses ability; *may* expresses possibility.
hopefully	Used as an adverb, as in the following sentence, the term is uncontested. EXAMPLE: We waited hopefully for the announcement of the election results last night. Some contest the use of *hopefully* as a disjunct; that is, as an adverb that expresses the speaker's comments on the content of a statement. EXAMPLE: Hopefully the candidate I like wins. Merriam–Webster's online dictionary says the second use is "entirely standard."
like, as if, as though	In formal situations, avoid using *like* for the conjunction *as if* or *as though* to introduce a subordinate clause. INFORMAL: I feel like I have the flu. FORMAL: I feel as if I have the flu.

continued

literally, figuratively	*Literally* means "in a strict sense." It is sometimes used in non-literal situations for emphasis, when *figuratively* is the more appropriate term. This type of use is contested. UNCONTESTED: I literally baked five-dozen cupcakes. CONTESTED: He literally went nuts. Usage experts for *The American Heritage Dictionary* suggest that the term is acceptable when used as an intensive adverb.
off, off of	Do not use *off* or *off of* for *from*. NONSTANDARD: I got some good advice off that mechanic. STANDARD: I got some good advice from that mechanic.
some, somewhat	In formal situations, avoid using *some* to mean "to some extent." Use *somewhat*. INFORMAL: Tensions between the nations began to ease some. FORMAL: Tensions between the nations began to ease somewhat.
who, whom	*Who* is used as a subject or a predicate nominative. *Whom* is used as a direct object, an indirect object or an object of a preposition. However, in spoken English, most people use *who* instead of *whom* in all cases.

The English language continues to change, and technology plays a part in that. The increasing use of texting as a means of communications has created a contested language all its own. Terms like *IMO (in my opinion)* and *LOL (laughing out loud)* have become a commonly used part of the vocabulary.

12 Using Reference Sources

12.1 DICTIONARIES

A **general dictionary** will tell you not only a word's definitions but also its pronunciation, its parts of speech, and its history and origin. A **specialized dictionary** focuses on terms related to a particular field of study or work. Use a dictionary to check the spelling of any word you are unsure of in your English class and other subjects as well.

12.2 THESAURI

A **thesaurus** (plural, thesauri) is a dictionary of synonyms. A thesaurus can be helpful when you find yourself using the same modifiers over and over again.

12.3 SYNONYM FINDERS

A **synonym finder** is often included in word-processing software. It enables you to highlight a word and be shown a display of its synonyms.

12.4 GLOSSARIES

A **glossary** is a list of specialized terms and their definitions. It is often found in the back of textbooks and sometimes includes pronunciations. In fact, this textbook has three glossaries: the **Glossary of Literary Informational Terms,** the **Glossary of Academic Vocabulary,** and the **Glossary of Vocabulary.** Use these glossaries to help you understand how terms are used in this textbook.

13 Spelling Rules

13.1 WORDS ENDING IN A SILENT *E*

Before adding a suffix beginning with a vowel or *y* to a word ending in a silent *e,* drop the *e* (with some exceptions).

    amaze + -ing = amazing

    love + -able = lovable

create + -ed = created

nerve + -ous = nervous

Exceptions: *change + -able = changeable; courage + -ous = courageous.*

When adding a suffix beginning with a consonant to a word ending in a silent **e,** keep the **e** (with some exceptions).

late + -ly = lately

spite + -ful = spiteful

noise + -less = noiseless

state + -ment = statement

Exceptions: *truly, argument, ninth, wholly, awful,* and others.

When a suffix beginning with **a** or **o** is added to a word with a final silent **e,** the final **e** is usually retained if it is preceded by a soft **c** or a soft **g.**

bridge + -able = bridgeable

peace + -able = peaceable

outrage + -ous = outrageous

advantage + -ous = advantageous

When a suffix beginning with a vowel is added to words ending in **ee** or **oe,** the final silent **e** is retained.

agree + -ing = agreeing

free + -ing = freeing

hoe + -ing = hoeing

see + -ing = seeing

13.2 WORDS ENDING IN Y

Before adding most suffixes to a word that ends in **y** preceded by a consonant, change the **y** to **i.**

easy + -est = easiest

crazy + -est = craziest

silly + -ness = silliness

marry + -age = marriage

Exceptions: *dryness, shyness,* and *slyness.*

However, when you add **-ing,** the **y** does not change.

empty + -ed = emptied   but

empty + -ing = emptying

When adding a suffix to a word that ends in **y** preceded by a vowel, the **y** usually does not change.

play + -er = player

employ + -ed = employed

coy + -ness = coyness

pay + -able = payable

13.3 WORDS ENDING IN A CONSONANT

In one-syllable words that end in one consonant preceded by one short vowel, double the final consonant before adding a suffix beginning with a vowel, such as **-ed** or **-ing.**

dip + -ed = dipped   set + -ing = setting

slim + -est = slimmest   fit + -er = fitter

The rule does not apply to words of one syllable that end in a consonant preceded by two vowels.

feel + -ing = feeling   peel + -ed = peeled

reap + -ed = reaped   loot + -ed = looted

In words of more than one syllable, double the final consonant when (1) the word ends with one consonant preceded by one vowel and (2) the word is accented on the last syllable.

be•gin′   per•mit′   re•fer′

In the following examples, note that in the new words formed with suffixes, the accent remains on the same syllable:

be•gin′ + -ing = be•gin′ ning = beginning

per•mit′ + -ed = per•mit′ ted = permitted

In some words with more than one syllable, though the accent remains on the same syllable when a suffix is added, the final consonant is nevertheless not doubled, as in the following examples:

tra′vel + -er = tra′vel•er = traveler

mar′ket + -er = mar′ket•er = marketer

In the following examples, the accent does not remain on the same syllable; thus, the final consonant is not doubled:

re•fer′ + -ence = ref′er•ence = reference

con•fer′ + -ence = con′fer•ence = conference

13.4 PREFIXES AND SUFFIXES

When adding a prefix to a word, do not change the spelling of the base word. When a prefix creates a double letter, keep both letters.

dis- + approve = disapprove

re- + build = rebuild

ir- + regular = irregular

mis- + spell = misspell

anti- + trust = antitrust

il- + logical = illogical

When adding **-ly** to a word ending in **l,** keep both **l**'s, and when adding **-ness** to a word ending in **n,** keep both **n's.**

careful + -ly = carefully

sudden + -ness = suddenness

final + -ly = finally

thin + -ness = thinness

13.5 FORMING PLURAL NOUNS

To form the plural of most nouns, just add **-s.**

prizes dreams circles stations

For most singular nouns ending in **o,** add **-s.**

solos halos studios photos pianos

When the singular noun ends in **s, sh, ch, x,** or **z,** add **-es.**

waitresses   brushes   ditches

axes   buzzes

When a singular noun ends in **y** with a consonant before it, change the **y** to **i** and add **-es.**

army—armies   candy—candies

baby—babies   diary—diaries

ferry—ferries   conspiracy—conspiracies

When a vowel (**a, e, i, o, u**) comes before the **y,** just add **-s.**

boy—boys   way—ways

array—arrays   alloy—alloys

weekday—weekdays   jockey—jockeys

For most nouns ending in **f** or **fe,** change the **f** to **v** and add **-es** or **-s.**

life—lives   calf—calves

knife—knives   thief—thieves

shelf—shelves   loaf—loaves

For some nouns ending in **f,** add **-s** to make the plural.

roofs chiefs reefs beliefs

Some nouns have the same form for both singular and plural.

deer sheep moose salmon trout

For some nouns, the plural is formed in a special way.

man—men   goose—geese

ox—oxen   woman—women

mouse—mice   child—children

For a compound noun written as one word, form the plural by changing the last word in the compound to its plural form.

stepchild—stepchildren firefly—fireflies

If a compound noun is written as a hyphenated word or as two separate words, change the most important word to the plural form.

brother-in-law—brothers-in-law

life jacket—life jackets

13.6 FORMING POSSESSIVES

If a noun is singular, add **'s.**

mother—my mother's car

Ross—Ross's desk

Exception: The **s** after the apostrophe is dropped after *Jesus', Moses',* and certain names in classical mythology (*Zeus'*). These possessive forms can be pronounced easily.

If a noun is plural and ends with **s,** just add an apostrophe.

parents—my parents' car

the Santinis—the Santinis' house

If a noun is plural but does not end in **s,** add **'s.**

people—the people's choice

women—the women's coats

13.7 SPECIAL SPELLING PROBLEMS

Only one English word ends in **-sede:** *supersede.* Three words end in **-ceed:** *exceed, proceed,* and *succeed.* All other verbs ending in the sound "seed" (except for the verb *seed*) are spelled with **-cede.**

concede precede recede secede

In words with *ie* or *ei,* when the sound is long *e* (as in *she*), the word is spelled *ie* except after *c* (with some exceptions).

i before *e*	thief	relieve	field
	piece	grieve	pier
except after c	conceit	perceive	ceiling
	receive	receipt	

Exceptions: *either, neither, weird, leisure, seize.*

14 Commonly Confused Words

Words	Definition	Example
accept/except	The verb *accept* means "to receive or believe"; *except* is usually a preposition meaning "excluding."	**Except** for some of the more extraordinary events, I can **accept** that the *Odyssey* recounts a real journey.
advice/advise	*Advise* is a verb; *advice* is a noun naming that which an *adviser* gives.	I **advise** you to take that job. Whom should I ask for **advice?**
affect/effect	As a verb, *affect* means "to influence." *Effect* as a verb means "to cause." If you want a noun, you will almost always want *effect*.	Did Circe's wine **affect** Odysseus's mind? It did **effect** a change in Odysseus's men. In fact, it had an **effect** on everyone else who drank it.
all ready/ already	*All ready* is an adjective meaning "fully ready." *Already* is an adverb meaning "before or by this time."	He was **all ready** to go at noon. I have **already** seen that movie.
allusion/ illusion	An *allusion* is an indirect reference to something. An *illusion* is a false picture or idea.	There are many **allusions** to the works of Homer in English literature. The world's apparent flatness is an **illusion.**
among/ between	*Between* is used when you are speaking of only two things. *Among* is used for three or more.	**Between** *Hamlet* and *King Lear,* I prefer the latter. Emily Dickinson is **among** my favorite poets.
bring/take	*Bring* is used to denote motion toward a speaker or place. *Take* is used to denote motion away from such a person or place.	**Bring** the books over here, and I will **take** them to the library.
fewer/less	*Fewer* refers to the number of separate, countable units. *Less* refers to bulk quantity.	We have **less** literature and **fewer** selections in this year's curriculum.
leave/let	*Leave* means "to allow something to remain behind." *Let* means "to permit."	The librarian will **leave** some books on display but will not **let** us borrow any.

continued

Words	Definition	Example
lie/lay	*Lie* means "to rest or recline." It does not take an object. *Lay* always takes an object.	Rover loves to **lie** in the sun. We always **lay** some bones next to him.
loose/lose	*Loose* (lo͞os) means "free, not restrained"; *lose* (lo͞oz) means "to misplace or fail to find."	Who turned the horses **loose?** I hope we won't **lose** any of them.
precede/ proceed	*Precede* means "to go or come before." Use *proceed* for other meanings.	Emily Dickinson's poetry **precedes** that of Alice Walker. You may **proceed** to the next section of the test.
than/then	Use *than* in making comparisons; use *then* on all other occasions.	Who can say whether Amy Lowell is a better poet **than** Denise Levertov? I will read Lowell first, and **then** I will read Levertov.
their/there/ they're	*Their* means "belonging to them." *There* means "in that place." *They're* is the contraction for "they are."	**There** is a movie playing at 9 P.M. **They're** going to see it with me. Sakara and Jessica drove away in **their** car after the movie.
two/too/to	*Two* is the number. *Too* is an adverb meaning "also" or "very." Use *to* before a verb or as a preposition.	Meg had to go to town, **too.** We had **too** much reading to do. **Two** chapters is **too** many.

Glossary of Literary and Informational Terms

Act An act is a major unit of action in a play, similar to a chapter in a book. Depending on their lengths, plays can have as many as five acts. Arthur Miller's play *The Crucible* has four acts.

See also Drama; Scene.

Allegory An allegory is a work with two levels of meaning, a literal one and a symbolic one. In such a work, most of the characters, objects, settings, and events represent abstract qualities. Personification is often used in traditional allegories. As in a fable or parable, the purpose of an allegory may be to convey truths about life, to teach religious or moral lessons, or to criticize social institutions.

Alliteration Alliteration is the repetition of consonant sounds at the beginnings of words. Poets use alliteration to impart a musical quality to their poems, to create mood, to reinforce meaning, to emphasize particular words, and to unify lines or stanzas. Note the examples of alliteration in the following sentence:

> <u>D</u>on't <u>d</u>oubt that I'll <u>d</u>o something
> <u>d</u>aring and jaw <u>d</u>ropping.

Allusion An allusion is an indirect reference to a person, place, event, or literary work with which the author believes the reader will be familiar.

Almanac *See* Reference Works.

Ambiguity Ambiguity is a technique in which a word, phrase, or event has more than one meaning or can be interepreted in more than one way. Some writers deliberately create this effect to give richness and depth of meaning. T. S. Eliot and Robert Frost are two poets known for their use of ambiguity.

Analogy An analogy is a point-by-point comparison between two things for the purpose of clarifying the less familiar of the two subjects.

Anapest *See* Meter.

Anaphora Anaphora is a repetition of a word or words at the beginning of successive lines, clauses, or sentences.

See also Repetition.

Anecdote An anecdote is a brief story that focuses on a single episode or event in a person's life and that is used to illustrate a particular point.

Antagonist An antagonist is usually the principal character in opposition to the protagonist, or hero of a narrative or drama. The antagonist can also be a force of nature.

See also Character; Protagonist.

Antihero An antihero is a protagonist who has the qualities opposite to those of a hero; he or she may be insecure, ineffective, cowardly, sometimes dishonest or dishonorable, or— most often—a failure. A popular antihero in contemporary culture is the cartoon character Homer Simpson.

Aphorism An aphorism is a brief statement, usually one sentence long, that expresses a general principle or truth about life.

Appeals by Association Appeals by association imply that one will gain acceptance or prestige by taking the writer's position.

Appeal to Authority An appeal to authority calls upon experts or others who warrant respect.

Appeal to Reason *See* Logical Appeal.

Archetype An archetype is a pattern in literature that is found in a variety of works from different cultures throughout the ages. An archetype can be a plot, a character, an image, or a setting. For example, the association of death and rebirth with winter and spring is an archetype common to many cultures.

Argument An argument is speech or writing that expresses a position on an issue or problem and supports it with reasons and evidence. An argument often takes into account other points of view, anticipating and answering objections that opponents of the position might raise.

See also Claim; Counterargument; Evidence; General Principle.

Aside In drama, an aside is a short speech directed to the audience, or another character, that is not heard by the other characters on stage.

See also **Soliloquy.**

Assonance Assonance is the repetition of vowel sounds within words. Both poets and prose writers use assonance to impart a musical quality to their works, to create mood, to reinforce meaning, to emphasize particular words, and to unify lines, stanzas, or passages. Note examples of assonance in the following sentence:

> The musician finished writing
> the lyrics to her next big hit.

See also **Alliteration; Consonance; Rhyme.**

Assumption An assumption is an opinion or belief that is taken for granted. It can be about a specific situation, a person, or the world in general. Assumptions are often unstated.

See also **General Principle.**

Atmosphere *See* **Mood.**

Audience Audience is the person or persons who are intended to read a piece of writing. The intended audience of a work determines its form, style, tone, and the details included.

Author's Message An author's message is the main idea or theme of a particular work.

See also **Main Idea; Theme.**

Author's Perspective An author's perspective is a unique combination of ideas, values, feelings, and beliefs that influences the way the writer looks at a topic. **Tone,** or attitude, often reveals an author's perspective.

Author's Position An author's position is his or her opinion on an issue or topic.

See also **Claim.**

Author's Purpose A writer usually writes for one or more of these purposes: to inform, to entertain, to express himself or herself, or to persuade readers to believe or do something. For example, the purpose of a news report (either in a newspaper or magazine) is primarily to inform; the purpose of a news editorial is to persuade the readers or audience to do or believe something.

Autobiographical Essay *See* **Essay.**

Autobiography An autobiography is the story of a person's life written by that person. Generally written from the first-person point of view, autobiographies can vary in style from straightforward chronological accounts to impressionistic narratives.

Ballad A ballad is a narrative poem that was originally meant to be sung. Ballads often contain dialogue and repetition and suggest more than they actually state. Traditional **folk ballads,** composed by unknown authors and handed down orally, are written in four-line stanzas with regular rhythm and rhyme. A **literary ballad** is one that is modeled on the folk ballads but written by a single author.

See also **Narrative Poem; Rhyme; Rhythm.**

Bias Bias is an inclination toward a particular judgment on a topic or issue. A writer often reveals a strongly positive or strongly negative opinion by presenting only one way of looking at an issue or by heavily weighting the evidence. Words with intensely positive or negative connotations are often a signal of a writer's bias.

Bibliography A bibliography is a list of books and other materials related to the topic of a text. Bibliographies can be good sources of works for further study on a subject.

See also **Works Consulted.**

Biography A biography is a type of nonfiction in which a writer gives a factual account of someone else's life. Written in the third person, a biography may cover a person's entire life or focus on only an important part of it. The poet Carl Sandburg wrote an acclaimed six-volume biography of Abraham Lincoln. Modern biography includes a popular form called **fictionalized biography,** in which writers use their imaginations to re-create past conversations and to elaborate on some incidents.

Blank Verse A poem written in blank verse consists of unrhymed lines of iambic pentameter. In other words, each line of blank verse has five pairs of syllables. In most pairs, an unstressed syllable is followed by a stressed syllable. The most versatile of poetic forms, blank verse imitates the natural rhythms of English speech.

See also **Iambic Pentameter; Meter; Rhythm.**

Business Correspondence Business correspondence includes all written business communications, such as business letters, e-mails, and memos. Business correspondence is to the point, clear, courteous, and professional.

Caesura A caesura is a pause or a break in a line of poetry. Poets use a caesura to emphasize the word or phrase that precedes it or to vary the rhythmical effects.

Cast of Characters The cast of characters is a list of all the characters in a play, usually in the order of appearance. This list is found at the beginning of a script.

Catalog A catalog is a list of people, things, or attributes. This technique, found in epics and in the Bible, also characterizes Whitman's style.

Cause and Effect A **cause** is an event or action that directly results in another event or action. An **effect** is the direct or logical outcome of an event or action. Basic **cause-and-effect relationships** include a single cause with a single effect, one cause with multiple effects, multiple causes with a single effect, and a chain of causes and effects. The concept of cause and effect also provides a way of organizing a piece of writing. It helps a writer show the relationships between events or ideas.

Central Idea *See* **Main Idea.**

Character Characters are the people, and sometimes animals or other beings, who take part in the action of a story or novel. Events center on the lives of one or more characters, referred to as **main characters.** The other characters, called **minor characters,** interact with the main characters and help move the story along.

Characters may also be classified as either static or dynamic. **Static characters** tend to stay in a fixed position over the course of the story. They do not experience life-altering moments and seem to act the same, even though their situations may change. In contrast, **dynamic**

characters evolve as individuals, learning from their experiences and growing emotionally.

See also **Antagonist; Characterization; Foil; Motivation; Protagonist.**

Characterization Characterization refers to the techniques a writer uses to develop characters. There are four basic methods of characterization:

- A writer may use physical description.
- The character's own actions, words, thoughts, and feelings might be presented.
- The actions, words, thoughts, and feelings of other characters provide another means of developing a character.
- The narrator's own direct comments also serve to develop a character.

See also **Character; Narrator.**

Chorus In the theater of ancient Greece, the chorus was a group of actors who commented on the **action** of the play. Between scenes, the chorus sang and danced to musical accompaniment, giving insights into the message of the play. The chorus is often considered a kind of ideal spectator, representing the response of ordinary citizens to the tragic events that unfold. Certain dramatists have continued to employ this classical convention as a way of representing the views of the society being depicted.

See also **Drama.**

Chronological Order Chronological order is the arrangement of events in their order of occurrence. This type of organization is used in both fictional narratives and in historical writing, biography, and autobiography.

Claim In an argument, a claim is the writer's position on an issue or problem. Although an argument focuses on supporting one claim, a writer may make more than one claim in a work.

Clarify Clarifying is a reading strategy that helps a reader to understand or make clear what he or she is reading. Readers usually clarify by rereading, reading aloud, or discussing.

Classification Classification is a pattern of organization in which objects, ideas, or information is presented in groups, or classes, based on common characteristics.

Cliché A cliché is an overused expression that has lost its freshness, force, and appeal. The phrase "happy as a lark" is an example of a cliché.

Climax In a plot structure, the climax, or turning point, is the moment when the reader's interest and emotional intensity reach a peak. The climax usually occurs toward the end of a story and often results in a change in the characters or a solution to the conflict.

See also Falling Action; Plot; Rising Action; Resolution.

Comedy A comedy is a dramatic work that is light and often humorous in tone, usually ending happily with a peaceful resolution of the main conflict. A comedy differs from a **farce** by having a more-believable plot, more-realistic characters, and less-boisterous behavior.

See also Drama; Farce.

Comic Relief Comic relief consists of humorous scenes, incidents, or speeches that are included in a serious drama to provide a reduction in emotional intensity. Because it breaks the tension, comic relief allows an audience to prepare emotionally for events to come.

Compare and Contrast To compare and contrast is to identify similarities and differences in two or more subjects. Compare-and-contrast organization can be used to structure a piece of writing, serving as a framework for examining the similarities and differences in two or more subjects.

Complication A complication is an additional factor or problem introduced into the rising action of a story to make the conflict more difficult. Often, a plot complication makes it seem as though the main character is getting further away from the thing he or she wants.

Conceit *See* Extended Metaphor.

Conclusion A conclusion is a statement of belief based on evidence, experience, and reasoning. A **valid conclusion** is a conclusion that logically follows from the facts or statements upon which it is based. A **deductive conclusion** is one that follows from a particular generalization or premise. An **inductive conclusion** is a broad conclusion or generalization that is reached by arguing from specific facts and examples.

Conflict A conflict is a struggle between opposing forces that is the basis of a story's plot. An **external conflict** pits a character against nature, society, or another character. An **internal conflict** is a conflict between opposing forces within a character.

See also Antagonist; Plot.

Connect Connecting is a reader's process of relating the content of a text to his or her own knowledge and experience.

Connotation Connotation is the emotional response evoked by a word, in contrast to its denotation, which is its literal meaning. *Kitten,* for example, is defined as "a young cat." However, the word also suggests, or connotes, images of softness, warmth, and playfulness.

Consonance Consonance is the repetition of consonant sounds within and at the ends of words.

> He ate most of the fruit in the kitchen yesterday.

See also Alliteration; Assonance.

Consumer Documents Consumer documents are printed materials that accompany products and services. They are intended for the buyers or users of the products or services and usually provide information about use, care, operation, or assembly. Some common consumer documents are applications, contracts, warranties, manuals, instructions, package inserts, labels, brochures, and schedules.

Context Clues When you encounter an unfamiliar word, you can often use context clues as aids for understanding. Context clues are the words and phrases surrounding the word that provide hints about the word's meaning.

Controlling Idea *See* Thesis Statement.

Counterargument A counterargument is an argument made to oppose another argument. A good argument anticipates opposing viewpoints and provides counterarguments to refute (disprove) or answer them.

Counterclaim *See* Counterargument.

Couplet *See* Sonnet.

Creation Myth *See* Myth.

Credibility *Credibility* refers to the believability or trustworthiness of a source and the information it contains.

Critical Essay *See* Essay.

Critical Review A critical review is an evaluation or critique by a reviewer or critic. Different types of reviews include film reviews, book reviews, music reviews, and art show reviews.

Cultural Hero A cultural hero is a larger-than-life figure who reflects the values of a people. Rather than being the creation of a single writer, this kind of hero evolves from the telling of folk tales from one generation to the next. The role of the cultural hero is to provide a noble image that will inspire and guide the actions of all who share that culture.

Dactyl *See* Meter.

Database A database is a collection of information that can be quickly and easily accessed and searched and from which information can be easily retrieved. It is frequently presented in an electronic format.

Debate A debate is an organized exchange of opinions on an issue. In academic settings, *debate* usually refers to a formal contest in which two opposing teams defend and attack a proposition.

See also Argument.

Deductive Reasoning Deductive reasoning is a way of thinking that begins with a generalization, presents a specific situation, and then advances with facts and evidence to a logical conclusion. The following passage has a deductive argument imbedded in it: "All students in the drama class must attend the play on Thursday. Since Ava is in the class,

she had better show up." This deductive argument can be broken down as follows: generalization—all students in the drama class must attend the play on Thursday; specific situation—Ava is a student in the drama class; conclusion—Ava must attend the play.

Denotation *See* Connotation.

Dénouement *See* Falling Action.

Description Description is writing that helps a reader to picture scenes, events, and characters. Effective description usually relies on imagery, figurative language, and precise diction.

See also Diction; Figurative Language; Imagery.

Dialect A dialect is the distinct form of a language as it is spoken in one geographical area or by a particular social or ethnic group. A group's dialect is reflected in characteristic pronunciations, vocabulary, idioms, and grammatical constructions. When trying to reproduce a given dialect, writers often use unconventional spellings to suggest the way words actually sound. Writers use dialect to establish setting, to provide local color, and to develop characters.

See also Local Color Realism.

Dialogue Dialogue is conversation between two or more characters in either fiction or nonfiction. In drama, the story is told almost exclusively through dialogue, which moves the plot forward and reveals characters' motives.

See also Drama.

Diary A diary is a writer's personal day-to-day account of his or her experiences and impressions. Most diaries are private and not intended to be shared. Some, however, have been published because they are well written and provide useful perspectives on historical events or on the everyday life of particular eras.

Diction A writer's or speaker's choice of words is called diction. Diction includes both vocabulary (individual words) and syntax (the order or arrangement of words). Diction can be formal or informal, technical or common, abstract or concrete.

Dictionary *See* Reference Works.

Drama Drama is literature in which plot and character are developed through dialogue and action; in other words, drama is literature in play form. It is performed on stage and radio and in films and television. Most plays are divided into acts, with each act having an emotional peak, or climax, of its own. The acts sometimes are divided into scenes; each scene is limited to a single time and place. Most contemporary plays have two or three acts, although some have only one act.

See also **Act; Dialogue; Scene; Stage Directions.**

Dramatic Irony *See* **Irony.**

Dramatic Monologue A dramatic monologue is a lyric poem in which a speaker addresses a silent or absent listener in a moment of high intensity or deep emotion, as if engaged in private conversation. The speaker proceeds without interruption or argument, and the effect on the reader is that of hearing just one side of a conversation. This technique allows the poet to focus on the feelings, personality, and motivations of the speaker.

See also **Lyric Poetry; Soliloquy.**

Draw Conclusions To draw a conclusion is to make a judgment or arrive at a belief based on evidence, experience, and reasoning.

Dynamic Character *See* **Character.**

Editorial An editorial is an opinion piece that usually appears on the editorial page of a newspaper or as part of a news broadcast. The editorial section of a newspaper presents opinions rather than objective news reports.

See also **Op-Ed Piece.**

Either/Or Fallacy An either/or fallacy is a statement that suggests that there are only two possible ways to view a situation or only two options to choose from. In other words, it is a statement that falsely frames a dilemma, giving the impression that no options exist but the two presented—for example, "Either we stop the construction of a new airport, or the surrounding suburbs will become ghost towns."

Elegy An elegy is a poem written in tribute to a person, usually someone who has died recently. The tone of an elegy is usually formal and dignified.

Emotional Appeals Emotional appeals are messages that evoke strong feelings—such as fear, pity, or vanity—in order to persuade instead of using facts and evidence to make a point. An **appeal to fear** is a message that taps into people's fear of losing their safety or security. An **appeal to pity** is a message that taps into people's sympathy and compassion for others to build support for an idea, a cause, or a proposed action. An **appeal to vanity** is a message that attempts to persuade by tapping into people's desire to feel good about themselves.

Encyclopedia *See* **Reference Works.**

Epic An epic is a long narrative poem on a serious subject presented in an elevated or formal style. An epic traces the adventures of a hero whose actions consist of courageous, even superhuman, deeds, which often represent the ideals and values of a nation or race. Epics typically address universal issues, such as good and evil, life and death, and sin and redemption. Homer's *Iliad* and *Odyssey* are famous epics from western civilization. The *Ramayana* is an epic from India.

Epic Hero An epic hero is a larger-than-life figure who embodies the ideals of a nation or race. Epic heroes take part in dangerous adventures and accomplish great deeds. Many undertake long, difficult journeys and display great courage and superhuman strength.

Epithet An epithet is a brief descriptive phrase that points out traits associated with a particular person or thing.

Essay An essay is a short work of nonfiction that deals with a single subject. Essays are often informal, loosely structured, and highly personal. They can be descriptive, informative, persuasive, narrative, or any combination of these.

An **autobiographical essay** focuses on an aspect of a writer's life. Generally, writers of autobiographical essays use the first-person point of view, combining objective description with the expression of subjective feelings.

Ethical Appeals Ethical appeals establish a writer's credibility and trustworthiness with an audience. When a writer links a claim to a widely accepted value, for example, the writer not only gains moral support for that claim but also establishes a connection with readers.

Evaluate To evaluate is to examine something carefully and judge its value or worth. Evaluating is an important skill for gaining insight into what you read. A reader can evaluate the actions of a particular character, for example, or can form an opinion about the value of an entire work.

Evidence Evidence is the specific pieces of information that support a claim. Evidence can take the form of facts, quotations, examples, statistics, or personal experiences, among others.

Exaggeration *See* Hyperbole.

Experimental Poetry Poetry described as experimental is often full of surprises—unusual word order, invented forms, descriptions of ordinary objects, and other distinctive elements not found in traditional verse forms. William Carlos Williams belonged to a group of experimental poets known as the Imagists. Their poems contain sharp, clear images of striking beauty, similar to the ones found in haiku.

Exposition Exposition is the part of a literary work that provides the background information necessary to understand characters and their actions. Typically found at the beginning of a work, the exposition introduces the characters, describes the setting, and summarizes significant events that took place before the action begins.

See also Plot; Rising Action.

Expository Essay *See* Essay.

Extended Metaphor Like any metaphor, an extended metaphor is a comparison between two essentially unlike things that nevertheless have something in common. It does not contain the word *like* or *as*. An extended metaphor compares two things at some length and in various ways. Sometimes the comparison is carried throughout a paragraph, a stanza, or an entire selection.

Like an extended metaphor, a **conceit** compares two apparently dissimilar things in several ways. The term usually implies a more elaborate, formal, and ingeniously clever comparison than the extended metaphor.

External Conflict *See* Conflict.

Eyewitness Account An eyewitness account is a firsthand report of an event written by someone who directly observed it or participated in it. As such, an eyewitness account is a primary source. Narrated from the first-person point of view, eyewitness accounts almost always include the following:

- objective facts about an event
- a chronological (time-order) pattern of organization
- vivid sensory details
- quotations from people who were present
- description of the writer's feelings and interpretations.

See also Primary Source.

Fable A fable is a brief tale that illustrates a clear, often directly stated, moral, or lesson. The characters in a fable are usually animals, but sometimes they are humans. The best-known fables—for example, "The Fox and the Crow" and "The Tortoise and the Hare" —are those of Aesop, a Greek slave who lived about 600 BC. Traditionally, fables are handed down from generation to generation as oral literature.

See also Oral Literature.

Fact versus Opinion A **fact** is a statement that can be proved or verified. An **opinion,** on the other hand, is a statement that cannot be proved because it expresses a person's beliefs, feelings, or thoughts.

See also Inference; Generalization.

Falling Action In a plot structure, the falling action, or resolution, occurs after the climax to reveal the final outcome of events and to tie up any loose ends.

See also Climax; Exposition; Plot; Rising Action.

Farce A farce is a type of exaggerated comedy that features an absurd plot, ridiculous situations, and humorous dialogue. The main purpose of a farce is to keep an audience laughing. The characters are usually **stereotypes,** or simplified examples of different traits or qualities. Comic devices typically used in farces include mistaken identity, deception, wordplay—such as puns and double meanings—and exaggeration.

See also Comedy; Stereotype.

Faulty Reasoning *See* Logical Fallacy.

Feature Article A feature article is a main article in a newspaper or a cover story in a magazine. A feature article is focused more on entertaining than informing. Features are lighter or more general than hard news and tend to be about human interest or lifestyles.

Fiction Fiction refers to works of prose that contain imaginary elements. Although fiction, like nonfiction, may be based on actual events and real people, it differs from nonfiction in that it is shaped primarily by the writer's imagination. The two major types of fiction are novels and short stories. The four basic elements of a work of fiction are character, setting, plot, and theme.

See also Novel; Short Story.

Figurative Language Figurative language is language that communicates ideas beyond the literal meaning of words. Figurative language can make descriptions and unfamiliar or difficult ideas easier to understand. The most common types of figurative language, called **figures of speech,** are **simile, metaphor, personification,** and **hyperbole**.

See also Hyperbole; Metaphor; Personification; Simile.

Figures of Speech *See* Figurative Language.

First-Person Point of View *See* Point of View.

Flashback A flashback is a scene that interrupts the action of a narrative to describe events that took place at an earlier time. It provides background helpful in understanding a character's present situation.

Foil A foil is a character whose traits contrast with those of another character. A writer might use a minor character as a foil to emphasize the positive traits of the main character.

See also Character.

Folk Tale A folk tale is a short, simple story that is handed down, usually by word of mouth, from generation to generation. Folk tales include legends, fairy tales, myths, and fables. Folk tales often teach family obligations or societal values.

See also Legend; Myth; Fable.

Foot *See* Meter.

Foreshadowing Foreshadowing is a writer's use of hints or clues to indicate events that will occur in a story. Foreshadowing creates suspense and at the same time prepares the reader for what is to come.

Form At its simplest, form refers to the physical arrangement of words in a poem—the length and placement of the lines and the grouping of lines into stanzas. The term can also be used to refer to other types of patterning in poetry—anything from rhythm and other sound patterns to the design of a traditional poetic type, such as a sonnet or dramatic monologue.

See also Genre; Stanza.

Frame Story A frame story exists when a story is told within a narrative setting, or "frame"; it creates a story within a story. This storytelling method has been used for over one thousand years and was employed in famous works such as *One Thousand and One Arabian Nights* and Geoffrey Chaucer's *The Canterbury Tales.*

Free Verse Free verse is poetry that does not have regular patterns of rhyme and meter. The lines in free verse often flow more naturally than do rhymed, metrical lines and thus achieve a rhythm more like that of everyday human speech. Walt Whitman is generally credited with bringing free verse to American poetry.

See also Meter; Rhyme.

Functional Documents *See* Consumer Documents; Workplace Documents.

Generalization A generalization is a broad statement about a class or category of people, ideas, or things, based on a study of only some of its members.

See also Overgeneralization.

General Principle In an argument, a general principle is an assumption that links the support to the claim. If one does not accept the general principle as a truth, then the support is inadequate because it is beside the point.

Genre Genre refers to the distinct types into which literary works can be grouped. The four main literary genres are fiction, poetry, nonfiction, and drama.

Gothic Literature Gothic literature is characterized by grotesque characters, bizarre situations, and violent events. Originating in Europe, gothic literature was a popular form of writing in the United States during the 19th century, especially in the hands of such notables as Edgar Allan Poe and Nathaniel Hawthorne. Interest in the gothic revived in the 20th century among southern writers such as William Faulkner and Flannery O'Connor.

Government Publications Government publications are documents produced by government organizations. Pamphlets, brochures, and reports are just some of the many forms these publications may take. Government publications can be good resources for a wide variety of topics.

Graphic Aid A graphic aid is a visual tool that is printed, handwritten, or drawn. Charts, diagrams, graphs, photographs, and maps can all be graphic aids.

Graphic Organizer A graphic organizer is a visual illustration of a verbal statement that helps a reader understand a text. Charts, tables, webs, and diagrams can all be graphic organizers. Graphic organizers and graphic aids can look the same. However, graphic organizers and graphic aids do differ in how they are used. Graphic aids are the visual representations that people encounter when they read informational texts. Graphic organizers are visuals that people construct to help them understand texts or organize information.

Haiku Haiku is a form of Japanese poetry in which 17 syllables are arranged in three lines of 5, 7, and 5 syllables. The rules of haiku are strict. In addition to the syllabic count, the poet must create a clear picture that will evoke a strong emotional response in the reader. Nature is a particularly important source of inspiration for Japanese haiku poets, and details from nature are often the subjects of their poems.

Hero *See* Cultural Hero; Tragic Hero.

Historical Context The historical context of a literary work refers to the social conditions that inspired or influenced its creation. To understand and appreciate some works, the reader must relate them to particular events in history. For example, to understand fully Lincoln's "Gettysburg Address," the reader must imaginatively re-create the scene—Lincoln addressing a war-weary crowd on the very site where a horrific battle had recently been fought.

Historical Documents Historical documents are writings that have played a significant role in human events or are themselves records of such events. The Declaration of Independence, for example, is a historical document.

Historical Narratives Historical narratives are accounts of real-life historical experiences, given either by a person who experienced those events or by someone who has studied or observed them.

See also Primary Sources; Secondary Sources.

Horror Fiction Horror fiction contains strange, mysterious, violent, and often supernatural events that create suspense and terror in the reader. Edgar Allan Poe is an author famous for his horror fiction.

How-To Book A how-to book is a book that is written to explain how to do something— usually an activity, a sport, or a household project.

Humor Humor is a term applied to a literary work whose purpose is to entertain and to evoke laughter. In literature, there are three basic types of humor, all of which may involve exaggeration or irony. **Humor of situation,** which is derived from the plot of a work, usually involves exaggerated events or situational irony. **Humor of character** is often based on exaggerated personalities or on characters who fail to recognize their own flaws, a form of dramatic irony. **Humor of language** may include sarcasm, exaggeration, puns, or verbal irony, which occurs when what is said is not what is meant.

See also Comedy; Farce; Irony.

Hyperbole Hyperbole is a figure of speech in which the truth is exaggerated for emphasis or for humorous effect. The expression "I'm so hungry I could eat a horse" is hyperbole.

See also Understatement.

Iamb *See* Meter.

Iambic Pentameter Iambic pentameter is a metrical pattern of five feet, or units, each of which is made up of two syllables, the first unstressed and the second stressed. Iambic pentameter is the most common meter used in English poetry; it is the meter used in blank verse and in the sonnet.

See also Blank Verse; Meter; Sonnet.

Idiom An idiom is a common figure of speech whose meaning is different from the literal meaning of its words. For example, the phrase "raining cats and dogs" does not literally mean that cats and dogs are falling from the sky; the expression means "raining heavily."

Imagery The descriptive words and phrases that a writer uses to re-create sensory experiences are called imagery. By appealing to the five senses, imagery helps a reader imagine exactly what the characters and experiences being described are like.

The term *synesthesia* refers to imagery that appeals to one sense when another is being stimulated.

See also Description; Kinesthetic Imagery.

Imagists *See* Experimental Poetry; Style.

Implied Main Idea *See* Main Idea.

Index The index of a book is an alphabetized list of important topics and details covered in the book and the page numbers on which they can be found. An index can be used to quickly find specific information about a topic.

Inductive Reasoning Inductive reasoning is the process of logical reasoning from observations, examples, and facts to a general conclusion or principle.

Inference An inference is a logical assumption that is based on observed facts and one's own knowledge and experience.

Informational Text Informational text is a category of writing that includes exposition, argument, and functional documents. These texts normally provide factual, historical, or technical information. However, the term also covers texts that make logical or emotional arguments in defense of a position. Examples include biographies, journalism, essays, narrative histories, instruction manuals, and speeches.

Interior Monologue *See* Monologue; Stream of Consciousness.

Internal Conflict *See* Conflict.

Interview An interview is a conversation conducted by a writer or reporter in which facts or statements are elicited from another person, recorded, and then broadcast or published.

Inverted Syntax Inverted syntax is a reversal in the expected order of words.

Irony Irony refers to a contrast between appearance and reality. **Situational irony** is a contrast between what is expected to happen and what actually does happen. **Dramatic irony** occurs when readers know more about a situation or a character in a story than the characters do. **Verbal irony** occurs when someone states one thing and means another.

Journal A journal is a periodical publication issued by a legal, medical, or other professional organization. Alternatively, the term may be used to refer to a diary or daily record.

See also Diary.

Kinesthetic Imagery Kinesthetic imagery re-creates the tension felt through muscles, tendons, or joints in the body.

See also Imagery.

Legend A legend is a story passed down orally from generation to generation and popularly believed to have a historical basis. While some legends may be based on real people or situations, most of the events are either greatly exaggerated or fictitious. Like myths, legends may incorporate supernatural elements and magical deeds. But legends differ from myths in that they claim to be stories about real human beings and are often set in a particular time and place.

Limited Point of View *See* Point of View.

Line The line is the core unit of a poem. In poetry, line length is an essential element of the poem's meaning and rhythm. There are a variety of terms to describe the way a line of poetry ends or is connected to the next line. Line breaks, where a line of poetry ends, may coincide with grammatical units. However, a line break may also occur in the middle of a grammatical or syntactical unit, creating pauses or emphasis. Poets use a variety of line breaks to play with meaning, thus creating a wide range of effects.

Literary Criticism Literary criticism refers to writing that focuses on a literary work or a genre, describing some aspect of it, such as its origin, its characteristics, or its effects.

Literary Letter A literary letter is a letter that has been published and read by a wider audience because it was written by a well-known public figure or provides information about the period in which it was written.

Literary Nonfiction Literary nonfiction is informational text that is recognized as being of artistic value or that is about literature. Autobiographies, biographies, essays, and eloquent speeches typically fall into this category.

Loaded Language Loaded language consists of words with strongly positive or negative connotations intended to influence a reader's or listener's attitude.

Local Color Realism Local color realism, especially popular in the late 18th century, is a style of writing that truthfully imitates ordinary life and brings a particular region alive by portraying the dialects, dress, mannerisms, customs, character types, and landscapes of that region. Mark Twain frequently uses local color realism in his writing for humorous effect.

See also Dialect.

Logical Appeal A logical appeal relies on logic and facts, appealing to people's reasoning or intellect rather than to their values or emotions. Flawed logical appeals—that is, errors in reasoning—are considered logical fallacies.

See also Logical Fallacy.

Logical Argument A logical argument is an argument in which the logical relationship between the support and the claim is sound.

Logical Fallacy A fallacy is an error in reasoning. Typically, a fallacy is based on an incorrect inference or a misuse of evidence. Some common logical fallacies are **circular logic, either/or fallacy, oversimplification, overgeneralization,** and **stereotyping.**

See also Either/Or Fallacy; Logical Appeal; Overgeneralization.

Lyric Poem A lyric poem is a short poem in which a single speaker expresses thoughts and feelings. In a love lyric, a speaker expresses romantic love. In other lyrics, a speaker may meditate on nature or seek to resolve an emotional crisis.

Magical Realism Magical realism is a style of writing that often includes exaggeration, unusual humor, magical and bizarre events, dreams that come true, and superstitions that prove warranted. Magical realism differs from pure fantasy in combining fantastic elements with realistic elements such as recognizable characters, believable dialogue, a true-to-life setting, a matter-of-fact tone, and a plot that sometimes contains historic events. This style characterizes some of the fiction of such influential South American writers as the late Jorge Luis Borges of Argentina and Gabriel García Márquez of Colombia.

Main Character *See* Character.

Main Idea A main idea is the central or most important idea about a topic that a writer or speaker conveys. It can be the central idea of an entire work or of just a paragraph. Often, the main idea of a paragraph is expressed in a topic sentence. However, a main idea may just be implied, or suggested, by details. A main idea and supporting details can serve as a basic pattern of organization in a piece of writing, with the central idea about a topic being supported by details.

Make Inferences *See* Inference.

Memoir A memoir is a form of autobiographical writing in which a person recalls significant events and people in his or her life. Most memoirs share the following characteristics: (1) they usually are structured as narratives told by the writers themselves, using the first-person point of view; (2) although some names may be changed to protect privacy, memoirs are true accounts of actual events; (3) although basically personal, memoirs may deal with newsworthy events having a significance beyond the confines of the writer's life; (4) unlike strictly historical accounts, memoirs often include the writers' feelings and opinions about historical events, giving the reader insight into the impact of history on people's lives.

Metaphor A metaphor is a figure of speech that compares two things that have something in common. Unlike similes, metaphors do not use the words *like* or *as* but make comparisons directly.

See also Extended Metaphor; Figurative Language; Simile.

Meter Meter is the repetition of a regular rhythmic unit in a line of poetry. Each unit, known as a **foot,** has one stressed syllable (indicated by a ´) and either one or two unstressed syllables (indicated by a ˘). The four basic types of metrical feet are the **iamb,** an unstressed syllable followed by a stressed syllable; the **trochee,** a stressed syllable followed by an unstressed syllable; the **anapest,** two unstressed syllables followed by a stressed syllable; and the **dactyl,** a stressed syllable followed by two unstressed syllables.

Two words are typically used to describe the meter of a line. The first word identifies the type of metrical foot—iambic, trochaic, anapestic, or dactylic—and the second word indicates the number of feet in a line: **monometer** (one foot), **dimeter** (two feet), **trimeter** (three feet), **tetrameter** (four feet), **pentameter** (five feet), **hexameter** (six feet), and so forth.

See also Rhythm; Scansion.

Minor Character *See* Character.

Mise en Scène *Mise en scène* is a term from the French that refers to the various physical aspects of a dramatic presentation, such as lighting, costumes, scenery, makeup, and props.

Modernism Modernism was a literary movement that roughly spanned the time period between the two world wars, 1914–1945. Modernist works are characterized by a high degree of experimentation and spare, elliptical prose. Modernist characters are most often alienated people searching unsuccessfully for meaning and love in their lives.

Monitor Monitoring is the strategy of checking your comprehension as you are reading and modifying the strategies you are using to suit your needs. Monitoring may include some or all of the following strategies: **questioning, clarifying, visualizing, predicting, connecting,** and **rereading.**

Monologue In a drama, the speech of a character who is alone on stage, voicing his or her thoughts, is known as a monologue. In a short story or a poem, the direct presentation of a character's unspoken thoughts is called an **interior monologue.** An interior monologue may jump back and forth between past and present, displaying thoughts, memories, and impressions just as they might occur in a person's mind.

See also Stream of Consciousness.

Mood Mood is the feeling or atmosphere that a writer creates for the reader. The writer's use of connotation, imagery, figurative language, sound and rhythm, and descriptive details all contribute to the mood.

See also Connotation; Description; Diction; Figurative Language; Imagery; Style.

Moral *See* Fable.

Motivation Motivation is the stated or implied reason behind a character's behavior. The grounds for a character's actions may not be obvious, but they should be comprehensible and consistent, in keeping with the character as developed by the writer.

See also Character.

Myth A myth is a traditional story, passed down through generations, that explains why the world is the way it is. Myths are essentially religious because they present supernatural events and beings and articulate the values and beliefs of a cultural group. A **creation myth** is a particular kind of myth that explains how the universe, the earth, and life on earth began.

Narrative A narrative is any type of writing that is primarily concerned with relating an event or a series of events. A narrative can be imaginary, as is a short story or novel, or factual, as is a newspaper account or a work of history. The word *narration* can be used interchangeably with *narrative,* which comes from the Latin word meaning "tell."

See also Fiction; Nonfiction; Novel; Plot; Short Story.

Narrative Poem A narrative poem is a poem that tells a story using elements of character, setting, and plot to develop a theme.

See also Ballad.

Narrator The narrator of a story is the character or voice that relates the story's events to the reader.

Naturalism An offshoot of realism, naturalism was a literary movement that originated in France in the late 1800s. Like the realists, the naturalists sought to render common people and ordinary life accurately. However, the naturalists emphasized how instinct and environment affect human behavior. Strongly influenced by Charles Darwin's ideas, the naturalists believed that the fate of humans is determined by forces beyond individual control.

News Article A news article is a piece of writing that reports on a recent event. In newspapers, news articles are usually written in a concise manner to report the latest news, presenting the most important facts first and then more detailed information. In magazines, news articles are usually more elaborate than those in newspapers because they are written to provide both information and analysis. Also, news articles in magazines do not necessarily present the most important facts first.

Nonfiction Nonfiction, or informational text, is writing about real people, places, and events. Unlike fiction, nonfiction is largely concerned with factual information, although the writer shapes the information according to his or her purpose and viewpoint. Biography, autobiography, and newspaper articles are examples of nonfiction.

See also Autobiography; Biography; Essay.

Novel A novel is an extended work of fiction. Like the short story, a novel is essentially the product of a writer's imagination. The most obvious difference between a novel and a short story is length. Because the novel is considerably longer, a novelist can develop a wider range of characters and a more complex plot.

Novella A novella is a work of fiction that is longer than a short story but shorter than a novel. A novella differs from a novel in that it concentrates on a limited cast of characters, a relatively short time span, and a single chain of events. The novella is an attempt to combine the compression of the short story with the development of a novel.

Octave *See* Sonnet.

Ode An ode is a complex lyric poem that develops a serious and dignified theme. Odes appeal to both the imagination and the intellect, and many commemorate events or praise people or elements of nature.

Off Rhyme *See* Slant Rhyme.

Omniscient Point of View *See* Point of View.

Onomatopoeia The word *onomatopoeia* literally means "name-making." It is the process of creating or using words that imitate sounds. The *buzz* of the bee, the *honk* of the car horn, the *peep* of the chick are all onomatopoetic, or echoic, words.

Onomatopoeia as a literary technique goes beyond the use of simple echoic words. Writers, particularly poets, choose words whose sounds suggest their denotative and connotative meanings: for example, *whisper, kick, gargle, gnash,* and *clatter.*

Op-Ed Piece An op-ed piece is an opinion piece that usually appears opposite ("op") the editorial page of a newspaper. Unlike editorials, op-ed pieces are written and submitted by named writers.

Open Letter An open letter is addressed to a specific person but published for a wider readership.

Oral Literature Oral literature is literature that is passed from one generation to another by performance or word of mouth. Folk tales, fables, myths, chants, and legends are part of the oral tradition of cultures throughout the world.

See also **Fable; Folk Tale; Legend; Myth.**

Organization *See* **Pattern of Organization.**

Overgeneralization An overgeneralization is a generalization that is too broad. You can often recognize overgeneralizations by the appearance of words and phrases such as *all, everyone, every time, any, anything, no one,* and *none.* Consider, for example, this statement: "None of the sanitation workers in our city really care about keeping the environment clean." In all probability, there are many exceptions. The writer can't possibly know the feelings of every sanitation worker in the city.

Overstatement *See* Hyperbole.

Overview An overview is a short summary of a story, a speech, or an essay. It orients the reader by providing a preview of the text to come.

Oxymoron An oxymoron is a special kind of concise paradox that brings together two contradictory terms, such as "venomous love" or "sweet bitterness."

Parable A parable is a brief story that is meant to teach a lesson or illustrate a moral truth. A parable is more than a simple story, however. Each detail of the parable corresponds to some aspect of the problem or moral dilemma to which it is directed. The story of the prodigal son in the Bible is a classic parable. In *Walden,* Thoreau's parable of the strong and beautiful bug that emerges from an old table is meant to show that, similarly, new life can awaken in human beings despite the deadness of society.

Paradox A paradox is a statement that seems to contradict itself but may nevertheless suggest an important truth.

A special kind of paradox is the oxymoron, which brings together two contradictory terms, as in the phrases "wise fool" and "feather of lead."

Parallelism Parallelism is the use of similar grammatical constructions to express ideas that are related or equal in importance.

Parallel Plot A parallel plot is a particular type of plot in which two stories of equal importance are told simultaneously. The story moves back and forth between the two plots.

Paraphrase Paraphrasing is the restating of information in one's own words.

See also **Summarize.**

Parody Parody is writing that imitates either the style or the subject matter of a literary work for the purpose of criticism, humorous effect, or flattering tribute.

Pattern of Organization A pattern of organization is a particular arrangement of ideas and information. Such a pattern may be used to organize an entire composition or a single paragraph within a longer work. The following are the most common organizational patterns: **cause-and-effect, chronological order, compare-and-contrast, classification, deductive, inductive, order of importance, problem-solution, sequential,** and **spatial.**

See also **Cause and Effect; Chronological Order; Classification; Compare and Contrast; Problem-Solution Order; Sequential Order.**

Periodical A periodical is a publication that is issued at regular intervals of more than one day. For example, a periodical may be a weekly, monthly, or quarterly journal or magazine. Newspapers and other daily publications generally are not classified as periodicals.

Persona *See* Speaker.

Personal Essay *See* Essay.

Personification Personification is a figure of speech in which an object, animal, or idea is given human characteristics.

> **Example:** In Emily Dickinson's poem "Because I could not stop for Death," death is personified as a gentleman of kindness and civility.

Persuasion Persuasion is the art of swaying others' feelings, beliefs, or actions. Persuasion normally appeals to both the intellect and the emotions of readers. **Persuasive techniques** are the methods used to influence others to adopt certain opinions or beliefs or to act in certain ways. Types of persuasive techniques include emotional appeals, ethical appeals, logical appeals, and loaded language. When used properly, persuasive techniques can add depth to writing that's meant to persuade. Persuasive techniques can, however, be misused to cloud factual information, disguise poor reasoning, or unfairly exploit people's emotions in order to shape their opinions.

See also **Appeals by Association; Appeal to Authority; Emotional Appeals; Ethical Appeals; Loaded Language; Logical Appeal.**

Persuasive Writing Persuasive writing is intended to convince a reader to adopt a particular opinion or to perform a certain action. Effective persuasion usually appeals to both the reason and the emotions of an audience.

Petrarchan Sonnet *See* **Sonnet.**

Plot The plot is the sequence of actions and events in a literary work. Generally, plots are built around a **conflict**—a problem or struggle between two or more opposing forces. Plots usually progress through stages: exposition, rising action, climax, and falling action.

The **exposition** provides important background information and introduces the setting, characters, and conflict. During the **rising action,** the conflict becomes more intense and suspense builds as the main characters struggle to resolve their problem. The **climax** is the turning point in the plot when the outcome of the conflict becomes clear, usually resulting in a change in the characters or a solution to the conflict. After the climax, the **falling action** occurs and shows the effects of the climax. As the falling action begins, the suspense is over but the results of the decision or action that caused the climax are not yet fully worked out. The **resolution**, which often blends with the falling action, reveals the final outcome of events and ties up loose ends.

See also **Climax; Conflict; Exposition; Falling Action; Rising Action.**

Poetry Poetry is language arranged in lines. Like other forms of literature, poetry attempts to re-create emotions and experiences. Poetry, however, is usually more condensed and suggestive than prose.

Poems often are divided into stanzas, or paragraph-like groups of lines. The stanzas in a poem may contain the same number of lines or may vary in length. Some poems have definite patterns of meter and rhyme. Others rely more on the sounds of words and less on fixed rhythms and rhyme schemes. The use of figurative language is also common in poetry.

The form and content of a poem combine to convey meaning. The way that a poem is arranged on the page, the impact of the images, the sounds of the words and phrases, and all the other details that make up a poem work together to help the reader grasp its central idea.

See also **Experimental Poetry; Form; Free Verse; Meter; Rhyme; Rhythm; Stanza.**

Point of View Point of view refers to the narrative perspective from which events in a story or novel are told. In the **first-person point of view,** the narrator is a character in the work who tells everything in his or her own words and uses the pronouns *I, me,* and *my.* In the **third-person point of view,** events are related by a voice outside the action, not by one of the characters. A third-person narrator uses pronouns such as *he, she,* and *they.* In the **third-person omniscient point of view,** the narrator is an all-knowing, objective observer who stands outside the action and reports what different characters are thinking. In the **third-person limited point of view,** the narrator stands outside the action and focuses on one character's thoughts, observations, and feelings.

In the **second-person point of view,** rarely used, the narrator addresses the reader intimately as *you.*

Predict Predicting is a reading strategy that involves using text clues to make a reasonable guess about what will happen next in a story.

Primary Sources Materials written or created by people who were present at events are called primary sources. Letters, diaries, speeches, autobiographies, and photographs are examples of primary sources, as are certain narrative accounts written by actual participants or observers.

See also **Secondary Sources; Sources.**

Prior Knowledge Prior knowledge is the knowledge a reader already possesses about a topic. This information might come from personal experiences, expert accounts, books, films, or other sources.

Problem-Solution Order Problem-solution order is a pattern of organization in which a problem is stated and analyzed and then one or more solutions are proposed and examined. Writers use words and phrases such as *propose, conclude, reason for, problem, answer,* and *solution* to connect ideas and details when writing about problems and solutions.

Procedural Documents *See* Consumer Documents.

Prologue A prologue is an introductory scene in a drama.

Prop Prop, an abbreviation of *property,* refers to a physical object that is used in a stage production. In Arthur Miller's *The Crucible,* an important prop is the small rag doll that Mary Warren brings from the court and gives to Elizabeth Proctor.

Propaganda Propaganda is a form of communication that may use distorted, false, or misleading information. It usually refers to manipulative political discourse.

Prose Generally, *prose* refers to all forms of written or spoken expression that are not in verse. The term, therefore, may be used to describe very different forms of writing—short stories as well as essays, for example.

Protagonist The protagonist is the main character in a work of literature, who is involved in the central conflict of the story. Usually, the protagonist changes after the central conflict reaches a climax. He or she may be a hero and is usually the one with whom the audience tends to identify.

See also Antagonist; Character; Tragic Hero.

Public Documents Public documents are documents that were written for the public to provide information that is of public interest or concern. They include government documents, speeches, signs, and rules and regulations.

See also Government Publications.

Purpose *See* Author's Purpose.

Quatrain A quatrain is a four-line stanza.

See also Poetry; Stanza.

Realism As a general term, *realism* refers to any effort to offer an accurate and detailed portrayal of actual life. Thus, critics talk about Shakespeare's realistic portrayals of his characters and praise the medieval poet Chaucer for his realistic descriptions of people from different social classes.

More specifically, realism refers to a literary method developed in the 19th century. The realists based their writing on careful observations of contemporary life, often focusing on the middle or lower classes. They attempted to present life objectively and honestly, without the sentimentality or idealism that had colored earlier literature. Typically, realists developed their settings in great detail in an effort to recreate a specific time and place for the reader. Kate Chopin and Mark Twain are considered realists.

See also Local-Color Realism; Naturalism.

Recurring Theme *See* Theme.

Reference Works General reference works are sources that contain facts and background information on a wide range of subjects. More specific reference works contain in-depth information on a single subject. Most reference works are good sources of reliable information because they have been reviewed by experts. The following are some common reference works: **encyclopedias, dictionaries, thesauri, almanacs, atlases, chronologies, biographical dictionaries,** and **directories.**

Reflective Essay *See* Essay.

Refrain In poetry, a refrain is part of a stanza, consisting of one or more lines that are repeated regularly, sometimes with changes, often at the ends of succeeding stanzas. Refrains are often found in ballads.

Regionalism Regionalism is a literary movement that arose from an effort to accurately represent the speech, manners, habits, history, folklore, and beliefs of people in specific geographic areas.

Repetition Repetition is a technique in which a sound, word, phrase, or line is repeated for emphasis or unity. Repetition often helps to reinforce meaning and create an appealing rhythm. The term includes specific devices associated with both prose and poetry, such as **alliteration** and **parallelism.**

See also **Alliteration; Parallelism; Sound Devices.**

Resolution *See* Falling Action.

Review *See* Critical Review.

Rhetorical Devices *See* Analogy; Repetition; Rhetorical Questions.

Rhetorical Questions Rhetorical questions are those that do not require a reply. Writers use them to suggest that their arguments make the answer obvious or self-evident.

Rhyme Rhyme is the occurrence of similar or identical sounds at the end of two or more words, such as *suite, heat,* and *complete.* Rhyme that occurs within a single line of poetry is called **internal rhyme.**

When rhyme comes at the end of a line of poetry, it is called **end rhyme.** The pattern of end rhyme in a poem is called the **rhyme scheme** and is charted by assigning a letter, beginning with the letter *a,* to each line. Lines that rhyme are given the same letter.

See also **Slant Rhyme.**

Rhyme Scheme *See* Rhyme.

Rhythm Rhythm refers to the pattern or flow of sound created by the arrangement of stressed and unstressed syllables, particularly in poetry. Some poems follow a regular pattern, or **meter,** of accented and unaccented syllables. Poets use rhythm to bring out the musical quality of language, to emphasize ideas, to create mood, and to reinforce subject matter.

See also **Meter.**

Rising Action Rising action is the stage of a plot in which the conflict develops and story events build toward a climax. During this stage, complications arise that make the conflict more intense. Tension grows as the characters struggle to resolve the conflict.

See also **Plot.**

Romanticism Romanticism was a movement in the arts that flourished in Europe and America throughout much of the 19th century. Romantic writers glorified nature and celebrated individuality. Their treatment of subjects was emotional rather than rational, intuitive rather than analytic.

Sarcasm Sarcasm, a type of verbal irony, refers to a critical remark expressed in a statement in which literal meaning is the opposite of actual meaning. Sarcasm is mocking, and its intention is to hurt.

See also **Irony.**

Satire Satire is a literary technique in which foolish ideas or customs are ridiculed for the purpose of improving society. Satire may be gently witty, mildly abrasive, or bitterly critical. Short stories, poems, novels, essays, and plays all may be vehicles for satire.

Scanning Scanning is the process of searching through writing for a particular fact or piece of information. When you scan, your eyes sweep across a page, looking for key words that may lead you to the information you want.

Scansion The process of determining meter is known as scansion. When you scan a line of poetry, you mark its stressed (´) and unstressed syllables (˘) in order to identify the rhythm.

See also **Meter.**

Scene In drama, a scene is a subdivision of an act. Each scene usually establishes a different time or place.

See also **Act; Drama.**

Scenery Scenery is a painted backdrop or other structures used to create the setting for a play.

Science Fiction Science fiction is prose writing that presents the possibilities of the past or the future, using known scientific data and theories as well as the creative imagination of the writer. Most science fiction comments on present-day society through the writer's fictional conception of a past or future society. Ray Bradbury and Kurt Vonnegut Jr. are two popular writers of science fiction.

Screenplay A screenplay is a script written for film.

Script The text of a play, film, or broadcast is called a script.

Secondary Sources Accounts written by people who were not directly involved in or witnesses to an event are called secondary sources. A history textbook is an example of a secondary source.

See also **Primary Sources; Sources.**

Sensory Details Sensory details are words and phrases that appeal to the reader's senses of sight, hearing, touch, taste, and smell. For example, the sensory detail "a fine film of rain" appeals to the senses of sight and touch. Sensory details stimulate the reader to create images in his or her mind.

See also **Imagery.**

Sequential Order A pattern of organization that shows the order in which events or actions occur is called sequential order. Writers typically use this pattern of organization to explain steps or stages in a process.

Sermon A sermon is a form of religious persuasion in which a speaker exhorts the audience to behave in a more spiritual and moral fashion.

Sestet *See* **Sonnet.**

Setting The setting of a literary work refers to the time and place in which the action occurs. A story can be set in an imaginary place, such as an enchanted castle, or a real place, such as New York City or Tombstone, Arizona. The time can be the past, the present, or the future. In addition to time and place, setting can include the larger historical and cultural contexts that form the background for a narrative. Setting is one of the main elements in fiction and often plays an important role in what happens and why.

Setting a Purpose The process of establishing specific reasons for reading a text is called setting a purpose.

Short Story A short story is a work of fiction that centers on a single idea and can be read in one sitting. Generally, a short story has one main conflict that involves the characters, keeps the story moving, and stimulates readers' interest.

See also **Fiction.**

Sidebar A sidebar is additional information set in a box alongside or within a news or feature article. Popular magazines often make use of sidebar information.

Signal Words Signal words are words and phrases that indicate what is to come in a text. Readers can use signal words to discover a text's pattern of organization and to analyze the relationships among the ideas in the text.

Simile A simile is a figure of speech that compares two things that have something in common, using a word such as *like* or *as*.

See also **Figurative Language; Metaphor.**

Situational Irony *See* **Irony.**

Slant Rhyme Rhyme that is not exact but only approximate is known as slant rhyme, or **off rhyme.**

See also **Rhyme.**

Slave Narrative A slave narrative is an autobiographical account written by someone who endured the miseries of slavery. These writers often use sensory details to re-create their experiences.

See also **Autobiography.**

Soliloquy *See* **Monologue.**

Sonnet A sonnet is a 14-line lyric poem, commonly written in iambic pentameter. The **Petrarchan sonnet** consists of two parts. The first eight lines, called the octave, usually have the rhyme scheme *abbaabba*. In the last six lines, called the sestet, the rhyme scheme may be *cdecde, cdcdcd,* or another variation. The **octave** generally presents a problem or raises a question, and the *sestet* resolves or comments on the problem. A **Shakespearean sonnet** is divided into three **quatrains** (groups of four lines) and a **couplet** (two rhyming lines). Its rhyme scheme is *abab cdcd efef gg*. The couplet usually expresses a response to the important issue developed in the three quatrains.

See also **Meter; Quatrain; Rhyme.**

Sound Devices *See* **Alliteration; Assonance; Consonance; Meter; Onomatopoeia; Repetition; Rhyme; Rhyme Scheme; Rhythm.**

Sources A source is anything that supplies information. **Primary sources** are materials written or created by people who were present at events, either as participants or as observers. Letters, diaries, autobiographies, speeches, and photographs are primary sources. **Secondary sources** are records of events that were created sometime after the events occurred; the writers were not directly involved or were not present when the events took place. Encyclopedias, textbooks, biographies, most newspaper and magazine articles, and books and articles that interpret or review research are secondary sources.

Spatial Order Spatial order is a pattern of organization that highlights the physical positions or relationships of details or objects. This pattern of organization is typically found in descriptive writing. Writers use words and phrases such as *on the left, to the right, here, over there, above, below, beyond, nearby,* and *in the distance* to indicate the arrangement of details.

Speaker The speaker of a poem, like the narrator of a story, is the voice that talks to the reader. In some poems, the speaker can be identified with the poet. In other poems, the poet invents a fictional character, or a persona, to play the role of the speaker. *Persona* is a Latin word meaning "actor's mask."

Speech A speech is a talk or public address. The purpose of a speech may be to entertain, to explain, to persuade, to inspire, or any combination of these aims.

Stage Directions Stage directions are the playwright's instructions for the director, performers, and stage crew. Usually set in italics, they are located at the beginning of and throughout a script. Stage directions usually tell the time and place of the action and explain how characters move and speak. They also describe scenery, props, lighting, costumes, music, or sound effects.

See also **Drama.**

Stanza A stanza is a group of lines that form a unit in a poem. A stanza is usually characterized by a common pattern of meter, rhyme, and number of lines. During the 20th century, poets experimented more freely with stanza form than did earlier poets, sometimes writing poems without any stanza breaks.

Static Character *See* **Character.**

Stereotype A stereotype is an over simplified image of a person, group, or institution. Sweeping generalizations about "all Southerners" or "every used-car dealer" are stereotypes. Simplified or stock characters in literature are often called stereotypes. Such characters do not usually demonstrate the complexities of real people.

Stereotyping Stereotyping is a dangerous type of overgeneralization. Stereotypes are broad statements made about people on the basis of their gender, ethnicity, race, or political, social, professional, or religious group.

Stream of Consciousness Stream of consciousness is a technique that was developed by modernist writers to present the flow of a character's seemingly unconnected thoughts, responses, and sensations. The term was coined by American psychologist William James to characterize the unbroken flow of thought that occurs in the waking mind.

See also **Modernism.**

Structure The structure of a literary work is the way in which it is put together—the arrangement of its parts. In poetry, structure refers to the arrangement of words and lines to produce a desired effect. A common structural unit in poetry is the stanza, of which there are numerous types. In prose, structure is the arrangement of larger units or parts of a selection. Paragraphs, for example, are a basic unit in prose, as are chapters in novels and acts in plays. The structure of a poem, short story, novel, play, or nonfiction selection usually emphasizes certain important aspects of content.

See also **Form; Stanza.**

Style Style is the distinctive way in which a work of literature is written. Style refers not so much to what is said but how it is said. Word choice, sentence length, tone, imagery, and use of dialogue all contribute to a writer's style. A group of writers might exemplify common stylistic characteristics; for example, the Imagists of the early 20th century wrote in a style that employs compression and rich sensory images.

Summarize To summarize is to briefly retell, or encapsulate, the main ideas of a piece of writing in one's own words.

See also **Paraphrase.**

Support Support is any material that serves to prove a claim. In an argument, support typically consists of reasons and evidence. In persuasive texts and speeches, however, support may include appeals to the needs and values of the audience.

See also **General Principle.**

Supporting Detail *See* **Main Idea.**

Surprise Ending A surprise ending is an unexpected plot twist at the end of a story.

> **Example:** "The Story of an Hour" ends with a surprise when Mrs. Mallard drops dead after her husband, presumed to be dead, reappears.

See also **Irony.**

Suspense Suspense is the excitement or tension that readers feel as they become involved in a story and eagerly await the outcome.

See also **Rising Action.**

Symbol A symbol is a person, place, or object that has a concrete meaning in itself and also stands for something beyond itself, such as an idea or feeling.

Synesthesia *See* **Imagery.**

Synthesize To synthesize information is to take information, combined with other pieces of information and prior knowledge, and make logical connections to gain a better understanding of a subject or to create a new product or idea.

Tall Tale A tall tale is a distinctively American type of humorous story characterized by exaggeration. Tall tales and practical jokes have similar kinds of humor. In both, someone gets fooled, to the amusement of the person or persons who know the truth.

See also **Humor; Hyperbole.**

Text Features Text features are design elements that indicate the organizational structure of a text and help make the key ideas and the supporting information understandable. Text features include headings, boldface type, italic type, bulleted or numbered lists, sidebars, and graphic aids such as charts, tables, timelines, illustrations, and photographs.

Theme A theme is an underlying message that a writer wants the reader to understand. It is a perception about life or human nature that the writer shares with the reader. In most cases, themes are not stated directly but must be inferred.

Recurring themes are themes found in a variety of works. For example, authors from varying backgrounds might convey similar themes having to do with the importance of family values. **Universal themes** are themes that are found throughout the literature of all time periods.

Thesaurus *See* **Reference Works.**

Thesis Statement In an argument, a thesis statement, or controlling idea, is an expression of the claim that the writer or speaker is trying to support. In an essay, a thesis statement is an expression, in one or two sentences, of the main idea or purpose of the piece of writing.

Third-Person Point of View *See* **Point of View.**

Title The title of a literary work introduces readers to the piece and usually reveals something about its subject or theme. Often, a poet uses the title to provide information necessary for understanding a poem.

Tone Tone is a writer's attitude toward his or her subject. A writer can communicate tone through diction, choice of details, and direct statements of his or her position. Unlike mood, which refers to the emotional response of the reader to a work, tone reflects the feelings of the writer. To identify the tone of a work of literature, you might find it helpful to read the work aloud, as if giving a dramatic reading before an audience. The emotions that you convey in an oral reading should give you hints as to the tone of the work.

See also **Connotation; Diction; Mood; Style.**

Topic Sentence The topic sentence of a paragraph states the paragraph's main idea. All other sentences in the paragraph provide supporting details.

Tragedy A tragedy is a dramatic work that presents the downfall of a dignified character who is involved in historically, morally, or socially significant events. The main character, or **tragic hero,** has a **tragic flaw,** a quality that leads to his or her destruction. The events in a tragic plot are set in motion by a decision that is often an error in judgment caused by the tragic flaw. Succeeding events are linked in a cause-and-effect relationship and lead inevitably to a disastrous conclusion, usually death. Arthur Miller's *The Crucible* could be classified as a tragedy.

Tragic Flaw *See* Tragedy.

Tragic Hero The ancient Greek philosopher Aristotle defined a tragic hero as a character whose basic goodness and superiority are marred by a tragic flaw that brings about or contributes to his or her downfall. The flaw may be poor judgment, pride, weakness, or an excess of an admirable quality. The tragic hero recognizes his or her own flaw and its consequences, but only after it is too late to change the course of events.

See also Character.

Traits *See* Character.

Transcendentalism The philosophy of transcendentalism, an American offshoot of German romanticism, was based on a belief that "transcendent forms" of truth exist beyond reason and experience. Ralph Waldo Emerson, the leader of the movement, asserted that every individual is capable of discovering this higher truth through intuition. Henry David Thoreau is another well-known transcendentalist writer.

See also Romanticism.

Transcript A transcript is a written record of words originally spoken aloud.

Trickster Tale A trickster tale is a folk tale about an animal or person who engages in trickery, violence, and magic. Neither all good nor all bad, a trickster may be foolish yet clever, greedy yet helpful, immoral yet moral.

See also Folk Tale.

Trochee *See* Meter.

Turning Point *See* Climax.

Understatement Understatement is a technique of creating emphasis by saying less than is actually or literally true. It is the opposite of **hyperbole,** or overstatement. One of the primary devices of **irony,** understatement can be used to develop a humorous effect, to create satire, or to achieve a restrained tone.

See also Hyperbole; Irony.

Unity of Effect When all elements of a story—plot, character, setting, imagery, and other literary devices—work together to create a single effect, it is known as unity of effect.

Universal Theme *See* Theme.

Verbal Irony *See* Irony.

Visualize Visualizing is the process of forming a mental picture based on written or spoken information.

Voice The term *voice* refers to a writer's unique use of language that allows a reader to "hear" a human personality in his or her writing. The elements of style that determine a writer's voice include sentence structure, diction, and tone. For example, some writers are noted for their reliance on short, simple sentences, while others make use of long, complicated ones. Certain writers use concrete words, such as *lake* or *cold,* which name things that you can see, hear, feel, taste, or smell. Others prefer abstract terms such as *memory,* which name things that cannot be perceived with the senses. A writer's tone also leaves its imprint on his or her personal voice. The term can be applied to the narrator of a selection, as well as the writer.

See also Diction; Tone.

Website A website is a collection of "pages" on the World Wide Web that is usually devoted to one specific subject. Pages are linked together and are accessed by clicking hyperlinks or menus, which send the user from page to page within the site. Websites are created by companies, organizations, educational institutions, branches of the government, the military, and individuals.

Word Choice *See* Diction.

Workplace Documents Workplace documents are materials that are produced or used within a work setting, usually to aid in the functioning of the workplace. They include job applications, office memos, training manuals, job descriptions, and sales reports.

Works Cited A list of works cited lists names of all the works a writer has referred to in his or her text. This list often includes not only books and articles but also nonprint sources.

Works Consulted A list of works consulted names all the works a writer consulted in order to create his or her text. It is not limited just to those works cited in the text.

See also **Bibliography.**

Using the Glossaries

The following glossaries list the Academic Vocabulary and Critical Vocabulary words found in this book in alphabetical order. Use these glossaries just as you would a dictionary—to determine the meanings, parts of speech, pronunciation, and syllabication of words. (Some technical, foreign, and more obscure words in this book are not listed here but are defined for you in the footnotes that accompany many of the selections.)

Many words in the English language have more than one meaning. These glossaries give the meanings that apply to the words as they are used in this book. Words closely related in form and meaning are listed together in one entry (for instance, **consumption** and **consume**), and the definition is given for the first form.

The following abbreviations are used to identify parts of speech of words:

adj. adjective   *adv.* adverb   *n.* noun   *v.* verb

Each word's pronunciation is given in parentheses. A guide to the pronunciation symbols appears in the Pronunciation Key below. The stress marks in the Pronunciation Key are used to indicate the force given to each syllable in a word. They can also help you determine where words are divided into syllables.

For more information about the words in these glossaries or for information about words not listed here, consult a dictionary.

Pronunciation Key

Symbol	Examples	Symbol	Examples	Symbol	Examples
ă	pat	m	mum	ûr	urge, term, firm, word, heard
ā	pay	n	no, sudden* (sud'n)		
ä	father	ng	thing	v	valve
âr	care	ŏ	pot	w	with
b	bib	ō	toe	y	yes
ch	church	ô	caught, paw	z	zebra, xylem
d	deed, milled	oi	noise	zh	vision, pleasure, garage
ĕ	pet	ŏŏ	took		
ē	bee	ōō	boot	ə	about, item, edible, gallop, circus
f	fife, phase, rough	ŏŏr	lure		
g	gag	ôr	core	ər	butter
h	hat	ou	out		
hw	which	p	pop	**Sounds in Foreign Words**	
ĭ	pit	r	roar	KH	German ich, ach; Scottish loch
ī	pie, by	s	sauce		
îr	pier	sh	ship, dish	N (bôn)	French, bon
j	judge	t	tight, stopped	œ	French feu, oeuf; German schön
k	kick, cat, pique	th	thin		
l	lid, needle* (nēd'l)	th	this	ü	French tu; German über
		ŭ	cut		

* In English the consonants *l* and *n* often constitute complete syllables by themselves.

Stress Marks

The relevant emphasis with which the syllables of a word or phrase are spoken, called stress, is indicated in three different ways. The strongest, or primary, stress is marked with a bold mark (´). An intermediate, or secondary, level of stress is marked with a similar but lighter mark (´). The weakest stress is unmarked. Words of one syllable show no stress mark.

Glossary of Academic Vocabulary

adapt (ə-dăpt´) *v.* to make something suitable for a particular situation; to adjust to an environment.

ambiguous (ăm-bĭg´yŏŏ-əs) *adj.* able to be interpreted in more than one way; uncertain.

analogy (ə-năl´ə-jē) *n.* a comparison that finds a similarity between things that are dissimilar.

clarify (klăr´ə-fī´) *v.* to make clearer or more understandable.

coherent (kō-hîr´ənt) *adj.* holding together in an orderly, logical, or consistent way.

confirm (kən-fûrm´) *v.* to establish the truth or certainty of something.

contemporary (kən-tĕm´pə-rĕr´ē) *adj.* coming from the same time period.

contrary (kŏn´trĕr´ē) *adj.* opposite or opposed in character or purpose.

definitely (dĕf´ə-nĭt-lē) *adv.* in an exact, certain, or precise way.

denote (dĭ-nōt´) *v.* to mean something specific; to name.

deny (dĭ-nī´) *v.* to refuse to see or to allow; to reject.

device (dĭ-vīs´) *n.* a literary technique used to achieve a certain effect; something made for a specific purpose.

displace (dĭs-plās´) *v.* to move or force from one place or position to another.

dynamic (dī-năm´ĭk) *adj.* characterized by change, movement, or activity.

format (fôr´măt´) *n.* the organization or arrangement of parts in a whole.

founder (foun´dər) *n.* someone who sets up, establishes, or provides the basis for something.

global (glō´bəl) *adj.* relating to the world as a whole.

ideological (ī´dē-ə-lŏj´ĭ-kəl) *adj.* based on ideas, beliefs, or doctrines.

implicit (ĭm-plĭs´ĭt) *adj.* not directly stated or obviously apparent.

infinite (ĭn´fə-nĭt) *adj.* without end or beyond measure.

publication (pŭb´lĭ-kā´shən) *n.* the act of making public in printed or electronic form; the product of this act.

quote (kwōt) *v.* to cite something word for word.

revise (rĭ-vīz´) *v.* to change or alter a text; reconsider.

revolution (rĕv´ə-lŏŏ´shən) *n.* the overthrow and replacement of a government, often through violent means.

simulated (sĭm´yə-lā´tĭd) *adj.* imitating something real.

somewhat (sŭm´wŏt´) *adv.* to a limited extent.

topic (tŏp´ĭk) *n.* the subject of a piece of writing or speech.

unify (yŏŏ´nə-fī´) *v.* to bring together into a cohesive whole.

unique (yŏŏ-nēk´) *adj.* one of a kind; unable to be compared.

virtual (vûr´chŏŏ-əl) *adj.* existing in essence or in a digital version but not in actual fact.

Glossary of Critical Vocabulary

abandonment (ə-băn´dən-mĕnt) *n.* a lack of restraint or inhibition.

abdicate (ăb´dĭ-kāt´) *v.* to relinquish or cede responsibility for.

abject (ăb´jĕkt´) *adj.* miserable and submissive.

abound (ə-bound´) *v.* occur or exist in great number.

affect (ə-fĕkt´) *v.* to cause or influence.

aggregate (ăg´rĭ-gĭt) *adj.* combined.

algorithm (ăl´gə-rĭ*th*´əm) *n.* instructions carried out in a specific sequence.

anomalous (ə-nŏm´ə-ləs) *adj.* unusual.

apportionment (ə-pôr´shən-mənt) *n.* distribution.

apprehension (ăp´rĭ-hĕn´shən) *n.* fear or anxiety; dread.

arrogate (ăr´ə-gāt´) *v.* to assume authority unjustly.

ascendant (ə-sĕn´dənt) *adj.* rising in influence; on an upward path.

ascendancy (ə-sĕn´dən-sē) *n.* a rise in power or influence.

atrocious (ə-trō´shəs) *adj.* evil or brutal.

autonomy (ô-tŏn´ə-mē) *n.* freedom from control; independence.

avert (ə-vûrt´) *v.* to turn away.

belatedly (bĭ-lā´tĭd-lē) *adv.* done too late or overdue.

blatantly (blāt´nt-lə) *adv.* in an offensively obvious, unashamed manner.

burgeoning (bûr´jən-ĭng) *adj.* rapidly increasing or growing.

caliber (kăl´ə-bər) *n.* level of ability.

capacity (kə-păs´i-tē) *n.* ability to hold or have somthing; function or role.

cardinal (kär´dn-əl) *adj.* most important; prime.

catalyst (kăt´l-ĭst) *n.* a substance that starts or speeds up a reaction.

cede (sēd) *v.* to yield or give away.

circulate (sûr´kyə-lāt´) *v.* to move or travel around or in a circular path.

circumvent (sûr´kəm-vĕnt´) *v.* to bypass or go around.

cleave (klēv) *v.* stick or adhere.

composed (kəm-pōzd´) *adj.* self-possessed; calm.

comprise (kəm-prīz´) *v.* contain.

congenial (kən-jēn´yəl) *adj.* agreeable; pleasant.

conjure (kŏn´jər) *v.* to produce from nothing, as if by magic.

copious (kō´pē-əs) *adj.* extensive.

cull (kŭl) *v.* to take from a large quantity.

defection (dĭ-fĕk´shŭn) *n.* the abandonment of one social or political group in favor of another.

deforestation (dē-fôr´ĭ-stā´shən) *n.* deliberate cutting down and clearing of trees and forests.

delinquency (dĭ-lĭng´kwən-sē) *n.* shortcoming or misbehavior.

denote (dĭ-nōt´) *v.* to name or give meaning to.

deprecate (dĕp´rĭ-kāt´) *v.* to express disapproval.

deteriorate (dĭ-tîr´ē-ə-rāt´) *v.* become worse; decline.

diligence (dĭl´ə-jəns) *n.* consistent, thorough effort and dedication.

disclaim (dĭs-klām´) *v.* to deny one's connection to; to distance oneself from.

discord (dĭs´kôrd´) *n.* disagreement or conflict.

disposition (dĭs´pə-zĭsh´ən) *n.* character or temperament.

disputatious (dĭs´pyə-tā´shəs) *adj.* argumentative; confrontational.

dissipation (dĭs´ə-pā´shən) *n.* wasteful self-indulgence.

distinction (dĭ-stĭngk´shən) *n.* difference in quality.

divergence (dĭ-vûr´jəns) *n.* a difference or variation.

divers (dī´vərz) *adj.* numerous.

efficacy (ĕf´ĭ-kə-sē) *n.* effectiveness.

elusive (ĭ-lōō´sĭv) *adj.* difficult to find.

emblem (ĕm´bləm) *n.* an identifying mark or symbol.

enclave (ĕn´klāv´) *n.* a distinct area within a larger area.

engross (ĕn-grōs´) *v.* to completely engage the attention or interest.

establish (ĭ-stăb´lĭsh) *v.* to formally set up; institute.

evidently (ĕv´ĭ-dənt-lē) *adv.* plainly, or obviously apparent from evidence or data.

evince (ĭ-vĭns´) *v.* reveal or give evidence of.

expedience (ĭk-spē´dē-əns) *n.* a self-interested means to an end.

extrapolation (ĭk-străp´ə-lā´shŭn) *n.* an estimate based on known information.

extremity (ĭk-strĕm´ĭ-tē) *n.* the outermost or farthest point or portion; the hand or foot.

façade (fə-säd´) *n.* false or misleading appearance.

faction (fak´shən) *n.* an organized subgroup that disagrees with the larger group as a whole.

factor (făk´tər) *n.* component or characteristic.

fecundity (fĭ-kŭn´dĭ-tē) *n.* fertility, productive capability.

ferment (fûr´mĕnt´) *n.* a state of violent, unpredictable change.

flux (flŭks) *n.* continual shift or change.

formidable (fôr´mĭ-də-bəl) *adj.* difficult and intimidating.

harbinger (här´bĭn-jər) *n.* a person or thing that signals a future occurrence.

illumination (ĭ-lōō´mə-nā´shən) *n.* awareness or enlightenment.

imminent (ĭm´ə-nənt) *adj.* about to happen; impending.

imperative (ĭm-pĕr´ə-tĭv) *adj.* of great importance; essential.

impose (ĭm-pōz´) *v.* to charge or apply.

indeterminate (ĭn´dĭ-tûr´mə-nĭt) *adj.* not precisely known.

infinitesimal (ĭn´fĭn-ĭ-tĕs´ə-məl) *adj.* extremely small; microscopic.

infringe (ĭn-frĭnj´) *v.* to interfere with; violate.

ingenious (ĭn-jēn´yəs) *adj.* cleverly inventive.

injunction (ĭn-jŭngk´shən) *n.* court order forbidding a specific action.

insuperable (ĭn-sōō´pər-ə-bəl) *adj.* impossible to overcome.

intangible (ĭn-tăn´jə-bəl) *adj.* unable to be defined or understood.

invest (ĭn-vĕst´) *v.* to grant or endow.

invocation (ĭn´və-kā´shən) *n.* prayer or incantation.

latent (lāt´nt) *adj.* underlying, hidden.

license (lī´səns) *n.* unacceptably unrestrained behavior.

lucid (lōō´sĭd) *adj.* easily understood.

mitigate (mĭt´ĭ-gāt´) *v.* to lessen.

mundane (mŭn-dān´) *adj.* ordinary; commonplace.

nascent (nā´sənt) *adj.* emerging; developing.

nemesis (nĕm´ĭ-sĭs) *n.* a bringer of destruction, often as vengeance.

oblige (ə-blīj´) *v.* to force or require.

obstinacy (ŏb´stə-nə-sē) *n.* stubbornness.

ostensibly (ŏ-stĕn´sə-blē) *adv.* seemingly or outwardly.

ostentatious (ŏs´tĕn-tā´shəs) *adj.* conspicuous and vulgar.

pale (pāl) *n.* boundary or enclosed area.

patent (păt´nt) *n.* an official document granting ownership.

pathos (pā´thŏs´) *n.* something that evokes pity or sympathy.

perennial (pə-rĕn´ē-əl) *adv.* enduring; long-lasting.

pertinacity (pûr´tn-ăs´ĭ-tē) *n.* firm, unyielding intent.

perturbation (pûr´tər-bā´shən) *n.* disturbance or agitation.

pervade (pər-vād´) *v.* to spread or exist throughout.

petulance (pĕch´ə-ləns) *n.* childish annoyance; sulkiness.

plaintive (plān´tĭv) *adj.* expressing sadness or sorrow.

plausibility (plô´zə-bĭl´ĭ-tē) *n.* likelihood; believability.

posterity (pŏ-stĕr´ĭ-tē) *n.* future generations.

precarious (prĭ-kâr´ē-əs) *adj.* unstable; uncertain.

precipitate (prĭ-sĭp´ĭ-tāt´) *v.* to cause to occur suddenly.

predominant (prĭ-dŏm´ə-nənt) *adj.* most important or prevalent.

prescribe (prĭ-skrīb´) *v.* to authorize or regulate.

pristine (prĭs´tēn´) *adj.* pure or unspoiled.

project (prə-jĕkt´) *v.* to communicate or put forth.

prostrate (prŏs´trāt´) *adj.* lying down with the head facing downward.

protrude (prō-trōōd´) *v.* to stick out or bulge.

provision (prə-vĭzh´ən) *n.* food supply.

purport (pər-pôrt´) *v.* to claim or pretend to be the case.

quicken (kwĭk´ən) *v.* to make alive or stimulate.

rampant (răm´pənt) *adj.* uncontrolled; without any restraint.

reciprocal (rĭ-sĭp´rə-kəl) *adj.* mutual or shared.

regimen (rĕj´ə-mən) *n.* a system or organized routine of behavior.

rendezvous (rän´dā-vōō´) *n.* meeting place.

reproach (rĭ-prōch´) *n.* a disgrace or a bad example.

resonance (rĕz´ə-nəns) *n.* richness of meaning; the ability to evoke emotion.

rudiment (rōō´də-mənt) *n.* basic form.

sceptical (skĕp´tĭ-kəl) *adj.* having doubts or reservations.

scrupulous (skrōō´pyə-ləs) *adj.* thorough and diligent.

sentinel (sĕn´tə-nəl) *n.* a lookout person or guard.

settlement (sĕt´l-mənt) *n.* a small community in a sparsely populated area.

stem (stĕm) *v.* to grow from or be caused by.

stoically (stō´ĭk-lē) *adv.* without showing emotion or feeling.

subtlety (sŭt´l-tē) *n.* nuance; fine detail.

succession (sək-sĕsh´ən) *n.* an ordered sequence.

succour (sŭk´ər) *n.* help and comfort.

sundry (sŭn´drē) *adj.* various or assorted.

supplant (sə-plănt´) *v.* to take the place of.

supposition (sŭp´ə-zĭsh´ən) *n.* a belief or assumption.

systematize (sĭs´tə-mə-tīz´) *v.* to form something into an organized plan or scheme.

taciturn (tăs´ĭ-tûrn´) *adj.* uncommunicative, withdrawn.

tangentially (tăn-jĕn´shəl-lē) *adv.* indirectly or peripherally connected.

tender (tĕn´dər) *v.* to offer or present.

tepid (tĕp´ĭd) *adj.* lukewarm; indifferent.

timidity (tĭ-mĭd´ĭ-tē) *n*. showing a lack of courage or confidence.

transcend (trăn-sĕnd´) *v*. to go beyond the limits or become independent of.

transient (trăn´zē-ənt) *adj*. temporary; short-term.

transition (trăn-zĭsh´ən) *n*. process of change.

tumultuous (tŏŏ-mŭl´chŏŏ-əs) *adj*. stormy, intense.

turbulence (tûr´byə-ləns) *n*. an unsettled or changeable state.

ubiquitous (yŏŏ-bĭk´wĭ-təs) *adj*. existing everywhere at once.

unalienable (ŭn-āl´yə-nə-bəl) *adj*. impossible to be taken away.

unfathomed (ŭn-făth´əmd) *adj*. located at the deepest place.

untenable (ŭn-tĕn´ə-bəl) *adj*. unsustainable, insupportable.

vacant (vā´kənt) *adj*. blank, expressionless.

venture (vĕn´chər) *v*. to risk or dare.

volatile (vŏl´ə-tl´) *adj*. liable to change suddenly or evaporate.

wring (rĭng) *v*. to obtain through force or pressure.

Index of Skills

A

abolitionist movement, 277
abstract nouns, R23
absurdity (element of satire), 379
Academic Vocabulary, 2, 103, 108, 170, 174, 268, 271, 276, 328, 406, 410, 602, 606
accept/except, R59
act (in play), R61
action verbs, R24, R33
active voice, 22, R35
activities
  media activity, 126, 168, 585
  speaking activity, 76, 101, 118, 158, 165, 185, 196, 247, 263, 282, 312, 316, 372, 380, 399, 486, 544, 566
  writing activity, 20, 33, 70, 75, 85, 94, 128, 148, 165, 205, 218, 231, 266, 292, 299, 322, 348, 357, 370, 394, 404, 435, 444, 454, 526, 541, 579, 600
adaptations, 298
adjective clauses, R42–R43
adjective phrases, R40
adjectives, R24, R36
  vs. adverbs, R36
  comparatives, R36–R37
  compound, 150
  hyphenated, 150
  predicate, R36
  proper, R29
  superlatives, R36–R37
adverb clauses, R43
adverb phrases, R40–R41
adverbs, R24, R36
  vs. adjectives, R36
  comparatives, R36–R37
  conjunctive, R39
  superlatives, R36–R37
advice/advise, R59
A&E® (Arts and Entertainment), 37, 167, 249
affect/effect, R59
affirmative side, in debates, R15
affixes, 206
African American writers, 412, 438–439
ain't, R55
allegory, R61
alliteration, 69, R61
all ready/already, R59
all right, R55
allusion/illusion, R59
allusions, 19, 85, 158, 294, 321, 322, 599, R61
ambiguity, 164, 247, 453
ambiguous references, R33

American literature
  19th century, 175–176
  colonial period, 109–110, 151–158
  early, 4
  Gothic, 263, 266, R69
  of Harlem Renaissance, 438–442, 444
  historical accounts, 5–19
  modern, 411, R72
  muckraking journalism, 330
  naturalism, 330, 347, 348, 350, 404
  realism, 347, 350, 372
  regionalism, 330
  Romanticism, 176, 234, 247, 263, 266, R77
  slave narratives, 277
Americas, exploration and settlement of, 3–4
among/between, R59
analogies, R54, R61. *See also* metaphors; similes
  analyzing, 578, 579
  arguments from, 594
  between central ideas, 218
  false, R20
analysis
  of debate, writing, 273
  media activity, 585
  thesis statement, R4
  writing activity, 205, 231, 266, 526
analytical essays
  draft of, 406
  elements of effective, 405
  exchanging with partner, 407
  organization, 406
  Performance Task Evaluation Chart, 408
  planning, 405–406
  revising, 407
  writing, 405–408
analyzing
  arguments, 281, R16–R17
  author's choices, 356
  author's point of view, 291, 578
  author's purpose, 298
  drama, 72, 75, 486, 504, 526, 540, 541, 544, 547
  events, 147, 195, 311
  foundational documents, 19, 117, 125, 128, 168
  historical accounts, 19
  ideas, 147, 195, 311
  interpretations of dramas, 72, 75, 544, 547
  language, 69, 100, 137, 204, 321, 369, 453, 599
  motivation, 434

poetry, 101, 158, 180, 182, 183, 185, 200, 201, 202, 203, 205, 322, 404, 444, 453, 454, 599, 600
point of view, 164
speeches, 291, 292
story elements, 434, 584
structure, 84, 93, 117, 147, 164, 184, 230, 247, 263, 321, 347, 404, 453, 594
style, 117, 196
Supreme Court decisions, 565, 566
text, 579, 585, 594, 600
theme, 85, 117
Analyzing the Media, 168
Analyzing the Text, 20, 33, 70, 85, 94, 101, 118, 126, 128, 138, 148, 158, 165, 178, 180, 182, 183, 185, 196, 200, 201, 202, 203, 205, 218, 231, 247, 263, 266, 282, 292, 299, 312, 316, 322, 348, 357, 370, 372, 380, 399, 404, 435, 444, 454, 486, 504, 526, 541, 566, 579, 585, 594, 600
Analyzing the Text and Media, 72, 75, 76, 394, 544, 547, 548
anapest, R72
anaphora, 382, R61
anecdotes, 93, R61
Annotate It!, 20, 33, 70, 85, 94, 118, 126, 138, 148, 158, 165, 185, 196, 205, 218, 231, 247, 263, 282, 292, 299, 312, 322, 348, 357, 370, 380, 394, 404, 435, 444, 454, 486, 504, 526, 541, 566, 579, 585, 594, 600
antagonist, 526, R61
antecedent, R30
  pronoun agreement with, R30–R31
antihero, R61
antithesis, 294
anti-transcendentalists, 176
antonyms, 436, R53
aphorism, R61
apostrophe, R27–R28
appeals
  by association, R17, R61
  to authority, R61
  bandwagon, R17
  emotional, R17, R66
  logical, R71
  to loyalty, R17
  to pity, fear, or vanity, R17, R66
appositive phrases, R41
appositives, R41
archaic vocabulary, 21
archetypes, R61
argumentative essays, 87–92, 103–106, 230, 601–604. *See also* arguments

arguments
  from analogy, 594
  analyzing, 281, R16–R17
  body of essay, 104
  building, 602
  claims, 93, 137, 281, 299, 566, 601, R2
  conclusions to, 104, R3
  counterarguments, 272, 602, R2, R16
  for debate, 272
  deductive, R18–R19
  definition of, R61
  delineating, 565
  draft of, 104–105, 602
  elements of effective, 103, 601
  evaluating, 565, 594, R21–R22
  evidence for, 281
  examples, 87–92, 129–136, 221–229, 569–577, 587–593
  exchanging with partner, 105, 603
  general principle, R68
  inductive, R18
  introduction to, 104
  linking ideas in, R3
  logical, R71
  logic and reasoning in, R18–R20
  organization, 104, 602
  parts of, 281
  peer feedback for, 105, 603
  Performance Task Evaluation Chart, 106, 604
  planning, 103–104, 601–602
  premises of, 137, 138, 281
  presenting, 105, 603
  purpose of, 137
  reading, R16–R22
  reasons in, 281
  recognizing persuasive techniques, R17
  revising, 105, 272, 603
  strategies for determining strong, R22
  structure of, 93
  style and tone for, R3
  use of transitions in, 140
  using quotations to support, 233
  writing, 103–106, 601–604, R2–R3
  writing activity, 33
Artful Sentences (Tufte), R3
articles
  citing, R11
  history, 141–146
  news, 357, R11, R73
asides, R62
as if, R55
assonance, R62
assumption, R62
as though, R55
As You Listen, 543
As You Read, 5, 23, 39, 77, 87, 97, 112, 121, 129, 141, 151, 159, 177, 187, 199, 207, 221, 235, 249, 279, 285,

295, 301, 317, 331, 352, 359, 373, 384, 391, 395, 401, 413, 439, 445, 458, 487, 505, 527, 549, 569, 581, 587, 597
As You View, 71, 73, 167, 315, 389, 392, 545
atmosphere, 263
attacking the person (faulty reasoning), R20
audience
  author's purpose and, 298
  for a work, R62
author's background, 5, 37, 77, 87, 97, 111, 129, 141, 151, 159, 177, 187, 199, 207, 221, 235, 249, 279, 285, 295, 301, 317, 331, 351, 373, 383, 395, 401, 413, 439, 445, 457, 569, 581, 597
author's choices, analyzing, 356
author's claim, R16. See also claims
author's message, R62
author's perspective, R62
author's point of view, analyzing, 291, 398, 578
author's position. See author's claim
author's purpose, 19, 372, R62
  analyzing, 298
  determining, 32, 93, 195, 217, 311, 356, 369
  evaluating, 380
  in satire, 379
  style and, 311
  tone and, 311
autobiographical essays, R66
autobiography, R62
auxiliary verbs, R24, R25, R47–R48

B
bad vs. badly, R37
balanced sentences, 284
ballads, R62
bandwagon appeals, R17
base words, R50
bias, R21, R62
biased tone, R3, R5
bibliography, R62. See also works cited
biography, R62
blank verse, 69, R62–R63
blocking, 72, 75, 547
book parts, citing, R10
books, citing, R10
brainstorming, 268
bring/take, R59
British colonies, 109–110
business correspondence, R63

C
caesura, R63
camera techniques, 547
can, may, R55
capitalization

first words, R29
  geographical names, R29
  organizations and events, R29
  people and titles, R29
  proper adjectives, R29
  quick reference, R29
captions, writing activity, 75, 548
cases
  nominative, R31
  objective, R31
  possessive, R31
casting, 72, 75, 547
cast of characters, R63
cataloguing, in free verse, 184
cause and effect, 316, R4, R63
CD-ROMs, citing, R11
central ideas. See also main idea; theme
  determining, 19, 217
  summarizing, 20, 218
characterization, R63
  direct, 540
  indirect, 540
characters, R63
  actions of, 540
  antagonist, 526
  dialogue of, 540, 542
  dynamic, R63
  foils, 526
  inferences about, 435, 541
  main, R63
  minor, R63
  motivations of, 434, R63, R72
  in poems, 453
  protagonist, 526
  static, R63
  theme and, 84
character traits, 434
chorus, R63
chronological order, 147, 311, R7, R63
circular logic, R19
circum-, 95
citations, R9, R10–R11
Cite Text Evidence, 20, 33, 70, 72, 75, 76, 85, 94, 101, 118, 126, 128, 138, 148, 158, 165, 168, 178, 180, 182, 183, 185, 196, 200, 201, 202, 203, 205, 218, 231, 247, 263, 266, 282, 292, 299, 312, 316, 322, 348, 357, 370, 372, 380, 394, 399, 404, 435, 444, 454, 486, 504, 526, 541, 544, 547, 548, 566, 579, 585, 594, 600
civil rights movement, 412
Civil War, 277–278
claims, 137, R63. See also arguments; thesis statement
  in arguments, 281, 299, 566, 601
  author's, R16
  counterclaims, R2, R16
  in debates, 272, R14–R15
  developing, R2

introducing, R2
linking ideas to, R3
making, 601
supporting, 93, 138, R14, R16, R80
vague, R2
clarify, R63
classical mythology, words from, R52
classification, 195, R63–R64
classroom discussions, R12–R13
clauses, R42–R43
adjective, R42–R43
adverb, R43
dependent (subordinate), 35
essential adjective, R43
independent, R42
nonessential adjective, R43
noun, R43
parallel, 120
subordinate, R42, R43
transitional, R3, R5
cliché, R64
climate change, 412
climax, 504, R7, R64, R75
coherence, 140
Cold War, 411
Collaborative Discussion, 18, 31, 68,
71, 74, 83, 92, 99, 116, 124, 136,
146, 156, 163, 167, 183, 194, 203,
216, 229, 246, 262, 280, 290, 297,
310, 315, 320, 346, 355, 368, 378,
388, 390, 391, 392, 397, 403, 433,
442, 452, 485, 503, 525, 539, 543,
546, 564, 577, 583, 593, 598
collaborative discussions, R12–R13
ground rules for, R12
moving forward in, R12
preparing for, R12
responding to ideas in, R13
collective nouns, R23, R48
collocations, 400
colloquial language, 455
colonial America, 109–110
colonial American poetry, 151–158
colons, 96, R27
comedy, R64
comic relief, R64
commas, R26
comma splices, R45
commonly confused words, R59–R60
common nouns, R23, R30
comparative form, R36–R37
Compare Anchor Texts, 111, 128
compare and contrast, 147, 148, R4,
R64
Compare Text and Media, 71, 72, 76,
383, 393, 543, 544, 548
Compare Texts, 151, 234, 247, 263,
266, 351, 372, 438, 439, 443
comparing
foundational documents, 128
interpretations of dramas, 72, 75,
76

poems, 158, 205
text, 196, 218, 348, 370
writers' styles, 568
comparison essay, writing activity,
299
comparisons
as context clues, R50
double, R37
illogical, R37
irregular, R37
regular, R36–R37
complements, R40
complete predicate, R25
complete subject, R25
complex sentences, 198, R44
complications, in plot, 504, R64
compound adjectives, 150
compound-complex sentences, 198,
R44
compound nouns, R23
compound numbers, 150
compound predicates, R40
compound sentences, 198, 265,
R43–R44
compound subjects, R40, R46
compound words, 150
conceit, 294
conclusions, R64
of arguments, 104, R3
deductive, R64
of essays, R5
inductive, R64
of narratives, R7
valid, R64
conclusions, drawing, 33, 69, 72, 94,
101, 118, 126, 299, 312, 322, 348,
357, 370, 394, 435, 454, 504, 566,
600, R66
concrete details, 596, R5
concrete nouns, R23
conflict, 504, R64, R75
conjunctions, R24, R38
coordinating, R24, R38–R39
correlative, R24, R39
subordinating, 35, R24, R39
conjunctive adverbs, R39
connect, R64
connotations, 32, 204, 248, R53–R54,
R64
consonance, R64
constitutional principles, 565
consumer documents, R64
content
determining author's point of view
from, 578
determining author's purpose
from, 195
context, historical, R69
context clues, R64
determining word meanings using,
86, 119, 219, 264, 313

types of, R49–R50
using, R49–R50
contrast, as context clue, 313, R50
controlling idea. *See* thesis statement
coordinating conjunctions, R24,
R38–R39
correlative conjunctions, R24, R39
costumes, 72, 75, 547
counterarguments, 272, 602, R16,
R65
counterclaims, R2, R16
credibility, R5, R65
credible sources, R8
criteria
for analytical essay, 405
for arguments, 103, 601
for debate, 271
for informative essay, 169
for narratives, 267
for panel discussions, 605
critical review, R65
Critical Vocabulary, 21, 34, 86, 95,
119, 127, 139, 149, 166, 197, 219,
232, 248, 264, 283, 293, 300, 313,
349, 358, 371, 381, 400, 436, 567,
580, 586, 595. *See also* Glossary
of Critical Vocabulary
critiques, 218, 394, 579
cultural hero, R65
cultural references, 321. *See also*
allusions

D

dactyl, R72
dangling participles, R41–R42
Dark Romantics, 234, 247
dashes, 371, 437, 509, R27
database, R65
debates, R65
affirmative side in, R15
analysis of, 273
building argument for, 272
collecting evidence for, 271
developing counterarguments, 272
evaluating, R15
format, R15
holding, 273, R15
moderators, R14
negative side in, R15
participants in, 271
Performance Task, 271–274
Performance Task Evaluation
Chart, 274
planning, 271, R14
practicing for, 272
preparing briefs and rebuttals for,
R14–R15
propositions in, R14
roles in, R14
speaking activity, 76, 316, 372, 566

structure of, 273, R14
teams for, R14
declarative sentences, R40
deductive conclusions, R64
deductive reasoning, 291, R18–R19, R65
definition, as context clue, 313, R49
delineation, of argument, 565
demonstrative pronouns, R24, R32
denotations, 139, 204, 248, R53–R54, R64
dénouement. *See* falling action
dependent clauses, 35
derivational suffixes, 206
description
  as narrative technique, R6–R7
  in writing, R65
  writing activity, 404
details
  concrete, 596, R5
  gathering, R6–R7
  sensory, 437
determining
  author's purpose, 32, 195, 217, 356
  central ideas, 19, 217
  theme, 84, 100, 128, 184, 204, 247, 263, 398
diagram, writing activity, 547
dialect, R65
dialogue, 437, 540, 542, 544, R6, R65
diary, R65
diction, 20, 148, 350, 356, 600, R65.
  See also word choice
dictionaries, 149, R56
dimeter, R72
direct characterization, 540
direct objects, R25, R40
direct quotations, R9
discussion
  Collaborative Discussion, 18, 31, 68, 72, 74, 83, 92, 99, 116, 124, 136, 146, 156, 163, 167, 183, 194, 203, 216, 229, 246, 262, 280, 290, 297, 310, 315, 320, 346, 355, 368, 378, 388, 390, 391, 392, 397, 433, 442, 452, 485, 503, 525, 539, 543, 546, 564, 577, 583, 593, 598
  speaking activity, 138, 158, 165, 196, 247, 263, 282, 312, 399, 486
discussions, collaborative
  ground rules for, R12
  moving forward in, R12–R13
  participating in, R12–R13
  preparing for, R12
  responding to ideas in, R13
documentary, 315
documents
  foundational, 117, 121–124, 128
  historical, R69
  public, 111–116, 295–297

seminal, 125, 137, 281
  workplace, R82
doesn't, R47–R48
domain-specific words, 119
don't, R47–R48
double comparisons, R37
double negatives, R37
drafts
  of analytical essay, 406
  of arguments, 602
  of essays, 170, 406, 602
  exchanging with partner, 269
  of informative essays, 170
  of narratives, 269
  revising, 105, 171, 269, 407, 603
  writing, 104–105, 170, 269, 602
drama, R66
  analyzing, 486, 504, 526, 540, 541, 544
  antagonist in, 526
  blocking, 72, 75
  casting, 72, 75
  characterization, 540
  characters in, 540
  climax in, 504
  comparing multiple interpretations of, 548
  complications in, 504
  conflict in, 504
  costumes, 72, 75
  The Crucible, 457–485, 487–503
  dialogue in, 540, 542, 544
  elements of, analyzing, 316, 486, 504, 526, 540
  foils in, 526
  interpretations of, 72, 543–548
  interpreting, 75, 541
  lighting, 72, 75
  modern American, 456
  plot in, 504
  protagonist in, 526
  resolution in, 504
  scenes, R77
  set design, 75
  Shakespearean, 36, 37–68
  sound in, 72
  stage directions in, 486, 540, 541
  timing in, 544
  tragedy, R81
  voice expression in, 544
dramatic irony, 398, 486, R70
dramatic monologue, 85, R66
dramatic tension, 263
drawing conclusions, 33, 69, 72, 94, 101, 118, 126, 299, 312, 322, 348, 357, 370, 394, 435, 454, 504, 566, 600, R66
dynamic characters, R63

E
early modern English, R53
eBook, 282, 292, 312, 322, 348, 357, 370, 394, 399, 404, 435, 454, 486, 504, 526, 541, 566, 579, 585, 594, 600
editorials, R66
effect, R63
effect/affect, R59
either/or fallacy, R19, R66
electronic publications, citing, R11
elegy, R66
Elizabethan England, 36
ellipsis, 102, R28
Emancipation Proclamation, 278
emotional appeals, R17, R66
encyclopedia articles, citing, R11
end rhyme, R77
English language
  early modern English, R53
  middle English, R53
  modern English, R53
  old English, R53
  preferred and contested usage, R55–R56
  proto-English, R52
  understanding, R52–R53
English settlers, 3
environment, 412
epic heroes, R66
epics, R66
epithet, R66
essays, R66
  analytical, 405–408
  argumentative, 87–92, 103–106, 230, 601–604
  autobiographical, R66
  citing, R10
  comparison and contrast, 147, 148, 299
  conclusion, R5
  drafts of, 104–105, 170, 406, 602
  examples, 187–194, 207–216, 373–378
  exchanging with partner, 105, 171, 407, 603
  explanatory, 70, 128
  informative, 169–172, 230, 393, 444, R4–R5
  narrative, 230
  presenting, 105, 603
  publishing online, 171
  reviews, 105
  revising, 171, 407, 603
  structure of, 230
  writing, 169–172, 405–408, 601–604
  writing activity, 128, 218, 322, 394, 444, 541
essential adjective clauses, R43
essential appositives, R41

ethical appeals, R66–R67
ethos, 291
etymology, 119, 349, 580, R51
European exploration, of the
   Americas, 3–4
European literature, 176, 234
evading the issue, R20
evaluating, R67
   arguments, 565, 594, R21–R22
   debates, R15
   evidence, R21–R22
   foundational documents, 118
   information, 393
   poetry, 205, 454
   purpose, 370, 380
   seminal texts, 125, 137, 281
   sources, R8–R9
   speeches, 282
   structure, 93, 230
   text, 20, 94, 148, 165, 218, 231, 247,
      263, 312, 348, 399, 435, 579
   video, 168, 394
evaluations, writing activity, 94
events
   analyzing, 195, 311
   sequence of, 147, 311, R7
evidence, R67
   in arguments, 281
   for debate, collecting, 271
   evaluating, R21–R22
   gathering, for panel discussion, 606
   to support claims, R2, R14, R16
   to support inferences, 69
   from text, 20, 33, 70, 72, 75, 76, 85,
      101, 118, 126, 128, 138, 148,
      158, 165, 178, 180, 182, 183,
      185, 196, 200, 201, 202, 203,
      218, 231, 247, 263, 266, 282,
      292, 299, 312, 316, 322, 348,
      357, 370, 372, 380, 394, 399,
      404, 435, 444, 454, 486, 541,
      544, 566, 579, 585, 594, 600, R5
   for theme, 100
exaggeration, 379
examples
   as context clues, 313, R50
   as support, R4–R5
except/accept, R59
exclamation points, 437, R26
exclamatory sentences, 437, R40
experimental poetry, R67
explanatory essay, writing activity,
   128
exploratory essay, writing activity, 70
exposition, R67, R75
extended metaphors, 204, 444, R67
external conflict, R64
extrinsic ethos, 291
eyewitness accounts, R67

F
fables, R67
facts, 596, R5
fact versus opinion, R67
fallacies, R19–R21, R71
falling action, R67, R75
false analogy, R20
false causation, R20
fantasy, 584
farce, R67, R69
farther/further, R37
faulty reasoning, R19–R20
fear, appeals to, R17, R66
feature article, R68
fewer/less, R59
fiction, R68. *See also* American
   literature; literature
   fantasy, 584
   Gothic, 234, 247
   horror, R69
   science, 411, 584, R77
   short stories, R78
   themes in, 84
fictionalized biography, R62
fictional narratives, 101, R68
   building suspense in, R7
   conclusions of, R7
   details for, R6–R7
   pacing, R7
   point of view for, R6
   sequencing of events in, R7
   writing, R6–R7
figurative language, 32, 100, R49, R68
   extended metaphors, 204, 444, R67
   hyperbole, 218
   metaphors, 100, 184, 185, 204, 217,
      443, R72
   pathos and, 291
   personification, 201, 217, 599, R74
   in poetry, 184, 444
   in Shakespeare, 69, 70
   similes, 32, 184, 217, R78
   use of, 217
figuratively, R56
figures of speech, 184
film
   adaptations, of dramas, 71–76,
      545–548
   blocking, 75, 547
   camera techniques, 547
   casting, 75, 547
   costumes, 75, 547
   documentary, 315
   lighting, 75, 547
   reviews, 72
   set design, 75, 547
first drafts. *See* drafts
first-person narrator, R6
first-person point of view, 164, 166,
   R75

flashbacks, 84, R7, R68
flash forwards, 84, 85
foils, 526, R68
folk ballads, R62
folk tales, R68
foot (metrical), R72
foreign words, R52
foreshadowing, R68
form, R68
formal debates, R14–R15
formal tone, 127, R3
foundational documents
   analyzing, 117, 125, 128, 168
   Bill of Rights, 122–124
   Declaration of Independence,
      111–116, 128
   Federalist Papers, 129–136
   U.S. Constitution, 128
   U.S. Constitution, preamble to, 121
foundational texts, 19
fragments, sentence, R44–R45
frame story, R68
free verse, 100, 184, R68
further/farther, R37
future perfect progressive tense, R35
future perfect tense, R34
future progressive tense, R34
future tense, R34
fyi, 2, 108, 276, 328, 410

G
general dictionary, R56
generalization, R68
   glittering generalities, R17
   hasty, R20
   overgeneralization, R19, R74
general principle, R68–R69
general references, R33
general reference works, 149
genre, R68–R69
gerund phrases, R42
gerunds, R42
Gilded Age, 329
glittering generalities, R17
globalization, 411
global violence, 412
glossaries, 149, R56
Glossary of Academic Vocabulary,
   R84
Glossary of Critical Vocabulary,
   R85–R88
Glossary of Literary and
   Informational Terms, R61–R82
good vs. *well*, R37
Gothic literature, 234, 247, 263, 266,
   R69
government publications, R69
grammar
   capitalization, R29
   handbook, R30–R48

parts of speech, R23–R24

punctuation, 96, 150, 371, 437, R26–R28

sentence parts, R25

graphic aids, R69

graphic organizers, 195, R69

creating, 602

semantic maps, 119

sequence charts, 311

word maps, 349

word webs, 95, 300, 358, 381, 595

graphics, R4

graphs, 393

Great Depression, 411

Great Migration, 438

Greek words, 291, 358, 580, R52

group discussions, R12–R13

H

haiku, R69

Harlem Renaissance, 438–442

hasty generalizations, R20

headings, R4

helping verbs, R25

heroes

cultural, R65

epic, R66

tragic, R81

heroism, 278

hexameter, R72

historical accounts, 5–19

historical context, R69

historical documents, R69

historical narratives, 311, R69

HISTORY®, 3, 5, 23, 109, 111, 129, 151, 277, 279, 285, 315, 317, 329, 383, 392, 457, 587

history articles, 141–146

history writing, examples, 23–31, 301–310

homonyms, R54

homophones, R54

hopefully, R55

horror fiction, R69

how-to books, R69

humor

of character, R69

of language, R69

and satire, 379

of situation, R69

hyperbole, 218, R69, R81

hyphenation, 150, R27

I

iamb, R72

iambic pentameter, 69, R62, R70

ideas

analyzing, 147, 195, 311

central, determining, 19, 217

central, summarizing, 20, 218

linking, in arguments, R3

main, R71

sharing, 169–170

identifying

allusions, 322

bias, R21

extended metaphors, 444

patterns, 126, 218

tone of speech, 282

idioms, 599, R49, R70

illogical comparisons, R37

imagery, R70

kinesthetic, R70

in poetry, 100, 158, 184, 599

and style, 32

synesthesia, R70

and word choice, 356

immigration, 329

imperative sentences, R40

indefinite pronouns, R24, R32, R46–R47

indefinite references, R33

independent clauses, 96, R42

index, R70

Indian Removal Act, 175

indirect characterization, 540

indirect objects, R25, R40

inductive conclusions, R64

inductive reasoning, 291, R18, R70

industrialization, 329

Industrial Revolution, 175

inferences, R70

about author's purpose, 217

about central idea, 19

about characters, 435, 541

about court opinions, 566

about figurative language, 69

about mood, 182

about poetry, 101, 178, 182, 205, 322, 444, 600

about purpose, 32, 356

about seminal texts, 138, 148

about Shakespearean drama, 70, 75

about speeches, 282, 292

supporting, 69, 434

about text, 33, 118, 126, 196, 218, 263, 299, 312, 357, 370, 380, 585

about theme, 84, 100, 204

infinitive phrases, R41

infinitives, R41

inflectional suffixes, 206

informal style, 127, 217, 455

informal tone, R3

information, 230, 393, 444

concrete details, 596

facts, 596

integrating and evaluating, 393

presentation formats, 393

types of, 596

informational texts, 301–310, 359–368, 384–388, 391, 569–577,

587–593, R70

informative essays, 230, 393, 444

drafts of, 170

exchanging with partner, 171

organization, 170

Performance Task Evaluation Chart, 172

planning, 169–170

publishing online, 171

revising, 171

writing, 169–172, R4–R5

informative writing, 596

intensive pronouns, R23, R32

interior monologue, R72

interjections, R24, R39

internal conflict, R64

internal rhyme, R77

Internet, 412

Internet documents, citing, R11

interpreting

allusions, 85

court opinions, 566

drama, 541

foundational documents, 126

poetry, 101, 158, 178, 180, 185, 200, 201, 322, 404, 453, 454, 600

seminal texts, 138, 148

symbolism, 247

text, 85, 94, 196, 218, 263, 299, 380, 435, 579

interrogative pronouns, R24, R32

interrogative sentences, R40

interviews, R70

citing, R11

interview summary, 454

intransitive verbs, R24

intrinsic ethos, 291

introduction, of arguments, 104

inverted sentences, R47

irony

analyzing, 165

author's purpose and use of, 93

contrast as, 85, 370

definition of, R70

dramatic, 398, 486, R70

and meaning, 93

sarcasm, R77

and satire, 379

situational, 398, R70

types of, 398

understatement, R81

verbal, 398, R70

irregular verbs, R34

italics, R28

J

jargon, R5

ject, 300

journal, R70

journal entries, 20

K

key terms, 137
kinesthetic imagery, R70

L

language
  ambiguous, 453
  analyzing, 69, 100, 137, 204, 321,
    369, 453, 599
  biased, R5, R21
  colloquial, 455
  figurative, 32, 69, 100, 217, 218, 291,
    599, R49, R68
  free verse, 100
  humor of, R69
  informal, 217, 455
  jargon, R5
  loaded, R21, R71
  propaganda, R21, R76
  sensory, R7
  Shakespearean, 69
  vivid, R7
Language and Style
  active and passive voice, 22
  anaphora, 382
  balanced sentences, 284
  colon use, 96
  comparing writers' styles, 568
  consistent tone, 350
  crafting effective sentences, 437
  dashes, 371
  dependent (subordinate) clauses, 35
  dialogue, 542
  formal style, 127
  hyphenation, 150
  informal style, 127, 455
  informative writing, 596
  misplaced modifiers, avoiding, 314
  parallel structure, 120, 186, 382
  point of view, 166
  quotations, 233
  rhetorical devices, 294
  rhetorical questions, 220
  semicolons, 265
  syntax in poetry, 102
  transitions, 140
  varying sentence structure, 198
language conventions. *See* Language
  and Style
Latin prefix *circum-*, 95
Latin root *ject*, 300
lay/lie, R60
leave/let, R59
lecture, speaking activity, 380
legal reasoning, 565
legal terminology, 567
legend, R70. *See also* myths
less/fewer, R59
letters
  literary, R71

open, R73
  writing activity, 20, 435
lie/lay, R60
lighting, 72, 75, 547
like, R55
limited narrator, 164, 398
line, R70–R71
linking verbs, R24, R33
lists, colons before, 96, R27
literally, R56
literary ballads, R62
literary criticism, 230, 231, R71
literary devices
  alliteration, R61, 69
  allusion, 19, 85, 158, 294, 321, 322,
    599, R61
  assonance, R62
  cliché, R64
  figurative language, 32, 69, 70, 100,
    204, 217, 218, 291, R49, R68
  foreshadowing, R68
  hyperbole, 218, R69, R81
  idioms, 599, R49, R70
  imagery, 32, 100, 158, 184, 356,
    599, R70
  irony, 85, 93, 165, R70, R81
  metaphors, 100, 184, 185, 204, 217,
    R72
  onomatopoeia, R73
  oxymoron, R74
  personification, 201, 217, 599, R74
  repetition, 19, 117, 180, 184
  rhetorical questions, 220, 294, R77
  sarcasm, R77
  similes, 32, 184, 217, R78
  symbolism, 184, 247, R80
literary letters, R71
literary nonfiction, R71
  examples, 5–18, 87–92, 112–116,
    121–124, 129–136 141–146,
    187–194, 207–216, 221–229,
    279–280, 285–290, 295–297,
    373–378
literary texts, 37–68, 77–83, 97–99,
    152–153, 154, 155–156, 159–163,
    177–183, 200–203, 235–246,
    249–262, 317–320, 331–346,
    352–355, 395–397, 401–403,
    413–433, 439–442, 445–452,
    456–539, 581–583, 597–598
literature. *See also* American
    literature; fiction; literary texts
  European, 176, 234
  Gothic, 263, 266
  modern, 411, R72
  naturalism in, 330, 347, 348, 350,
    404
  oral, R73–R74
  realism in, 347, 350, 372
  Romanticism, 176, 234, 247, 263,
    266, R77

loaded language, R21, R71
local color realism, R71
logic
  analyzing, in arguments, R18–R20
  circular, R19
logical appeals, R71
logical arguments, R71
logical fallacies, R19–R20, R71
logos, 291
loose/lose, R60
loyalty, appeals to, R17
lyric poetry, R71

M

magazine articles, citing, R11
magical realism, R71
main characters, R63
main idea, R71. *See also* central ideas;
    thesis statement
main verb, R25
manifest destiny, 175
A Manual for Writers (Turabian), R9
may, can, R55
media. *See also* film; video
  analyzing, 72, 75, 76, 168, 394,
    544, 547
  comparing with text, 543–548
media activity
  analysis, 585
  presentation, 126, 168, 504, 594
Media Analysis, 71, 167, 315, 543
memoirs, R71–R72
metaphors, 100, 184, 185, 217, 443,
    R72
  extended, 204, 444, R67
meter, 69, R72, R77
Mexican-American War, 175
middle English, R53
minor characters, R63
mise en scène, R72
misplaced modifiers, avoiding, 314
missions, 4
MLA citation guidelines, R10–R11
*MLA Handbook for Writers of
    Research Papers* (MLA), R9
moderators, debate, R14
modern drama, 456
modern English, R53
modernism, R72
Modern Language Association
    (MLA), R9
modern literature, 411
modifiers, R35
  adjectives, R36
  adverbs, R36
  comparisons, R36
  dangling, R38
  definition of, 314
  misplaced, 314, R37–R38
  problems with, R37–R38

monitor, R72
monologue, R72
monometer, R72
mood, R72
motivations, of characters, 434, R63, R72
muckrakers, 330
multimedia links, R5
multimedia presentations, 126, 504, 594
multiple-meaning words, 204, 293, R54
multiple plot lines, R7
*my*Notebook, 103, 169, 267, 271, 405, 601, 605
myths, R72
*my*WriteSmart, 72, 75, 76, 101, 104, 105, 128, 170, 171, 269, 272, 282, 292, 312, 322, 348, 357, 370, 372, 394, 399, 404, 406, 407, 435, 454, 486, 504, 526, 541, 544, 547, 566, 579, 594, 600, 602, 603, 606, 607

N

name-calling (faulty reasoning), R20
narration, and point of view, 164, 166
narrative poetry, 453, R73
narratives, 230, 231, R73
    conclusions of, R7
    drafts of, 269
    elements of effective, 267
    exchanging with partner, 269
    historical, 311, R69
    inspiration for, 267
    organization, 268
    Performance Task Evaluation Chart, 270
    planning, 267–268
    revising, 269
    sharing, 269
    slave, R78
    writing, 267–270, R6–R7
    writing activity, 348, 370
narrative techniques, R6–R7. *See also literary devices*
    flashbacks, 84
    flash forwards, 84, 85
narrator, R6, R73
    limited, 164, 398
    omniscient, 164, 398
Native Americans, 3, 4, 175
naturalism, 330, 347, 348, 350, 404, R73
negatives, double, R37
negative side, in debates, R15
news articles, R73
    citing, R11
    writing activity, 357
New Spain, 4
New World, 3–4, 36

nominative pronouns, R31
nonessential adjective clauses, R43
nonessential appositives, R41
nonfiction, R71, R73
non sequitur, R20
North America
    British colonies in, 109–110
    exploration and settlement of, 3–4
note taking, 406
noun clauses, R43
nouns, R23, R30
    abstract, R23
    collective, R23, R48
    common, R23, R30
    compound, R23
    concrete, R23
    plural, R23, R30, R58
    possessive, R23, R30, R58
    predicate, R40
    proper, R23, R30
    singular, R23, R30
novellas, R73
novels, R73, 356
nuances, 139, 248, 381, 586

O

objective pronouns, R31
objective tone, R3, R5
objects
    direct, R25, R40
    indirect, R25, R40
observations, identifying, in writing narratives, R6
odes, R73
off, off of, R56
off rhyme, R78
old English, R53
omniscient narrator, 164, 398
online sources, citing, R11
onomatopoeia, R73
op-ed pieces, R73
open letters, R73
oral defense, speaking activity, 185
oral literature, R73–R74
oral presentations, 101
organization
    for analytical essay, 406
    for arguments, 104, 602
    for informative essay, 170
    for narratives, 268
    for panel discussions, 605
    pattern of, R74
organizational patterns, 147, R4, R74
    chronological order, 147, 311
    classification, 195
    comparison and contrast, 147
    spatial order, R79
outlines
    for analytical essay, 406
    for arguments, 104

writing activity, 292
overgeneralization, R19, R74
oversimplification, R19
overview, R74
oxymoron, R74

P

pacing, 544, R7
panel discussions
    elements for effective participation in, 605
    gathering evidence for, 606
    outlining ideas for, 606
    participating in, 605–608
    Performance Task Evaluation Chart, 608
    planning, 605–606
    practicing for, 606
    reinforcing ideas for, 607
    summarizing, 607
parables, R74
paradox, 205, R74
parallelism, 102, 117, 120, 186, 198, 382, R44, R74
parallel plots, R74
paraphrasing, 19, 202, R9, R74
parataxis, 102
parentheses, R27
parenthetical citations, R9
parody, R74
participle phrases, R41
participles, R41
    dangling, R41–R42
    misplaced, R41–R42
parts of speech, 232, R23–R24. *See also specific parts of speech*
passive voice, 22, R35
pastoral poetry, 411
past participles, R33–R34
past perfect progressive tense, R35
past perfect tense, R34
past principal part, R33–R34
past progressive tense, R34
past tense, R34
pathos, 291
patterns
    identifying, 126, 218
    of organization, 147, 195, R74, R79
    of word changes, 197, 595
peer feedback, 105, 171, 269, 407, 603
pentameter, R72
Performance Task, end of collection, 323–326
    debating an issue, 271–274
    participating in panel discussion, 605–608
    Plan, Produce, Revise, Present, 103–105, 169–171, 267–269, 271–273, 323–326, 405–407, 601–603, 605–607

writing an analytical essay, 405–408
writing an argument, 103–106, 601–604
writing a narrative, 267–270
writing an informative essay, 169–172
Performance Task, selection
  media activity, 126, 168, 504, 585, 594
  speaking activity, 76, 101, 118, 138, 158, 165, 185, 196, 247, 263, 282, 312, 316, 372, 380, 399, 486, 544, 566
  writing activity, 20, 33, 70, 72, 75, 85, 94, 128, 148, 165, 205, 218, 231, 266, 292, 299, 322, 348, 357, 370, 394, 404, 435, 444, 454, 526, 541, 547, 548, 579, 600
Performance Task Evaluation Chart
  analytical essay, 408
  argument, 106, 604
  debate, 274
  informative essay, 172
  narrative, 270
  panel discussion, 608
periods, R26
personal pronouns, 166, R23, R30, R46
personification, 201, 217, 599, R74
persuasion, R74–R75
persuasive techniques, R17, R74
persuasive texts, R75. *See also* arguments
  analyzing, R16–R17
  evaluating, R21–R22
  reading, R16–R22
Petrarchan sonnet, 444, R78
photographs, 389–390, 393, 394
phrases, R40
  adjective, R40
  adverb, R41
  appositives, R41
  determining meanings of, 32
  gerund, R42
  infinitive, R41
  parallel, 120
  participle, R41
  prepositional, R25, R38, R40–R41
  verbal, R41–R42
pity, appeals to, R17, R66
plagiarism, R9
Plan, Produce, Revise, Present. *See under* Performance Task, end of collection
plays. *See also* drama
  citing, R11
plot, R75
  complications in, 504, R64
  in drama, 504

falling action in, R67, R75
multiple plot lines, R7
parallel, R74
rising action in, R75, R77
theme and, 84
plural nouns, R23, R30, R58
poems/poetry, R75
  allusions in, 158, 321, 322, 599
  analyzing, 101, 157, 158, 178, 180, 182, 183, 185, 200, 201, 202, 203, 205, 322, 444, 454, 599, 600
  cataloguing, 184
  characters in, 453
  citing, R10
  colonial, 110, 151–158
  comparing and contrasting, 205, 454
  determining theme of, 184, 204
  direct statements in, 184
  evaluating, 205, 454
  examples, 97–99, 177–183, 317–320, 401–403, 446–452, 597–598
  experimental, R67
  figurative language in, 100, 443
  free verse, 100, 184
  of Harlem Renaissance, 438–442
  imagery in, 100, 158, 184, 599
  inferences about, 205, 444, 600
  interpreting, 158, 180, 185, 200, 201, 322, 404, 453, 454, 600
  lines, R71–R72
  lyric, R71
  metaphors in, 184, 185, 443, 444
  modern, 411
  narrative, 453, R73
  19th century, 176–183, 199–203
  odes, R73
  parallelism in, 186
  pastoral, 411
  personification in, 201
  Petrarchan sonnet, 444
  quatrain, R76
  refrain, R76
  repetition, 180, 184
  rhyme, R77
  rhythm, 321, R77
  scansion, R77
  similes in, 184
  sonnet, R78
  speaker in, R79
  stanza, R79
  structure, 184, 321, 453
  summarizing, 444
  symbolism in, 180, 184
  syntax, 102
  textual details, 157
  theme in, 157, 443
  topic of, 157, 443
point of view, 85, R75
  analyzing, 164, 291, 398, 578

author's, 291, 398, 578
establishing, R6
first-person, 164, 166, R75
second-person, 164, 166
third-person, 164, 166, 357, 398, R75
policy statements, R14
political pamphlets, 110
political science, 119
pollution, 412
possessive nouns, R23, R30, R58
possessive pronouns, R31
precede/proceed, R60
precise usage (vocabulary strategy), 436
precise words and phrases, 437
predicate
  adjectives, R36
  complete, R25
  compound, R40
  nominatives, R40, R47
  nouns, R40
  pronouns, R40
predict, R75
prefixes, 206, 358, 595, R50, R57–R58
  circum-, 95
premises, 137, 138, 281
prepositional phrases, R25, R38, R40–R41
prepositions, R24, R38
presentations
  media activity, 168, 504, 585, 594
  multimedia, 126, 504, 594
  oral, 101
present participles, R33–R34
present perfect progressive tense, R35
present perfect tense, R34
present principal part, R33–R34
present progressive tense, R34
present tense, R34
primary sources, 19, R8, R75, R79
prior knowledge, R75–R76
problems, identifying, in writing narratives, R6
problem-solution order, R76
progressive movement, 330
prologue, R76
pronouns, R23, R30
  antecedent agreement, R30–R31
  cases, R31
  demonstrative, R24, R32
  indefinite, R24, R32, R46–R47
  intensive, R23, R32
  interrogative, R24, R32
  nominative, R31
  objective, R31
  personal, 166, R23, R30, R46
  possessive, R31
  predicate, R40
  reference problems, R33

reflexive, R23, R31–R32
relative, R24, R32–R33, R43, R48
pronunciation, 283
pronunciation key, R83
propaganda, R21, R76
proper adjectives, R29
proper nouns, R23, R30
propositions, R14
props, R76
prose, R76
protagonists, 526, R76
proto-English, R52
public documents, R76
    Declaration of Independence,
      111–116
    Declaration of Sentiments, 295–299
punctuation
    apostrophes, R27–R28
    colons, 96, R27
    commas, R26
    dashes, 371, 437, R27
    ellipses, 102, R28
    exclamation points, 437, R26
    hyphenation, 150
    hyphens, R27
    parentheses, R27
    periods, R26
    question marks, R26
    quick reference, R26–R28
    quotation marks, R28
    semicolons, 265, R26–R27
purpose, 19
    analyzing author's, 298
    of argument, 137
    determining author's, 32, 93, 195,
      217, 356, 369
    evaluating, 281, 370
    of foundational documents, 125,
      128
    of text, 124

Q

quatrains, R76, R78
question marks, R26
questions
    research, R8
    rhetorical, 220, 294, R77
quotation marks, R28
quotations
    direct, R9
    introducing, with colon, 96, R27
    use of, 233

R

readers' theater, 544
reading, persuasive texts, R16–R22
realism, 330, 347, 350, 372, R76
    local color, R71
reasoning
    circular, R19
    deductive, 291, R18–R19, R65

faulty, R19–R20
inductive, 291, R18, R70
reasons
    in arguments, 281
    to support claims, R2
rebuttals, in debates, R14–R15
Reconstruction era, 277–278
recurring themes, R80
reference works, R76
    bibliographies, R62
    dictionaries, 149, R56
    general, 149
    glossaries, R56
    for preferred and contested usage,
      R55–R56
    specialized, 149, R56
    synonym finders, R56
    thesaurus, 436, R56
    using, 119, 149, R56
reflexive pronouns, R23, R31–R32
refrain, R76
regionalism, 330, R76
regular verbs, R33–R34
relative pronouns, R24, R32–R33,
    R43, R48
repetition, 19, 117, 180, 184, 382, 437,
    R77
rereading, 76, 101, 102, 105, 117, 148,
    157, 169, 196, 218, 292, 348, 399,
    400, 407, 435, 454, 486, 504, 541,
    548, 568, 579
research
    conducting, R8–R9
    focus of, R8
    formulating question for, R8
research questions, R8
research report, writing activity, 579
resolution (plot), 504, R64, R67, R75.
      See also falling action
reviews, film, 72
Revolutionary War, 109
rhetoric, 93, 291
rhetorical devices, 294, 578
rhetorical features, 19, 117, 125, 128,
    294, 298, 578
rhetorical questions, 220, 294, R77
rhyme, R77
    slant, R78
rhyme scheme, R77
rhythm, 321, R77
rising action, R75, R77
Romanticism, 176, 234, 247, 263, 266,
    R77
roots, R50
    determining meaning from, 358
    Latin root *ject*, 300
rough drafts. *See* drafts
rubric. *See* Performance Task
    Evaluation Chart
run-on sentences, R45

S

sarcasm, R77
satire, 379, R77
scanning, R77
scansion, R77
scene, R77
scenery, R77
science fiction, 411, 584, R77
screenplays, R77
scripts, R78
secondary sources, R8, R78, R79
second-person point of view, 164, 166
semantic maps, 119
semicolons, 265, R26–R27
seminal texts, evaluating, 125, 137,
    281
sensory details, 437, R78
sensory language, R7
sentence fragments, 198, R44–R45
sentences
    balanced, 284
    complements, R40
    complete, writing, R44–R45
    complex, 198, R44
    compound, 198, 265, R43–R44
    compound-complex, 198, R44
    compound subjects and predicates,
      R40
    crafting effective, 437
    declarative, R40
    exclamatory, 437, R40
    imperative, R40
    interrogative, R40
    inverted, R47
    parallel, 120, R44
    parts of, R25, R39–R40
    with predicate nominatives, R47
    run-on, R45
    simple, 198, R43
    subject-verb agreement, R45–R48
    topic, R81
    types of, R40
sentence structure, R43–R44
    comparing, 568
    and style, 578
    varying, 198
sequence, 147, 311
sequence charts, 311
sequential order, R78
series
    introducing, with colon, 96
    semicolons to separate items in,
      265
sermons, R78
set design, 75, 547
setting, R78
setting a purpose, R78
Shakespearean drama, 37
    alliteration in, 69
    blank verse, 69

figurative language in, 69
film interpretations of, 71–76
language in, 69
meter of, 69
The Tempest, 37–68
Shakespearean sonnet, R78
short stories, R78
analyzing, 399
citing, R10
examples, 77–83, 159–163,
235–246, 249–262, 331–346,
395–397, 413–433, 581–583
sidebars, R78
signal words, 311, R78
similarities, as context clues, 313
similes, 32, 184, 217, R78
simple sentences, 198, R43
singular nouns, R23, R30
situational humor, R69
situational irony, 398, R70
situations, identifying, in writing
narratives, R6
slang, R49
slant rhyme, R77, R78
slave narratives, 277, R78
snob appeal, R17
some, somewhat, R56
sonnets, R78
sound, 72
sources, R79
citing, R9, R10–R11
credible, R8
evaluating, R8–R9
incorporating into research paper,
R9
locating, R8
MLA citation guidelines, R10–R11
online, R11
primary, 19, R8, R79
secondary, R8, R78, R79
for *The Tempest*, 36
South America, exploration and
settlement of, 3–4
Spanish settlers, 4
spatial order, R79
speaker, in poem, R79
speaking activity
debate, 76, 316, 372, 566
discussion, 138, 158, 165, 196, 247,
263, 282, 312, 399, 486
lecture, 380
oral defense, 185
oral presentations, 101
readers' theater, 544
speech, 118
specialized dictionaries, R56
specialized reference works, 149, R56
specialized vocabulary, 34, 369, R55
speeches, R79
analyzing, 291, 292
evaluating, 282

examples, 279–280, 285–290
presenting, 323–326
speaking activity, 118
tone of, 282
spelling, R49, R56–R60
spelling rules
plural nouns, forming, R58
possessives, forming, R58
prefixes, R57–R58
special spelling problems, R58–R59
suffixes, R57–R58
words ending in a consonant, R57
words ending in silent *e*, R56–R57
words ending in *y*, R57
stage directions, 486, 540, 541, R79
stanza, R79
static characters, R63
stereotyping, R19, R79
story elements, analyzing, 584
story structure, 84
stream of consciousness, R79
stress, word, 544
structure, R79. *See also*
organizational patterns
ambiguity and, 164
analyzing, 84, 93, 117, 147, 164, 184,
230, 247, 263, 321, 347, 404,
453, 594
anaphora, 382
of arguments, 93
comparison and contrast, 147
for debate, 273
evaluating, 93, 118, 230
free verse, 184
meaning and, 263
overall, 578
parallel, 102, 117, 120, 186, 198, 382
poetic, 184, 321, 453
rhythm, 321
sentence, 198, 568, 578
suspense and, 164
style, 32, R79–R80. *See also* Language
and Style
analyzing, 117
for arguments, R3
balanced, 284
comparing writers' styles, 568
determining author's point of view
from, 578
determining author's purpose
from, 195, 217, 311
elements of, 217
formal, 127
informal, 127, 217, 455
for informative essay, R5
punctuation and, 265
syntax, 117, 120, 198, 284, 437
tone, 117, 195
word choice and, 196, 578
style manuals, R9
subject complements, R40

subjects
collective nouns as, R48
complete, R25
compound, R40, R46
indefinite pronouns as, R46–R47
personal pronouns as, R46
relative pronouns as, R48
subject-verb agreement
basic, R45
with *be*, R46
with collective nouns, R48
with compound subjects, R46
don't and *doesn't* as auxiliary verbs,
R47–R48
with indefinite pronouns, R46–R47
inverted sentences, R47
with personal pronouns, R46
with predicate nominatives, R47
with relative pronouns, R48
with words between subject and
verb, R46
subordinate clauses, 35, R42, R43
subordinating conjunctions, 35, R24,
R39
suffixes, 206, R50–R51, R57–R58
derivational, 206
inflectional, 206
patterns of word changes and, 197,
595
word families and, 358
summaries, 292, 600, R9
summarizing, R80. *See also*
paraphrasing
central ideas, 19, 217, 218
foundational documents, 126
panel discussions, 607
poetry, 202, 445
text, 312, 380, 579, 585
superlative form, R36–R37
support
for claims, R16, R80
types of, R4–R5
Supreme Court decisions, 549–568
surprise endings, R80
suspense, 164, R7, R80
symbolism, 180, 247, 404, R80
interpreting, 247
in poetry, 184
synonym finders, R56
synonyms, 436, R53
syntactical elements
ellipsis, 102
parallelism, 102
parataxis, 102
in poetry, 102
syntax, 35, 102, 117, 120, 198, 284,
437, 455
synesthesia, R70
synthesize, R80

T

tables, 393, 394
take/bring, R59
tall tales, R80
technical terms, 32, 369
technology, 412
The Tempest (Shakespeare)
  analyzing, 69–70
  excerpt from, 37–68
  introduction to, 36
  media versions of, 71–76
  sources for, 36
tense, verb, R34–R35
tension, dramatic, 263
terrorism, 412
testimonials, R17
tetrameter, R72
text
  analyzing, 20, 33, 70, 72, 75, 76, 85,
    94, 101, 103, 118, 126, 128, 138,
    148, 158, 165, 169, 178, 180,
    182, 183, 185, 196, 201, 202,
    203, 218, 231, 247, 263, 266,
    282, 292, 299, 312, 322, 348,
    357, 370, 372, 380, 394, 399,
    404, 435, 444, 454, 486, 504,
    541, 566, 579, 585, 594, 600
  comparing, 151, 196, 348, 370
  evaluating, 20, 94, 148, 165, 218,
    231, 247, 263, 312, 348, 399,
    435, 579
  evidence from, 20, 33, 70, 72, 75, 76,
    85, 101, 118, 126, 128, 138, 148,
    158, 165, 178, 180, 182, 183,
    185, 196, 200, 201, 202, 203,
    218, 231, 247, 263, 266, 282,
    292, 299, 312, 316, 322, 348,
    357, 370, 372, 380, 394, 399,
    404, 435, 444, 454, 541,
    544, 566, 579, 585, 594, 600
  inferences about, 33, 69, 118, 126,
    196, 218, 263, 299, 312, 357,
    370, 380, 585
  interpreting, 85, 94, 196, 218, 263,
    299, 380, 435, 579
  making connections between, 372
  paraphrasing, 19
  persuasive, reading, R16–R22
  summarizing, 312, 380, 579, 585
text features, R80
textual details, 157
textual evidence, R5
than/then, R60
their/there/they're, R60
theme, 19, 117, 298, R80. *See also*
  central ideas
  in American Romanticism, 266
  analyzing, 85, 117
  definition of, 125
  determining, 84, 100, 128, 184, 204,
    247, 263, 398

  making connections between, 348
  of poem, 157, 184, 444
  recurring, R80
  textual evidence for, 100
  universal, R80
thesaurus, 149, 436, R56
thesis statement, R4, R80
third-person limited, R75
third-person narrator, R6
third-person omniscient, R75
third-person point of view, 164, 166,
  357, 398, R75
time-order signal words, 311
time travel, 584
timing, of dialogue, 544
titles, R80
tokenism, 292
tone, 32, 117, R80
  analyzing, 231
  of argument, R3
  author's purpose and, 195
  biased, R3, R5
  comparing, 568
  consistent, 350
  determining author's point of view
    from, 578
  determining author's purpose
    from, 311
  formal, 127, R3
  informal, R3
  for informative essay, R5
  irony and, 93
  objective, R3, R5
  of speech, 282
  word choice and, 204, 350
topic, 157
  developing, R4–R5
  introducing, R4
  of poem, 444
  research, R8
topic sentence, R81
traditional ballads, R62
tragedy, R81
tragic flaw, R81
tragic heroes, R81
transcendentalism, 176, 218, R81
transcontinental railroad, 278, 329
transcript, R81
transfer technique, R17
transitions, 140, R3, R4–R5
transitive verbs, R24
trickster tales, R81
trimeter, R72
trochee, R72
Tufte, Virginia, R3
Turabian, Kate L., R9
two/too/to, R60

U

understatement, R81
United States

  19th century, 175–176
  territorial expansion, 175
unity of effect, R81
universal themes, R80
urbanization, 329
usage. *See* commonly confused
  words; reference works
U.S. Constitution, 110, 121–125, 128

V

valid conclusions, R64
valid reasons, to support claims, R14
vanity, appeals to, R17, R66
verbal irony, 93, 398, R70
verbal phrases, R41–R42
verbals, R41–R42
verbs, R24, R33
  action, R24, R33
  active and passive voice, 22
  active voice, R35
  auxiliary, R24, R25, R47–R48
  gerunds, R42
  helping, R25
  intransitive, R24
  irregular, R34
  linking, R24, R33
  main, R25
  participles, R41
  passive voice, R35
  principal parts, R33–R34
  progressive forms, R34–R35
  regular, R33–R34
  subject-verb agreement, R45–R48
  tenses, R34–R35
  transitive, R24
video, 167, 392. *See also* film
  analyzing, 168, 316
  citing, R11
  evaluating, 394
  to present information, 393
visualizing, R81
vivid language, R7
vocabulary
  Academic Vocabulary, 2, 103, 108,
    170, 174, 268, 271, 276, 328,
    406, 410, 602, 606
  archaic vocabulary, 21
  commonly confused words, R59–
    R60
  Critical Vocabulary, 21, 34, 86, 95,
    119, 127, 149, 149, 166, 197, 219,
    232, 248, 264, 283, 293, 300,
    313, 349, 358, 371, 381, 400,
    436, 567, 580, 586, 595
  specialized vocabulary, 34, 369,
    R55
  strategies for understanding,
    R49–R56
Vocabulary Strategy
  affixes, 206
  archaic vocabulary, 21

consulting general and specialized reference works, 149
context clues, 86, 219, 264, 313, R49–R50
Critical Vocabulary, 149
domain-specific words, 119
etymology, 349, 580
evaluating nuances in meaning, 139
Latin prefix *circum-*, 95
Latin root *ject*, 300
legal terminology, 567
multiple-meaning words, 293
nuances in word meanings, 248, 381, 586
parts of speech, 232
patterns of word changes, 197, 595
precise usage, 436
pronunciation, 283
specialized vocabulary, 34
word collocations, 400
word families, 358
voice, 22, R81
voice expression, 544
volume, 544

W

War of 1812, 175
websites, R81
westward expansion, 175

who/whom, R56
word choice, 148, 196, 204, 291, 350, 356, 542, 568, 578, 600
word collocations, 400
word families, 358, R52
word maps, 349
word meanings
    determining, 32, 119, 219, 264, 313
    nuances in, 139, 248, 381, 586
word origins, R51–R52
word webs, 95, 300, 358, 595
workplace documents, R82
works cited, R9, R10, R82
works consulted, R82
World War I, 411
World War II, 411
writing
    analytical essays, 405–408
    arguments, 601–604, R2–R3
    complete sentences, R44–R45
    drafts, 104–105, 170, 269, 406
    essays, 169–172, 405–408, 601–604, R4–R5
    informative essays, 169–172, R4–R5
    narratives, 267–270, R6–R7
writing activity
    analysis, 205, 231, 266, 526
    argument, 33
    captions, 75, 548
    comparison, 299

description, 404
diagram, 547
discussion, 165
dramatic monologue, 85
essay, 128, 148, 218, 322, 394, 444, 541
evaluation, 94
exploratory essay, 70
interview summary, 454
journal entries, 20
letters, 20, 435
narrative, 348, 370
news articles, 357
outline and summary, 292
research report, 579
reviews, 72
summary, 600
writing style. *See* Language and Style; style

Index of Titles and Authors

A

Against Nature, 221
AMERICA The Story of Us: Jacob
　Riis, 392

B

Balboa, 77
*"Blaxicans" and Other Reinvented
　Americans,* 87
Because I could not stop for Death,
　201
Bishop, Elizabeth, 401
Black Man Talks of Reaping, A, 442
Bontemps, Arna, 439, 442
Bradford, William, 5
Brin, David, 581
*Building the Transcontinental
　Railroad* (excerpt from *The
　Chinese in America*), 301

C

Chang, Iris, 301
Chernow, Ron, 141
Child Mortality Rates, 391
Chopin, Kate, 395
*Coming Merging of Mind and
　Machine, The,* 569
Coming of Age in the Dawnland
　(excerpt from *1491*), 23
Crucible, The, 457
Crucible, The, 543 (audio version)
Crucible, The, 545 (production
　images)
Cullen, Countee, 439, 441

D

Declaration of Independence, The, 111
Declaration of Sentiments, 295
Death of the Hired Man, The, 447
Diamond, Jared, 587
Dickinson, Emily, 199–203
Douglass, Frederick, 285

E

*Ends of the World as We Know Them,
　The,* 587

F

Federalist No. 10, The, 129
54th Massachusetts, The, 315
Fish, The, 401
Fitzgerald, F. Scott, 413
Food Product Design (excerpt from
　Fast Food Nation), 359
Freneau, Philip, 151, 155
From the Dark Tower, 441
Frost, Robert, 445, 446, 448

G

Genesis of the Tenement (excerpt
　from *How the Other Half Lives*),
　384
Growing Up Asian in America, 187

H

Harjo, Joy, 97
Hawthorne, Nathaniel, 235
Hayden, Robert, 317

J

Jefferson, Thomas, 111
Johnson, Charles, 159
Jungle, The (excerpt), 352

K

Kurzweil, Ray, 569

L

Lincoln, Abraham, 279
London, Jack, 331
Lowest Animal, The, 373

M

Madison, James, 129
Mann, Charles C., 23
Mending Wall, 446
Miller, Arthur, 457
Minister's Black Veil, The, 235
Much Madness is divinest Sense, 202
Murray, Sabina, 77

N

New Orleans, 97
Noda, Kesaya E., 187

O

Oates, Joyce Carol, 221
Of Plymouth Plantation (excerpt), 5
*On Being Brought from Africa to
　America,* 154
*On the Emigration to America and
　Peopling the Western Country,*
　155

P

Patrick Henry: Voice of Liberty, 167
Pit and the Pendulum, The, 249
Poe, Edgar Allan, 249

R

Reality Check, 581
Riis, Jacob, 383, 384, 389, 392
Rodriguez, Richard, 87
Runagate Runagate, 317

S

Second Inaugural Address, 279
Schlosser, Eric, 359
Shakespeare, William, 37
Sinclair, Upton, 352
Smith, Tracy K., 597
Soldier for the Crown, A, 159
Song of the Son, 440
Song of Myself, 177
Soul selects her own Society, The, 200
Stanton, Elizabeth Cady, 295
Story of an Hour, The, 395
Supreme Court of the United States,
　549

T

Tell all the truth but tell it slant, 203
Tempest, The (excerpt), 37
Tempest, The, 71 (film version)
Tempest, The, 73 (production images)
Tenement Photos, 389
*Thomas Jefferson: The Best of
　Enemies,* 141
Thoreau, Henry David, 207
*Tinker v. Des Moines Independent
　Community School District,* 549
To Build a Fire, 331
*To the Right Honourable William,
　Earl of Dartmouth,* 152
Toomer, Jean, 439, 440
Twain, Mark, 373

U

United States Constitution, The
　(excerpt), 121
Universe as Primal Scream, The, 597

W

Walden (excerpt), 207
*What to the Slave Is the Fourth of
　July?* 285
Wheatley, Phillis, 151, 152, 154
Whitman, Walt, 177–183
Winter Dreams, 413

Acknowledgments

"Against Nature" by Joyce Carol Oates originally published in *The Ontario Review,* 1986. Text copyright © 1986 by The Ontario Review. Reprinted by permission of John Hawkins & Associates, Inc.

Excerpt from *The American Heritage Dictionary of the English Language, Fifth Edition.* Text copyright © 2011 by Houghton Mifflin Harcourt. Adapted and reprinted by permission of Houghton Mifflin Harcourt Publishing Company.

"Balboa" from *Tales of the New World* by Sabina Murray. Text copyright © 2011 by Sabina Murray. Reprinted by permission of Grove/Atlantic Inc.

"Because I could not stop for Death" from *The Poems of Emily Dickinson* by Emily Dickinson, Thomas H. Johnson, ed. Text copyright © 1951, 1955, 1979, 1983 by the President and Fellows of Harvard College. Reprinted by permission of Harvard University Press and the Trustees of Amherst College.

"A Black Man Talks of Reaping" from *Personals* by Arna Bontemps. Text copyright © 1963 by Arna Bontemps. Reprinted by permission of Harold Ober Associates, Inc.

"'Blaxicans' and other Reinvented Americans" by Richard Rodríguez from *The Chronicle of Higher Education,* September 12, 2003. Text copyright © 2003 by Richard Rodríguez. Reprinted by permission of Georges Borchardt, Inc., on behalf of the author.

"Building the Transcontinental Railroad" from *The Chinese in America: A Narrative History* by Iris Chang. Text copyright © 2003 by Iris Chang. Reprinted by permission of Viking Penguin, a division of Penguin Group (USA) Inc.

"The Coming Merging of Mind and Machine" from *Scientific American* by Ray Kurzweil, March 23, 2009. Text copyright © 2009 by Scientific American, a Division of Nature America, Inc. Reprinted by permission of Scientific American.

Excerpt from "Coming of Age in the Dawnland" from *1491: New Revelations of the Americas Before Columbus* by Charles C. Mann, first published in Great Britain by Granta Books. Text copyright © 2005 by Charles C. Mann. Reprinted by permission of Alfred A. Knopf, a division of Random House, Inc., Granta Books and Ward & Balkin Agency on behalf of the author. Any third party use of this material, outside of this publication, is prohibited. Interested parties must apply directly to Random House, Inc. for permission.

The Crucible by Arthur Miller. Text copyright © 1952, 1953, 1954, renewed © 1980, 1981, 1982 by Arthur Miller. Reprinted by permission of Viking Penguin, a division of Penguin Group (USA) Inc. and The Wylie Agency, Inc.

"The Death of the Hired Man" by Robert Frost from *The Poetry of Robert Frost,* edited by Edward Connery Lathem. Text copyright © 1930, 1939, 1969 by Henry Holt and Company, LLC. Text copyright © 1958 by Robert Frost. Text copyright © 1967 by Lesley Frost Ballantine. Reprinted by permission of Henry Holt and Company, LLC.

"The Ends of the World as We Know Them" by Jared Diamond from *The New York Times,* January 1, 2005. Text copyright © 2005 by The New York Times. Reprinted by permission of PARS International on behalf of the New York Times. All rights reserved.

Excerpt from *Fast Food Nation* by Eric Schlosser. Text copyright © 2001 by Eric Schlosser. Reprinted by permisison of Random House Audio, a division of Random House, Inc., Houghton Mifflin Harcourt Publishing Company and Penguin Books Ltd. Any third party use of this material outside of this publication is prohibited. Interested parties must apply directly to Random House, Inc. for permission.

"The Fish" from *The Complete Poems 1927-1979* by Elizabeth Bishop. Text copyright © 1979, 1983 by Alice Helen Methfessel. Reprinted by permission of Farrar, Straus and Giroux, LLC.

"From the Dark Tower" by Countee Cullen. Text copyright © 1927, 1947 by Countee Cullen. Reprinted by permission of Thompson and Thompson.

"Growing Up Asian in America" by Kesaya E. Noda from *Making Waves: An Anthology of Writings By and About Asian American Women,* edited by Asian Women United of California. Text copyright © 1989 by Asian Women United of California. Reprinted by permission of Asian Women United of California.

"The Lowest Animal" from *Letters from the Earth* by Mark Twain, edited by Bernard DeVoto. Text copyright © 1938, 1944, 1946, 1959, 1962 by The Mark Twain Company. Text copyright © 1942 by The President and Fellows of Harvard College. Reprinted by permission of HarperCollins Publishers.

"Mending Wall" by Robert Frost from *The Poetry of Robert Frost,* edited by Edward Connery Lathem. Text copyright © 1930, 1939, 1969 by Henry Holt and Company, LLC. Text copyright © 1958 by Robert Frost. Text copyright © 1967 by Lesley Frost Ballantine. Reprinted by permission of Henry Holt and Company, LLC.

"Much madness is divinest sense" from *The Poems of Emily Dickinson* by Emily Dickinson, Thomas H. Johnson, ed. Text copyright © 1951, 1955, 1979, 1983 by the President and Fellows of Harvard College. Reprinted by permission of Harvard University Press and the Trustees of Amherst College.

"New Orleans" from *She Had Some Horses* by Joy Harjo. Text copyright © 2008, 1983 by Joy Harjo. Reprinted by permission of W. W. Norton & Company, Inc.

From *Of Plymouth Plantation, 1620-1647* by William Bradford, edited by Samuel Eliot Morison. Text copyright © 1952 by Samuel Eliot Morison. Text copyright renewed © 1980 by Emily M. Beck. Reprinted by permission of Alfred A. Knopf, a division of Random House, Inc. Any third party use of this material, outside of this publication, is prohibited. Interested parties must apply directly to